SEARS LIST OF
SUBJECT HEADINGS

Sears List

of

Subject

Headings

11th Edition

Edited by

BARBARA M. WESTBY

New York

The H. W. Wilson Company

1977

Printed in the United States of America

Library of Congress Cataloging in Publication Data

Sears, Minnie Earl, 1873-1933.
    Sears list of subject headings.

    First-5th ed. published under title: List of subject
headings for small libraries.
    Bibliography: p. xxxiii-xxxiv.
    1. Subject headings. I. Westby, Barbara Marietta.
II. Title. III. Title: List of subject headings.
Z695.S43   1977   025.3'3   77-807
ISBN 0-8242-0610-X

TABLE OF CONTENTS

Preface

Minnie Earl Sears prepared the first edition of this work in response to demands for a list of subject headings that was more suitable to the needs of the small library than the A.L.A. and the Library of Congress lists. Published in 1923 the *List of Subject Headings for Small Libraries* was based on the headings used by nine small libraries that were known to be well cataloged. However, Minnie Sears early recognized the need for uniformity, and she followed the form of the Library of Congress subject headings with few exceptions. This decision was important and foresighted because it allowed a library to add Library of Congress headings as needed when not provided by the Sears List and to graduate to the full use of Library of Congress headings when collections grew too large for a limited subject heading list.

Minnie Sears used only *See* and "refer from" references in the first edition. In the second (1926) edition she added *See also* references at the request of teachers of cataloging who were using the List as a textbook. To make the List more useful as a textbook she wrote a chapter on "Practical Suggestions for the Beginner in Subject Heading Work" for the third edition (1933).

Isabel Stevenson Monro edited the fourth (1939) and fifth (1944) editions. A new feature of the fourth edition was the inclusion of Dewey Decimal Classification numbers as adapted for the *Standard Catalog for Public Libraries*. The new subjects added to the List were based on those used in the Standard Catalog Series and on the catalog cards issued by The H. W. Wilson Company. Therefore, the original subtitle "Compiled from Lists used in Nine Representative Small Libraries" was dropped. Another new feature was the printing in italics of those subdivisions that had a more general application.

The sixth (1950), seventh (1954), and eighth (1959) editions were prepared by Bertha M. Frick. In recognition of the pioneering and fundamental contributions made by Minnie Sears the title was changed to *Sears List of Subject Headings* with the sixth edition. Since the List was being used by medium-sized libraries as well as small ones, the phrase "for Small Libraries" was deleted from the title. The symbols *x* and *xx* were substituted for the *See* and "refer from" phrases to conform to the format adopted by the Library of Congress.

The ninth edition (1965), the first to be prepared by the present editor, continued the policies of the earlier editions, with one major exception. The Dewey Decimal Classification numbers were dropped by the publisher. Many users of Sears had called to the attention of the publisher the inconsistency of including classification numbers and at the same time instructing the cataloger to consult the *Dewey Decimal Classification* for numbers. Moreover, it was the expressed opinion of these users that the inclusion of numbers often led to a misuse of the publication due to a misunderstanding of the relationship between subject headings and classification. Although the merits of these complaints were arguable, the publisher decided to omit the Dewey numbers from the ninth and tenth editions.

In the 12 years since the numbers were discontinued, larger library systems in particular have been drawing increasingly upon the resources of networks and computerized cataloging. Computerized cataloging is, however, still expensive and beyond the reach, and even the need, of many medium to small-sized libraries. With present restricted budgets and reduced staffs, these libraries—or more precisely their librarians —have been left with little or no assistance in the classification of their collections. It is largely in response to the needs of these librarians that suggested Dewey Decimal

Classification numbers are reintroduced in this eleventh edition. The numbers have been assigned by the editor of the Standard Catalog Department of The H. W. Wilson Company.

The classification numbers are taken from the tenth edition of the *Abridged Dewey Decimal Classification and Relative Index* (1971), published by Forest Press, Inc. In most cases only one number is assigned to a subject heading. There are instances, however, where a given subject is susceptible to more than one point of view, and one number is consequently inadequate for the subject heading. In these cases more than one number may be appropriate, for example: **Food additives 614.3, 641.4, and 664.** In the Relative Index these numbers represent the viewpoints of public health control, technology, and commercial processing, respectively. Occasionally, certain subjects are given the number of an entire class: **Languages, Modern (400's); and Literature (800's).** No classification numbers are assigned to some very general subject headings, e.g. **Charters, Exhibitions, Gifts, Hallmarks, National Characteristics, Identifications,** and **Indexes.** These headings cannot be classified unless a specific application is identified.

Few of the numbers in the tenth edition of "Abridged Dewey" are carried out more than four places beyond the decimal point. Except for libraries with large collections, where more detailed numbers may be required, the numbers in this edition of Sears should be adequate. The need for more detailed classification can often be satisfied by the addition of form and geographic subdivisions, as given in the Dewey schedules. Libraries for whom even relatively brief numbers are too long should consult the section entitled "Reduction" (p.27) in the Introduction to the Dewey volume.

The "Practical Suggestions for the Beginner in Subject Heading Work" has been a continuing feature since it was written by Minnie Sears. The chapter as revised by Bertha Frick was reprinted in the ninth edition. The present editor revised this chapter for the tenth edition and has made further changes in the eleventh. A new section on audio-visual and other materials has also been included. The chapter has been retitled to emphasize "Principles."

The headings added to the eleventh edition were suggested by librarians representing various sizes and types of libraries and by the catalogers at The H. W. Wilson Company who are responsible for the headings in the Standard Catalog Series and *Book Review Digest.* In addition, selections were made from *Library of Congress Subject Headings,* 8th edition, and from the *Hennepin County Library Cataloging Bulletin.* The *Legislative Indexing Vocabulary,* issued by the Library of Congress Congressional Research Service, was also consulted. While the new headings added to the ninth edition were chiefly from the fields of science and technology, those suggested and selected for the tenth edition reflected the interest in social and environmental problems. The selections for the present edition cover many areas. The swift developments in knowledge, the fluctuating popularity of interests, and the interrelationships of subjects increase the difficulty of the selection and wording of headings. Biology, psychology, and mathematics, for example, are being applied to almost every subject. No list can hope to keep completely abreast of the information explosion, nor can it provide for every idea, object, process, and relationship. With patterns established and examples provided, the cataloger can add new headings as needed. Guides for the wording of new headings may be found in the works themselves as well as in periodical literature and indexes. Although daily newspaper terminology may be too colloquial for use as headings, it does provide a clue to the way in which a patron may ask for materials, and it also suggests terms to be used as cross references.

The successive editors of the Sears List have followed the policy established by Minnie Sears to use the Library of Congress form of subject headings with some modifications for current terminology and spelling. Further modifications, introduced to meet the needs of smaller collections, include the simplification of phrasing (e.g. **City planning** rather than Cities and towns—Planning) and, in some cases, a broadening of specificity. Thus, closely related headings have been combined to create one **Sears** heading from two Library of Congress headings (e.g. **Bacteriology** for Bacteria and Bacteriology; **Cotton manufacture and trade** for Cotton manufacture and Cotton trade).

In accord with a suggestion of the Cataloging of Children's Materials Committee of A.L.A., modifications of Library of Congress headings are kept to a minimum; but choice often poses a dilemma. On the one hand, Library of Congress headings, devised for the largest collection in the country, are not always practical for a small collection. On the other hand, the increase of centralized, cooperative, and commercial cataloging and processing services make standardization not only desirable but virtually mandatory. Acting on a further suggestion of the Committee, the editor incorporated the headings from *Subject Headings for Children's Literature* (Library of Congress) into the Sears List. Some of the headings were not included specifically because they fell into the category of headings that can be added to Sears as needed; others were omitted because they already existed in Sears in a slightly different form. Since the Sears List is intended for both adult and juvenile collections, two similar headings for the same subject could not be used. Therefore, when Library of Congress has chosen different headings for adult and juvenile use of the same subject, a choice was made for Sears. In cases where the Sears List uses the adult form, the cataloger of children's materials may prefer to use the form found in *Subject Headings for Children's Literature.*

An appendix of black subject headings was included in the tenth edition for use by those libraries that preferred to change the Negro headings. The Library of Congress has since decided to cancel the heading Negroes, replacing it with two headings: Afro-Americans (for black people in the United States) and Blacks (for those in other geographic areas). For most users of Sears this distinction would probably be unnecessary. With this in mind, the editor has decided to use the heading **Blacks** for black people regardless of geographic area and to incorporate the appendix of the tenth edition into the main list.

In this edition terms considered by the editor to be sexist, racist or pejorative have been changed or eliminated. One exception is the heading **Man,** which is to be used only in an anthropological and generic sense.

For spelling, hyphenization, and definition the editor consulted *Webster's Third New International Dictionary of the English Language, Unabridged* (1961). Capitalization and the forms of corporate entries used as examples are based on the *Anglo-American Cataloging Rules.* Because a second edition of the rules is in progress, and decisions are still not final as of this writing, a number of examples of corporate names included in previous editions have been deleted.

Filing of entries in Sears continues to follow Rule 35, subject arrangement 2, in the *ALA Rules for Filing Catalog Cards* (1942) with a slight modification for parenthetical qualifiers. The straight alphabetical arrangement of the second edition (1968), which disregards all punctuation, would have separated the subdivisions under a particular heading by the interfiling of non-related headings. The editor feels that a list of subject headings serves a different purpose from a dictionary catalog. In using a list of headings the cataloger, concentrating on one subject and its subdivisions, would be distracted by extraneous subjects.

A common criticism of any list concerns the degree of specificity in its headings. Specificity is relative and depends on the size of a library, its function, the nature of its collection, and its patrons. Practicality rather than theory should determine the degree of specificity, and a balanced blend of theory and practice has been the philosophy of Sears. In a small collection the use of too many specific headings can result in the scattering of like materials. Sears, by example or directive, suggests over 200 classes of headings that may be added by the cataloger when more specific subject headings are needed. Combinations of related materials under one heading and the use of subdivisions also affect specificity.

Two "key" headings (**English language** and **United States**) with subdivisions applicable to a similar class of headings were provided in the first edition. Their number has steadily increased. The "key" for individual presidents, provided in the ninth edition, was deleted in the tenth edition in favor of an expansion of the subdivisions applicable to presidents individually and collectively under **Presidents—U.S.** Most of the subdivisions under **World War, 1914-1918** have been omitted because they also appear under **World War, 1939-1945**. The latter heading has been made a "key" for all wars. For a list of "key" headings see p xxxix.

Every heading in the List that may be used as a subject heading is printed in boldface type whether it is in the main file, in a *See also* paragraph, in a "refer from" reference, or an example for an explanation. If a term is not printed in boldface, it is not to be used as a heading.

The list of *See also, x,* and *xx* references follows the format used by the Library of Congress. For a full explanation of cross-referencing see p xxvi-xxxi.

As editor I wish to express my gratitude and heartfelt thanks to the catalogers who responded to my request for suggestions for headings to be added to this edition, in particular the catalogers of the Montgomery County (Md.) Public Schools. Special thanks are due to Frederick J. Rosenthal, Congressional Research Service, and to Edward J. Blume and Eugene T. Frosio, Subject Cataloging Division, Library of Congress, for answering questions on subject headings, and to Paul W. Winkler, editor, *Anglo-American Cataloging Rules,* 2d edition, for advice on the form of corporate entries. Special thanks are also due to Sister Claudia Carlen, St. John's Provincial Seminary Library, Plymouth, Mich., for advice on Catholic headings. Last, but not least, my thanks to The H. W. Wilson Company, especially Estelle A. Fidell and Barbara E. Dill of the Standard Catalog Department, and Thomas E. Sullivan, Associate Director of Indexing Services, for specific suggestions, constructive criticism, and editorial assistance.

The publisher, The H. W. Wilson Company, acknowledges its thanks to Forest Press, Inc., of the Lake Placid Education Foundation, for permission to use the tenth edition (1971) of the *Abridged Dewey Decimal Classification and Relative Index.*

This edition is submitted with the editor's hope that it will prove helpful and practical. Continued consumer reaction will aid in its improvement. An invitation is hereby extended to users and readers to submit requests at any time for new or revised headings and to forward constructive criticism. All suggestions will be received with gratitude and will receive serious consideration and study.

Barbara M. Westby

Chief, Catalog Management Division
Processing Department
Library of Congress

January 1977

Principles of the Sears List of Subject Headings

This chapter considers some principles and practices of subject cataloging that must be understood before an attempt is made to assign subject headings to library materials. Most of the illustrations refer to the Sears List of Subject Headings but the principles are applicable to other lists of subject headings as well, particularly the one issued by the Library of Congress on which the headings in this List are based.

Purpose of Subject Cataloging. The purpose of subject cataloging is to list under one uniform word or phrase all of the materials on a given subject that a library has in its collection. A subject is the theme or topic treated in a book, filmstrip, or other work. A subject heading is the word or phrase used in the library catalog to express this theme or topic. A subject entry is the catalog card with the subject heading placed at the top as the filing medium.

Library materials are given subject entries in the catalog in order to show what information the library has on a given subject, just as author entries are made to show the works that the library has by a given author. Properly made, the subject entry is a very important supplement to the reference tools in the library because it may enable the reader or librarian to find quickly and surely the material needed to answer a question on a subject. Subject entries are sometimes also the fastest way of finding a particular book. Ordinarily one consults the author entry for a specific work, but, if there is uncertainty about the author's name, one may find the individual piece more rapidly under a subject entry. Smith's *Basic Mathematics* would be difficult to find quickly if one did not know the author's first name and had to consult all the cards in the catalog under Smith. What if the author's name were really spelled Smyth? In either case, the book could be found readily under the subject **Mathematics.**

A printed list of subject headings, such as the Sears List, incorporates the thought and experience of many minds in various types of libraries. By using the List as a base, the cataloger has a source on which to rely. Consistency in both the specificity and the form of subject headings for the present and for the future is attained by working from an accepted list of subject headings where the choice among possible wordings has been made and recorded. By following the patterns of headings printed in the List, the catalogers will be able to add new headings that will be consistent with the List.

Determining the Subject of the Work. The first step in subject cataloging is to ascertain the real subject of the material and the purpose for which it was produced. Sometimes this is readily determined, e.g. **Butterflies** is obviously the subject of the book titled *Butterfly Book*. In other cases, the subject is not so easy to ascertain because it may be a complex one or the author may not express it in a manner clear to someone unfamiliar with the subject. The subject of a work cannot always be determined from the title alone. The title information is often misleading and undue dependence on it can result in error. A book entitled *Great Masters in Art* immediately suggests the subject **Artists** but closer examination reveals the book to be about painters specifically, not artists in general. Therefore, the more exact subject is **Painters,** not **Artists.** Another illustration is "Fundamentals of Instrumentation," part 1 of a *Manual of Instrumentation.* This title may suggest a treatise on musical instruments or music, but actually it is a book on engineering instruments.

The steps to follow in determining the subject of a work are the same whether one is considering its value for a reader, classifying it, or assigning subject headings to it. After reading the title page of a book to be cataloged, examine the table of contents, and read the preface and introduction. Then, if the theme of the book is still not clear, examine the text carefully and read parts of it, if necessary. For nonbook materials examine the container, the label, any accompanying guides, etc., and view or listen to the contents. The cataloger will be in a position to determine the subject of the item in hand *only* after this preliminary examination has been made. If the meaning of a subject is not clearly understood, one should consult reference sources, not only an unabridged dictionary and general encyclopedias, but also specialized reference books as well. Only when the cataloger has decided on the subject content of the work and *identified it with explicit words,* can the Sears List be used to advantage. The cataloger's own phrasing of the subject must be adapted to the terminology of the List. The library catalog will be more useful if the cataloger considers materials from the reader's point of view. The reader's profile depends on age, background, education, occupation, and geographical location as well as the type of library —school, public, university, or special. When examining a work the cataloger should ask "If I wanted material on this subject, under what words would I look in the catalog?" In choosing these words, that is, assigning the proper subject headings, there are certain principles that should be followed. These are considered in the next five sections.

Specific Entry. Appreciation of the principle of specific entry is fundamental both in using and in making a modern subject catalog. The rule of specific entry is to enter an item under the most specific term, i.e. subject heading, which accurately and precisely represents its content. This word serves as a succinct abstract of the work. If a reader wants information about bridges, the direct approach is to consult the catalog under the heading **Bridges,** not under the large topic **Engineering,** or even the more restricted field, **Civil engineering.** Or, consider the principle of specific entry from the cataloger's point of view. If one is examining a work about penguins, it is not sufficient to dismiss it as belonging under the subject **Birds,** or even under **Water birds.** It must be entered under the most specific heading that expresses the content, that is **Penguins.** If the work is entered under **Birds,** a reader would have to look through many entries in order to find information on penguins. Having found the most specific entry that will fit the item do not then make subject entries under both the specific and the general subject headings. A book with the title *Birds of the Ocean* should not be entered under both **Birds** and **Water birds** but only under **Water birds.** To eliminate this duplication, a network of *See also* references directs the reader from the broader subject headings to the more specific ones, e.g. **Birds.** *See also* . . . **Water birds;** and names of specific birds. . . . In many cases the most specific entry may be a general subject, e.g. *Song Birds of the World* will have the subject heading **Birds.** The specific term, as can be seen, refers to the exact word that summarizes the subject of the book for the user of the catalog. Specificity is relative and depends on the size of the library, the nature of its collection, its function, and its patrons. The heading should be as specific as possible for the topic it is intended to cover.

If the name of a specific object is not found in the List, the name of the larger group to which it belongs should be consulted. For example, in assigning subject headings to a work discussing elm and ash trees, the cataloger would find neither **Elm** nor **Ash** listed. However, under the broader subject, **Trees,** the following directions are given: "Names of trees are not included in this list but are to be added as needed, in the singular form." The cataloger thus has the authority to use the two headings, **Elm** and **Ash.** (Further directions for adding headings can be found on p xxxviii).

Materials should be considered in categories. The word or phrase chosen as a subject must fit not only the items being cataloged but also apply to a group of items on the same subject. The cataloger must consider not only the one piece in hand but also the other book and nonbook materials that discuss the same subject, albeit under different titles, in order to select a subject heading that will serve the entire group in the catalog with relation to other groups. In cataloging *Everybody's Cook Book* the inexperienced cataloger might think first of Cook books as the heading that will give the best description. But there are two other works that belong in the same group: *How's and Why's of Cooking* and *Cooking for Profit.* These contain not only recipes but also other material on cooking. **Cookery** fits the three closely related items better than Cook books and it also fits well with the related subject **Cookery for the sick.**

Common Usage. The word or words used to express a subject must represent common usage. In American libraries this means current American spelling and terminology: **Labor** not Labour; **Color** not Colour; **Elevator** not Lift. In British libraries these words would be reversed. Foreign terms are not used unless they have been incorporated into the English language, e.g. Laissez faire. By the same token contemporary words are to be used: **Home economics** not Domestic economy. Today a more current term might be Homemaking, or Household management, but changing a heading is not always possible or advisable. There may be too many cards to change or, as in the case of **Home economics,** the term is still being used and newer usage may not have stabilized.

A general rule is to use a popular or common, rather than a scientific or technical, name where there is a choice. Subject headings are chosen to fit the needs of the people who are likely to use the catalog. A reader in a small public library will look under **Birds,** not Ornithology, or **Cancer,** not Carcinoma. In a scientific library Ornithology and Carcinoma might be more appropriate. After deciding on the common name as entry word, the cataloger should make a reference from the scientific name to the form used. Such references will be discussed later. A term in common usage and expressed in the language of the user will be understood by that person and will pass the test of comprehensibility.

A decision must be made whether the form of the heading is to be in a singular or plural form. Plural is the most prevalent but in practice both are used. Abstract ideas are usually stated in the singular. A concept or action is singular (**Theater**) whereas objects and things are plural (**Theaters**). The names of fruit trees are stated in the singular so that they can represent either the fruit or the tree. In this case, singular is more inclusive than the plural. In other cases, plural will have the broader coverage (**Art; Arts**).

Some descriptive phrases also carry different connotations, e.g. Arab, Arabian, and Arabic. Their use in headings appears to be inconsistent, but they are used in the following ways: Arab relating to the people; Arabian referring to the geographical area; and Arabic for the language, script, or literature. These subject headings should be consistent, with distinction being made between ethnic, geographical, and linguistic terms.

Uniformity. Another factor to be considered is that of uniformity. One uniform term must be selected from several synonyms and this term must be applied consistently to all works on the topic. China, Chinaware, and Porcelain are all entered under **Porcelain.** This example also illustrates the fact that the subject heading must be inclusive and cover the topic. The heading chosen must be unambiguous. If several meanings attach to one word, that word must be qualified: **Masks (Facial); Masks (Plays); Masks (Sculpture).** When variant spellings are in use, one must be selected and uniformly applied: **Rhyme,** not Rime.

Form Headings. In addition to the subject headings that interpret the content of various materials, there are headings of another kind, usually known as form headings, or form subject headings, that have the same appearance as regular subject headings but refer to the literary or artistic form of a work and not to its subject matter, e.g. **Essays, Poetry, Fiction, Hymns, Songs,** etc. Literary form headings are used for collections rather than works of an individual. For example, the form heading **Essays** is used not for works of an individual author but for collections of essays by authors of different nationalities. If the collection includes essays only by American authors, then the more specific heading **American essays** would be used. While the use of form entries for works of individual authors might be helpful, the result in most libraries would not be worth the effort because such entries usually duplicate subject approaches already available in reference sources in the library. The proliferation of entries would be an extra cost and would increase the size of the catalog unnecessarily. Materials of this type are generally classified and arranged on the shelves according to their literary forms, and the reader often has access to the shelves or to the shelf list. Ordinarily individual works of literature are remembered in association with an author, and a reader consults the author or title entry in the catalog for such works.

For a work about the essay as a literary form, e.g. the appreciation of the essay or how to write it, the heading **Essay** represents a true subject and not a form heading. The distinction between form headings and subject headings can sometimes be made by using the singular form for the true subject heading and the plural for the form heading, e.g. **Short story; Short stories.** But the peculiarities of language do not always permit this. For example, the heading **English poetry** is used for a book about English poetry but in order to show that a book is a collection of poetry by several English authors the subdivision *Collections* must be added, i.e. **English poetry—Collections.** (Note that *Collected works* is used for non-artistic and non-literary headings).

In addition to the literary form headings there are some other useful form headings that are determined by the general format of the material and the purpose of the work, e.g. **Almanacs; Dictionaries; Encyclopedias; Filmstrips; Yearbooks.**

Classification and Subject Headings. The cataloger should now recognize a fundamental difference between classification and subject headings for the dictionary catalog. In a system of classification, which determines the arrangement of works on the shelves and groups together materials on one subject, an item can obviously stand in only one place. But in the catalog, cards representing the item can appear, if necessary, under more than one subject. The cataloger does not have to decide on one subject to the exclusion of all others, but can make the item useful with cards for as many different points of view as there are distinct subjects in the item (usually, however, not more than three).

Theoretically, there is no limit to the number of subject cards that could be made for one item, but practically such a policy not only would be expensive but also inefficient for the user of the catalog. For many works, one subject heading will represent the contents accurately. A book such as *Guide to the Trees* is fully and specifically covered by the subject heading **Trees.** Frequently two are necessary as in the title *Field Book of American Trees and Shrubs* to which one would assign both **Trees** and **Shrubs.** Occasionally three are required to do justice to the work. More than three should be considered very carefully. The need for more than three may be due to the cataloger's inability to identify precisely the single heading that would cover all the topics in the work.

The practice may be stated as follows: As many as three specific subject headings in a given area may be assigned, but if a work treats of more than three, then the next larger inclusive heading is adopted and the specific headings are omitted. A work about lemons and limes would be entered under **Lemon** and **Lime.** If the work also included material on oranges, a third card with the heading **Orange** would be made for the catalog. But if the work discusses grapefruit and citron as well, the only subject heading assigned would be **Citrus fruit.**

Do not assign both a general heading and one of its specific aspects to the same work. In the example cited above, the material may have discussed the orange in more detail than the other fruits, but **Citrus fruit** and **Orange** would not be assigned simultaneously.

The following statistics give a practical demonstration of the proportion of books requiring more than one subject entry. Minnie Sears in one of her early editions reported on books cataloged for a high school library, the books having the same characteristics as those in the collections of small public libraries. Of 1241 titles belonging in the first seven classes of the Dewey Decimal Classification, 788, or 63 per cent, required only one subject heading; 358, or 29 per cent, required two subjects; 76, or 6 per cent, received three subjects, and the remaining 2 per cent had received four or five headings. This study showed that the average number of subject cards for each title was 1.46. An interesting comparison may be made with a similar study made by the Technical Processes Research Office at the Library of Congress which revealed that 1.2 subject headings are assigned to each title cataloged.

The cataloger is now aware of another difference between classification and subject cataloging, one particularly significant for small libraries where the classification is by broader subjects and so is not as closely subdivided as the subject entries for the catalog. Materials on birds, water birds, and all the special kinds of water birds are classed together in **598.2.** Another example is found in the treatment of fruit. A book on fruits in general, one on citrus fruits, and one on oranges will all three be classified in one number in a library, while in the catalog each book will have its own specific subject heading: **Fruit; Citrus fruit; Orange.**

It is well to remember this essential difference in the two processes; otherwise, the rule for classifying by broad subject in a small library (large libraries are not considered here) may cause confusion when the librarian assigns subject headings which must be specific in order to achieve maximum usefulness.

The cataloger has learned that subject headings are used for materials that have definite, definable subjects. However, there are a few works in which the subject is so indefinite that it is better not to assign a heading. If a cataloger cannot find a definite subject, the reader may not find the item under a make-shift or general heading. Do not use vague terms. They are a disservice to the reader. A book titled *Appreciation* received the heading **Human behavior** from one cataloger while another assigned the word **Happiness.** In reality neither was correct. The book was a personal account of one of the sources of the author's pleasure in life.

Now that certain principles of subject headings have been considered, the cataloger should understand the structure of subject headings.

Grammar of Subject Headings. (1) *Single Noun.* The simplest form of subject heading consists of a single noun and is the ideal type when the language supplies it. Such terms are not only the simplest in form but often the easiest to comprehend. Most of the large fields of knowledge can be expressed by single words (**Art; Agriculture; Education; Religion;** etc.) as can many specific objects (**Apple; Chairs; Pottery; Trees; Violin;** etc.). But many words have synonyms from which a choice has to be made, and conversely a word may have two or more quite different meanings; for others there is a choice in spelling; another consideration is the use of the singular or plural form. For example, in the case of **Pottery,** other words that might be used are: Crockery; Earthenware; Faience; Fayency; Stoneware. In the Sears List, the term chosen is **Pottery** and references are made from the other terms. On the other hand, the word Date may mean a fruit, an historical period, or a social engagement, Files may refer to an arrangement of material or a tool; Forging may mean counterfeiting or metalwork; Bridge may refer among other things to a game or an engineering structure. In the latter case, using the plural removes the possibility of the game but the singular form has to be qualified: **Bridge (Game).** Also the plural **Bridges (Dentistry)** must be distinguished from the engineering structure.

Whenever identical words with different meanings are used in the catalog one of them must be qualified, that is, defined more specifically. In the example of the book on lemons and limes, neither heading is listed in Sears but may be added when needed, as instructed under both **Fruit** or **Citrus fruit.** However, in adding Lime to the List the cataloger finds **Lime** used in relation to **Cement.** The plural Limes should not be used because Sears states that the name of all fruit should be in the singular form. The cataloger would therefore add a qualifier to Lime, i.e. **Lime (Fruit).** With **Seals (Animals)** and **Seals (Numismatics)** already in the List, any subject that must be added to the List but uses the same word must be defined, e.g. **Seals (Christmas, etc.)** or **Seals (Law).**

Whether to use the singular or the plural or both sometimes depends on the peculiarities of the language since the two forms may express quite different concepts. In many cases, the singular connotes the general, and the plural the specific aspects. Or stated another way, the singular expresses abstract ideas and the plural refers to things. Thus, **Theater** means the art while **Theaters** refers to the buildings. (According to the latest Library of Congress policy the singular form will be used for art headings, e.g. **Painting** will be used for both the art and the object.) The same parallel exists in the terms, **Essay** and **Essays, Short story** and **Short stories.** In all these cases, both forms are necessary, but in general if only one form is required, the plural has been adopted. However, the singular form has been chosen for the names of most fruits and nuts so that the more general term (**Apple; Pecan;** etc.) can be used to include works that consider the fruit or the tree or both.

(2) *Compound Headings.* Using two nouns joined by "and" usually groups together under one heading closely related material which cannot be separated easily in concept and which is usually treated together in books (**Boats and boating; Cities and towns; Publishers and publishing**), or two different subjects that are treated in their relation to each other (**Aeronautics and civilization; Religion and science; Television and children**), or two subjects that are opposites but are usually discussed together (**Belief and doubt; Good and evil; Joy and sorrow**).

The problem in forming such headings is word order. There is no rule to cover all situations although catalogers have been prone to follow the alphabetic when there is no common usage. Whichever order is chosen, reference must be made from the opposite order.

(3) *Adjective with Noun.* Often a specific concept is best expressed by qualifying the noun with an adjective (**American literature; Electric engineering; Tropical fish**). Sometimes the expression is inverted (**Flies, Artificial; Philosophy, Modern**). The reasons for inversion are twofold: 1) an assumption is made that the reader will think first of the noun; or, 2) the noun is placed first in order to keep all aspects of a broad subject together when that result is deemed desirable. Inversion can be made when the first element qualifies the second and the second is an independent unit.

Art, Abstract	**Education, Elementary**	**Insurance, Accident**
Art, American	**Education, Higher**	**Insurance, Fire**
Art, Decorative	**Education, Secondary**	**Insurance, Health**

In formulating this kind of heading it is difficult to decide whether to use the normal order followed in speaking and writing or the inverted order; some users of the catalog will think of it one way, others in the opposite. A reference is usually required from the order not chosen for the subject heading. The best principle is to stress the key word and to avoid scattering material on the same subject throughout the alphabet. It should be noted that some adjective noun phrases could never be inverted because the noun has no significance without the adjective, e.g. **International relations.**

(4) *Phrase Headings.* Some concepts which involve two areas of knowledge can be expressed only by more or less complex phrases. These are the least satisfactory headings as they offer the greatest variation in wording, are often the longest, and may not be thought of readily by either the maker or the user of the catalog—but the English language seems to offer no more compact terminology. Examples are: **Freedom of information; Geographical distribution of animals and plants; Information storage and retrieval systems.** Sometimes the phrase is inverted to place the important word first, or to facilitate the filing of related subjects together, although this results in an awkward appearance: **Cities and towns, Ruined, extinct, etc.**

Subdivisions. There are other means by which the scope of the List can be enlarged far beyond the actual headings printed. This is through the use of subdivisions of headings. The principle of specific entry can be achieved in some cases only by subdividing a general subject by words or phrases which indicate special aspects.

Birds	**Music**	**Water**
Birds—Eggs and nests	**Music—Acoustics and**	**Water—Analysis**
Birds—Migration	**physics**	**Water—Pollution**
Birds—Protection	**Music—Theory**	**Water—Purification**

In each of the specific fields above, the subdivisions are characteristic of it and those used under one are not applicable to the other two listed here. However, the subdivision *Analysis* would be applicable to a number of other topics besides **Water;** such as **Air; Blood; Food;** etc. Some terms or phrases used as subdivisions are applicable to so many different topics that the subdivisions are not printed under all possible headings. Some are referred to in their alphabetic places with directions for their use. They vary in kind and in value to an individual library.

(1) *Subdivisions by Physical Form.* Some materials present a subject not in expository or narrative form but as lists, outlines, or tables; or, graphically as maps,

pictures, or filmstrips. The work may be a directory of chemists, a bibliography of children's literature, a dictionary of psychology, a collection of geological maps, a Bible picture book. In such cases, it is important to show the user of the catalog that they are not works *about* chemists, or children's literature, or psychology, or geology, or the Bible, respectively. If the reader wants a bibliography or dictionary or maps or pictures, etc., it is equally important for him to be able to locate this directly without having to read through all the cards under the main heading. Standard terms known as "form divisions" are the most common subdivisions and may be used whenever appropriate. Since they show what the material *is*, rather than what it is *about*, they are as necessary for a small library as for a large one. Some examples of form divisions are:

Bibliography	*Gazeteers*	*Portraits*
Catalogs	*Indexes*	*Registers*
Dictionaries	*Maps*	*Statistics*
Directories	*Pictorial works*	*Terminology*

Some of these terms are used alone as actual subject headings, but as subdivisions they are usually called form headings. In either case, each of these terms is listed in its alphabetic place in the List with directions for use; for example (entry shortened):

Bibliography

See also **Archives** . . . also names of persons, places and subjects with the subdivision *Bibliography*, e.g. **Shakespeare, William—Bibliography; U.S. —Bibliography; Agriculture—Bibliography;** etc.

Comparable statements are included under each of the other form headings. Applying these directions to the types of materials cited above, the headings would be:

Chemists—Directories   **Geology—Maps**
Children's literature—Bibliography   **Bible—Pictorial works**
Psychology—Dictionaries

None of these headings appears in this form in the List, unless it has been cited as an example. Therefore, the *See* or *See also* under the name of the form is to be interpreted as directions for use. Only when a heading has been established and added can the words *See* or *See also* be interpreted literally.

(2) *Subdivisions That Show Noncomprehensive Treatment.* Some works though literary in composition and general in subject are not comprehensive in scope. Random essays on a topic, if they do not present a connected and extensive review; yearbooks on a subject; or periodicals in a particular field are representative of this type of treatment. The standard terms for such noncomprehensive material, which may be used as subdivisions of general subject headings, are:

Addresses and essays	*Societies*
Laboratory guides	*Yearbooks*
Periodicals	

By following directions under these terms, subject headings such as those listed below could be formulated:

Architecture—Addresses and essays
Chemistry—Laboratory guides
Engineering—Periodicals
Commerce—Yearbooks

This kind of subdivision is particularly valuable under headings for the large fields of knowledge which are represented by many cards in the catalog. The cataloger must be guided by the character of the content, not by the title. Many works whose titles begin with such expressions as "Outlines of," "Handbook of," "Manual of" are in fact comprehensive works. For example, Wells' *Outline of History*, Locke's *Essay Concerning Human Understanding*, and Rose's *Handbook of Latin Literature* are comprehensive, lengthy treatises and to use the form divisions that the titles suggest would be inaccurate and ridiculous! Other so-titled "Outlines" or "Manuals" or "Handbooks" may prove to be bibliographies, dictionaries, or statistics of the subject.

(3) *Subdivisions That Show Special Aspects.* A general subject may be presented from a particular point of view. The work may be a history of the subject, the most common of the special aspects; or it may deal with the philosophy of the subject, research in the field, the laws about it, or how to study and teach it. These concepts applied to general subjects are expressed by such headings as:

Education—History **Radio—Law and legislation**
Religion—Philosophy **Mathematics—Study and teaching**
Aeronautics—Research

(4) *Subdivisions That Show Chronology.* In any catolog, large or small, there will be many works on American history. If they are all entered under the general heading, the library patron must look through many cards to find a specific era. However, with chronological subdivisions corresponding to generally accepted periods of a country's history or to the spans of time most frequently treated in materials, a search can be narrowed to **U.S.—History—1945-1953,** etc. If a chronological era has been given a specific name, this is included in the heading with dates, e.g., **U.S.—History—Revolution, 1775-1783.** The current trend is to use dates in preference to names. This facilitates filing both in the manual and machine modes.

The List includes period subdivisions only for those countries for which a library is apt to acquire so many works about their history (United States, Great Britain, France, Germany, Italy and a few others) that it is necessary to separate them into groups according to the period treated. Although some countries have a longer history than any of these, period subdivisions of history are not needed because the library acquires so little material about them. Regardless of the period treated all the material would be assigned the general heading, e.g. **India—History.**

Some of the subject and form subdivisions that are applicable to a considerable number of subjects are listed in their alphabetic places in the List and are also gathered together in one list on p xl-xli. There the cataloger can see readily what possibilities of subdivision are available. History subdivisions, however, are different for each country and so cannot be listed in one place. (The cataloger may wish to consult *LC Period Subdivisions Under Names of Places,* 2d. ed. 1975).

Geographic Names. Many works limit the discussion of an otherwise general subject to a specific country, state, city, or other region. This is such a common method of treatment that the List has provided directions for many subjects that may be so treated. Other subjects not so identified can be subdivided by the cataloger if this is needed or is desirable.

(1) *Subject Subdivided by Place.* Various subject headings, especially in the fields of science, technology, and economics are followed by a parenthetic statement giving permission to subdivide the heading geographically, such as: "**Agriculture (May subdiv. geog.).**" In application this means that if the work in hand deals with agriculture in general, only the heading **Agriculture** is used; but if it deals with agriculture in Iowa or in France, for example, then the cataloger may assign the heading **Agriculture—Iowa** or **Agriculture—France.**

The unit may be the name of a country, state, city, or other political or geographic area, depending on the nature of the subject and its treatment in the work. There are, however, some topics which would not apply to cities, in which case the note will read: "(May subdiv. geog. country or state)."

If the subject is in the field of art or music, then the wording varies slightly since we think of Spanish art, for example (rather than art in Spain), or German music (rather than music in Germany). The List reads "**Art** (May subdiv. geog. adjective form, e.g. **Art, French**)" and "**Music** (May subdiv. geog. adjective form, e.g. **Music, American**)." From these directions the work on Spanish art would be assigned the heading **Art, Spanish** and that on German music, **Music, German.**

Observe that the parenthetic note is permissive not mandatory. If the library has only a few works on a subject for which geographic treatment is suggested, perhaps it would be easier for the user of the catalog to find these under the main heading without geographic subdivision. Some small libraries limit the use of geographic subdivision to countries other than the United States and to nationalities other than American since most of their material, general or special, will be concerned with the United States. The Sears List historically has never distinguished between French art or Art in France (which is not necessarily French). Should a library have sufficient material to warrant such a distinction, **Art—France** could be established in addition to **Art, French** which is suggested. One of the fundamentals of cataloging is to use one's judgment based on the materials on hand and the purpose and needs of the library.

The use of direct and indirect subdivisions must also be considered. The Sears List prefers the direct place subdivision as the most useful to the reader. In the direct form the name of the place discussed in the work is used directly as the subdivision, e.g. **Theater—Paris** or **Agriculture—Iowa.** The indirect form of place subdivision interposes the name of the country (the larger geographic area) between the subject and the smaller area that may be mentiond in the work, e.g. Theater—France—Paris and Agriculture—U.S.—Iowa. In the Sears List United States is abbreviated, but in the Library of Congress List it is no longer used in the abbreviated form.

(2) *Names of Places Subdivided by Subject.* A different procedure is followed for most topics in the fields of history, geography, politics and social sciences, which are treated from a regional point of view. In works discussing the history of California, a census of Peru, the government of Italy, the boundaries of Bolivia, the population of Paris, or the climate of Alaska, the area treated is the unique factor and its name is the most specific heading for the work, with the particular subject as a subdivision. Directions for formulating the headings are given under the general subjects in the same way that subject subdivisions are indicated, for example:

Census
    See also names of countries, cities, etc. with the subdivision *Census*, e.g. **U.S.
    —Census;** etc.

The *See also* is to be interpreted as a direction for formulating a heading for the specific area needed and when placed in the card catalog is a guide to the reader. Similar directions appear under **Boundaries; Climate; Population;** etc., which, applied to the topics cited above, would result in the headings:

California—History	**Bolivia—Boundaries**
Peru—Census	**Paris—Population**
Italy—Politics and government	**Alaska—Climate**

The name of any country, state, city, or other area could have been used if needed. However, some topics are applicable to countries only (e.g. *Commercial policy; Diplomatic and consular service*); others are used only under names of cities (e.g. *Harbor; Streets; Suburbs and environs*). The subdivision *Description and travel* is used for countries, states, and other large areas but is modified to the single word *Description* when applied to cities; therefore, **New Orleans—Description**, but **Louisiana —Description and travel.**

Headings that represent types of instiutions, such as hospitals, libraries and schools, are used as subdivisions under names of cities but if the discussion covers a larger area, then the order is reversed, for example:

> **Chicago—Churches** but **Churches—U.S.**
> **Cleveland—Hospitals** but **Hospitals—Ohio**
> **Baltimore—Libraries** but **Libraries—Maryland**

In such cases, the general heading will limit the subdivision to country and state while the *See also* directions will indicate its use for cities:

> **Hospitals** (May subdiv. geog. country or state)
> *See also* . . . names of cities with the subdivision *Hospitals*, e.g. **Chicago— Hospitals; etc.**

In addition, a list of subject subdivisions which may be used under the name of any city is given in the List under **Chicago;** those that may be used under the name of any state are listed under **Ohio;** while under the **United States** are those that may be used under the name of any country or region, except the subdivisions of history. Since each country's history is unique, its periods of history are individual.

Local materials are an exception to these rules if the library wishes to keep all of the home town or area materials together. Then (1) and (2) above can be ignored and all materials listed under the name of the locality with all aspects as subdivisions.

There are no definite rules on subdividing by place or by subject. In general, subject headings in the field of science, technology, economics, education, and the arts are subdivided by place, while history, geography, politics, and the social sciences are made subdivisions under place. But there are exceptions. That aspect of the subject that is most important or has the primary interest is the criterion for decision. When one reads about social life and customs, one asks where the social life exists, e.g. **U.S. —Social life and customs.** However, one aspect of social life is the **Family.** This is the subject of importance and one asks secondarily where the family is located. (Note that **Family** is not subdivided by place in Sears as it is in the Library of Congress, but if a library has much material on the subject it might be advisable, and is permissible, to do so).

In general, the cataloger would enter under place and subdivide by subject those topics whose predominant interest is focused on area or people as history, geography, or government. One would enter under subject and subdivide by place those topics that are primarily of interest for the subject matter regardless of place. In the field of the social sciences the decision must be made in each instance on the element of predominance because no general rule applies.

Some headings in the subject areas of biography, language, and literature require subdivisions relevant to their areas, but others do not. Since knowing when not to subdivide is as important as when to use subdivision, the editor has treated these areas in some detail.

Biography. Works in the field of biography are of two different categories: those in which biography as a form of writing is discussed, a relatively small class covered adequately by the subject heading **Biography (as a literary form);** and lives of persons, a very large class which must be considered in two groups—individual biography and collective biography.

(1) *Individual Biography.* Usually the only subject heading needed for the life of an individual is the name of the person, established in the same way as an author entry. If the work is an autobiography, some catalogers do not make a subject card for it since the author and the subject are the same. However, since readers have been trained to look under subject entries it seems reasonable to make both an author and a subject card, especially if there are many other entries as author or if there are subject entries by other authors, or if the library has a divided catalog.

Occasionally a biography will include so much material about the field in which the individual was working that a second subject heading is required in addition to the personal name. A life of Mary Baker Eddy, for example, may include a valuable account of the development of Christian Science that would require the subject heading, **Christian Science—History.** It must be emphasized that such second subject headings should be used only when there is a substantial amount of material included and when the book tells more about a person's work than his personal life. It is not used just because the biographee was prominent in the field.

There are a few individuals about whom there is a large amount of material that is other than biographical, such as works about their writings or other activities. In such cases, subdivisions are added to the individual's name to separate various aspects treated, among which is *Biography.* The two outstanding individuals are Jesus Christ and William Shakespeare. The List includes these names with subdivisions appropriate to material written about them. The subdivisions listed under Shakespeare may be used, if needed, under the names of other authors about whom there is a large amount of varied literature, notably Dante and Goethe. Subdivisions listed under **Presidents—U.S.** are to be used where appropriate under the name of any president. It must be noted that this represents the exceptional, not the usual treatment. For most individual biographies only the name is needed. That is, do not use the subdivision *Biography.*

(2) *Collective Biography.* This term refers usually to works containing more than three biographies, for if there are no more than three, each subject will be given a heading, consisting of the person's name, as in individual biography. (Some catalogers will treat even larger collections as a group of individual biographies). There are several varieties of collective biography, each requiring a separate kind of treatment.

General. Collections of biographies not limited to any area or to any class of people are assigned the heading **Biography.** Sometimes the work includes many individuals, such as *International Who's Who;* sometimes a small group, such as *Ten Biographies of Famous Men and Women.*

Local Biography. Very common are the biographies devoted to persons of a particular area, such as *Who's Who in Asia, Who's Who in Latin America, Dictionary of American Biography, Eminent Californians, Leaders in London;* or to ethnic groups, such as *Prominent Jews.* In such works the subject heading is the name of the area or ethnic group with the subdivision *Biography:*

Asia—Biography	**California—Biography**
Latin America—Biography	**London—Biography**
U.S.—Biography	**Jews—Biography**

If there are many cards under any such heading, the literary works (that is, those designed for continuous reading) may be separated from the reference works which list a large number of names in alphabetic order, by adding to the heading for the latter, the subdivision *Dictionaries*. The heading for such a work as *Who's Who in America* may be, therefore, **U.S.—Biography—Dictionaries.**

Classes of Persons. Collective biographies that are devoted to lives of persons of a particular occupation or profession are entered under the term applied to its members, such as **Artists; Authors; Engineers; Librarians; Musicians; Poets; Radiologists, Scientists;** etc., with the subdivision *Biography*.

In a field where there is no adequate term to express its members, or when the name of the class or group refers to the subject in general not to individuals, the heading used for the specific field is subdivided by the term *Biography*:

Catholic Church—Biography   **U.S.—History—Civil War, 1861-1865—**
Religions—Biography   **Biography**
                                           Women—Biography

N.B. The headings for areas, classes and groups are used for collective biographies only and not for the life of an individual American, artist, author, Jew, woman, etc. However, reference to names of individuals should be made under the class names, for example: "Artists. See also names of individual artists."

Language and Literature. These fields are closely related, but they differ considerably in the amount of material published and in their treatment in the subject catalog. Any general library has proportionately a large number of works on literature, often its largest field of interest, and a comparatively small number of works on language. In both areas, but more particularly in language, the major interest is not in the general treatment but in the national aspect, that is, French language or English literature, German grammar or Italian drama, Spanish dictionaries or Hebrew poetry, etc.

Language. The subject heading for a general work about a specific language is the direct phrase: **English language; French language; German language.** If the work deals with a particular aspect or form of that language, terms representing them are used as subdivisions of the name of the language. Examples are:

English language—Etymology   **German language—Grammar**
French language—Dictionaries   **Spanish language—Terms and phrases**

Some of the general form and subject subdivisions will be needed also under names of languages, for example, **Italian language—History.**

Names of some languages are included in this List (and others are to be added as needed) but no subdivisions are listed except under **English language.** This serves as a guide or "key" to the subdivisions that may be used under the name of any language.

Literature. The field of literature includes two classes of material which must be distinguished carefully: (1) works about literature, a relatively small group; (2) examples of literature, that is *belles-lettres,* or the literature itself, a very large group. In the first we are dealing with actual subjects; in the second with literary forms, not subjects.

(1) *Works about Literature.* The subject headings for works about the various literary forms are their specific names, e.g. **Drama; Essay; Fiction; Poetry.** Works about the major literary forms of national literatures are entered also under the direct phrase, not, as in language, as subdivisions; e.g. **Irish drama; Italian poetry; Russian**

fiction. Specific aspects are expressed by subdivisions, as for other subjects; e.g. **Drama —Technique; English literature—Dictionaries; Poetry—Indexes; German literature— History and criticism.** It should be noted that the subdivision *History and criticism* is always used in its entirety and corresponds to the subdivision *History* used with other than literature, film, and music subjects.

Names of some national literatures are included in the List (and others are to be added as needed) but the full list of subdivisions which may be used under them are listed only under **English literature** which thus serves as the "key" to subdivisions that may be used under the name of any national literature. The major literary forms may be used for any national literature by substituting its name for the word "English."

(2) *Examples of Literature, i.e. Belles-lettres.* This large class of material must be separated into two categories whose treatment is entirely different.

Individual Authors. In general, the literary works of individual authors receive no subject entry. Literature is known by author and title and readers usually want a specific novel, or a certain play, or poetry by a specific author—material which can be located in the catalog by author and title entries.

Collections of Several Authors. Because collections containing works of several authors are entered in the catalog under the name of the compiler editor, or title, a device has been adopted to locate such works in the subject catalog by giving them a heading representing the form of literature in the collection. Since such headings are used also for actual subjects, distinction must be made between the headings for works *describing* a particular literary form and *examples* of it. The singular form is used as an actual subject heading. If it has an acceptable plural, this can be used to represent collections, but if there is no true plural then the subdivision *Collections* must be added to the name of the literary form:

Subject Heading	Form Heading for Collections
Essay	**Essays; American essays; etc.**
Parody	**Parodies**
Short story	**Short stories**
Drama	**Drama—Collections**
French drama	**French drama—Collections**
Fiction	**Fiction—Collections**
Russian fiction	**Russian fiction—Collections**
Literature	**Literature—Collections**
German literature	**German literature—Collections**
Poetry	**Poetry—Collections**
Japanese poetry	**Japanese poetry—Collections**

Minor literary forms, such as parodies, satire, and short stories, are not listed under the national adjective. If national treatment is needed, the adjective is added after the name of the form, e.g. **Satire, English.** These headings are used not only for collections by several authors but also for works of individual authors and for works about such forms. This departure in treatment from that given to the major literary forms is due to the small number of books involved. If the number of books for any of them is large the heading may be subdivided to separate the works about them from the literature itself, e.g. **Satire, English—History and criticism.**

N.B. Catalogers frequently give novels, poems and plays based on historical events or lives of famous persons a subject entry. Such headings must be distinguished from the headings which are assigned to factual accounts by adding the subdivision *Drama; Fiction;* or *Poetry,* as the case may be:

> **Slavery in the U.S.—Drama**
> **Lincoln, Abraham—Fiction**
> **Bunker Hill, Battle of, 1775—Poetry**

Nonbook materials. The assignment of subject headings for audio-visual and special instructional materials should follow the same principles that are applied to books. The heading most specifically describing the contents of the material should be used, and the same headings should be applied to book and nonbook materials alike. This is especially important if the catalog integrates all media. One integrated catalog would seem to be preferable because this would bring all materials on one subject together regardless of format. For this edition of the List almost all of the subjects and subdivisions which include the word book have been changed to make them applicable to all materials. Two exceptions are *Handbooks, manuals, etc.* and *Yearbooks.*

Because nonbook materials often concentrate on very small aspects of larger subjects, the cataloger may not find in the List the specific heading that should be used. In such instances the cataloger should be generous in adding new subjects (see p xxxii-xxxiii). It may also be necessary to use a form heading for the format of the material, as well as a subject heading for the content. **Short films,** for example, could be created as a subject if needed to describe a specific type of film.

Subject headings for nonbook materials may need special form subdivisions to describe physical format. If they are used they should be based on the general material designations listed in the *Anglo-American Cataloging Rules,* 2d edition. These designations may also be found in: *Anglo-American Cataloging Rules, Chapter 12, revised: Audiovisual Media and Special Instructional Materials* (A.L.A. 1975). The use of these subdivisions is optional and is dependent on the size and the physical organization of the library's collection. For small collections, the general material designation, placed at the end of the title, may be sufficient to indicate the format of the material. In an omnimedia catalog form subdivisions for nonbook materials may be necessary. If separate catalogs are maintained this type of subdivision may be superfluous. In some libraries the specific subject heading with the general subdivision *Audio-visual aids* may be all that is required.

A multi-item set or a multi-subject item may need subject headings for each part in addition to subjects for the work as a whole. For example, a filmstrip set titled *Africa* may consist of eight filmstrips, each of which illustrates a different country. In this case **Africa** would be used as the heading for the set as a whole, but subject headings should also be made for each of the eight countries.

Terminology. The subject headings for the general fields of knowledge and for concrete objects are simple to comprehend, but terms for abstract ideas may offer some difficulty. By looking through the *See also* references under a given heading, or noting the *See* references to it, a cataloger may often find how the term is used.

Sometimes two or more terms may seem to cover the same subject, unless the exact meaning and limitations of each is appreciated. Some headings in the List are accompanied by a scope note explaining their limitations as an aid to differentiating between overlapping subjects. For example, the headings **Alcoholism; Liquor problem; Liquor industry; Prohibition; Temperance** overlap to a certain degree, but because of doubt in their distinctions one should not use all of them for any one book. By means of the scope notes included with these terms, it is understood that **Alcoholism** is used for medical works and works on drunkenness; **Liquor problem** includes works of an administrative or local character; **Liquor industry** is used for works on the liquor industry and trade; **Prohibition** for works dealing with the legal prohibition of liquor traffic and liquor manufacture; and **Temperance** is used for general works on the temperance question and the temperance movement.

A cataloger must consult the library's own catalog in order to see how a subject heading has been used. Printed catalogs such as the *Cumulative Book Index* and the "Standard Catalog Series" are also of value in order to see what kind of works are included under a given subject. Other cataloging aids are the *Weekly Record* and its monthly and annual cumulations the *American Book Publishing Record, Subject Guide to Books in Print,* and the *Library of Congress Catalogs: Subject Catalog.* Aid in interpreting the scope and meaning of a subject heading may be found by looking up its classification number or numbers in the *Dewey Decimal Classification.* There the topic can be studied in its relation to other topics, a development usually impossible to see directly in an alphabetic arrangement.

Each cataloger will have individual problems in interpretation of subjects. Whenever a decision has been made on the scope of a term where there has been doubt, a definition or explanation should be recorded for future use. Such notes are a necessity for catalogers and they may be helpful also to users of the catalog. Whenever it is felt that such an explanation would be of general value, it may be typed on a card and filed in the catalog preceding the entries under the subject heading. Of course, the wording may have to be adapted slightly from that in the List which is addressed to catalogers.

References. After an item has been assigned a subject heading, attention must be directed to insuring that the reader who is searching for this material will not fail to find it because of insufficient references to the proper heading. The following is a summary of the types, methods of formulation, and use of references.

(1) *Specific "See" References.* These refer the reader from terms or phrases not used as subject headings to terms or phrases that are used. They are, therefore, absolutely essential to the success of the catalog. The reader must be directed from variant spellings and terminology to the one word or phrase that has been selected to represent the subject. While a subject heading may be used on as many cards as the library has works on the subject, the *See* reference is made on one card only. For example, the first time the heading **Agriculture** is used, the cataloger (following the suggestion in the *x* paragraph under **Agriculture** in the List) will make a card for the catalog that reads: "Farming. See Agriculture." This will not be made again, no matter how many times the heading **Agriculture** is used, and no work will ever be assigned the word Farming as a heading.

See references are made:

(1) from synonyms or from terms so nearly synonymous that they would cover the same kind of material

(2) from the second part of a compound heading, e.g. **Prejudices and antipathies** requires a reference from Antipathies

(3) from the second part of an inverted heading, e.g. **Chemistry, Technical** requires a reference from Technical chemistry

(4) sometimes from an inverted heading to normal order, e.g. **Adult education** requires a reference from Education, Adult. (Note the number of used headings that begin with the word Education)

(5) from variant spellings to the spelling used, e.g. **Rhyme** requires a reference from Rime

(6) from opposites when they are included without being specifically mentioned, e.g. **Temperance** requires a reference from Intemperance

(7) from the singular to the plural when the two forms would not file together in the catalog, e.g. **Mice** requires a reference from Mouse; **Cats** requires a reference from Cat. (Note the long list of headings between the singular and the plural of each of these two words)

It is not always necessary to make every *See* reference indicated in the List; for example, under the heading **Prisons,** a *See* reference from Dungeons is indicated but this should not be made unless the works listed under **Prisons** contain something about ancient prisons, that is, Dungeons. On the other hand, the cataloger may need to make additions to the *See* references in order to include local terminology.

(2) *Specific "See also" References.* The *See* references are concerned mainly with terminology, guiding the reader from words he may think of to those actually used for subject headings. But the *See also* references are concerned entirely with guiding the reader from headings where he has found information to other headings which list materials on related or more specific aspects of the subject. Consequently such references cannot be made without knowing whether the library has material under the other subjects.

In general, *See also* references are made from the general subject to more specific parts of it, and not ordinarly from the specific to the general. For example, "Science. See also Mathematics," but not the other way around. Proceeding one step at a time to the next more specific topic would result in: "Mathematics. See also Arithmetic"; and "Arithmetic. See also Business arithmetic." *See also* references are also made between related subjects of more or less equal specificity, for example, "Drawing. See also Painting."

See also references are much more difficult than *See* references both to make and to understand, and their value is not so unquestioned. They have been included freely under headings (in the *xx* paragraph) in the List but only knowledge of the library's collection can determine whether any of these suggestions should be followed. For example, a work that discusses both inventions and patents will be entered in the catalog under **Inventions** and under **Patents.** The List suggests the reference, "Inventions. See also Patents," but it must not be made if the only material that is to be found in the catalog under **Patents** is this work which is already listed under **Inventions.** If there is a choice between two headings, the predominant one should be chosen.

(3) *General References.* In addition to specific references, there are general *See* and *See also* references which, instead of referring to many individual headings, serve as blanket references to all headings of a particular group. Some references are a combination of specific and general. It is the general references which give the cataloger directions for adding specific headings that have been omitted from the List, as explained previously. Their use and value in the public catalog are somewhat different. The most common types of general references are ones to:

(1) Common names of different species of a class, **e.g.**

Flowers

   See also **Annuals (Plants)** . . . also names of flowers, e.g. **Roses; etc.**

(2) Names of individual persons, e.g.

Artists

   See also **Architects** . . . also names of individual artists

(3) Names of particular institutions, buildings, societies, etc., e.g.

Abbeys
See also **Cathedrals** . . . also names of individual abbeys, e.g. **Westminster Abbey**; etc.

Labor unions
See also **Arbitration, Industrial** . . . also names of individual labor unions, e.g. **United Steelworkers of America**; etc.

(4) Names of particular geographic features, e.g.

Mountains
See also **Mountaineering** . . . also names of mountain ranges (e.g. **Rocky Mountains**; etc.); and names of mountains, e.g. **Elk Mountain, Wyo.**; etc.

(5) Geographic treatment of a general subject, e.g.

Population
See also **Birth control** . . . also names of countries, cities, etc. with the subdivision *Population*, e.g. **U.S.—Population; Chicago—Population**; etc.

(6) Form divisions, e.g.

Glossaries. *See* name of language or subject with the subdivision *Dictionaries*, e.g. **English language—Dictionaries; Chemistry—Dictionaries**; etc.

(7) National literatures, e.g.

Poetry
See also **Ballads** . . . also **American poetry; English poetry**; etc.

It is apparent that the general references in the List save an enormous amount of space both in the List and the library catalog. If all the headings for which directions are given were formulated they would be innumerable. In an individual library relatively few of these headings are used so that it may be preferable to formulate specific references when specific headings are added, particularly if there are only a few in the class. That is, if the cataloger uses the headings **Azaleas; Parakeets; Pineapple** (none of which is in the printed List), these names would be added to the *See also* references under the respective groups represented. For example, assuming that the headings **Fruit; Berries;** and **Citrus fruit** had been used for materials in the library, the reference in the List and in the catalog would now read: "Fruit. See also Berries; Citrus fruit; Pineapple."

However, when there is a long list of specific headings, catalogers disagree on the policy of adding them to the reference. For example, the heading **Artists** in the List, reads: "*See also* . . . names of individual artists." Some catalogers, in preparing this reference for the catalog, would omit the phrase, "names of individual artists," and instead, add the names of all the artists that have been used as subject headings in the library's catalog; other catalogers expect the reader to recall the individual, and the reference is left as printed. Each library must determine this on the basis of the number of specific references that would be needed. But under headings where the individual names may not be numerous or well-known, it is feasible for the cataloger and useful to the reader to list the names rather than to rely on the general reference. However, in the example in the preceding paragraph, the cataloger would be advised to make the reference as follows: "Fruit. See also Berries, Citrus fruit; also names of fruit, e.g., Pineapple, etc."

The cataloger should note that under a *See* reference there is never a subject entry for a work, while under *See also* references there are always entries. Reading the reference structure in the List always poses a problem for beginners as does the making of the references for the library catalog. Below is a heading from the List and its reading:

> **Birds** (May subdiv. geog.) **598.2**
>> Names of birds are not included in this list but are to be added as needed, in the plural form e.g. **Canaries; Robins;** etc.
>> *See also* classes of birds, e.g. **Birds of prey; Cage birds; Game and game birds; State birds; Water birds;** and names of specific birds, e.g. **Canaries; Robins;** etc.
>> *x* Bird; Ornithology
>> *xx* **Vertebrates; Zoology**

Note that the *See also* references read in direct order from top to bottom: **Birds.** *See also* **Birds of prey; Cage birds; Game and game birds;** . . . .The *See* references read in the reverse order, from bottom to top, that is, from the word opposite the *x* up to the heading: Bird. *See* **Birds.** Ornithology. *See* **Birds.** "*See also* from" references also read from the bottom to the top, that is, from the word opposite the *xx* up to the heading: **Vertebrates.** *See also* **Birds. Zoology.** *See also* **Birds.**

To maintain a subject authority file on cards rather than checking in the book as described on p xxxvi-xxxvii the cataloger would make cards and include on each card all the instructions and scope notes printed in the List.

The set of cards on the next page illustrates one type of spacing.

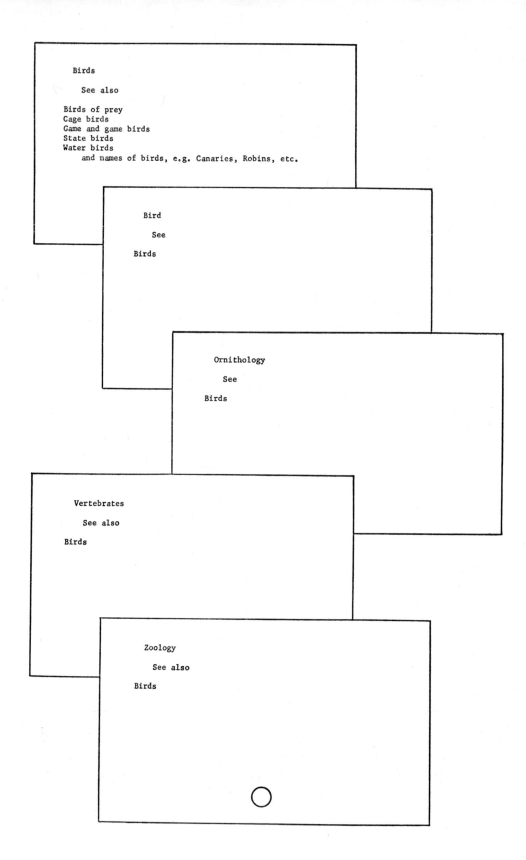

Birds

　　See also

Birds of prey
Cage birds
Game and game birds
State birds
Water birds
　　and names of birds, e.g. Canaries, Robins, etc.

Bird

　　See

Birds

Ornithology

　　See

Birds

Vertebrates

　　See also

Birds

Zoology

　　See also

Birds

The directions and scope notes printed in the List for the guidance of the cataloger should be modified for the card catalog if the cataloger feels that a note is needed for the patron. Following is an example of a rewording:

As it appears in the List for the cataloger:

> **Air lines**
> Use for materials dealing with systems of
> aerial transportation and with com-
> panies engaged in this business.
> Materials dealing with the routes
> along which the planes are flown
> are entered under **Airways**
> *See also* **Airways**
> *x* Airlines
> *xx* **Aeronautics, Commercial; Airways**

As it appears in the card catalog for the reader:

Air lines

    Here are listed materials dealing with the
systems of aerial transportation and with
companies engaged in this business.

    Materials on the routes along which the
planes are flown are entered under Airways.

New Terminology for Old Subjects. The English language is changing constantly so that from time to time new terms appear for subjects which are not new. Through the years many changes have had to be made: **Child welfare** was formerly *Children—Charities, protection, etc.;* **Radio advertising** started out as *Radio broadcasting—Business applications; House decoration* was in use before the present **Interior decoration;** and *Profession, Choice of* before **Vocational guidance.**

It is impossible for the subject headings to reflect all the newest language styles, particularly in fields whose terminology fluctuates frequently, for a term that is current today may soon be superseded by another, or a term considered passé may return to favor. But at least new terms can be represented in the catalog by *See* references to the heading used.

Of course, if a heading is found to be incorrect or is no longer in common usage, or suddenly assumes a pejorative or biased connotation, changes must be made. The adoption of a new term means changing not only all the old entries to the new form but also the various references to and from it. It is impossible to state at what stage in the development of the language such changes should be made. Each heading must be considered individually. If change is desirable but the number of cards to be changed is prohibitive, one can accomplish the change by *See also* reference cards. Using one of the aforementioned changes as an example, the cataloger would make the following cards substituting for (date) the calendar year in which the change is made:

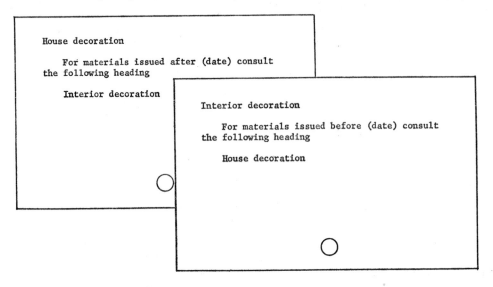

These reference cards could also assume the following format. A guide card that protrudes above the other cards in the tray is more readily seen by the user of the catalog.

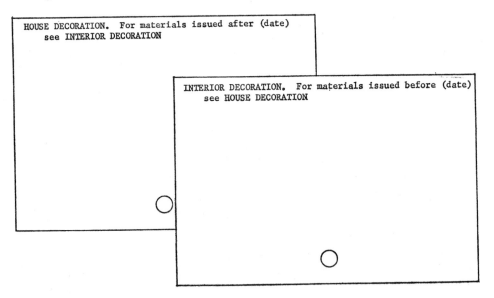

New Subjects. No printed list of subject headings can be entirely up to date. There are constantly new ideas, new inventions, or new countries being created. Headings for these new topics of current interest will have to be added by the cataloger as needed. They should be constructed in the same way as headings for related topics and as the cataloger has been shown in this text.

First aid is supplied by the periodical indexes, such as the *Readers' Guide to Periodical Literature, Applied Science & Technology Index,* etc., since their editors must assign subject headings to material as soon as it is published. As the new subject develops, some change in the heading may be made in succeeding issues of the index. By the time a book is written about a new subject, the terminology may have changed and become stabilized since the first periodical index article appeared. Therefore, the catalogs of new works such as *Booklist, Cumulative Book Index,* and *Book Review Digest* are valuable aids. The Library of Congress includes headings for new subjects in the quarterly supplements to its list of subject headings. The *Weekly Record* publishes Library of Congress cataloging information which is cumulated in monthly and annual issues of the *American Book Publishing Record.* Through the Cataloging in Publication program the Library of Congress cataloging information will usually appear on the verso of the title page in books of those publishers cooperating in the program.

It is not always possible to decide at once on the permanent form for a new subject heading, but the cataloger cannot always wait for the subject to develop before giving headings to new material. Tentative headings can be assigned, perhaps written in pencil on the cards, and used until the terminology becomes standardized. A list of these tentative headings should be kept (it will never be long) so that they can be reconsidered later and either adopted permanently or changed, as the case may be, and added to the List. One must be sure that the new term is not merely a new name or a colloquialism for a subject already in the catalog.

Recording Headings and References. The cataloger should keep a list of subject headings used and references made for them. This may be kept on cards and filed in the catalog department or a copy of the Sears List may be checked whenever a heading is used for the first time. Additions to the List should be written in and references should be recorded as needed. Detailed directions for checking the List and a Sample Page illustrating them will be found on p xxxvi-xxxvii.

Materials for Further Reference

Akers, Susan Grey
    Akers' Simple Library Cataloging. 6th ed. Completely rev. and rewritten by Arthur Curley and Jana Varlejs. Metuchen, N.J., Scarecrow Press, 1977. (Chapter 2)

Bakewell, K. G. B. A Manual of Cataloguing Practice. Oxford, Elmsford, N.Y., Pergamon, 1972. (Chapter 5)

Canadian Library Association. Committee on Canadian Subject Headings
    A List of Canadian Subject Headings. Ottawa, CLA, 1968. (A new edition is in preparation)

Coates, E. J. Subject Catalogues; Headings and Structure. London, Library Association, 1960.

Dewey, Harry
    An Introduction to Library Cataloging and Classification. 4th ed. rev. and enl. Madison, Wis., Capital Press [c1957] (Chapters 10-13 and 15)

Dunkin, Paul S.
    Cataloging USA. Chicago, ALA, 1969. (Chapter 5)

Eaton, Thelma
    Cataloging and Classification; an Introductory Manual. 4th ed. Ann Arbor, Mich., Edwards, 1967. (Chapters 5-6)

Foskett, A. C.
  The Subject Approach to Information. Hamden, Conn., Archon Books, 1969.
  (Chapters 3-4, 16-17)
  Chiefly a study on classification but the above chapters are pertinent

Frarey, Carlyle James
  Subject Headings. New Brunswick, N.J., Graduate School of Library Service,
    Rutgers University, 1960. (The State of the library art, v. 1, pt. 2)
    A review and evaluation of the literature on subject headings

Harris, Jessica L.
  Subject Analysis; Computer Implications of Rigorous Definition. Metuchen, N.J.,
    Scarecrow Press, 1970

Haykin, David Judson
  Subject Headings; a Practical Guide. Reprint of 1951 ed. Boston, Gregg, 1972.

HCL [Hennepin County Library] Cataloging Bulletin. Edina, Minn.

Library Literature; a Bimonthly Index to Books, Periodicals and Theses on Library
    Science and Librarianship, New York, The H. W. Wilson Co.
    Refers to many articles on subject headings

Mann, Margaret
  Introduction to Cataloging and the Classification of Books. 2d ed. Chicago, ALA,
    1943. (Chapters 9-10)

Pettee, Julia
  Subject Headings; the History and Theory of the Alphabetical Subject Approach
    to Books. New York, The H. W. Wilson Co., 1946 (Out-of-print)

Piercy, Esther J.
  Commonsense Cataloging; a Manual for the Organization of Books and Other
    Materials in School and Small Public Libraries. Rev. by Marian Sanner.
    New York, The H. W. Wilson Co., 1974. (Chapter 7)

Tauber, Maurice Falcolm
  Technical Services in Libraries: Acquisitions, Cataloging, Classification, Binding,
    Photographic Reproduction, and Circulation Operations. New York, Colum-
    bia University Press, 1954. (Chapter 10)

Wynar, Bohdan S.
  Introduction to Cataloging and Classification. 4th rev. ed. Littleton, Colo., Libraries
    Unlimited, 1972. (Chapters 13-15)

CHECKING AND ADDING HEADINGS

See Sample Page opposite

1. *Check the subject heading used.* When the subject heading **Birds** is used for the first time, a check mark is placed in front of it.

2. *Make and check "See" references to the heading.* The *x* terms under **Birds** are considered and the cataloger decides to make a reference from Bird and from Ornithology as suggested. Cards are made for the catalog reading: "Bird. See Birds" and "Ornithology. See Birds." The terms Bird and Ornithology are checked both in their alphabetic places in the List and in the *x* references under **Birds**.

3. *Make and check "See also" references to the heading.* The *xx* headings given under **Birds** are examined to see whether they have been used in the catalog. The heading **Vertebrates** has a check mark beside it showing that it has been used. The cataloger decides to place a reference card in the catalog reading: "Vertebrates. See also Birds." It is recorded in the List:

   under **Birds,** in the *xx* paragraph, **Vertebrates** is checked
   under **Vertebrates,** in the *See also* paragraph, **Birds** is checked

   For purposes of this explanation assumption is made that **Zoology** has not been used yet.

4. *Adding headings to the List.* The library acquires a book about ostriches. The term is not in the List but the directions given in the note under **Birds** tell the cataloger that the heading **Ostriches** may be added. It is written in the margin in its alphabetic place and checked. To the public catalog is added the reference card: "Birds. See also Ostriches." It is recorded in the List:

   under **Birds,** to the *See also* paragraph is added, **Ostriches,** and checked
   under **Ostriches,** is added, *xx* **Birds**, and checked

   The library acquires a book on birds of the Gaspé Peninsula. Following the permission given with the heading **Birds,** "(May subdiv. geog.)," the cataloger uses the heading, **Birds—Gaspé Peninsula,** writing it in the margin in its alphabetic place and checking it. Since the library has very little material about this region, it is decided to make a reference for the catalog reading, "Gaspé Peninsula—Birds. See Birds—Gaspé Peninsula." This reference is added also to the List and traced under the new heading by adding, *x* Gaspé Peninsula—Birds.

5. *Canceled subjects.* If all cards for a subject are withdrawn from the catalog, turn to the subject heading in the List, find what references have been made and remove the cards (if they are individual references) or cancel the heading (if other references are on the card). At the same time, erase or cross off the check marks in the List to show that the subject and its references are not now used.

*Abbreviated entries taken from various pages of the Sears List. A check (∨)
indicates that the heading or reference has been used in the library's catalog,
marginal notes show how subjects may be added when needed*

✓**Birds** (May subdiv. geog.) **598.2**

Names of birds are not included in this
list but are to be added as needed,
in the plural form, e.g. **Canaries;
Robins;** etc.

See also classes of birds, e.g. **Birds of
prey; Cage birds; Game and game
birds; State birds; Water birds;** and
names of specific birds, e.g. **Canaries; Robins;** etc. _____ → ✓Ostriches

x Bird; Ornithology

xx ✓**Vertebrates; Zoology**

Birds—Flight 598.2 _____ → ✓Birds–Gaspé Peninsula

Birds—Habits and behavior 598.2   x ✓Gaspé Peninsula–Birds

✓Gaspé Peninsula –Birds. See
Gasoline engines. *See* **Gas and oil engines**   Birds–Gaspé Peninsula

Gastronomy. *See* **Cookery; Dinners and
dining; Food; Menus**

Ornamental plants. *See* **Plants, Ornamental**

✓Ornithology. *See* **Birds**

Orphanages 362.7

See also **Child Welfare**

x Charitable institutions; Homes (Institutions)

xx **Charities; Child welfare; Children—
Institutional care; Institutional care;
Public welfare**

Osteopathy 615

See also **Massage**

xx **Massage; Medicine; Medicine—Practice**   ✓Ostriches

Ostrogoths. *See* **Teutonic peoples**   xx ✓Birds

Versification 416; 426

See also **Poetry; Rhyme**

x English language—Versification; Meter; Prosody

xx **Authorship; Poetics; Rhythm**

✓**Vertebrates 596**

See also **Amphibians;** ✓**Birds; Fishes;
Mammals; Reptiles**

xx **Animals; Zoology**

HEADINGS TO BE ADDED BY THE CATALOGER

It is neither possible nor necessary to enter all proper, common, and corporate names in a subject heading list such as Sears. If a specific name is not included in the List, the cataloger must establish a heading for it, using available reference sources.

A. PROPER NAMES

1. Names of persons
2. Names of families
3. Names of places
    a. Political units: countries, states, cities, provinces, counties, etc.
    b. Groups of states or countries: e.g. **Atlantic States; Baltic States;** etc.
    c. Geographic features: Mountain ranges and individual mountains; island groups and individual islands; river valleys and individual rivers; regions; oceans; lakes; etc.
4. Names of nationalities
5. Names of national languages and literatures
6. Names of wars and battles
7. Names of treaties
8. Names of Indian tribes

B. CORPORATE NAMES

1. Names of associations, societies, clubs, etc.
2. Names of institutions: colleges, libraries, hospitals, etc.
3. Names of church denominations
4. Names of government bodies
5. Names of buildings, parks, ships, etc.

C. COMMON NAMES

1. Names from such categories as:

animals	fruits	tools
birds	games	trees
fishes	musical instruments	vegetables
flowers	nuts	

2. Names of diseases
3. Names of organs and regions of the body
4. Names of chemicals
5. Names of minerals

N.B. Wherever the List cites, "*See also* [or *See*] names of . . . ," the specific name may be added even though not included in the List

"KEY" HEADINGS

To enable the cataloger to see the full display of possible subdivisions that may be used with some of the more popular categories, the editor has provided certain prominent names in the List to serve as "keys":

Persons:

> **Presidents—U.S.** (to illustrate subdivisions which may be used under any president)
>
> **Shakespeare, William** (to illustrate subdivisions which may be used under any voluminous author)

Places:

> **United States** (or **U.S.**); **Ohio; Chicago** (to illustrate subdivisions under geographic names, except for historical periods)

Languages and Literatures:

> **English language** (to illustrate subdivisions which may be used with any language)
>
> **English literature** (to illustrate subdivisions which may be used with any literature)
>
> N.B. Most of the principal languages and literatures will be found in the List

Wars:

> **World War, 1939-1945,** (to illustrate subdivisions which may be used under any war or battle)

LIST OF SUBDIVISIONS

In addition to the subdivisions which may be used under the "keys" above, the following general subdivisions may be used as needed:

Addresses and essays
Anecdotes, facetiae, satire, etc.
Automation
Bibliography
Bio-bibliography
Biography
Cartoons and caricatures
Case studies
Catalogs
Dictionaries
Directories
Discography
Encyclopedias
Exhibitions
Fiction
Guides

Handbooks, manuals, etc.
History (for all works except literature, film, and music)
History and criticism (for literature, film, and music)
Indexes
Outlines, syllabi, etc.
Periodicals
Philosophy
Pictorial works
Psychology
Research
Societies
Statistics
Study and teaching
Yearbooks

Although not quite as general in application as those listed above, the subdivisions listed below may also be used under subjects where appropriate. The list is not all inclusive, but the subdivisions are recorded here for convenient and rapid reference:

Accidents
Accounting
Air conditioning
Analysis
Anatomy
Assassination
Attitude
Audio-visual aids
Care and treatment
Censorship
Citizen participation
Civil rights
Collected works (except literature and art)
Collectibles
Collection and preservation
Collections (for literature and art)
Collectors and collecting
Colonies
Competitions
Computer programs
Conservation and restoration
Correspondence
Diseases
Diseases and pests

Documentation
Drama
Economic aspects
Education
Employment
Entrance requirements
Environmental aspects
Equipment and supplies
Estimates
Examinations, questions, etc.
Experiments
Finance
Fuel consumption
Habits and behavior
Heating and ventilation
Housing
Identification
Institutional care
International cooperation
Jargon
Laboratory guides
Law and legislation
Maintenance and repair
Malpractice
Maps

SEARS LIST OF SUBJECT HEADINGS

ABC. *See* **Alphabet**

ABM. *See* **Antimissile missiles**

A.D.C. *See* **Child welfare**

Abacus 513.028

Abandoned towns. *See* **Cities and towns, Ruined, extinct, etc.**

Abbeys 271; 726

 See also **Cathedrals; Convents; Monasteries;** also names of individual abbeys, e.g. **Westminster Abbey;** etc.

 xx **Church architecture; Church history; Convents; Monasteries**

Abbreviations 423

 See also **Acronyms; Ciphers; Code names; Shorthand; Signs and symbols**

 x Contractions; Symbols

 xx **Ciphers; Shorthand; Signs and symbols; Writing**

Ability 153.9

 See also types of ability, e.g. **Creative ability; Executive ability; Leadership; Musical ability;** etc.

 xx **Success**

Ability—Testing 153.9; 371.2

 x Aptitude testing

 xx **Educational tests and measurements; Mental tests**

Ability grouping in education 371.2

 See also **Nongraded schools**

 x Grouping by ability

 xx **Grading and marking (Students)**

Abnormal children. *See* **Exceptional children; Handicapped children**

Abnormal psychology. *See* **Psychology, Pathological**

Abolition of slavery. *See* **Abolitionists; Slavery**

Abolitionists 326; 923

 x Abolition of slavery

 xx **Slavery in the U.S.**

Aborigines *See* **Ethnology**

Abortion 179; 613.9

 x Fetal death; Miscarriage; Right to live

 xx **Birth control**

Abrasives 553; 621.9; 668

Absence from school. *See* **School attendance**

Absenteeism (Labor) 331.2; 658.31

 See also **Employee morale**

 x Employee absenteeism; Labor absenteeism

 xx **Labor and laboring classes; Personnel management**

1

Absenteeism (School). *See* **School attendance**

Abstinence. *See* **Fasting; Temperance**

Abstract art. *See* **Art, Abstract**

Abuse of animals. *See* **Animals—Treatment**

Academic degrees. *See* **Degrees, Academic**

Academic dissertations. *See* **Dissertations, Academic**

Academic freedom 371.1; 378.1

> *See also* **Church and education**
>
> *x* Freedom of teaching; Teaching, Freedom of
>
> *xx* **Church and education; Civil rights; Intellectual freedom; Toleration**

Accelerated reading. *See* **Rapid reading**

Accident insurance. *See* **Insurance, Accident**

Accidents 614.8

> *See also*

Disasters	**Poisons**
Explosions	**Shipwrecks**
Fires	**Traffic accidents**
First aid	
Occupations, Dangerous	

> also subjects with the subdivision *Accidents,* e.g. **Aeronautics—Accidents; Railroads—Accidents;** etc.
>
> *x* Emergencies; Injuries
>
> *xx* **Disasters; First aid**

Accidents—Prevention 614.8; 658.38

> *See also* **Safety appliances; Safety education;** also subjects with the subdivision *Safety appliances* or *Safety measures,* e.g. **Aeronautics—Safety measures; Railroads—Safety appliances;** etc.
>
> *x* Prevention of accidents; Safety measures
>
> *xx* **Safety appliances; Safety education**

Accidents, Space craft. *See* **Astronautics—Accidents**

Acclimatization. *See* **Adaptation (Biology); Man—Influence of environment; Plant introduction**

Accompaniment, Musical. *See* **Musical accompaniment**

Accountants 920; 923

> *x* Bookkeepers; Certified public accountants

Accounting 657

> *See also* **Auditing; Bookkeeping; Cost accounting;** also names of industries, professions, etc. with the subdivison *Accounting,* e.g. **Corporations—Accounting;** etc.
>
> *x* Financial accounting
>
> *xx* **Auditing; Bookkeeping; Business; Business arithmetic; Business education**

Accounting machines. *See* **Calculating machines**

2

Accounts, Collecting of. *See* **Collecting of accounts**

Acculturation 301.24

　See also **East and West; Intercultural education**

　xx **Anthropology;　Civilization;　Culture; East and West; Ethnology; Race relations**

Acetate silk. *See* **Rayon**

Achievement tests. *See* **Examinations**

Acids 546; 547; 661

　Names of acids are not included in this list but are to be added as needed, e.g. **Carbolic acid;** etc.

　See also names of acids, e.g. **Carbolic acid;** etc.

　xx **Chemicals; Chemistry**

Acne 616.5; 618.9

　xx **Skin—Diseases**

Acoustics. *See* **Architectural acoustics; Hearing; Music—Acoustics and physics; Sound**

Acquisitions (Libraries). *See* **Libraries—Acquisitions**

Acrobats and acrobatics 791.3; 796.4; 927

　See also **Gymnastics;** also names of acrobatic feats, e.g. **Tumbling;** etc.

　xx **Circus; Gymnastics**

Acronyms 421

　x English language—Acronyms; Initialisms

　xx **Abbreviations; Code names**

Acting 791.4; 791.43-45; 792

　Use for general materials on the art and technique of acting in any medium (stage, televsion, etc.), in the presentation of plays, and on acting as a profession. Materials limited to presentation of plays are entered under **Amateur theatricals** or, if professional actors are involved, under **Theater—Production and direction.** Materials about members of the profession are entered under **Actors and actresses**

　See also **Actors and actresses; Drama in education;　Pageants;　Pantomimes; Theater**

　x Dramatic art; Histrionics; Stage

　xx **Actors and actresses; Amateur theatricals; Drama; Drama in education; Public speaking; Theater**

Acting—Costume. *See* **Costume**

Action, Social. *See* **Social action**

Activism, Social. *See* **Social action**

Activity schools. *See* **Education—Experimental methods**

Actors and actresses (May subdiv. geog. adjective form, e.g. **Actors and actresses, American)　920; 927**

　See also **Acting; Black actors and actresses;**

Actors and actresses—*Continued*
>> **Comedians; Theater;** also names of individual actors and actresses

> *x* Actresses; Stage
> *xx* **Acting; Entertainers; Theater**

Actors and actresses, American   920; 927
> *x* American actors and actresses; U.S.—Actors and actresses

Actresses. *See* **Actors and actresses**

Acupuncture   615
> *xx* **Medicine**

Adages. *See* **Proverbs**

Adaptability (Psychology). *See* **Adjustment (Psychology)**

Adaptation (Biology)   574.5; 581.5; 591.5
> *See also* **Man—Influence of environment**
> *x* Acclimatization
> *xx* **Biology; Ecology; Evolution; Genetics; Variation (Biology)**

Adaptation (Psychology). *See* **Adjustment (Psychology)**

Adding machines. *See* **Calculating machines**

Additives, Food. *See* **Food additives**

Addresses. *See* **Lectures and lecturing; Orations; Speeches, addresses, etc.;** and general subjects with the subdivision *Addresses and essays,* e.g. **Agriculture—Addresses and essays; U.S.—History —Addresses and essays;** etc.

Adhesives   620.1; 668; 691
> *See also* names of adhesives, e.g. **Cement; Glue; Mortar;** etc.

Adjustment (Psychology)   155.2; 155.4; 155.67
> *x* Adaptability (Psychology); Adaptation (Psychology); Coping behavior; Maladjustment (Psychology)
> *xx* **Psychology**

Adjustment, Social. *See* **Social adjustment**

Administration. *See* **Civil service; Management; Political science; Public administration; The State;** and names of countries, cities, etc. with the subdivision *Politics and government,* e.g. **U.S.—Politics and government;** etc.

Administration of criminal justice. *See* **Criminal justice, Administration of**

Administration of justice. *See* **Justice, Administration of**

Administrative ability. *See* **Executive ability**

Administrative law   342.6
> *See also* **Civil service; Constitutional law; Local government; Public administration**
> *x* Law, Administrative
> *xx* **Constitutional law; Law; Public administration**

Administrators and executors. *See* **Executors and administrators**

Admirals   920; 923

4

Adolescence 155.5; 301.43
> *x* Teen age
> *xx* **Youth**

Adolescent psychiatry 155.5
> *x* Psychiatry, Adolescent
> *xx* **Child psychiatry; Psychiatry**

Adolescent psychology 155.5
> *x* Psychology, Adolescent
> *xx* **Psychology**

Adolescents. *See* **Youth**

Adoption 346.1; 362.7
> *See also* **Foster home care**
> *x* Children—Adoption
> *xx* **Foster home care**

Adoption, Interracial 362.7
> *x* Interracial adoption

Adult education 374
> *See also* **Agricultural extension work; Evening and continuation schools; Prisoners—Education**
> *x* Education, Adult; Education of adults
> *xx* **Continuing education; Education; Education, Higher; Education, Secondary; Evening and continuation schools; University extension**

Adulteration of food. *See* **Food adulteration and inspection**

Adults, Runaway. *See* **Runaways**

Adventure and adventurers 904; 910.4; 920; 923
> *See also* **Discoveries (in geography); Escapes; Explorers; Frontier and pioneer life; Heroes and heroines; Sea stories; Seafaring life; Shipwrecks; Underwater exploration; Voyages and travels**
> *xx* **Voyages and travels**

Advertisement writing. *See* **Advertising copy**

Advertising 659.1
> May be subdivided by topic, e.g. **Advertising—Libraries;** etc.
> *See also*

Commercial art	**Publicity**
Electric signs	**Radio advertising**
Mail-order business	**Selling**
Marketing	**Show windows**
Packaging	**Sign painting**
Posters	**Signs and sign-**
Printing—Specimens	**boards**
Propaganda	**Television advertis-**
Public relations	**ing**

> *xx* **Business; Propaganda; Public relations; Publicity; Retail trade; Selling**

Advertising, Art in. *See* **Commercial art**

Advertising, Fraudulent 343.8
> *x* Deceptive advertising; False advertising; Fraudulent advertising; Misleading advertising; Truth in advertising

5

Advertising—Libraries 021.7

    x Libraries—Advertising; Library advertising

Advertising, Pictorial. *See* **Commercial art; Posters**

Advertising, Radio. *See* **Radio advertising**

Advertising, Television. *See* **Television advertising**

Advertising copy 659.13

    x Advertisment writing; Copy writing

    xx **Authorship**

Advertising layout and typography 659.13

    xx **Printing; Type and type founding**

Aerial bombs. *See* **Bombs**

Aerial navigation. *See* **Navigation (Aeronautics)**

Aerial photography. *See* **Photography, Aerial**

Aerial rockets. *See* **Rockets (Aeronautics)**

Aerial spraying and dusting. *See* **Aeronautics in agriculture**

Aerobiology. *See* **Air—Microbiology**

Aerodromes. *See* **Airports**

Aerodynamics 533; 629.132

    See also **Aeronautics; Ground cushion phenomena**

    x Streamlining

    xx **Aeronautics; Air; Dynamics; Pneumatics**

Aerodynamics, Supersonic 629.132

    See also **Aerothermodynamics**

    x High speed aerodynamics; Speed, Supersonic; Supersonic aerodynamics

    xx **High speed aeronautics**

Aeronautical instruments 629.135

    See also **Airplanes—Electric equipment;** also names of specific instruments, e.g. **Gyroscope;** etc.

    x Airplanes—Instruments; Instruments, Aeronautical

    xx **Scientific apparatus and instruments**

Aeronautical sports 797.5

    See also names of specific sports, e.g. **Airplane racing; Skydiving;** etc.

    xx **Aeronautics; Sports**

Aeronautics 629.13

    Use for materials on the scientific aspects of aircraft and their construction and operation; or for materials that treat collectively various types of aircraft

    See also

Aerodynamics	**Helicopters**
Aeronautical sports	**High speed aeronau-**
Airplanes	**tics**
Airships	**Kites**
Astronautics	**Meteorology in**
Balloons	**aeronautics**
Flight	**Navigation (Aero-**
Flying saucers	**nautics)**
Gliders (Aeronau-	**Parachutes**
tics)	**Radio in aeronautics**

Aeronautics—*Continued*
>   Rocketry   Rockets (Aeronau-
>   tics)
>   *x* Aviation; Locomotion
>   *xx* **Aerodynamics; Airships; Balloons; En-
>   gineering; Flight**

Aeronautics—Accidents   387.7; 629.13
>   *See also* **Survival (after airplane accidents,
>   shipwrecks, etc.)**
>   *x* Air crashes; Airplane accidents; Air-
>   planes—Accidents
>   *xx* **Accidents**

Aeronautics, Commercial   387.7
>   *See also* **Air lines; Air mail service; Air-
>   plane industry and trade**
>   *x* Air cargo; Air freight; Air transport;
>   Commercial aeronautics; Commercial
>   aviation
>   *xx* **Freight and freightage; Transportation**

Aeronautics, Commercial—Chartering   387.7
>   *x* Air lines—Chartering; Airplanes—Char-
>   tering; Air charters; Charter flights

Aeronautics, Commercial—Hijacking. *See* **Hi-
>   jacking of airplanes**

Aeronautics—Flights   387.7; 629.13
>   *See also* **Space Flight**
>   *x* Aeronautics—Voyages; Flights around
>   the world; Transatlantic flights
>   *xx* **Voyages and travels**

Aeronautics, High speed. *See* **High speed aero-
>   nautics**

Aeronautics—Medical aspects. *See* **Aviation
>   medicine**

Aeronautics, Meteorology in. *See* **Meteorol-
>   ogy in aeronautics**

Aeronautics, Military   358.4
>   *See also* **Air bases; Air defenses; Air
>   power; Air raid shelters; Aircraft car-
>   riers; Airplanes, Military; Parachute
>   troops;** also names of wars with the
>   subdivision *Aerial operations,* e.g.
>   **World War, 1939-1945—Aerial oper-
>   ations;** etc.
>   *x* Aeronautics, Naval; Air raids—Protec-
>   tive measures; Air warfare; Military
>   aeronautics; Naval aeronautics
>   *xx* **Military art and science; War**

Aeronautics, Naval. *See* **Aeronautics, Military**

Aeronautics—Navigation. *See* **Navigation
>   (Aeronautics)**

Aeronautics—Piloting. *See* **Airplanes—Pilot-
>   ing**

Aeronautics, Radio in. *See* **Radio in aeronau-
>   tics**

Aeronautics—Safety measures   387.7; 629.134
>   *x* Safety measures
>   *xx* **Accidents—Prevention**

Aeronautics—Songs and music   784.6
>   *xx* **Music; Songs**

Aeronautics—Study and teaching 629.1307
   See also **Airplanes—Piloting**
   x Flight training
Aeronautics—Voyages. *See* **Aeronautics—
   Flights**
Aeronautics and civilization 301.24
   See also **Astronautics and civilization**
   x Civilization and aeronautics
   xx **Civilization**
Aeronautics in agriculture 631
   Use same form for aeronautics in other
      fields of endeavor
   x Aerial spraying and dusting; Airplanes
      in agriculture; Crop dusting
   xx **Agricultural pests; Agriculture; Insects,
      Injurious and beneficial; Spraying and
      dusting**
Aeroplanes. *See* **Airplanes**
Aerosols
   xx **Air—Pollution**
Aerospace industries 338.4
   See also **Airplane industry and trade**
   x Aircraft production
Aerospace law. *See* **Space law**
Aerospace medicine. *See* **Aviation medicine;
   Space medicine**
Aerothermodynamics 629.132; 629.4
   x Thermoaerodynamics
   xx **Aerodynamics, Supersonic; Astronautics;
      High speed aeronautics; Thermody-
      namics**
Aesthetics. *See* **Esthetics**
Affection. *See* **Friendship; Love**
Affirmative action programs 331.1; 658.31
   xx **Discrimination in employment; Person-
      nel management**
Affliction. *See* **Joy and sorrow**
Africa 916; 960
   See also **Pan-Africanism**
Africa—History 960
Africa—History—1960-   960
Africa, Central 916.7; 967
   x Central Africa
Africa, East 916.7; 967
   A general term covering roughly Uganda,
      Kenya and Tanzania
   x East Africa
Africa, Eastern 916.7; 967
   A term covering the area extending from
      Sudan and Ethiopia to Mozambique
Africa, French-speaking Equatorial 916.7; 967
   A general term covering Central African
      Republic, Chad, Congo (Brazzaville,
      and Gabon)
   x French Equatorial Africa
Africa, French-speaking West 916.6; 966
   A general term covering Dahomey,
      Guinea, Ivory Coast, Mali, Mauri-
      tania, Niger, Senegal, and Upper
      Volta

Africa, French-speaking West—*Continued*
  x French West Africa
Africa, North 916.1; 961
  A general term for the area including Mo-
    rocco, Algeria, Tunisia, and Libya
  x Barbary States; North Africa
Africa, Northeast 916; 960
  A general term covering Sudan, Ethiopia,
    Somalia, and the French Territory of
    Afars and Issas
Africa, Northwest 916.6; 966
  A general term for the area extending
    eastward from Morocco, Spanish Sa-
    hara, and Mauritania to include Libya
    and Chad
Africa, South. *See* **South Africa**
Africa, Southern 916.8; 916.89; 968; 968.9
  Use for materials on the area south of
    Zaire and Tanzania
  x Southern Africa
Africa, Southwest 916.8; 968
  Use for materials on the territory of South
    West Africa
Africa, West 916.6; 966
  A general term covering the area South of
    the Sahara from Senegal to Nigeria
  x West Africa
African Americans. *See* **Blacks**
African civilization. *See* **Civilization, African**
African relations. *See* **Pan-Africanism**
African songs. *See* **Songs, African**
Africans 572.896
  x Native peoples
Afro-American studies. *See* **Black studies**
Afro-Americans. *See* **Blacks**
After-dinner speeches 808.5; 808.85
  See also **Speeches, addresses, etc.; Toasts**
  xx **Orations; Speeches, addresses, etc.;
    Toasts**
Age. *See* **Middle age; Old age; Youth**
Age—Physiological effect. *See* **Aging**
Age and employment 331.3
  See also **Child labor**
  x Employment and age
  xx **Discrimination in employment; Middle
    age; Old age**
Age discrimination 301.44
  x Discrimination, Age
  xx **Discrimination**
Aged. *See* **Elderly**
Agents, Sales. *See* **Sales personnel**
Aggregates. *See* **Set theory**
Aggressiveness (Psychology) 152.4; 155.2
  See also **Assertiveness (Psychology); Vio-
    lence**
  xx **Psychology**
Aging 612.6
  x Age—Physiological effect
  xx **Elderly; Gerontology; Middle age; Old
    age**

Agnosticism 149; 211

   See also **Atheism; Belief and doubt; Positivism; Rationalism; Skepticism**

   xx **Atheism; Belief and doubt; Faith; Free thought; God; Positivism; Rationalism; Religion; Skepticism; Truth**

Agrarian question. *See* **Agriculture—Economic aspects; Agriculture and state; Land tenure**

Agreements. *See* **Contracts**

Agribusiness 338.1

   x Agricultural industries

   xx **Agriculture—Economic aspects**

Agricultural bacteriology. *See* **Bacteriology, Agricultural**

Agricultural botany. *See* **Botany, Economic**

Agricultural chemicals 631.8

   See also types of chemicals, e.g. **Insecticides; Pesticides;** etc.; also names of individual chemicals

   xx **Agricultural Chemistry**

Agricultural chemistry 630.1

   See also **Agricultural chemicals; Chemurgy; Fertilizers and manures; Soils**

   x Chemistry, Agricultural

   xx **Chemistry; Fertilizers and manures; Soils**

Agricultural clubs. *See* **Agriculture—Societies**

Agricultural cooperation. *See* **Agriculture, Cooperative**

Agricultural credit 332.7

   x Credit, Agricultural; Farm credit; Rural credit

   xx **Agriculture—Economic aspects; Banks and banking; Credit; Mortgages**

Agricultural economics. *See* **Agriculture—Economic aspects**

Agricultural education. *See* **Agriculture—Study and teaching**

Agricultural engineering 631.3

   See also **Drainage; Electricity in agriculture; Irrigation**

   x Farm mechanics

   xx **Agricultural machinery; Engineering; Farm engines**

Agricultural experiment stations 630.7

   See also **Agricultural extension work**

   x Experimental farms; Farms, Experimental

   xx **Agriculture—Research; Agriculture — Study and teaching; Agriculture and state**

Agricultural extension work (May subdiv. geog. by state) **630.7**

   Use for general materials and for materials on agricultural extension work in the U.S. Materials dealing with agricultural extension work in particular states or localities are entered under this heading with local subdi-

10

Agricultural extension work—*Continued*
    vision, e.g. **Agricultural extension work—Ohio;** etc.
  See also **Agriculture—Study and teaching; County agricultural agents**
  x Extension work, Agricultural
  xx **Adult education; Agricultural experiment stations; Agriculture—Study and teaching; Agriculture and state**
Agricultural industries. *See* **Agribusiness**
Agricultural laborers 331.7
  See also **Migrant labor; Peasantry**
  x Farm laborers; Laborers
  xx **Labor and laboring classes; Peasantry**
Agricultural machinery 631.3
  See also **Agricultural engineering; Electricity in agriculture; Farm engines;** also names of farm machinery, e.g. **Harvesting machinery; Plows; Tractors;** etc.
  x Agricultural tools; Farm implements; Farm machinery; Farm mechanics; Implements, utensils, etc.
  xx **Machinery; Tools**
Agricultural pests 632
  See also **Aeronautics in agriculture; Fungi; Insects, Injurious and beneficial; Pests —Control; Plants—Diseases; Spraying and dusting; Weeds;** also names of crops, etc., with the subdivision *Diseases and pests,* e.g. **Fruit—Diseases and pests;** etc.
  x Diseases and pests; Garden pests
  xx **Insects, Injurious and beneficial; Pests; Zoology, Economic**
Agricultural pests—Biological control. *See* **Pests—Biological control**
Agricultural policy. *See* **Agriculture and state**
Agricultural products. *See* **Farm produce**
Agricultural research. *See* **Agriculture—Research**
Agricultural societies. *See* **Agriculture—Societies**
Agricultural tools. *See* **Agricultural machinery**
Agriculture (May subdiv. geog.) **630**
  See also

Aeronautics in agriculture	**Gardening**
Aquaculture	**Horticulture**
Botany, Economic	**Land tenure**
Dairying	**Land use**
Domestic animals	**Organiculture**
Dry farming	**Pastures**
Farms	**Plant breeding**
Forests and forestry	**Reclamation of land**
Fruit culture	**Rotation of crops**
	Soils

  also names of agricultural products, (e.g. **Corn;** etc.); and headings beginning with the words **Agricultural** and **Farm**

11

Agriculture—*Continued*
> *x* Agronomy; Farming; Planting
> *xx* **Life sciences**

Agriculture—Addresses and essays 630
> *x* Addresses
> *xx* **Essays; Lectures and lecturing; Speeches, addresses, etc.**

Agriculture—Bibliography 016.63
> *xx* **Bibliography**

Agriculture, Cooperative 334
> Use for materials dealing with cooperation in the production and disposal of agricultural products
> *x* Agricultural cooperation; Collective farms; Cooperative agriculture; Farmers' cooperatives
> *xx* **Cooperation**

Agriculture—Documentation 630.2
> *xx* **Documentation**

Agriculture—Economic aspects 338.1
> *See also* **Agribusiness; Agricultural credit; Farm management; Farm produce—Marketing; Land tenure**
> *x* Agrarian question; Agricultural economics
> *xx* **Economics; Farm management; Farm produce—Marketing**

Agriculture—Research 630.7
> *See also* **Agricultural experiment stations**
> *x* Agricultural research
> *xx* **Research**

Agriculture—Societies 630.6
> *See also* names of agricultural societies, e.g. **4-H clubs; Grange;** etc.
> *x* Agricultural clubs; Agricultural societies; Boys' agricultural clubs; Girls' agricultural clubs
> *xx* **Country life; Societies**

Agriculture, Soilless. *See* **Plants—Soilless culture**

Agriculture—Statistics 338.1021; 630.2
> *x* Crop reports
> *xx* **Statistics**

Agriculture—Study and teaching 630.7
> *See also* **Agricultural experiment stations; Agricultural extension work; County agricultural agents**
> *x* Agricultural education
> *xx* **Agricultural extension work; Vocational education**

Agriculture—Tenant farming. *See* **Farm tenancy**

Agriculture—Tropics 630.913
> *xx* **Tropics**

Agriculture—U.S. 630.973
> *x* U.S.—Agriculture

Agriculture and state 338.1
> *See also* **Agricultural experiment stations; Agricultural extension work**

12

Agriculture and state—*Continued*

    x Agrarian question; Agricultural policy; State and agriculture

    xx **Industry and state**

Agronomy. *See* **Agriculture**

Ague. *See* **Malaria**

Aid to dependent children. *See* **Child welfare**

Aid to developing areas. *See* **Economic assistance; Technical assistance**

Air 533; 546

    Use for materials treating of air as an element and of its chemical and physical properties. Materials treating of the body of air surrounding the earth are entered under **Atmosphere**

    See also **Aerodynamics; Atmosphere; Ventilation**

    xx **Atmosphere; Hygiene; Meteorology**

Air, Compressed. *See* **Compressed air**

Air—Microbiology 576

    x Aerobiology

    xx **Microbiology**

Air—Pollution (May subdiv. geog.) **614.7; 628.5**

    See also **Air—Quality;** also names of air pollutants, e.g. **Aerosols;** etc.

    x Air pollution; Atmosphere—Pollution; Pollution of air

    xx **Air—Quality; Pollution**

Air—Pollution—U.S. 614.7; 628.5973

    x U.S.—Air—Pollution

Air—Quality 614.7

    See also **Air—Pollution**

    x Air quality; Quality

    xx **Air—Pollution; Quality control**

Air bases 358.4

    x Air stations, Military; Air stations, Naval; Military air bases; Naval air bases

    xx **Aeronautics, Military; Airports**

Air bearing lift. *See* **Ground cushion phenomena**

Air bearing vehicles. *See* **Ground effect machines**

Air cargo. *See* **Aerononautics, Commercial**

Air charter. *See* **Aeronautics, Commercial—Chartering**

Air conditioning 613.5; 644; 697.9

    See also **Refrigeration and refrigerating machinery; Ventilation;** also subjects with the subdivision *Air conditioning,* e.g. **Automobiles—Air conditioning;** etc.

    xx **Refrigeration and refrigerating machinery; Ventilation**

Air crashes. *See* **Aeronautics—Accidents**

Air cushion vehicles. *See* **Ground effect machines**

Air defenses 363.3

    Use for materials on civilian defense against air attack. Materials on mili-

Air defenses—*Continued*

tary defense against air raids are entered under **Aeronautics, Military.** General materials on civilian defense are entered under **Civil defense**

See also **Air raid shelters; Ballistic missile early warning system; Radar defense networks**

x Air raids—Protective measures; Air warfare; Defenses, Air

xx **Aeronautics, Military; Civil defense**

Air freight. *See* **Aeronautics, Commercial**

Air hostesses. *See* **Air lines—Flight attendants**

Air lines 387.7

Use for materials dealing with systems of aerial transportation and with companies engaged in this business. Materials dealing with the routes along which the planes are flown are entered under **Airways**

See also **Airways**

x Airlines

xx **Aeronautics, Commercial; Airways**

Air lines—Chartering. *See* **Aeronautics, Commercial—Chartering**

Air lines—Flight attendants 387.7

x Air hostesses; Air lines—Hostesses; Air stewardesses; Air stewards; Airplane hostesses; Flight attendants; Hostesses, Air line; Stewardesses, Air line; Stewards, Air line

Air lines—Hijacking. *See* **Hijacking of airplanes**

Air lines—Hostesses. *See* **Air lines—Flight attendants**

Air mail service 383

xx **Aeronautics, Commercial; Postal service**

Air navigation. *See* **Navigation (Aeronautics)**

Air pilots 920; 926

See also **Astronauts; Women air pilots**

x Airplanes—Pilots; Aviators; Pilots, Airplane; Test pilots

Air piracy. *See* **Hijacking of airplanes**

Air planes. *See* **Airplanes**

Air pollution. *See* **Air—Pollution**

Air ports. *See* **Airports**

Air power 358.4

xx **Aeronautics, Military**

Air quality. *See* **Air—Quality**

Air raid shelters 363.3

x Bomb shelters; Fallout shelters; Public shelters; Shelters, Air raid

xx **Aeronautics, Military; Air defenses; Civil defense**

Air raids—Protective measures. *See* **Aeronautics, Military; Air defenses**

Air rights law. *See* **Airspace law**

Air routes. *See* **Airways**

Air-ships. *See* **Airships**

Air space law. *See* **Airspace law**

Air stations, Military. *See* **Air bases**

Air stations, Naval. *See* **Air bases**

Air stewardesses. *See* **Air lines—Flight attendants**

Air stewards. *See* **Air lines—Flight attendants**

Air surfing. *See* **Gliding and soaring**

Air terminals. *See* **Airports**

Air traffic control   387.7

    x Airports—Traffic control

Air transport. *See* **Aeronautics, Commercial**

Air warfare. *See* **Aeronautics, Military; Air defenses; Airplanes, Military; Chemical warfare;** and names of wars with the subdivision *Aerial operations,* e.g. **World War, 1939-1945—Aerial operations;** etc.

Aircraft. *See* **Airplanes; Airships; Gliders (Aeronautics); Helicopters**

Aircraft carriers   359.3; 623.82

    x Airplane carriers; Carriers, Aircraft

    xx **Aeronautics, Military; Warships**

Aircraft production. *See* **Airplane industry and trade; Aerospace industries**

Airdromes. *See* **Airports**

Airlines. *See* **Air lines**

Airplane accidents. *See* **Aeronautics—Accidents**

Airplane carriers. *See* **Aircraft carriers**

Airplane engines. *See* **Airplanes—Engines**

Airplane hijacking. *See* **Hijacking of airplanes**

Airplane hostesses. *See* **Air lines—Flight attendants**

Airplane industry and trade   338.4; 387.7

    x Aircraft production

    xx **Aeronautics, Commercial; Aerospace industries**

Airplane racing   797.5

    x Airplanes—Racing

    xx **Aeronautical sports**

Airplane spotting. *See* **Airplanes—Identification**

Airplanes   387.7; 629.133

    See also **Gliders (Aeronautics); Propellers, Aerial;** also types of airplanes and special makes of airplanes, e.g. **Bombers; Helicopters; Vertically rising airplanes;** etc.

    x Aeroplanes; Air planes; Aircraft; Biplanes; Monoplanes

    xx **Aeronautics**

Airplanes—Accidents. *See* **Aeronautics—Accidents**

Airplanes—Chartering. *See* **Aeronautics, Commercial—Chartering**

Airplanes—Design and construction   629.134

Airplanes—Electric equipment   629.135

    x Airplanes—Instruments

    xx **Aeronautical instruments**

Airplanes—Engines 629.134

    See also **Jet propulsion**

    x Airplane engines; Airplanes—Motors

    xx **Engines; Gas and oil engines**

Airplanes—Flight testing. *See* **Airplanes—Testing**

Airplanes—Hijacking. *See* **Hijacking of airplanes**

Airplanes—Identification 623.7402; 629.13302

    x Airplane spotting; Airplanes—Recognition

    xx **Identification**

Airplanes—Inspection 387.7; 629.133

Airplanes—Instruments. *See* **Aeronautical instruments; Airplanes—Electric equipment**

Airplanes, Jet propelled. *See* **Jet planes**

Airplanes—Maintenance and repair 629.134

    x Airplanes—Repair

Airplanes—Materials 629.134

Airplanes, Military 623.74

    See also types of military airplanes, e.g. **Bombers;** etc.

    x Air warfare; Airplanes, Naval; Military airplanes; Naval airplanes

    xx **Aeronautics, Military**

Airplanes—Models 629.133

    x Miniature objects; Model airplanes; Models

    xx **Machinery—Models; Models and model making**

Airplanes—Motors. *See* **Airplanes—Engines**

Airplanes, Naval. *See* **Airplanes, Military**

Airplanes—Noise 629.134

    xx **Noise; Noise—Pollution**

Airplanes—Operation. *See* **Airplanes—Piloting**

Airplanes—Piloting 629.132

    Use for materials on instruction in the mechanics of flying

    See also types and names of airplanes with the subdivision *Piloting,* e.g. **Helicopters—Piloting;** etc.

    x Aeronautics—Piloting; Airplanes—Operation; Flight training; Piloting (Aeronautics)

    xx **Aeronautics—Study and teaching; Navigation (Aeronautics)**

Airplanes—Pilots. *See* **Air pilots**

Airplanes—Propellers. *See* **Propellers, Aerial**

Airplanes—Racing. *See* **Airplane racing**

Airplanes—Recognition. *See* **Airplanes—Identification**

Airplanes—Repair. *See* **Airplanes—Maintenance and repair**

Airplanes, Rocket propelled. *See* **Rocket planes**

Airplanes—Testing 629.134

    x Airplanes—Flight testing; Test pilots

Airplanes, Vertically rising. *See* **Vertically rising airplanes**

Airplanes in agriculture. *See* **Aeronautics in agriculture**

Airports   629.136

See also **Air bases; Heliports**

x Aerodromes; Air ports; Air terminals; Airdromes

Airports—Traffic control. *See* **Air traffic control**

Airships   629.133

Use for materials on lighter than air craft, mechanically driven

See also **Aeronautics; Balloons**

x Air-ships; Aircraft; Balloons, Dirigible; Blimps; Dirigible balloons; Lighter than air craft; Zeppelins

xx **Aeronautics**

Airspace law   341.4

x Air rights law; Air space law

xx **Space law**

Airways   387.7

Use for materials dealing with routes along which planes are flown and where aids to navigation are maintained such as landing fields, beacons, etc. Materials dealing with the companies engaged in aerial transportation are entered under **Air lines**

See also **Air lines**

x Air routes

xx **Air lines**

Alaska Highway   388.1; 917.98

Alchemy   540.1

Use for materials on the medieval chemical science which sought to transmute baser metals into gold. Modern materials on the transmutation of metals are entered under **Transmutation (Chemistry)**

See also **Transmutation (Chemistry)**

x Hermetic art and philosophy; Metals, Transmutation of; Philosophers' stone; Transmutation of metals

xx **Chemistry; Occult sciences; Superstition**

Alcohol   547; 661

See also **Alcoholism; Distillation; Liquor industry; Liquor problem; Liquors and liqueurs; Temperance**

x Intoxicants

xx **Distillation; Stimulants**

Alcohol, Denatured   661

x Alcohol, Industrial; Denatured alcohol; Industrial alcohol

Alcohol, Industrial. *See* **Alcohol, Denatured**

Alcohol—Physiological effect   613.8; 616.8

x Physiological effect

xx **Alcoholism; Temperance**

Alcohol and teen agers. *See* **Alcohol and youth**

Alcohol and youth   613.8; 616.8

Use same form for alcohol and other groups of people

x Alcohol and teen agers; Drinking and youth; Teen age drinking; Teen agers and alcohol; Youth and alcohol

xx **Alcoholism**

Alcoholics   616.8

x Drunkards; Inebriates

xx **Alcoholism**

Alcoholism   616.8

Use chiefly for medical materials, including works on drunkenness, dipsomania, etc.

See also **Alcohol—Physiological effect; Alcohol and youth; Alcoholics; Liquor problem; Temperance**

x Dipsomania; Drinking; Drunkenness; Intemperance; Intoxication

xx **Alcohol; Drug abuse; Liquor problem; Temperance**

Alfalfa   633

xx **Hay**

Algae   561; 589.3

x Sea mosses; Seaweeds

xx **Marine plants**

Algebra   512

See also **Logarithms; Number theory; Probabilities**

xx **Mathematical analysis; Mathematics**

Algebra, Boolean   511

x Boolean algebra

xx **Logic, Symbolic and mathematical; Set theory**

Algebras, Linear   512

See also **Topology**

x Linear algebras

xx **Mathematical analysis; Topology**

Alienation (Social psychology)   301.6

x Estrangement (Social psychology); Rebels (Social psychology); Social alienation

xx **Social psychology**

Aliens   323.6; 325

See also **Citizenship; Naturalization; Refugees;** and phrase headings such as **Mexicans in the U.S.;** etc.

x Foreigners

xx **Citizenship; Immigration and emigration; International law; Naturalization**

Alkoran.   *See* **Koran**

All Fools' Day.   *See* **April Fools' Day**

All Hallows' Eve.   *See* **Halloween**

All terrain vehicles   629.2

See also types of vehicles, e.g. **Snowmobiles;** etc.

xx **Vehicles**

Allegories   808.88

Use for collections of allegories

See also **Fables; Parables**

Allegories—*Continued*
    xx **Fiction; Parables; Symbolism in litera-
        ture**
Allegory 704.94; 808
    Use for materials on allegory as a literary
        form
Allergy 616.9
    xx **Immunity**
Alleys. *See* **Streets**
Allied health personnel 610.69
    See also types of personnel, e.g. **Medical
        technologists;** etc.
    x Paramedical personnel
Alligators 598.1
    Use for materials on the American croco-
        dile. General materials are entered
        under **Crocodiles**
    xx **Crocodiles**
Alloys 669
    See also **Brass; Metallurgy; Pewter;** also
        names of alloys, e.g. **Aluminum al-
        loys;** etc.
    xx **Chemistry, Technical; Metallurgy;
        Metals; Solder and soldering**
Allusions 808.88
Almanacs 310
    See also **Calendars; Nautical almanacs;
        Yearbooks**
    x Annuals
    xx **Astronomy; Calendars; Yearbooks**
Alphabet 411
    Use for materials dealing with the series
        of characters which form the elements
        of a written language and for mate-
        rials teaching children the ABCs. Ma-
        terials dealing with the styles of al-
        phabets used by artists, etc., are
        entered under **Alphabets**
    See also **Alphabets; Writing**
    x ABC; Letters of the alphabet
    xx **Writing**
Alphabet—Filmstrips 411
    xx **Audio-visual materials**
Alphabet—Texts 411
    xx **Audio-visual materials**
Alphabeting. *See* **Files and filing**
Alphabets 745.6
    See note under **Alphabet**
    See also **Illumination of books and manu-
        scripts; Initials; Lettering; Monograms**
    xx **Alphabet; Decoration and ornament; Ini-
        tials; Lettering; Sign painting**
Alpine plants 581; 635.9
    x Mountain plants
    xx **Geographical distribution of animals and
        plants; Plants**
Alternating current machinery. *See* **Electric
        machinery—Alternating current**
Alternating currents. *See* **Electric currents,
        Alternating**

Alternative life style. *See* **Counter culture; Life styles**

Alternative press. *See* **Underground press**

Alternative schools. *See* **Free schools**

Alternative universities. *See* **Free universities**

Altitude, Influence of. *See* **Man—Influence of environment**

Aluminum 669; 673

   See also **Aluminum foil**

Aluminum—Recycling 604.6; 673

   xx **Recycling (Waste, etc.)**

Aluminum alloys 669; 673

   xx **Alloys**

Aluminum foil 673

   xx **Aluminum; Packaging**

Ama. *See* **Pearl diving and divers**

Amateur motion pictures 778.5

   x Motion pictures, Amateur; Personal films

   xx **Motion picture photography**

Amateur radio stations 621.3841

   x Ham radio stations; Radio stations, Amateur

   xx **Radio, Short wave**

Amateur theatricals 792

   Use for materials on the production of plays by non-professional groups. Collections of plays for such groups are entered under **Drama—Collections; American drama—Collections;** and similar subjects

   See also **Acting; Charades; Children's plays; College and school drama; Drama in education; Makeup, Theatrical; One act plays; Pantomimes; Shadow pantomimes and plays; Theater—Production and direction**

   x Play production; Private theatricals; Theatricals, Amateur

   xx **Amusements; Drama in education; Theater**

Ambassadors. *See* **Diplomats**

America 917; 970

   Use for general materials on the western hemisphere or the two Americas

   See also **Central America; Latin America; North America; South America;** and names of separate countries of these areas

America—Antiquities 917

America—Exploration 970.01; 973.1

   See also **Explorers; Northwest Passage; U.S.—Exploring expeditions**

   x Canada—Exploration; Conquistadores; Explorations; North America—Exploration; South America—Exploration; U.S.—Exploration

   xx **Discoveries (in geography); Explorers**

America—History 970; 973

   x American history

America—Politics and government   970; 973
> Use for general materials on politics and government in the western hemisphere or in three or more countries of the two Americas

> *See also* **Pan-Americanism**

> *xx* **Pan-Americanism**

American actors and actresses.   *See* **Actors and actresses, American**

American   architecture.   *See*   **Architecture, American**

American art.   *See* **Art, American**

American artificial satellites.   *See* **Artificial satellites, American**

American artists.   *See* **Artists, American**

American arts.   *See* **Arts, American**

American authors.   *See* **Authors, American**

American ballads.   *See* **Ballads, American**

American Bicentennial.   *See* **American Revolution Bicentennial, 1776–1976**

American bison.   *See* **Bison**

American characteristics.   *See* **National characteristics, American**

American Civil War.   *See* **U.S.—History—Civil War, 1861–1865**

American civilization.   *See* **Civilization, American; U.S.—Civilization**

American colleges.   *See* **Colleges and universities—U.S.**

American colonies.   *See* **U.S.—History—Colonial period, 1600–1775**

American color prints.   *See* **Color prints, American**

American composers.   *See* **Composers, American**

American decoration and ornament.   *See* **Decoration and ornament, American**

American drama   812
> *xx* **Drama**

American drama—Collections   812.08
> *xx* **Drama—Collections**

American drama—History and criticism   812.09
> *xx* **Drama—History and criticism**

American dramatists.   *See* **Dramatists, American**

American drawing.   *See* **Drawing, American**

American engraving.   *See* **Engraving, American**

American environmental policy.   *See* **Environmental policy—U.S.**

American espionage.   *See* **Espionage, American**

American essays   814.08
> *xx* **Essays**

American ethics.   *See* **Ethics, American**

American fiction   813; Fic
> *x* Fiction, American
> *xx* **Fiction**

American flag.   *See* **Flags—U.S.**

American folk art.   *See* **Folk art, American**

American folk dancing. *See* **Folk dancing, American**

American folk music. *See* **Folk music, American**

American folk songs. *See* **Folk songs—U.S.**

American furniture. *See* **Furniture, American**

American government. *See* **U.S.—Politics and government**

American graphic arts. *See* **Graphic arts, American**

American historians. *See* **Historians, American**

American history. *See* **America—History; U.S. —History**

American illustrators. *See* **Illustrators, American**

American Indians. *See* **Indians; Indians of North America; Indians of South America;** etc.

American labor unions. *See* **Labor unions— U.S.**

American letters 816
> *xx* **Letters**

American literature 810
> May be subdivided by the name of a state or region, e.g. **American literature— Massachusetts; American literature— Southern States**
>
> May use same subdivisions and literary forms as for **English literature**
>
> *See also* **Authors, American; Ballads, American; Canadian literature; Latin American literature;** also various forms of American literature, e.g. **American poetry; Satire, American**
>
> *x* U.S.—Literature

American literature—American Indian authors 897
> *x* Indian literature (American); Indians of North America—Literature

American literature—Black authors 810
> Use same pattern for other forms of literature
>
> *x* Black literature (American)

American literature—Collections 810.8
> Use for collections of both poetry and prose by several American authors. Collections consisting of prose only are entered under **American prose literature;** collections of poetry are entered under **American poetry—Collections**

American Loyalists 973.3
> *x* Loyalists, American; Tories, American
>
> *xx* **U.S.—History—Revolution, 1775–1783**

American military assistance. *See* **Military assistance, American**

American music. *See* **Music, American**

American musicians. *See* **Musicians, American**

American names. *See* **Names, Personal—U.S.**

22

American national characteristics. *See* **National characteristics, American**

American national songs. *See* **National songs, American**

American newspapers 071
xx **Newspapers**

American novelists. *See* **Novelists, American**

American orations 815.08
Use for collections of orations by several authors
xx **Orations**

American painters. *See* **Painters, American**

American painting. *See* **Painting, American**

American periodicals 051
xx **Periodicals**

American philosophers. *See* **Philosophers, American**

American philosophy. *See* **Philosophy, American**

American poetry 811
xx **American literature; Poetry**

American poetry—Black authors 811
x Black poetry

American poetry—Collections 811.08
xx **Poetry—Collections**

American poetry—History and criticism 811.09
xx **Poetry—History and criticism**

American poets. *See* **Poets, American**

American politicians. *See* **Politicians, American**

American politics. *See* **U.S.—Politics and government**

American pottery. *See* **Pottery, American**

American prints. *See* **Prints, American**

American propaganda. *See* **Propaganda, American**

American prose literature 818
Use for collections of prose writings by several American authors which may include a variety of literary forms such as essays, fiction, orations, etc.
x Prose literature, American

American refugees. *See* **Refugees, American**

American Revolution. *See* **U.S.—History—Revolution, 1775–1783**

American Revolution Bicentennial, 1776–1976 973.3
See also names of special bicentennial events, e.g. **Operation Sail, 1976;** etc.
x American Bicentennial; Bicentennial celebrations—U.S.—1976; U.S.—Bicentennial celebrations; U.S.—History —Revolution, 1775–1783—Centennial celebrations, etc.
xx **U.S.—Centennial celebrations, etc.**

American Revolution Bicentennial, 1776–1976 —Collectibles 973.3
x Collectibles; Collections of objects
xx **Collectors and collecting**

American satire. *See* **Satire, American**

American science. *See* **Science—U.S.**

American sculptors. *See* **Sculptors, American**

American sculpture. *See* **Sculpture, American**

American songs. *See* **Songs, American**

American-Spanish War, 1898. *See* **U.S.—History—War of 1898**

American travelers. *See* **Travelers, American**

American wit and humor 817.08; 817.09
>   *x* Tall tales
>   *xx* **Wit and humor**

American youth. *See* **Youth—U.S.**

Americanisms 427
>   Use for materials dealing with usage of words and expressions peculiar to the United States
>   *x* English language—Americanisms
>   *xx* **English language—Dialects**

Americanization 325.73
>   *See also* **Naturalization; U.S.—Foreign population; U.S.—Immigration and emigration**

Americans in foreign countries 325
>   *See also* **Americans in Greece;** and similar headings

Americans in Greece 325.495
>   Use same form for Americans in other countries, areas, etc., e.g. **Americans in Europe;** etc.
>   *xx* **Americans in foreign countries**

Amerindians. *See* **Indians; Indians of North America; Indians of South America**

Amish 289.7
>   *xx* **Mennonites**

Ammunition 623.4
>   *See also* types of ammunition, e.g. **Bombs; Gunpowder;** etc.
>   *xx* **Explosives; Gunpowder; Projectiles**

Amnesty 355.1; 364.6
>   *See also* **Pardon**
>   *xx* **Desertion, Military; Pardon**

Amphibians 567; 597
>   *See also* names of amphibians, e.g. **Frogs; Salamanders;** etc.
>   *x* Batrachia
>   *xx* **Vertebrates**

Amplifiers (Electronics) 621.381
>   *See also* special types of amplifiers, e.g. **Amplifiers, Vacuum tube; Masers;** etc.
>   *xx* **Electronics**

Amplifiers, Vacuum tube 621.3815
>   *xx* **Amplifiers (Electronics); Radio—Apparatus and supplies; Vacuum tubes**

Amusement parks 791.06
>   *See also* names of specific parks, e.g. **Disneyland;** etc.
>   *x* Carnivals (Circus)
>   *xx* **Parks**

Amusements 790
>   Use for materials about various kinds of

24

Amusements—*Continued*

entertainment and pastimes. All types of amusements are not listed below. Add as needed.

See also

Amateur theatricals	**Motion pictures**
Charades	**Play**
Church entertain-	**Puzzles**
ments	**Recreation**
Circus	**Riddles**
Concerts	**Scientific recrea-**
Dancing	**tions**
Entertaining	**Sports**
Fortune telling	**Theater**
Games	**Toys**
Hobbies	**Vaudeville**
Indoor games	**Ventriloquism**
Magic	
Mathematical recrea-	
tions	

x Entertainments; Pastimes

xx **Entertaining; Games; Indoor games; Play; Recreation; Sports**

Anaesthetics. *See* **Anesthetics**

Analysis (Chemistry). *See* **Chemistry, Analytic;** and names of substances with the subdivision *Analysis,* e.g. **Food—Analysis;** etc.

Analysis (Mathematics). *See* **Calculus; Mathematical analysis**

Analysis, Microscopic. *See* **Metallography; Microscope and microscopy**

Analysis, Spectrum. *See* **Spectrum**

Analysis of food. *See* **Food—Analysis; Food adulteration and inspection**

Analysis situs. *See* **Topology**

Analytical chemistry. *See* **Chemistry, Analytic**

Analytical geometry. *See* **Geometry, Analytic**

Anarchism and anarchists 320.5; 335

See also **Terrorism**

xx **Freedom; Political crimes and offenses; Political science; Syndicalism**

Anatomy 574.4; 611

See also **Anatomy, Comparative; Anatomy, Human; Bones; Nervous system; Physiology;** also subjects with the subdivision *Anatomy,* e.g. **Birds—Anatomy; Botany—Anatomy;** etc.

x Morphology

xx **Biology; Medicine; Physiology**

Anatomy, Artistic 704.94; 743

See also **Figure drawing; Figure painting**

x Art anatomy; Artistic anatomy; Human figure in art

xx **Art; Drawing**

Anatomy, Comparative 591.4

See also **Man—Origin and antiquity**

x Comparative anatomy; Morphology

xx **Anatomy; Evolution; Man—Origin and antiquity; Zoology**

25

Anatomy, Dental. *See* **Teeth**

Anatomy, Human   611

   See also names of organs and regions of
      the body, e.g. **Heart;** etc.

   x Body, Human; Human anatomy; Human
      body

   xx **Anatomy**

Anatomy, Vegetable. *See* **Botany—Anatomy**

Anatomy of plants. *See* **Botany—Anatomy**

Ancestor worship   291.2; 291.3

   x The dead, Worship of

   xx **Funeral rites and ceremonies; Shinto;
      Worship**

Ancestry. *See* **Genealogy; Heredity**

Ancient architecture. *See* **Architecture, An-
      cient**

Ancient art. *See* **Art, Ancient**

Ancient civilization. *See* **Civilization, Ancient**

Ancient geography. *See* **Geography, Ancient**

Ancient history. *See* **History, Ancient**

Ancient philosophy. *See* **Philosophy, Ancient**

Anecdotes   808.88; 818; etc.

   See also subjects with the subdivision *An-
      ecdotes, facetiae, satire, etc.,* e.g. **Mu-
      sic—Anecdotes, facetiae, satire, etc.;**
      etc.

   x Facetiae; Stories

   xx **Wit and humor**

Anesthetics   615; 617

   x Anaesthetics

   xx **Materia medica; Pain; Surgery**

Angina pectoris. *See* **Heart—Diseases**

Anglican Church. *See* **Church of England**

Angling. *See* **Fishing**

Anglo-French intervention in Egypt, 1956. *See*
      Sinai Campaign, 1956

Anglo-Saxon language   429

   May be subdivided like **English language**

   x English language—To 1100; Old En-
      glish language

Anglo-Saxon literature   829

   May use same subdivisions and names of
      literary forms as for **English literature**

   x English literature—To 1100; Old En-
      glish literature

Anglo-Saxons   572.9362; 941.01

   x Saxons

   xx **Gt. Brit.—History—To 1066; Teutonic
      peoples**

Animal babies. *See* **Animals—Infancy**

Animal behavior. *See* **Animals—Habits and
      behavior**

Animal camouflage. *See* **Camouflage (Biology)**

Animal chemistry. *See* **Physiological chemis-
      try**

Animal coloration. *See* **Color of animals**

Animal communication   591.5

   x Animal language; Animals—Language;
      Communication among animals

Animal distribution. *See* **Geographical distribution of animals and plants**

Animal drawing. *See* **Animal painting and illustration**

Animal homes. *See* **Animals—Habitations**

Animal husbandry. *See* **Livestock**

Animal industry. *See* **Domestic animals; Livestock**

Animal instinct. *See* **Instinct**

Animal intelligence 156

> *See also* **Animals—Habits and behavior; Instinct; Learning, Psychology of; Psychology, Comparative;** also names of animals with the subdivision *Psychology,* e.g. **Dogs—Psychology;** etc.
>
> *x* Animal psychology; Intelligence of animals
>
> *xx* **Animals—Habits and behavior; Instinct; Psychology, Comparative**

Animal kingdom. *See* **Zoology**

Animal language. *See* **Animal communication**

Animal light. *See* **Bioluminescence**

Animal locomotion 591.1

> *x* Animals—Movements;   Locomotion; Movements of animals

Animal lore. *See* **Animals, Mythical; Animals in literature; Natural history**

Animal magnetism. *See* **Hypnotism**

Animal migration. *See* **Animals—Migration**

Animal oils. *See* **Oils and fats**

Animal painting and illustration 704.94; 743; 758

> Use for materials on the art and methods of painting and drawing animals. Materials about representations of animals in works of art (painting, sculpture, etc.), or reproductions of them, are entered under **Animals in art.** Materials consisting of photographs or illustrations of animals are entered under **Animals—Pictorial works**
>
> *See also* **Animals—Pictorial works; Animals in art; Photography of animals**
>
> *x* Animal drawing
>
> *xx* **Animals—Pictorial works; Animals in art; Painting; Photography of animals**

Animal parasites. *See* **Parasites**

Animal photography. *See* **Photography of animals**

Animal physiology. *See* **Zoology**

Animal pictures. *See* **Animals—Pictorial works**

Animal products. *See* names of special products, e.g. **Hides and skins; Ivory; Wool;** etc.

Animal psychology. *See* **Animal intelligence; Psychology, Comparative**

Animal stories. *See* **Animals—Fiction**

Animal training. *See* **Animals—Training**

Animals (May subdiv. geog.) **590; 591**

    Use for descriptive and non-systematic or non-technical material. Subdivisions under this heading may be used under names of orders and classes of the animal kingdom and with names of individual animals

    See also **Color of animals; Desert animals; Domestic animals; Fresh water animals; Furbearing animals; Game and game birds; Geographical distribution of animals and plants; Marine animals; Natural history; Pets; Poisonous animals; Zoological gardens; Zoology;** also names of orders and classes of the animal kingdom (e.g. **Vertebrates; Mammals; Primates;** etc.); and names of individual animals, e.g. **Monkeys;** etc.

    x Beasts; Fauna; Wild animals

    xx **Zoology**

Animals, Aquatic. *See* **Fresh water animals; Marine animals**

Animals—Camouflage. *See* **Camouflage (Biology)**

Animals—Color. *See* **Color of animals**

Animals—Courtship 156; 591.3

    x Courtship of animals

    xx **Animals—Habits and behavior**

Animals, Cruelty to. *See* **Animals—Treatment**

Animals—Diseases 636.089

    See also names of animals with the subdivision *Diseases*, e.g., **Cattle—Diseases;** etc.

    x Diseases of animals; Domestic animals—Diseases

    xx **Diseases; Veterinary medicine**

Animals, Domestic. *See* **Domestic animals**

Animals, Extinct. *See* **Extinct animals**

Animals—Fiction Fic

    See also names of animals with the subdivision *Fiction*, e.g., **Dogs—Fiction;** etc.

    x Animal stories; Animals—Stories

    xx **Animals in literature; Fables; Fiction**

Animals, Fictitious. *See* **Animals, Mythical**

Animals, Fossil. *See* **Fossils**

Animals, Fresh water. *See* **Fresh water animals**

Animals—Geographical distribution. *See* **Geographical distribution of animals and plants**

Animals—Habitations 591.5

    x Animal homes; Habitations of animals; Houses of animals

Animals—Habits and behavior 156; 591.1; 591.5

    See also **Animal intelligence; Instinct; Nature study; Tracking and trailing;** also types of specific behavior, e.g. **Animals—Courtship; Animals—Hiberna-**

Animals—Habits and behavior—*Continued*
tion; **Animals—Migration;** etc. and
names of animals with the subdivision
Habits and behavior, e.g. **Primates—
Habits and behavior; Monkeys—Habits and behavior;** etc.
x Animal behavior; Behavior; Habits of
animals
xx **Animal intelligence; Nature study**
Animals—Hibernation 591.5
x Hibernation of animals
xx **Animals—Habits and behavior**
Animals, Imaginary. *See* **Animals, Mythical**
Animals—Infancy 591
x Animal babies; Baby animals
Animals—Language. *See* **Animal communication**
Animals, Marine. *See* **Marine animals**
Animals—Migration 591.5
See also names of animals with the subdivision *Migration,* e.g. **Birds—Migration;** etc.
x Animal migration; Migration of animals
xx **Animals—Habits and behavior; Geographical distribution of animals and plants**
Animals—Movements. *See* **Animal locomotion**
Animals, Mythical 398.2; Fic
See also names of mythical animals, e.g.
Dragons; Giants; Mermaids; Unicorns; etc.
x Animal lore; Animals, Fictitious; Animals, Imaginary; Creatures, Imaginary; Fictitious animals; Imaginary animals; Mythical animals
xx **Mythology**
Animals—Photography. *See* **Photography of animals**
Animals—Pictorial works 591.022; 743; 778.9
See note under **Animal painting and illustration**
See also **Animal painting and illustration; Animals in art; Photography of animals**
x Animal pictures; Illustrations; Pictorial works
xx **Animal painting and illustration; Animals in art; Photography of animals; Pictures**
Animals—Poetry 808.81; 811.08; etc.
See also **Animals in literature**
xx **Animals in literature; Poetry**
Animals, Prehistoric. *See* **Fossils**
Animals—Protection. *See* **Animals—Treatment**
Animals, Rare. *See* **Rare animals**
Animals, Sea. *See* **Marine animals**
Animals—Stories. *See* **Animals—Fiction**

Animals—Training   636.08

    See also names of animals with the subdivision *Training,* e.g., **Dogs—Training; Horses—Training;** etc.

    x Animal training; Training of animals

    xx **Circus**

Animals—Treatment   179

    See also **Vivisection**

    x Abuse of animals; Animals, Cruelty to; Animals—Protection; Cruelty to animals; Kindness to animals; Prevention of cruelty to animals; Protection of animals

    xx **Domestic animals; Vivisection**

Animals—U.S.   591.9

    x U.S.—Animals

Animals, Useful and harmful.   *See* **Zoology, Economic**

Animals, War use of   355.4

    See also **Dogs, War use of**

Animals in art   704.94

    See note under **Animal painting and illustration**

    See also **Animal painting and illustration; Animals—Pictorial works**

    xx **Animal painting and illustration; Animals—Pictorial works; Art**

Animals in literature   808.8; 809

    Use for materials that discuss animals in literature. Poems or stories about animals are entered under **Animals—Poetry; Animals—Fiction**

    See also **Animals—Fiction; Animals—Poetry; Bible—Natural history;** also phrase headings of specific animals in literature, e.g. **Dogs in literature;** etc.

    x Animal lore

    xx **Animals—Poetry; Nature in literature**

Animated cartoons.   *See* **Motion picture cartoons**

Annapolis Naval Academy.   *See* **United States Naval Academy, Annapolis**

Anniversaries.   *See* **Holidays;** and names of special days, e.g. **Fourth of July;** etc.

Annual income.   *See* **Wages—Annual wage**

Annual wage plans.   *See* **Wages—Annual wage**

Annuals.   *See* **Almanacs; Calendars; Yearbooks;** and general subjects and names of organizations with the subdivision *Yearbooks,* e.g. **Literature—Yearbooks; United Nations—Yearbooks;** etc.

Annuals (Plants)   582; 635.9

    xx **Flower gardening; Flowers; Plants, Cultivated**

Annuities   368.3

    See also **Insurance, Life; Pensions**

    x Retirement income

Annuities—*Continued*

    xx **Insurance, Life; Investments**

Annulment of marriage. *See* **Marriage—Annulment**

Anonyms. *See* **Pseudonyms**

Answers to questions. *See* **Questions and answers**

Ant. *See* **Ants**

Antarctic expeditions. *See* **Antarctic regions;** and names of expeditions, e.g. **Byrd Antarctic Expedition, 1st, 1928–1930;** etc.

Antarctic regions 919.8; 998

    See also **Scientific expeditions; South Pole;** also names of explorers and exploring expeditions

    x Antarctic expeditions; Expeditions, Antarctic and Arctic; Polar expeditions

    xx **Discoveries (in geography); Earth; Polar regions; Scientific expeditions; South Pole; Voyages and travels**

Antenuptial contracts. *See* **Marriage contracts**

Anthracite coal. *See* **Coal**

Anthropogeography 572.9

    See also **Geopolitics; Man—Influence of environment**

    x Biogeography; Geographical distribution of people; Geography, Social

    xx **Anthropology; Ethnology; Geography; Geopolitics; History; Human ecology; Immigration and emigration**

Anthropology 301.2; 573

    See also

Acculturation	**Language and languages**
Anthropogeography	
Anthropometry	**Man**
Archeology	**National characteristics**
Civilization	
Color of people	**Physical anthropology**
Ethnology	
Ethnopsychology	**Social change**
Eugenics	

    also names of races and peoples (e.g. **Semitic peoples; Ojibwe Indians;** etc.); and names of countries, cities, etc. with the subdivision *Race relations,* e.g. **U.S.—Race relations**

    x Human race

    xx **Civilization; Ethnology; Man**

Anthropology, Physical. *See* **Physical anthropology**

Anthropometry 573

    See also **Fingerprints**

    x Skeletal remains

    xx **Anthropology; Ethnology; Man**

Anti-Americanism. *See* **U.S.—Foreign opinion**

Antiballistic missiles. *See* **Antimissile missiles**

Antibiotics 615

    See also names of specific antibiotics, e.g.
        Penicillin; etc.

    xx **Chemotherapy**

Antibusing. *See* **Busing (School integration)**

Anticommunist movements 322.4

    x Underground, Anticommunist

    xx **Communism**

Anticorrosive paint. *See* **Corrosion and anticorrosives**

Antimissile missiles 623.4

    x ABM; Antiballistic missiles

    xx **Guided missiles**

Antipathies. *See* **Prejudices and antipathies**

Anti-poverty programs. *See* **Economic assistance, Domestic**

Antiques 745.1

    See also **Art objects; Collectors and col-
lecting**

Antiquities. *See* **Archeology; Bible—Antiquities; Christian antiquities; Classical antiquities; Indians of North America—
Antiquities; Jews—Antiquities; Man—
Origin and antiquity; Man, Prehistoric;** and names of countries, cities,
etc. with the subdivision *Antiquities,*
e.g. **U.S.—Antiquities;** etc.

Antiquities, Biblical. *See* **Bible—Antiquities**

Antiquities, Christian. *See* **Christian antiquities**

Antiquities, Classical. *See* **Classical antiquities**

Antiquities, Ecclesiastical. *See* **Christian antiquities**

Anti-Reformation. *See* **Reformation**

Antisemitism. *See* **Jews and Gentiles**

Antiseptics 615

    See also **Disinfection and disinfectants**

    xx **Disinfection and disinfectants; Surgery;
Therapeutics**

Antislavery. *See* **Slavery**

Antitrust law 343.7

    x Trusts, Industrial—Law and legislation

    xx **Commercial law; Trusts, Industrial**

Antivivisection. *See* **Vivisection**

Antiwar movements. *See* names of wars with
the subdivision *Protest movements,*
e.g., **World War, 1939–1945—Protest
movements;** etc.

Antonyms. *See* names of languages with the
subdivision *Synonyms and antonyms,*
e.g. **English language—Synonyms and
antonyms;** etc.

Ants 595.7

    x Ant; Hymenoptera

    xx **Insects**

Anxiety. *See* **Fear; Stress (Psychology); Worry**

Apartheid. *See* **Segregation; South Africa—
Race relations**

Apartment houses 647; 728.3

    See also **Condominiums**

Apartment houses—*Continued*

    x Flats

    xx **Architecture, Domestic; Houses; Housing; Landlord and tenant**

Apiculture. *See* **Bees**

Apollo project 629.45

    See also headings beginning with **Lunar** and **Moon**

    x Project Apollo

    xx **Life support systems (Space environment); Orbital rendezvous (Space flight); Space flight to the moon**

Apologetics 239

    See also **Natural theology; Religion and science**

    x Christianity—Apologetic works; Christianity—Evidences; Evidences of Christianity; Fundamental theology

Apostles 920; 922

    x Disciples, Twelve

    xx **Christian saints; Church history—Early church, ca. 30–600**

Apostles' Creed 238

    xx **Creeds**

Apostolic Church. *See* **Church history—Early church, ca. 30–600**

Apparatus, Chemical. *See* **Chemical apparatus**

Apparatus, Electric. *See* **Electric apparatus and appliances**

Apparatus, Electronic. *See* **Electronic apparatus and appliances**

Apparatus, Scientific. *See* **Scientific apparatus and instruments**

Apparitions 133.1

    See also **Demonology; Ghosts; Hallucinations and illusions; Miracles; Spiritualism; Visions**

    x Phantoms; Specters; Spirits

    xx **Demonology; Ghosts; Hallucinations and illusions; Psychical research; Spiritualism; Superstition; Visions**

Apperception 153.7

    See also **Attention; Consciousness; Knowledge, Theory of; Perception**

    xx **Educational psychology; Knowledge, Theory of; Perception; Psychology**

Apple 582; 634

    xx **Fruit**

Appliances, Electric. *See* **Electric apparatus and appliances; Household appliances, Electric**

Appliances, Electronic. *See* **Electronic apparatus and appliances**

Applications for positions 331.1

    See also **Interviewing; Resumés (Employment)**

    x Employment applications; Employment references; Job applications; Letters

Applications for positions—*Continued*
> of recommendation; Recommendations for positions

> *xx* **Personnel management**

Applied art. *See* **Art industries and trade**

Applied mechanics. *See* **Mechanics, Applied**

Applied psychology. *See* **Psychology, Applied**

Applied science. *See* **Technology**

Apportionment (Election law) 324; 328
> *x* Legislative reapportionment; Reapportionment (Election law)

> *xx* **Representative government and representation**

Appraisal. *See* **Assessment; Valuation**

Appraisal of books. *See* **Books—Reviews; Books and reading; Books and reading—Best books; Criticism; Literature —History and criticism**

Appreciation of art. *See* **Art appreciation**

Appreciation of music. *See* **Music—Analysis, appreciation**

Apprentices 331.5
> *See also* **Employees—Training**

> *xx* **Child labor; Employees—Training; Labor and laboring classes; Technical education**

April Fools' Day 394.2
> *x* All Fools' Day

Aptitude testing. *See* **Ability—Testing**

Aquaculture 639
> *See also* **Fisheries**

> *x* Aquiculture; Fresh water aquaculture; Mariculture; Marine aquaculture; Ocean farming; Sea farming

> *xx* **Agriculture; Food supply; Marine Resources**

Aquanauts 920; 925
> *x* Oceanauts

> *xx* **Undersea research stations; Underwater exploration**

Aquariums 639
> *See also* **Fish culture; Goldfish; Marine aquariums;** also names of specific aquariums

> *xx* **Fishes; Fresh water animals; Fresh water biology; Fresh water plants; Natural history**

Aquariums, Saltwater. *See* **Marine aquariums**

Aquatic animals. *See* **Fresh water animals; Marine animals**

Aquatic birds. *See* **Water birds**

Aquatic plants. *See* **Fresh water plants; Marine plants**

Aquatic sports. *See* **Water sports**

Aqueducts 628.1
> *x* Conduits; Water conduits

> *xx* **Civil engineering; Hydraulic structures; Water supply**

Aquiculture. *See* **Aquaculture**

Arab civilization. *See* **Civilization, Arab**

Arab countries   915.6; 956
>   *xx* Middle East
Arab-Israel War, 1948–1949.   *See* **Israel-Arab
      War, 1948–1949**
Arab-Israel War, 1956.   *See* **Sinai campaign,
      1956**
Arab-Israel War, 1967–   . *See* **Israel-Arab
      War, 1967–**
Arab-Israel War, 1973.   *See* **Israel-Arab War,
      1973**
Arab-Israeli relations.   *See* **Israeli-Arab rela-
      tions**
Arabic art.   *See* **Art, Islamic**
Arabs   572.917; 909
>   *See also* names of specific Arab peoples,
      e.g. **Bedouins; Moors;** etc.
Arachnida.   *See* **Spiders**
Arbitration, Industrial   331.89
>   *See also* **Collective bargaining; Strikes and
      lockouts**
>   *x* Conciliation, Industrial; Industrial arbi-
      tration; Industrial conciliation; Labor
      arbitration; Labor negotiations; Medi-
      ation, Industrial; Trade agreements
      (Labor)
>   *xx* **Collective bargaining; Industrial rela-
      tions; Labor and laboring classes; La-
      bor disputes; Labor unions; Strikes
      and lockouts**
Arbitration, International   341.5
>   *See also* **Disarmament; League of Nations;
      Peace; United Nations**
>   *x* International arbitration
>   *xx* **Disarmament; International cooperation;
      International law; International rela-
      tions; Peace; Security, International;
      Treaties**
Arboriculture.   *See* **Forests and forestry; Fruit
      culture; Trees**

Arc light.   *See* **Electric lighting**

Arc welding.   *See* **Electric welding**

Archaeology.   *See* **Archeology**

Archeologists   920; 923
>   *xx* **Historians**

Archeology   913
>   *See also*

Architecture, An-cient	**Cliff dwellers and cliff dwellings**
Arms and armor	**Ethnology**
Bible—Antiquities	**Excavations**
Brasses	**(Archeology)**
Bronze age	**Funeral rites and**
Bronzes	**ceremonies**
Christian antiquities	**Gems**
Christian art and symbolism	**Heraldry**
	Historic sites
Cities and towns, Ruined, extinct, etc.	**Indians of North America—Antiqui-**
Classical antiquities	**ties**

35

Archeology—*Continued*

Inscriptions	**Pyramids**
Iron age	**Radiocarbon dating**
Man, Prehistoric	**Religious art and**
Mounds and mound	**symbolism**
builders	**Stone age**
Mummies	**Stone implements**
Numismatics	**Temples**
Obelisks	**Tombs**
Pottery	

also names of regions, countries, cities, etc. with the subdivision *Antiquities,* e.g. **U.S.–Antiquities;** etc.

x Antiquities; Archaeology; Prehistory; Ruins

xx **Anthropology; Art; Bronze age; Civilization; Classical antiquities; Ethnology; History; History, Ancient; Iron age**

Archeology, Biblical. *See* **Bible—Antiquities**

Archeology, Christian. *See* **Christian antiquities**

Archeology, Classical. *See* **Classical antiquities**

Archery 799.3

See also **Bow and arrow**

xx **Bow and arrow; Shooting**

Architects 920; 927

xx **Artists**

Architectural acoustics 729

See also **Soundproofing**

x Acoustics

xx **Sound**

Architectural decoration and ornament. *See* **Decoration and ornament, Architectural**

Architectural design. *See* **Architecture—Details**

Architectural designs. *See* **Architecture—Designs and plans**

Architectural details. *See* **Architecture—Details**

Architectural drawing 720.28

See also **Architecture—Designs and plans; Architecture—Details**

x Drawing, Architectural; Plans

xx **Drawing; Mechanical drawing**

Architectural engineering. *See* **Building; Building, Iron and steel; Strains and stresses; Strength of materials; Structures, Theory of**

Architectural metalwork 721

x Metalwork, Architectural

xx **Metalwork**

Architectural orders. *See* **Architecture—Orders**

Architectural perspective. *See* **Perspective**

Architecture (May subdiv. geog. adjective form, e.g. **Architecture, Greek;** etc.) All types of architecture and buildings are

Architecture—*Continued*
>
> not included in this list. Add as needed
>
> **720**
>
> *See also*

Building	**Obelisks**
Building materials	**Palaces**
Castles	**Public buildings**
Cathedrals	**School buildings**
Church architecture	**Skyscrapers**
Concrete construc-	**Spires**
tion	**Strains and stresses**
Decoration and orna-	**Strength of materials**
ment, Architectural	**Structural engineer-**
Farm buildings	**ing**
Industrial buildings	**Synagogues**
Library architecture	**Temples**
Monuments	**Theaters**
Mosques	**Tombs**
Naval architecture	

> *also* styles of architecture, e.g., **Architec-
> ture, Byzantine;** etc., and types of
> buildings; and headings beginning
> with the word **Architectural**
>
> *x* Construction
>
> *xx* **Art; Building; Women—Employment**

Architecture, American   720.973

> *x* American architecture; U.S.—Architec-
> ture

Architecture, Ancient   722

> *See also* **Architecture, Greek; Architec-
> ture, Roman; Pyramids; Temples**
>
> *x* Ancient architecture
>
> *xx* **Archeology**

Architecture, Asian   722

> *See also* **Mosques; Temples**
>
> *x* Asian architecture; Oriental architec-
> ture

Architecture, Baroque   724

> *x* Baroque architecture

Architecture, Byzantine   723

> *x* Byzantine architecture
>
> *xx* **Architecture**

Architecture, Church. *See* **Church architecture**

Architecture, Colonial   724

> *See also* names of countries, cities, etc
> with the subdivision *Historic build-
> ings, etc.,* e.g. **Chicago—Historic build-
> ings, etc.;** etc.
>
> *x* Colonial architecture

**Architecture—Composition,   proportion,   etc.
729**

> *x* Architecture—Proportion;   Proportion
> (Architecture)
>
> *xx* **Composition (Art)**

**Architecture—Conservation   and   restoration
690; 720**

> *See also* **Buildings—Maintenance and re-
> pair**

Architecture—Conservation and restoration— *Continued*

    x Architecture—Restoration; Buildings, Restoration of; Conservation of buildings; Preservation of buildings; Restoration of buildings

  xx **Buildings—Maintenance and repair**

Architecture—Decoration and ornament. *See* **Decoration and ornament, Architectural**

Architecture—Designs and plans   721; 729

    See also **Architecture, Domestic—Designs and plans**

    x Architectural designs; Architecture—Plans; Designs, Architectural

  xx **Architectural drawing**

Architecture—Details   729

    See also **Chimneys; Doors; Fireplaces; Floors; Foundations; Roofs; Windows; Woodwork**

    x Architectural design; Architectural details; Design, Architectural; Details, Architectural

  xx **Architectural drawing**

Architecture, Domestic   728

    See also **Apartment houses; Farm buildings; Houses; Prefabricated houses; Solar homes**

    x Architecture, Rural; Country houses; Domestic architecture; Dwellings; Habitations, Human; Residences; Rural architecture; Suburban homes; Summer homes; Villas

Architecture, Domestic—Designs and plans   728

    x Home designs; House plans

  xx **Architecture—Designs and plans**

Architecture, Ecclesiastical. *See* **Church architecture**

Architecture, Gothic   723

    See also **Cathedrals; Church architecture**

    x Gothic architecture

  xx **Cathedrals; Christian antiquities; Church architecture**

Architecture, Greek   722

    x Greek architecture

  xx **Architecture, Ancient**

Architecture, Medieval   723

    See also **Architecture, Romanesque; Castles; Cathedrals**

    x Medieval architecture

  xx **Middle Ages**

Architecture, Modern—20th century   724.9

    x Modern architecture

Architecture, Naval. *See* **Naval architecture; Shipbuilding**

Architecture—Orders   729

    x Architectural orders; Orders, Architectural

Architecture—Plans. *See* **Architecture—Designs and plans**

Architecture—Proportion. *See* **Architecture— Composition, proportion, etc.**

Architecture, Renaissance 724
    xx **Renaissance**

Architecture—Restoration. *See* **Architecture— Conservation and restoration**

Architecture, Roman 722
    x Roman architecture
    xx **Architecture, Ancient**

Architecture, Romanesque 723
    x Romanesque architecture
    xx **Architecture, Medieval**

Architecture, Rural. *See* **Architecture, Domestic; Farm buildings**

Architecture and the handicapped 720
    Use same form for architecture and other groups of people
    x Handicapped and architecture

Archives (May subdiv. geog.) **025.17**
    See also **Charters; Libraries; Manuscripts**
    x Documents; Government records—Preservation; Historical records—Preservation; Preservation of historical records; Public records—Preservation; Records—Preservation
    xx **Bibliography; Charters; Documentation; History—Sources; Libraries**

Archives—U.S. 025.17973
    x U.S.—Archives

Arctic expeditions. *See* **Arctic regions;** and names of special expeditions

Arctic regions 919.8; 998
    See also **North Pole; Northeast Passage; Northwest Passage; Scientific expeditions;** also names of explorers and exploring expeditions
    x Arctic expeditions; Expeditions, Antarctic and Arctic; Polar expeditions
    xx **Discoveries (in geography); Earth; North Pole; Polar regions; Scientific expeditions**

Ardennes, Battle of the, 1944–1945 940.54
    x Bastogne, Battle of; Battle of the Bulge; Bulge, Battle of the
    xx **Battles; World War, 1939–1945; World War, 1939–1945—Campaigns and battles**

Area studies 914-919
    See also names of specific area studies, e.g. **Black studies;** etc.
    x Foreign area studies
    xx **Education**

Arena theater 725
    x Round stage; Theater-in-the-round
    xx **Theater**

Argentine rummy. *See* **Canasta (Game)**

Argumentation. *See* **Debates and debating; Logic**

Aristocracy 301.44

> See also **Democracy; Nobility; Upper classes**
>
> xx **Democracy; Equality; Nobility; Political science; Social classes; Sociology**

Arithmetic 513

> See also **Business arithmetic**
>
> xx **Mathematics; Set theory; Textbooks**

Arithmetic, Commercial. See **Business arithmetic**

Arithmetic—Study and teaching 372.7; 513.07

> See also **Counting; Number games**

Armada, 1588 942.05

> x Spanish Armada
>
> xx **Gt. Brit.—History—Tudors, 1485–1603**

Armaments. See **Armies; Disarmament; Industrial mobilization; Munitions; Navies**

Armed forces. See **Armies; Navies; Sailors; Soldiers;** and names of countries and international organizations with the subdivision *Armed Forces,* e.g. **U.S.—Armed Forces;** etc.

Armies 355.3

> See also **Disarmament; Military art and science; Military service, Compulsory; Military service, Voluntary; Navies; Soldiers; War; World War, 1939–1945 —Human resources;** also names of countries with the subhead *Army* (e.g. **U.S. Army;** etc.); and headings beginning with the word **Military**
>
> x Armaments; Armed forces; Army; Military forces; Military power
>
> xx **Military art and science; Navies; Soldiers; Strategy; War**

Armies—Medical and sanitary affairs 355.3

> See also **Medicine, Military; Military hygiene;** also names of wars with the subdivision *Medical and sanitary affairs,* e.g. **World War, 1939–1945—Medical and sanitary affairs;** etc.
>
> xx **Medicine, Military; Military hygiene**

Armistice Day. See **Veterans Day**

Armor. See **Arms and armor**

Armored cars (Tanks). See **Tanks (Military science)**

Arms, Coats of. See **Heraldry**

Arms aid. See **Military assistance**

Arms and armor 355.8; 623.4; 739.7

> See also **Firearms; Ordnance; Rifles**
>
> x Armor; Weapons and weaponry
>
> xx **Archeology; Costume; Military art and science**

Arms control. See **Disarmament**

Army. See **Armies; Military art and science;** and names of countries with the subhead *Army,* e.g. **U.S. Army;** etc.

Army desertion. See **Desertion, Military**

Army life. *See* **Soldiers;** and names of armies with the subdivision—*Military life* e.g. **U.S. Army—Military life;** etc.

Army posts. *See* **Military posts**

Army schools. *See* **Military education**

Army tests. *See* **U.S. Army—Examinations**

Army vehicles. *See* **Vehicles, Military**

Aromatic plant products. *See* **Essences and essential oils**

Arrow. *See* **Bow and arrow**

Art (May subdiv. geog. adjective form, e.g. **Art, French;** etc.) **700**

Names of all types of art are not included in this list but are to be added as needed

Subdivisions listed under this heading may be used under other art media where applicable

See also

Anatomy, Artistic	**Folk art**
Animals in art	**Forgery of works of**
Archeology	**art**
Architecture	**Futurism (Art)**
Art objects	**Gems**
Arts and crafts	**Graphic arts**
Blacks in literature	**Illumination of**
and art	**books and manu-**
Brasses	**scripts**
Bronzes	**Illustration of books**
Children in litera-	**Painting**
ture and art	**Photography,**
Christian art and	**Artistic**
symbolism	**Pictures**
Collage	**Plants in art**
Collectors and col-	**Portraits**
lecting	**Religious art and**
Commercial art	**symbolism**
Composition (Art)	**Sculpture**
Design, Decorative	**Surrealism**
Drawing	**Symbolism**
Engraving	**Women in literature**
Esthetics	**and art**
Etching	

x Iconography

xx **Civilization; Humanities**

Art, Abstract   709.04

See also types of abstract art, e.g. **Kinetic art;** etc.

x Abstract art; Art, Nonobjective; Nonobjective art; Painting, Abstract

xx **Art, Modern—20th century**

Art, American   709.73

x American art; U.S.—Art

Art—Analysis, interpretation, appreciation. *See* **Art appreciation; Art—Study and teaching; Art criticism**

Art, Ancient   709.01

See also **Classical antiquities**

x Ancient art

41

Art, Applied. *See* **Art industries and trade;
Design, Industrial**

Art, Arabic. *See* **Art, Islamic**

Art, Asian   709.5
 x Art, Oriental; Asian art; Oriental art

Art, Baroque   709.03
 x Baroque art

Art, Black. *See* **Black art**

Art, Buddhist   709.17
 x Buddhist art

Art, Byzantine   709.02
 x Byzantine art
 xx **Art, Medieval**

Art, Christian. *See* **Christian art and symbolism**

Art, Classical. *See* **Art, Greek; Art, Roman**

Art, Commercial. *See* **Commercial art**

Art—Composition. *See* **Composition (Art)**

Art—Criticism. *See* **Art criticism**

Art, Decorative   745
 Use for general materials on the decoration and use of artistic objects. Materials limited to the line or form that
these objects may take are entered
under **Design.** Materials limited to the
external ornamentation of objects are
entered under **Design, Decorative**
 See also

Bronzes	**Illustration of**
Decoration and or-	**books**
nament	**Mosaics**
Design, Decorative	**Mural painting and**
Enamel and enamel-	**decoration**
ing	**Needlework**
Furniture	**Pottery**

 x Decorative art; Decorative arts
 xx **Decoration and ornament; Design, Decorative**

Art, Ecclesiastical. *See* **Christian art and symbolism**

Art—Education. *See* **Art—Study and teaching**

Art, Erotic. *See* **Erotic art**

Art—Exhibitions   708
 x Art exhibitions
 xx **Exhibitions**

Art—Forgeries. *See* **Forgery of works of art**

Art—Galleries and museums   708; 727
 Use for general materials only
 See also names of countries, cities, etc.
with the subdivision *Galleries and
museums* (e.g. **U.S.—Galleries and
museums; Chicago—Galleries and museums;** etc.); and names of individual galleries and museums
 x Art galleries; Art museums; Galleries
(Art); Picture galleries
 xx **Museums**

Art, Graphic. *See* **Graphic arts**

Art, Greek 709.38; 709.495

    x Art, Classical; Classical art; Greek art

    xx **Classical antiquities**

Art—History 709

    xx **History**

Art, Immoral. *See* **Erotic art**

Art, Indian. *See* **Indians of North America—Art**

Art, Islamic 709.17

    x Arabic art; Art, Arabic; Art, Mohammedan; Art, Moorish; Mohammedan art; Moorish art; Moslem art

Art, Kinetic. *See* **Kinetic art**

Art, Medieval 709.02

    See also **Art, Byzantine; Art, Romanesque; Illumination of books and manuscripts**

    x Medieval art; Religious art

    xx **Civilization, Medieval; Middle Ages**

Art, Modern 709.03

    x Modern art

Art, Modern—19th century 709.03

    See also **Postimpressionism (Art)**

Art, Modern—20th century 709.04

    See also names of modern art, e.g. **Art, Abstract; Kinetic art;** etc.

    x Contemporary art

Art, Mohammedan. *See* **Art, Islamic**

Art, Moorish. *See* **Art, Islamic**

Art, Municipal 711

    See also **City planning; Public buildings**

    x Civic art; Municipal art; Municipal improvement

    xx **Cities and towns; City planning**

Art, Nonobjective. *See* **Art, Abstract**

Art, Oriental. *See* **Art, Asian**

Art—Prices 702

    xx **Prices**

Art, Renaissance 709.02

    xx **Renaissance**

Art, Roman 709.37

    x Art, Classical; Classical art; Roman art

    xx **Classical antiquities**

Art, Romanesque 709.02

    See also **Painting, Romanesque**

    x Romanesque art

    xx **Art, Medieval**

Art—Study and teaching 707

    x Art—Analysis, interpretation, appreciation; Art—Education; Art education; Art schools

    xx **Study, Method of**

Art—Technique 702.8

Art—Thefts. *See* **Art thefts**

Art anatomy. *See* **Anatomy, Artistic**

Art and mythology 704.94

    Use same form for art and other subjects

    x Mythology in art

    xx **Art and religion; Mythology**

Art and religion   704.948

> *See also* **Art and mythology; Religious art and symbolism**
>
> *x* Religion and art
>
> *xx* **Art and society; Religious art and symbolism**

Art and society   701

> *See also* **Art and religion; Art and state; Art industries and trade; Folk art**
>
> *x* Society and art

Art and state   701

> *x* State and the arts; State encouragement of the arts
>
> *xx* **Art and society**

Art appreciation   701

> *x* Appreciation of art; Art—Analysis, interpretation, appreciation
>
> *xx* **Art criticism; Esthetics**

Art criticism   701

> *See also* **Art appreciation**
>
> *x* Art—Analysis interpretation, appreciation; Art—Criticism
>
> *xx* **Criticism**

Art education.   *See* **Art—Study and teaching**

Art exhibitions.   *See* **Art—Exhibitions**

Art forgeries.   *See* **Forgery of works of art**

Art galleries.   *See* **Art—Galleries and museums**

Art in advertising.   *See* **Commercial art**

Art in motion.   *See* **Kinetic art**

Art industries and trade. (May subdiv. geog.) **680**

> Use for materials dealing with decorative art in industry, peasant art, etc. and the production for commercial purposes of handicrafts and objects having an artistic value or interest
>
> *See also* **Arts and crafts; Commercial art; Design, Industrial; Folk art;** also special industries, trades, etc., e.g. **Glass painting and staining; Leather work;** etc.
>
> *x* Applied art; Art, Applied; Decorative arts; Industry and art; Peasant art
>
> *xx* **Art and society; Folk art; Industrial arts**

Art industries and trade—U.S.   680

> *x* U.S.—Art industries and trade

Art metalwork   739; 745.56

> *See also* kinds of art metalwork, e.g. **Bronzes; Goldwork; Jewelry; Silverwork;** etc.
>
> *x* Decorative metalwork; Metalwork, Art
>
> *xx* **Metalwork**

Art museums.   *See* **Art—Galleries and museums**

Art objects   745.1

> Use for general materials about articles of artistic merit such as snuff boxes, brasses, pottery, needlework, glassware, etc.

Art objects—*Continued*

  See also classes of art objects, e.g. **Furniture; Pottery;** etc.

  xx **Antiques; Art**

Art objects, Forgery of. *See* **Forgery of works of art**

Art robberies. *See* **Art thefts**

Art schools. *See* **Art—Study and teaching**

Art thefts   704

  x Art robberies; Art—Thefts; Thefts, Art

Artesian wells. *See* **Wells**

Arthritis   616.7

  xx **Gout; Rheumatism**

Articles of war. *See* **Military law**

Articulation (Education)   371.2

  Use for materials that discuss the integration of various elements of the school system so as to provide for continuous progress by the student. This may be the adjustments and relationships between different levels (e.g. elementary and secondary schools, high school and college); the integration between subjects (e.g. humanities and social studies); or the relationship between the school's program and outside factors (e.g. church, scouts, welfare agencies)

  x Integration in education

  xx **Education—Curricula; School administration and organization**

Artificial flies. *See* **Flies, Artificial**

Artificial flowers   745.59

  x Flowers, Artificial

Artificial food. *See* **Food, Artificial**

Artificial fuels. *See* **Synthetic fuels**

Artificial heart   617

  xx **Artificial organs**

Artificial insemination   176; 618.1; 636.08

  x Impregnation, Artificial; Insemination, Artificial

Artificial insemination, Human   618.1

Artificial intelligence   001.53

  x Brain, Electronic; Electronic brains; Intelligence, Artificial; Machine intelligence

  xx **Bionics**

Artificial islands   624

  x Drilling platforms; Islands, Artificial; Offshore structures; Platforms, Drilling; Structures, Offshore

Artificial organs   617

  See also names of artificial organs, e.g. **Artificial heart;** etc.

  x Organs, Artificial; Prosthesis

Artificial respiration   614.8

  x Respiration, Artificial

  xx **First aid**

Artificial rubber. *See* **Rubber, Artificial**

Artificial satellites (May subdiv. geog. adjective
form) **629.43; 629.46**

 See also types of satellites, e.g., **Meteorological satellites; Space stations; Space
vehicles;** etc., also names of specific
satellites, e.g., **Explorer (Artificial satellite);** etc.

 x Orbiting vehicles; Satellites, Artificial

 xx **Astronautics; Space vehicles**

Artificial satellites, American 629.43

 x American artificial satellites; U.S.—Artificial satellites

Artificial satellites–Control systems 629.8

Artificial satellites–Launching 629.47

 x Launching of satellites

 xx **Rockets (Aeronautics)**

Artificial satellites—Law and legislation. *See*
 Space law

Artificial satellites–Orbits 629.43

Artificial satellites, Russian 629.43

 x Russian artificial satellites; Sputniks

Artificial satellites–Tracking 629.43

 x Tracking of satellites

**Artificial satellites in telecommunication
621.38**

 See also names of specific satellites or projects, e.g., **Telstar project;** etc.

 x Communications relay satellites; Global
satellite communications systems;
Satellite communication system

 xx **Telecommunication**

Artificial silk. *See* **Rayon**

Artificial weather control. *See* **Weather—Control**

Artillery 355.7

 See also **Ordnance**

Artistic anatomy. *See* **Anatomy, Artistic**

Artistic photography. *See* **Photography, Artistic**

Artists (May subdiv. geog. adjective form, e.g.
Artists, French; etc.) **920; 927**

 See also

Architects	**Illustrators**
Black artists	**Painters**
Children as artists	**Potters**
Engravers	**Sculptors**
Etchers	**Women artists**

 also names of individual artists

 xx **Painters**

Artists, American 920; 927

 x American artists; U.S.—Artists

Artists, Black. *See* **Black artists**

Artists' materials 741.2; 751.2

 x Drawing materials; Painters' materials

Arts (May subdiv. geog. adjective form) **700**

 Use for materials on the arts in general,
including the visual arts, literature,
and the performing arts. For materials
on the visual arts only (architecture,
painting, etc.) use **Art**

Arts—*Continued*

  x Arts, Fine; Fine arts
Arts, American 709.73
  x American arts
Arts, Fine. *See* **Arts**
Arts, Graphic. *See* **Graphic arts**
Arts, Useful. *See* **Industrial arts; Technology**
Arts and crafts 745

  All types and specific kinds of crafts are
    not included in this list. Add as needed
  See also

Basket making	**Jewelry**
Beadwork	**Lacquer and**
Bookbinding	**lacquering**
China painting	**Leather work**
Decoration and or-	**Metalwork**
nament	**Modeling**
Design, Decorative	**Mosaics**
Enamel and enamel-	**Mural painting and**
ing	**decoration**
Folk art	**Needlework**
Glass painting and	**Pottery**
staining	**Rugs**
Goldwork	**Silverwork**
Handicraft	**Stencil work**
Illumination of	**Weaving**
books and manu-	**Wood carving**
scripts	
Industrial arts	
education	

  x Crafts; Decorative arts
  xx **Art; Art industries and trade; Folk art;**
    Industrial arts; Industrial arts educa-
    tion
Asbestos 620.1; 666; 691
  xx **Geology, Economic**
Asceticism 248
  xx **Fasting; Religious orders**
Asia 915; 950
  See also areas of Asia, e.g. **Asia, Southeast;**
    Far East; Middle East; etc.
  x East; Orient
Asia—Politics and government 950
  x Politics
Asia, Southeast 915.9; 959

  Use for materials on Southeast Asia in-
    cluding Burma, Thailand, Malaysia,
    Singapore, Indonesia, Vietnam, Cam-
    bodia, Laos, and the Philippine Islands
  x Southeast Asia
  xx **Asia**
Asian architecture. *See* **Architecture, Asian**
Asian art. *See* **Art, Asian**
Asian civilization. *See* **Civilization, Asian**
Asphalt 625.8; 665
  xx **Concrete; Pavements**
Asphyxiating gases. *See* **Gases, Asphyxiating**
    and poisonous
Assassination 364.1

  See also **Murder; Terrorism;** also names of

Assassination—*Continued*

persons and groups of persons with the subdivision *Assassination,* e.g. Presidents—U.S.—Assassination; etc.

xx Crime; Murder; Offenses against the person; Political crimes and offenses

Assault, Criminal. *See* Rape

Assembly, Right of. *See* Freedom of assembly

Assembly programs, School. *See* School assembly programs

Assertiveness (Psychology) 152.4; 155.2

xx Aggressiveness (Psychology); Psychology

Assessment 336.2

Use for general materials only. Materials on the assessment of a given locality are entered under Taxation followed by the appropriate geographical division

See also Taxation; Valuation

x Appraisal

xx Taxation

Assessments, Political. *See* Campaign funds

Assistance to developing areas. *See* Economic assistance; Technical assistance

Associations 060; 366

See also Clubs; Community life; Cooperation; Societies; also names of types of associations, e.g. Trade and professional associations; etc.; and subjects with the subdivision *Societies,* e.g. Agriculture—Societies; etc.; and names of specific associations

x Organizations; Voluntary associations

xx Societies

Associations, International. *See* International agencies

Astrobiology. *See* Life on other planets; Space biology

Astrodynamics 521; 629.41

See also Astronautics; Navigation (Astronautics); Space flight

xx Astronautics; Dynamics; Space flight

Astrogeology 523.9

See also Lunar geology; also names of planets with the subdivision *Geology,* e.g. Mars (Planet)—Geology; etc.

xx Geology

Astrology 133.5

See also Occult sciences; Horoscopes

x Hermetic art and philosophy

xx Astronomy; Divination; Fortune telling; Occult sciences; Prophecies (Occult sciences); Stars; Superstition

Astronautical accidents. *See* Astronautics—Accidents

Astronautical communication systems. *See* Astronautics—Communication systems

Astronautical instruments 629.4

See also Astronautics—Communication systems

Astronautical instruments—*Continued*

    x Instruments, Astronautical; Space ve-
hicles—Instruments

    xx **Astronautics–Communication systems;
Navigation (Astronautics)**

Astronautics (May subdiv. geog.) **629.4**

    See also **Aerothermodynamics; Artificial
satellites; Astrodynamics; Interplanetary voyages; Navigation (Astronautics); Outer space; Rocketry; Space
flight; Space flight to the moon; Space
sciences; Space ships; Space stations;
Space vehicles**

    xx **Aeronautics; Astrodynamics; Space sci-
ences; Space vehicles**

Astronautics–Accidents 629.4

    x Accidents, Spacecraft; Asronautical acci-
dents; Space ships—Accidents; Space
vehicles—Accidents

Astronautics–Communication systems 629.47

    See also **Astronautical instruments; Radio
in astronautics; Television in astronautics**

    x Astronautical communication systems;
Space communication

    xx **Astronautical instruments; Interstellar
communication; Telecommunication**

Astronautics–International cooperation 629.4

    x International space cooperation

    xx **International cooperation**

Astronautics—Law and legislation. *See* **Space
law**

Astronautics, Photography in. *See* **Space photography**

Astronautics–U.S. 629.4

    x U.S.—Astronautics

Astronautics and civilization 301.24

    See also **Religion and astronautics; Space
colonies; Space law**

    x Civilization and astronautics; Outer
space and civilization; Space age;
Space power

    xx **Aeronautics and civilization; Civilization**

Astronautics and religion. *See* **Religion and
astronautics**

Astronauts 920; 926

    See also **Space vehicles–Piloting**

    x Cosmonauts; Space ships—Pilots

    xx **Air pilots; Space flight**

Astronauts–Clothing 629.47

    x Pressure suits; Space suits

    xx **Life support systems (Space environment)**

Astronauts–Food 629.47

    x Meals for astronauts; Menus for space
flight

    xx **Astronauts–Nutrition**

Astronauts–Nutrition 629.47

    See also **Astronauts–Food**

    x Space nutrition

    xx **Nutrition**

Astronavigation. *See* **Navigation (Astronautics)**

Astronomers 920; 925
 xx **Scientists**
Astronomical instruments 522
 See also **Astronomical photography;** and names of instruments, e.g. **Telescope;** etc.
 x Instruments, Astronomical
 xx **Scientific apparatus and instruments**
Astronomical observatories 522
 x Observatories, Astronomical
Astronomical photography 522
 x Photography, Astronomical
 xx **Astronomical instruments; Photography**

Astronomical physics. *See* **Astrophysics**

Astronomical spectroscopy. *See* **Astrophysics; Spectrum**

Astronomy 520-523
 See also

Almanacs	**Planets,** and names
Astrology	of planets
Astrophysics	**Quasars**
Bible—Astronomy	**Radio astronomy**
Comets	**Seasons**
Eclipses, Lunar	**Solar system**
Eclipses, Solar	**Space environment**
Life on other planets	**Space sciences**
Meteorites	**Spectrum**
Meteors	**Stars**
Moon	**Sun**
Nautical astronomy	**Tides**
Outer space	**Zodiac**

 also headings beginning with the word **Astronomical**
 x Constellations
 xx **Science; Space sciences; Stars; Universe**

Astronomy—Atlases. *See* **Stars—Atlases**

Astronomy—Collected works 508
 x Collections of literature
Astronomy—Mathematics 521
 xx **Mathematics**

Astronomy, Nautical. *See* **Nautical astronomy**

Astrophysics 523.01
 x Astronomical physics; Astronomical spectroscopy; Physics, Astronomical
 xx **Astronomy; Physics; Stars**

Astros. *See* **Houston Astros**

Asylum, Right of 341.48
 See also **Refugees, Political**
 x Political asylum; Right of asylum; Sanctuary (Law)
 xx **International law**

Asylums. *See* **Institutional care;** also classes of people with the subdivision *Institutional care;* e.g. **Blind—Institutional care; Deaf—Institutional care; Mentally ill—Institutional care;** etc.

Atheism 211

See also **Agnosticism; Deism; Rationalism; Skepticism; Theism**

xx **Agnosticism; Deism; Faith; God; Rationalism; Religion; Theism; Theology**

Athletes 920; 927

Athletes, Black. *See* **Black athletes**

Athletic coaching. *See* **Coaching (Athletics)**

Athletics 796

See also

Coaching (Athletics)	Physical education and training
Olympic games	Sports

also names of specific athletic activities, e.g. **Boxing; Gymnastics; Rowing; Track athletics;** etc.

x College athletics; Intercollegiate athletics

xx **Physical education and training; Sports**

Atlantic cable. *See* **Cables, Submarine**

Atlantic Ocean 551.4; 909.63; 910.163

xx **Ocean**

Atlantic States 917.4; 917.5; 974; 975

x Eastern Seaboard; Middle Atlantic States; South Atlantic States

xx **United States**

Atlas (Missile) 623.4; 629.47

xx **Ballistic missiles; Intercontinental ballistic missiles**

Atlases 912

See also **Bible—Geography;** also names of subjects with the subdivision *Atlases*, e.g. **Stars—Atlases;** etc.; and countries, cities, etc. with the subdivision *Maps*, e.g. **U.S.—Maps;** etc.

x Geographical atlases

xx **Geography; Maps**

Atlases, Astronomical. *See* **Stars—Atlases**

Atlases, Historical 911

x Geography, Historical—Maps; Historical atlases; Historical geography; History—Atlases; Maps, Historical

Atmosphere 551.5

Use for materials treating of the body of air surrounding the earth as distinguished from the upper rarefied air. Materials dealing with air as an element and of its chemical and physical properties are entered under **Air**

See also **Air; Meteorology**

xx **Air; Earth; Meteorology**

Atmosphere—Pollution. *See* **Air—Pollution**

Atmosphere, Upper 551.5

See also **Stratosphere**

x Upper atmosphere

Atolls. *See* **Coral reefs and islands**

Atom smashing. *See* **Cyclotron**

Atomic bomb 623.4

See also **Hydrogen bomb; Radioactive fallout**

Atomic bomb—*Continued*

 xx **Atomic energy; Atomic warfare; Atomic weapons; Bombs; Hydrogen bomb**

Atomic bomb–Physiological effect   616.9

 See also **Radiation–Physiological effect**

 xx **Radiation–Physiological effect**

Atomic bomb–Testing   623.4

Atomic energy   539.7; 621.48

 See also **Atomic bomb; Nuclear engineering; Nuclear propulsion; Nuclear reactors**

 x Atomic power; Nuclear energy; Nuclear power

 xx **Atomic theory; Nuclear physics**

Atomic medicine.   *See* **Nuclear medicine**

Atomic nuclei.   *See* **Nuclear physics**

Atomic piles.   *See* **Nuclear reactors**

Atomic power.   *See* **Atomic energy**

Atomic power plants   621.48

 x Power plants, Atomic; Nuclear power plants

 xx **Power plants**

Atomic power plants–Environmental aspects   621.48

 x Environmental aspects

 xx **Environment**

Atomic power plants–Fires and fire prevention   621.48

 xx **Fire prevention; Fires**

Atomic power plants–Security measures   621.48

 x Security measures

 xx **Burglary protection**

Atomic powered vehicles.   *See* **Nuclear propulsion**

Atomic submarines   623.82

 x Nuclear submarines; Submarines, Atomic

 xx **Nuclear propulsion; Submarines**

Atomic theory   539; 549

 See also **Atomic energy; Quantum theory**

 xx **Chemistry, physical and theoretical; Quantum theory**

Atomic warfare   355.02

 See also **Atomic bomb; Atomic weapons; Hydrogen bomb**

 x Nuclear warfare

Atomic weapons   623.4

 See also types of atomic weapons, e.g. **Atomic bomb; Ballistic missiles; Intercontinental ballistic missiles; Hydrogen bomb;** etc.

 x Nuclear weapons; Weapons, Atomic

 xx **Atomic warfare; Ordnance**

Atomic weapons and disarmament.   *See* **Disarmament**

Atoms   539; 541

 See also **Cyclotron; Electrons; Nuclear physics; Transmutation (Chemistry)**

 xx **Chemistry, Physical and theoretical; Neutrons; Protons**

Atonement 299

   x Redemption

   xx **Sacrifice; Salvation; Sin; Theology**

Atonement, Christian 232; 234

   x Jesus Christ—Atonement

   xx **Jesus Christ**

Atrocities 179

   See also **Persecution**

   xx **Crime; Cruelty**

Atrocities, Military. *See* names of wars with the subdivision *Atrocities*, e.g. **World War, 1939-1945–Atrocities;** etc.; and names of specific atrocities

Attendance, School. *See* **School attendance**

Attention 153.7

   See also **Listening**

   x Concentration

   xx **Apperception; Educational psychology; Listening; Memory; Psychology; Thought and thinking**

Attitude (Psychology) 152.4

   See also **Conformity; Job satisfaction; Public opinion;** also names of groups of individuals with the subdivision *Attitudes*, e.g. **Youth–Attitudes;** etc.

   x Frustration

   xx **Emotions; Psychology; Public opinion; Social psychology**

Attorneys. *See* **Lawyers**

Auction bridge. *See* **Bridge (Game)**

Auctions 658.8

   x Sales, Auction

Audio-visual education 371.33

   See also **Audio-visual materials; Motion pictures in education; Radio in education; Sound recordings; Television in education;** also subjects with the subdivision *Audio-visual aids*, e.g. **Library education–Audio-visual aids;** etc.

   x Visual instruction

   xx **Education**

Audio-visual materials 025.17; 371.33

   See also names of specific materials, e.g. **Filmstrips; Motion pictures; Sound recordings;** etc. and subjects with the subdivision *Audio-visual aids*, e.g. **Library education–Audio-visual aids;** etc.; or with the subdivision indicating the specific medium designators, e.g. **Alphabet–Texts; Cowhands–Filmstrips; Sculpture–Motion pictures;** etc.

   x Multi-media materials; Nonbook materials; Nonprint materials

   xx **Audio-visual Education; Teaching–Aids and devices**

Audio-visual materials centers. *See* **Instructional materials centers**

Audiodiscs. *See* **Sound recordings**

Audiorecords. *See* **Sound recordings**

53

Auditing   657

    See also **Accounting**

    xx **Accounting; Bookkeeping**

Aurora borealis.   *See* **Auroras**

Auroras   523.01; 538; 551.4

    x Aurora borealis; Northern lights; Polar lights

    xx **Geophysics; Meteorology**

Author and publisher.   *See* **Authors and publishers**

Authoritarianism.   *See* **Fascism; Totalitarianism**

Authors (May subdiv. geog. adjective form, e.g. **Authors, English;** etc.)   **920; 928**

    See also **Literature—Bio-bibliography; Literature—History and criticism;** also **Children as authors; Black authors; Pseudonyms; Women authors;** also classes of writers (e.g. **Dramatists; Novelists; Poets;** etc.); and names of individual authors

    x Writers

    xx **Books; Literature—Bio-bibliography; Literature—History and criticism**

Authors, American   920; 928

    x American authors; U.S.—Authors

    xx **American literature**

Authors, Black.   *See* **Black authors**

Authors—Correspondence   92

    x Correspondence

Authors, English   920; 928

    See also **English literature—Bio-bibliography**

    x English authors

    xx **English literature**

Authors—Homes and haunts.   *See* **Literary landmarks**

Authors and publishers   070.5

    Use for materials on the relations between author and publisher

    See also **Copyright**

    x Author and publisher; Publishers and authors

    xx **Authorship;   Contracts;   Copyright; Publishers and publishing**

Authorship   808

    Use for general materials treating of the means of becoming an author. Materials concerning the composition of special types of literature are entered under more specific headings such as **Fiction—Technique; Short story;** etc.

    See also

Advertising copy	**Drama—Technique**
Authors and publishers	**Fiction—Technique**
	Journalism
Biography (as a literary form)	**Plots (Drama, fiction, etc.)**
Copyright	**Radio authorship**

Authorship—*Continued*
  Report writing   **Television author-**
  Short story   **ship**
  Technical writing   **Versification**
    x Writing (Authorship)
    xx **Literature**
Authorship—Handbooks, manuals, etc. 808.02
    See also **Printing—Style manuals**
    xx **Printing—Style manuals**
Auto courts. *See* **Hotels, motels, etc.**
Autobiographies 920
    Use for collections of autobiographies
    x Diaries; Memoirs
    xx **Biography**
Autocodes. *See* **Programming languages**
    (Electronic computers)
Autographs 929.8
    See also **Manuscripts**
    x Handwriting
    xx **Biography; Manuscripts; Writing**
Automata 629.8
    Use for materials on robots in non-human
      form. Materials on automata in hu-
      man form are entered under **Robots**
    See also **Robots**
    xx **Mechanical movements; Robots**
Automated information networks. *See* **Infor-**
    mation networks
Automatic computers. *See* **Computers**
Automatic control. *See* **Automation; Cyber-**
    netics; Electric controllers; Servo-
    mechanisms
Automatic data processing. *See* **Electronic data**
    processing
Automatic information retrieval. *See* **Informa-**
    tion storage and retrieval systems
Automatic programming languages. *See* **Pro-**
    gramming languages (Electronic com-
    puters)
Automatic teaching. *See* **Teaching machines**
Automation 301.24; 629.8
    See also **Feedback control systems; Servo-**
      mechanisms; Systems engineering; also
      subjects with the subdivision *Automa-*
      tion, e.g. **Libraries—Automation;** etc.
    x Automatic control; Computer control;
      Machinery, Automatic
    xx **Machinery in industry**
Automobile accidents. *See* **Traffic accidents**
Automobile driver education. *See* **Automobile**
    drivers—Education
Automobile drivers 629.28
    x Automobile driving; Automobiles—Driv-
      ing; Drivers, Automobile
Automobile drivers—Education 629.28
    x Automobile driver education; Driver ed-
      ucation
    xx **Education**
Automobile driving. *See* **Automobile drivers**

55

Automobile engines. *See* **Automobiles—Engines**

Automobile guides. *See* **Automobiles—Road guides**

Automobile industry and trade   338.4; 388.34

Automobile insurance. *See* **Insurance, Automobile**

Automobile parts. *See* **Automobiles—Parts**

Automobile pools. *See* **Car pools**

Automobile racing   796.7

> *See also* **Karts and karting;** also names of types of automobile races and names of specific races
>
> *x* Automobiles—Racing; Racing

Automobile repairs. *See* **Automobiles—Maintenance and repair**

Automobile touring. *See* **Automobiles—Touring**

Automobile trailers. *See* **Automobiles—Trailers**

Automobile transmission. *See* **Automobiles—Transmission devices**

Automobile trucks. *See* **Trucks**

Automobiles   629.2

> *See also* **Buses; Sports cars; Trucks;** also names of specific makes and models of automobiles, e.g. **Ford automobile;** etc.
>
> *x* Cars (Automobiles); Locomotion; Motor cars
>
> *xx* **Transportation; Transportation, Highway; Vehicles**

Automobiles—Accidents. *See* **Traffic accidents**

Automobiles—Air conditioning   629.2

> *xx* **Air conditioning**

Automobiles—Brakes   629.2

> *xx* **Brakes**

Automobiles, Compact   629.2

> *See also* names of specific makes and models
>
> *x* Compact automobiles; Compact cars

Automobiles—Design and construction   629.2

Automobiles, Diesel   629.2

> *x* Diesel automobiles

Automobiles—Driving. *See* **Automobile drivers**

Automobiles, Electric   629.22

> *x* Electric automobiles

Automobiles—Electric equipment   629.2

> *x* Electric equipment of automobiles

Automobiles—Engines   629.2

> *x* Automobile engines; Automobiles—Motors
>
> *xx* **Engines; Gas and oil engines**

Automobiles, Foreign   629.22

> *See also* names of specific makes and models
>
> *x* Foreign automobiles

Automobiles—Fuel consumption   629.28

> *xx* **Energy consumption; Fuel**

Automobiles—Gearing. *See* **Automobiles—Transmission devices**

Automobiles—Law and legislation 343.9; 629.2026

   See also **Traffic regulations**

   x Laws

   xx **Law; Legislation; Traffic regulations**

Automobiles—Maintenance and repair 629.28

   See also **Automobiles—Restoration**

   x Automobile repairs; Automobiles—Repairing

   xx **Repairing**

Automobiles—Models 629.22

   x Model cars

   xx **Machinery—Models**

Automobiles—Motors. *See* **Automobiles—Engines**

Automobiles—Parts 629.28

   x Automobile parts

Automobiles—Pollution control devices 629.2

   x Pollution control devices (Motor vehicles)

Automobiles—Pools. *See* **Car pools**

Automobiles—Racing. *See* **Automobile racing**

Automobiles—Repairing. *See* **Automobiles—Maintenance and repairs**

Automobiles—Restoration 629.28

   x Restoration of automobiles

   xx **Automobiles—Maintenance and repair**

Automobiles—Road guides 910.2

   See also **Road maps**

   x Automobile guides

   xx **Maps; Road maps**

Automobiles—Service stations 629.28

   x Filling stations; Gas stations; Service stations, Automobile

Automobiles—Touring 796.7

   x Automobile touring; Motoring

   xx **Travel**

Automobiles—Trailers 629.22

   See also **Travel trailers and campers**

   x Automobile trailers; Trailers

Automobiles—Transmission devices 629.2

   x Automobile transmission; Automobiles—Gearing; Transmissions, Automobile

   xx **Gearing**

Autosuggestion. *See* **Hypnotism; Mental suggestion**

Autumn 525

   x Fall

   xx **Seasons**

Avant-garde churches. *See* **Noninstitutional churches**

Avant-garde films. *See* **Experimental films**

Avant-garde theater. *See* **Experimental theater**

Aviation. *See* **Aeronautics**

Aviation medicine 616.9

   See also **Space medicine**

   x Aeronautics—Medical aspects; Aero-

Aviation medicine—*Continued*
        space medicine; Medicine, Aviation
   xx **Medicine; Space medicine**
Aviators. *See* **Air pilots**
Awards. *See* **Rewards (Prizes, etc.);** and
        names of awards
Awards, Literary. *See* **Literary prizes**
Axiology. *See* **Values**
Aztecs 980.3
   xx **Indians of Mexico**
BMEWS. *See* **Ballistic missile early warning**
        system
B-52 bomber 623.74
   xx **Bombers**
Babies. *See* **Infants**
Baby animals. *See* **Animals—Infancy**
Baby sitters 649
   xx **Children—Care and hygiene; Infants—**
       Care and hygiene
Bacilli. *See* **Bacteriology; Germ theory of**
       disease
Back packing. *See* **Backpacking**
Backpacking 796.5
   x Back packing; Pack transportation
   xx **Camping; Hiking**
Bacon-Shakespeare controversy. *See* **Shake-**
       speare, William—Authorship
Bacon's Rebellion, 1676 973.2
   xx **U.S.—History—Colonial period, 1600-**
       1775
Bacteria. *See* **Bacteriology**
Bacterial warfare. *See* **Biological warfare**
Bacteriology 589.9
   See also **Disinfection and disinfectants;**
       Fermentation; Germ theory of dis-
       ease; Immunity; Microorganisms;
       also subjects with the subdivision *Bac-*
       teriology, e.g. **Cheese—Bacteriology;**
       etc.
   x Bacilli; Bacteria; Disease germs;
       Germs; Medicine, Preventive; Mi-
       crobes; Preventive medicine
   xx **Communicable diseases; Fermentation;**
       Fungi; Germ theory of disease; Med-
       icine; Microorganisms; Microbiol-
       ogy; Parasites; Pathology; Science
Bacteriology, Agricultural 630.1
   See also **Soils—Bacteriology;** also names
       of crops, etc. with the subdivision *Dis-*
       eases and pests, e.g. **Fruit—Diseases**
       and pests; etc.
   x Agricultural bacteriology; Diseases and
       pests
   xx **Soils—Bacteriology**
Badges of honor. *See* **Decorations of honor;**
       Insignia; Medals
Bahaism 297
   x Baha'i Faith
   xx **Islam; Religions**

Baking   641.7

    See also names of baked products, e.g. **Bread; Cake; Pastry;** etc.

    xx **Cookery**

Balance of nature.   *See* **Ecology**

Balance of payments   382.1

    xx **International economic relations**

Balance of power   327

    x Power politics

Ball bearings.   *See* **Bearings (Machinery)**

Ball games   796.3

    See also names of games, e.g. **Baseball; Soccer;** etc.; also names of competitions

    xx **Games**

Ballads (May subdiv. geog. adjective form*)* **808.81; 811.08; etc.**

    Use for collections of ballads, and for materials about ballads. Materials treating of the folk tunes associated with these ballads, and collections which include both words and music, are entered under **Folk songs**

    See also **Folk songs**

    xx **Literature; Folk songs; Poetry; Songs**

Ballads, American   811.08

    x American ballads; U.S.—Ballads

    xx **American literature**

Ballet   792.8

    See also **Pantomimes**

    xx **Dancing; Drama; Opera; Performing arts; Theater**

Ballet, Water.   *See* **Synchronized swimming**

Ballet dancers   792.8

    xx **Dancers**

Ballets   792.8

Ballets—Stories, plots, etc.   792.8

    x Stories

    xx **Plots (Drama, fiction, etc.)**

Ballistic missile early warning system   621.3848

    x BMEWS; Early warning system, Ballistic missile

    xx **Air defenses; Radar defense networks**

Ballistic missiles   623.4

    See also types of ballistic missiles, e.g. **Intercontinental ballistic missiles;** etc.; also names of specific missiles, e.g. **Atlas (Missile);** etc.

    x Missiles, Ballistic

    xx **Atomic weapons; Guided missiles; Rocketry; Rockets (Aeronautics)**

Balloons   623.74; 629.133

    See also **Aeronautics**

    xx **Aeronautics; Airships**

Balloons, Dirigible.   *See* **Airships**

Ballot.   *See* **Elections**

Band music   785.1

    xx **Instrumental music; Military music**

Bandages and bandaging   614.8

    xx **First aid**

Bandits. *See* **Robbers and outlaws**
Bandmasters. *See* **Conductors (Music)**
Bands (Music) 785.06
 >   *See also* **Conducting; Drum majoring;
 >   Instrumentation and orchestration;
 >   Orchestra; Wind instruments;** and
 >   names of types of bands
 >   *xx* **Conducting; Orchestra; Wind instruments**
Banking. *See* **Banks and banking**
Bankruptcy 332.7; 346.7
 >   *x* Business failures; Failure (in business);
 >   Insolvency
 >   *xx* **Commercial law; Debtor and creditor;
 >   Finance**
Banks and banking (May subdiv. geog.) **332.1**
 >   *See also*

Agricultural credit	**Investments**
Consumer credit	**Money**
Credit	**Negotiable instru-**
Federal Reserve	**ments**
banks	**Savings and loan**
Foreign exchange	**associations**
Interest (Economics)	**Trust companies**
Investment trusts	

 >   *x* Banking; Savings banks
 >   *xx* **Business; Capital; Commerce; Credit;
 >   Finance; Money; Trust companies**
Banks and banking, Cooperative 334
 >   *x* Cooperative banks; Credit unions; Peo-
 >   ple's banks
 >   *xx* **Cooperation; Cooperative societies**
Banks and banking—Data processing 332.1028
 >   *x* Data processing
 >   *xx* **Electronic data processing**
Banks and banking—U.S. 332.1
 >   *x* U.S.—Banks and banking
Banned books. *See* **Books—Censorship**
Banners. *See* **Flags**
Banquets. *See* **Dinners and dining**
Baptism 234; 265
 >   *x* Christening; Immersion, Baptismal
 >   *xx* **Rites and ceremonies; Sacraments;
 >   Theology**
Baptists 920; 922
 >   *See also* **Church of the Brethren; Men-
 >   nonites**
Bar. *See* **Lawyers**
Barbary corsairs. *See* **Pirates**
Barbary States. *See* **Africa, North**
Barbecue cooking. *See* **Cookery, Outdoor**
Barns 631.2
 >   *xx* **Farm buildings**
Barometer 551.5028
 >   *xx* **Meteorological instruments**
Baronage. *See* **Nobility**
Baroque architecture. *See* **Architecture, Ba-
 roque**
Baroque art. *See* **Art, Baroque**
Barristers. *See* **Lawyers**
Barrows. *See* **Mounds and mound builders**

Bars and restaurants. *See* **Restaurants, bars, etc.**
Baseball 796.357
See also **Little league baseball; Softball**
xx **Ball games; College sports; Sports**
Baseball clubs 796.357
See also names of individual clubs, e.g. **Houston Astros;** etc.
Basements 721
x Cellars
xx **Foundations**
Bases (Chemistry) 661
xx **Chemistry**
Bashfulness 152.4
x Shyness
xx **Emotions**
Basket making 746.4
xx **Arts and crafts; Industrial arts education; Weaving**
Bastogne, Battle of. *See* **Ardennes, Battle of the, 1944–1945**
Bat. *See* **Bats**
Baths 613; 615
See also **Hydrotherapy**
x Cleanliness
xx **Hydrotherapy; Hygiene; Physical therapy**
Bathyscaphe 623.8
xx **Oceanography—Research; Submersibles**
Batik 746.6
xx **Dyes and dyeing**
Baton twirling 785.06
See also **Drum majoring**
xx **Drum majoring**
Batrachia. *See* **Amphibians**
Bats 599
x Bat
xx **Mammals**
Battered child syndrome. *See* **Child abuse**
Batteries, Electric. *See* **Electric batteries; Storage batteries**
Battle of the Bulge. *See* **Ardennes, Battle of the, 1944–1945**
Battle ships. *See* **Warships**
Battle songs. *See* **War songs**
Battles 355.4; 904
Names of battles are not included in this list but are to be added as needed, e.g. **Ardennes, Battle of the, 1944–1945;** etc.
See also **Naval battles;** also names of wars with the subdivision *Campaigns and battles* (e.g. **U.S.—History—Civil War, 1861–1865—Campaigns and battles; World War, 1939–1945—Campaigns and battles;** etc.) and names of individual battles, e.g. **Ardennes, Battle of the, 1944–1945;** etc.
x Fighting; Sieges
xx **Military art and science; Military history; Naval battles; War**

Battleships. *See* **Warships**

Bay of Pigs invasion. *See* **Cuba—History—Invasion, 1961**

Bazaars. *See* **Fairs**

Beaches 551.4
> *xx* **Seashore**

Beadwork 746.5
> *xx* **Arts and crafts; Crocheting; Embroidery; Weaving**

Bearings (Machinery) 621.8
> *See also* **Lubrication and lubricants**
> *x* Ball bearings; Journals (Machinery)
> *xx* **Lubrication and lubricants; Machinery**

Beasts. *See* **Animals**

Beat generation. *See* **Bohemianism**

Beatniks. *See* **Bohemianism**

Beautification of the landscape. *See* **Landscape protection**

Beauty. *See* **Esthetics**

Beauty shops 646.7
> *See also* **Cosmetics**

Beavers 599
> *xx* **Fresh water animals; Furbearing animals**

Bedouins 572.917
> *xx* **Arabs**

Bedspreads 746.9
> *x* Coverlets
> *xx* **Interior decoration**

Bee. *See* **Bees**

Beef 641.3; 664
> *xx* **Meat**

Beef cattle. *See* **Cattle**

Bees 595.7; 638
> *See also* **Honey**
> *x* Apiculture; Bee; Hymenoptera
> *xx* **Honey; Insects**

Begging 362.5; 301.44
> *See also* **Tramps**
> *x* Mendicancy
> *xx* **Tramps**

Beginning reading materials. *See* **Easy reading materials**

Behavior. *See* **Animals—Habits and behavior; Human behavior**

Behavior modification 152
> *xx* **Human behavior; Psychology, Applied**

Behavior problems (Children). *See* **Problem children**

Belief and doubt 121
> Use for materials treating the subject from the philosophical standpoint. Materials on religious belief are entered under **Faith**
> *See also* **Agnosticism; Rationalism; Skepticism; Truth**
> *x* Certainty; Doubt
> *xx* **Agnosticism; Emotions; Knowledge, Theory of; Philosophy; Rationalism; Religion; Skepticism**

Bell System Telstar satellite. *See* **Telstar project**

Belles-lettres. *See* **Literature**

Bells   621.389; 789
> *x* Carillons; Chimes; Church bells

Belts and belting   621.8
> *See also* **Power transmisison**
> *x* Chain belting
> *xx* **Machinery; Power transmission**

Benevolent institutions. *See* **Institutional care**

Bequests. *See* **Gifts; Inheritance and succession; Wills**

Bereavement   152.4
> *See also* **Sympathy**
> *xx* **Death; Sympathy**

Bermuda triangle   001.9
> *x* Devil's triangle; Graveyard of the Atlantic

Berries   634
> Names of berries are not included in this list but are to be added as needed, in the plural form, e.g. **Strawberries;** etc.
> *See also* names of berries, e.g. **Strawberries;** etc.
> *xx* **Fruit; Fruit culture**

Best books. *See* **Books and reading—Best books**

Best sellers   028
> *x* Books—Best sellers
> *xx* **Books and reading**

Betting. *See* **Gambling**

Bevel gearing. *See* **Gearing**

Beverages   613.3; 641.3; 641.8; 663
> *See also* names of types of beverages, e.g. **Liquors and liqueurs;** also names of specific beverages, e.g. **Cocoa; Coffee;** etc.
> *x* Drinks
> *xx* **Diet; Food**

Bible   220
> The subject subdivisions under **Bible** may be used also for any part of the Bible, under the same form of entry as for the texts of such parts, e.g. **Bible. O.T.—Biography; Bible. O.T. Pentateuch—Commentaries; Bible. O.T. Psalms—History; Bible. N.T. Gospels—Inspiration;** etc.
> *x* Holy Scriptures; Scriptures, Holy
> *xx* **Hebrew literature; History, Ancient; Jewish literature; Sacred books**

Bible—Animals. *See* **Bible—Natural history**

Bible—Antiquities   220.9
> *See also* **Christian antiquities**
> *x* Antiquities; Antiquities, Biblical; Archeology, Biblical; Biblical archeology
> *xx* **Archeology**

Bible—Astronomy   220.8
> *xx* **Astronomy**

Bible—Biography 220.9

> *See also* **Christianity—Biography; Women in the Bible**
>
> *x* Biblical characters

Bible—Birds. *See* **Bible—Natural history**

Bible—Botany. *See* **Bible—Natural history**

Bible—Catechisms, question books 238

> *x* Bible—Question books
>
> *xx* **Bible—Study; Catechisms**

Bible—Chronology 220.9

> *x* Chronology, Biblical

Bible—Commentaries 220.7

> *x* Bible—Interpretation;   Commentaries, Biblical

Bible—Concordances 220.2

> *x* Bible—Indexes; Concordances
>
> *xx* **Bible—Dictionaries**

Bible—Criticism, interpretation, etc. 220.6

> *x* Bible—Exegesis;   Bible—Hermeneutics; Bible—Interpretation; Exegesis, Biblical; Hermeneutics, Biblical; Higher criticism
>
> *xx* **Bible as literature; Criticism**

Bible—Dictionaries 220.3

> *See also* **Bible—Concordances**
>
> *x* Bible—Indexes

Bible—Drama 808.2; 808.82; 812; etc.

> *See also* **Mysteries and miracle plays**
>
> *x* Bible plays; Plays, Bible
>
> *xx* **Religious drama**

Bible—Evidences, authority, etc. 220.1

> *See also* **Miracles (Christianity)**
>
> *x* Evidences of the Bible
>
> *xx* **Free thought**

Bible—Exegesis. *See* **Bible—Criticism, interpretation, etc.**

Bible—Fiction. *See* **Bible—History of Biblical events—Fiction**

Bible—Flowers. *See* **Bible—Natural history**

Bible—Gardens. *See* **Bible—Natural history**

Bible—Geography 220.9

> *x* Bible—Maps; Geography, Biblical
>
> *xx* **Atlases**

Bible—Hermeneutics. *See* **Bible—Criticism, interpretation, etc.**

Bible—History 220.9

> Use for materials on the origin, authorship and composition of the Bible as a book. Materials dealing with historical events as described in the Bible are entered under **Bible—History of Biblical events**

Bible—History of Biblical events 220.9

> See note under **Bible—History**
>
> *x* History, Biblical

Bible—History of Biblical events—Fiction Fic

> See note under **Bible stories**
>
> *x* Bible—Fiction

Bible—Illustrations. *See* **Bible—Pictorial works**

Bible—Indexes. *See* **Bible—Concordances; Bible—Dictionaries**

Bible—Inspiration 220.1
    x Inspiration, Biblical
Bible—Interpretation. *See* **Bible—Commentaries; Bible—Criticism, interpretation, etc.**
Bible—Introductions. *See* **Bible—Study**
Bible—Language, style, etc. *See* **Bible as literature**
Bible—Literary character. *See* **Bible as literature**
Bible—Maps. *See* **Bible—Geography**
Bible—Miracles. *See* **Miracles (Christianity)**
Bible—Natural history 220.8
    x Bible—Animals; Bible—Birds; Bible—Botany; Bible—Flowers; Bible—Gardens; Bible—Plants; Bible—Zoology; Botany of the Bible; Natural history, Biblical; Zoology of the Bible
    xx **Animals in literature; Birds in literature**
Bible—Parables. *See* **Jesus Christ—Parables**
Bible—Pictorial works 220.22
    x Bible—Illustrations
    xx **Christian art and symbolism; Jesus Christ—Art**
Bible—Plants. *See* **Bible—Natural history**
Bible—Prophecies 220.1
    See also **Jesus Christ—Prophecies**
    x Prophecies (Bible)
Bible—Psychology 220.8
    x Psychology, Biblical
Bible—Question books. *See* **Bible—Catechisms, question books**
Bible—Reading 220.5
Bible—Science. *See* **Bible and science**
Bible—Stories *See* **Bible stories**
Bible—Study 220.07
    See also **Bible—Catechisms, question books**
    x Bible—Introductions; Bible classes; Bible study
    xx **Christian education; Sunday schools**
Bible—Use 220.6
    Use for materials that show how the Bible is used as a guide to living, to cultivation of a spiritual life, and to problems of doctrine
Bible—Versions 220; 220.5
    Use for history of versions, including materials on both the Old Testament and the New Testament
Bible—Women. *See* **Women in the Bible**
Bible—Zoology. *See* **Bible—Natural history**
Bible. New Testament 225
    Use same subject subdivisions as those given under **Bible.** They may be used also for groups of books (e.g. **Bible. N.T. Gospels;** etc.) and for single books (e.g. **Bible. N.T. Matthew;** etc.)
    x New Testament

Bible. Old Testament 221

> Use same subject subdivisions as those given under **Bible.** They may be used also for groups of books (e.g. **Bible. O.T. Pentateuch;** etc. and for single books (e.g. **Bible. O.T. Psalms;** etc.)

> *x* Old Testament

Bible and science 220.8

> *x* Bible—Science; Science and the Bible

> *xx* **Religion and science**

Bible as literature 220.6

> *See also* **Bible—Criticism, interpretation, etc.; Religious literature**

> *x* Bible—Language, style, etc.; Bible—Literary character

> *xx* **Religious literature**

Bible classes. *See* Bible—Study; Sunday schools; Summer schools, Religious

Bible in literature 809

> Use for materials that discuss the effect of the Bible on literature in general, on a national literature or on an individual author. A second subject heading is necessary for the name of the literature or the name of the author discussed

> *See also* **Religion in literature**

> *xx* **Literature; Religion in literature**

Bible in the schools. *See* **Religion in the public schools**

Bible plays. *See* **Bible—Drama; Mysteries and miracle plays**

Bible stories 220.9

> Use for materials that retell or adapt stories from the Bible. Not to be used for fiction in which characters and settings are taken from the Bible. Enter these under **Bible—History of Biblical events—Fiction**

> *x* Bible—Stories; Stories

Bible study. *See* **Bible—Study**

Biblical archeology. *See* **Bible—Antiquities**

Biblical characters. *See* **Bible—Biography**

Bibliographic control 029

> *See also* **Cataloging; Indexing; Information storage and retrieval systems; MARC system**

> *x* Universal bibliographic control

> *xx* **Documentation**

Bibliography 010-016

> *See also*

Archives	**Indexing**
Bookbinding	**Information storage**
Books	**and retrieval**
Cataloging	**systems**
Classification—	**Library science**
Books	**Manuscripts**
Indexes	**Printing**

> *also* names of persons, places and subjects with the subdivision *Bibliography,* e.g.

Bibliography—*Continued*
> Shakespeare, William—Bibliography; U.S.—Bibliography; Agriculture—Bibliography; etc.

> *xx* **Books; Cataloging; Documentation; Library science**

Bibliography—Best books. *See* **Books and reading—Best books**

Bibliography—Editions   016.094
> *See also* **Paperback books**

> *x* Bibliography—Reprints; Editions; Reprints

Bibliography—First editions   016.094
> *x* Books—First editions; First editions

Bibliography—Reprints. *See* **Bibliography—Editions**

Bibliomania. *See* **Book collecting**

Bibliophily. *See* **Book collecting**

Bicentennial celebrations—U.S.—1976. *See* **American Revolution Bicentennial, 1776–1976**

Biculturalism (May subdivide geog. except U.S.) **301.24**
> *xx* **Civilization; Culture**

Biculturalism—Canada   301.24
> *x* Canada—Biculturalism
> *xx* **Canada—English-French relations**

Bicycle racing   796.6
> *x* Racing
> *xx* **Bicycles and bicycling**

Bicycles and bicycling   629.22; 796.6
> *See also* **Bicycle racing; Motorcycles**
> *x* Biking; Cycling; Tricycles

Bigotry. *See* **Prejudices and antipathies; Toleration**

Biking. *See* **Bicycles and bicycling**

Bilingual books (May subdivide by languages)

Bilingual education. *See* **Education, Bilingual**

Bilingualism (May subdivide geog. except U.S.) **410**
> *See also* **Education, Bilingual**
> *xx* **Language and languages**

Bilingualism—Canada   409.71
> *x* Canada—Bilingualism

Bill of rights. *See* **U.S. Constitution—Amendments**

Billboards. *See* **Signs and signboards**

Bills and notes. *See* **Negotiable instruments**

Bills of credit. *See* **Credit; Negotiable instruments; Paper money**

Bills of fare. *See* **Menus**

Bimetallism. *See* **Gold; Monetary policy; Silver**

Binary system (Mathematics)   513
> *x* Pair system
> *xx* **Mathematics**

Binding of books. *See* **Bookbinding**

Bioastronautics. *See* **Space biology; Space medicine**

67

Bio-bibliography. *See* names of persons, subjects and names of countries, cities, etc. with the subdivision *Bio-bibliography,* e.g. **English literature—Bio-bibliography; U.S.—Bio-bibliography;** etc.

Biochemistry 574.1

See also **Metabolism; Molecular biology; Physiological chemistry**

x Biological chemistry; Chemistry, Biological

xx **Chemistry; Physiological chemistry**

Bioethics 174

See also **Medical ethics; Transplantation of organs, tissues, etc.—Moral and religious aspects**

x Biological ethics; Biology—Ethics; Biomedical ethics; Ethics, Biological; Life sciences ethics

xx **Social ethics**

Biofeedback training 153.1

x Visceral learning

xx **Feedback (Psychology); Learning, Psychology of**

Biogeography. *See* **Anthropogeography; Geographical distribution of animals and plants**

Biography 920; 921-928

Use for collections of biographies which are not limited to one country or to one class of people. Materials that deal with the writing of biography are entered under **Biography (as a literary form)**

See also

Autobiographies	**Genealogy**
Autographs	**Heraldry**
Christianity—Biography	**Obituaries**
Epitaphs	**Portraits**

also names of countries, cities, etc. and subjects with the subdivision *Biography* (e.g. **U.S.—Biography; Chicago—Biography; Men—Biography; Musicians—Biography; Religions—Biography; Women—Biography;** etc.) and names of persons for biographies of individuals

x Memoirs

xx **Genealogy; History**

Biography—Dictionaries 920.03

Use for collections of biographies, which are not limited to one country or to one class of people, that are arranged in dictionary form

Biography (as a literary form) 808

Use for materials that deal with the writing of biography

xx **Authorship; Literature**

Biological anthropology. *See* **Physical anthropology**

Biological chemistry. *See* **Biochemistry**

Biological clocks. *See* **Biology—Periodicity**

Biological control of pests. *See* **Pests—Biological control**

Biological ethics. *See* **Bioethics**

Biological oceanography. *See* **Marine biology; Marine ecology**

Biological physics. *See* **Biophysics**

Biological rhythms. *See* **Biology—Periodicity**

Biological warfare 358; 623.4
  x Bacterial warfare; Germ warfare
  xx **Communicable diseases; Military art and science; Tactics**

Biologists 920; 925
  xx **Naturalists**

Biology 574
  See also

Adaptation (Biology)	Heredity
	Life (Biology)
Anatomy	Marine biology
Biomathematics	Microbiology
Botany	Natural history
Cells	Physiology
Color of animals	Protoplasm
Cryobiology	Radiobiology
Death	Reproduction
Embryology	Sex
Evolution	Space biology
Fresh water biology	Variation (Biology)
Genetics	Zoology

  x Morphology
  xx **Evolution; Life (Biology); Life sciences; Natural history; Science**

Biology—Ecology. *See* **Ecology**

Biology, Economic. *See* **Botany, Economic; Zoology, Economic**

Biology—Ethics. *See* **Bioethics**

Biology, Marine. *See* **Marine biology**

Biology, Molecular. *See* **Molecular biology**

Biology—Periodicity 574.1
  x Biological clocks; Biological rhythms; Biorhythms
  xx **Periodicity**

Bioluminescence 574.1
  x Animal light; Luminescence, Animal
  xx **Phosphorescence**

Biomathematics 510
  xx **Biology; Mathematics**

Biomechanics. *See* **Human engineering**

Biomedical ethics. *See* **Bioethics**

Bionics 001.53
  Use for materials on the science of technological systems which function in the manner of living systems
  See also **Artificial intelligence; Optical data processing**
  x Biotechnology
  xx **Biophysics; Cybernetics; Systems engineering**

Biophysics 574.1

> *See also* **Bionics; Cells; Molecular biology; Radiobiology**
>
> *x* Biological physics; Molecular physiology; Physics, Biological; Physiology, Molecular
>
> *xx* **Physics**

Biorhythms. *See* **Biology—Periodicity**

Biosciences. *See* **Life sciences**

Biotechnology. *See* **Bionics; Cybernetics; Human engineering**

Biplanes. *See* **Airplanes**

Bird. *See* **Birds**

Bird houses 598.2

Bird photography. *See* **Photography of birds**

Bird song 598.2

> *x* Birds—Song

Bird watching 598.2

Birdbanding 598.2

> *x* Birds—Banding; Birds—Marking

Birds (May subdiv. geog.) **598.2**

> Names of birds are not included in this list but are to be added as needed, in the plural form, e.g. **Canaries; Robins;** etc.
>
> *See also* classes of birds, e.g. **Birds of prey; Cage birds; Game and game birds; State birds; Water birds;** etc.; and names of specific birds, e.g. **Canaries; Robins;** etc.
>
> *x* Bird; Ornithology
>
> *xx* **Vertebrates; Zoology**

Birds—Anatomy 598.2

> *xx* **Anatomy**

Birds, Aquatic. *See* **Water birds**

Birds—Banding. *See* **Birdbanding**

Birds—Collection and preservation 579

> *x* Collections of natural specimens; Specimens, Preservation of
>
> *xx* **Collectors and collecting; Taxidermy; Zoological specimens—Collection and preservation**

Birds—Eggs and nests 598.2

> *x* Birds' eggs; Birds' nests; Nests
>
> *xx* **Eggs**

Birds—Flight 598.2

Birds—Habits and behavior 598.2

Birds—Marking. *See* **Birdbanding**

Birds—Migration 598.2

> *x* Migration of birds
>
> *xx* **Animals—Migration; Geographical distribution of animals and plants**

Birds—Photography. *See* **Photography of birds**

Birds—Protection 333.9

> *See also* **Game protection**
>
> *x* Protection of birds
>
> *xx* **Game protection; Wildlife—Conservation**

Birds, Rare. *See* **Rare birds**

Birds—Song. *See* **Bird song**

Birds—U.S. 598.2

> *x* U.S.—Birds

Birds' eggs. *See* **Birds—Eggs and nests**
Birds in literature   809
    See also **Bible—Natural history**
    xx **Nature in literature**
Birds' nests. *See* **Birds—Eggs and nests**
Birds of prey   598.2
    See also names of birds of prey, e.g.
        Eagles; etc.
    xx **Birds**
Birth. *See* **Childbirth**
Birth control   176; 344.4; 613.9
    See also **Birth rate;** also methods of birth
        control, e.g. **Abortion; Sterilization**
        (Birth control); etc.
    x Conception—Prevention; Contraception;
        Family planning; Planned parenthood
    xx **Birth rate; Eugenics; Population; Sexual**
        ethics; Sexual hygiene
Birth control—Moral and religious aspects   241;
    261.8
    x Moral and religious aspects
    xx **Ethics**
Birth, Multiple   618.2
    See also names of multiple births, e.g.
        Twins; etc.
    x Multiple birth
Birth rate   301.32
    See also **Birth control; Population**
    xx **Birth control; Population**
Birth records. *See* **Registers of births, etc.**
Birthdays   392
    x Days
Births, Registers of. *See* **Registers of births,**
    etc.
Bison   599; 636.2
    x American bison; Buffalo, American
Bituminous coal. *See* **Coal**
Black actors and actresses   920; 927
    xx **Actors and actresses**
Black Americans. *See* **Blacks**
Black art   704
    See also **Black artists**
    x Art, Black; Blacks—Art
    xx **Black artists**
Black art (Magic). *See* **Witchcraft**
Black artists   920; 927
    See also **Black art**
    x Artists, Black
    xx **Artists; Black art**
Black athletes   920; 927
    x Athletes, Black
Black authors   920; 928
    x Authors, Black
    xx **Authors**
Black business people   920; 923
    x Business people, Black
    xx **Blacks—Employment**
Black death. *See* **Plague**
Black folk songs. *See* **Black songs**
Black folklore. *See* **Folklore, Black**

Black friars. *See* **Dominicans**
Black Hawk War, 1832   973.5
   xx **Indians   of   North   America—Wars;**
      U.S.—History—1815—1861
Black lead. *See* **Graphite**
Black librarians   920; 923
   See also **Libraries and blacks**
   x Librarians, Black
   xx **Libraries and blacks**
Black literature (American). *See* **American**
      literature—Black authors
Black magic (Witchcraft). *See* **Witchcraft**
Black minstrels   791.1
   x Minstrels, Black
Black music   781.7
   See also **Black songs; Blacks—Songs and**
      music; Spirituals (Songs)
   x Music, Black
   xx **Blacks—Songs and music**
Black musicians   920; 927
   x Musicians, Black
Black Muslims   572.917
   x Nation of Islam; Muslims, Black
   xx **Black nationalism; Blacks—Religion; U.S.**
      —Race relations
Black nationalism   301.45
   See also **Black Muslims**
   x Black   separatism;   Nationalism,   Black;
      Separatism, Black
   xx **Blacks—Political   activity;   Blacks—Race**
      identity
Black   poetry.   *See*   **American   poetry—Black**
      authors
Black power   322.4
   xx **Blacks—Civil   rights;   Blacks—Economic**
      conditions; Blacks—Political activity
Black separatism. *See* **Black nationalism**
Black songs   784.7
   See also **Blacks—Songs and music; Blues**
      (Songs, etc.); Spirituals (Songs)
   x Black   folk   songs;   Folk   songs,   Black
      (American)
   xx **Black music; Music, American; Songs;**
      Songs, American; Spirituals (Songs)
Black spirituals. *See* **Spirituals (Songs)**
Black studies   301.4507
   x Afro-American studies
   xx **Area studies; Blacks—Education; Blacks—**
      Race identity
Black suffrage. *See* **Blacks—Suffrage**
Blackboard drawing. *See* **Chalk talks; Crayon**
      drawings
Blackouts, Electric power. *See* **Electric power**
      failures
Blackouts in war. *See* **Civil defense**
Blacks   301.45; 909
   Use for general materials on the blacks in
      the U.S. If limited to a particular area
      in the U.S. may use geog. subdivision,
      e.g., **Blacks—Arkansas;   Blacks—Chi-**

Blacks—*Continued*

cago; **Blacks–Southern States**; etc. Materials dealing with blacks in other countries are entered under **Blacks– Africa; Blacks–France;** etc.

See also **Slavery in the U.S.**

x African-Americans; Afro-Americans; Black Americans; Blacks—U.S.; Negroes

xx **Ethnology; Slavery in the U.S.**

Blacks–Africa   572.896

Blacks—Art.   *See* **Black art**

Blacks–Biography   920

Blacks–Civil rights   323.4

See also **Black power**

x Demonstrations for black civil rights —U.S.; Freedom marches—U.S.; Marches for black civil rights—U.S.

xx **Blacks–Political activity; Civil rights**

Blacks–Economic conditions   330.973

See also **Black power**

xx **Economic conditions**

Blacks–Education   370.19

See also **Black studies; School integration; Segregation in education**

xx **Education**

Blacks–Employment   331.6

See also **Black business people**

x Blacks—Occupations

xx **Discrimination in employment; Employment**

Blacks–Folklore.   *See* **Folklore, Black**

Blacks–Housing   301.5

x Housing, Black

xx **Housing**

Blacks–Integration   301.45

See also **School integration**

x Integration, Racial

Blacks–Libraries.   *See* **Libraries and blacks**

Blacks–Occupations.   *See* **Blacks–Employment**

Blacks–Political activity   324

See also **Black nationalism; Black power; Blacks–Civil rights**

Blacks–Race identity   301.2; 301.45

See also **Black studies; Black nationalism**

x Negritude; Race identity; Racial identity

xx **Race awareness**

Blacks–Religion   277.3

See also **Black Muslims**

xx **Religion**

Blacks–Segregation   301.45

See also **Segregation in education**

xx **Segregation**

Blacks–Social conditions   301.45; 309.173

xx **Social conditions**

Blacks–Social life and customs   301.45; 917.3

Blacks–Songs and music   784.7

See also **Black music**

xx **Black music; Black songs**

Blacks—Suffrage 324
    x Black suffrage
    xx **Suffrage**
Blacks—U.S. *See* **Blacks**
Blacks and libraries. *See* **Libraries and blacks**
Blacks in art. *See* **Blacks in literature and art**
Blacks in literature and art 704; 809
    Use for materials treating of blacks in
    literature and blacks depicted in works
    of art. For works of black authors or
    artists see **American literature—Black
    authors; Black art.** For materials
    about black authors or artists see
    Black authors; Black artists
    x Blacks in art
    xx **Art; Characters and characteristics in
    literature**
Blacksmithing 682
    See also **Forging; Welding**
    x Farriering; Horseshoeing
    xx **Forging; Ironwork**
Blast furnaces 669
    xx **Furnaces; Smelting**
Bleaching 667
    See also **Dyes and dyeing**
    xx **Chemistry, Technical; Cleaning; Dyes
    and dyeing; Textile industry**
Blimps. *See* **Airships**
Blind 362.4
    xx **Physically handicapped; Vision disorders**
Blind, Books for the 027.6
    See also **Large print books; Talking books**
    x Books for the blind; Braille books
Blind, Dogs for the. *See* **Guide dogs**
Blind—Education 371.9
    x Blind—Rehabilitation; Education of the
    blind
    xx **Vocational education; Vocational guid-
    ance**
Blind—Institutional care 362.4
    x Asylums; Charitable institutions; Homes
    (Institutions)
    xx **Institutional care**
Blind—Rehabilitation. *See* **Blind—Education**
Blizzards 551.5
    xx **Storms**
Block printing. *See* **Color prints; Linoleum
    block printing; Textile printing; Wood
    engraving; Woodcuts**
Block signal systems. *See* **Railroads—Signaling**
Blood 612
    xx **Physiology**
Blood—Circulation 612
    See also **Blood pressure**
    x Circulation of the blood
    xx **Blood pressure; Heart**
Blood—Diseases 616.1; 616.9
    See also names of blood diseases, e.g. **Leu-
    kemia;** etc.
    x Diseases of the blood

Blood—Groups. *See* **Blood groups**
Blood—Pressure. *See* **Blood pressure**
Blood—Transfusion   615
  x Blood transfusion
  xx **Blood groups**
Blood groups   612
  See also **Blood—Transfusion**
  x Blood—Groups; Rh factor
  xx **Heredity**
Blood pressure   612
  See also **Blood—Circulation**
  x Blood—Pressure
  xx **Blood—Circulation**
Blood transfusion. *See* **Blood—Transfusion**
Blue prints. *See* **Blueprints**
Blueprints   604.2; 692
  x Blue prints
Blues (Songs, etc.)   784.7
  xx **Black songs; Jazz music; Music, Popular
    (Songs, etc.); Spirituals (Songs)**
Boarding houses. *See* **Hotels, motels, etc.**
Boarding schools. *See* **Private schools**
Boards of education. *See* **School boards**
Boards of health. *See* **Health boards**
Boards of trade. *See* **Chambers of commerce**
Boat building. *See* **Boatbuilding**
Boat racing   797.1
  See also names of races
  x Motorboat racing; Racing; Yacht racing
  xx **Boats and boating**
Boatbuilding   623.8
  See also **Shipbuilding; Yachts and yachting**
  x Boat building
  xx **Boats and boating; Naval architecture;
    Shipbuilding**
Boating. *See* **Boats and boating**
Boats, Submarine. *See* **Submarines; Submer-
    sibles**
Boats and boating   797.1
  See also

Boat racing	**Motorboats**
Boatbuilding	**Rowing**
Canoes and canoe-	**Sailing**
ing	**Ships**
Catamarans	**Steamboats**
Houseboats	**Submarines**
Iceboats	**Yachts and yachting**
Marinas	

  x Boating; Locomotion
  xx **Sailing; Ships; Water sports**
Body, Human. *See* **Anatomy, Human; Physi-
    ology**
Body and mind. *See* **Mind and body**
Body language   153; 153.7
  xx **Nonverbal communication**
Body weight control. *See* **Reducing**
Boer War, 1899-1902. *See* **South African War,
    1899-1902**
Bogs. *See* **Marshes**

Bohemianism 301.44

    See also **Hippies**

    x Beat generation; Beatniks

    xx **Collective settlements; Counter culture; Manners and customs**

Bolshevism. *See* **Communism**

Bomb shelters. *See* **Air raid shelters**

Bombers 358.4; 623.7

    See also names of bombers, e.g. **B-52 bomber;** etc.

    xx **Airplanes; Airplanes, Military**

Bombs 623.4

    Use for materials on bombs in general and those to be launched from aircraft.

    See also names of types of bombs, e.g. **Atomic bomb; Guided missiles; Hydrogen bomb; Incendiary bombs;** etc.

    x Aerial bombs

    xx **Ammunition; Ordnance; Projectiles**

Bombs, Flying. *See* **Guided missiles**

Bombs, Incendiary. *See* **Incendiary bombs**

Bonds 332.6

    See also **Debts, Public; Stocks**

    xx **Debts, Public; Finance; Investments; Negotiable instruments; Securities; Stock exchange; Stocks**

Bones 611; 612

    See also **Fractures**

    x Osteology

    xx **Anatomy; Physiology**

Bonsai 635.9

    x Kamuti

    xx **Dwarf trees**

Bonus, Soldiers'. *See* **Pensions, Military**

Book awards. *See* **Literary prizes,** and names of awards, e.g. **Caldecott Medal books;** etc.

Book buying (Libraries). *See* **Libraries—Acquisitions**

Book catalogs. *See* **Catalogs, Book**

Book collecting 020.75

    x Bibliomania; Bibliophily

    xx **Book selection; Collectors and collecting**

Book fairs. *See* **Book industries and trade—Exhibitions**

Book illustration. *See* **Illustration of books**

Book industries and trade 686

    See also **Bookbinding; Booksellers and bookselling; Paper making and trade; Printing; Publishers and publishing**

    x Book trade

    xx **Booksellers and bookselling; Paper making and trade; Publishers and publishing**

Book industries and trade—Exhibitions 686.074

    See also **Printing—Exhibitions**

    x Book fairs; Books—Exhibitions

    xx **Printing—Exhibitions**

Book lending. *See* **Libraries—Circulation, loans**

Book numbers, Publishers' standard. *See* Pub-
lishers' standard book numbers
Book plates. *See* Bookplates
Book prices. *See* Books—Prices
Book prizes. *See* Literary prizes; and names
of prizes, e.g. Caldecott Medal books;
etc.
Book rarities. *See* Rare books
Book reviews. *See* Books—Reviews
Book sales. *See* Books—Prices
Book selection 025.2
Use for materials that discuss the principles
of book appraisal, and how to select
books for libraries. Lists of recom-
mended books are entered under Books
and reading—Best books
See also Book collecting; Books and read-
ing—Best books
x Books—Appraisal; Books—Selection;
Choice of books
xx Books and reading—Best books; Libraries
—Acquisitions; Libraries—Collection
development
Book trade. *See* Book industries and trade;
Booksellers and bookselling; Publishers and publishing
Book Week 021.7
Bookbinding 025.7; 686.3
x Binding of books
xx Arts and crafts; Bibliography; Book
industries and trade; Industrial arts;
Leather industry and trade
Bookkeepers. *See* Accountants
Bookkeeping 657
See also Accounting; Auditing; Cost accounting; Office equipment and supplies; also names of industries, professions, etc. with the subdivision *Accounting,* e.g. Corporations—Accounting; etc.
xx Accounting; Business; Business arithmetic; Business education
Bookmobiles 027.4
xx Library extension
Bookplates 025.7
x Book plates; Ex libris
Books 001.54; 028.7
See also

Authors	Illustration of books
Bibliography	Libraries
Cataloging	Literature
Classification— Books	Manuscripts Paperback books
Illumination of books and manu- scripts	Printing Publishers and pub- lishing

also headings beginning with the word
Book
xx Bibliography; Literature; Printing; Publishers and publishing

Books—Appraisal. *See* **Books—Reviews; Book selection; Books and reading; Books and reading—Best books; Criticism; Literature—History and criticism**

Books—Best sellers. *See* **Best sellers**

Books—Catalogs. *See* **Catalogs, Book; Catalogs, Booksellers'; Catalogs, Publishers'**

Books—Censorship   323.44

    x Banned books; Index librorum prohibitorum; Prohibited books

    xx **Censorship; Freedom of the press**

Books—Copyright. *See* **Copyright—Books**

Books—Exhibitions. *See* **Book industries and trade—Exhibitions;   Printing—Exhibitions**

Books—First editions. *See* **Bibliography—First editions**

Books—Large print. *See* **Large print books**

Books, Paperback. *See* **Paperback books**

Books—Prices   338.402

    x Book prices; Book sales; Manuscripts—Prices

    xx **Booksellers and bookselling; Prices**

Books, Rare. *See* **Rare books**

Books—Reviews   028.1; 808

    x Appraisal of books; Book reviews; Books—Appraisal; Evaluation of literature; Literature—Evaluation; Reviews

    xx **Books and reading; Criticism**

Books, Sacred. *See* **Sacred books**

Books—Selection. *See* **Book selection**

Books, Talking. *See* **Talking books**

Books and reading   028

    Use for general materials on reading for information and culture, advice to readers, and surveys of reading habits

    See also **Best sellers; Books—Reviews; Children's literature; Libraries; Literature; Reference books**

    x Appraisal of books; Books—Appraisal; Choice of books; Evaluation of literature; Literature—Evaluation; Reading interests

    xx **Communication; Education; Reading**

Books and reading—Best books   028.52

    Use for lists of recommended books

    See also **Book selection**

    x Appraisal of books; Best books; Bibliography—Best books; Books—Appraisal; Choice of books; Evaluation of literature; Literature—Evaluation

    xx **Book selection; Reference books**

Books for children. *See* **Children's literature**

Books for sight saving. *See* **Large print books**

Books for the blind. *See* **Blind, Books for the**

Booksellers and bookselling   658.8

    See also **Book industries and trade; Books—Prices; Catalogs, Booksellers'; Publishers and publishing**

Booksellers and bookselling—*Continued*

 x Book trade

 xx **Book industries and trade; Publishers and publishing; Sales personnel; Selling**

Booksellers' catalogs. *See* **Catalogs, Booksellers'**

Boolean algebra. *See* **Algebra, Boolean**

Boots. *See* **Shoes and shoe industry**

Border life. *See* **Frontier and pioneer life**

Boring 622

 Use for materials on the operation of cutting holes in earth or rock. Materials dealing with workshop operations in metal, wood, etc. are entered under **Drilling and boring**

 See also **Wells**

 x Drilling and boring (Earth and rocks); Shaft sinking; Well boring

 xx **Gas, Natural; Hydraulic engineering; Mining engineering; Petroleum; Tunnels; Water supply engineering; Wells**

Boring (Metal, wood, etc.). *See* **Drilling and boring**

Boss rule. *See* **Corruption in politics**

Botanical chemistry 581.1

 See also **Plants—Chemical analysis**

 x Chemistry, Botanical; Plant chemistry

 xx **Chemistry; Plants—Chemical analysis**

Botanical gardens 580.74

 See also names of botanical gardens

 xx **Gardens; Parks**

Botanical specimens—Collection and preservation. *See* **Plants—Collection and preservation**

Botanists 920; 925

 xx **Naturalists**

Botany (May subdiv. geog.) **580**

 See also

Bulbs	**Plants, Fossil**
Flower gardening	**Seeds**
Flowers	**Shrubs**
Fruit	**Trees**
Grafting	**Variation (Biology)**
Leaves	**Vegetables**
Plant physiology	**Weeds**
Plants	

 x Flora; Vegetable kingdom

 xx **Biology; Natural history; Nature study; Science**

Botany, Agricultural. *See* **Botany, Economic**

Botany—Anatomy 581.4

 x Anatomy, Vegetable; Anatomy of plants; Botany—Structure; Morphology; Plant anatomy; Plants—Anatomy; Structural botany; Vegetable anatomy

 xx **Anatomy**

Botany—Ecology 581.5

 See also **Desert plants**

 x Plants—Ecology; Symbiosis

 xx **Ecology; Forest influences**

Botany, Economic   581.6

> *See also* **Cotton; Forest products; Grain; Grasses; Plant introduction; Plants, Edible; Poisonous plants; Weeds**
>
> *x* Agricultural botany; Biology, Economic; Botany, Agricultural; Economic botany; Plants, Useful
>
> *xx* **Agriculture**

Botany, Fossil.   *See* **Plants, Fossil**

Botany—Geographical distribution.   *See* **Geographical distribution of animals and plants**

Botany, Medical   581.6

> *x* Herbals; Herbs, Medical; Medical botany; Medicinal plants; Plants, Medicinal
>
> *xx* **Medicine; Pharmacy**

Botany—Nomenclature.   *See* **Botany—Terminology; Plant names, Popular**

Botany—Pathology.   *See* **Plants—Diseases**

Botany—Physiology.   *See* **Plant physiology**

Botany—Structure.   *See* **Botany—Anatomy**

Botany—Terminology   580.3

> Use for materials on scientific names of plants, etc. Materials on popular names are entered under **Plant names, Popular**
>
> *See also* **Plant names, Popular**
>
> *x* Botany—Nomenclature; Nomenclature; Plant names, Scientific; Terminology
>
> *xx* **Plant names, Popular**

Botany—U.S.   581.973

> *x* U.S.—Botany

Botany of the Bible.   *See* **Bible—Natural history**

Boulder Dam.   *See* **Hoover Dam**

Boundaries   320.1; 341.42

> *See also* **Geopolitics;** also names of wars with the subdivision *Territorial questions* (e.g. **World War, 1939–1945—Territorial questions;** etc.) and names of countries, cities etc. with the subdivision *Boundaries,* e.g. **U.S.—Boundaries;** etc.
>
> *x* Frontiers; Geography, Political; Political boundaries; Political geography
>
> *xx* **Geography; Geopolitics; International law; International relations**

Bounties.   *See* **Subsidies**

Bourgeoisie.   *See* **Middle classes**

Bow and arrow   799.2; 799.3

> *See also* **Archery**
>
> *x* Arrow
>
> *xx* **Archery**

Bowed instruments.   *See* **Stringed instruments**

Bowling   794.6; 796.31

> *x* Tenpins

Boxing   796.8

Boxing—*Continued*
> *x* Fighting; Prize fighting; Pugilism; Sparring
> *xx* **Athletics; Self-defense**

Boy Scouts 369.43
> *x* Cub Scouts
> *xx* **Boys; Boys' clubs; Scouts and scouting**

Boycott 322.4; 331.89
> *xx* **Passive resistance**

Boys 155.4; 301.43
> *See also* **Boy Scouts; Children; Young men; Youth**
> *xx* **Children; Men; Young men; Youth**

Boys—Clubs. *See* **Boys' clubs**
Boys—Employment. *See* **Child labor**
Boys—Societies. *See* **Boys' clubs**
Boys' agricultural clubs. *See* **Agriculture—Societies; Boys' clubs; 4-H clubs**

Boys' clubs 369.42
> *See also* **Boy Scouts; 4-H clubs**
> *x* Boys' agricultural clubs; Boys—Clubs; Boys—Societies
> *xx* **Clubs; Men—Societies; Social settlements; Societies**

Boys' towns. *See* **Children—Institutional care**
Brahmanism 294.5
> *See also* **Caste; Hinduism**
> *xx* **Buddhism; Hinduism; Religions**

Braille books. *See* **Blind, Books for the**
Brain 611; 612
> *See also* **Dreams; Head; Memory; Mind and body; Nervous system; Phrenology; Psychology; Sleep**
> *xx* **Head; Nervous system**

Brain—Diseases 616.8
> *See also* **Cerebral palsy**

Brain, Electronic. *See* **Artificial intelligence; Computers**
Brain storming. *See* **Problem solving, Group**
Brainwashing 153.8
> *x* Will
> *xx* **Mental suggestion**

Brakes 625.2; 629.2
> *See also* subjects with the subdivision *Brakes,* e.g. **Automobiles—Brakes;** etc.
> *xx* **Railroads—Safety appliances**

Branch stores. *See* **Chain stores**
Brand names. *See* **Trademarks**
Brass 669; 673
> *See also* **Brasses**
> *xx* **Alloys; Founding; Zinc**

Brass instruments. *See* **Wind instruments**
Brasses 739
> *x* Monumental brasses; Sepulchral brasses
> *xx* **Archeology; Art; Brass; Inscriptions; Sculpture; Tombs**

Bravery. *See* **Courage**
Brazilian literature 869
> May use same subdivisions and names of literary forms as for **English literature**

Brazilian literature—*Continued*

 See also **Portuguese literature**

 xx **Latin American literature; Portuguese literature**

Brazing. *See* **Solder and soldering**

Bread 641.8; 664

 xx **Baking; Cookery; Food**

Breadstuffs. *See* **Flour; Grain; Wheat**

Breakfast cereals. *See* **Cereals, Prepared**

Breathing. *See* **Respiration**

Breeder reactors. *See* **Nuclear reactors**

Breeding. *See* **Livestock; Plant breeding**

Bricklaying 693.2

 See also **Masonry**

 xx **Bricks; Building; Masonry**

Bricks 666; 691

 See also **Bricklaying; Tiles**

 xx **Building materials; Clay; Clay industries**

Bridal customs. *See* **Marriage customs and rites**

Bridge (Game) 795.4

 x Auction bridge; Contract bridge; Duplicate bridge

 xx **Card games**

Bridges 624.2

 See also names of cities and rivers with the subdivision *Bridges* (e.g. **Chicago—Bridges; Hudson River—Bridges;** etc.) also names of bridges, e.g. **Golden Gate Bridge;** etc.

 x Suspension bridges; Viaducts

 xx **Building, Iron and steel; Civil engineering; Masonry; Transportation**

Brigands. *See* **Robbers and outlaws**

Bright children. *See* **Gifted children**

British Commonwealth of Nations. *See* **Commonwealth of Nations**

British Dominions. *See* **Commonwealth of Nations**

British in India 325.954

 Use same form for British in other countries, states, etc., e.g. **British in France;** etc.

 x English in India

Broadcasting 384.5

 See also **Radio broadcasting; Television broadcasting**

 xx **Telecommunication**

Bronze age 913

 See also **Archeology; Iron age**

 x Prehistory

 xx **Archeology; Iron age; Man, Prehistoric**

Bronzes 739

 xx **Archeology; Art; Art, Decorative; Art metalwork; Decoration and ornament; Metalwork; Sculpture**

Brownouts. *See* **Electric power failures**

Brutality. *See* **Cruelty**

Bubonic plague. *See* **Plague**

Buccaneers. *See* **Pirates**

Buddhism 294.3

    See also **Brahmanism; Theosophy; Zen Buddhism**

    xx **Religions; Theosophy**

Buddhist art. *See* **Art, Buddhist**

Budget (May subdiv. geog.) **351.7**

    Use for materials on the budget or reports on the appropriations and expenditures of a government

    See also **Finance**

    xx **Finance**

Budget—U.S. 353.007

    See also **U.S.—Appropriations and expenditures**

    x Federal budget; U.S.—Budget

Budgets, Business 658.1

    x Business—Budget

    xx **Business**

Budgets, Household 640

    x Domestic finance; Family budget; Finance, Household; Home economics —Accounting; Household budget; Household finances

    xx **Cost of living; Finance, Personal**

Budgets, Personal. *See* **Finance, Personal**

Buffalo, American. *See* **Bison**

Buffing. *See* **Grinding and polishing**

Bugging, Electronic. *See* **Eavesdropping**

Building 690

    See also

Architecture	**Foundations**
Bricklaying	**Masonry**
Carpentry	**Roofs**
Chimneys	**Sanitary engineering**
Concrete construction	**Strength of materials**
Doors	**Walls**
Engineering	**Windows**
Floors	

    x Architectural engineering; Construction

    xx **Architecture; Carpentry; Houses; Structural engineering; Structures, Theory of; Technology**

Building, Concrete. *See* **Concrete construction**

Building—Contracts and specifications 692

    x Building—Specifications; Building contracts

    xx **Contracts**

Building—Estimates 692

    x Estimates

Building, Iron and steel 693

    See also **Bridges; Roofs; Skyscrapers; Steel, Structural; Strains and stresses; Strength of materials; Structures, Theory of**

    x Architectural engineering; Iron and steel building; Steel construction

    xx **Iron; Steel; Steel, Structural**

Building—Materials. *See* **Building materials**

Building—Repair and reconstruction. *See* **Buildings—Maintenance and repair**

Building—Specifications. *See* **Building—Contracts and specifications**

Building and loan associations. *See* **Savings and loan associations**

Building contracts. *See* **Building—Contracts and specifications**

Building materials   691

All types of building materials are not included in this list. Add as needed

See also

Bricks	**Strength of materials**
Cement	
Concrete	**Structural engineering**
Concrete, Reinforced	
Glass construction	**Stucco**
Steel, Structural	**Terra cotta**
Stone	**Tiles**
	Wood

x Building—Materials; Structural materials

xx **Architecture; Materials; Strength of materials**

Building repair. *See* **Buildings—Maintenance and repair**

Building security. *See* **Burglary protection**

Buildings   690; 720

See also names of types of buildings and construction, e.g. **Buildings, Prefabricated; Farm buildings; Industrial buildings; School buildings;** etc.; also names of cities and names of institutions with the subdivision *Buildings,* e.g. **Chicago—Buildings; Colleges and universities—Buildings;** etc.; also names of specific buildings

Buildings, College. *See* **Colleges and universities—Buildings**

Buildings, Farm. *See* **Farm buildings**

Buildings, Historic. *See* **Historic buildings, etc.**

Buildings, Industrial. *See* **Industrial buildings**

Buildings, Library. *See* **Library architecture**

Buildings—Maintenance and repair   690

See also **Architecture—Conservation and restoration; Houses—Maintenance and repair**

x Building—Repair and reconstruction; Building repair; Buildings—Remodeling; Remodeling of buildings

xx **Architecture—Conservation and restoration; Repairing**

Buildings, Office. *See* **Office buildings**

Buildings, Prefabricated   693.9

See also **Prefabricated houses**

xx **Buildings**

Buildings, Public. *See* **Public buildings;** and names of countries, cities, etc. with the subdivision *Public buildings,* e.g. **Chicago—Public buildings;** etc.

Buildings—Remodeling. *See* **Buildings—Maintenance and repair**

Buildings, Restoration of. *See* **Architecture—Conservation and restoration**

Buildings, School. *See* **School buildings**

Buildings—Security. *See* **Burglary protection**

Built-in furniture 684.1; 749
  x Furniture, Built-in
  xx **Furniture**

Bulbs 581.3; 635.9
  xx **Botany; Flower gardening; Gardening**

Bulge, Battle of the. *See* **Ardennes, Battle of the, 1944–1945**

Bullets. *See* **Projectiles**

Bullfights 791.8
  x Fighting

Bullion. *See* **Gold; Money; Silver**

Bunker Hill, Battle of, 1775—Poetry 811
  xx **Poetry**

Bureaucracy 350-352
  See also **Civil service**
  xx **Civil service; Political science; Public administration**

Burglar alarms 621.389
  xx **Burglary protection; Electric apparatus and appliances**

Burglars. *See* **Robbers and outlaws**

Burglary protection 621.389
  See also types of protective devices, e.g. **Burglar alarms; Locks and keys;** etc.; also types of buildings with the subdivision *Security measures,* e.g. **Atomic power plants—Security measures;** etc.

  x Building security; Buildings—Security; Houses—Security; Protection against burglary; Residential security

Burial. *See* **Catacombs; Cemeteries; Cremation; Cryonics; Epitaphs; Funeral rites and ceremonies; Mounds and mound builders; Mummies; Tombs**

Burial statistics. *See* **Mortality; Registers of births, etc.; Vital statistics** and names of countries, cities, etc. with the subdivision *Statistics,* e.g. **U.S.—Statistics;** etc.

Buried cities. *See* **Cities and towns, Ruined, extinct, etc.**

Buried treasure 910.4
  x Hidden treasure; Sunken treasure; Treasure trove

Burying grounds. *See* **Cemeteries**

Buses 388.4; 629.22
  x Motor buses
  xx **Automobiles; Local transit; Transportation; Transportation, Highway**

Bush survival. *See* **Wilderness survival**

Business 650

See also

Accounting	Instalment plan
Advertising	Mail-order business
Banks and banking	Manufactures
Bookkeeping	Marketing
Budgets, Business	Markets
Commercial law	Merchants
Competition	Occupations
Corporations	Office management
Credit	Profit
Department stores	Real estate business
Economic conditions	Selling
Efficiency, Industrial	Small business
Industrial manage-	Trust companies
ment	

x Trade

xx **Commerce; Economics; Industrial management; Success**

Business—Budget. See **Budgets, Business**

Business, Choice of. See **Vocational guidance**

Business—International aspects. See **International business enterprises**

Business—Political activity. See **Business and
politics**

Business, Small. See **Small business**

Business and government. See **Industry and
state**

Business and politics 658

x Business—Political activity; Politics and
business

xx **Politics, Practical**

Business arithmetic 513

See also **Accounting; Bookkeeping; Interest
(Economics)**

x Arithmetic, Commercial; Commercial
arithmetic

xx **Arithmetic**

Business colleges. See **Business education**

Business combinations. See **Conglomerate corporations; Trusts, Industrial**

Business correspondence. See **Business letters**

Business cycles 338.5

See also names of types of business cycles,
e.g. **Depressions, Economic;** etc.

x Business depressions; Cycles, Business;
Economic cycles; Stabilization in industry

xx **Economic conditions**

Business depressions. See **Business cycles; Depressions, Economic; Economic conditions**

Business education 650.7

Use for materials on how to teach business
and for description of business operations

See also **Accounting; Bookkeeping; Commercial law; Penmanship; Secretaries;
Shorthand; Typewriting**

x Business colleges; Business schools;

86

Business education—*Continued*
> Clerical work—Training; Commercial education; Commercial schools; Education, Business; Office work—Training; Schools, Commercial

xx **Education**

Business English. *See* **English language—Business English**

Business enterprises, International. *See* **International business enterprises**

Business ethics   174
> *See also* **Competition; Honesty; Success**
> *xx* **Ethics; Honesty; Professional ethics**

Business failures. *See* **Bankruptcy**

Business forecasting   338.5
> *xx* **Forecasting**

Business law. *See* **Commercial law**

Business letters   651.7
> *See also* **English language—Business English**
> *x* Business correspondence; Commercial correspondence: Correspondence
> *xx* **English language—Business English; Letter writing**

Business libraries   026
> *x* Libraries, Business
> *xx* **Libraries; Libraries, Special**

Business machines. *See* **Office equipment and supplies**

Business people, Black. *See* **Black business people**

Business schools. *See* **Business education**

Busing (School integration) (May subdiv. geog. state or city)   **344.7; 370.19**
> *x* Antibusing; Racial balance in schools; School busing
> *xx* **School children—Transportation; Segregation in education**

Butter   637; 641.3
> *See also* **Margarine**
> *xx* **Dairy products; Milk**

Butter, Artificial. *See* **Margarine**

Butterflies   595.7
> *See also* **Caterpillars; Moths**
> *x* Cocoons; Lepidoptera
> *xx* **Insects; Moths**

Buttons   391; 687
> *xx* **Clothing and dress**

Buyers' guides. *See* **Consumer education; Shopping**

Buying   351.7; 352; 658.7
> Use for materials on buying by government agencies and commercial and industrial enterprises. Materials on buying by the consumer are entered under **Consumer education; Shopping.** See notes under these headings
> *See also* **Consumer education; Instalment plan; Shopping**
> *x* Purchasing

87

Buying—*Continued*
    xx **Consumer education; Industrial management; Shopping**
By-products. *See* **Waste products**
Byrd Antarctic Expedition, 1st, 1928–1930
        919.8
    x Antarctic expeditions; Expeditions, Antarctic and Arctic
Byzantine architecture. *See* **Architecture, Byzantine**
Byzantine art. *See* **Art, Byzantine**
Byzantine Empire 914.95; 949.5
    x Eastern Empire
CATV. *See* **Community antenna television**
CB radio. *See* **Citizens band radio**
CRT. *See* **Cathode ray tubes**
Cabinet officers 920; 923
    x Ministers of state
Cabinet work 684
    See note under **Carpentry**
    See also **Veneers and veneering; Woodwork**
    xx **Carpentry; Furniture; Woodwork**
Cabins. *See* **Log cabins**
Cable codes. *See* **Cipher and telegraph codes**
Cable television. *See* **Community antenna television**
Cables 384.6
    xx **Power transmission; Rope**
Cables, Submarine 384.6; 621.382
    x Atlantic cable; Ocean cables; Pacific cable; Submarine cables; Submarine telegraph; Telegraph, Submarine
    xx **Telecommunication; Telegraph**
Cactus 635.9
    xx **Desert plants**
Cafeterias. *See* **Restaurants, bars, etc.**
Cage birds 636.6
    See also names of cage birds, e.g. **Canaries;** etc.
    xx **Birds**
Cake 641.8; 664
    xx **Baking; Cookery**
Cake decorating 641.8
    xx **Confectionery**
Calculating machines 510.28; 651.8; 681
    See also **Computers; Cybernetics; Slide rule**
    x Accounting machines; Adding machines; Calculators; Pocket calculators
    xx **Computers; Office equipment and supplies**
Calculators. *See* **Calculating machines**
Calculus 515
    x Analysis (Mathematics); Integral calculus
    xx **Mathematical analysis; Mathematics**
Caldecott Medal books 028.5
    x Book awards; Book prizes; Literary awards; Literature—Prizes
    xx **Children's literature; Illustration of books; Literary prizes**

88

Calendars 529
    See also **Almanacs**
    x Annuals
    xx **Almanacs; Time; Yearbooks**
California—Gold discoveries 979.4
    x Gold rush
Calisthenics. *See* **Gymnastics; Physical education and training**
Calligraphy 745.6
    xx **Penmanship; Writing**
Calvinism 284
    See also **Congregationalism; Predestination; Puritans**
    xx **Congregationalism; Puritans; Reformation**
Cambistry. *See* **Foreign exchange; Weights and measures**
Camels 599; 636.2
    x Dromedaries
    xx **Desert animals**
Cameras 771.3
    See also names of types of cameras and of individual makes of cameras, e.g. **Motion picture cameras; Kodak camera;** etc.
    xx **Photography; Photography—Equipment and supplies**
Camouflage (Biology) 591.5
    See also **Color of animals**
    x Animal camouflage; Animals—Camouflage
    xx **Color of animals**
Camouflage (Military) 355.4; 359.4; 623.7
    xx **Military art and science; Naval art and science**
Camp cooking. *See* **Cookery, Outdoor**
Camp Fire Girls 369.47
    xx **Girls' clubs**
Camp sites. *See* **Campgrounds**
Campaign funds (May subdiv. geog.) **329**
    x Assessments, Political; Elections—Finance; Political assessments; Political parties—Finance
    xx **Corruption in politics; Elections; Politics, Practical**
Campaign funds—U.S. 329
    x Elections—U.S.—Finance; U.S.—Campaign funds
Campaign literature (May subdivide by date and party) **329**
    xx **Politics, Practical**
Campaigns, Political. *See* **Politics, Practical**
Campaigns, Presidential—U.S. *See* **Presidents —U.S.—Election**
Campbellites. *See* **Disciples of Christ**
Campers and trailers. *See* **Travel trailers and campers**
Campgrounds 796.54
    See also **Trailer parks**
    x Camp sites

Camping   796.54

See note under **Camps**

See also **Backpacking; Cookery, Outdoor; Outdoor life; Tents; Travel trailers and campers; Wilderness survival**

xx **Outdoor life; Outdoor recreation**

Camps   796.54

Use for materials on camps with a definite program of activities. Materials on the technique of camping are entered under **Camping**

x Summer camps

Camps (Military)   355.7

See also **Concentration camps**

x Military camps

xx **Military art and science**

Campus disorders. *See* **College students—Political activity**

Canada   917.1; 971

See also **Northwest, Canadian;** also names of individual provinces

Canada—Biculturalism. *See* **Biculturalism—Canada**

Canada—Bilingualism. *See* **Bilingualism—Canada**

Canada—English-French relations   301.24; 917.1

See also **Biculturalism—Canada; Quebec (Province)—History—Autonomy and independence movements**

x Canada—French-English relations

Canada—Exploration. *See* **America—Exploration**

Canada—French-English relations. *See* **Canada—English-French relations**

Canada—History—To   1763   (New   France)   971.01

x New France—History

Canada—History—1763–1791   971.02

Canada—History—19th century   971.03-971.05

Canada—History—1914–1945   971.06

Canada—History—1945–   971.06

Canada, Northwest. *See* **Northwest, Canadian**

Canadian Indians. *See* **Indians of North America—Canada**

Canadian Invasion, 1775–1776   973.3

xx **U.S.—History—Revolution, 1775–1783**

Canadian literature   810; 819

May use same subdivisions and names of literary forms as for **English literature**

See also **French Canadian literature**

xx **American literature**

Canadian literature, French. *See* **French Canadian literature**

Canadian Northwest. *See* **Northwest, Canadian**

Canadians   917.1

See also **French Canadians**

Canals   386; 627

See also **Inland navigation;** also names of canals, e.g. **Panama Canal;** etc.

Canals—*Continued*
    xx Civil engineering; Hydraulic structures;
        Inland navigation; Transportation;
        Waterways
Canaries   598.2; 636.6
    xx Birds; Cage birds
Canasta (Game)   795.4
    x Argentine rummy
    xx Card games
Cancer   616.9
    x Carcinoma
    xx Tumors
Cancer—Chemotherapy   616.9
    xx Chemotherapy
Candles   665
    xx Lighting
Candy. *See* Confectionery
Caning of chairs. *See* Chair caning
Canned goods. *See* Canning and preserving
Cannibalism   291.3; 394
    xx Ethnology
Canning and preserving   641.4; 644
    x Canned goods; Food, Canned; Fruit—
        Canning; Pickling; Preserving; Vege-
        tables—Canning
    xx Chemistry, Technical; Cookery; Food—
        Preservation
Cannon. *See* Ordnance
Canoes and canoeing   797.1
    xx Boats and boating; Water sports
Canon law. *See* Ecclesiastical law
Cantatas   783.4
    See also Choral music
    xx Vocal music
Canvas embroidery. *See* Needlepoint
Capital   332
    See also Banks and banking; Capitalism;
        Interest (Economics); Investments; La-
        bor and laboring classes; Monopolies;
        Profit; Trusts, Industrial; Wealth
    xx Capitalism; Economics; Finance; Income;
        Money; Wealth
Capital and labor. *See* Industrial relations
Capital punishment   179; 364.6
    x Death penalty; Executions; Hanging
    xx Crime; Criminal law; Murder; Punish-
        ment
Capitalism   330.1; 339
    See also Capital; Socialism
    xx Capital; Economics; Labor and laboring
        classes; Monopolies; Profit; Socialism;
        Trusts, Industrial
Capitalists and financiers   920; 923
    See also Millionaires
    x Financiers
    xx Wealth
Capitalization (Finance). *See* Corporations—
        Finance; Railroads—Finance; Securi-
        ties; Valuation

Capitals (Cities)   910-918; 930-998
> Use for materials on the capital cities of several countries or states

Capitols   725

Car pools   388.3
> *x* Automobile pools; Automobiles—Pools; Carpools
> *xx* Traffic engineering; Transportation

Car wheels.   *See* **Wheels**

Carbines.   *See* **Rifles**

Carbolic acid   546; 547; 661
> *xx* Acids; Chemicals

Carbon   546; 547; 661; 662
> *See also* **Charcoal; Coal; Diamonds; Graphite**

Carbon 14 dating.   *See* **Radiocarbon dating**

Carburetors   621.43
> *xx* Gas and oil engines

Carcinoma.   *See* **Cancer**

Card catalogs.   *See* **Catalogs, Card**

Card games   795.4
> *See also* **Card tricks;** also names of card games, e.g. **Bridge (Game); Canasta (Game);** etc.
> *x* Cards, Playing; Playing cards
> *xx* Gambling; Games

Card tricks   795.4
> *xx* Card games; Magic; Tricks

Cardiac diseases.   *See* **Heart—Diseases**

Cardinals   920; 922

Cards, Greeting.   *See* **Greeting cards**

Cards, Playing.   *See* **Card games**

Career education.   *See* **Vocational education**

Careers.   *See* **Occupations; Professions; Vocational guidance**

Caricatures.   *See* **Cartoons and caricatures**

Carillons.   *See* **Bells**

Carnivals.   *See* **Festivals**

Carnivals (Circus).   *See* **Amusement parks**

Carols   783.6
> *See also* names of individual carols
> *x* Christmas carols
> *xx* Christmas—Poetry; Church music; Folk songs; Hymns; Religious poetry; Songs; Vocal music

Carpentry   694
> Use for materials dealing with the constructing of a wooden building or the wooden portion of any building. Materials that treat of the making and finishing of fine woodwork, such as furniture or interior details, are entered under **Cabinet work**
> *See also* **Building; Cabinet work; Doors; Floors; Roofs; Turning; Walls; Woodwork**
> *xx* Building; Industrial arts education; Woodwork

Carpentry—Tools 694
>*See also* names of tools, e.g. **Saws;** etc.
>*xx* **Tools**

Carpetbag rule. *See* **Reconstruction (1865–1876)**

Carpets 645; 746.7; 747
>*See also* **Rugs; Weaving**
>*xx* **Decoration and ornament; Interior decoration; Rugs; Textile industry; Weaving**

Carpools. *See* **Car pools**

Carriages and carts 388.3; 688.6
>*x* Carts; Coaches, Stage; Stagecoaches; Wagons
>*xx* **Transportation**

Carriers, Aircraft. *See* **Aircraft carriers**

Cars (Automobiles). *See* **Automobiles**

Cars, Armored (Tanks). *See* **Tanks (Military science)**

Cartels. *See* **Trusts, Industrial**

Cartography. *See* **Charts; Map drawing; Maps**

Cartoons and caricatures 741.5
>Use for general collections of, and materials about, caricatures and cartoons
>*See also* **Comic books, strips, etc.; Motion picture cartoons;** also subjects with the subdivision *Cartoons and caricatures,* e.g. **Computers—Cartoons and caricatures;** and names of wars with the subdvision *Humor, caricatures, etc.,* e.g. **World War, 1939–1945—Humor, caricatures, etc.;** etc.
>*x* Caricatures; Humorous pictures; Illustrations, Humorous; Pictures, Humorous
>*xx* **Comic books, strips, etc.; Pictures; Portraits**

Carts. *See* **Carriages and carts**

Carving (Meat, etc.) 642
>*xx* **Dinners and dining**

Carving, Wood. *See* **Wood carving**

Case studies. *See* subjects with the subdivision *Case studies,* e.g. **Juvenile delinquency—Case studies;** etc.

Case work, Social. *See* **Social case work**

Cassette books. *See* **Talking books**

Cassette recorders and recording. *See* **Magnetic recorders and recording**

Castaways. *See* **Survival (after airplane accidents, shipwrecks, etc.)**

Caste 294.5; 301.44
>*See also* **Social classes**
>*xx* **Brahmanism; Hinduism; Manners and customs**

Casting. *See* **Founding; Plaster casts**

Castles 728.8
>*x* Chateaux
>*xx* **Architecture; Architecture, Medieval**

Casts, Plaster. *See* **Plaster casts**

Casualty insurance. *See* **Insurance, Casualty**

Cat. *See* **Cats**

Catacombs 272; 394; 726

    See also **Church history—Early church, ca. 30–600**

    x Burial

    xx **Cemeteries; Christian antiquities; Christian art and symbolism; Church history—Early church, ca. 30–600; Tombs**

Cataloging 025.3

    See also **Bibliography; Classification—Books; Indexing; Subject headings**

    x Cataloguing

    xx **Bibliographic control; Bibliography; Books; Documentation; Indexing; Libraries—Technical services; Library science**

Cataloging—Music 025.3

    Use same form for the cataloging of other types of materials

    x Music—Cataloging

Catalogs. *See* **Catalogs, Booksellers'; Catalogs, Publishers'; Library catalogs;** and subjects with the subdivision *Catalogs,* e.g. **Motion pictures—Catalogs;** etc.

Catalogs, Book 010

    x Book catalogs; Books—Catalogs; Catalogs in book form

    xx **Library catalogs**

Catalogs, Booksellers' 017-019

    x Books—Catalogs; Booksellers' catalogs; Catalogs

    xx **Booksellers and bookselling**

Catalogs, Card 017-019

    x Card catalogs

    xx **Library catalogs**

Catalogs, Classified 017

    See also **Classification—Books**

    x Catalogs, Systematic; Classed catalogs Classified catalogs

    xx **Classification—Books; Library catalogs**

Catalogs, Library. *See* **Library catalogs**

Catalogs, Publishers' 015

    x Books—Catalogs; Catalogs; Publishers' catalogs

    xx **Publishers and publishing**

Catalogs, Subject 017

    See also **Subject headings**

    xx **Library catalogs**

Catalogs, Systematic. *See* **Catalogs, Classified**

Catalogs in book form. *See* **Catalogs, Book**

Cataloguing. *See* **Cataloging**

Catalysis 541; 547; 660

    xx **Chemistry, Physical and theoretical**

Catamarans 623.82; 797.1

    xx **Boats and boating**

Catastrophes. *See* **Disasters**

Catechisms 238; 268

    See also **Bible—Catechisms, question books; Creeds**

Catechisms—*Continued*

> *xx* **Christian education; Creeds; Theology—Study and teaching**

Caterers and catering   642

> *See also* **Desserts; Dinners and dining; Luncheons; Menus**
> *xx* **Cookery; Menus**

Caterpillars   595.7

> *x* Cocoons
> *xx* **Butterflies; Moths**

Cathedrals (May subdiv. geog.)   726

> *See also* **Architecture, Gothic;** also names of individual cathedrals
> *xx* **Abbeys; Architecture; Architecture, Gothic; Architecture, Medieval; Christian art and symbolism; Church architecture; Churches**

Cathedrals—U.S.   726

> *x* U.S.—Cathedrals

Cathode ray tubes   537.5; 621.3815

> *x* CRT
> *xx* **Vacuum tubes**

Catholic Church   282

> *See also* subjects with the subdivision *Catholic Church*, e.g. **Church and state—Catholic Church;** etc.
> *x* Roman Catholic Church
> *xx* **Christianity; Papacy**

Catholic Church—Clergy   253

> *See also* **Ex-priests; Priests**
> *xx* **Clergy**

Catholic Church—Converts. *See* **Converts, Catholic**

Catholic Church—Foreign relations. *See* **Catholic Church—Relations (Diplomatic)**

Catholic Church—Missions   266

> *xx* **Missions, Christian**

Catholic Church—Relations   282

> Use for materials on relations between the Catholic Church and other churches and religions

Catholic Church—Relations (Diplomatic)   282

> *See also* **Holy See**
> *x* Catholic Church—Foreign relations
> *xx* **International relations**

Catholic Church in the U.S.   282.73

> Use same form for Catholic Church, and for other churches, in other countries, states, etc., e.g. **Catholic Church in France;** etc.

Catholic converts. *See* **Converts, Catholic**

Catholic ex-priests. *See* **Ex-priests**

Catholic literature   208

> *x* Index librorum prohibitorum
> *xx* **Literature; Religious literature**

Catholics in the U.S.   301.45

> Use same form for Catholics in other countries, cities, etc., e.g. **Catholics in Boston;** etc.

Cats   599; 636.8
>   *x* Cat
>   *xx* **Domestic animals; Pets**

Cattle   636.2
>   Use for general materials and for materials on beef cattle. Materials limited to dairy cattle are entered under **Cows**
>   *See also* **Cows; Dairying; Livestock; Pastures**
>   *x* Beef cattle
>   *xx* **Dairying; Domestic animals; Livestock**

Cattle—Diseases   636.2
>   *x* Cows—Diseases
>   *xx* **Animals—Diseases; Veterinary medicine**

Cattle brands   636.2

Cave drawings   743; 759.01
>   *xx* **Mural painting and decoration; Picture writing**

Cave dwellers   913
>   *xx* **Man, Prehistoric**

Caves   551.4; 796.5
>   *x* Grottoes; Speleology

Celery   633; 635
>   *xx* **Vegetables**

Celibacy   176; 253
>   *xx* **Marriage; Religious orders**

Cellars.   *See* **Basements**

Cello.   *See* **Violoncello**

Cells   574.8; 581.8; 591.8
>   *See also* **DNA; Embryology; Protoplasm; Protozoa**
>   *x* Cytology
>   *xx* **Biology; Biophysics; Embryology; Physiological chemistry; Physiology; Protoplasm; Reproduction**

Cells, Electric.   *See* **Electric batteries**

Celtic legends.   *See* **Legends, Celtic**

Celts   572.9364; 936.4
>   *See also* **Druids and Druidism**
>   *x* Gaels
>   *xx* **France—History—To 1328; Gt. Brit.—History—To 1066**

Cement   620.1; 666; 691
>   *See also* **Concrete; Pavements**
>   *x* Hydraulic cement
>   *xx* **Adhesives; Building materials; Ceramics; Concrete; Lime; Masonry; Plaster and plastering**

Cemeteries   393; 718
>   *See also* **Catacombs; Epitaphs; Tombs;** also names of cities with the subdivision *Cemeteries* (e.g. **Chicago—Cemeteries;** etc.); and names of cemeteries
>   *x* Burial; Burying grounds; Churchyards; Graves; Graveyards
>   *xx* **Public health; Sanitation; Tombs**

Censorship   301.15
>   Use for general materials on freedom of expression in various fields

Censorship—*Continued*

See *also* **Free speech; Freedom of information; Freedom of the press;** also subjects with the subdivision *Censorship,*
e.g. **Books—Censorship; Motion pictures—Censorship; Television—Censorship;** etc.

xx **Freedom of information; Intellectual
freedom**

Census 312

See *also* names of countries, cities, etc.
with the subdivision *Census,* e.g. **U.S.
—Census;** etc.

xx **Population; Statistics; Vital statistics**

Centers for the performing arts 725

See *also* **Theaters;** also names of individual
centers

xx **Performing arts**

Central Africa. *See* **Africa, Central**

Central America 917.28; 972.8

xx **America**

Central Europe 914.3; 943

Use for materials on the area included in
the basins of the Danube, Elbe and
Rhine rivers

x Europe, Central

Central States. *See* **Middle West**

Centralization of schools. *See* **Schools—Centralization**

Centralized processing (Libraries). *See* **Libraries—Technical services**

Ceramic industries 338.4

See *also* Types of ceramic industries, e.g.
Glass manufacture

Ceramic materials 666; 738.1

See *also* names of individual materials, e.g.
Clay; etc.

Ceramics 666

Use for materials on the technology of
fired earth products or clay products
intended for industrial use. Earthenware, chinaware, porcelain are entered
under **Pottery** and **Porcelain**

See *also* **Cement; Glass; Glazes; Pottery;
Tiles**

x Keramics

Cereals. *See* **Cereals, Prepared; Grain**

Cereals, Prepared 641.3; 664

x Breakfast cereals; Cereals

Cerebral palsy 616.8

x Palsy, Cerebral; Paralysis, Cerebral;
Paralysis, Spastic; Spastic paralysis

xx **Brain—Diseases**

Ceremonies. *See* **Etiquette; Manners and customs; Rites and ceremonies**

Certainty. *See* **Belief and doubt; Probabilities;
Truth**

Certified public accountants. *See* **Accountants**

Chain belting. *See* **Belts and belting**

Chain stores 658.8
    x Branch stores; Stores
    xx **Retail trade**
Chair caning 684.1
    x Caning of chairs
Chairs 684.1; 749
    xx **Furniture**
Chalk talks 741.2
    x Blackboard drawing
Chamber music 785.7
    xx **Instrumental music; Music; Orchestral music**
Chambers of commerce 381
    x Boards of trade; Trade, Boards of
    xx **Commerce**
Change, Social. *See* **Social change**
Change of life in men. *See* **Climacteric, Male**
Change of life in women. *See* **Menopause**
Change of sex. *See* **Transexuality**
Chanties. *See* **Sea songs**
Chants (Plain, Gregorian, etc.) 783.5
    x Gregorian chant; Plain chant; Plainsong
    xx **Church music**
Chaplains 253
    See also names of bodies or institutions having chaplains, with the subdivision *Chaplains*, e.g. **U.S. Army—Chaplains;** etc.
    xx **Clergy**
Character 155.2
    See also **Human behavior; Temperament**
    xx **Personality; Temperament**
Character education 370.11; 649
    x Education, Character; Education, Ethical; Education, Moral; Ethical education; Moral education
    xx **Education; Ethics; Religious education**
Characteristics, National. *See* **National characteristics**
Characters and characteristics in literature 809; 810.9; 820.9; etc.
    See also **Blacks in literature and art; Children in literature and art; Children in poetry; Drama—Technique; Plots (Drama, fiction, etc.); Women in literature and art;** also names of prominent authors with the subdivision *Characters*, e.g. **Shakespeare, William—Characters;** etc.; and names of individual characters in literature
    x Literary characters
    xx **Literature**
Charades 793.2
    xx **Amateur theatricals; Amusements; Riddles**
Charcoal 662
    xx **Carbon; Fuel**
Charitable institutions. *See* **Charities; Institutional care; Orphanages;** also classes of people with the subdivision *Institu-*

Charitable institutions—*Continued*
> *tional care*, e.g. **Blind—Institutional care; Deaf—Institutional care; Mentally ill—Institutional care;** etc.

Charities 361.7-361.8
> Use for materials on privately supported welfare activities. Materials on tax supported welfare activities are entered under **Public welfare.** Materials on the methods employed in welfare work, public or private, are entered under **Social work**

> *See also*

Charities, Medical	**Institutional care**
Charity organiza-	**Orphanages**
tion	**Public welfare**
Child care	**Red Cross**
centers	**Social settlements**
Child welfare	**Unemployed**
Endowments	

> *also* names of cities with the subdivision *Charities* (e.g. **Chicago—Charities;** etc.); and names of wars with the subdivision *Civilian relief,* e.g. **World War, 1939–1945—Civilian relief;** etc.

> *x* Charitable institutions; Endowed charities; Homes (Institutions); Institutions, Charitable and philanthropic; Philanthropy; Poor relief; Social welfare; Welfare agencies; Welfare work

> *xx* **Charity organization; Endowments; Poverty; Public welfare; Social problems; Social work**

Charities, Legal. *See* **Legal aid**

Charities, Medical 362
> *See also* **Hospitals; Institutional care**
> *x* Medical charities; Socialized medicine
> *xx* **Charities; Medical care; Medicine, State; Public health**

Charities, Public. *See* **Public welfare**

Charity 177
> *xx* **Ethics; Human behavior**

Charity organization 361
> *See also* **Charities**
> *x* Philanthropy
> *xx* **Charities**

Charlatans. *See* **Impostors and imposture**

Charms 133.4
> *x* Spells; Talismans
> *xx* **Demonology; Folklore; Superstition; Witchcraft**

Charter flights. *See* **Aeronautics, Commercial—Chartering**

Charters
> *See also* **Archives; Manuscripts**
> *x* Documents
> *xx* **Archives; History—Sources; Manuscripts**

Chartography. *See* **Charts; Map drawing; Maps**

Charts   912
  See also **Maps**
  x Cartography; Chartography
  xx **Maps**
The chase.   *See* **Hunting**
Chateaux.   *See* **Castles**
Chattel mortgages.   *See* **Mortgages**
Checkers   794.2
  x Draughts
Cheers and cheerleading   371.8
Cheese   637; 641.3
  xx **Dairy products; Milk**
Cheese—Bacteriology   637
  xx **Bacteriology**
Chemical analysis.   *See* **Chemistry, Analytic;**
    and names of substances with the sub-
    division *Analysis,* e.g. **Water—Anal-**
    ysis; etc.
Chemical apparatus   542
  x Apparatus, Chemical; Chemistry—Ap-
    paratus
  xx **Scientific apparatus and instruments**
Chemical elements   546
  See also **Periodic law;** also names of ele-
    ments, e.g. **Hydrogen;** etc.
  x Elements, Chemical
Chemical engineering   660.2
  See also **Chemistry, Technical; Metallurgy**
  x Chemistry, Industrial; Industrial chem-
    istry
  xx **Chemistry,   Technical;   Engineering;**
    Metallurgy
Chemical equations   540.21
  x Equations, Chemical
  xx **Chemical reactions**
Chemical geology.   *See* **Geochemistry**
Chemical industries   338.4; 660
  Use for materials about industries based
    mainly on chemical processes. Mate-
    rials on the manufacture of chemicals
    as such are entered under **Chemicals**
  See also names of industries, e.g. **Paper**
    making and trade; etc.
  x Chemistry, Industrial; Industrial chem-
    istry; Industries, Chemical
  xx **Chemicals; Chemistry, Technical**
Chemical reactions   540-547
  See also **Chemical equations**
  x Reactions, Chemical
Chemical societies.   *See* **Chemistry—Societies**
Chemical technology.   *See* **Chemistry, Techni-**
    cal
Chemical warfare   358
  See also **Gases, Asphyxiating and poison-**
    ous—War use; Incendiary weapons
  x Air warfare
  xx **Military art and science; War**
Chemicals   661
  Use for general materials on chemicals, in-

Chemicals—*Continued*

cluding their manufacture. See note under **Chemical industries**

See also **Chemical industries; Chemistry, Technical;** also names of groups of chemicals (e.g. **Acids;** etc.); and names of individual chemicals, e.g. **Carbolic acid;** etc.

xx **Chemistry, Technical**

Chemiculture. *See* **Plants—Soilless culture**

Chemistry 540

See also

Acids	**Fire**
Agricultural chem-	**Geochemistry**
istry	**Microchemistry**
Alchemy	**Pharmacy**
Bases (Chemistry)	**Photographic chem-**
Biochemistry	**istry**
Botanical chemistry	**Physiological chem-**
Color	**istry**
Combustion	**Poisons**
Explosives	**Spectrum**
Fermentation	

also headings beginning with the word **Chemical**

xx **Science**

Chemistry, Agricultural. *See* **Agricultural chemistry**

Chemistry, Analytic 543-545

See also names of substances with the subdivision *Analysis,* e.g. **Water—Analysis;** etc.

x Analysis (Chemistry); Analytical chemistry; Chemical analysis; Qualitative analysis; Quantitative analysis

Chemistry, Animal. *See* **Physiological chemistry**

Chemistry—Apparatus. *See* **Chemical apparatus**

Chemistry, Biological. *See* **Biochemistry**

Chemistry, Botanical. *See* **Botanical chemistry**

Chemistry—Dictionaries 540.3

x Glossaries

xx **Dictionaries**

Chemistry—Experiments 540.7

x Experiments, Scientific; Scientific experiments

xx **Science—Experiments**

Chemistry, Industrial. *See* **Chemical engineering; Chemical industries; Chemistry, Technical**

Chemistry, Inorganic 546

See also **Metals**

x Inorganic chemistry

Chemistry—Laboratory guides 540.28

x Laboratory guides

Chemistry, Medical and pharmaceutical 615

See also **Disinfection and disinfectants; Drugs; Materia medica; Pharmacy; Poisonous plants; Poisons**

Chemistry, Medical and pharmaceutical—
Continued

    x Chemistry, Pathological; Chemistry, Pharmaceutical; Medical chemistry; Pathological chemistry; Pharmaceutical chemistry

    xx **Medicine; Pharmacy; Physiological chemistry; Therapeutics**

Chemistry, Organic 547

    x Organic chemistry

    xx **Physiological chemistry**

Chemistry, Organic—Synthesis 547

    See also **Plastics; Polymers and polymerization; Synthetic products**

    x Chemistry, Synthetic; Synthetic chemistry

    xx **Plastics**

Chemistry, Pathological. *See* **Chemistry, Medical and pharmaceutical; Physiological chemistry**

Chemistry, Pharmaceutical. *See* **Chemistry, Medical and pharmaceutical**

Chemistry, Photograhic. *See* **Photographic chemistry**

Chemistry, Physical and theoretical 541

    See also

Atomic theory	**Nuclear physics**
Atoms	**Periodic law**
Catalysis	**Polymers and**
Colloids	**polymerization**
Crystallography	**Quantum theory**
Electrochemistry	**Radiochemistry**
Molecules	**Thermodynamics**

    x Physical chemistry; Theoretical chemistry

    xx **Nuclear physics; Physics; Quantum theory**

Chemistry, Physiological. *See* **Physiological chemistry**

Chemistry—Problems, exercises, etc. 540.76

    x Problems, exercises, etc.

Chemistry—Societies 540.6

    x Chemical societies

Chemistry, Synthetic. *See* **Chemistry, Organic —Synthesis**

Chemistry, Technical 660

    See also

Alloys	**Corrosion and anti-**
Bleaching	**corrosives**
Canning and pre-	**Electrochemistry**
serving	**Food—Analysis**
Chemical engineer-	**Gums and resins**
ing	**Synthetic products**
Chemical industries	**Tanning**
Chemicals	**Textile chemistry**
Chemurgy	**Waste products**

    also names of specific industries and products, e.g. **Clay industries; Dyes and dyeing;** etc.

Chemistry, Technical—*Continued*

  x Chemical technology; Chemistry, Industrial; Industrial chemistry; Technical chemistry

  xx **Chemical engineering; Chemicals; Metallurgy; Technology**

Chemistry, Textile. *See* **Textile chemistry**

Chemistry of food. *See* **Food—Analysis**

Chemists 920; 925

  xx **Scientists**

Chemotherapy 615

  See also **Antibiotics;** also names of diseases with the subdivision *Chemotherapy,* e.g. **Cancer—Chemotherapy;** etc.

  x Drug therapy; Pharmacotherapy

  xx **Pharmacology**

Chemurgy 660.2

  Use for materials that deal with the advancement of the industrial use of farm products by means of applied science

  See also **Synthetic products**

  xx **Agricultural chemistry; Chemistry, Technical; Synthetic products**

Chess 794.1

  xx **Games**

Chicago 917.73; 977.3

  Subdivisions have been given under this subject to serve as a guide to the subdivisions that may be used under the name of any city. They are examples of the application of directions given in the general references under various headings throughout the list. References are given only for those headings that are cited specifically under the general references. The subdivisions under **United States** may be consulted as a guide for formulating other references that may be needed.

Chicago—Antiquities 917.73

Chicago—Bibliography 016.9773

Chicago—Bio-bibliography 016.92

Chicago—Biography 920

  xx **Biography**

Chicago—Biography—Portraits 920

Chicago—Boundaries 917.73; 977.3

Chicago—Bridges 624.2; 917.73

  xx **Bridges**

Chicago—Buildings 720.9773

  xx **Buildings**

Chicago—Cemeteries 917.73

  xx **Cemeteries**

Chicago—Census 317.73

Chicago—Charities 361-362

  xx **Charities**

Chicago—Churches 277.73

  xx **Churches**

Chicago—Climate 551.6

Chicago—Commerce 381

Chicago—Correctional institutions 365
　xx **Correctional institutions**
Chicago—Demonstrations 322.4
　xx **Demonstrations**
Chicago—Description 917.73
　x Description
Chicago—Description—Guides 917.73
　x Chicago—Guides; Guides
Chicago—Description—Maps. *See* **Chicago—**
　　Maps
Chicago—Description—Views 917.73
　x Chicago—Pictures;　Chicago—Views;
　　Scenery
　xx **Pictures; Views**
Chicago—Directories 977.3025
　　Use for lists of names and addresses. Lists
　　of names without addresses are en-
　　tered under **Chicago—Registers**
　　See also **Chicago—Registers**
　xx **Chicago—Registers**
Chicago—Directories—Telephone 384.6025
　x Directories—Telephone; Telephone—Di-
　　rectories; Telephone directories
Chicago—Economic conditions 330.9773
Chicago—Fires and fire prevention 614.8
　xx **Fire prevention; Fires**
Chicago—Floods 551.4
　xx **Floods**
Chicago—Foreign population 301.45; 325.773
　x Foreign population; Population, Foreign
Chicago—Galleries and museums 708
　xx **Art—Galleries and museums**
Chicago—Government. *See* **Chicago—Politics**
　　and government
Chicago—Government publications 015.773
Chicago—Guides. *See* **Chicago—Description—**
　　Guides
Chicago—Harbor 386
　xx **Harbors**
Chicago—Historic buildings, etc. 917.73
　xx **Architecture, Colonial**
Chicago—History 977.3
Chicago—History—Societies 977.306
Chicago—Hospitals 362.1
　xx **Hospitals**
Chicago—Hotels, motels, etc. 647
　xx **Hotels, motels, etc.**
Chicago—Industries 338.9773
　x Chicago—Manufactures
　xx **Manufactures**
Chicago—Intellectual life 917.73
Chicago—Libraries 027
　xx **Libraries; Public libraries**
Chicago—Lighting 621.32; 628.9
　xx **Lighting; Streets—Lighting**
Chicago—Manufactures. *See* **Chicago—Indus-**
　　tries
Chicago—Maps 912
　x Chicago—Description—Maps
　xx **Chicago—Streets; Maps; Road maps**

Chicago—Moral conditions   309.1773
Chicago—Occupations   331.7
  xx **Occupations**
Chicago—Office buildings   725; 917.73
  xx **Office buildings**
Chicago—Officials and employees   352.09773
  x Employees and officials; Municipal employees; Officials
  xx **Civil service**
Chicago—Parks   711-712; 917.73
  xx **Parks**
Chicago—Pictures.   *See* **Chicago—Description—Views**
Chicago—Poetry   808.81; 811; 811.08; etc.
  xx **Poetry**
Chicago—Police   352
  xx **Police**
Chicago—Politics and government   977.3
  x Chicago—Government; Politics
  xx **Municipal government**
Chicago—Poor   309.1773
  xx **Poor; Poverty**
Chicago—Population   301.32; 312
  xx **Population**
Chicago—Public buildings   725; 917.73
  x Buildings, Public
  xx **City planning; Public buildings**
Chicago—Public schools.   *See* **Chicago—Schools**
Chicago—Public works   363.5
  x Municipal improvements
  xx **City planning; Public works**
Chicago—Race relations   301.45
  xx **Race relations**
Chicago—Registers   977.3025
  Use for lists of names without addresses. Lists of names that include addresses are entered under **Chicago—Directories**
  See also **Chicago—Directories**
  xx **Chicago—Directories**
Chicago—Restaurants, bars, etc.   647
  xx **Restaurants, bars, etc.**
Chicago—Riots   301.6
  xx **Riots**
Chicago—Schools   379.773
  x Chicago—Public schools
  xx **High schools; Public schools; Schools**
Chicago—Social conditions   309.1773
  xx **Social conditions**
Chicago—Social life and customs   917.73
Chicago—Social policy   309.2
Chicago—Statistics   317.73
  xx **Statistics**
Chicago—Streets   388.4; 917.73
  See also **Chicago—Maps**
  xx **Streets**
Chicago—Suburbs and environs   917.73
  See also **Chicago metropolitan area**
  xx **Suburban life**
Chicago—Synagogues   726
  xx **Synagogues**

105

Chicago—Transit systems   388.4
  x Transit systems
  xx **Local transit**
Chicago—Urban renewal. *See* **Urban renewal
    —Chicago**
Chicago—Views. *See* **Chicago—Description—
    Views**
Chicago—Water supply   628.1
  xx **Water supply**
Chicago metropolitan area   917.73
  xx **Chicago—Suburbs and environs; Metro-
    politan areas**
Chicago metropolitan area—Politics and gov-
    ernment   977.3
  xx **Metropolitan government**
Chicago metropolitan area—Transit systems
    388.4
  x Transit systems
  xx **Local transit**
Chicanos. *See* **Mexican Americans**
Chief justices. *See* **Judges**
Child abuse   362.7
  x Battered child syndrome; Child batter-
    ing; Child neglect; Children, Cruelty
    to; Cruelty to children
  xx **Child welfare; Parent and child**
Child and parent. *See* **Parent and child**
Child artists. *See* **Children as artists**
Child authors. *See* **Children as authors**
Child battering. *See* **Child abuse**
Child birth. *See* **Childbirth**
Child care centers   362.7
  See also **Nursery schools**
  x Day care centers; Day nurseries; Nur-
    series, Day
  xx **Charities; Child welfare; Children—Insti-
    tutional care; Nursery schools**
Child development   155.4; 612.6
  See also **Child psychology; Children—
    Growth**
  x Child study; Children—Development
  xx **Children**
Child labor (May subdiv. geog.)   **331.3**
  See also **Apprentices; Hours of labor**
  x Boys—Employment; Children—Employ-
    ment; Employment of children; Girls
    —Employment; Working boys; Work-
    ing girls
  xx **Age and employment; Child welfare;
    Education, Compulsory; Hours of
    labor; Labor and laboring classes;
    Labor supply; School attendance;
    Social problems**
Child labor—U.S.   331.3
  x U.S.—Child labor
Child neglect. *See* **Child abuse**
Child psychiatry   616.8
  See also **Adolescent psychiatry; Child psy-
    chology; Mentally handicapped chil-**

Child psychiatry—*Continued*
>> dren; **Mentally ill children; Mentally retarded children**

> *x* Children—Mental health; Pediatric psychiatry; Psychiatry, Child

> *xx* **Psychiatry**

Child psychology 155.4

> *See also* **Educational psychology; Learning, Psychology of; Mental tests**

> *x* Child study; Children—Psychology; Psychology, Child

> *xx* **Child development; Child psychiatry; Educational psychology; Psychology**

Child study. *See* **Child development; Child psychology**

Child welfare 362.7

> Use for materials on the aid, support, and protection of children, by the state or by private welfare organizations

> *See also*

Child abuse	**Children's hospitals**
Child care centers	**Foster home care**
Child labor	**Juvenile delin-**
Children—Care and	**quency**
hygiene	**Mothers' pensions**
Children—Institu-	**Orphanages**
tional care	**Playgrounds**

> *x* A.D.C.; Aid to dependent children; Children—Charities, protection, etc.; Dependent children; Protection of children

> *xx* **Charities; Children's hospitals; Juvenile delinquency; Mothers' pensions; Orphanages; Public welfare**

Childbirth 618.2

> *See also* **Natural childbirth; Pregnancy**

> *x* Birth; Child birth; Labor (Childbirth) Midwifery; Obstetrics

> *xx* **Medicine—Practice; Pregnancy**

Children 301.43

> The term is popularly applied to any age up to fifteen or even later. Materials limited to the first two years of a child's life are entered under **Infants**

> *See also*

Boys	**Kindergarten**
Child development	**Motion pictures**
Education, Ele-	**and children**
mentary	**Orphans**
Exceptional chil-	**Play**
dren	**Playgrounds**
Girls	**Runaways**
Heredity	**Television and chil-**
Indians of North	**dren**
America—Chil-	**World War, 1939–**
dren	**1945—Children**
Infants	**Youth**

> *xx* **Boys; Family; Girls; Infants; Youth**

Children, Abnormal. *See* **Exceptional children; Handicapped children**

Children—Adoption. *See* **Adoption**

Children—Care and hygiene   649; 618.9

Use for general materials on the physical care of children. Materials limited to their physical care in school are entered under **School hygiene**

See also **Baby sitters; Children—Diseases; Children's hospitals; Children—Nutrition; Health education; Infants—Care and hygiene; Nursing; School children—Food; School hygiene; School nurses**

x Children—Health; Health of children; Pediatrics

xx **Child welfare; Hygiene; Nursing**

Children—Charities, protection, etc. *See* **Child welfare**

Children—Civil rights   344

Children—Clothing. *See* **Children's clothing**

Children—Costume   391

Use for descriptive and historical materials on children's costume among various nations and at different periods. Materials dealing with children's clothing from a practical standpoint are entered under **Children's clothing**

xx **Costume**

Children, Crippled. *See* **Physically handicapped children**

Children, Cruelty to. *See* **Child abuse**

Children, Delinquent. *See* **Juvenile delinquency**

Children—Development. *See* **Child development**

Children—Diseases   618.9

See also **Children's hospitals;** also names of diseases, e.g. **Diphtheria;** etc.

x Children's diseases; Diseases of children; Medicine, Pediatric; Pediatrics

xx **Children—Care and hygiene; Children's hospitals; Diseases; Medicine—Practice**

Children—Education. *See* **Education, Elementary; Education, Preschool**

Children, Emotionally disturbed. *See* **Problem children**

Children—Employment. *See* **Child labor**

Children, Exceptional. *See* **Exceptional children**

Children—Food   641.5

x Children's food

xx **Children—Nutrition**

Children, Gifted. *See* **Gifted children**

Children—Growth   612.6

xx **Child development; Growth**

Children—Health. *See* **Children—Care and hygiene; School hygiene**

Children—Hospitals. *See* **Children's hospitals**

Children, Hyperactive. *See* **Hyperactive children**

Children—Institutional care   362.7

 See also **Child care centers; Foster home care; Orphanages; Reformatories**

  x Boys' towns; Children's homes; Homes (Institutions); Institutions, Charitable and philanthropic

  xx **Child welfare; Foster home care; Institutional care**

Children—Language   155.4

  xx **Language and languages**

Children—Mental health.   *See* **Child psychiatry**

Children—Nutrition   641.1; 649

  See also **Children—Food**

  xx **Children—Care and hygiene; Nutrition**

Children—Placing out.   *See* **Foster home care**

Children—Psychology.   *See* **Child psychology**

Children, Retarded.   *See* **Mentally retarded children; Slow learning children**

Children, Runaway.   *See* **Runaways**

Children and motion pictures.   *See* **Motion pictures and children**

Children and television.   *See* **Television and children**

Children as artists   704; 920; 927

  Use for books about children as artists and for works of art by children

  See also **Finger painting**

  x Child artists

  xx **Artists; Gifted children**

Children as authors   028.5; 920; 928

  Use for books written by children and for books about children as authors

  x Child authors

  xx **Authors; Gifted children**

Children as consumers.   *See* **Young consumers**

Children in art.   *See* **Children in literature and art**

Children in literature and art   704.94; 809

  Use for materials treating of children in literature, and children depicted in works of art. Materials about children as authors and books written by children are entered under **Children as authors.** Materials about child artists are entered under **Children as artists**

  See also **Children in poetry**

  x Children in art

  xx **Art; Characters and characteristics in literature; Children in poetry; Literature**

Children in poetry   809.1

  See also **Children in literature and art**

  xx **Characters and characteristics in literature; Children in literature and art; Poetry**

Children in the U.S.   301.43

  Use same form for children in other countries, e.g. **Children in India**; etc.

Children's books.   *See* **Children's literature**

Children's clothing   646; 649

  See note under **Children—Costume**

Children's clothing—*Continued*

    x Children—Clothing

    xx **Clothing and dress**

Children's courts. *See* **Juvenile courts**

Children's diseases. *See* **Children—Diseases**

Children's food. *See* **Children—Food**

Children's homes. *See* **Children—Institutional care**

Children's hospitals 362.7

    See also **Child welfare; Children—Diseases**

    x Children—Hospitals

    xx **Child welfare; Children—Care and hygiene; Children—Diseases; Hospitals; Public welfare**

Children's libraries. *See* **Libraries, Children's; School libraries**

Children's literature 028.5

    Use for materials on the development of juvenile literature, discussions of good books for children, etc. Materials written by children and books about children as authors are entered under **Children as authors**

    See also **Caldecott Medal books; Children's plays; Children's poetry; Easy reading materials; Fairy tales; Libraries, Children's; Libraries and schools; Picture books for children; Reading materials; Storytelling**

    x Books for children; Children's books; Children's reading; Children's stories; Juvenile literature

    xx **Books and reading; Libraries, Children's; Libraries and schools; Literature; School libraries**

Children's plays 808.82; 812; 812.08; etc.

    Use for collections of plays for children by one or more authors

    x Plays for children; School plays

    xx **Amateur theatricals; Children's literature; Drama—Collections; Theater**

Children's poetry 808.81; 811; 811.08; etc.

    Use for collections of poetry for children by one or more authors. Materials on poetry written by children are entered under **Children as authors**

    See also **Children's songs; Lullabies; Nursery rhymes**

    x Poetry for children

    xx **Children's literature; Poetry—Collections**

Children's reading. *See* **Children's literature; Reading**

Children's songs 784.6

    See also **Lullabies; Nursery rhymes**

    xx **Children's poetry; School songbooks; Songs**

Children's stories. *See* **Children's literature; Fairy tales**

Chills and fever. *See* **Malaria**

Chimes. *See* **Bells**

Chimneys 697; 729

    x Smoke stacks

    xx **Architecture—Details; Building; Fireplaces; Heating; Ventilation**

China 915.1; 951

    Note: All subdivisions used under China should be divided with same dates as **China—History**

    x China (People's Republic of China, 1949–   ); People's Republic of China

China—History 951

China—History—1912–1949 951.04

China—History—1949–1976 951.05

China—History—1976–   951.05

China (People's Republic of China, 1949–   ). *See* **China**

China (Porcelain). *See* **Porcelain**

China (Republic of China, 1949–   ). *See* **Taiwan**

China painting 738.2

    x Porcelain painting

    xx **Arts and crafts; Painting; Porcelain**

Chinaware. *See* **Porcelain**

Chinese-Americans 301.45

Chinese in the U.S. 301.45

    Use same form for Chinese in other countries, states, etc., e.g. **Chinese in Russia; etc.**

Chinese satellite countries. *See* **Communist countries**

Chipmunks 599

    xx **Squirrels**

Chippewa Indians. *See* **Ojibwe Indians**

Chiropody. *See* **Podiatry**

Chivalry 394

    See also **Civilization, Medieval; Crusades; Feudalism; Heraldry; Knights and knighthood; Romances**

    xx **Civilization, Medieval; Crusades; Feudalism; Heraldry; Knights and knighthood; Manners and customs; Middle Ages**

Chivalry—Romances. *See* **Romances**

Chocolate 633; 641.3

    See also **Cocoa**

    xx **Cocoa**

Choice, Freedom of. *See* **Free will and determinism**

Choice of books. *See* **Book selection; Books and reading; Books and reading—Best books**

Choice of profession. *See* **Vocational guidance**

Choirs (Music) 783.8

    See also **Choral music; Choral societies; Conducting, Choral; Singing**

    xx **Choral music; Choral societies; Church music; Conducting, Choral; Singing**

Choral conducting. *See* **Conducting, Choral**

Choral music 783.8

 See also **Choirs (Music); Choral societies; Conducting, Choral**

 x Music, Choral

 xx **Cantatas; Choirs (Music); Choral societies; Church music; Conducting, Choral; Vocal music**

Choral societies 783.806

 See also **Choirs (Music); Choral music**

 x Singing societies

 xx **Choirs (Music); Choral music; Societies**

Choral speaking 808.5

 x Unison speaking

Christ. *See* **Jesus Christ**

Christening. *See* **Baptism**

Christian antiquities 225.9; 270

 See also **Architecture, Gothic; Catacombs; Christian art and symbolism; Church architecture; Church furniture; Fasts and feasts**

 x Antiquities; Antiquities, Christian; Antiquities, Ecclesiastical; Archeology, Christian; Church antiquities; Ecclesiastical antiquities

 xx **Archeology; Bible—Antiquities; Christian art and symbolism**

Christian art and symbolism 246

 See also

Bible—Pictorial works	**Church furniture**
Catacombs	**Illumination of books and manuscripts**
Cathedrals	**scripts**
Christian antiquities	**Jesus Christ—Art**
Church architecture	**Mary, Virgin—Art**

 x Art, Christian; Art, Ecclesiastical; Christian symbolism; Ecclesiastical art; Iconography; Sacred art

 xx **Archeology; Art; Christian antiquities; Jesus Christ—Art; Religious art and symbolism; Symbolism**

Christian biography. *See* **Christianity—Biography**

Christian Church (Disciples). *See* **Disciples of Christ**

Christian civilization. *See* **Civilization, Christian**

Christian doctrine. *See* **Theology, Doctrinal**

Christian education 268

 See note under **Church and education**

 See also **Bible—Study; Catechisms; Church and education; Theology—Study and teaching**

 x Education, Christian

 xx **Christian life; Religious education; Theology—Study and teaching**

Christian ethics 241; 248

 See also **Christian life; Christianity and economics; Conscience; Love (Theology); Psychology, Pastoral; Sin; Social ethics**

Christian ethics—*Continued*

    x Ethics, Christian; Christian moral the-
       ology; Moral theology, Christian

    xx **Christian life; Ethics; Social ethics**

Christian life   248

    See also **Christian education; Christian
       ethics; Conversion; Revivals**

    x Life, Christian

    xx **Christian ethics; Religious life; Spiritual
       life**

Christian literature, Early   281

    Use for materials about the writings of
       Christian authors to the time of
       Gregory the Great in the West and
       John of Damascus in the East. Collec-
       tions of such writings are entered
       under this heading with subdivision
       Collections

    See also **Church history—Early church,
       ca. 30–600**

    x Early Christian literature

    xx **Latin literature; Literature; Literature,
       Medieval; Religious literature**

Christian ministry.   *See* **Ministry, Christian**

Christian missions.   *See* **Missions, Christian**

Christian moral theology.   *See* **Christian ethics**

Christian names.   *See* **Names, Personal**

Christian saints   920; 922

    See also **Apostles**

    xx **Saints**

Christian Science   289.5

    See also **Faith healing; Mental healing**

    x Church of Christ, Scientist; Divine heal-
       ing; Mind cure

    xx **Faith healing; Medicine and religion;
       Mental healing**

Christian sociology.   *See* **Sociology, Christian**

Christian symbolism.   *See* **Christian art and
    symbolism**

Christian unity   262; 270.8

    Use for materials on the worldwide move-
       ment towards bringing all Christian
       faiths into cooperation, fellowship and
       eventually one organization.

    See also **Community churches; Interfaith
       relations**

    x Church unity; Ecumenical movement

    xx **Church**

Christianity   200

    See also

Church	**Jesus Christ**
Civilization, Chris-	**Miracles (Christianity)**
tian	**Missions, Christian**
Councils and synods	**Protestantism**
Deism	**Reformation**
God (Christianity)	**Theology**

    also names of Christian churches and sects
       (e.g. **Catholic Church; Huguenots;**
       etc.) and headings beginning with the
       words **Christian** and **Church**

Christianity—*Continued*

  xx **Church; Deism; God (Christianity); Jesus Christ; Religions; Theism; Theology**

Christianity—Apologetic works. *See* **Apologetics**

Christianity—Biography 920; 922

  x Christian biography; Church biography; Ecclesiastical biography; Religious biography

  xx **Bible—Biography; Biography; Religions—Biography**

Christianity—Evidences. *See* **Apologetics**

Christianity—History. *See* **Church history**

Christianity—Origin. *See* **Church history—Early church, ca. 30–600**

Christianity—Philosophy 201

  x Theology—Philosophy

Christianity and economics 261.8

  See also **Church and labor**

  x Economics and Christianity

  xx **Christian ethics; Church and labor; Communism and religion; Economics; Sociology, Christian**

Christianity and other religions 261.2

  See also **Paganism**

  x Comparative religion

Christianity and politics 261.7

  x Politics and Christianity

  xx **Church and state; Religion and politics**

Christianity and war. *See* **War and religion**

Christmas (May subdiv. geog.) **263; 394.2**

  See also **Christmas entertainments; Christmas—Poetry; Jesus Christ—Nativity; Santa Claus**

  x Days; Religious festivals

  xx **Jesus Christ—Nativity**

Christmas—Drama 394.2; 791; 808.82; 812.08; etc.

  x Christmas plays; Plays, Christmas

  xx **Christmas entertainments; Religious drama**

Christmas—Poetry 808.81; 811; etc.

  See also **Carols**

  x Christmas poetry

  xx **Christmas; Poetry—Collections**

Christmas—U.S. 394.2

  x U.S.—Christmas

Christmas cards. *See* **Greeting cards**

Christmas carols. *See* **Carols**

Christmas decorations 745.59

Christmas entertainments 394.2

  See also **Christmas—Drama**

  x Entertainments

  xx **Christmas**

Christmas plays. *See* **Christmas—Drama**

Christmas poetry. *See* **Christmas—Poetry**

Christology. *See* **Jesus Christ**

Chromosomes 574.8

  See also **Genetics**

Chromosomes—*Continued*

    xx **Genetics**

Chronology, Biblical. *See* **Bible—Chronology**

Chronology, Historical 902

    Use for materials in which events are arranged by date

    x Dates, Historical; Historical chronology; History—Chronology; U.S.—History —Chronology

Church 260

    See also **Christian unity; Christianity**

    xx **Christianity; Theology**

Church, Apostolic. *See* **Church history—Early church, ca. 30–600**

Church and education 261.1

    Use for materials on the relation of the church to education in general, and for materials on the history of the part that the church has taken in secular education. Materials on church supported and controlled elementary and secondary schools are entered under **Church schools.** Materials on the instruction of religion in schools and private life are entered under **Religious education,** and on Christian religion under **Christian education**

    See also **Academic freedom; Religion in the public schools; Theology—Study and teaching**

    x Education and church; Education and religion; Religion and education

    xx **Academic freedom; Christian education; Church and state; Education; Theology—Study and teaching**

Church and labor 261.8

    See also **Christianity and economics**

    x Labor and the church

    xx **Christianity and economics; Labor and laboring classes**

Church and race relations 261.8

    x Integrated churches; Race relations and the church

Church and social problems 261.1; 261.8

    Use for materials dealing with the practical treatment of social problems from the point of view of the church. For materials on social theory from a Christian point of view use **Sociology, Christian**

    See also **Church work**

    x Religion and social problems; Social problems and the church

    xx **Church work**

Church and state 261.7; 322

    See also **Christianity and politics; Church and education; Ecclesiastical law; Freedom of conscience; Popes—Temporal power; Religion in the public schools; Religious freedom**

115

Church and state—*Continued*

    x Religion and state; State and church; State church

    xx **Church history; Political science; Popes— Temporal power; Religious freedom**

Church and state—Catholic Church   282

    xx **Catholic Church**

Church and state in Latin America   278

    Use same form for church and state in other countries, e.g. **Church and state in France;** etc.

Church and war. *See* **War and religion**

Church antiquities. *See* **Christian antiquities**

Church architecture   726

    See also **Abbeys; Architecture, Gothic; Cathedrals; Churches; Mosques; Spires; Temples**

    x Architecture, Church; Architecture, Ecclesiastical; Ecclesiastical architecture; Religious art

    xx **Architecture; Architecture, Gothic; Christian antiquities; Christian art and symbolism; Churches**

Church attendance. *See* **Public worship**

Church bells. *See* **Bells**

Church biography. *See* **Christianity—Biography**

Church councils. *See* **Councils and synods**

Church denominations. *See* **Sects;** and names of particular denominations and sects

Church entertainments   259

    x Church sociables; Entertainments; Socials

    xx **Amusements; Church work**

Church festivals. *See* **Fasts and feasts**

Church finance   254.8

    See also **Tithes**

    x Finance, Church

    xx **Finance**

Church furniture   247; 729

    x Ecclesiastical furniture

    xx **Christian antiquities; Christian art and symbolism; Furniture**

Church history   209; 270

    Use for materials treating of the development of Christianity and church organization

    See also

Abbeys	**Missions, Christian**
Church and state	**Papacy**
Convents	**Persecution**
Councils and synods	**Popes**
Creeds	**Protestant churches**
Jews	**Protestantism**
Martyrs	**Reformation**
Miracles (Christianity)	**Revivals**
	Sects

    also names of countries, states, etc. with the subdivision *Church history* (e.g. **U.S.—Church history;** etc.); names of

Church history—*Continued*
> denominations, sects, churches, etc.;
> and headings beginning with the word
> **Christian**
>
> *x* Christianity—History; Ecclesiastical history; History, Church; Religious history
>
> *xx* **History**

Church history—Early church, ca. 30–600   209; 270.1-270.2
> *See also* **Apostles; Catacombs; Gnosticism; Persecution**
>
> *x* Apostolic Church; Christianity—Origin; Church, Apostolic; Primitive Christianity
>
> *xx* **Catacombs; Christian literature, Early**

Church history—Middle Ages, 600–1500   270.2; 270.5
> *See also* **Crusades; Papacy; Popes—Temporal power**
>
> *xx* **Middle Ages**

Church history—Modern period, 1500–   270.8

Church history—Reformation, 1517–1648. *See* **Reformation**

Church law. *See* **Ecclesiastical law**

Church libraries. *See* **Libraries, Church**

Church music   783
> *See also* **Carols; Chants (Plain, Gregorian, etc.); Choirs (Music); Choral music; Hymns; Liturgies; Oratorios; Organ music**
>
> *x* Music, Sacred; Psalmody; Religious music; Sacred music
>
> *xx* **Devotional exercises; Hymns; Music**

Church of Christ (Disciples). *See* **Disciples of Christ**

Church of Christ, Scientist. *See* **Christian Science**

Church of England   283
> *See also* **Puritans**
>
> *x* Anglican Church; England, Church of; Episcopal Church
>
> *xx* **Puritans**

Church of Jesus Christ of Latter-Day Saints   289.3
> *x* Latter-Day Saints; Mormon Church
>
> *xx* **Mormons and Mormonism**

Church of the Brethren   286
> *x* Dunkards; Dunkers; German Baptist Brethren
>
> *xx* **Baptists**

Church schools   377
> *See* note under **Church and education**
>
> *x* Denominational schools; Nonpublic schools; Parochial schools; Schools, Parochial
>
> *xx* **Private schools; Schools**

Church service books. *See* **Liturgies**

Church settlements. *See* **Social settlements**

Church sociables. *See* **Church entertainments**

Church unity. *See* **Christian unity**

Church work 250

> *See also*

Church and social problems	**Psychology, Pastoral**
Church entertainments	**Revivals**
	Rural churches
Evangelistic work	**Sunday schools**
Missions, Christian	

> *xx* **Church and social problems; Pastoral work**

Church work, Rural. *See* **Rural churches**

Church work with children. *See* **Church work with youth**

Church work with the sick 361.7

> Use same form for church work with other groups of people

Church work with youth 259

> *x* Church work with children
> *xx* **Youth**

Churches (May subdiv. geog. country or state)
270; 280

> Use for general descriptive and historical materials on churches which cannot be entered under **Church architecture.** Materials relating to the churches of a city are entered under the name of the city with the subdivision *Churches*
> *See also* **Cathedrals; Church architecture;** also names of cities with the subdivision *Churches* (e.g. **Chicago— Churches;** etc.); and names of individual churches
> *xx* **Church architecture**

Churches, Avant-garde. *See* **Noninstitutional churches**

Churches, Community. *See* **Community churches**

Churches, Country. *See* **Rural churches**

Churches, Noninstitutional. *See* **Noninstitutional churches**

Churches, Rural. *See* **Rural churches**

Churches, Undenominational. *See* **Community churches**

Churches—U.S. 277.3; 280; 726

> *x* U.S.—Churches

Churchyards. *See* **Cemeteries**

Cicadas 595.7; 632

> *x* Locusts, Seventeen-year; Seventeen-year locusts

Cigarettes 679

> *xx* **Smoking**

Cigars 679

> *xx* **Smoking**

Cinema. *See* **Motion pictures**

Cinematography. *See* **Motion picture photography**

Cipher and telegraph codes   621.382

    x Cable codes; Codes, Telegraph; Morse code; Telegraph codes

    xx **Telegraph**

Ciphers   652

    See also **Abbreviations; Cryptography; Writing**

    x Contractions

    xx **Abbreviations; Cryptography; Signs and symbols; Writing**

Ciphers (Lettering).   *See* **Monograms**

Circuits, Electric.   *See* **Electric circuits**

Circulation of the blood.   *See* **Blood—Circulation**

Circumnavigation.   *See* **Voyages around the world**

Circus   791.3

    See also **Acrobats and acrobatics; Animals —Training; Clowns**

    xx **Amusements**

Cities and towns (May subdiv. geog.)   **301.34**

    Use for general materials on cities and towns. For materials on large cities and their surrounding areas use **Metropolitan areas.** General materials on the government of cities are entered under **Municipal government;** general materials on local government other than that of cities are entered under **Local government**

    See also **Art, Municipal; City life; Markets; Parks; Sociology, Urban; Streets; Tenement houses; Villages;** also headings beginning with the word **Municipal;** and names of individual cities and towns

    x Municipalities; Towns; Urban areas

    xx **Local government; Metropolitan areas; Municipal government; Sociology; Sociology, Urban**

Cities and towns—Civic improvement   309.2

    See also **City planning; Community centers**

    x Civic improvement; Municipal improvements

Cities and towns—Lighting.   *See* **Streets—Lighting**

Cities and towns—Planning.   *See* **City Planning**

Cities and towns, Ruined, extinct, etc.   913

    See also **Excavations (Archeology)**

    x Abandoned towns; Buried cities; Extinct cities; Ghost towns; Ruins; Sunken cities

    xx **Archeology**

Cities and towns—U.S.   301.34; 917.3; 973

    x U.S.—Cities and towns

Citizen participation.   *See* subjects with the subdivision *Citizen participation,* e.g. **City planning—U.S.—Citizen participation;** etc.

Citizens band radio 621.3845
>*x* CB radio; Citizens radio service
>*xx* **Radio, Shortwave**

Citizens radio service. *See* **Citizens band radio**

Citizenship 172; 323.6
>*See also* **Aliens; Naturalization; Patriotism;
>   Suffrage**
>*x* Civics; Foreigners; Franchise; Nation-
>   ality (Citizenship)
>*xx* **Aliens; Constitutional law; Naturaliza-
>   tion; Political ethics; Political science;
>   Social ethics**

Citrus fruit 634
>Names of fruits are not included in this list
>   but are to be added as needed, in the
>   singular form, e.g. **Orange;** etc.
>*See also* names of citrus fruits, e.g. **Orange;**
>   etc.
>*xx* **Fruit**

City and town life. *See* **City life**

City government. *See* **Municipal government**

City life 301.34
>*See also* **Community life**
>*x* City and town life; Town life; Urban life
>*xx* **Cities and towns; Community life; So-
>   ciology, Urban**

City manager. *See* **Municipal government by
>   city manager**

City planning (May subdiv. geog.) **309.2; 711**
>*See also* **Art, Municipal; Housing; Social
>   surveys; Urban renewal; Zoning;** also
>   names of cities with the subdivisions
>   *Public buildings* and *Public works,*
>   e.g. **Chicago—Public buildings; Chi-
>   cago—Public works;** etc.
>*x* Cities and towns—Planning; Municipal
>   planning; Planning, City; Town plan-
>   ning; Urban planning
>*xx* **Art, Municipal; Cities and towns—Civic
>   improvement; Housing; Regional plan-
>   ning; Tenement houses; Urban renewal**

City planning—U.S. 309.2; 711
>*x* U.S.—City planning

**City planning—U.S.—Citizen participation
>   301.34; 309.2**
>*x* Citizen participation; Civic involvement
>*xx* **Social action**

City planning—Zone system. *See* **Zoning**

City traffic 388.3
>*x* Local traffic; Street traffic; Traffic, City;
>   Urban traffic
>*xx* **Streets; Traffic engineering**

City transit. *See* **Local transit**

Civic art. *See* **Art, Municipal**

Civic improvement. *See* **Cities and towns—
>   Civic improvement**

Civic involvement. *See* subjects with the sub-
>   division *Citizen participation*, e.g. **City
>   planning—U.S.—Citizen participation**

120

Civics. *See* **Citizenship; Political science; U.S. —Politics and government**

Civil defense   363.3

See note under **Air defenses**

See also **Air defenses; Air raid shelters; Disaster relief; Rescue work; World War, 1939–1945–Evacuation of civilians**

x Blackouts in war; Civilian defense; Defense, Civil; World War, 1939–1945—Civilian defense

xx **Disaster relief; Military art and science**

Civil disobedience. *See* **Government, Resistance to; Passive resistance**

Civil disorders. *See* **Riots**

Civil engineering   624

See also

Aqueducts	**Mining engineering**
Bridges	**Public works**
Canals	**Railroad engineering**
Dams	**Reclamation of land**
Drainage	**Rivers**
Dredging	**Roads**
Excavation	**Sanitary engineering**
Foundations	
Harbors	**Steel, Structural**
Highway engineering	**Streets**
	Strength of materials
Hydraulic engineering	
	Structural engineering
Irrigation	
Marine engineering	**Subways**
Masonry	**Surveying**
Mechanical engineering	**Tunnels**
	Walls
Military engineering	**Water supply**

xx **Engineering**

Civil government. *See* **Political science; U.S.—Politics and government**

Civil liberty. *See* **Freedom**

Civil rights   323.4

See also **Academic freedom; Free speech; Freedom; Freedom of assembly; Freedom of information; Freedom of movement; Freedom of the press; Religious freedom;** also names of groups of people with the subdivision *Civil rights*, e.g. **Blacks–Civil rights; Men–Civil rights; Women–Civil rights;** etc.

x Human rights; Natural law; Rights, Civil

xx **Constitutional law; Discrimination; Freedom; Political science**

Civil service (May subdiv. geog.) **350-352**

Use for general materials on the history and development of public service. Materials on public personnel administration, including the duties of civil service employees, their salaries, pensions, etc., are entered under the name

121

Civil service—*Continued*
> of the country, state or city with the subdivision *Officials and employees*
>
> *See also* **Bureaucracy;** also names of countries, cities, etc. with the subdivision *Officials and employees,* **e.g. Chicago—Officials and employees;** etc.
>
> *x* Administration; Employees and officials; Government employees; Government service; Municipal employees; Office, Tenure of; Officials; Tenure of office
>
> *xx* **Administrative law; Bureaucracy; Political science; Public administration**

Civil service—Examinations 351.3
> *xx* **Examinations**

Civil service—U.S. 350.973
> *See also* **U.S.—Officials and employees**
>
> *x* U.S.—Civil service
>
> *xx* **U.S.—Officials and employees**

Civil War—England. *See* **Gt. Brit.—History—Civil War and Commonwealth, 1642–1660**

Civil War—U.S. *See* **U.S.—History—Civil War, 1861–1865**

Civilian defense. *See* **Civil defense**

Civilian evacuation. *See* **World War, 1939–1945—Evacuation of civilians**

Civilization 901.9
> Use for materials dealing with civilization in general and with the development of socal customs, art, industry, religion, etc. of several countries or peoples. Materials confined to the civilization of one country are entered under the name of the country with the subdivision *Civilization.* Materials on peoples whose culture spread beyond their own boundaries are entered under such headings as **Civilization, Asian; Civilization, Greek; Civilization, Occidental; Civilization, Scandinavian;** etc.
>
> *See also*

Acculturation	**Learning and scholarship**
Aeronautics and civilization	**Manners and customs**
Anthropology	**Progress**
Archeology	**Religions**
Art	**Science and civilization**
Astronautics and civilization	**Social problems**
Biculturalism	**Society, Nonliterate folk**
Culture	**Technology and civilization**
Education	**War and civilization**
Ethics	
Ethnology	
Industry	
Inventions	

> *also* names of countries, states, etc. with the subdivision *Civilization,* e.g. **U.S.—Civilization;** etc.

Civilization—*Continued*

    xx **Anthropology; Culture; Ethnology; History; History—Philosophy; Progress; Sociology**

Civilization, African

    x African civilization

Civilization, American 917; 918

    Use for general materials on the civilization of the western hemisphere or of Latin America, and for materials on ancient American civilization, including that of the Mayas, Aztecs, etc. Materials limited to the civilization of the United States are entered under **U.S. —Civilization**

    x American civilization

Civilization, Ancient 913; 930

    See also **Man, Prehistoric**

    x Ancient civilization

    xx **History, Ancient**

Civilization, Arab 909

    x Arab civilization

Civilization, Asian 915

    x Asian civilization; Civilization, Oriental; Oriental civilization

    xx **East and West**

Civilization, Christian 200.9

    x Christian civilization

    xx **Christianity**

Civilization, Greek 913.38

    Use same form for materials dealing with the culture of people not confined to one country, e.g. **Civilization, Arab; Civilization, Oriental;** etc.

    See also **Hellenism**

    x Greece—Civilization; Greek civilization

Civilization, Jewish. *See* **Jews—Civilization**

Civilization, Medieval 901.92

    See also **Art, Medieval; Chivalry; Feudalism; Middle Ages; Monasticism**

    x Medieval civilization

    xx **Chivalry; Middle Ages; Middle Ages—History; Renaissance**

Civilization, Modern 901.93-901.94

    Use for materials covering the period after 1453

    See also **History, Modern; Renaissance**

    x Modern civilization

    xx **History, Modern**

Civilization, Modern, 1950– 901.94

Civilization, Occidental 909

    x Occidental civilization; Western civilization

    xx **East and West**

Civilization, Oriental. *See* **Civilization, Asian**

Civilization, Scandinavian 914.8

    x Scandinavian civilization

Civilization and aeronautics. *See* **Aeronautics and civilization**

123

Civilization and astronautics. *See* **Astronautics and civilization**

Civilization and science. *See* **Science and civilization**

Civilization and technology. *See* **Technology and civilization**

Civilization and war. *See* **War and civilization**

Clairvoyance 133.8

 See also **Divination; Extrasensory perception; Fortune telling; Hypnotism; Mind reading; Thought transference**

 xx **Divination; Fortune telling; Mind reading; Occult sciences; Psychical research; Spiritualism; Thought transference**

Clans and clan system 301.44; 390; 941

 See also **Tartans**

 x Highland clans; Scottish clans

 xx **Family; Feudalism**

Class conflict. *See* **Social conflict**

Class distinction. *See* **Social classes**

Class struggle. *See* **Social conflict**

Classed catalogs. *See* **Catalogs, Classified**

Classes (Mathematics). *See* **Set theory**

Classical antiquities 913.37-913.38

 See also **Archeology; Art, Greek; Art, Roman; Mythology, Classical;** also names of countries, cities, etc. with the subdivision *Antiquities,* e.g. **Greece—Antiquities;** etc.

 x Antiquities; Antiquities, Classical; Archeology, Classical; Classical archeology; Greek antiquities; Roman antiquities

 xx **Archeology; Art, Ancient**

Classical archeology. *See* **Classical antiquities**

Classical art. *See* **Art, Greek; Art, Roman**

Classical biography. *See* **Greece—Biography; Rome—Biography**

Classical dictionaries 913.3803

 x Dictionaries, Classical

 xx **History, Ancient**

Classical education 370.11

 See also **Colleges and universities; Humanism; Humanities**

 x Education, Classical

 xx **Colleges and universities; Education; Education, Higher; Humanism; Humanities**

Classical geography. *See* **Geography, Ancient**

Classical languages. *See* **Greek language; Latin language**

Classical literature 880

 See also **Greek literature; Latin literature**

 x Literature, Classical

 xx **Greek literature; Latin literature; Literature**

Classical mythology. *See* **Mythology, Classical**

124

Classification—Books 025.4
    Use same form for classification of other
       library materials
    See also **Catalogs, Classified; Classification,**
       Dewey Decimal
    x Libraries—Classification; Library classi-
       fication
    xx **Bibliography; Books; Cataloging; Cata-**
       logs, Classified; Documentation; Li-
       braries—Technical services; Library
       science; Subject headings
Classification, Dewey Decimal 025.4
    x Dewey Decimal Classification
    xx **Classification—Books**
Classified catalogs. *See* **Catalogs, Classified**
Classroom management 371.1
    xx **School discipline; Teaching**
Clay 553; 666; 738.1
    See also **Bricks; Modeling**
    xx **Ceramic materials; Soils**
Clay industries 338.2; 666
    See also **Bricks; Pottery; Tiles**
    xx **Chemistry, Technical**
Clay modeling. *See* **Modeling**
Cleaning 648; 667
    See also **Bleaching; Cleaning compounds;**
       Dry cleaning; Dyes and dyeing;
       House cleaning; Laundry; Soap;
       Street cleaning
Cleaning compounds 648; 667
    See also **Detergents, Synthetic; Soap**
    xx **Cleaning**
Cleanliness. *See* **Baths; Hygiene; Sanitation**
Clearing of land. *See* **Reclamation of land**
Clergy 253
    See also **Chaplains; Priests;** also church
       denominations with the subdivision
       Clergy, e.g. **Catholic Church—Clergy;**
       etc.
    x Curates; Ministers of the gospel; Pas-
       tors; Preachers; Rectors
    xx **Pastoral work**
Clergy—Office. *See* **Ministry**
Clerical employees. *See* **Clerks**
Clerical work—Training. *See* **Business educa-**
       tion
Clerks 331.7
    See also **Sales personnel**
    x Clerical employees; Commercial employ-
       ees; Employees, Clerical; Office em-
       ployees
    xx **Sales personnel**
Clerks (Retail trade). *See* **Sales personnel**
Cliff dwellers and cliff dwellings 917; 970.4
    See also **Mounds and mound builders**
    xx **Archeology; Indians of North America**
Climacteric, Female. *See* **Menopause**
Climacteric, Male 612.6
    x Change of life in men; Male climacteric

Climate   551.6

Use for materials on climate as it relates to man and to plant and animal life, including the effects of changes of climate. Materials limited to the climate of a particular region are entered under the name of the place with the subdivision *Climate*. Materials on the state of the atmosphere at a given time and place with respect to heat or cold, wetness or dryness, calm or storm, are entered under **Weather.** Scientific materials on the atmosphere, especially weather factors, are entered under **Meteorology**

See also **Forest influences; Meteorology; Rain and rainfall; Seasons; Weather;** also names of countries, cities, etc. with the subdivision *Climate*, e.g. **U.S. —Climate;** etc.

x Climatology

xx **Earth sciences; Meteorology; Physical geography; Weather**

Climate and forests. *See* **Forest influences**

Climatology. *See* **Climate**

Climbing plants   582; 635.9

x Vines

xx **Gardening; Plants**

Clipper ships   387.2; 623.82

xx **Ships**

Clippings (Books, newspapers, etc.)   025.17

x Newspaper clippings; Press clippings

xx **Newspapers**

Clocks and watches   681

See also **Sundials**

x Horology; Watches

xx **Time**

Clog dancing   793.3

xx **Dancing; Tap dancing**

Cloisters. *See* **Convents; Monasteries**

Closed-circuit television   384.55

See also **Television in education**

x Television, Closed-circuit

xx **Intercommunication systems; Microwave communication systems; Television; Television in education**

Closed shop. *See* **Open and closed shop**

Cloth. *See* **Fabrics**

Clothiers. *See* **Clothing trade**

Clothing, Leather. *See* **Leather garments**

Clothing, Men's. *See* **Men's clothing**

Clothing and dress   646

Use for materials dealing with clothing from a practical standpoint including the art of dress. Descriptive and historical materials on the costume of particular countries or periods are entered under **Costume.** Materials describing mode or style of dress are entered under **Fashion**

Clothing and dress—*Continued*

> *See also* **Children's clothing; Costume; Dress accessories;. Dressmaking; Fashion; Men's clothing; Tailoring; Women's clothing;** etc.; also names of articles of clothing and accessories, e.g. **Buttons; Hats; Hosiery; Leather garments; Shoes and shoe industry;** etc.

> *x* Dress

> *xx* **Costume; Fashion; Hygiene; Manners and customs**

Clothing and dress—Dry cleaning. *See* **Dry cleaning**

Clothing and dress—Repairing 646.2; 646.4

Clothing trade 338.4; 687

> *See also* **Tailoring**

> *x* Clothiers

Cloud seeding. *See* **Weather—Control**

Clouds 551.5

> *xx* **Meteorology**

Clowns 791.3; 920; 927

> *xx* **Circus; Entertainers**

Clubs 367

> *See also* **Boys' clubs; Girls' clubs; Men—Societies; Societies; Women—Societies**

> *xx* **Associations; Societies**

Coaches, Stage. *See* **Carriages and carts**

Coaching (Athletics) 796

> For the coaching of individual sports see the name of the sport in the phrase **Football coaching** and similar phrases

> *x* Athletic coaching; Sports coaching

> *xx* **Athletics; College sports; Physical education and training; School sports; Sports**

Coal 553

> *See also* **Coal mines and mining**

> *x* Anthracite coal; Bituminous coal

> *xx* **Carbon; Fuel; Geology, Economic**

Coal gas. *See* **Gas**

Coal gasification 622

> *x* Gasification of coal

Coal miners 920; 926

> *xx* **Miners**

Coal mines and mining 622

> *See also* **Mining engineering**

> *xx* **Coal; Mines and mineral resources**

Coal oil. *See* **Petroleum**

Coal tar products 547; 661

> *See also* **Gas; Oils and fats**

> *xx* **Gas; Petroleum**

Coast pilot guides. *See* **Pilot guides**

Coastal signals. *See* **Signals and signaling**

Coats of arms. *See* **Heraldry**

Cocoa 613.3; 633; 641.8

> *See also* **Chocolate**

> *xx* **Beverages; Chocolate**

Cocoons. *See* **Butterflies; Caterpillars; Moths; Silkworms**

Code names
    See also **Acronyms**
    xx **Abbreviations; Names**
Codes, Telegraph. *See* **Cipher and telegraph codes**
Codetermination (Industrial relations). *See* **Employees' representation in management**
Coeducation 376
    See also **Education; Men—Education; Women—Education**
    xx **Colleges and universities; Education; Men—Education; Women—Education**
Coffee 613.3; 633; 641.8
    xx **Beverages**
Coffee houses 647
    xx **Restaurants, bars, etc.**
Cog wheels. *See* **Gearing**
Cognition. *See* **Knowledge, Theory of**
Cohabitation. *See* **Unmarried couples**
Coin collecting. *See* **Coins**
Coinage 332.4
    Use for materials on the processing and history of metal money. Lists of coins and materials about coins and coin collecting are entered under **Coins**
    See also **Counterfeits and counterfeiting; Gold; Mints; Monetary policy; Money; Silver**
    xx **Gold; Mints; Money; Silver**
Coinage of words. *See* **Words, New**
Coins 737.4
    Use for lists of coins, materials about coins and coin collecting. Materials on coins from the point of view of art and archeology are entered under **Numismatics;** materials on the processing of metal money are entered under **Coinage**
    See also **Numismatics**
    x Coin collecting
    xx **Money; Numismatics**
Cold 551.5
    See also **Cryobiology; Ice; Low temperatures**
    xx **Low temperatures**
Cold—Physiological effect 613.1
    xx **Cryobiology**
Cold—Therapeutic use 615
    See also **Cryosurgery**
Cold (Disease) 616.2
    See also **Influenza**
    x Common cold
Cold storage 641.4; 664
    See also **Compressed air; Refrigeration and refrigerating machinery**
    xx **Food—Preservation; Meat industry and trade; Refrigeration and refrigerating machinery**

Cold war. *See* **Psychological warfare; World politics—1945–1965; World politics, 1965–**

Collaborationists. *See* **Treason**

Collage   745.59; 751.4

   xx **Art**

Collectibles. *See* names of events with the subdivision *Collectibles,* e.g. **American Revolution Bicentennial, 1776–1976—Collectibles;** etc.; and names of objects collected with the subdivision *Collectors and collecting,* e.g. **Postage stamps—Collectors and collecting;** etc. **—Collected works;** etc.

Collecting. *See* **Collectors and collecting**

Collecting of accounts   658.8

   x Accounts, Collecting of

   xx **Commercial law; Credit; Debtor and creditor**

Collection development (Libraries). *See* **Libraries—Collection development**

Collections of art, painting, etc. *See* types of art with the subdivision *Collections,* e.g. **Painting—Collections;** etc.

Collections of literature. *See* **Essays; Short stories;** etc.; and names of literatures and literary forms with the subdivision *Collections,* e.g. **English literature—Collections; Poetry—Collections;** etc. For other collections of writings see names of authors, literary or otherwise, or subjects with the subdivision *Collected works,* e.g. **Shakespeare, William—Collected works; Astronomy —Collected works;** etc.

Collections of natural specimens. *See* **Zoological specimens—Collection and preservation;** and names of specimens with the subdivision *Collection and preservation,* e.g. **Birds—Collection and preservation;** etc.

Collections of objects. *See* **Collectors and collecting;** and names of objects collected with the subdivision *Collectors and collecting,* e.g. **Postage stamps—Collectors and collecting;** etc.; and names of events with the subdivision *Collectibles,* e.g. **American Revolution Bicentennial, 1776–1976—Collectibles;** etc.

Collective bargaining   331.8; 331.89; 658.31

   May be subdivided by topic, e.g. **Collective bargaining—Librarians;** etc.

   See also **Arbitration, Industrial; Employees' representation in management; Labor contract; Labor unions; Strikes and lockouts**

   x Labor negotiations

   xx **Arbitration, Industrial; Employees' representation in management; Industrial relations; Labor and laboring classes;**

129

Collective bargaining—*Continued*
>> Labor contract; Labor disputes; Labor unions; Strikes and lockouts

Collective bargaining—Librarians 331.89
> *x* Librarians—Collective bargaining; Libraries—Collective bargaining

Collective farms. *See* Agriculture, Cooperative

Collective labor agreements. *See* Labor contract

Collective security. *See* Security, International

Collective settlements (May subdiv. geog.) 335
> *See also* Bohemianism; Counter culture; also names of individual communes
> *x* Communal living; Communes; Group living
> *xx* Counter culture

Collective settlements—Israel 335
> *x* Israel—Collective settlements; Kibbutz

Collective settlements—U.S. 335
> *x* U.S.—Collective settlements

Collectivism. *See* Communism; Socialism

Collectors and collecting 790.13
> *See also* Book collecting; also names of objects collected with the subdivision *Collectors and collecting,* e.g. Postage stamps—Collectors and collecting; etc.; names of events with the subdivision *Collectibles,* e.g. American Revolution Bicentennial, 1776–1976—Collectibles; etc.; and names of natural specimens with the subdivision *Collection and preservation,* e.g. Birds—Collection and preservation; Zoological specimens—Collection and preservation; etc.
> *x* Collecting; Collections of objects
> *xx* Antiques; Art; Hobbies

Collects. *See* Prayers

College and school drama 371.8
> Use for materials about college and school drama. Collections of plays for production in colleges and schools are entered under College and school drama —Collections
> *See also* Drama in education
> *x* College drama; School drama; Theatricals, College
> *xx* Amateur theatricals; Drama; Drama in education; Student activities

College and school drama—Collections 808.82; 812.08; etc.
> *x* College plays; Plays, College; School plays
> *xx* Drama—Collections

College and school journalism 371.8
> *x* College journalism; College periodicals; School journalism; School newspapers
> *xx* Journalism; Student activities

College athletics. *See* Athletics; College sports

College costs 378.3
    x Tuition
    xx **Colleges and universities—Finance**
College degrees. *See* **Degrees, Academic**
College drama. *See* **College and school drama**
College entrance requirements. *See* **Colleges and universities—Entrance requirements;** and names of individual colleges and universities with the subdivision *Entrance requirements*
College fraternities. *See* **Fraternities and sororities**
College journalism. *See* **College and school journalism**
College libraries. *See* **Libraries, College and university**
College life. *See* **College students**
College periodicals. *See* **College and school journalism**
College plays. *See* **College and school drama—Collections**
College songs. *See* **Students' songs**
College sororities. *See* **Fraternities and sororities**
College sports 371.8
    See also **Coaching (Athletics);** also names of individual sports, e.g. **Baseball; Football; Rowing; Soccer; Track athletics;** etc.
    x College athletics; Intercollegiate athletics; Varsity sports
    xx **School sports; Sports**
College students 378.1
    x College life; Colleges and universities—Students; Undergraduates; University students
    xx **Students**
College students—Political activity 378.1
    x Campus disorders
    xx **Politics, Practical**
College students—Sexual behavior 378.1
    xx **Sexual behavior**
College teachers. *See* **Colleges and universities—Faculty; Educators; Teachers**
Colleges and universities (May subdiv. geog.) 378.1
    See also

Classical education	**Free universities**
Coeducation	**Junior colleges**
Commencements	**Libraries, College**
Degrees, Academic	**and university**
Dissertations, Academic	**Scholarships, fellowships, etc.**
Education, Higher	**Teachers colleges**
Fraternities and sororities	**University extension**

    also headings beginning with the word **College** and names of individual institutions

Colleges and universities—*Continued*

  x Universities

  xx **Classical education; Education; Education, Higher; Professional education; Schools**

Colleges and universities–Buildings 727

  x Buildings, College

  xx **Buildings**

Colleges and universities–Curricula 378.1

  x Core curriculum; Courses of study; Curriculum (Courses of study); Schools—Curricula; Study, Courses of

  xx **Education–Curricula**

Colleges and universities–Entrance requirements 378.1

  See also names of individual colleges and universities with the subdivision *Entrance requirements*

  x College entrance requirements; Entrance requirements for colleges and universities

  xx **Examination; Free universities**

Colleges and universities–Faculty 378.1

  x College teachers; Faculty (Education)

College and universities–Finance 378

  See also **College costs; Federal aid to education**

  x Tuition

College and universities–Students. *See* **College students**

Colleges and universities–U.S. 378.73

  x American colleges; U.S.—Colleges and universities; U.S.—Universities

Collies 636.7

  xx **Dogs**

Collisions, Railroad. *See* **Railroads–Accidents**

Colloids 541; 547

  xx **Chemistry, Physical and theoretical**

Colonial architecture. *See* **Architecture, Colonial**

Colonial furniture (U.S.). *See* **Furniture, American**

Colonial history (U.S.) *See* **U.S.–History–Colonial period, 1600–1775**

Colonial life and customs (U.S.). *See* **U.S.–History–Colonial period, 1600–1775; U.S.–Social life and customs–Colonial period, 1600–1775**

Colonialism. *See* **Colonies; Imperialism**

Colonies 325

  Use for materials on general colonial policy. Materials on the policy of settling immigrants or nationals in unoccupied areas are entered under **Colonization.** Materials on migration from one country to another are entered under **Immigration and emigration.** Materials on the movement of population within a country for permanent settle-

132

Colonies—*Continued*

ment are entered under **Migration, Internal**

See also **Colonization; Immigration and emigration; Land settlement; National liberation movements; Penal colonies;** also names of countries with the subdivision *Colonies,* e.g. **Gt. Brit.—Colonies; U.S.—Colonies;** etc.

x Colonialism; Dependencies

xx **Colonization**

Colonies, Space. *See* **Space colonies**

Colonization 325

See note under **Colonies**

See also **Colonies; Immigration and emigration; Jews—Colonization; Migration, Internal; Penal colonies;** also names of countries with the subdivision *Immigration and emigration,* e.g. **U.S.—Immigration and emigration;** etc.

x Dependencies

xx **Colonies; History; Immigration and emigration; Land settlement**

Color 535.6; 752

See also **Dyes and dyeing;** also names of individual colors, e.g. **Red;** etc.

x Colour

xx **Chemistry; Esthetics; Light; Optics; Painting; Photometry**

Color—Psychology 152.1

x Psychology of color

xx **Color sense; Psychology**

Color blindness 617.7

xx **Color sense; Vision disorders**

Color etchings. *See* **Color prints**

Color of animals 591.1

See also **Camouflage (Biology)**

x Animal coloration; Animals—Color; Pigmentation

xx **Animals; Biology; Camouflage (Biology) Evolution; Variation (Biology)**

Color of people 573

x Human color; Man—Color; Pigmentation; Skin, Color of

xx **Anthropology; Ethnology; Evolution; Man—Influence of environment; Physical anthropology**

Color photography 778.6

x Color slides; Photography, Color

xx **Photography**

Color printing 686.2

Use for materials on typographic printing in color. Materials on pictures printed in color from engraved metal, wood or stone are entered under **Color prints**

See also **Illustration of books; Lithography; Silk screen printing**

xx **Printing**

133

Color prints (May subdiv. geog. adjective form) 769

See note under **Color printing**

See also **Linoleum block printing**

x Block printing; Color etchings; Painting —Color reproductions

Color prints, American 769

x American color prints

Color prints, Japanese 769

x Japanese color prints; Japanese prints

Color sense 152.1

See also **Color blindness; Color—Psychology**

xx **Psychology, Physiological; Senses and sensation; Vision**

Color slides. *See* **Color photography; Slides (Photography)**

Color television 621.388

x Television, Color

xx **Television**

Colorado River—Hoover Dam. *See* **Hoover Dam**

Colour. *See* **Color**

Columnists. *See* **Journalists**

Combinations, Industrial. *See* **Trusts, Industrial**

Combustion 541; 544; 545

See also **Fire; Fuel; Heat**

x Spontaneous combustion

xx **Chemistry; Fire; Heat**

Comedians 920; 927

xx **Actors and actresses; Entertainers**

Comedy 792.2

x Comic literature

xx **Drama; Wit and humor**

Comets 523.6

xx **Astronomy; Solar system**

Comic books, strips, etc. 741.5

See also **Cartoons and caricatures**

x Comic strips; Funnies; Humorous pictures

xx **Cartoons and caricatures**

Comic literature. *See* **Comedy; Parody; Satire**

Comic opera. *See* **Opera; Operetta**

Comic strips. *See* **Comic books, strips, etc.**

Commandments, Ten. *See* **Ten commandments**

Commencements 371.2

x Graduation

xx **Colleges and universities; High schools; School assembly programs**

Commentaries, Biblical. *See* **Bible—Commentaries**

Commerce 380-382

Use for general materials on foreign and domestic commerce. Materials limited to commerce between states are entered under **Interstate commerce**

134

Commerce—*Continued*

See also

Banks and bank- ing	**Interstate com- merce**
Business	**Markets**
Chambers of com- merce	**Merchants**
	Monopolies
Competition	**Prices**
Contracts	**Profit sharing**
Cooperation	**Retail trade**
Exchange	**Stock exchange**
Free trade and pro- tection	**Stocks**
	Tariff
Geography, Com- mercial	**Trade routes**
	Trademarks
Insurance, Marine	**Transportation**
International business enterprises	**Trusts, Industrial**

> *also* names of countries, cities, etc. with the subdivision *Commerce* (e.g. **U.S.—Commerce;** etc.); names of articles of commerce (e.g. **Cotton;** etc.); and headings beginning with the word **Commercial**

> *x* Distribution (Economics); Exports; Foreign trade; Imports; International trade; Trade

> *xx* **Economics; Exchange; Finance; Transportation**

Commerce, Interstate. *See* **Interstate commerce**

Commercial aeronautics. *See* **Aeronautics, Commercial**

Commercial arithmetic. *See* **Business arithmetic**

Commercial art 741.6

> Use for general materials on the application of art to business, i.e. in advertising layout, fashion design, lettering, etc.

> *See also* **Fashion design; Posters; Textile design**

> *x* Advertising, Art in; Advertising, Pictorial; Art, Commercial; Art in advertising

> *xx* **Advertising; Art; Art industries and trade; Drawing**

Commercial aviation. *See* **Aeronautics, Commercial**

Commercial correspondence. *See* **Business letters**

Commercial education. *See* **Business education**

Commercial employees. *See* **Clerks**

Commercial geography. *See* **Geography, Commercial**

Commercial law 346.7

> *See also*

Antitrust law	**Bankruptcy**

Commercial law—*Continued*

Collecting of accounts	Landlord and tenant
Contracts	Maritime law
Corporation law	Mortgages
Debtor and creditor	Negotiable instruments

    x Business law; Law, Business; Law, Commercial; Mercantile law

   xx **Business; Business education; Law; Maritime law**

Commercial paper. *See* **Negotiable instruments**

Commercial photography. *See* **Photography, Commercial**

Commercial policy 380.1; 381-382

    Use for general materials on the various regulations by which governments seek to protect and increase the commerce of a country such as subsidies, tariffs, free ports, etc.

    See also **Free trade and protection; Tariff;** also names of countries with the subdivision *Commercial policy*, e.g. **U.S. —Commercial policy;** etc.

    x Government regulation of commerce; Reciprocity; Trade barriers; World economics

   xx **Economic policy; International economic relations**

Commercial products 380.1

    See also **Forest products; Geography, Commercial; Manufactures; Marine resources; Raw materials;** also names of individual products

    x Consumer goods; Consumer products; Merchandise; Products, Commercial

Commercial schools. *See* **Business education**

Commercial travelers. *See* **Sales personnel**

Commercials, Radio. *See* **Radio advertising**

Commercials, Television. *See* **Television advertising**

Commission government. *See* **Municipal government by commission**

Commission government with city manager. *See* **Municipal government by city manager**

Common cold. *See* **Cold (Disease)**

Common law marriage. *See* **Unmarried couples**

Common market. *See* **European Economic Community**

Common schools. *See* **Public schools**

The Commonwealth. *See* **Political science; Republics; The State**

Commonwealth of England. *See* **Gt. Brit.— History—Civil War and Commonwealth, 1642–1660**

Commonwealth of Nations   942.06

Use for materials that deal collectively with Great Britain and the self-governing dominions

See also **Gt. Brit.—Colonies**

x British Commonwealth of Nations; British Dominions

xx **Great Britain**

Communal living.   *See* **Collective settlements**

Communes.   *See* **Collective settlements**

Communicable diseases   616.9

See also **Bacteriology; Biological warfare; Disinfection and disinfectants; Epidemics; Fumigation; Germ theory of disease; Immunity; Insects as carriers of disease; Vaccination;** also names of communicable diseases, e.g. **Smallpox;** etc.

x Contagion and contagious diseases; Contagious diseases; Diseases, Communicable; Diseases, Contagious; Diseases, Infectious; Infection and infectious diseases; Quarantine

xx **Diseases; Epidemics; Immunity; Medicine—Practice; Public health**

Communicable diseases—Prevention   614.4

Communication   001.54; 301.16

Use for general materials on communication in its broadest sense, including the spoken and written word

See also

Books and reading	**Newspapers**
Cybernetics	**Nonverbal communication**
Information science	
Language and languages	**Postal service**
	Telecommunication
Language arts	**Writing**
Mass media	

x Mass communication

Communication among animals.   *See* **Animal communication**

Communication arts.   *See* **Language arts**

Communications relay satellites.   *See* **Artificial satellites in telecommunication**

Communion.   *See* **Lord's Supper**

Communism (May subdiv. geog.) 320.5; 321.9; 335.4

See also **Anticommunist movements; Socialism**

x Bolshevism; Collectivism; Marxism

xx **Cooperation; Individualism; Labor and laboring classes; Political science; Socialism; Sociology; Syndicalism; Totalitarianism**

Communism—Russia   947.084-947.085

x Russia—Communism; Russian communism

Communism—U.S.   335.4; 973.91-973.92

x U.S.—Communism

Communism and literature 335.4; 809; 810.9; etc.

    Use same form for Communism and other subjects, e.g. **Communism and religion;** etc.

    x Literature and communism

Communism and religion 261.7; 335.4

    See also **Christianity and economics**

    x Religion and communism

Communist countries 947

    x Chinese satellite countries; Iron curtain countries; People's democracies; Russian satellite countries; Soviet bloc

Communities, Space. *See* **Space colonies**

Community and libraries. *See* **Libraries and community**

Community and school 370.19

    Use for materials on ways in which the community at large, as distinct from government, may aid the school program

    See also **Parents' and teachers' associations**

    x School and community

    xx **Community life**

Community antenna television 384.55

    x CATV; Cable television; Television, Cable

    xx **Television broadcasting**

Community centers 374.2; 790

    See also **Playgrounds**

    x Play centers; Recreation centers; School buildings as recreation centers; Schools as social centers; Social centers

    xx **Cities and towns—Civic improvement; Community life; Community organization; Playgrounds; Recreation; Social problems; Social settlements**

Community chests. *See* **Fund raising**

Community churches 254

    Use for materials on local churches that have no denominational affiliations

    x Churches, Community; Churches, Undenominational; Nondenominational churches; Undenominational churches; Union churches

    xx **Christian unity**

Community colleges. *See* **Junior colleges**

Community councils. *See* **Community organization**

Community health services 362

    xx **Community services; Public health**

Community life 301.34

    See also **City life; Community and school; Community centers; Community organization**

    x Neighborhood

    xx **Associations; City life**

Community organization 301.34

    See also **Community centers; Local government; Urban renewal**

Community organization—*Continued*
    x Community councils
    xx **Community life; Social work; Urban renewal**
Community schools. *See* **Schools**
Community services 361
    See also types of services, e.g. **Community health services;** etc.
Community songbooks. *See* **Songbooks**
Community surveys. *See* **Social surveys**
Community theater. *See* **Theater—Little theater movement**
Compact automobiles. *See* **Automobiles, Compact**
Compact cars. *See* **Automobiles, Compact**
Companies. *See* **Corporations**
Companies, Trust. *See* **Trust companies**
Company symbols. *See* **Trademarks**
Comparative anatomy. *See* **Anatomy, Comparative**
Comparative government 350; 351
    See also names of countries, cities, etc. with the subdivision *Politics and government*, e.g. **U.S.—Politics and government;** etc.
    x Government, Comparative
    xx **Political science**
Comparative librarianship 020
    x Librarianship, Comparative
    xx **International education; Library science**
Comparative linguistics. *See* **Language and languages**
Comparative literature. *See* **Literature, Comparative**
Comparative philology. *See* **Philology, Comparative**
Comparative physiology. *See* **Physiology, Comparative**
Comparative psychology. *See* **Psychology, Comparative**
Comparative religion. *See* **Christianity and other religions; Religions**
Compass 538.028; 623.89
    x Magnetic needle; Marine's compass
    xx **Magnetism; Navigation**
Compassion. *See* **Sympathy**
Compensation. *See* **Pensions; Wages; Workers' compensation**
Competition 338.6
    See also **Monopolies; Trusts, Industrial**
    xx **Business; Business ethics; Commerce; Monopolies; Trusts, Industrial**
Competition, Unfair 338.6
    x Fair trade; Unfair competition
Competitions. *See* **Rewards (Prizes, etc.);** and subjects with the subdivision *Competitions*, e.g. **Literature—Competitions;** etc.

139

Composers (May subdiv. geog. adjective form)
920; 927

xx **Musicians**

Composers, American 920; 927

x American composers; U.S.—Composers

Composition (Art) 701

See also **Architecture—Composition, proportion, etc.; Painting**

x Art—Composition

xx **Art; Painting**

Composition (Music) 781.6

See also **Counterpoint; Fugue; Harmony; Instrumentation and orchestration; Music, Popular (Songs, etc.)—Writing and publishing; Musical accompaniment**

x Music—Composition; Musical composition; Song writing

xx **Music; Music—Study and teaching; Music—Theory**

Composition (Printing). *See* **Typesetting**

Composition (Rhetoric). *See* **Rhetoric;** and names of languages with the subdivision *Composition and exercises,* e.g. **English language—Composition and exercises;** etc.

Compost 631.8

xx **Fertilizers and manures; Soils**

Comprehensive health care organizations. *See* **Health maintenance organizations**

Compressed air 621.5

x Air, Compressed; Pneumatic transmission

xx **Cold storage; Foundations; Pneumatics; Power (Mechanics)**

Compulsory education. *See* **Education, Compulsory**

Compulsory labor. *See* **Convict labor; Peonage; Slavery**

Compulsory military service. *See* **Military service, Compulsory**

Compulsory school attendance. *See* **Education, Compulsory; School attendance**

Computer control. *See* **Automation**

Computer program languages. *See* **Programming languages (Electronic computers)**

Computer programming. *See* **Programming (Electronic computers)**

Computer programs 001.6; 651.8

See also subjects with the subdivision *Computer programs,* e.g. Oceanography—**Computer programs;** etc.

x Computer software; Programs, Computer; Software, Computer

xx **Programming (Electronic computers)**

Computer software. *See* **Computer programs; Programming (Electronic computers); Programming languages (Electronic computers)**

Computers 338.4; 621.3819

    Use for materials on modern electronic computers developed after 1945. Materials on calculating machines and mechanical computers made before 1945 are entered under **Calculating machines**

    See also **Calculating machines; Electronic data processing; Information storage and retrieval systems;** also names of types and of specific computers, e.g. **Microcomputers; Minicomputers; IBM 7090 (Computer);** etc.

    x Automatic computers; Brain, Electronic; Computers, Electronic; Computing machines (Electronic); Electronic brains; Electronic calculating machines; Electronic computers; Mechanical brains

    xx **Calculating machines; Cybernetics; Electronic apparatus and appliances**

Computers—Cartoons and caricatures 338.4; 621.3819; 741.5

    xx **Cartoons and caricatures**

Computers, Electronic. *See* **Computers**

Computers—Programming. *See* **Programming (Electronic computers)**

Computing machines (Electronic). *See* **Computers**

Con games. *See* **Swindlers and swindling**

Concentration. *See* **Attention**

Concentration camps 365

    See also **Prisoners of war;** also names of individual camps; and names of wars with the subdivision *Prisoners and prisons,* e.g. **World War, 1939–1945—Prisoners and prisons;** etc.

    x Internment camps

    xx **Camps, Military; Political crimes and offenses; Prisoners of war**

Conception—Prevention. *See* **Birth control**

Concepts 153.2

    See also types of concepts and images, e.g. **Size and shape;** etc.

    xx **Perception**

Concerto 785.6

    xx **Musical form**

Concertos 785.6

    xx **Musical form; Orchestral music**

Concerts 780.73

    See also **Music festivals**

    xx **Amusements; Music**

Conchology. *See* **Shells**

Conciliation, Industrial. *See* **Arbitration, Industrial**

Concordances. *See* **Bible—Concordances;** and names of authors with the subdivision *Concordances,* e.g. **Shakespeare, William—Concordances;** etc.

Concrete 691; 693.5

See also **Asphalt; Cement; Pavements**

xx **Building materials; Cement; Foundations; Masonry; Plaster and plastering**

Concrete—Testing 691

xx **Strength of materials**

Concrete, Reinforced 693.5

x Reinforced concrete

xx **Building materials**

Concrete construction 693.4; 693.5

x Building, Concrete; Construction, Concrete

xx **Architecture; Building**

Condemnation of land. *See* **Eminent domain**

Condensers (Electricity) 621.31

x Electric condensers

xx **Induction coils**

Condensers (Steam) 621.1

xx **Steam engines**

Condominiums 647

xx **Apartment houses**

Conduct of life. *See* **Human behavior**

Conducting 781.6

Use for materials on orchestral conducting or a combination of orchestral and choral conducting. Materials limited to choral conducting are entered under **Conducting, Choral**

See also **Bands (Music); Conducting, Choral; Conductors (Music); Orchestra**

xx **Bands (Music); Conductors (Music); Music—Study and teaching; Orchestra**

Conducting, Choral 784.9

See note under **Conducting**

See also **Choirs (Music); Choral music; Conductors (Music)**

x Choral conducting

xx **Choirs (Music); Choral music; Conducting; Conductors (Music)**

Conductors, Electric. *See* **Electric conductors**

Conductors (Music) 920; 927

See also **Conducting; Conducting, Choral**

x Bandmasters; Music conductors

xx **Conducting; Conducting, Choral; Musicians; Orchestra**

Conduits. *See* **Aqueducts**

Confectionery 641.8; 664

See also **Cake decorating**

x Candy

xx **Cookery; Ice cream, ices, etc.**

Confederacies. *See* **Federal government**

Confederate States of America 973.7

xx **U.S.—History—Civil War, 1861–1865**

Confederation of American colonies. *See* **U.S. —History—1783–1809**

Conferences. *See* **Congresses and conventions**

Confessions of faith. *See* **Creeds**

Confidence game. *See* **Swindlers and swindling**

142

Configuration (Psychology). *See* **Gestalt psychology**

Conflict, Social. *See* **Social conflict**

Conflict of generations   301.42
>   See also **Parent and child**
>   *x* Generation gap
>   *xx* **Human relations; Parent and child; Social conflict**

Conflict of interests   351.9
>   *See also* **Corruption in politics; Misconduct in office**
>   *xx* **Political ethics**

Conformity   301.15
>   *See also* **Dissent; Individuality; Social Values**
>   *x* Nonconformity; Social conformity
>   *xx* **Attitude (Psychology); Individuality**

Confucianism   299
>   *xx* **Religions**

Conglomerate corporations   338.8
>   *x* Business combinations; Consolidation and merger of corporations; Corporations, Conglomerate; Industrial mergers; Mergers, Conglomerate
>   *xx* **Corporations**

Congregationalism   285
>   *See also* **Calvinism; Friends, Society of; Puritans; Unitarianism**
>   *xx* **Calvinism; Puritans**

Congress—U.S. *See* **U.S. Congress**

Congresses and conventions   060
>   *See also* **International organization; Treaties;** also names of specific congresses
>   *x* Conferences; Conventions (Congresses); International conferences
>   *xx* **Intellectual cooperation; International cooperation**

Congressional investigations. *See* **Governmental investigations**

Conjuring. *See* **Magic**

Conquistadores. *See* **America—Exploration**

Conscience   171; 241
>   *See also* **Freedom of conscience**
>   *xx* **Christian ethics; Duty; Ethics**

Conscientious objectors   343.1; 355.2
>   *See also* **Military service, Compulsory—Draft resisters; Pacifism;** also names of wars with the subdivision *Conscientious objectors,* e.g. **World War, 1939–1945—Conscientious objectors;** etc.
>   *xx* **Freedom of conscience; Military service, Compulsory—Draft resisters; Pacifism; War and religion**

Consciousness   126; 153
>   *See also* **Gestalt psychology; Individuality; Knowledge, Theory of; Personality; Self; Subconsciousness**
>   *xx* **Apperception; Mind and body; Perception; Psychology; Subconsciousness**

Conscription, Military. *See* **Military service, Compulsory**

Conservation of buildings. *See* **Architecture—Conservation and restoration**

Conservation of energy. *See* **Energy conservation; Force and energy**

Conservation of forests. *See* **Forests and forestry**

Conservation of natural resources   333.7-333.9; 639

　　See also **Energy conservation; Nature conservation**

　　x Preservation of natural resources; Resource management

　　xx **Environmental policy; Natural resources**

Conservation of nature. *See* **Nature conservation**

Conservation of power resources. *See* **Energy conservation**

Conservation of the soil. *See* **Soil conservation**

Conservation of water. *See* **Water conservation**

Conservation of wildlife. *See* **Wildlife—Conservation**

Conservation of works of art, books, etc. *See* subjects with the subdivision *Conservation and restoration,* e.g. **Painting—Conservation and restoration**; etc.

Conservatism   320.5

　　See also **Right and left (Political science)**

　　xx **Right and left (Political science)**

Consolation. *See* **Sympathy**

Consolidation and merger of corporations. *See* **Conglomerate corporations**

Consolidation of schools. *See* **Schools—Centralization**

Consortia, Library. *See* **Library cooperation; Library information networks**

Constellations. *See* **Astronomy; Stars**

Constitution. *See* names of countries and states with the subhead *Constitution,* e.g. **U.S. Constitution**; etc.

Constitutional amendments—U.S. *See* **U.S. Constitution—Amendments**

Constitutional history   342.2

　　See also **Democracy; Monarchy; Political science; Representative government and representation; Republics;** also names of countries, states, etc. with the subdivision *Constitutional history,* e.g. **U.S.—Constitutional history**; etc.

　　x Constitutional law—History; History, Constitutional

　　xx **Constitutions; History; Political science**

Constitutional law   342

　　See also

Administrative law	**Democracy**
Citizenship	**Eminent domain**
Civil rights	**Executive power**
Constitutions	**Federal government**

144

Constitutional law—*Continued*

    Injunctions
    Legislation
    Legislative bodies
    Monarchy
    Political science
    Proportional repre-
        sentation
    Referendum

    Representative gov-
        ernment and rep-
        resentation
    Republics
    Separation of
        powers
    Suffrage

    also names of countries with the subdivision *Constitutional law,* e.g. **U.S.— Constitutional law;** etc.

    x Law, Constitutional

    xx **Administrative law; Constitutions; Law; Political science**

Constitutional law—History. *See* **Constitutional history**

Constitutions 342.2

    See also **Constitutional history; Constitutional law; Representative government and representation;** also names of countries, states, etc. with the subhead *Constitution,* e.g. **U.S. Constitution;** etc.

    xx **Constitutional law; Political science; Representative government and representation**

Constitutions, State 342.2

    See also **State governments;** also names of states with the subhead *Constitution,* e.g. **Ohio. Constitution;** etc.

    x State constitutions

    xx **Political science; State governments**

Construction. *See* **Architecture; Building; Engineering**

Construction, Concrete. *See* **Concrete construction**

Construction of roads. *See* **Roads**

Consulates. *See* **Diplomatic and consular service**

Consuls. *See* **Diplomats**

Consumer behavior. *See* **Consumers**

Consumer credit 332.7

    See also **Instalment plan**

    x Credit, Consumer

    xx **Banks and banking; Credit; Finance, Personal**

Consumer education 640.73

    Use for materials on the selection and most efficient use of consumer goods and services, including methods of educating the consumer. Materials on the economic theory of consumption are entered under **Consumption (Economics)**

    See also **Buying; Shopping**

    x Buyers' guides; Consumers' guides; Shoppers' guides

    xx **Buying; Home economics; Shopping**

145

Consumer goods. *See* **Commercial products; Manufactures**

Consumer organizations. *See* **Cooperative societies**

Consumer price index. *See* **Cost of living**

Consumer products. *See* **Commercial products; Manufactures**

Consumer protection 343.7

Use for materials on governmental and private activities which guard the consumer against dangers to his health, safety, or economic well-being

See also **Drugs—Adulteration and analysis; Food adulteration and inspection**

x Consumerism

Consumerism. *See* **Consumer protection**

Consumers 658.8

Use for materials on consumer behavior

See also **Young consumers**

x Consumer behavior

xx **Shopping**

Consumers' cooperative societies. *See* **Cooperative societies**

Consumers' guides. *See* **Consumer education**

Consumption (Economics) 339.4

See note under **Consumer education**

See also **Prices**

xx **Economics**

Consumption of energy. *See* **Energy consumption**

Contact lenses 617.7

xx **Eyeglasses; Lenses**

Contagion and contagious diseases. *See* **Communicable diseases**

Contagious diseases. *See* **Communicable diseases**

Contaminated food. *See* **Food contamination**

Contamination of environment. *See* **Pollution**

Contemporary art. *See* **Art, Modern—20th century**

Continental drift 551.4

See also **Plate tectonics**

x Drifting of continents

xx **Continents; Plate tectonics**

Continental shelf 551.4

See also **Territorial waters**

xx **Territorial waters**

Continents 551.4

See also **Continental drift**

Continuation schools. *See* **Evening and continuation schools**

Continuing education 374.8

See also **Adult education**

x Education, Continuing; Lifelong education; Permanent education; Recurrent education

xx **Education**

Contraband trade. *See* **Smuggling**

Contraception. *See* **Birth control**

Contract bridge. *See* **Bridge (Game)**

146

Contract labor 331.5

    See also **Convict labor; Peonage; Slavery**

    xx **Labor and laboring classes; Peonage**

Contractions. *See* **Abbreviations; Ciphers**

Contracts 346.2

    See also **Authors and publishers;** also types of contracts, e.g. **Labor contract; Mortgages; Negotiable instruments;** and subjects with the subdivision *Contracts and specifications,* e.g. **Building–Contracts and specifications;** etc.

    x Agreements

    xx **Commerce; Commercial law**

Control. *See* subjects with the subdivision *Control,* e.g. **Pests–Control; Weather –Control;** etc.

Conundrums. *See* **Riddles**

Conventions (Congresses). *See* **Congresses and conventions**

Conventions, Political. *See* **Political conventions**

Convents 271

    See also **Abbeys; Monasteries; Religious orders for women**

    x Cloisters; Nunneries

    xx **Abbeys; Church history; Monasteries**

Conversation 808.56

    x Discussion; Table talk; Talking

    xx **Language and languages**

Conversation in foreign languages. *See* **Languages, Modern–Conversations and phrases;** and names of foreign languages with the subdivision *Conversation and phrase books,* e.g. **French language–Conversations and phrases;** etc.

Conversion 248

    See also **Converts, Catholic; Grace (Theology); Salvation**

    xx **Christian life; Evangelistic work; Theology**

Conversion of waste products. *See* **Recycling (Waste, etc.); Salvage (Waste, etc.)**

Converts 248

    Use for materials on converts from one religion or denomination to another. For persons affiliating with a particular denomination or religion use adjective form, e.g. **Converts, Catholic;** etc.

Converts, Catholic 282

    x Catholic Church—Converts; Catholic converts

    xx **Conversion; Converts**

Conveying machinery 621.8

    See also **Hoisting machinery**

    xx **Hoisting machinery**

Convict labor 331.5; 365

    See also **Peonage; Prisons**

Convict labor—*Continued*

>   *x* Compulsory labor; Convicts; Forced labor; Prison labor

>   *xx* **Contract labor; Criminals; Labor and laboring classes; Peonage; Prisons**

Convicts. *See* **Convict labor; Criminals; Penal colonies; Prisoners**

Cook books. *See* **Cookery**

Cookery 641.5

>   Use for general materials on cookery, including American cookery. If limited to a particular area in the U.S. may use geog. subdiv., e.g. **Cookery—Maine; Cookery—Southern States;** etc. For materials on foreign cookery, use geog. subdiv. adjective form, e.g. **Cookery, French;** etc. For types of cooking, use adjective form, e.g. **Cookery, Microwave;** etc.

>   *See also*

Baking	**Diet**
Bread	**Dinners and dining**
Cake	**Flavoring essences**
Canning and preserving	**Food**
Caterers and catering	**Luncheons**
	Menus
Confectionery	**Pastry**
Cookery for the sick	**Salads**
	Sandwiches
Desserts	**Soups**

>   *x* Cook books; Cooking; Gastronomy; Recipes

>   *xx* **Diet; Dinners and dining; Food; Home economics**

Cookery, Microwave 641.5

>   *x* Microwave cookery

Cookery, Outdoor 641.5; 641.7

>   *x* Barbecue cooking; Camp cooking; Outdoor cookery

>   *xx* **Camping**

Cookery, Quantity 641.5

>   *x* Cookery for institutions, etc.; Quantity cookery

Cookery—Vegetables 641.6

>   Use same form for the cooking of other foods

>   *x* Vegetarian cooking

>   *xx* **Vegetables**

Cookery for institutions, etc. *See* **Cookery, Quantity**

Cookery for the sick 641.5

>   *See also* names of diets, e.g. **Salt free diet;** etc.

>   *x* Food for invalids; Invalid cookery

>   *xx* **Cookery; Diet in disease; Nursing; Sick**

Cooking. *See* **Cookery**

Cooking utensils. *See* **Household equipment and supplies**

Cooling appliances. *See* **Refrigeration and re-frigerating machinery**

Cooperation 334

Use for general materials on the theory and history of cooperation and the cooperative movement. Materials dealing specifically with cooperative enterprises are entered under **Cooperative societies**

See also

Agriculture, Co-operative	**International co-operation**
Banks and bank-ing, Cooperative	**Labor unions**
Communism	**Profit sharing**
Cooperative so-cieties	**Savings and loan associations**
	Socialism

x Cooperative distribution; Distribution, Cooperative; Rochdale system

xx **Associations; Commerce; Economics; Profit sharing**

Cooperation, Intellectual. *See* **Intellectual co-operation**

Cooperation, International. *See* **International cooperation**

Cooperation, Library. *See* **Library cooperation**

Cooperative agriculture. *See* **Agriculture. Co-operative**

Cooperative banks. *See* **Banks and banking, Cooperative**

Cooperative building associations. *See* **Savings and loan associations**

Cooperative distribution. *See* **Cooperation; Cooperative societies**

Cooperative societies 334; 658.8

See note under **Cooperation**

See also types of cooperative societies, e.g. **Banks and banking, Cooperative; Savings and loan associations;** etc.

x Consumer organizations; Consumers' co-operative societies; Cooperative distri-bution; Cooperative stores; Distribu-tion, Cooperative; Societies, Coopera-tive; Stores

xx **Cooperation; Corporations; Societies**

Cooperative stores. *See* **Cooperative societies**

Coping behavior. *See* **Adjustment (Psychol-ogy)**

Copper engraving. *See* **Engraving**

Copperwork 673; 739

xx **Metalwork**

Copy writing. *See* **Advertising copy**

Copybooks. *See* **Penmanship**

Copying processes and machines 686.4

See also names of specific processes, e.g. **Xerography;** etc.

x Duplicating processes; Photocopying machines; Reproduction processes; Reprography

Copyright 341.7; 346.47

    May be subdivided by topic, e.g. **Copyright —Books;** etc.

    See also **Authors and publishers; Fair use (Copyright); Publishers and publishing**

    x Intellectual property; International copyright; Literary property; Property, Literary

    xx **Authors and publishers; Authorship; Publishers and publishing**

Copyright—Books 341.7; 346.47

    x Books—Copyright

Coral reefs and islands 551.4

    x Atolls

    xx **Geology; Islands**

Corals 563; 593

    xx **Invertebrates; Marine animals**

Core curriculum. *See* **Education—Curricula;** also types of education and schools with the subdivision *Curricula,* e.g. **Library education—Curricula; Colleges and universities—Curricula;** etc.

Corn 633

    x Maize

    xx **Agriculture; Forage plants; Grain**

Coronary heart diseases. *See* **Heart—Diseases**

Corporate symbols. *See* **Trademarks**

Corporation law 346.6

    See also **Public service commissions; Public utilities; Trusts, Industrial**

    x Law, Corporation

    xx **Commercial law; Corporations; Law; Monopolies; Public utilities**

Corporations 338.7; 658.1

    See also

Conglomerate corporations	**Municipal ownership**
Cooperative societies	**Public service commissions**
Corporation law	**Public utilities**
Government ownership	**Trust companies**
International business enterprises	**Trusts, Industrial**

    x Companies

    xx **Business; Public utilities; Stocks; Trusts, Industrial**

Corporations—Accounting 657; 658.1

    xx **Accounting; Bookkeeping**

Corporations, Conglomerate. *See* **Conglomerate corporations**

Corporations—Finance 658.1

    x Capitalization (Finance)

Corporations, International. *See* **International business enterprises**

Corporations, Multinational. *See* **International business enterprises**

Corpulence. *See* **Obesity**

150

Correctional institutions 365

    See also types of correctional institutions, e.g. **Prisons; Reformatories;** etc.; also names of cities with the subdivision *Correctional institutions,* e.g. **Chicago —Correctional institutions;** etc.

    x Penal institutions

Correspondence. *See* **Business letters; Letter writing; Letters;** also subjects with the subdivision *Correspondence,* e.g. **Authors—Correspondence;** etc.

Correspondence schools and courses 374

    x Home education; Home study courses; Self-instruction

    xx **Education; Technical education; University extension**

Corrosion and anticorrosives 620.1

    See also **Paint**

    x Anticorrosive paint; Rust; Rustless coatings

    xx **Chemistry, Technical; Paint**

Corruption, Police. *See* **Police corruption**

Corruption in politics 324; 329

    See also **Campaign funds; Lobbying; Misconduct in office;** also names of specific incidents, e.g. **Watergate Affair, 1972– ;** etc.

    x Boss rule; Graft in politics; Political corruption; Political scandals; Politics, Corruption in; Spoils system

    xx **Conflict of interests; Lobbying; Misconduct in office; Political crimes and offenses; Political ethics; Politics, Practical**

Corsairs. *See* **Pirates**

Cosmetic surgery. *See* **Surgery, Plastic**

Cosmetics 646.7; 668

    See also **Perfumes**

    x Makeup (Cosmetics); Toilet preparations

    xx **Beauty shops; Costume**

Cosmic rays 539.7

    x Millikan rays

    xx **Nuclear physics; Radiation; Radioactivity; Space environment**

Cosmobiology. *See* **Space biology**

Cosmogony. *See* **Universe**

Cosmogony, Biblical. *See* **Creation**

Cosmography. *See* **Universe**

Cosmology. *See* **Universe**

Cosmology, Biblical. *See* **Creation**

Cosmonauts. *See* **Astronauts**

Cost accounting 657

    See also **Efficiency, Industrial**

    xx **Accounting; Bookkeeping**

Cost of living 339.4

    See also **Budgets, Household; Prices; Saving and thrift; Standard of living; Wages**

Cost of living—*Continued*

    x Consumer price index; Food, Cost of; Household finances; Living, Cost of

    xx **Economics; Home economics; Labor and laboring classes; Prices; Saving and thrift; Social conditions; Standard of living; Wages**

Cost of medical care. *See* **Medical care—Costs**

Costume   391; 792

    Use for descriptive and historical materials on the costume of particular countries or periods and for materials on fancy costume and theatrical costumes. Materials dealing with clothing from a practical standpoint, including the art of dress, are entered under **Clothing and dress.** Materials describing the prevailing mode or style in dress are entered under **Fashion**

    See also

Arms and armor	**Indians of North**
Children—Costume	**America—Cos-**
Clothing and dress	**tume and adorn-**
Cosmetics	**ment**
Fans	**Makeup, Theatrical**
Fashion	**Millinery**
Hats	**Uniforms, Military**
	Wigs

    x Acting—Costume; Fancy dress; Style in dress; Theatrical costume

    xx **Clothing and dress; Ethnology; Fashion; Manners and customs**

Costume, Military. *See* **Uniforms, Military**

Costume design. *See* **Fashion design**

Cottages. *See* **Houses**

Cotton   633

    See also **Fibers**

    xx **Botany, Economic; Commerce; Fibers; Yarn**

Cotton manufacture and trade   677

    xx **Textile industry**

Councils and synods   262

    See also names of special councils and synods, e.g. **Vatican Council, 2d, 1962–1965;** etc.

    x Church councils; Ecumenical councils; Synods

    xx **Christianity; Church history**

Counseling   361; 371.4

    Use for materials that treat of principles or practices used in various types of guidance work—students, employment, veterans, personnel

    See also **Crisis centers; Interviewing; Social case work;** also types of counseling, e.g. **Educational counseling; Hotlines (Telephone counseling); Marriage counseling;** etc.

    x Guidance

Counseling—*Continued*

   xx **Interviewing; Personnel management; Psychology, Applied; Social case work; Welfare work in industry**

Counter culture   301.44

   See also **Bohemianism; Collective settlements**

   x Alternative life style; Counterculture; Escape life style; Noncomformity

   xx **Collective settlements; Life styles; Social conditions**

Counter-Reformation.   *See* **Reformation**

Counterculture.   *See* **Counter culture**

Counterespionage.   *See* **Intelligence service**

Counterfeits and counterfeiting   332.9; 364.1

   xx **Coinage; Crime; Forgery; Impostors and imposture; Money; Swindlers and swindling**

Counterintelligence.   *See* **Intelligence service**

Counterpoint   781.4

   See also **Fugue**

   xx **Composition (Music); Music—Theory**

Counting   513; E

   See also **Number games**

   xx **Arithmetic—Study and teaching**

Country churches.   *See* **Rural churches**

Country houses.   *See* **Architecture, Domestic**

Country life (May subdiv. geog.)   **630.1**

   Use for descriptive, popular and literary materials on living in the country. Materials dealing with social organization and conditions in rural communities are entered under **Sociology, Rural**

   See also **Agriculture—Societies; Farm life; Outdoor life; Sociology, Rural**

   x Rural life

   xx **Farm life; Outdoor life; Sociology, Rural**

Country life—U.S.   630.1

   x U.S.—Country life

Country schools.   *See* **Rural schools**

County agricultural agents   630.7

   xx **Agricultural extension work; Agriculture—Study and teaching**

County government   352

   x County officers

   xx **Local government**

County libraries.   *See* **Libraries, County**

County officers.   *See* **County government**

County planning.   *See* **Regional planning**

Coups d'état.   *See* **Revolutions**

Courage   179

   See also **Fear; Heroes and heroines; Morale**

   x Bravery; Heroism

   xx **Fear; Heroes and heroines; Human behavior**

Courses of study.   *See* **Education—Curricula;** also types of education and schools with the subdivision *Curricula*, e.g. **Library education—Curricula; Colleges and universities—Curricula;** etc.

Court life. *See* **Courts and courtiers**

Court martial. *See* **Courts martial and courts of inquiry**

Courtesy 177; 395

    See also **Etiquette; Human behavior**

    x Manners; Politeness

    xx **Etiquette; Human behavior**

Courtiers. *See* **Courts and courtiers**

Courting. *See* **Dating (Social customs)**

Courts (May subdiv. geog.) **347.1**

    See also **Courts martial and courts of inquiry; Criminal procedure; Judges; Jury; Justice, Administration of; Juvenile courts**

    x Judiciary

    xx **Judges; Justice, Administration of; Law**

Courts–U.S. 347.1

    x Federal courts; U.S.—Courts

Courts and courtiers 390; 929.7

    See also **Kings and rulers; Queens**

    x Court life; Courtiers

    xx **Kings and rulers; Manners and customs; Queens**

Courts martial and courts of inquiry 343.1

    See also **Military law**

    x Court martial; Military courts

    xx **Courts; Military law; Trials**

Courtship. *See* **Dating (Social customs)**

Courtship of animals. *See* **Animals—Courtship**

Covens. *See* **Witches**

Coverlets. *See* **Bedspreads; Quilts**

Cow. *See* **Cows**

Cowboys. *See* **Cowhands**

Cowgirls. *See* **Cowhands**

Cowhands 917.8; 978

    See also **Rodeos**

    x Cowboys; Cowgirls; Gauchos

    xx **Frontier and pioneer life; Ranch life**

Cowhands–Filmstrips 917.802; 978.02

    xx **Audio-visual materials**

Cowhands–Songs and music 784.7

    xx **Music; Songs**

Cows 636.2

    See also **Dairying; Milk**

    x Cow; Dairy cattle

    xx **Cattle; Dairying; Livestock**

Cows—Diseases. *See* **Cattle—Diseases**

Crabs 565; 595

    xx **Crustacea**

Cradle songs. *See* **Lullabies**

Crafts. *See* **Arts and crafts; Handicraft**

Cranes, derricks, etc. 621.8

    x Derricks

    xx **Hoisting machinery**

Crayon drawing 741.2

    See also **Pastel drawing**

    x Blackboard drawing

    xx **Drawing; Pastel drawing; Portrait painting**

Creation 213; 233

    See also **Earth; Evolution; Geology; God; Man; Mythology; Theology; Universe**

    x Cosmogony, Biblical; Cosmology, Biblical

    xx **Earth; Evolution; Geology; God; Man; Natural theology; Religion and science; Universe**

Creation (Literary, artistic, etc.) 153.3

    See also **Creative ability**

    x Inspiration

    xx **Creative ability; Genius; Imagination; Intellect; Inventions**

Creative ability 153.3; 701; 801

    See also **Creation (Literary, artistic, etc.); Creative thinking**

    x Creativity

    xx **Ability; Creation (Literary, artistic, etc.); Creative thinking**

Creative movement 152.3

    x Motor coordination; Movement education

    xx **Creative thinking**

Creative thinking 153.4

    See also **Creative ability; Creative movement**

    xx **Creative ability**

Creativity. *See* **Creative ability**

Creatures, Imaginary. *See* **Animals, Mythical**

Credibility. *See* **Truthfulness and falsehood**

Credit 332.7

    See also **Agricultural credit; Banks and banking; Collecting of accounts; Consumer credit; Debtor and creditor; Debts, Public; Instalment plan; Loans; Negotiable instruments**

    x Bills of credit; Letters of credit

    xx **Banks and banking; Business; Debtor and creditor; Economics; Finance; Money**

Credit, Agricultural. *See* **Agricultural credit**

Credit, Consumer. *See* **Consumer credit**

Credit unions. *See* **Banks and banking, Cooperative**

Creeds 238

    See also **Apostles' Creed; Catechisms; Nicene Creed**

    x Confessions of faith; Faith, Confessions of

    xx **Catechisms; Church history; Theology**

Cremation 393; 614

    See also **Funeral rites and ceremonies**

    x Burial; Incineration; Mortuary customs

    xx **Funeral rites and ceremonies; Public health; Sanitation**

Creoles 917.6; 976

Crests. *See* **Heraldry**

Crewelwork 746.4

    xx **Embroidery**

Crime (May subdiv. geog.) **364**

> All types of crime are not included in this list. Add as needed
>
> *See also*

Assassination	**Organized crime**
Atrocities	**Parole**
Capital punishment	**Police**
Counterfeits and	**Prisons**
counterfeiting	**Prostitution**
Crime prevention	**Punishment**
Crimes without	**Racketeering**
victims	**Rape**
Criminal law	**Reformatories**
Criminals	**Riots**
Forgery	**Smuggling**
Justice, Administra-	**Swindlers and swin-**
tion of	**dling**
Juvenile delin-	**Treason**
quency	**Trials**
Lynching	**Vigilance commit-**
Murder	**tees**

> *x* Crimes; Criminology; Felony; Vice
>
> *xx* **Criminal justice, Administration of; Justice, Administration of; Police; Prisons; Punishment; Social ethics; Social problems; Trials**

Crime—U.S. 364

> *x* U.S.—Crime

Crime and narcotics. *See* **Narcotics and crime**

Crime prevention 364.4

> *See also* **Criminal psychology**
>
> *x* Prevention of crime
>
> *xx* **Crime**

Crime syndicates. *See* **Organized crime; Racketeering**

Crimean War, 1853–1856 947

> *x* Gt. Brit.—History—Crimean War, 1853–1856; Russo-Turkish War, 1853–1856

Crimes. *See* **Crime**

Crimes, Military. *See* **Military offenses**

Crimes, Political. *See* **Political crimes and offenses**

Crimes against public safety. *See* **Offenses against public safety**

Crimes against the person. *See* **Offenses against the person**

Crimes without victims 364.1

> *See also* names of crimes, e.g. **Drug abuse; Gambling**; etc.
>
> *x* Non-victim crimes; Victimless crimes
>
> *xx* **Crime; Criminal law**

Criminal assault. *See* **Rape**

Criminal investigation 364.12

> *See also* **Criminals—Identification; Detectives; Eavesdropping; Fingerprints; Medical jurisprudence; Police; Wiretapping**
>
> *xx* **Detectives; Police**

Criminal justice, Administration of 345

   See also **Crime; Pardon; Parole; Prisons; Punishment**

   x Administration of criminal justice

   xx **Criminal law**

Criminal law 345

   See also **Capital punishment; Crimes without victims; Criminal justice, administration of; Criminal procedure; Jury; Medical jurisprudence; Military offenses; Misconduct in office; Offenses against public safety; Offenses against the person; Probation; Punishment; Trials; Vigilance committees;** also names of crimes, e.g. **Murder;** etc.

   x Law, Criminal; Misdemeanors (Law); Penal codes; Penal law

   xx **Crime; Criminal procedure; Law; Prisons; Punishment**

Criminal procedure 345.5

   See also **Criminal law**

   xx **Courts; Criminal law**

Criminal psychology 364.3

   See also **Psychology, Pathological**

   x Psychology, Criminal

   xx **Crime prevention; Psychology, Pathological**

Criminals 364.1

   See also **Convict labor; Penal colonies; Pirates; Prisoners; Robbers and outlaws Swindlers and swindling**

   x Convicts; Delinquents; Gangs; Reform of criminals

   xx **Crime**

Criminals—Identification 364.12

   See also **Fingerprints**

   xx **Criminal investigation; Identification**

Criminals and drugs. *See* **Drugs and criminals**

Criminology. *See* **Crime**

Crippled children. *See* **Physically handicapped children**

Crippled people. *See* **Physically handicapped**

Crisis centers

   See also **Hotlines (Telephone counseling)**

   x Crisis intervention centers

   xx **Counseling; Hotlines (Telephone counseling); Social work**

Crisis counseling. *See* **Hotlines (Telephone counseling)**

Crisis intervention centers. *See* **Crisis centers**

Crisis intervention telephone service. *See* **Hotlines (Telephone counseling)**

Criticism 801

   Use for materials on the history, principles, methods, etc. of criticism in general and of literary criticism in particular. Criticism in a specific field is entered under the subject in variant forms as listed below. Criticism of the work of an individual author, artist, composer, etc. is entered under his/her name as subject; only in the case of voluminous authors is it necessary to add the subdivision *Criticism, interpretation, etc.* Criticism of a single work is entered under the person's name followed by the title of the work

See *also* **Art criticism; Bible—Criticism, interpretation, etc.; Books—Reviews; Dramatic criticism; Shakespeare, William—Criticism, interpretation, etc.; Style, Literary;** also literature, film, and music subjects with the subdivision *History and criticism,* e.g. **English literature—History and criticism; English poetry—History and criticism; Music—History and criticism;** etc.

x Appraisal of books; Books—Appraisal; Evaluation of literature; Literary criticism; Literature—Evaluation

xx **Esthetics; Literature; Literature—History and criticism; Rhetoric; Style, Literary**

Crocheting 746.4

See *also* **Beadwork; Lace and lace making**

Crockery. *See* **Pottery**

Crocodiles 598.1

For the American crocodiles use **Alligators**
See *also* **Alligators**
xx **Reptiles**

Cro-Magnons 573
xx **Man, Prehistoric**

Crop dusting. *See* **Aeronautics in agriculture**

Crop reports. *See* **Agriculture—Statistics**

Crop rotation. *See* **Rotation of crops**

Crops. *See* **Farm produce**

Crops, Rotation of. *See* **Rotation of crops**

Cross-country running. *See* **Track athletics**

Cross-examination. *See* **Witnesses**

Crossword puzzles 793.73
xx **Puzzles; Word games**

Crowds 301.18
See *also* **Demonstrations; Riots—Control; Social psychology**
x Mobs
xx **Riots; Social psychology**

Crucifixion of Christ. *See* **Jesus Christ—Crucifixion**

Crude oil. *See* **Petroleum**

Cruelty 179
See *also* **Atrocities**
x Brutality
xx **Ethics**

Cruelty to animals. *See* **Animals—Treatment**

Cruelty to children. *See* **Child abuse**

Crusades 909.07
See *also* **Chivalry**
xx **Chivalry; Church history—Middle Ages, 600–1500; Middle Ages—History**

Crustacea   565; 595

    See also names of shellfish, e.g. **Crabs; Lobsters;** etc.

    xx **Invertebrates; Shellfish**

Cryobiology   574.1

    See also **Cold—Physiological effect**

    x Freezing; Low temperature biology

    xx **Biology; Cold; Low temperatures**

Cryogenic internment.   *See* **Cryonics**

Cryogenic surgery.   *See* **Cryosurgery**

Cryogenics.   *See* **Low temperatures**

Cryonics   621.5

    x Burial; Cryogenic internment; Freezing of human bodies; Human cold storage

Cryosurgery   617

    x Cryogenic surgery

    xx **Cold—Therapeutic use; Surgery**

Cryptography   652

    See also **Ciphers**

    x Secret writing

    xx **Ciphers; Signs and symbols; Writing**

Crystal gazing.   *See* **Divination**

Crystalline rocks.   *See* **Rocks**

Crystallization.   *See* **Crystallography**

Crystallography   548

    See also **Mineralogy**

    x Crystallization; Crystals

    xx **Chemistry, Physical and theoretical; Petrology; Rocks; Science**

Crystals.   *See* **Crystallography**

Cub Scouts.   *See* **Boy Scouts**

Cuba   917.291; 972.91

    xx **Islands**

Cuba—History   972.91

Cuba—History—Revolution, 1958–1959   972.91

Cuba—History—1959–   972.91

Cuba—History—Invasion, 1961   972.91

    x Bay of Pigs invasion; Operation Pluto; Pluto operation

Cubism   709.04; 759.06

    See also **Postimpressionism (Art)**

    xx **Painting; Postimpressionism (Art)**

Cults and sects.   *See* **Sects**

Cultural change.   *See* **Social change**

Cultural relations   301.24; 341.7

    See also **Exchange of persons programs**

    x Intercultural relations

    xx **Intellectual cooperation; International cooperation; International relations**

Culturally deprived.   *See* **Socially handicapped**

Culturally deprived children.   *See* **Socially handicapped children**

Culturally handicapped.   *See* **Socially handicapped**

Culturally handicapped children.   *See* **Socially handicapped children**

Culture   301.2; 901.9

    Use for general discussions of refinement in manners, taste, etc. and the intellectual content of civilization. Ma-

159

Culture—*Continued*

terials limited to the culture of individual nations are entered under names of countries with subdivisions *Civilization* or *Social life and customs*

See also **Acculturation; Biculturalism; Civilization; Education; Humanism; Learning and scholarship**

x Intellectual life

xx **Civilization; Education; Learning and scholarship**

Curates. *See* **Clergy**

Curiosities and wonders   001.9

See also subjects with the subdivision *Miscellanea*, e.g. **Medicine—Miscellanea; Music—Miscellanea;** etc.

x Enigmas; Oddities; Wonders

Currency. *See* **Money**

Currency devaluation. *See* **Monetary policy**

Current events   909.82

Use for materials on the study and teaching of current events. Periodicals and yearbooks devoted to the events themselves are entered under **History—Periodicals; History—Yearbooks**

xx **History, Modern—Study and teaching**

Currents, Alternating. *See* **Electric currents, Alternating**

Currents, Electric. *See* **Electric currents**

Curricula (Courses of study). *See* **Education —Curricula;** also types of education and schools with the subdivision *Curricula*, e.g. **Library education—Curricula; Colleges and universities— Curricula;** etc.

Curriculum materials centers. *See* **Instructional materials centers**

Curtains. *See* **Drapery**

Customs (Tariff). *See* **Tariff**

Customs, Social. *See* **Manners and customs;** and names of ethnic groups, countries, cities, etc. with the subdivision *Social life and customs*, e.g. **Indians of North America—Social life and customs; Jews—Social life and customs; U.S.— Social life and customs;** etc.

Cybernetics   001.53

See also **Bionics; Computers; System analysis; Systems engineering**

x Automatic control; Biotechnology; Mechanical brains

xx **Calculating machines; Communication; Electronics**

Cycles. *See* **Periodicity**

Cycles, Business. *See* **Business cycles**

Cycles, Motor. *See* **Motorcycles**

Cycling. *See* **Bicycles and bicycling; Motorcycles**

160

Cyclones 551.5

>   Materials on the cylonic storms of the
>   West Indies are entered under **Hurri-**
>   **canes.** Storms of the China Seas and
>   the Phillippines are entered under
>   **Typhoons**

>   *xx* **Hurricanes; Meteorology; Storms; Tor-**
>   **nadoes; Winds**

Cyclopedias. *See* **Encyclopedias**

Cyclotron 539.7; 621.48

>   *x* Atom smashing; Magnetic resonance ac-
>   celerator

>   *xx* **Atoms; Nuclear physics; Transmutation**
>   **(Chemistry)**

Cytology. *See* **Cells**

Czechoslovakia 914.37; 943.7

Czechoslovakia—History—Intervention, 1968–
943.7

>   *x* Russian intervention in Czechoslovakia;
>   Soviet invasion of Czechoslovakia

D Day. *See* **Normandy, Attack on, 1944**

DDT (Insecticide) 668

>   *x* Dichloro-diphenyl-trichloroethane
>   *xx* **Insecticides**

DNA 574.8

>   *x* Deoxyribonucleic acid; Desoxyribonu-
>   cleic acid
>   *xx* **Cells; Heredity**

Dairies. *See* **Dairying**

Dairy cattle. *See* **Cows**

Dairy products 637; 641.3

>   *See also* **Dairying;** also names of dairy
>   products, e.g. **Butter; Cheese; Milk;**
>   etc.
>   *x* Products, Dairy
>   *xx* **Dairying**

Dairying 637

>   *See also* **Cattle; Cows; Dairy products; Milk**
>   *x* Dairies
>   *xx* **Agriculture; Cattle; Cows; Dairy prod-**
>   **ucts; Home economics; Livestock**

Dams 627

>   *See also* names of dams, e.g. **Hoover Dam;**
>   etc.
>   *xx* **Civil engineering; Floods—Control; Hy-**
>   **draulic structures; Irrigation; Rivers;**
>   **Water power; Water supply**

Dance music 781.5; 785.4

>   *See also* **Jazz music; Music, Popular (Songs,**
>   **etc.)**
>   *xx* **Dancing; Instrumental music; Music**

Dancers 920; 927

>   *See also* types of dancers, e.g. **Ballet**
>   **dancers;** etc.
>   *xx* **Entertainers**

Dancing (May subdiv. geog.) **793.3**

>   *See also* **Dance music;** also types of dances
>   and dancing, e.g. **Ballet; Clog dancing;**

Dancing—*Continued*

    Folk dancing; Modern dance; Tap dancing; etc.

  xx **Amusements; Etiquette**

Dancing—U.S. 793.3

  x U.S.—Dancing

Dangerous occupations. *See* **Occupations, Dangerous**

Danish language 439.8

  May be subdivided like **English language**

  xx **Norwegian language; Scandinavian languages**

Danish literature 839.8

  May use same subdivisions and names of literary forms as for **English literature**

  xx **Scandinavian literature**

Dark Ages. *See* **Middle Ages**

Darkroom technique in photography. *See* **Photography—Processing**

Darwinism. *See* **Evolution**

Data processing. *See* **Electronic data processing; Information storage and retrieval systems;** and subjects with the subdivision *Data processing,* e.g. **Banks and banking—Data processing;** etc.

Data storage and retrieval systems. *See* **Information storage and retrieval systems**

Date etiquette. *See* **Dating (Social customs)**

Dates, Historical. *See* **Chronology, Historical**

Dating, Radiocarbon. *See* **Radiocarbon dating**

Dating (Social customs) 301.41; 392

  See also **Love**

  x Courting; Courtship; Date etiquette

  xx **Etiquette; Love; Marriage**

Day care centers. *See* **Child care centers**

Day dreams. *See* **Fantasy**

Day nurseries. *See* **Child care centers**

Days. *See* **Birthdays; Fasts and feasts; Festivals; Holidays;** and names of special days, e.g. **Christmas; Memorial Day;** etc.

The dead, Worship of. *See* **Ancestor worship**

Dead Sea scrolls 229

  x Qumran texts

Deaf 362.4

  xx **Physically handicapped**

Deaf—Education 371.9

  x Education of the deaf

  xx **Education; Vocational education; Vocational guidance**

Deaf—Institutional care 362.4

  x Asylums; Charitable institutions; Homes (Institutions)

Deaf—Means of communication 419

  x Finger alphabet; Lip reading; Sign language

Deafness   362.4; 617.8
   See also **Ear; Hearing; Hearing aids**
   xx **Hearing**
Death   128; 236
   See also **Bereavement; Future life; Heaven;
      Hell; Mortality; Terminal care**
   xx **Biology; Eschatology; Life; Mortality**
Death, Mercy.   *See* **Euthanasia**
Death masks.   *See* **Masks (Sculpture)**
Death notices.   *See* **Obituaries**
Death penalty.   *See* **Capital punishment**
Death rate.   *See* **Mortality; Vital statistics**
Deaths, Registers of.   *See* **Registers of births,
      etc.**
Debates and debating   808.53
   See also **Discussion groups; Parliamentary
      practice; Radio addresses, debates, etc.**
   x Argumentation; Discussion; Speaking
   xx **Public speaking; Rhetoric**
Debtor and creditor   332.7; 346.7
   Use for economic and statistical materials
      about debt as well as for legal ma-
      terials involving debtor and creditor
   See also **Bankruptcy; Collecting of ac-
      counts; Credit**
   xx **Commercial law; Credit**
Debts, Public (May subdiv. geog.)   336.3
   See also **Bonds;** and names of wars with
      the subdivision *Finance,* e.g. **World
      War, 1939–1945–Finance;** etc.
   x National debts; Public debts; State
      debts; War debts
   xx **Bonds; Credit; Economics; Finance;
      Loans**
Debts, Public–U.S.   336.973
   x U.S.—Debts, Public; U.S.—Public debts
Decalogue.   *See* **Ten commandments**
Decentralization of schools.   *See* **Schools–De-
      centralization**
Deceptive advertising.   *See* **Advertising, Fraud-
      ulent**
Decision making   153.8; 658.4
Declamations, Musical.   *See* **Monologues with
      music**
Declaration of Independence.   *See* **U.S. Decla-
      ration of Independence**
Decoration, Interior.   *See* **Interior decoration**
Decoration and ornament (May subdiv. geog.
      adjective form, e.g. **Decoration and
      ornament, Mexican;** etc.)   745; 745.4
   Use for materials dealing with the forms
      and styles of decoration in various
      fields of fine arts or applied art; the
      history of such styles of ornament as
      Empire, Louis XV, etc.; and with
      manifestation in different countries
      or periods, as Chinese, Renaissance.
      Materials limited to the decoration
      of houses are entered under **Interior
      decoration.** Materials limited to the

Decoration and ornament—*Continued*
> application of decoration to objects
> are entered under **Design, Decorative**

See also

Alphabets	**Interior decoration**
Art, Decorative	**Ironwork**
Bronzes	**Jewelry**
Carpets	**Leatherwork**
Design	**Lettering**
Design, Decorative	**Metalwork**
Enamel and enam-	**Mosaics**
eling	**Painting**
Flower arrange-	**Plants in art**
ment	**Pottery**
Furniture	**Sculpture**
Gems	**Stencil work**
Holiday decora-	**Stucco**
tions	**Table setting and**
Illumination of	**decoration**
books and manu-	**Tapestry**
scripts	**Terra cotta**
Illustration of books	**Wood carving**

> *x* Decorative arts; Ornament
> *xx* **Art, Decorative; Arts and crafts; Design,**
> **Decorative**

Decoration and ornament, American 745; 745.4
> *x* American decoration and ornament;
> U.S.—Decoration and ornament

Decoration and ornament, Architectural   729
> Use same form for other types of decora-
> tion and ornament
> *x* Architectural decoration and ornament;
> Architecture—Decoration and orna-
> ment
> *xx* **Architecture**

Decoration Day.   *See* **Memorial Day**

Decorations, Holiday.   *See* **Holiday decora-**
tions

Decorations of honor   355.1; 929.7
> *See also* **Heraldry; Insignia; Medals**
> *x* Badges of honor; Emblems
> *xx* **Heraldry; Insignia; Medals**

Decorative art.   *See* **Art, Decorative**

Decorative arts.   *See* **Art, Decorative; Art in-**
dustries and trade; Arts and crafts;
Decoration and ornament; Design,
Decorative; Interior decoration; and
the subjects referred to under these
headings

Decorative metalwork.   *See* **Art metalwork**

Decoupage   745.54
> *xx* **Paper crafts**

Deduction (Logic).   *See* **Logic**

Deep diving vehicles.   *See* **Submersibles**

Deep sea diving.   *See* **Diving, Submarine**

Deep sea technology.   *See* **Oceanography**

Deep sea vehicles.   *See* **Submersibles**

Deep submergence vehicles.   *See* **Submersibles**

Deer   599
   See also **Reindeer**
   xx **Game and game birds**
Defamation.   *See* **Libel and slander**
Defective speech.   *See* **Speech disorders**
Defective vision.   *See* **Vision disorders**
Defectors, Military.   *See* **Desertion, Military**
Defense, Civil.   *See* **Civil defense**
Defense policy.   *See* **Military policy**
Defenses, Air.   *See* **Air defenses**
Defenses, National.   *See* **Industrial mobilization;** and names of countries with the subdivision *Defenses,* e.g. **U.S.—Defenses;** etc.
Defenses, Radar.   *See* **Radar defense networks**
Degrees, Academic   378
   x Academic degrees; College degrees; Doctors' degrees; Honorary degrees; University degrees
   xx **Colleges and universities**
Degrees of latitude and longitude.   *See* **Geodesy; Latitude; Longitude**
Dehydrated foods.   *See* **Food, Dried**
Dehydrated milk.   *See* **Milk, Dried**
Deism   211
   See also **Atheism; Christianity; Free thought; God; Positivism; Rationalism; Theism**
   xx **Atheism; Christianity; God; Pantheism; Rationalism; Religion; Theism; Theology**
Deities.   *See* **Gods**
Delinquency, Juvenile.   *See* **Juvenile delinquency**
Delinquents.   *See* **Criminals; Juvenile delinquency**
Delusions.   *See* **Hallucinations and illusions; Superstition; Witchcraft**
Democracy   321.4; 321.8
   See also

Aristocracy	**Referendum**
Equality	**Representative government and representation**
Federal government	
Freedom	**Republics**
Middle classes	**Socialism**
Monarchy	**Suffrage**

   x Popular government; Self-government
   xx **Aristocracy; Constitutional history; Constitutional law; Equality; Federal government; Monarchy; Political science; Representative government and representation; Republics**
Democratic Party   329.3
   xx **Political parties**
Demoniac possession   133.4
   See also **Devil; Exorcism**
   xx **Devil; Exorcism**

Demonology   133.4

See also **Apparitions; Charms; Devil; Exorcism; Occult sciences; Superstition; Witchcraft**

x Evil spirits; Spirits

xx **Apparitions; Devil; Exorcism; Ghosts; Occult sciences; Superstition; Witchcraft**

Demonstrations (May subdiv. geog. country or state)   **322.4**

Use for materials on large public gatherings, marches, etc. organized for non-violent protest even though incidental disturbances or incipient rioting may occur

See also **Riots; Youth movement;** also cities and institutions with the subdivision *Demonstrations,* e.g. **Chicago— Demonstrations;** etc.

x Marches (Demonstrations); Protest marches and rallies; Protests; Public demonstrations

xx **Crowds; Riots**

Demonstrations—U.S.   **322.4**

x U.S.—Demonstrations

Demonstrations for black civil rights—U.S. See **Blacks—Civil rights**

Demountable houses.   See **Prefabricated houses**

Denatured alcohol.   See **Alcohol, Denatured**

Denominational schools.   See **Church schools**

Denominations, Religious.   See **Sects;** and names of particular denominations and sects

Dentistry   **617.6**

See also **Teeth**

x Medicine, Dental

xx **Teeth**

Deoxyribonucleic acid.   See **DNA**

Department stores   **658.8**

See also **Selling**

x Stores

xx **Business; Retail trade**

Dependencies.   See **Colonies; Colonization**

Dependent children.   See **Child welfare; Orphans**

Depressions, Economic   **338.5**

x Business depressions; Economic depressions; Panics, Economic

xx **Business cycles; Economics**

Derailments.   See **Railroads—Accidents**

Dermatitis.   See **Skin—Diseases**

Derricks.   See **Cranes, derricks, etc.**

Descent.   See **Genealogy; Heredity**

Description.   See names of cities with the subdivision *Description* (e.g. **Chicago— Description;** etc.); names of modern countries, states and regions with the subdivision *Description and travel* (e.g. **U.S.—Description and travel;** etc.); and names of ancient countries with

Description—*Continued*

the subdivision *Description and geography,* e.g. **Greece—Description and geography;** etc.

Descriptive geometry. *See* **Geometry, Descriptive**

Desegregated schools. *See* **School integration**

Desegregation in education. *See* **School integration**

Desert animals 591.5

See also names of desert animals, e.g. **Camels;** etc.

xx **Animals; Deserts; Geographical distribution of animals and plants**

Desert plants 581.5

See also names of desert plants, e.g. **Cactus;** etc.

xx **Botany—Ecology; Deserts; Geographical distribution of animals and plants; Plants**

Desertion, Military (May subdiv. geog.) **355.1**

See also **Amnesty; Military service, Compulsory—Draft resisters;** also names of wars with the subdivision *Desertions,* e.g., **World War, 1939–1945—Desertions;** etc.

x Army desertion; Defectors, Military; Military desertion

xx **Military offenses; Military service, Compulsory—Draft resisters**

Desertion, Military—U.S. 355.1

x U.S. Army—Desertions

Desertion and nonsupport 173; 301.42

x Nonsupport

xx **Divorce**

Deserts 551.4

See also **Desert animals; Desert plants**

Design 745.4

Use for materials on the theory of design

See also **Fashion design; Pattern making; Textile design**

xx **Decoration and ornament; Pattern making**

Design, Architectural. *See* **Architecture—Details**

Design, Decorative 745; 745.4

Use for materials dealing with purely ornamental features of design, e.g. design applied externally to objects. Materials dealing with practical applications of the line, form or mass which objects may take are entered under **Design, Industrial**

See also **Art, Decorative; Decoration and ornament; Drawing; Illumination of books and manuscripts; Lettering; Tapestry; Textile design**

x Decorative arts; Designs, Floral; Floral design; Flowers in art; Nature in or-

167

Design, Decorative—*Continued*
  nament; Ornamental design; Plant forms in design
  xx **Art; Art, Decorative; Arts and crafts; Decoration and ornament; Drawing**
Design, Industrial **745.2**
  See also **Human engineering; Systems engineering**
  x Art, Applied; Industrial design
  xx **Art industries and trade**
Designs, Architectural. *See* **Architecture—Designs and plans**
Designs, Floral. *See* **Design, Decorative; Flower arrangement**
Desoxyribonucleic acid. *See* **DNA**
Desserts **641.8**
  See also names of desserts, e.g. **Ice cream, ices, etc.;** etc.
  xx **Caterers and catering; Cookery; Dinners and dining**
Destiny. *See* **Fate and fatalism**
Destitution. *See* **Poverty**
Details, Architectural. *See* **Architecture—Details**
Detective stories. *See* **Mystery and detective stories**
Detectives **351.7; 363.2**
  See also **Criminal investigation; Police; Secret service**
  xx **Criminal investigation; Police; Secret service**
Detergent pollution of rivers, lakes, etc. **614.7; 628.1**
  x Water—Detergent pollution
  xx **Detergents, Synthetic; Water—Pollution**
Detergents, Synthetic **668**
  See also **Detergent pollution of rivers, lakes, etc.**
  x Synthetic detergents
  xx **Cleaning compounds; Soap**
Determinism and indeterminism. *See* **Free will and determinism**
Deuterium oxide **546**
  x Heavy water; Water—Heavy water
Devaluation of currency. *See* **Monetary policy**
Developing areas **330.9**
  See also **Economic assistance; States, New; Technical assistance**
  x Developing countries; Third World; Underdeveloped areas
  xx **Economic assistance; Economic conditions; Industrialization; Technical assistance**
Developing countries. *See* **Developing areas**
Development. *See* **Embryology; Evolution**
Devices (Heraldry). *See* **Heraldry; Insignia; Symbolism**
Devil **235**
  See also **Demoniac possession; Demonology**

Devil—*Continued*

    x Satan

    xx **Demoniac possession; Demonology; Folklore**

Devil's triangle. *See* **Bermuda triangle**

Devotion. *See* **Devotional exercises; Prayer; Worship**

Devotional exercises 242; 248

    See also **Church music; Hymns; Liturgies; Prayer**

    x Devotion; Family devotions; Family prayers; Theology, Devotional

    xx **Prayer; Worship**

Devotional literature 242

    xx **Literature**

Dewey Decimal Classification. *See* **Classification, Dewey Decimal**

Diagnosis 616

    See also **Pain; Pathology**

    x Symptoms

    xx **Medicine—Practice; Pathology**

Diagrams, Statistical. *See* **Statistics—Graphic methods**

Dialectics. *See* **Logic**

Dialects. *See* names of languages with the subdivision *Dialects,* e.g. **English language—Dialects;** etc.

Diamonds 553

    xx **Carbon; Precious stones**

Diaries. *See* **Autobiographies**

Dichloro-diphenyl-trichloroethane. *See* **DDT (Insecticide)**

Dictators 920; 923

    xx **Kings and rulers; Totalitarianism**

Dictionaries 403; 413; etc.

    See also **Dictionaries, Polyglot;** and names of languages and subjects with the subdivision *Dictionaries,* e.g. **English language—Dictionaries; Chemistry—Dictionaries; English literature—Dictionaries; U.S.—Biography—Dictionaries;** etc.

Dictionaries, Classical. *See* **Classical dictionaries**

Dictionaries, Polyglot 413

    x Polyglot dictionaries

    xx **Dictionaries**

Dies (Metalworking) 621.9; 671.2

    xx **Metalwork**

Diesel automobiles. *See* **Automobiles, Diesel**

Diesel engines 621.43

    xx **Engines; Gas and oil engines**

Diet 613.2

    See also **Beverages; Cookery; Digestion; Food, Dietetic; Menus; Nutrition; School children—Food; Vegetarianism;** also names of diets, e.g. **Salt free diet;** etc.

    x Dietetics

    xx **Cookery; Digestion; Hygiene; Nutrition**

Diet in disease   615

    See also **Cookery for the sick;** also names
        of diets, e.g. **Salt free diet;** etc.

    x Diet therapy; Dieting

    xx **Therapeutics**

Diet therapy.   *See* **Diet in disease**

Dietetic food.   *See* **Food, Dietetic**

Dietetics.   *See* **Diet**

Dieting.   *See* **Diet in disease; Reducing**

Digestion   574.1; 612

    See also **Diet; Food; Indigestion; Nutrition**

    xx **Diet; Nutrition; Physiological chemistry;
        Physiology; Stomach**

Diners.   *See* **Restaurants, bars, etc.**

Dinners and dining   642

    See also **Carving (Meat, etc.); Cookery;
        Desserts; Food; Menus**

    x Banquets; Eating; Gastronomy

    xx **Caterers and catering; Cookery; Enter-
        taining; Etiquette; Food; Menus**

Dinosaurs   568

    xx **Reptiles, Fossil**

Dioptrics.   *See* **Refraction**

Diphtheria   616.9

    xx **Children–Diseases; Diseases**

Diplomacy   327; 341.3

    See also **Diplomatic and consular service;
        Diplomats; Treaties;** also names of
        countries with the subdivision *Foreign
        relations,* e.g. **U.S.–Foreign relations;**
        etc.

    xx **Diplomatic and consular service; Inter-
        national relations**

Diplomatic and consular service   341.3

    See also **Diplomacy; Diplomats;** also names
        of countries with the subdivision *Dip-
        lomatic and consular service,* e.g. **U.S.
        –Diplomatic and consular service;** etc.

    x Consulates; Embassies; Foreign service;
        Legations

    xx **Diplomacy; Diplomats; International re-
        lations**

Diplomats   920; 923

    See also **Diplomatic and consular service**

    x Ambassadors; Consuls; Ministers (Diplo-
        matic agents)

    xx **Diplomacy; Diplomatic and consular
        service; International relations; Poli-
        ticians**

Dipsomania.   *See* **Alcoholism**

Diptera.   *See* **Flies; Mosquitoes**

Direct current machinery.   *See* **Electric ma-
    chinery–Direct current**

Direct legislation.   *See* **Referendum**

Direct primaries.   *See* **Primaries**

Direct taxation.   *See* **Income tax; Taxation**

Directing (Theater).   *See* **Theater–Production
    and direction**

Direction sense.   *See* **Orienteering**

Directories 025

Use for materials about directories and for bibliographies of directories

See also subjects and names of countries, cities, etc. with the subdivision *Directories,* e.g. **Junior colleges—Directories; Physicians—Directories; U.S.—Directories;** etc.

Directories—Telephone. *See* names of cities with the subdivision *Directories—Telephone,* e.g. **Chicago—Directories—Telephone;** etc.

Directory, French, 1795–1799. *See* **France—History—Revolution, 1789–1799**

Dirigible balloons. *See* **Airships**

Disability insurance. *See* **Insurance, Accident; Insurance, Health**

Disabled. *See* **Handicapped**

Disadvantaged. *See* **Socially handicapped**

Disadvantaged children. *See* **Socially handicapped children**

Disarmament 327; 341.73

See also **Arbitration, International; Peace; Sea power; Security, International**

x Armaments; Arms control; Atomic weapons and disarmament; Limitation of armament; Military power; Nonproliferation of nuclear weapons; Nuclear test ban

xx **Arbitration, International; Armies; International relations; Military art and science; Navies; Peace; Sea power; Security, International; War**

Disaster relief 361.5

See also **Civil defense**

x Emergency relief

xx **Civil defense**

Disasters 904

See also types of disasters, e.g. **Accidents; Fires; Natural disasters; Railroads—Accidents; Shipwrecks;** etc.; also names of particular disasters, e.g. **New England—Hurricane, 1938; San Francisco—Earthquake and fire, 1906;** etc.

x Catastrophes

xx **Accidents**

Disciples, Twelve. *See* **Apostles**

Disciples of Christ 286

x Campbellites; Christian Church (Disciples); Church of Christ (Disciples)

Discipline of children. *See* **School discipline**

Discography. *See* **Sound recordings;** and subjects and names of persons with the subdivision *Discography,* e.g. **Music—Discography; Shakespeare, William—Discography;** etc.

Discoverers. *See* **Discoveries (in geography); Explorers**

Discoveries (in geography)   910

See also **America—Exploration; Antarctic regions; Arctic regions; Explorers; Northeast Passage; Northwest Passage; Scientific expeditions; Voyages and travels;** also names of countries with the subdivision Description and travel, e.g. **U.S.—Description and travel;** etc.

x Discoverers; Discoveries, Maritime; Explorations; Maritime discoveries; Navigators

xx **Adventure and adventurers; Explorers; Geography; History; Voyages and travels**

Discoveries (in science).   See **Inventions; Patents; Science**

Discoveries, Maritime.   See **Discoveries (in geography)**

Discrimination   177; 301.44-301.45

Use for general materials on discrimination by race, religion, sex, age, social status, or other factors

See also **Age discrimination; Civil rights; Minorities; Race discrimination; Segregation; Sex discrimination; Toleration**

xx **Blacks; Human relations; Minorities; Race relations; Segregation; Social problems; Toleration**

Discrimination, Age.   See **Age discrimination**

Discrimination, Racial.   See **Race discrimination**

Discrimination, Sex.   See **Sex discrimination**

Discrimination in education   370.19

See also **Segregation in education**

x Education, Discrimination in

xx **Segregation in education; Race discrimination**

Discrimination in employment   331.1

See also **Affirmative action programs; Age and employment; Equal pay for equal work;** also names of groups of people with the subdivision Employment, e.g. **Blacks—Employment; Men—Employment; Women—Employment;** etc.

x EEO; Employment discrimination; Equal employment opportunity; Equal opportunity in employment; Fair employment practice; Job discrimination; Right to work

Discrimination in housing   301.5

x Fair housing; Housing, Discrimination in; Open housing; Segregation in housing

Discrimination in public accommodations 301.6

x Public accommodations, Discrimination in; Segregation in public accommodations

Discussion.   See **Conversation; Debates and debating**

Discussion groups 374.2

    x Forums (Discussions); Great books program; Group discussion; Panel discussions

    xx **Debates and debating**

Disease (Pathology). *See* **Pathology**

Disease germs. *See* **Bacteriology; Germ theory of disease**

Diseases 614.4; 616

    See also **Epidemics; Medicine—Practice;** also names of diseases and groups of diseases (e.g. **Diphtheria; Communicable diseases;** etc.); and subjects with the subdivision *Diseases,* e.g. **Animals —Diseases; Children—Diseases; Skin— Diseases;** etc.

Diseases, Communicable. *See* **Communicable diseases**

Diseases, Contagious. *See* **Communicable diseases**

Diseases, Industrial. *See* **Occupational diseases**

Diseases, Infectious. *See* **Communicable diseases**

Diseases, Mental. *See* **Mental illness; Psychology, Pathological**

Diseases, Occupational. *See* **Occupational diseases**

Diseases, Tropical. *See* **Tropics—Diseases and hygiene**

Diseases and pests. *See* **Agricultural pests; Bacteriology, Agricultural; Fungi; Household pests; Insects, Injurious and beneficial; Parasites; Plants—Diseases;** names of individual pests (e.g. **Locusts;** etc.); and names of crops, etc. with the subdivision *Diseases and pests,* e.g. **Fruit—Diseases and pests;** etc.

Diseases of animals. *See* **Animals—Diseases**

Diseases of children. *See* **Children—Diseases**

Diseases of occupation. *See* **Occupational diseases**

Diseases of plants. *See* **Plants—Diseases**

Diseases of the blood. *See* **Blood—Diseases**

Diseases of women. *See* **Women—Diseases**

Dishes. *See* **Glassware; Porcelain; Pottery**

Dishonesty. *See* **Honesty**

Disinfection and disinfectants 614.7; 648

    See also **Antiseptics; Fumigation**

    x Germicides

    xx **Antiseptics; Bacteriology; Chemistry, Medical and pharmaceutical; Communicable diseases; Fumigation; Hygiene; Public health; Sanitation**

Disneyland 791.06

    xx **Amusement parks**

Disobedience. *See* **Obedience**

Displaced persons. *See* **Refugees; Refugees, Political;** and names of wars with the subdivision *Displaced persons,* e.g.

Displaced persons—*Continued*
  World War, 1939–1945–Displaced persons; etc.
Disposal of refuse. *See* **Refuse and refuse disposal**
Disputes, Labor. *See* **Labor disputes**
Dissent 322.4
  x Noncomformity; Protest
  xx **Conformity**
Dissertations, Academic 378.1
  Use for materials about theses and dissertations
  x Academic dissertations; Doctoral theses; Theses
  xx **Colleges and universities**
Distillation 641.2; 663
  See also **Alcohol; Essences and essential oils; Liquors and liqueurs**
  x Stills
  xx **Alcohol; Liquors and liqueurs**
Distribution (Economics). *See* **Commerce; Marketing**
Distribution, Cooperative. *See* **Cooperation; Cooperative societies**
Distribution of animals and plants. *See* **Geographical distribution of animals and plants**
Distribution of wealth. *See* **Economics; Wealth**
District libraries. *See* **Libraries, Regional**
District nurses. *See* **Nurses**
District schools. *See* **Rural schools**
Districting (in city planning). *See* **Zoning**
Dividends. *See* **Securities; Stocks**
Divination 133.3
  See also **Astrology; Clairvoyance; Dreams; Fortune telling; Occult sciences; Oracles; Palmistry; Prophecies (Occult sciences); Superstition**
  x Crystal gazing; Necromancy; Soothsaying
  xx **Clairvoyance; Occult sciences; Oracles; Prophecies (Occult sciences); Supernatural; Superstition**
Divine healing. *See* **Christian Science; Faith healing; Miracles**
Diving 797.2
  See also **Scuba diving; Skin diving**
  xx **Swimming; Water sports**
Diving, Scuba. *See* **Scuba diving**
Diving, Skin. *See* **Skin diving**
Diving, Submarine 627.7
  See also **Scuba diving; Skin diving; Underwater exploration**
  x Deep sea diving; Submarine diving
  xx **Oceanography–Research; Underwater exploration**
Divinity of Christ. *See* **Jesus Christ–Divinity**
Division of powers. *See* **Separation of powers**
Divorce 173; 301.42; 346.1

Divorce—*Continued*

 See also **Desertion and non-support; Marriage; Marriage—Annulment**

 x Separation (Law)

 xx **Domestic relations; Family; Marriage; Marriage—Annulment; Men—Social conditions; Social problems; Women—Social conditions**

Docks **386; 387.1; 627**

 See also **Harbors**

 xx **Harbors; Hydraulic structures; Marinas**

Doctoral theses. *See* **Dissertations, Academic**

Doctors. *See* **Physicians**

Doctors' degrees. *See* **Degrees, Academic**

Doctrinal theology. *See* **Theology, Doctrinal**

Documentary films. *See* **Motion pictures, Documentary**

Documentation **029**

 See also **Archives; Bibliographic control; Bibliography; Cataloging; Classification—Books; Information storage and retrieval systems; Library science;** also subjects with the subdivision *Documentation*, e.g. **Agriculture—Documentation;** etc.

 xx **Information science**

Documents. *See* **Archives; Charters; Government publications**

Dog. *See* **Dogs**

Dog guides. *See* **Guide dogs**

Dogmatic theology. *See* **Theology, Doctrinal**

Dogs **599; 636.7**

 See also classes of dogs, e.g. **Guide dogs;** etc.; also names of specific breeds, e.g. **Collies;** etc.

 x Dog

 xx **Pets**

Dogs—Fiction **FIC E SC**

 xx **Animals—Fiction**

Dogs—Psychology **156**

 xx **Animal intelligence; Psychology, Comparative**

Dogs—Training **636.7**

 xx **Animals—Training**

Dogs, War use of **355.4**

 xx **Animals, War use of**

Dogs for the blind. *See* **Guide dogs**

Dogs in literature **809**

 xx **Animals in literature**

Doll. *See* **Dolls**

Dollhouses **688.7**

 x Miniature objects

 xx **Toys**

Dolls **688.7**

 x Doll

 xx **Toys**

Domesday book **942.02**

 x Doomsday book

Domestic animals **636**

Use for general materials on farm animals.

Domestic animals—*Continued*

Materials limited to animals as pets are entered under **Pets.** Materials on stock raising as an industry are entered under **Livestock.** Names of all animals are not included in this list but are to be added as needed

See also **Animals—Treatment; Livestock;** and names of domestic animals, e.g. **Cats; Cattle; Pets; Poultry; Reindeer;** etc.

x Animal industry; Animals, Domestic; Farm animals

xx **Agriculture; Animals; Livestock; Pets; Zoology, Economic**

Domestic animals—Diseases. *See* **Animals— Diseases**

Domestic appliances. *See* **Household appliances, Electric; Household equipment and supplies**

Domestic architecture. *See* **Architecture, Domestic**

Domestic arts. *See* **Home economics**

Domestic finance. *See* **Budgets, Household**

Domestic relations 301.42

See also **Divorce; Family; Marriage; Parent and child**

x Family relations

xx **Family; Marriage**

Domestic workers. *See* **Household employees**

Dominicans 271

x Black Friars; Friars, Black; Friars preachers; Jacobins (Dominicans); Mendicant orders; Preaching Friars; St. Dominic, Order of

xx **Religious orders for men, Catholic**

Dominion of the sea. *See* **Sea power**

Donations. *See* **Gifts**

Doomsday book. *See* **Domesday book**

Door to door selling. *See* **Peddlers and peddling**

Doors 729

xx **Architecture—Details; Building; Carpentry**

Double stars. *See* **Stars**

Doubt. *See* **Belief and doubt**

Draft, Military. *See* **Military service, Compulsory**

Draft dodgers. *See* **Military service, Compulsory—Draft resisters**

Draft evaders. *See* **Military service, Compulsory—Draft resisters**

Draft resisters. *See* **Military service, Compulsory—Draft resisters**

Drafting, Mechanical. *See* **Mechanical drawing**

Dragons 398.2

xx **Animals, Mythical**

Drainage   631.6

Use for materials on land drainage. Materials on house drainage are entered under **Drainage, House**

See also **Marshes; Sewerage**

x Land drainage

xx **Agricultural engineering; Civil engineering; Hydraulic engineering; Municipal engineering; Reclamation of land; Sanitary engineering; Sewerage; Soils**

Drainage, House   728

See also **Plumbing; Sanitary engineering; Sewerage**

x House drainage

xx **Plumbing; Sanitation, Household**

Drama   808.2

Use for general materials on the drama. Materials on the history and criticism of the drama as literature are entered under **Drama—History and criticism.** Materials on criticism of the drama as presented on the stage are entered under **Dramatic criticism.** Materials on the presentation of plays are entered under **Acting; Amateur theatricals; Theater—Production and direction.** Materials on how to write plays are entered under **Drama—Technique.** Collections of plays are entered under **Drama—Collections; American drama —Collections; English drama—Collections;** etc.

See also

Acting	**One act plays**
Ballet	**Opera**
College and school drama	**Pantomimes**
	Passion plays
Comedy	**Plots (Drama, fiction, etc.)**
Dramatic criticism	
Dramatists	**Puppets and puppet plays**
Folk drama	
Masks (Plays)	**Radio plays**
Morality plays	**Religious drama**
Motion picture plays	**Television plays**
	Theater
Mysteries and miracle plays	**Tragedy**

also **American drama; English drama;** etc.; and names of special subjects, historical events and famous persons with the subdivision *Drama,* e.g. Easter—Drama; U.S.—History—Civil War, 1861–1865—Drama; Napoléon I, Emperor of the French—Drama; etc.

x Stage

xx **Literature; Theater**

Drama—Collections   808.82

Use for collections of plays by several authors

Drama–Collections—*Continued*

> *See also* **American drama–Collections; English drama–Collections;** etc.; also **Children's plays; College and school drama–Collections**
>
> *x* Plays

Drama–History and criticism   809.2

> *See also* **American drama–History and criticism; English drama–History and criticism;** etc.

Drama–Plots.   *See* **Plots (Drama, fiction, etc.)**

Drama, Religious.   *See* **Religious drama**

Drama–Technique   808.2

> *See also* **Motion picture plays–Technique; Radio plays–Technique; Television plays–Technique**
>
> *x* Play writing; Playwriting
>
> *xx* **Authorship; Characters and characteristics in literature**

Drama in education   372.6

> *See also* **Acting; Amateur theatricals; College and school drama; Religious drama; Theater**
>
> *xx* **Acting; Amateur theatricals; College and school drama; School assembly programs**

Dramatic art.   *See* **Acting**

Dramatic criticism   792.9

> Use for materials on criticism of the drama as presented on the stage. Materials on criticism of the drama as a literary form are entered under **Drama–History and criticism; American drama–History and criticism;** etc.
>
> *See also* **Motion picture plays–History and criticism**
>
> *x* Theater criticism
>
> *xx* **Criticism; Drama; Theater**

Dramatic music.   *See* **Opera; Operetta**

Dramatic plots.   *See* **Plots (Drama, fiction, etc.)**

Dramatists (May subdiv. geog. adjective form, e.g. **Dramatists, American;** etc.)   **920; 927**

> Use for materials dealing largely with the personal lives of several playwrights. Materials treating of their literary work are entered under **Drama–History and criticism; English drama–History and criticism;** etc.
>
> *x* Playwrights; Writers
>
> *xx* **Authors; Drama; Poets**

Dramatists, American   920; 927

> *x* American dramatists; U.S.—Dramatists

Drapery   684.3

> *x* Curtains
>
> *xx* **Interior decoration; Upholstery**

Draughts.   *See* **Checkers**

Drawing (May subdiv. geog. adjective form, e.g. **Drawing, American;** etc.)   **741; 743**

Drawing—*Continued*

See also

Anatomy, Artistic	**Landscape drawing**
Architectural draw-	**Mechanical draw-**
ing	**ing**
Commercial art	**Painting**
Crayon drawing	**Pastel drawing**
Design, Decorative	**Pen drawing**
Figure drawing	**Pencil drawing**
Geometrical draw-	**Perspective**
ing	**Shades and**
Graphic methods	**shadows**
Illustration of	**Topographical**
books	**drawing**

    x Drawings; Sketching

    xx **Art; Design, Decorative; Graphic arts; Illustration of books; Perspective**

Drawing, American 741.09; 741.9

    x American drawing; U.S.—Drawing

Drawing, Architectural. *See* **Architectural drawing**

Drawing materials. *See* **Artists' materials**

Drawings. *See* **Drawing**

Dreams 154.6

    See also **Fantasy; Psychoanalysis; Sleep**

    xx **Brain; Divination; Fortune telling; Mind and body; Psychical research; Psychoanalysis; Psychology, Physiological; Sleep; Subconsciousness; Superstition; Visions**

Dredging 627.7

    xx **Civil engineering; Hydraulic engineering**

Dress. *See* **Clothing and dress**

Dress accessories 646

    xx **Clothing and dress**

Dressing of ores. *See* **Ore dressing**

Dressmaking 646.4; 687

    See also **Needlework; Sewing; Tailoring**

    x Garment making

    xx **Clothing and dress; Fashion; Needlework; Sewing; Tailoring**

Dressmaking—Patterns 646.4; 687

    x Patterns

Dried flowers. *See* **Flowers, Drying**

Dried foods. *See* **Food, Dried**

Dried milk. *See* **Milk, Dried**

Drifting of continents. *See* **Continental drift**

Drill and minor tactics 355.5

    See also **Military art and science**

    x Military drill; Minor tactics

    xx **Military art and science**

Drill (Nonmilitary) 613.7

    x Marches (Exercises)

    xx **Physical education and training**

Drilling and boring 621.9

    Use for materials relating to workshop operations in metal, wood, etc. Materials relating to the operation of cutting

Drilling and boring—*Continued*
　　　　holes in earth or rock are entered
　　　　under **Boring**
　　x Boring (Metal, wood, etc.)
Drilling and boring (Earth and rocks). *See*
　　　　Boring
Drilling platforms. *See* **Artificial islands**
Drink question. *See* **Liquor problem**
Drinking. *See* **Alcoholism**
Drinking and youth. *See* **Alcohol and youth**
Drinks. *See* **Beverages; Liquors and liqueurs**
Driver education. *See* **Automobile drivers—**
　　　　Education
Drivers, Automobile. *See* **Automobile drivers**
Dromedaries. *See* **Camels**
Drop forging. *See* **Forging**
Dropouts 371.2
　　x School dropouts; School withdrawals
　　xx **Educational counseling; School attend-**
　　　　ance; Youth
Droughts 551.5; 632
　　See also **Dust storms; Rain and rainfall**
　　xx **Meterology; Rain and rainfall**
Drug abuse 613.8; 616.8
　　　　Use for materials on the misuse of drugs
　　　　in a broad sense. Materials limited to
　　　　addiction to hard drugs such as opium,
　　　　heroin, etc. are entered under **Narcotic**
　　　　habit
　　See also **Drugs and youth;** also types of
　　　　drug abuse, e.g. **Alcoholism; Narcotic**
　　　　habit; etc.
　　x Drug addiction; Drug habit; Drugs—
　　　　Abuse; Drugs—Misuse
　　xx **Crimes without victims**
Drug abuse—Personal narratives 613.8; 616.8
　　x Personal narratives
Drug addiction. *See* **Drug abuse; Narcotic**
　　　　habit
Drug addicts. *See* **Narcotic addicts**
Drug habit. *See* **Drug abuse; Narcotic habit**
Drug pushers. *See* **Narcotic traffic**
Drug therapy. *See* **Chemotherapy**
Drug traffic. *See* **Narcotic traffic**
Drugs 615
　　See also **Materia medica; Pharmacology;**
　　　　Pharmacy; Poisons; also names of
　　　　groups of drugs, e.g. **Narcotics;** etc.;
　　　　and names of individual drugs
　　x Pharmaceuticals
　　xx **Chemistry, Medical and pharmaceutical;**
　　　　Materia medica; Pharmacology; Phar-
　　　　macy; Therapeutics
Drugs—Abuse *See* **Drug abuse**
Drugs—Adulteration and analysis 614.3
　　xx **Consumer protection**
Drugs—Misuse. *See* **Drug abuse**
Drugs—Physiological effect 613.8

Drugs—Psychological aspects 615
   xx **Psychology, Applied**
Drugs and criminals 364.1
   x Criminals and drugs
Drugs and teen agers. *See* **Drugs and youth**
Drugs and youth 613.8
   Use same form for drugs and other groups
      of people and subjects, e.g. Drugs and
      criminals
   x Drugs and teen agers; Teen agers and
      drugs; Youth and drugs
   xx **Drug abuse; Juvenile delinquency; Nar-**
      cotics and youth
Druids and Druidism 299
   xx **Celts; Religions**
Drum 789
   xx **Musical instruments; Percussion instru-**
      ments
Drum majoring 371.8; 785.06
   See also **Baton twirling**
   xx **Bands (Music); Baton twirling**
Drunkards. *See* **Alcoholics**
Drunkenness. *See* **Alcoholism; Liquor prob-**
      lem; Temperance
Dry cleaning 646.6; 667
   x Clothing and dress—Dry cleaning
   xx **Cleaning**
Dry farming 631.5
   x Farming, Dry
   xx **Agriculture; Irrigation**
Dry goods. *See* **Fabrics**
Ducks 636.5
   xx **Poultry**
Ductless glands. *See* **Glands, Ductless**
Dueling 179; 394
   See also **Fencing**
   x Fighting
   xx **Fencing; Manners and customs**
Dunes. *See* **Sand dunes**
Dungeons. *See* **Prisons**
Dunkards. *See* **Church of the Brethren**
Dunkers. *See* **Church of the Brethren**
Duplicate bridge. *See* **Bridge (Game)**
Duplicating processes. *See* **Copying processes**
      and machines
Dust, Radioactive. *See* **Radioactive fallout**
Dust storms 551.5
   xx **Droughts; Erosion; Storms**
Duties. *See* **Tariff; Taxation**
Duty 170
   See also **Conscience; Ethics**
   xx **Ethics; Human behavior**
Dwarf trees 582; 635.9
   See also names of dwarf trees; e.g. **Bonsai;**
      etc.
   xx **Trees**
Dwarfs 398.2; 573
   x Midgets
Dwellings. *See* **Architecture, Domestic;**
      Houses; Prefabricated houses; also

Dwellings—*Continued*
>> classes of people with the subdivision *Housing,* e.g. **Physically handicapped—Housing;** etc.

Dyes and dyeing   667; 746.6
> *See also* **Bleaching;** also types of dyeing, e.g. **Batik; Tie dyeing;** etc.
> *xx* **Bleaching; Chemistry, Technical; Cleaning; Color; Pigments; Textile chemistry; Textile industry; Wool**

Dying patient.   *See* **Terminal care**

Dynamics   531
> *See also*

Aerodynamics	**Motion**
Astrodynamics	**Physics**
Force and energy	**Quantum theory**
Hydrodynamics	**Statics**
Kinematics	**Thermodynamics**
Matter	

> *x* Kinetics
> *xx* **Force and energy; Mathematics; Mechanics; Physics; Statics**

Dynamite   662
> *xx* **Explosives**

Dynamos.   *See* **Electric generators**

Dyspepsia.   *See* **Indigestion**

EEO.   *See* **Discrimination in employment**

ESP.   *See* **Extrasensory perception**

Eagles   598.2
> *xx* **Birds of prey**

Ear   611; 612
> *See also* **Hearing**
> *xx* **Deafness; Head; Hearing**

Early Christian literature.   *See* **Christian literature, Early**

Early warning system, Ballistic missile.   *See* **Ballistic missile early warning system**

Earth   525; 550
> Use for general materials on the whole planet. Materials limited to the structure and composition of the earth and the physical changes which it has undergone and is still undergoing are entered under **Geology**
> *See also*

Antarctic regions	**Glacial epoch**
Arctic regions	**Latitude**
Atmosphere	**Longitude**
Creation	**Meterology**
Earthquakes	**Ocean**
Geodesy	**Oceanography**
Geography	**Physical geography**
Geology	**Universe**
Geophysics	

> *x* World
> *xx* **Creation; Geology; Physical geography; Solar system; Universe**

Earth—Age   551.7

Earth—Chemical composition.   *See* **Geochemistry**

Earth—Crust 551.1
    See also **Plate tectonics**
Earth, Effect of man on. *See* **Man—Influence on nature**
Earth—Internal structure 551.1
Earth—Photographs from space 778.3
    xx **Space photography**
Earth sciences 550
    See also **Climate; Geochemistry; Geography; Geology; Geophysics; Meteorology; Oceanography; Water**
    x Geoscience
    xx **Science**
Earthenware. *See* **Pottery**
Earthquakes (May subdiv. geog.) 551.2
    See also **Volcanoes**
    x Seismography; Seismology
    xx **Earth; Geology; Natural disasters; Physical geography**
Earthquakes—U.S. 551.2
    x U.S.—Earthquakes
Earthwork. *See* **Soils (Engineering)**
Earthworks (Archeology). *See* **Excavations (Archeology)**
East. *See* **Asia**
East Africa. *See* **Africa, East**
East and West 301.29; 301.29181; 901.9
    Use for materials on both acculturation and cultural conflict between Asian and Occidental civilizations
    See also **Acculturation; Civilization, Occidental; Civilization, Asian**
    xx **Acculturation**
East (Far East). *See* **Far East**
East Germany. *See* **Germany, East**
East Indians 915.4; 954
    See also **Hindus**
    x Indians (of India)
    xx **Hindus**
East (Near East). *See* **Middle East**
Easter 263; 394.2
    x Ecclesiastical fasts and feasts; Religious festivals
    xx **Holy Week; Lent**
Easter—Drama 808.82; 812; etc.
    xx **Drama**
Eastern churches 281
    See also **Orthodox Eastern Church**
Eastern Empire. *See* **Byzantine Empire**
Eastern Europe 914.7; 947
    x Europe, Eastern
Eastern Seaboard. *See* **Atlantic States**
Easy reading materials
    x Beginning reading materials; Preprimers; Primers; Preschool reading materials
    xx **Children's literature; Reading materials**
Eating. *See* **Dinners and dining**
Eavesdropping 364.12
    See also **Wiretapping**

183

Eavesdropping—*Continued*

    x Bugging, Electronic; Electronic bugging; Electronic eavesdropping; Electronic listening devices; Listening devices; Surveillance, Electronic

   xx **Criminal investigation; Privacy, Right of; Wiretapping**

Ecclesiastical antiquities. *See* **Christian antiquities**

Ecclesiastical architecture. *See* **Church architecture**

Ecclesiastical art. *See* **Christian art and symbolism**

Ecclesiastical biography. *See* **Christianity—Biography**

Ecclesiastical fasts and feasts. *See* **Fasts and feasts;** and names of special fasts and feasts, e.g. **Easter; Lent;** etc.

Ecclesiastical furniture. *See* **Church furniture**

Ecclesiastical history. *See* **Church history**

Ecclesiastical law 262.9

   See also **Tithes**

   x Canon law; Church law; Law, Ecclesiastical

   xx **Church and state; Law**

Ecclesiastical rites and ceremonies. *See* **Liturgies; Rites and ceremonies; Sacraments;** and special rites and ceremonies, e.g. **Funeral rites and ceremonies; Lord's Supper;** etc.

Echo ranging. *See* **Sonar**

Eclipses, Lunar 523.3

   x Lunar eclipses; Moon—Eclipses

   xx **Astronomy**

Eclipses, Solar 523.7

   x Solar eclipses; Sun—Eclipses

   xx **Astronomy**

Ecology 574.5

   See also **Adaptation (Biology); Botany—Ecology; Food chains (Ecology); Geographical distribution of animals and plants;** and types of ecology, e.g. **Marine ecology;** etc.

   x Balance of nature; Biology—Ecology; Ecosystems

   xx **Environment**

Ecology, Human. *See* **Human ecology**

Ecology, Marine. *See* **Marine ecology**

Ecology, Social. *See* **Human ecology**

Economic assistance 338.91

   Use for general materials on international economic aid given in the form of gifts, loans, relief grants, or technical assistance. Materials limited to the latter are entered under **Technical assistance**

   See also **Developing areas; Reconstruction (1939–1951); Technical assistance; World War, 1939–1945—Civilian relief**

Economic assistance—*Continued*

    x Aid to developing areas; Assistance to developing areas; Foreign aid program

    xx **Developing areas; Economic policy; International cooperation; International economic relations; Reconstruction (1939–1951)**

Economic assistance, Domestic   338.93-338.99

    See also **Poverty; Public works; Subsidies; Unemployed**

    x Antipoverty programs; Poor relief

    xx **Economic policy; Unemployed**

Economic botany.   *See* **Botany, Economic**

Economic conditions   330.9

    Use for general materials on some or all of the following: natural resources, business, commerce, industry, labor, manufactures, financial conditions; and for the history of the economic development of several countries

    See also **Business cycles; Developing areas; Economic policy; Geography, Commercial; Labor supply; Natural resources; Quality of life;** also classes of people and names of countries, cities, areas, etc. with the subdivision *Economic conditions*, e.g. **Blacks—Economic conditions; U.S.—Economic conditions;** etc.

    x Business depressions; Economic development; Economic history; Stabilization in industry; World economics

    xx **Business; Economics; Geography, Commercial; Social conditions; Wealth**

Economic cycles.   *See* **Business cycles**

Economic depressions.   *See* **Depressions, Economic**

Economic development.   *See* **Economic conditions**

Economic entomology.   *See* **Insects, Injurious and beneficial**

Economic geography.   *See* **Geography, Commercial**

Economic geology.   *See* **Geology, Economic**

Economic history.   *See* **Economic conditions**

Economic mobilization.   *See* **Industrial mobilization**

Economic planning.   *See* **Economic policy**

Economic policy   338.9-338.91

    Use for materials on the policy of governments towards economic problems

    See also **Commercial policy; Economic assistance; Economic assistance, Domestic; Fiscal policy; Free trade and protection; Government ownership; Human resources policy; Industrial mobilization; Industrialization; Industry and state; International economic relations; Municipal ownership;**

Economic policy—*Continued*

National security; Social policy; Subsidies; Tariff; Technical assistance; also names of countries and states with the subdivision *Economic policy* (e.g. **U.S.–Economic policy; Ohio–Economic policy;** etc.); and names of countries with the subdivision *Commercial policy*, e.g. **U.S.–Commercial policy;** etc.

x Economic planning; National planning; Planning, Economic; Planning, National; Welfare state; World economics

xx **Economic conditions; Economics; Industry and state; National security; Social policy**

Economic relations, Foreign. *See* **International economic relations**

Economic zoology. *See* **Zoology, Economic**

Economics   330

See also

Business	**Government ownership**
Capital	
Capitalism	**Income**
Christianity and economics	**Industry**
Commerce	**Labor and laboring classes**
Consumption (Economics)	**Land use**
Cooperation	**Money**
Cost of living	**Monopolies**
Credit	**Population**
Debts, Public	**Prices**
Depressions, Economic	**Profit**
Economic conditions	**Property**
	Saving and thrift
Economic policy	**Socialism**
Finance	**Statistics**
Free trade and protection	**Trusts, Industrial**
	Wages
	Waste (Economics)
	Wealth

also subjects with the subdivision *Economic aspects*, e.g. **Agriculture– Economic aspects;** etc.

x Distribution of wealth; Political economy; Production

xx **Social sciences**

Economics–History   330.1

Use for materials describing the development of economic theories. Materials on the economic conditions and development of countries are entered under **Economic conditions**

Economics, Medical. *See* **Medical economics**

Economics and Christianity. *See* **Christianity and economics**

Economics of war. *See* **War–Economic aspects**

Economy. *See* **Saving and thrift**

186

Ecosystems. *See* **Ecology**

Ecumenical councils. *See* **Councils and synods**

Ecumenical movement. *See* **Christian unity**

Eddas 839

 xx **Icelandic and Old Norse literature; Poetry; Scandinavian literature**

Eden 222

 x Garden of Eden

Edible plants. *See* **Plants, Edible**

Editions. *See* **Bibliography—Editions**

Editors and editing. *See* **Journalism; Journalists; Publishers and publishing**

Education (May subdiv. geog.) **370**

 Subdivisions listed under this heading may be used under other education headings where applicable

 See also

Adult education	**Learning and scholarship**
Area studies	
Audio-visual education	**Libraries**
	Library education
Books and reading	**Military education**
Business education	**Naval education**
Character education	**Physical education and training**
Church and education	
	Professional education
Classical education	
Coeducation	**Religious education**
Colleges and universities	**Scholarships, fellowships, etc.**
Continuing education	**Schools** and references under that heading
Correspondence schools and courses	
	Study, Method of
Culture	**Teachers**
Education and state	**Teaching**
Educators	**Technical education**
Evening and continuation schools	**Vocational education**
Illiteracy	
International education	

 also names of classes of people and social and ethnic groups with the subdivision *Education*, (e.g. **Automobile drivers—Education; Deaf—Education; Blacks—Education;** etc.) subjects with the subdivision *Study and teaching* (e.g. **Science—Study and teaching;** etc.) and headings beginning with the words **Education** and **Educational**

 x Instruction; Pedagogy

 xx **Civilization; Coeducation; Culture; Learning and scholarship; Schools; Teaching**

Education, Adult. *See* **Adult education**

Education—Aims and objectives 370.11

Education—Associations. *See* **Educational associations**

Education, Bilingual   371.9
> *x* Bilingual education
> *xx* **Bilingualism; Intercultural education**

Education, Business.   *See* **Business education**
Education, Character.   *See* **Character education**
Education, Christian.   *See* **Christian education**
Education, Classical.   *See* **Classical education**
Education, Compulsory   379
> *See also* **Child labor; Evening and continu-
> ation schools; School attendance**
> *x* Compulsory   education;   Compulsory
> school attendance
> *xx* **School attendance**

Education, Continuing.   *See* **Continuing educa-
> tion**
Education—Curricula   375
> *See   also* **Articulation   (Education);** also
> types of education and schools with
> the subdivision *Curricula*, e.g. **Library
> education—Curricula;   Colleges   and
> universities—Curricula;** etc.
> *x* Core   curriculum;   Courses   of   study;
> Curricula (Courses of study); Schools
> —Curricula; Study, Courses of

Education, Discrimination in.   *See* **Discrimina-
> tion in education**
Education, Elementary   372
> Use for general materials on education of
> children below the secondary school
> level
> *See   also* **Exceptional   children;   Kinder-
> garten; Montessori method of educa-
> tion; Nursery schools**
> *x* Children—Education;   Education,   Pri-
> mary; Education of children; Elemen-
> tary   education;   Grammar   schools;
> Primary education
> *xx* **Children**

Education, Ethical.   *See* **Character education;
> Religious education**
Education—Experimental methods   371.307
> *See also* types of experimental methods,
> e.g. **Free schools; Non-graded schools;
> Open plan schools;** etc.
> *x* Activity schools; Experimental methods
> in education; Progressive education;
> Teaching—Experimental methods

Education—Federal aid.   *See* **Federal aid to
> education**
Education—Finance   379
> *See also* **Federal aid to education; State aid
> to education**
> *x* School finance; School taxes; Tuition
> *xx* **Finance**

Education, Higher   378
> Use for general consideration of education
> above the secondary level, i.e. for ma-
> terials on college education, profes-
> sional education, etc. Use for mate-

Education, Higher—*Continued*

rials not specific enough to be entered under **Colleges and universities**

See also **Adult education; Classical education; Colleges and universities; Junior colleges; Professional education; Technical education; University extension**

x Higher education

xx **Colleges and universities**

Education, Industrial. *See* **Industrial arts education; Technical education**

Education, Integration. *See* **School integration**

Education, Intercultural. *See* **Intercultural education**

Education, International. *See* **International education**

Education, Medical. *See* **Medicine—Study and teaching**

Education, Military. *See* **Military education**

Education, Moral. *See* **Character education**

Education, Multicultural. *See* **Intercultural education**

Education, Musical. *See* **Music—Study and teaching**

Education, Naval. *See* **Naval education**

Education—Personnel service. *See* **Educational counseling**

Education, Physical. *See* **Physical education and training**

Education, Preschool   372.21

See also **Kindergarten; Nursery schools**

x Children—Education;   Infants—Education; Preschool education

xx **Kindergarten; Nursery schools**

Education, Primary. *See* **Education, Elementary**

Education, Professional. *See* **Professional education**

Education, Religious. *See* **Religious education**

Education, Scientific. *See* **Science—Study and teaching**

Education, Secondary   373

A more inclusive subject than **High schools**

See also **Adult education; Evening and continuation schools; High schools; Junior high schools; Private schools; Public schools**

x High school education; Secondary education; Secondary schools

xx **High schools**

Education, Segregation in. *See* **Segregation in education**

Education—State aid. *See* **State aid to education**

Education—Statistics   370.21

Education—Study and teaching   370.7

Use for materials on the study and teaching of education as a science. Materials limited to the methods of training teachers are entered under **Teachers—**

Education—Study and teaching—*Continued*
　　Training. Materials on the methods of teaching are entered under **Teaching**
　　See also **Teachers—Training; Teachers colleges**
　　x Pedagogy
Education, Technical.　*See* **Technical education**
Education, Theological.　*See* **Religious education; Theology—Study and teaching**
Education—U.S.　370
　　x U.S.—Education
Education, Vocational.　*See* **Vocational education**
Education and church.　*See* **Church and education**
Education and radio.　*See* **Radio in education**
Education and religion.　*See* **Church and education**
Education and state　379
　　See also **Federal aid to education; Scholarships, fellowships, etc.; State aid to education**
　　x Educational policy; State and education
　　xx **Education**
Education and television.　*See* **Television in education**
Education associations.　*See* **Educational associations**
Education for librarianship.　*See* **Library education**
Education of adults.　*See* **Adult education**
Education of children.　*See* **Education, Elementary**
Education of criminals.　*See* **Prisoners—Education**
Education of men.　*See* **Men—Education**
Education of prisoners.　*See* **Prisoners—Education**
Education of the blind.　*See* **Blind—Education**
Education of the deaf.　*See* **Deaf—Education**
Education of veterans.　*See* **Veterans—Education**
Education of women.　*See* **Women—Education**
Education of workers.　*See* **Labor and laboring classes—Education**
Educational administration.　*See* **School administration and organization**
Educational associations　370.6
　　See also **Parents' and teachers' associations**
　　x Education—Associations; Education associations
　　xx **Societies; Teachers**
Educational counseling　371.4
　　See also **Dropouts; School psychologists; Vocational guidance**
　　x Education—Personnel service; Educational guidance; Guidance; Personnel service in education; Student guidance; Students—Counseling
　　xx **Counseling; Vocational guidance**

190

Educational films. *See* **Libraries and motion pictures; Motion pictures in education**

Educational guidance. *See* **Educational counseling**

Educational measurements. *See* **Educational tests and measurements**

Educational policy. *See* **Education and state**

Educational psychology 370.15

> *See also* **Apperception; Attention; Child psychology; Imagination; Memory; Mental tests; Perception; Psychology, Applied; Thought and thinking**
>
> *x* Psychology, Educational
>
> *xx* **Child psychology; Psychology; Teaching**

Educational sociology 370.19

> *x* Social problems in education; Sociology, Educational
>
> *xx* **Sociology**

Educational surveys 370.21

> *x* School surveys; Surveys
>
> *xx* **Social surveys**

Educational television. *See* **Television in education**

Educational tests and measurements 371.2

> *See also* **Ability—Testing; Examinations; Grading and marking (Students); Mental tests**
>
> *x* Educational measurements; Tests
>
> *xx* **Mental tests**

Educators 920; 923

> *See also* **Teachers**
>
> *x* College teachers; Faculty (Education)
>
> *xx* **Education; Teachers**

Efficiency, Household. *See* **Home economics**

Efficiency, Industrial 658

> Use for materials dealing with specific means of increasing efficiency and output in business and industries. Such materials include time and motion studies, and the application of psychological principles
>
> *See also* **Executive ability; Factory management; Job analysis; Motion study; Office management; Personnel management; Time study**
>
> *x* Industrial efficiency
>
> *xx* **Business; Cost accounting; Engineering; Executive ability; Factory management; Industrial management; Industry; Management; Personnel management**

Eggs 598.2; 636.5

> *See also* **Birds—Eggs and nests**

Egypt 916.2; 962

Egypt—Antiquities 913.32

> *x* Egyptology

Egypt—History 932; 962

> *See also* **Sinai Campaign, 1956**

Egypt—History—1970– 962

Egyptology. *See* **Egypt—Antiquities**

191

Eight-hour day. *See* **Hours of labor**

Eighteenth century   901.93; 909.7
>   See note under **Nineteenth century**

Elderly (May subdiv. geog.)   155.67; 301.43
>   *See also* **Aging**
>   *x* Aged; Older people; Senior citizens
>   *xx* **Gerontology; Old age**

Elderly—Care and hygiene   362.6; 618.9
>   *See also* **Nursing homes**

Elderly—Diseases   618.9
>   *x* Geriatrics

Elderly—Housing   362.6
>   *x* Homes for the elderly; Housing for the
>   elderly; Old age homes

Elderly—Library service. *See* **Libraries and
>   the elderly**

Elderly—Medical care   362.6; 618.9
>   *See also* **Medicare**
>   *x* Medical care for the elderly
>   *xx* **Medical care**

Elderly—Recreation   790.19
>   *xx* **Recreation**

Elderly—Societies   367; 790.19

Elderly—U.S.   301.43
>   *x* U.S.—Elderly

Election (Theology). *See* **Predestination**

Electioneering. *See* **Politics, Practical**

Elections (May subdiv. geog.)   324
>   *See also* **Campaign funds; Presidents—U.S.
>   —Election;   Primaries;   Referendum;
>   Representative government and rep-
>   resentation; Suffrage**
>   *x* Ballot; Franchise; Polls, Election; Vot-
>   ing
>   *xx* **Politics, Practical; Primaries; Propor-
>   tional representation; Representative
>   government and representation**

Elections—Finance. *See* **Campaign funds**

Elections, Primary. *See* **Primaries**

Elections—U.S.   324.73
>   *x* U.S.—Elections

Elections—U.S.—Finance. *See*   **Campaign
>   funds—U.S.**

Electoral college. *See* **Presidents—U.S.—Elec-
>   tion**

Electric apparatus and appliances   621.3; 644
>   *See also* names of electric apparatus and
>   appliances, e.g. **Burglar alarms; Elec-
>   tric   batteries;   Electric   generators;
>   Electric lamps;** etc.
>   *x* Apparatus, Electric; Appliances, Electric;
>   Electric appliances
>   *xx* **Electric engineering; Scientific apparatus
>   and instruments**

Electric apparatus and appliances, Domestic.
>   *See* **Household appliances, Electric**

Electric appliances. *See* **Electric apparatus and
>   appliances;   Household   appliances,
>   Electric**

192

Electric automobiles. *See* **Automobiles, Electric**

Electric batteries   621.35
See also **Solar batteries; Storage batteries**
x Batteries, Electric; Cells, Electric
xx **Electric apparatus and appliances; Electrochemistry; Storage batteries**

Electric circuits   621.319
See also **Electronic circuits**
x Circuits, Electric

Electric communication. *See* **Telecommunication**

Electric condensers. *See* **Condensers (Electricity)**

Electric conductors   621.319
See also **Radio, Short wave**
x Conductors, Electric

Electric controllers   629.8
x Automatic control

Electric currents   537.6; 621.31
See also **Electric measurements; Electric transformers**
x Currents, Electric

Electric currents, Alternating   537.6; 621.31
x Alternating currents; Currents, Alternating

Electric distributions. *See* **Electric lines; Electric power distribution**

Electric engineering   621.3
See also **Electric apparatus and appliances; Electric lighting; Electric machinery; Electric power distribution; Electric railroads; Electricity in mining; Radio; Telegraph; Telephone**
xx **Mechanical engineering**

Electric equipment of automobiles. *See* **Automobiles—Electric equipment**

Electric eye. *See* **Photoelectric cells**

Electric generators   621.313
x Dynamos; Generators, Electric
xx **Electric apparatus and appliances; Electric machinery**

Electric heating   621.39; 644; 697
x Electricity in the home
xx **Heating**

Electric household appliances. *See* **Household appliances, Electric**

Electric industries   338.4
See also **Radio industry and trade**
x Electric utilities; Industries, Electric
xx **Public utilities**

Electric lamps   621.32; 644
See also **Electric lighting**
x Incandescent lamps
xx **Electric apparatus and appliances; Electric lighting; Lamps**

Electric light. *See* **Electric lighting; Photometry; Phototherapy**

Electric lighting   621.32
See also **Electric lamps**

Electric lighting—*Continued*

    x Arc light; Electric light; Electricity in the home; Light, Electric

    xx **Electric engineering; Electric lamps; Electric wiring; Lighting**

Electric lighting, Fluorescent. *See* **Fluorescent lighting**

Electric lines 621.319

    Use for materials on general transmission systems

    See also **Electric wiring**

    x Electric distribution; Electric power transmission; Electric transmission; Electricity—Distribution; Power transmission, Electric; Transmission of power

    xx **Electric power distribution**

Electric machinery 621.31

    Use for discussions of more than one kind or class of machines. Materials treating of the smaller machines and appliances are entered under **Electric apparatus and appliances**

    See also **Electric generators; Electric motors; Electric transformers**

    xx **Electric engineering; Machinery**

Electric machinery—Alternating current 621.319

    x Alternating current machinery

Electric machinery—Direct current 621.319

    x Direct current machinery

Electric measurements 621.37

    See also **Electric meters; Electric testing**

    x Measurements, Electric

    xx **Electric currents; Electric testing; Weights and measures**

Electric meters 621.37

    x Meters, Electric

    xx **Electric measurements**

Electric motors 621.4

    See also **Electric transformers**

    x Induction motors; Motors

    xx **Electric machinery**

Electric power 621.31

    xx **Power (Mechanics); Power resources**

Electric power—Interruptions. *See* **Electric power failures**

Electric power distribution 621.319

    See also **Electric lines; Electric wiring**

    x Electric distribution; Electric power transmission; Electric transmission; Electricity—Distribution; Power transmission, Electric; Rural electrification; Transmission of power

    xx **Electric engineering; Power transmission**

Electric power failures 621.319

    x Blackouts, Electric power; Brownouts; Electric power—Interruptions; Electric power interruptions; Power blackouts; Power failures

Electric power in mining. *See* **Electricity in mining**

Electric power interruptions. *See* **Electric power failures**

Electric power plants 621.312

    x Electric utilities; Power plants, Electric

    xx **Power plants**

Electric power transmission. *See* **Electric lines; Electric power distribution**

Electric railroads 621.33; 625.1

    See also **Railroads–Electrification; Street railroads**

    x Interurban railroads; Railroads, Electric

    xx **Electric engineering; Public utilities; Railroads; Railroads–Electrification; Street railroads; Transportation**

Electric signs 621.32; 659.13

    See also **Neon tubes**

    x Signs (Advertising); Signs, Electric

    xx **Advertising; Signs and signboards**

Electric smelting. *See* **Electrometallurgy**

Electric switches. *See* **Electric switchgear**

Electric switchgear 621.31

    x Electric switches; Switches, Electric

Electric testing 621.37

    See also **Electric measurements**

    xx **Electric measurements**

Electric toys 688.7

    xx **Toys**

Electric transformers 621.31

    x Transformers, Electric

    xx **Electric currents; Electric machinery; Electric motors**

Electric transmission. *See* **Electric lines; Electric power distribution**

Electric utilities. *See* **Electric industries; Electric power plants; Public utilities;** and names of specific utilities

Electric waves 537.1; 621.381

    See also **Electromagnetic waves; Microwaves; Radio, Short wave**

    x Hertzian waves; Radio waves

    xx **Waves**

Electric welding 671.5

    x Arc welding; Resistance welding; Spot welding; Welding, Electric

    xx **Welding**

Electric wiring 621.319; 621.32

    See also **Electric lighting; Telegraph; Telephone**

    x Wiring, Electric

    xx **Electric lines; Electric power distribution**

Electrical. *See* headings beginning with the word **Electric**

Electricity 537; 621.3

    See also **Electrons; Lightning; Magnetism; Radioactivity; Telegraph; Telephone; X rays;** also headings beginning with **Electric** and **Electro**

    xx **Magnetism; Physics**

Electricity—Distribution. *See* **Electric lines; Electric power distribution**

Electricity, Medical. *See* **Electrotherapeutics**

Electricity in agriculture 631.3

Use same form for electricity in other endeavors, e.g. **Electricity in mining;** etc.

x Electricity on the farm; Rural electrification

xx **Agricultural engineering; Agricultural machinery**

Electricity in medicine. *See* **Electrotherapeutics**

Electricity in mining 622

See also **Mining engineering**

x Electric power in mining; Mining, Electric

xx **Electric engineering; Mining engineering**

Electricity in the home. *See* **Electric heating; Electric lighting; Household appliances, Electric**

Electricity on the farm. *See* **Electricity in agriculture**

Electrification of railroads. *See* **Railroads— Electrification**

Electrochemistry 541; 660

See also **Electric batteries; Electrometallurgy; Electroplating; Electrotyping**

xx **Chemistry, Physical and theoretical; Chemistry, Technical**

Electromagnetic waves 537.1

See also **Heat; Light; Microwaves; Ultraviolet rays; X-rays**

x Waves, Electromagnetic

xx **Electric waves; Radiation**

Electromagnetism 537; 621.3

See also **Masers**

xx **Magnetism**

Electromagnets 538

x Magnet winding

xx **Magnetism; Magnets**

Electrometallurgy 669

See also **Electroplating; Electrotyping**

x Electric smelting

xx **Electrochemistry; Electroplating; Electrotyping; Metallurgy; Smelting**

Electron microscope and microscopy 578

xx **Microscope and microscopy**

Electron tubes. *See* **Vacuum tubes**

Electronic apparatus and appliances 621.381

See also names of electronic apparatus and appliances, e.g. **Computers; Intercommunication systems;** etc.

x Apparatus, Electronic; Appliances, Electronic

xx **Electronics; Scientific apparatus and appliances**

Electronic brains. *See* **Artificial intelligence; Computers**

Electronic bugging. *See* **Eavesdropping**

196

Electronic calculating machines. *See* **Computers**

Electronic circuits   621.381

  xx **Electric circuits; Electronics**

Electronic computers. *See* **Computers**

Electronic data processing   001.6

  See also **On line data processing; Optical data processing; Programming (Electronic computers); Programming languages (Electronic computers);** also subjects with the subdivision *Data processing,* e.g. **Banks and banking—Data processing;** etc.

  x Automatic data processing; Data processing

  xx **Computers; Information science; Information storage and retrieval systems**

Electronic eavesdropping. *See* **Eavesdropping**

Electronic listening devices. *See* **Eavesdropping**

Electronic music   789.9

  x Music, Electronic; Synthesizer music; Tape recorder music

  xx **Music**

Electronic musical instruments. *See* **Musical instruments, Electronic**

Electronics   537.5; 621.381

  See also **Amplifiers (Electronics); Cybernetics; Electronic apparatus and appliances; Electronic circuits; High-fidelity sound systems; Microelectronics; Semiconductors; Transistors**

  xx **Electrons; Photoelectric cells; Vacuum tubes**

Electrons   539.7

  See also **Electronics**

  xx **Atoms; Electricity; Neutrons; Nuclear physics; Physics; Protons; Radioactivity**

Electroplating   671.7

  See also **Electrometallurgy**

  xx **Electrochemistry;   Electrometallurgy; Metalwork**

Electrotherapeutics   615

  See also **Radiotherapy**

  x Electricity, Medical; Electricity in medicine; Medical electricity

  xx **Massage; Physical therapy; Therapeutics**

Electrotyping   686.2

  See also **Electrometallurgy**

  xx **Electrochemistry;   Electrometallurgy; Printing**

Elementary education. *See* **Education, Elementary**

Elements, Chemical. *See* **Chemical elements**

Elephants   569; 599

  xx **Mammals**

Elevators   621.8

  x Lifts

  xx **Hoisting machinery**

Elizabeth II, Queen of Great Britain 92
  xx **Kings and rulers; Queens**
Elk Mountain, Wyo. 917.87; 978.7
  xx **Mountains**
Elocution. *See* **Public speaking**
Elves. *See* **Fairies**
Emancipation of slaves. *See* **Slavery; Slavery in the U.S.**
Emancipation of women. *See* **Women—Civil rights**
Embassies. *See* **Diplomatic and consular service**
Emblems. *See* **Decorations of honor; Heraldry; Insignia; Mottoes; Seals (Numismatics); Symbolism**
Embroidery 746.4
  See also types of embroidery, e.g. **Beadwork; Crewelwork; Needlepoint;** etc.
  xx **Needlework; Sewing**
Embryology 574.3; 612
  See also **Cells; Protoplasm; Reproduction**
  x Development
  xx **Biology; Cells; Evolution; Protoplasm; Reproduction; Zoology**
Emergencies. *See* **Accidents; First aid**
Emergency relief. *See* **Disaster relief**
Emigration. *See* **Immigration and emigration**
Eminent domain 333.1
  x Condemnation of land; Expropriation; Land, Condemnation of
  xx **Constitutional law; Land use; Property; Railroads; Real estate**
Emotional stress. *See* **Stress (Psychology)**
Emotionally disturbed children. *See* **Mentally ill children; Problem children**
Emotions 152.4
  See also **Attitude (Psychology); Bashfulness; Belief and doubt; Fear; Horror; Joy and sorrow; Laughter; Love; Pain; Pleasure; Prejudices and antipathies; Sympathy;** and names of other emotions
  x Feelings; Frustration; Passions
  xx **Psychology; Psychology, Physiological**
Emperors. *See* **Kings and rulers; Roman emperors;** and names of emperors, kings, etc.
Empiricism 146
  See also **Pragmatism**
  x Experience
  xx **Knowledge, Theory of; Philosophy; Pragmatism; Reality**
Employee absenteeism. *See* **Absenteeism (Labor)**
Employee morale 331.2; 658.3
  See also **Job satisfaction**
  xx **Absenteeism (Labor); Morale; Personnel management; Psychology, Applied; Work**
Employees 920

Employees, Clerical. *See* **Clerks**

Employees—Dismissal   658.31

   xx **Personnel management**

Employees—Training   331.2

     See also **Apprentices; Retraining, Occupational; Technical education**

     x Factories—Training departments; Factory schools; In-service training; Training of employees

   xx **Apprentices; Occupational training; Personnel management; Technical education; Vocational education**

Employees and officials. *See* **Civil service;** and names of countries, cities, etc. and organizations with the subdivision *Officials and employees*, e.g. **Chicago—Officials and employees; United Nations—Officials and employees;** etc.

Employees' representation in management   331.89

     See also **Collective bargaining**

     x Codetermination (Industrial relations); Industrial councils; Labor representation in regulation of industry; Management, Employees' representation in; Shop committees; Participatory management; Workers participation in management; Workshop councils

   xx **Collective bargaining; Factory management; Industrial relations; Labor and laboring classes; Personnel management**

Employer-employee relations. *See* **Industrial relations**

Employers' liability. *See* **Workers' compensation**

Employment   331.1

     See also **Human resources; Labor supply; Vocational guidance;** also names of groups of people with the subdivision *Employment*, e.g. **Blacks—Employment; Veterans—Employment;** etc.

   xx **Labor and laboring classes; Vocational guidance**

Employment, Part time   331.2

     x Part time employment

   xx **Unemployed**

Employment, Temporary   331.2

     x Temporary employment

Employment agencies   331.1

     See also **Labor supply**

     x Jobs

   xx **Labor and laboring classes; Labor supply; Labor turnover; Personnel management; Recruiting of employees; Unemployed**

Employment and age. *See* **Age and employment**

Employment applications. *See* **Applications for positions**

199

Employment discrimination. *See* **Discrimination in employment**

Employment management. *See* **Personnel management**

Employment of children. *See* **Child labor**

Employment of veterans. *See* **Veterans—Employment**

Employment of women. *See* **Women—Employment**

Employment references. *See* **Applications for positions**

Empresses. *See* **Queens**

Enamel and enameling   738.4

    x Porcelain enamels

    xx **Art, Decorative; Arts and crafts; Decoration and ornament**

Encounter groups. *See* **Group relations training**

Encyclicals, Papal   262.9

    x Papal encyclicals

Encyclopedias   030; 031; etc.

    See also subjects with the subdivision *Encyclopedias,* e.g. **Sports—Encyclopedias;** etc.

    x Cyclopedias

    xx **Reference books**

End of the world   236; 291.2

    x World, End of the

    xx **Eschatology**

Endangered animals. *See* **Rare animals**

Endangered birds. *See* **Rare birds**

Endocrinology   616.4

    See also **Glands, Ductless; Hormones**

Endowed charities. *See* **Charities; Endowments**

Endowments   361.6-361.7

    See also **Charities; Scholarships, fellowships, etc.**

    x Endowed charities; Foundations (Endowments); Hospital endowments; Philanthropy; School endowments

    xx **Charities**

Endurance, Physical. *See* **Physical fitness**

Energy. *See* **Force and energy; Power resources**

Energy and state. *See* **Energy policy**

Energy conservation   333.7

    See also **Energy consumption; Energy policy;** also types of energy conservation, e.g. **Recycling (Waste, etc.);** etc.

    x Conservation of energy; Conservation of power resources; Power resources conservation

    xx **Conservation of natural resources; Energy consumption; Energy policy; Power resources**

Energy consumption   333.7-333.9

    See also **Energy conservation;** also subjects with the subdivision *Fuel consumption,* e.g. **Automobiles—Fuel consumption;** etc.

Energy consumption—*Continued*

 x Consumption of energy

 xx **Energy conservation; Power resources**

Energy policy 333

 See also **Energy conservation**

 x Energy and state; Power resources and state; State and energy

 xx **Energy conservation; Power resources**

Energy resources. *See* **Power resources**

Enforcement of law. *See* **Law enforcement**

Engineering 620

 See also **Aeronautics; Efficiency, Industrial; Engineers; Mechanics;** also types of engineering, e.g. **Agricultural engineering; Chemical engineering; Civil engineering;** etc.

 x Construction

 xx **Building; Mechanics; Technology**

Engineering—Periodicals 620.5

 xx **Periodicals**

Engineering—Study and teaching 620.7

 xx **Technical education**

Engineering, Structural. *See* **Structural engineering**

Engineering drawing. *See* **Mechanical drawing**

Engineering instruments 620.28

 x Instruments, Engineering

 xx **Scientific apparatus and instruments**

Engineering materials. *See* **Materials**

Engineers 920; 926

 See also **Inventors**

 xx **Engineering**

Engines 621.4

 See also

Airplanes—Engines	**Gas and oil engines**
Automobiles—Engines	**Heat engines**
Diesel engines	**Marine engines**
Farm engines	**Pumping machinery**
Fire engines	**Solar engines**
Fuel	**Steam engines**
	Turbines

 x Motors

 xx **Machinery; Mechanical engineering**

England 914.2

 Use with the subdivisions *Description and travel; Historic buildings, etc.; Industries; Intellectual life; Social life and customs* for works limited to England

 xx **Great Britain**

England, Church of. *See* **Church of England**

England—History. *See* **Gt. Brit.—History**

English as a foreign language. *See* **English as a second language**

English as a second language 428

 See also **English language—Conversations and phrases**

 x English as a foreign language; English for foreigners; English language—Study and teaching, Foreign; English

English as a second language—*Continued*
　　　　language—Texts for foreigners; English language as a second language
English authors. *See* **Authors, English**
English composition. *See* **English language—Composition and exercises**
English drama 822
　　See also **Morality plays; Mysteries and miracle plays**
　　xx **Drama; English literature**
English drama—Collections 822.08
　　xx **Drama—Collections**
English drama—History and criticism 822.09
　　xx **Drama—History and criticism**
English essays 824.08
　　Use for collections of literary essays by several authors
　　xx **English literature; Essays**
English fiction 823; Fic
　　x Fiction, English
　　xx **English literature; Fiction**
English fiction—History and criticism 823.09
English for foreigners. *See* **English language—Conversations and phrases; English as a second language**
English grammar. *See* **English language—Grammar**
English history. *See* **Gt. Brit.—History**
English in India. *See* **British in India**
English language 420
　　Subdivisions used under this heading may be used under other languages unless otherwise specified
　　xx **Language and languages**
English language—Acronyms. *See* **Acronyms**
English language—Americanisms. *See* **Americanisms**
English language—Antonyms. *See* **English language—Synonyms and antonyms**
English language—Business English 808
　　See also **Business letters**
　　x Business English
　　xx **Business letters**
English language—Composition and exercises 808
　　See also **Rhetoric**
　　x Composition (Rhetoric); English composition
　　xx **Rhetoric**
English language—Conversations and phrases 427; 428
　　x English for foreigners
　　xx **English as a second language**
English language—Dialects 427
　　See also **Americanisms**
　　x Dialects
English language—Dictionaries 423
　　For dictionaries of English and another language use the name of the foreign language as a further subdivision un-

English language—Dictionaries—*Continued*
der *Dictionaries,* e.g. **English language —Dictionaries—French;** etc.

See also **English language—Terms and phrases**

x Glossaries

xx **Dictionaries; English language—Terms and phrases**

English language—Dictionaries—French 443
Use for English-French dictionaries. For French-English dictionaries use **French language—Dictionaries—English.** Use both headings for an English-French and French-English dictionary

English language—Errors 428

English language—Etymology 422
x Etymology

English language—Examinations, questions, etc. 420.76
xx **Examinations**

English language—Foreign words and phrases 422
x Foreign language phrases

English language—Grammar 425
See also **English language—Usage**
x English grammar
xx **Grammar**

English language—History 420.9
xx **History**

English language—Homonyms 423
x Homonyms

English language—Idioms 427
See also **English language—Provincialisms; English language—Usage**
x Idioms
xx **English language—Provincialisms**

English language—Jargon 427
x Jargon

English language—Orthography. *See* **English language—Spelling**

English language—Phonetics. *See* **English language—Pronunciation**

English language—Phrases and terms. *See* **English language—Terms and phrases**

English language—Programmed instruction 420.7
x Self-instruction
xx **Programmed instruction**

English language—Pronunciation 421
x English language—Phonetics; Phonology; Pronunciation
xx **Phonetics**

English language—Provincialisms 427
See also **English language—Idioms**
x Localism; Provincialism
xx **English language—Idioms**

English language—Punctuation. *See* **Punctuation**

English language—Reading materials. *See* **Reading materials**

203

English language—Reading materials—*Cont'd*
    Use subdivision *Reading materials* for languages other than English, e.g. **French language—Reading materials**; etc.
English language—Rhetoric. *See* **Rhetoric**
English language—Rhyme 426
    xx **Rhyme**
English language—Slang 427
    x Slang
English language—Social aspects 420
    x Social aspects
English language—Spelling 421
    See also **Spellers; Spelling reform**
    x English language—Orthography; Orthography; Spelling
English language—Spelling reform. *See* **Spelling reform**
English language—Study and teaching 420.7
English language—Study and teaching, Foreign. *See* **English as a second language**
English language—Synonyms and antonyms 423
    x Antonyms; English language—Antonyms; Synonyms; Thesauri
English language—Terms and phrases 427
    Use for general lists of words and phrases which are applicable to certain situations (curious expressions, public speaking phrases, etc.) rather than to a specific subject. If the list is limited to a special field use name of that subject with the subdivision *Dictionaries,* e.g. **Chemistry—Dictionaries**; etc.
    See also **English language—Dictionaries**
    x English language—Phrases and terms
    xx **English language—Dictionaries**
English language—Texts for foreigners. *See* **English as a second language**
English language—To 1100. *See* **Anglo-Saxon language**
English language—Usage 428
    xx **English language—Grammar; English language—Idioms**
English language—Versification. *See* **Versification**
English language as a second language. *See* **English as a second language**
English letters 826
    xx **English literature; Letters**
English literature 820
    Subdivisions used under this heading may be used under other literatures
    See also **Authors, English; English drama; English essays; English fiction; English letters; English newspapers; English orations; English periodicals; English poetry; English prose literature; English wit and humor; Parodies; Satire, English; Short stories**
    xx **Literature**
English literature—Bibliography 016.82

English literature—Bio-bibliography 016.82
   x Bio-bibliography
   xx **Authors, English**
English literature—Collections 820.8
      Use for collections of poetry and prose by
         several authors. Collections of prose
         are entered under **English prose liter-**
         ature. Collections of poetry are en-
         tered under **English poetry—Collec-**
         tions
   See also **English poetry—Collections; En-**
      glish prose literature
   x Collections of literature
   xx **Literature—Collections**
English literature—Criticism. *See* **English lit-**
      erature—History and criticism
English literature—Dictionaries 820.3
   See also **English literature—Indexes**
   xx **Dictionaries; English literature—Indexes**
English literature—Examinations, questions, etc.
      820.76
   xx **English literature—Study and teaching**
English literature—History and criticism 820.9
   x English literature—Criticism
   xx **Criticism; History**
English literature—Indexes 820.1
   See also **English literature—Dictionaries**
   xx **English literature—Dictionaries**
English literature—Outlines, syllabi, etc. 820.2
   See also **English literature—Study and**
      teaching
   x Outlines, syllabi, etc.
   xx **English literature—Study and teaching;**
      Literature—Outlines, syllabi, etc.
English literature—Study and teaching 820.7
   See also **English literature—Examinations,**
      questions, etc.; English literature—Out-
      lines, syllabi, etc.
   xx **English literature—Outlines, syllabi, etc.**
English literature—To 1100. *See* **Anglo-Saxon**
      literature
English newspapers 072
   xx **English literature; Newspapers**
English orations 825
   xx **English literature; Orations**
English parodies. *See* **Parodies**
English periodicals 052
   xx **English literature; Periodicals**
English poetry 821
   xx **English literature; Poetry**
English poetry—Collections 821.08
   xx **English literature—Collections; Poetry—**
      Collections
English poetry—History and criticism 821.09
   xx **Criticism; Poetry—History and criticism**
English prose literature 820.8; 828
      Use for collections of prose writings which
         may include several literary forms
         such as essays, fiction, orations, etc.
   x Prose literature, English

English prose literature—*Continued*

    xx **English literature; English literature— Collections**

English satire. *See* **Satire, English**

English wit and humor 827.08

    Use for collections of several authors. May be used also for materials about **English wit and humor**

    xx **English literature; Wit and humor**

Engravers 920; 927

    See also **Etchers; Lithographers**

    xx **Artists**

Engraving (May subdiv. geog. adjective form, e.g. **Engraving, American;** etc.) 760; 765

    See also **Etching; Gems; Linoleum block printing; Mezzotint engraving; Photoengraving; Wood engraving**

    x Copper engraving; Engravings; Line engraving; Steel engraving

    xx **Art; Etching; Graphic arts; Illustration of books; Pictures**

Engraving, American 760; 769

    x American engraving; U.S.—Engraving

Engravings. *See* **Engraving**

Enigmas. *See* **Curiosities and wonders; Riddles**

Enlarging (Photography). *See* **Photography— Enlarging**

Enlistment. *See* **U.S. Army—Recruiting, enlistment, etc.; U.S. Navy—Recruiting, enlistment, etc.**

Ensembles (Mathematics). *See* **Set theory**

Ensigns. *See* **Flags**

Ensilage. *See* **Silage and silos**

Enteric fever. *See* **Typhoid fever**

Entertainers 920; 927

    See also **Actors and actresses; Clowns; Comedians; Dancers**

Entertaining 395; 642

    Use for materials that treat of the art and skill of entertaining and hospitality

    See also **Amusements; Dinners and dining; Etiquette; Games; Luncheons; Parties**

    x Guests; Hospitality

    xx **Amusements; Etiquette; Home economics**

Entertainments. *See* **Amusements; Christmas entertainments; Church entertainments; Skits**

Entomology. *See* **Insects**

Entomology, Economic. *See* **Insects, Injurious and beneficial**

Entomology, Medical. *See* **Insects as carriers of disease**

Entozoa. *See* **Parasites**

Entrance requirements for colleges and universities. *See* **Colleges and universities— Entrance requirements;** and names of individual colleges and universities

Entrance requirements for colleges and universities—*Continued*

with the subdivision *Entrance requirements*

Environment 301.31

See also **Ecology;** and subjects with subdivision *Environmental aspects*, e.g. **Atomic power plants—Environmental aspects;** etc.

Environment, Space. *See* **Space environment**

Environment and pesticides. *See* **Pesticides—Environmental aspects**

Environment and state. *See* **Environmental policy**

Environmental aspects. *See* subjects with the subdivision *Environmental aspects*, e.g. **Atomic power plants—Environmental aspects;** etc.

Environmental policy (May subdiv. geog.) **301.31**

See also **Conservation of natural resources; Human ecology; Man—Influence on nature; Natural resources; Pollution**

x Environment and state; State and environment

xx **Human ecology; Man—Influence on nature**

Environmental policy—International cooperation 301.3

xx **International cooperation**

Environmental policy—U.S. **301.31**

x American environmental policy; U.S.—Environmental policy

Environmental pollution. *See* **Pollution**

Enzymes **547; 574.1**

See also **Fermentation**

Eolithic period. *See* **Stone age**

Ephemerides. *See* **Nautical almanacs**

Epic poetry **808.1; 808.81; 811.08; etc.**

See also **Romances**

xx **Poetry**

Epidemics **614.4**

See also **Communicable diseases;** also names of contagious diseases, e.g. **Smallpox;** etc.

x Pestilences

xx **Communicable diseases; Diseases; Public health**

Epigrams **808.88; 818; etc.**

See also **Proverbs; Quotations; Toasts**

x Sayings

xx **Proverbs; Wit and humor**

Epigraphy. *See* **Inscriptions**

Epilepsy **616.8**

xx **Nervous system—Diseases**

Episcopal Church. *See* **Church of England; Protestant Episcopal Church in the U.S.A.**

Epistemology. *See* **Knowledge, Theory of**

207

Epitaphs 929

>   *x* Burial; Graves

>   *xx* **Biography; Cemeteries; Inscriptions; Tombs**

Epithets. *See* **Names; Nicknames**

Epizoa. *See* **Parasites**

Equal employment opportunity. *See* **Discrimination in employment**

Equal opportunity in employment. *See* **Discrimination in employment**

Equal pay for equal work 331.1

>   *xx* **Discrimination in employment; Wages; Women—Employment**

Equality 323.4

>   *See also* **Aristocracy; Democracy; Individualism; Social classes; Socialism**

>   *x* Inequality; Social equality

>   *xx* **Democracy; Freedom; Socialism; Sociology**

Equations, Chemical. *See* **Chemical equations**

Equestrianism. *See* **Horseback riding**

Equipment and supplies. *See* appropriate subjects with the subdivision *Equipment and supplies*, e.g. **Sports—Equipment and supplies**; etc.

Ergonomics. *See* **Human engineering**

Erosion 551.3; 631.4

>   *See also* **Dust storms; Soil conservation**; also types of erosion, e.g. **Soil erosion**; etc.

Erotic art 700

>   *x* Art, Erotic; Art, Immoral; Immoral art; Sex in art

>   *xx* **Erotica**

Erotic literature 800

>   *x* Immoral literature; Literature, Erotic; Literature, Immoral

>   *xx* **Erotica**

Erotica

>   *See also* **Pornography**; also types of erotica, e.g. **Erotic art; Erotic literature**; etc.

>   *xx* **Pornography**

Errors 001.9

>   Use for materials on errors of judgment, errors of observation, scientific errors, popular misconceptions, etc. Errors in language are entered under names of languages with the subdivision *Errors*, e.g. **English language—Errors**; etc.

>   *See also* **Superstition**

>   *x* Fallacies; Mistakes

>   *xx* **Superstition**

Eruptions. *See* **Geysers; Volcanoes**

Escape life style. *See* **Counter culture**

Escapes 365; 904

>   *x* Prison escapes

>   *xx* **Adventure and adventurers; Prisons**

Eschatology 236; 291.2

>   *See also* **Death; End of the world; Future life; Heaven; Hell; Immortality; Mil-**

Eschatology—*Continued*

　　　lennium; Second Advent

　　x Intermediate state

　　xx **Theology**

Eskimos　970.1

　　x Esquimaux; Inuits

Eskimos—Folklore.　*See* **Folklore, Eskimo**

Esperanto　499

　　xx **Language, Universal**

Espionage (May subdiv. geog. adj. form)　**327;
　　355.3**

　　See also **Spies**

　　xx **Intelligence service; Secret service; Sub-
　　　versive activities**

Espionage, American　327; 355.3

　　x American espionage

Esquimaux.　*See* **Eskimos**

Essay　808.4

　　Use for materials on the appreciation of
　　　the essay and on writing the essay

　　xx **Literature**

Essays　808.84

　　Use for collections of literary essays by
　　　authors of different nationalities. Col-
　　　lections of literary essays by American
　　　authors are entered under **American
　　　essays;** by English authors, under **Eng-
　　　lish essays;** etc. Essays limited to a
　　　particular subject, by one or more au-
　　　thors, are entered under that subject.
　　　If it is not treated comprehensively,
　　　add the subdivision *Addresses and es-
　　　says*

　　See also **American essays; English essays;**
　　　etc.; also general subjects with the
　　　subdivision *Addresses and essays,* e.g.
　　　**Agriculture—Addresses and essays;
　　　U.S.—History—Addresses and essays;**
　　　etc.

　　x Collections of literature

　　xx **Literature—Collections**

Essences and essential oils　664; 668

　　See also **Flavoring essences; Perfumes**

　　x Aromatic plant products; Oils, Essential;
　　　Vegetable oils; Volatile oils

　　xx **Distillation; Oils and fats**

Estate planning　332.024; 343.4

　　See also **Inheritance and transfer tax; In-
　　　surance; Investments; Taxation**

　　xx **Finance, Personal**

Estate tax.　*See* **Inheritance and transfer tax**

Esthetics　111.8; 701

　　See also **Art appreciation; Color; Criticism;
　　　Painting; Poetry; Rhythm; Romanti-
　　　cism; Sculpture; Values**

　　x Aesthetics; Beauty; Taste (Esthetics)

　　xx **Art**

Estimates.　*See* appropriate technical subjects
　　　with the subdivision *Estimates,* e.g.
　　　Building—Estimates; etc.

Estrangement (Social psychology). *See* **Aliena-**
    tion (Social Psychology)

Etchers   920; 927
    xx **Artists; Engravers**

Etching   767
    See also **Engraving**
    x Etchings
    xx **Art; Engraving; Pictures**

Etchings. *See* **Etching**

Eternal life. *See* **Future life**

Eternal punishment. *See* **Hell**

Eternity   115
    Use for materials on the philosophical con-
        cept of eternity. Materials dealing
        with the character and form of a
        future life are entered under **Future**
        life
    See also **Future life**
    xx **Future life**

Ethical education. *See* **Character education;**
    Religious education

Ethics (May subdiv. geog. adjective form, e.g.
    Ethics, Japanese; Ethics, Jewish; etc.)
    170
    See also

Character education	**Honesty**
Charity	**Human behavior**
Conscience	**Joy and sorrow**
Cruelty	**Justice**
Duty	**Sin**
Free will and de-	**Spiritual life**
terminism	**Stoics**
Friendship	**Utilitarianism**
Good and evil	**Values**
Happiness	

    also types of ethics, e.g. **Business ethics;**
        Christian ethics; etc. and subjects with
        the subdivision *Moral and religious*
        aspects, e.g. **Birth control—Moral and**
        religious aspects; etc.
    x Moral philosophy; Morality; Morals;
        Natural law; Philosophy, Moral
    xx **Civilization; Duty; Human behavior;**
        Life; Philosophy; Theology

Ethics, American   170
    x American ethics; U.S.—Ethics

Ethics, Biological. *See* **Bioethics**

Ethics, Christian. *See* **Christian ethics**

Ethics, Legal. *See* **Legal ethics**

Ethics, Medical. *See* **Medical ethics**

Ethics, Political. *See* **Political ethics**

Ethics, Professional. *See* **Professional ethics**

Ethics, Sexual. *See* **Sexual ethics**

Ethics, Social. *See* **Social ethics**

Ethiopian-Italian War, 1935–1936. *See* **Italo-**
    Ethiopian War, 1935–1936

Ethnic groups   301.45
    For materials on several groups in a region
        use **Ethnology** subdivided geog.; for

Ethnic groups—*Continued*
    individual groups use their names,
    e.g. **Mexican Americans;** etc.
  See also **Minorities; Race relations**
  x Groups, Ethnic
  xx **Ethnology**

Ethnic psychology. *See* **Ethnopsychology**
Ethnography. *See* **Ethnology**

Ethnology (May subdiv. geog.)   **572**
  See also

Acculturation	**Man, Nonliterate**
Anthropogeography	**Man, Prehistoric**
Anthropology	**Manners and cus-**
Anthropometry	**toms**
Archeology	**Physical anthro-**
Cannibalism	**pology**
Civilization	**Race**
Color of people	**Race relations**
Costume	**Sacrifice**
Ethnic groups	**Society, Nonliterate**
Ethnopsychology	**folk**
Folklore	**Totems and totem-**
Language and lan-	**ism**
guages	

  also names of peoples, e.g. **Blacks; Teu-
    tonic peoples;** etc.; and names of
    countries with the subdivision *Social
    life and customs,* e.g. **U.S.—Social life
    and customs;** etc.
  x Aborigines; Ethnography; Geographical
    distribution of people; Native peoples;
    Races of people
  xx **Anthropology; Archeology; Civilization;
    Geography; History; Man; Science**

Ethnology—U.S.   **572.973**
  See also names of individual ethnic groups,
    e.g. **Indians of North America; Mex-
    ican Americans;** etc.
  x U.S.—Ethnology; U.S.—Peoples

Ethnopsychology   **155.8**
  See also **National characteristics; Social
    psychology**
  x Ethnic psychology; Folk psychology;
    National psychology; Psychology,
    Ethnic; Psychology, National; Psy-
    chology, Racial; Race psychology
  xx **Anthropology; Ethnology; National
    characteristics; Psychology; Social
    psychology; Sociology**

Etiquette   **395**
  See also **Courtesy; Dancing; Dating (So-
    cial customs); Dinners and dining; En-
    tertaining; Letter writing; Manners
    and customs;** and types of etiquette as
    in phrases, e.g. **Table etiquette;** etc.
    also names of countries with the sub-
    division *Social life and customs*
  x Ceremonies; Manners; Politeness; Sal-
    utations

Etiquette—*Continued*

    xx **Courtesy; Entertaining; Human behavior; Manners and customs**

Etymology. *See* names of languages with the subdivision *Etymology*, e.g. **English language—Etymology**; etc.

Eucharist. *See* **Lord's Supper**

Eugenics 573.2; 575.1

    See also **Birth control; Heredity**

    xx **Anthropology; Family; Genetics; Heredity; Population; Social problems**

Europe, Central. *See* **Central Europe**

Europe, Eastern. *See* **Eastern Europe**

Europe—History 940

Europe—History—To 476 936-937

Europe—History—476–1492 940.1-940.2

    See also **Holy Roman Empire; Hundred Years' War, 1339–1453; Middle Ages —History; Thirteenth century**

    xx **Middle Ages—History**

Europe—History—1492–1789 940.2

    See also names of wars, e.g. **Seven Years' War, 1756–1763; Spanish Succession, War of, 1701–1714; Thirty Years' War, 1618–1648**; etc.

    xx **Reformation; Seven Years' War, 1756–1763**

Europe—History—1789–1900 940.2

    x Europe—History—19th century; Napoleonic Wars

Europe—History—19th century. *See* **Europe —History—1789–1900**

Europe—History—20th century 940.5

Europe—History—1914–1945 940.5

    See also **World War, 1914–1918; World War, 1939–1945**

Europe—History—1945– 940.55

Europe—Politics and government 940

    May be subdivided by period using the same subdivisions as under **Europe— History**, e.g. **Europe—Politics and government—1789–1900**

    See also **European federation**

European common market. *See* **European Economic Community**

European Economic Community 382

    x Common market; European common market

European federation 301.24; 940

    x Federation of Europe; Paneuropean federation; United States of Europe (proposed)

    xx **Europe—Politics and government; Federal government; International organization**

European War, 1914–1918. *See* **World War, 1914–1918**

European War, 1939–1945. *See* **World War, 1939–1945**

212

Euthanasia 174
>   *x* Death, Mercy; Killing, Mercy; Mercy
    killing; Right to die; Right to live
>   *xx* **Homicide; Medical ethics**

Evacuation of civilians. *See* names of wars
    with the subdivision *Evacuation of
    civilians,* e.g. **World War, 1939–1945
    —Evacuation of civilians;** etc.

Evaluation of literature. *See* **Books—Reviews;
    Books and reading; Books and read-
    ing—Best books; Criticism; Literature
    —History and criticism**

Evangelistic work 253.7
>   *See also* **Conversion; Missions, Christian;
    Revivals; Salvation Army**
>   *xx* **Church work; Missions, Christian; Re-
    vivals**

Evening and continuation schools 374.8
>   *See also* **Adult education**
>   *x* Continuation schools; Evening schools;
    Night schools
>   *xx* **Adult education; Education; Education,
    Compulsory; Education, Secondary;
    Public schools; Technical education**

Evening schools. *See* **Evening and continua-
    tion schools**

Evergreens 585
>   *xx* **Landscape gardening; Shrubs; Trees**

Evidences of Christianity. *See* **Apologetics**
Evidences of the Bible. *See* **Bible—Evidences,
    authority, etc.**
Evil. *See* **Good and evil**
Evil spirits. *See* **Demonology**
Evolution 573.2; 575
>   *See also*

Adaptation (Biol-ogy)	**Man—Influence of environment**
Anatomy, Compar-ative	**Man—Origin and antiquity**
Biology	**Mendel's law**
Color of animals	**Natural selection**
Color of people	**Religion and sci-ence**
Creation	
Embryology	**Social change**
Heredity	**Variation (Biology)**
Life—Origin	

>   *x* Darwinism; Development; Mutation
    (Biology); Origin of species
>   *xx* **Biology; Creation; Genetics; Heredity;
    Man—Origin and antiquity; Natural
    selection; Philosophy, Modern; Re-
    ligion and science; Variation (Biol-
    ogy); Zoology**

Ex libris. *See* **Bookplates**
Examinations 371.2
>   Use for general materials about examina-
    tions, their value, etc. Materials dis-
    cussing the requirements for examina-
    tions in particular branches of study,
    or compilations of questions and an-

213

Examinations—*Continued*

swers for such examinations, are entered under the subject with the subdivision *Examinations, questions, etc.,* e.g. **English language—Examinations, questions, etc.;** etc.

See also **Civil service—Examinations; Colleges and universities—Entrance requirements; Mental tests;** also particular branches of study with the subdivision *Examinations, questions, etc.,* e.g. **English language—Examinations, questions, etc.; Music—Examinations, questions, etc.;** etc.

x Achievement tests; Objective tests; Tests

xx **Educational tests and measurements; Teaching**

Ex-Catholic priests. *See* **Ex-priests**

Excavation 624

xx **Civil engineering; Tunnels**

Excavations (Archeology) (May subdiv. geog.) **913**

See also **Mounds and mound builders**

x Earthworks (Archeology); Ruins

xx **Archeology; Cities and towns, Ruined, extinct, etc.; Mounds and mound builders**

Excavations (Archeology)—U.S. 917.3

x U.S.—Excavations (Archeology)

Exceptional children 155.4

See also **Gifted children; Handicapped children; Problem children; Slow learning children**

x Abnormal children; Children, Abnormal; Children, Exceptional

xx **Children; Education, Elementary**

Exchange 332.4; 332.6

See also **Commerce; Foreign exchange; Money; Stock exchange**

xx **Commerce**

Exchange of persons programs 301.24

See also classes of persons participating in an exchange; e.g. **Teachers, Interchange of;** etc.

x Interchange of visitors; Specialists exchange programs; Visitors' exchange programs

xx **Cultural relations; International cooperation**

Exchange of prisoners of war. *See* **Prisoners of war**

Exchange of teachers. *See* **Teachers, Interchange of**

Executions. *See* **Capital punishment**

Executive ability 658.4

See also **Efficiency, Industrial; Leadership**

x Administrative ability

xx **Ability; Efficiency, Industrial**

214

Executive departments. *See* names of countries, states, etc. with the subdivision *Executive departments,* e.g. **U.S.—Executive departments;** etc.

Executive investigations. *See* **Governmental investigations**

Executive power (May subdiv. geog.) **351.04; 353.03**

Use for materials that discuss the duties, rights and abuses of the highest administrative authority of a country, often as compared or contrasted with the legislative power

See also **Monarchy; Presidents; Separation of powers**

x Presidents—Powers and duties

xx **Constitutional law; Political science; Presidents**

Executive power—U.S. 353.03

x Presidents—U.S.—Power; U.S.—Executive power

Executors and administrators 346.5

See also **Wills**

x Administrators and executors

xx **Inheritance and succession; Wills**

Exegesis, Biblical. *See* **Bible—Criticism, interpretation, etc.**

Exercise 613.7; 796.4

See also **Gymnastics; Physical education and training; Physical fitness;** also names of special exercises and physical activities, e.g. **Rowing;** etc.

xx **Hygiene; Physical education and training; Reducing**

Exhaustion. *See* **Fatigue**

Exhibitions

See also **Fashion shows; Flower shows;** etc.; also subjects with the subdivision *Exhibitions,* e.g. **Art—Exhibitions; Printing—Exhibitions;** etc.; and names of exhibitions, e.g. **Expo '70;** etc.

x Expositions; Industrial exhibitions; International exhibitions; World's fairs

xx **Fairs**

Exiles. *See* **Refugees**

Existentialism 142

xx **Metaphysics; Philosophy, Modern; Phenomenology**

Exobiology. *See* **Life on other planets; Space biology**

Exorcism 133.4

See also **Demoniac possession; Demonology; Witchcraft**

xx **Demoniac possession; Demonology; Superstition**

Expeditions, Antarctic and Arctic. *See* **Arctic regions; Antarctic regions;** and names of expeditions, e.g. **Byrd Antarctic Expedition, 1st, 1928–1930;** etc.

215

Expeditions, Scientific. *See* **Scientific expeditions**

Experience. *See* **Empiricism**

Experimental farms. *See* **Agricultural experiment stations**

Experimental films 791.4

  x Avant-garde films; Films; Motion pictures, Experimental; Personal films; Underground films

  xx **Motion pictures**

Experimental methods in education. *See* **Education—Experimental methods**

Experimental psychology. *See* **Psychology, Physiological**

Experimental schools. *See* **Free schools**

Experimental theater 792

  x Avant-garde theater

  xx **Theater**

Experimental universities. *See* **Free universities**

Experiments, Scientific. *See* **Science—Experiments;** and particular branches of science with the subdivision *Experiments,* e.g. **Chemistry—Experiments;** etc.

Exploration, Space. *See* **Outer space—Exploration**

Exploration, Submarine. *See* **Underwater exploration**

Exploration, Underwater. *See* **Underwater exploration**

Explorations. *See* **America—Exploration; Discoveries (in geography); Explorers;** and names of countries with the subdivision *Exploring expeditions,* e.g. **U.S.—Exploring expeditions;** etc.

Explorer (Artificial satellite) 629.46

  xx **Artificial satellites**

Explorers 920; 923

  See also **America—Exploration; Discoveries (in geography); Travelers; Voyages and travels;** also names of countries with the subdivisions *Description and travel* and *Exploring expeditions,* e.g. **U.S.—Description and travel; U.S.—Exploring expeditions;** etc.; and names of individual explorers

  x Discoverers; Explorations; Navigators; Voyagers

  xx **Adventure and adventurers; America—Exploration; Discoveries (in geography); Heroes and heroines; Travelers; Voyages and travels**

Exploring expeditions. *See* names of countries with the subdivision *Exploring expeditions* (e.g. **U.S.—Exploring expeditions;** etc.); and names of expeditions, e.g. **Lewis and Clark Expedition;** etc.

Explosions 904

  xx **Accidents**

Explosives   623.4; 662

> *See also* types of explosives and explosive
>> devices, e.g. **Ammunition; Dynamite;**
>> **Gunpowder; Torpedoes;** etc.

> *xx* **Chemistry**

Expo '70   607.4

> *x* Japan World's Exposition, Osaka, 1970;
>> Osaka. World's Fair, 1970

> *xx* **Exhibitions; Fairs**

Exports.   *See* **Commerce; Tariff**

Expositions.   *See* **Exhibitions**

Express highways   625.7

> *x* Freeways; Limited access highways;
>> Motorways; Parkways; Superhigh-
>> ways; Turnpikes (Modern); Toll
>> roads

> *xx* **Roads; Traffic engineering**

Express service   380.5

> *See also* **Pony express**

> *xx* **Railroads; Transportation**

Expression.   *See* **Nonverbal communication**

Expressionism (Art)   759.06

> *See also* **Postimpressionism (Art)**

> *xx* **Painting; Postimpressionism (Art)**

Ex-priests   253

> *x* Catholic ex-priests; Ex-Catholic priests

> *xx* **Catholic Church—Clergy; Priests**

Expropriation.   *See* **Eminent domain**

Ex-service men   *See* **Veterans**

Extension work, Agricultural.   *See* **Agricul-**
> **tural extension work**

Extermination of pests.   *See* **Pests—Control**

Extinct animals   560; 562-569

> *See also* **Rare animals;** also names of ex-
>> tinct animals, e.g. **Mastodon;** etc.

> *x* Animals, Extinct

> *xx* **Fossils; Rare animals**

Extinct cities.   *See* **Cities and towns, Ruined,**
> **extinct, etc.**

Extinct plants.   *See* **Plants, Fossil**

Extracurricular activities.   *See* **Student activ-**
> **ities**

Extragalactic nebulae.   *See* **Galaxies**

Extrasensory perception   133.8

> *x* ESP

> *xx* **Clairvoyance;   Psychical   research;**
> **Thought transference**

Extraterrestrial bases   629.44

> Use for materials on installations set up on
>> other planets for specific purposes
>> other than colonization

> *See also* **Space colonies**

> *xx* **Space colonies**

Extraterrestrial communication.   *See* **Interstel-**
> **lar communication**

Extraterrestrial environment.   *See* **Space envi-**
> **ronment**

Extraterrestrial life.   *See* **Life on other planets;**
> **Space biology**

217

Extravehicular activity (Space flight)   629.45

   x Space vehicles—Extravehicular activity; Space walk; Walking in space

   xx **Space flight**

Extremism (Political science). *See* **Radicals and radicalism; Right and left (Political science)**

Eye   611; 612

   See also **Optometry; Vision**

   xx **Head; Optometry; Vision**

Eyeglasses   617.7; 681

   See also kinds of eyeglasses, e.g. **Contact lenses;** etc.

   x Spectacles

FM Radio.   *See* **Radio frequency modulation**

FORTRAN   (Computer   program   language)   001.6

   x Formula translation (Computer program language); Fortran (Computer program language)

   xx **Programming languages (Electronic computers)**

Fables   398.2

   Use for materials in which animals or inanimate objects speak and act like human beings. Also used for materials about fables

   See also **Animals—Fiction; Folklore; Parables**

   x Tales

   xx **Allegories; Fiction; Folklore; Legends; Literature; Parables**

Fabrics   677

   See also names and types of fabrics, e.g. **Linen; Nylon; Synthetic fabrics;** etc.

   x Cloth; Dry goods; Textiles

Fabrics, Synthetic.   *See* **Synthetic fabrics**

Face   611; 612

   See also **Nose; Physiognomy**

   xx **Head; Physiognomy**

Facetiae.   *See* **Anecdotes; Wit and humor**

Factories   725

   See also kinds of factories, e.g. **Mills and millwork;** etc.; also headings beginning with the word **Factory**

   x Industrial plants; Mill and factory buildings

   xx **Industrial buildings; Mills and millwork**

Factories—Management.   *See* **Factory management**

Factories—Training departments.   *See* **Employees—Training**

Factory and trade waste.   *See* **Industrial wastes**

Factory management   658.5

   Use for materials on the technical problems of manufacturing processes. Materials on general principles of management of industries are entered under **Industrial management**

218

Factory management—*Continued*
  See also Efficiency, Industrial; Employees'
    representation in management; Job
    analysis; Motion study; Office man-
    agement; Personnel management; Su-
    pervisors; Time study
  x Factories—Management; Production en-
    gineering; Shop management
  xx Efficiency, Industrial; Industrial manage-
    ment; Management; Personnel man-
    agement
Factory schools. *See* Employees—Training
Factory waste. *See* Industrial wastes
Faculty (Education). *See* Colleges and uni-
    versities—Faculty; Educators; Teachers
Faience. *See* Pottery
Failure (in business). *See* Bankruptcy
Fair employment practice. *See* Discrimination
    in employment
Fair housing. *See* Discrimination in housing
Fair trade. *See* Competition, Unfair
Fair trade (Tariff). *See* Free trade and pro-
    tection
Fair trial and free press. *See* Freedom of the
    press and fair trial
Fair use (Copyright) 341.47
  xx Copyright
Fairies 398
  See also Fairy tales
  x Elves; Gnomes; Goblins
  xx Folklore; Superstition
Fairs 607.4
  See also Exhibitions; Markets; also names
    of fairs; e.g. Expo '70; etc.
  x Bazaars; Trade fairs; World's fairs
  xx Markets
Fairy tales 398.2
  See also Folklore
  x Children's stories; Stories; Tales
  xx Children's literature; Fairies; Fiction;
    Folklore; Legends; Literature
Faith 234
  Use for materials treating of religious faith
    and doubt. Materials treating of doubt
    from the philosophical standpoint are
    entered under Belief and doubt
  See also Agnosticism; Atheism; Salvation;
    Skepticism; Truth
  x Religious belief
  xx Religion; Spiritual life; Theology
Faith, Confessions of. *See* Creeds
Faith healing 615
  See also Christian Science; Mental healing;
    Miracles; Therapeutics, Suggestive
  x Divine healing; Mind cure; Spiritual
    healing
  xx Christian Science; Medicine and religion;
    Mental healing; Mind and body; Sub-
    consciousness; Therapeutics, Sugges-
    tive

219

Faithfulness. *See* **Loyalty**
Falconry 799.2
    x Hawking
    xx **Game and game birds; Hunting**
Fall. *See* **Autumn**
Fallacies. *See* **Errors; Logic**
Falling stars. *See* **Meteors**
Fallout, Radioactive. *See* **Radioactive fallout**
Fallout shelters. *See* **Air raid shelters**
False advertising. *See* **Advertising, Fraudulent**
Falsehood. *See* **Truthfulness and falsehood**
Family 301.42
    See also

Clans and clan	**Home**
system	**Marriage**
Divorce	**Parent and child**
Domestic relations	**Single parent fam-**
Eugenics	**ily**
Family life	
Family life educa-	
tion	

    also names of members of the family, e.g.
        Children; Fathers; Mothers; etc.
    xx **Domestic relations; Home; Human rela-**
        tions; Marriage; Sociology
Family—Religious life 249
    x Family devotions; Family prayers; Fam-
        ily worship
    xx **Religious life**
Family budget. *See* **Budgets, Household**
Family devotions. *See* **Devotional exercises;**
        Family—Religious life
Family histories. *See* **Genealogy**
Family life 301.42
    x Family relations; Home life
    xx **Family**
Family life education 301.42; 362.8
    See also **Finance, Personal; Home econom-**
        ics; Human relations; Marriage coun-
        seling; Sex education
    xx **Family; Human behavior; Marriage**
Family names. *See* **Names, Personal**
Family planning. *See* **Birth control**
Family prayers. *See* **Devotional exercises;**
        Family—Religious life
Family relations. *See* **Domestic relations;**
        Family life
Family social work. *See* **Social case work**
Family trees. *See* **Genealogy**
Family worship. *See* **Family—Religious life**
Famines (May subdiv. geog.) **904**
    xx **Food supply**
Famines—U.S. 904
    x U.S.—Famines
Fancy dress. *See* **Costume**
Fans 391
    xx **Costume**
Fantastic fiction 808.3; Fic
    See also **Science fiction**
    xx **Fiction**

Fantasy 153.3

   x Day dreams

   xx **Dreams; Imagination**

Far East 915; 950

   Use for materials on the Far East includ-
      ing China, Japan, Korea, Formosa,
      Hongkong and Macao

   x East (Far East); Orient

   xx **Asia**

Farm animals. *See* **Domestic animals; Live-
      stock**

Farm buildings 631.2; 728.6

   See also names of specific farm buildings,
      e.g. **Barns;** etc.

   x Architecture, Rural; Buildings, Farm;
      Rural architecture

   xx **Architecture; Architecture, Domestic;
      Buildings**

Farm credit. *See* **Agricultural credit**

Farm crops. *See* **Farm produce**

Farm engines 631.3

   See also **Agricultural engineering; Tractors**

   xx **Agricultural machinery; Engines; Gas
      and oil engines; Steam engines**

Farm implements. *See* **Agricultural machinery**

Farm laborers. *See* **Agricultural laborers**

Farm life (May subdiv. geog.) **630.1; 301.43**

   See also **Country life; Ranch life; Sociol-
      ogy, Rural**

   x Rural life

   xx **Country life; Sociology, Rural**

Farm life—U.S. 630.1

   x U.S.—Farm life

Farm machinery. *See* **Agricultural machinery**

Farm management 631

   See also **Agriculture—Economic aspects**

   xx **Agriculture—Economic aspects; Farms;
      Management**

Farm mechanics. *See* **Agricultural engineering;
      Agricultural machinery**

Farm produce 633

   See also names of farm products, e.g. **Hay;**
      etc.

   x Agricultural products; Crops; Farm
      crops

   xx **Food; Raw materials**

Farm produce—Marketing 338.1

   See also **Agriculture—Economic aspects**

   x Fruit—Marketing; Marketing of farm
      produce; Vegetables—Marketing

   xx **Agriculture—Economic aspects; Market-
      ing; Prices**

Farm tenancy 333.5

   Use for materials on the economic and so-
      cial aspects of farm tenancy. Materials
      that treat of the legal aspect are en-
      tered under **Landlord and tenant**

   x Agriculture—Tenant farming; Farming
      on shares; Sharecropping; Tenant
      farming

Farm tenancy—*Continued*

　　xx **Farms; Land tenure; Landlord and tenant**

Farmers' cooperatives. *See* **Agriculture, Cooperative**

Farming. *See* **Agriculture**

Farming, Dry. *See* **Dry farming**

Farming on shares. *See* **Farm tenancy**

Farms 631.2

　　See also **Farm management; Farm tenancy**

　　xx **Agriculture; Land use; Real estate**

Farms, Experimental. *See* **Agricultural experiment stations**

Farriering. *See* **Blacksmithing**

Fascism (May subdiv. geog.) **320.5; 321.9; 335.6**

　　See also **National socialism**

　　x Authoritarianism

　　xx **National socialism; Totalitarianism**

Fascism—Germany. *See* **National socialism**

Fascism—U.S. 973.9

　　x U.S.—Fascism

Fashion 391

　　Use for materials describing the prevailing mode or style in dress. Historical information on styles of particular countries or periods are entered under **Costume**

　　See also **Clothing and dress; Costume; Dressmaking; Tailoring**

　　x Style in dress

　　xx **Clothing and dress; Costume**

Fashion design 741.67; 746.9

　　x Costume design

　　xx **Commercial art; Design**

Fashion models. *See* **Models, Fashion**

Fashion shows 391.074; 659.1

　　xx **Exhibitions**

Fashionable society. *See* **Upper classes**

Fast breeder reactors. *See* **Nuclear reactors**

Faster reading. *See* **Rapid reading**

Fasting 178

　　See also **Asceticism; Fasts and feasts**

　　x Abstinence

Fasts and feasts 263; 394.2

　　Use for materials on religious fasts and feasts in general. May be subdiv. by religion, e.g. **Fasts and feasts—Judaism;** etc. Materials on secular festivals are entered under **Festivals**

　　See also **Festivals; Holidays;** also names of individual fasts and feasts

　　x Church festivals; Days; Ecclesiastical fasts and feasts; Feasts; Fiestas; Religious festivals

　　xx **Christian antiquities; Fasting; Festivals; Holidays; Rites and ceremonies**

Fasts and feasts—Judaism 296.4

　　See also names of individual fasts and feasts, e.g. **Yom Kippur;** etc.

Fasts and feasts—Judaism—*Continued*
    x Festivals—Jews; Jewish holidays; Jews
        —Festivals
Fat.   *See* Oils and fats
Fate and fatalism   149
    See also Free will and determinism; Pre-
        destination
    x Destiny; Fortune
    xx Philosophy
Fathers   301.42
    xx Family; Men
Fatigue   613.7
    See also Rest
    x Exhaustion; Weariness
    xx Physiology; Rest
Fatness.   *See* Obesity
Fats.   *See* Oils and fats
Fauna.   *See* Animals; Zoology
Fayence.   *See* Pottery
Fear   131; 152.4
    See also Courage; Horror
    x Anxiety
    xx Courage; Emotions; Nervous system—
        Diseases; Neuroses
Feasts.   *See* Fasts and feasts
Federal aid to education   379
    Use same form for federal aid to other
        subjects
    x Education—Federal aid
    xx Colleges and universities—Finance; Edu-
        cation—Finance; Education and state
Federal aid to libraries   021.8
    x Libraries—Federal aid
    xx Libraries and state; Library finance
Federal budget.   *See* Budget—U.S.
Federal courts.   *See* Courts—U.S.
Federal government   351
    See also Democracy; European federation;
        State governments
    x Confederacies
    xx Constitutional law; Democracy; Political
        science; Republics; State governments
Federal libraries.   *See* Libraries, Governmental
Federal reserve banks   332.1
    xx Banks and banking
Federal revenue sharing.   *See* Revenue sharing
Federal-state tax relations.   *See* Intergovern-
        mental tax relations
Federation, International.   *See* International or-
        ganization
Federation of Europe.   *See* European federa-
        tion
Feedback control systems   629.8
    See also Servomechanisms
    xx Automation
Feedback (Psychology)   153.1
    See also Biofeedback training
    xx Learning, Psychology of

223

Feeds 633
    See also **Forage plants; Hay; Root crops; Silage and silos;** also names of feeds, e.g. **Oats;** etc.
    x Fodder
    xx **Grasses; Hay; Root crops**
Feeling. *See* **Perception; Touch**
Feelings. *See* **Emotions**
Feet. *See* **Foot**
Fellowships. *See* **Scholarships, fellowships, etc.**
Felony. *See* **Crime**
Female climacteric *See* **Menopause**
Female role. *See* **Sex role**
Feminine psychology. *See* **Women—Psychology**
Feminism 301.41; 323.4
    See also **Women—Civil rights; Women's liberation movement**
    x Women—Rights; Women's rights
    xx **Women—Civil rights; Women's liberation movement**
Fencing 796.8
    See also **Dueling**
    x Fighting
    xx **Dueling; Physical education and training**
Fermentation 547; 663
    See also **Bacteriology; Wine and wine making; Yeast**
    xx **Bacteriology; Chemistry; Enzymes; Wine and wine making**
Ferns 587; 635.9
    xx **Plants**
Fertilization of plants 581.1
    x Plants—Fertilization; Pollination
    xx **Flowers; Insects; Plant breeding; Plant physiology; Plants**
Fertilizers and manures 631.8; 668
    See also **Agricultural chemistry; Compost; Lime; Nitrates; Phosphates; Potash**
    x Manures
    xx **Agricultural chemistry; Soils**
Festivals (May subdiv. geog.) 394.2
    See note under **Fasts and feasts**
    See also **Fasts and feasts; Holidays; Music festivals; Pageants**
    x Carnivals; Days; Fiestas
    xx **Fasts and feasts; Manners and customs; Pageants**
Festivals—Jews. *See* **Fasts and feasts—Judaism**
Festivals—U.S. 394.2
    x U.S.—Festivals
Fetal death. *See* **Abortion**
Feudalism 321.3
    See also **Chivalry; Clans and clan system; Middle Ages; Peasantry**
    x Fiefs; Vassals
    xx **Chivalry; Civilization, Medieval; Land tenure; Land use; Middle Ages—History**

Fever   616
> *See also* names of fevers, e.g. **Malaria;** etc.
>
> *xx* **Medicine—Practice; Therapeutics**

Fiat money.   *See* **Paper money**

Fibers   677
> *See also* **Cotton; Flax; Hemp; Linen; Paper;
>   Silk; Wool**
>
> *x* Textile fibers
>
> *xx* **Cotton; Hemp**

Fibers, Glass.   *See* **Glass fibers**

Fiction   808.3
> Use for fiction as a literary form
> *See also*

Allegories	**Plots (Drama, fic-**
Fables	**tion, etc.)**
Fairy tales	**Romances**
Folklore	**Romanticism**
Legends	**Short story**
Novelists	

> *also* **American fiction; English fiction;** etc.;
>   and subjects with the subdivision *Fic-
>   tion,* e.g. **Animals—Fiction; Slavery in
>   the U.S.—Fiction; Napoléon I, Em-
>   peror of the French—Fiction;** etc.; and
>   such phrase headings that do not lend
>   themselves to subdivision, e.g. **Fan-
>   tastic fiction; Historical fiction; Mys-
>   tery and detective stories; Science
>   fiction;** etc.
>
> *x* Novels; Stories
>
> *xx* **Literature**

Fiction, American; Fiction, English; etc.   *See*
>   **American fiction; English fiction;** etc.

Fiction, Historical.   *See* **Historical fiction**

Fiction—History and criticism   809.3

Fiction—Plots.   *See* **Plots (Drama, fiction, etc.)**

Fiction—Technique   808.3
> *x* Technique
>
> *xx* **Authorship**

Fictitious animals.   *See* **Animals, Mythical**

Fictitious names.   *See* **Pseudonyms**

Fiddle.   *See* **Violin**

Fiefs.   *See* **Feudalism; Land tenure**

Field athletics.   *See* **Track athletics**

Field hockey   796.35
> *x* Hockey

Field hospitals.   *See* **Hospitals, Military; Medi-
>   cine, Military**

Field trips   371.3
> *x* School excursions; School trips

Fiestas.   *See* **Fasts and feasts; Festivals**

Fifth column.   *See* **Subversive activities**

Fighting.   *See* **Battles; Boxing; Bullfights; Duel-
>   ing; Fencing; Gladiators; Military art
>   and science; Naval art and science;
>   Self-defense; War**

Figure drawing   743
> *See also* **Figure painting**
>
> *x* Human figure in art

Figure drawing—*Continued*
  xx **Anatomy, Artistic; Drawing; Figure painting**
Figure painting 757
  See also **Figure drawing; Portrait painting**
  x Human figure in art
  xx **Anatomy, Artistic; Figure drawing; Painting; Portrait painting**
Figure skating. *See* **Ice skating; Roller skating**
Files and filing 025.3; 651.5
  See also **Indexing**
  x Alphabeting; Filing systems
  xx **Indexing**
Filing systems. *See* **Files and filing**
Filling stations. *See* **Automobiles—Service stations**
Films. *See* types of films, e.g. **Experimental films; Filmstrips; Microfilms; Motion pictures;** etc.; also subjects with the subdivision *Motion pictures,* e.g. **Sculpture—Motion pictures;** etc.
Filmstrips 371.33; 778.2
  See also **Slides (Photography)**
  x Films; Strip films
  xx **Audio-visual materials; Photography; Slides (Photography)**
Finance (May subdiv. geog.) 332; 336
  See also

Bankruptcy	**Interest (Economics)**
Banks and banking	**Internal revenue**
Bonds	**Investments**
Budget	**Metropolitan**
Capital	**finance**
Church finance	**Monetary policy**
Commerce	**Money**
Credit	**Municipal finance**
Debts, Public	**Paper money**
Finance, Personal	**Prices**
Fiscal policy	**Securities**
Foreign exchange	**Speculation**
Income	**Stock exchange**
Income tax	**Tariff**
Inflation (Finance)	**Taxation**
Insurance	**Wealth**

  also subjects with the subdivision *Finance,* e.g. **Education—Finance;** etc.
  x Finance, Public; Funds; Public finance
  xx **Budget; Economics; Monetary policy**
Finance, Church. *See* **Church finance**
Finance, Household. *See* **Budgets, Household**
Finance, Municipal. *See* **Municipal finance**
Finance, Personal 332.024
  See also **Budgets, Household; Consumer credit; Estate planning; Insurance; Investments; Saving and thrift**
  x Budgets, Personal; Personal finance
  xx **Family life education; Finance**
Finance, Public. *See* **Finance**
Finance—U.S. 336.973
  x U.S.—Finance

226

Financial accounting. *See* **Accounting**
Financiers. *See* **Capitalists and financiers**
Fine arts. *See* **Arts**
Finger alphabet. *See* **Deaf—Means of communication**
Finger games. *See* **Finger play**
Finger marks. *See* **Fingerprints**
Finger painting 751.4
   x Painting, Finger
   xx **Children as artists; Painting**
Finger play 796.1
   x Finger games
   xx **Play**
Finger prints. *See* **Fingerprints**
Fingerprints 364.12
   x Finger marks; Finger prints
   xx **Anthropometry; Criminal investigation; Identification**
Finishes and finishing. *See* **Lacquer and lacquering; Paint; Painting, Industrial; Varnish and varnishing; Wood finishing**
Finno-Russian War, 1939–1940. *See* **Russo-Finnish War, 1939–1940**
Fire 536
   See also **Combustion; Fires; Fuel; Heat; Heating**
   xx **Chemistry; Combustion; Heat**
Fire balls. *See* **Meteors**
Fire bombs. *See* **Incendiary bombs**
Fire departments 628.9
Fire engines 621.2; 628.9
   xx **Engines; Fire fighting**
Fire fighters 920; 920.9
   x Firemen and firewomen
Fire fighting 628.9
   See also **Fire engines**
   xx **Fire prevention; Fires**
Fire insurance. *See* **Insurance, Fire**
Fire prevention 614.8
   See also **Fire fighting; Fireproofing;** also subjects and names of cities with the subdivision *Fires and fire prevention,* e.g. **Atomic power plants—Fires and fire prevention; Chicago—Fires and fire prevention;** etc.
   x Prevention of fire
   xx **Fires**
Firearms 623.4
   See also **Gunpowder; Ordnance; Shooting;** also types of firearms, e.g. **Pistols; Rifles; Shotguns;** etc.
   x Guns; Small arms; Weapons and weaponry
   xx **Arms and armor; Shooting**
Firearms—Control. *See* **Firearms—Law and legislation**
Firearms—Law and legislation 344.5
   x Firearms—Control; Guns—Control

Firearms industry and trade 338.4; 683

> Use for materials on the small arms industry. Materials on heavy firearms are entered under **Ordnance**

Firemen and firewomen. *See* **Fire fighters**

Fireplaces 697; 729

> *See also* **Chimneys**
>
> *xx* **Architecture–Details; Heating**

Fireproofing 628.9; 693.8

> *xx* **Fire prevention; Insurance, Fire**

Fires 614.8; 904

> *See also* **Fire fighting; Fire prevention; Forest fires; Insurance, Fire;** also subjects and names of cities with the subdivision *Fires and fire prevention,* e.g. **Atomic power plants–Fires and fire prevention; Chicago–Fires and fire prevention;** etc.
>
> *xx* **Accidents; Disasters; Fire**

Fireworks 662

First aid 614.8

> *See also* **Accidents; Artificial respiration; Bandages and bandaging; Lifesaving**
>
> *x* Emergencies; Injuries; Wounded, First aid to
>
> *xx* **Accidents; Hospitals, Military; Lifesaving; Medicine, Military; Nursing; Rescue work; Sick**

First editions. *See* **Bibliography–First editions**

First ladies—U.S. *See* **Presidents–U.S.–Wives**

Fiscal policy (May subdiv. geog.) **336.3**

> *See also* **Monetary policy**
>
> *xx* **Economic policy; Finance; Monetary policy**

Fiscal policy–U.S. 336.973

> *x* U.S.—Fiscal policy

Fish. *See* **Fishes**

Fish as food. *See* **Sea food**

Fish culture 639

> *x* Fish hatcheries
>
> *xx* **Aquariums; Fishes**

Fish hatcheries. *See* **Fish culture**

Fisheries (May subdiv. geog.) **639**

> Use for materials on the fishing industry
>
> *See also* **Fishes; Pearlfisheries; Whaling**
>
> *x* Fishing industry; Sea fisheries
>
> *xx* **Aquaculture; Fishes; Marine resources; Natural resources**

Fisheries–U.S. 639

> *x* U.S.—Fisheries

Fishes (May subdiv. geog.) **567; 597**

> Names of fishes are not included in this list but are to be added as needed, e.g. **Salmon;** etc.
>
> *See also* **Aquariums; Fish culture; Fisheries; Fishing; Sea food; Tropical fish;** also names of fishes, e.g. **Salmon;** etc.
>
> *x* Fish; Ichthyology
>
> *xx* **Fisheries; Marine animals; Vertebrates**

228

Fishes—Geographical distribution. *See* **Geographical distribution of animals and plants**

Fishes—Photography. *See* **Photography of fishes**

Fishes–U.S. 597

    x U.S.—Fishes

Fishing (May subdiv. geog.) **799.1**

    Use for materials on fishing as a sport. Materials on fishing as an industry are entered under **Fisheries**

    See also **Flies, Artificial;** also types of fishing, e.g. **Fly casting; Spear fishing; Trout fishing;** etc.

    x Angling

    xx **Fishes; Water sports**

Fishing—Equipment and supplies 799.1

    x Fishing tackle

Fishing–U.S. 799.1

    x U.S.—Fishing

Fishing flies. *See* **Flies, Artificial**

Fishing industry. *See* **Fisheries**

Fishing tackle. *See* **Fishing—Equipment and supplies**

Five-day work week. *See* **Hours of labor**

Flags (May subdiv. geog.) **929.9**

    See also **Signals and signaling**

    x Banners; Ensigns

    xx **Heraldry; Signals and signaling**

Flags–U.S. 929.9

    x American flag; U.S.—Flags

Flats. *See* **Apartment houses**

Flatware, Silver. *See* **Silverware**

Flavoring essences 664

    xx **Cookery; Essences and essential oils; Food**

Flax 633; 677

    See also **Linen**

    xx **Fibers; Linen; Yarn**

Flexible hours of labor. *See* **Hours of labor**

Flexitime. *See* **Hours of labor**

Flies 595.7

    See also names of flies; e.g., **Fruit flies;** etc.

    x Diptera; Fly; House flies

    xx **Household pests; Insects as carriers of disease; Pests**

Flies, Artificial 688.7; 799.1

    See also **Fly casting**

    x Artificial flies; Fishing flies

    xx **Fishing**

Flight 629.132

    See also **Aeronautics**

    x Flying; Locomotion

    xx **Aeronautics**

Flight attendants. *See* **Air lines—Flight attendants**

Flight to the moon. *See* **Space flight to the moon**

Flight training. *See* **Aeronautics—Study and teaching; Airplanes—Piloting**

Flights around the world. *See* **Aeronautics—Flights**

Flint implements. *See* **Stone implements**

Floats (Parades). *See* **Parades**

Flood control. *See* **Floods—Control**

Flood prevention. *See* **Floods—Control**

Floods 551.4; 551.5; 904

>*See also* **Reclamation of land; Rivers;** also names of rivers, cities, etc. with the subdivision *Floods,* e.g. **Chicago—Floods;** etc.
>
>*xx* **Meteorology; Natural disasters; Rain and rainfall; Rivers; Water**

Floods—Control 627

>*See also* **Dams; Forest influences; Rivers**
>
>*x* Flood control; Flood prevention
>
>*xx* **Forest influences; Hydraulic engineering**

Floods and forests. *See* **Forest influences**

Floors 694; 721

>*xx* **Architecture—Details; Building; Carpentry**

Flora. *See* **Botany; Plants**

Floral decoration. *See* **Flower arrangement**

Floral design. *See* **Design, Decorative**

Floriculture. *See* **Flower gardening**

Florists' designs. *See* **Flower arrangement**

Flour 664

>*See also* **Grain; Wheat**
>
>*x* Breadstuffs
>
>*xx* **Wheat**

Flour mills 664

>*x* Grist mills; Milling (Flour)
>
>*xx* **Mills and millwork**

Flower arrangement 745.92

>Use for materials on the artistic arrangement of flowers, including decoration of houses, churches, etc. with flowers
>
>*x* Designs, Floral; Floral decoration; Florists' designs; Flowers—Arrangement
>
>*xx* **Decoration and ornament; Flowers; Table setting and decoration**

Flower gardening 635.9

>Use for practical materials on the cultivation of flowering plants for either commercial or private purposes
>
>*See also*

Annuals (Plants)	**Perennials**
Bulbs	**Plant breeding**
Flowers	**Plant propagation**
Greenhouses	**Plants, Ornamental**
House plants	**Window gardening**

>*also* names of flowers, e.g. **Roses;** etc.
>
>*x* Floriculture
>
>*xx* **Botany; Flowers; Gardening; Horticulture; Plants**

230

Flower painting and illustration   758

   x Flowers in art

   xx **Flowers; Painting; Plants in art**

Flower shows   635.9074

   x Flowers—Exhibitions

   xx **Exhibitions**

Flowers (May subdiv. geog.)   **582**

   Use for general materials on the botanical characteristics of flowers, guides for studying and classifying them or for study of flowers from the artistic point of view. Materials limited to the cultivation of flowers are entered under **Flower gardening**

   Names of flowers are not included in this list but are to be added as needed, in the plural form; e.g. **Roses;** etc.

   See also

Annuals (Plants)	**Perennials**
Fertilization of	**Plants**
plants	**State flowers**
Flower arrange-	**Wild flowers**
ment	**Window gardening**
Flower gardening	
Flower painting and	
illustration	

   also names of flowers, e.g. **Roses;** etc.

   xx **Botany; Flower gardening; Plants**

Flowers—Arrangement. *See* **Flower arrangement**

Flowers, Artificial. *See* **Artificial flowers**

Flowers, Drying   745.92

   x Dried flowers

Flowers—Exhibitions. *See* **Flower shows**

Flowers, State. *See* **State flowers**

Flowers—U.S.   582

   x U.S.—Flowers

Flowers, Wild. *See* **Wild flowers**

Flowers in art. *See* **Design, Decorative; Flower painting and illustration; Plants in art**

Flu. *See* **Influenza**

Fluorescent lighting   621.32

   x Electric lighting, Fluorescent; Light, Electric

   xx **Lighting**

Fluoridation of water. *See* **Water—Fluoridation**

Flute   788

   xx **Wind instruments**

Fly. *See* **Flies**

Fly casting   799.1

   xx **Fishing; Flies, Artificial**

Flying. *See* **Flight**

Flying bombs. *See* **Guided missiles**

Flying saucers   001.9

   x UFO; Unidentified flying objects

   xx **Aeronautics**

Fodder. *See* **Feeds**

Fog   551.5

   xx **Meteorology; Water**

Fog signals. *See* **Signals and signaling**

Foliage. *See* **Leaves**

Folk art (May subdiv. geog. adjective form, e.g. **Folk art, Swedish;** etc.)   **745**

Use for general and historical materials on peasant and popular art in the fields of decorative arts, music, dancing, theater, etc.

See also **Art industries and trade; Arts and crafts**

x Peasant art

xx **Art; Art and society; Art industries and trade; Arts and crafts**

Folk art, American   745

x American folk art; U.S.—Folk art

Folk dancing (May subdiv. geog. adjective form, e.g. **Folk dancing, Swedish;** etc.) **793.3**

See also **Indians of North America—Dances; Square dancing**

x National dances

xx **Dancing; Folk music**

Folk dancing, American   793.3

x American folk dancing; U.S.—Folk dancing

Folk drama   808.82; 812; etc.

See also **Puppets and puppet plays**

x Folk plays

xx **Drama**

Folk lore. *See* **Folklore**

Folk medicine   616

x Folklore, Medical; Medical folklore

xx **Medicine, Popular**

Folk music (May subdiv. geog. adj. form) **784.4**

See also **Folk dancing**

xx **Music**

Folk music, American   784.4

x American folk music; U.S.—Folk music

Folk plays. *See* **Folk drama**

Folk psychology. *See* **Ethnopsychology**

Folk society, Nonliterate. *See* **Society, Nonliterate folk**

Folk songs (May subdiv. geog. adjective form, except for the U.S. and states and regions of the U.S. where the noun form is used, e.g. **Folk songs, French;** etc.; but **Folk songs—U.S.; Folk songs—Ohio;** etc.) **784.4**

See note under **Ballads**

See also **Ballads; Carols; Folklore; National songs**

xx **Ballads; Folklore; National songs; Songs; Vocal music**

Folks songs, African. *See* **Songs, African**

Folk songs, American. *See* **Folk songs—U.S.**

Folk songs, Black (African). *See* **Songs, African**

Folk songs, Black (American). *See* **Black songs**

232

Folk songs—U.S. 784.4

   x American folk songs; Folk songs, American; U.S.—Folk songs

  xx **Songs, American**

Folk tales. *See* **Folklore**

Folklore (May subdiv. geog. noun form (e.g. **Folklore—Ireland;** etc.) or, where country subdivision is not applicable, use ethnic subdivision, adjective form, e.g. **Folklore, Jewish;** etc.) **398; 398.2**

Use for a discussion of folklore in general and also for a story or a collection of stories based on spoken rather than written traditions

  See also

Charms	**Legends**
Devil	**Mythology**
Fables	**Nursery rhymes**
Fairies	**Plant lore**
Fairy tales	**Proverbs**
Folk songs	**Sagas**
Ghosts	**Superstition**
Grail	**Weather lore**
Halloween	**Witchcraft**

   x Folk lore; Folk tales; Tales; Tall tales; Traditions

  xx **Ethnology; Fables; Fairy tales; Fiction; Folk songs; Legends; Mythology; Superstition**

Folklore, Black 398.2

   x Black folklore; Blacks—Folklore

Folklore, Eskimo 398.2

   x Eskimos—Folklore

Folklore, Indian 398.2

Use for materials on folklore of American Indians. Collections of Indian legends, myths, tales, etc. are entered under **Indians of North America—Legends**

  See also **Indians of North America—Legends**

   x Indian folklore; Indians of North America—Folklore; Indians of North America—Mythology

  xx **Indians of North America—Legends**

Folklore, Jewish 398.2

   x Jews—Folklore

Folklore, Medical. *See* **Folk medicine**

Folklore—U.S. 398.2

   x U.S.—Folklore

Folklore of plants. *See* **Plant lore**

Folkways. *See* **Manners and customs**

Food 641; 664

  See also

Beverages	**Grain**
Cookery	**Markets**
Dinners and dining	**Nutrition**
Farm produce	**Vegetarianism**
Flavoring essences	**Vitamins**

Food—*Continued*

　　also names of foods, e.g. **Bread; Fruit; Meat; Vegetables;** etc.; *also* types of food, e.g. **Food, Artificial; Food, Dietetic; Food, Natural;** etc.; and subjects with the subdivision *Food,* e.g. **School children—Food;** etc.

　　x Gastronomy

　　xx **Cookery; Digestion; Dinners and dining; Home economics; Hygiene; Nutrition**

Food—Analysis   543

　　See also **Food additives**

　　x Analysis (Chemistry); Analysis of food; Chemistry of food; Food chemistry

　　xx **Chemistry, Technical**

Food, Artificial   641.3; 664

　　x Artificial food; Synthetic food

　　xx **Food**

Food, Canned. *See* **Canning and preserving**

Food—Contamination. *See* **Food contamination**

Food—Control. *See* **Food supply**

Food, Cost of. *See* **Cost of living**

Food, Dehydrated. *See* **Food, Dried**

Food, Dietetic   641.3; 664

　　x Dietetic food

　　xx **Diet; Food**

Food, Dried   641.4; 664

　　See also **Food, Freeze dried**

　　x Dehydrated foods; Dried foods; Food, Dehydrated

　　xx **Food—Preservation**

Food, Freeze dried   641.4; 664

　　x Freeze dried food

　　xx **Food, Dried**

Food, Frozen   641.4; 664

　　See also **Ice cream, ices, etc.**

　　x Frozen food

　　xx **Food—Preservation**

Food, Health. *See* **Food, Natural**

Food—Law and legislation   641.026

　　See also **Food adulteration and inspection**

　　x Food laws; Laws

　　xx **Food adulteration and inspection; Law; Legislation**

Food, Natural   641

　　x Food, Health; Health food; Natural food; Organic food

　　xx **Food**

Food—Preservation   641.4; 664

　　See also **Canning and preserving; Cold storage; Food, Dried; Food, Frozen; Food additives**

　　x Food preservation; Preservation of food

　　xx **Food supply**

Food additives   614.3; 641.4; 664

　　x Additives, Food

　　xx **Food—Analysis; Food—Preservation**

234

Food adulteration and inspection   614.3
>   *See also* **Food—Law and legislation; Meat inspection; Milk supply**
>
>   *x* Adulteration of food; Analysis of food; Food inspection; Inspection of food; Pure food
>
>   *xx* **Consumer protection; Food—Law and legislation; Public health**

Food chains (Ecology)   574.5
>   *xx* **Ecology**

Food chemistry.   *See* **Food—Analysis**

Food contamination   614.3
>   *x* Contaminated food; Food—Contamination

Food for invalids.   *See* **Cookery for the sick**

Food for school children.   *See* **School children —Food**

Food inspection.   *See* **Food adulteration and inspection**

Food laws.   *See* **Food—Law and legislation**

Food plants.   *See* **Plants, Edible**

Food-poisoning   615.9

Food preservation.   *See* **Food—Preservation**

Food supply   338.1
>   *See also* **Aquaculture; Famines; Food— Preservation; Meat industry and trade**
>
>   *x* Food—Control

Foot   611
>   *x* Feet; Toes

Foot—Care and hygiene.   *See* **Podiatry**

Football   796.33
>   *See also* **Soccer**
>
>   *xx* **College sports; Sports**

Football coaching   796.33
>   *xx* **Coaching (Athletics)**

Forage plants   633
>   *See also* **Grasses; Pastures; Silage and silos;** also names of specific forage plants, e.g. **Corn; Hay; Soybean;** etc.
>
>   *xx* **Feeds; Grasses; Pastures; Plants**

Force and energy   531
>   *See also* **Dynamics; Mechanics; Motion; Quantum theory**
>
>   *x* Conservation of energy; Energy
>
>   *xx* **Dynamics; Mechanics; Motion; Power (Mechanics); Quantum theory**

Force pumps. *See* **Pumping machinery**

Forced labor.   *See* **Convict labor; Peonage; Slavery**

Ford automobile   629.22
>   *xx* **Automobiles**

Forecasting
>   *See also* types of forecasting, e.g. **Business forecasting; Weather forecasting;** etc.
>
>   *x* Future; Predictions

Foreign aid program.   *See* **Economic assistance; Technical assistance**

Foreign area studies.   *See* **Area studies**

Foreign automobiles.   *See* **Automobiles, Foreign**

Foreign economic relations. *See* **International economic relations**

Foreign exchange   332.4
  x Cambistry; International exchange
  xx **Banks and banking; Exchange; Finance; Money; Stock exchange**

Foreign investments. *See* **Investments, Foreign**

Foreign language laboratories. *See* **Language laboratories**

Foreign language phrases. *See* **Languages, Modern—Conversations and phrases;** and names of languages with the subdivision *Conversations and phrases,* e.g. **French language—Conversations and phrases;** etc. For materials on foreign words and phrases incorporated into languages see names of languages with the subdivision *Foreign words and phrases, e.g.* **English language—Foreign words and phrases;** etc.

Foreign Legion (French Army). *See* **France. Army. Foreign Legion**

Foreign missions, Christian. *See* **Missions, Christian**

Foreign opinion. *See* names of countries with the subdivision *Foreign opinion,* or *Foreign opinion* subdivided geog. adjective form, e.g. **U.S.—Foreign opinion; U.S.—Foreign opinion, French;** etc.

Foreign policy. *See* names of countries with the subdivision *Foreign relations,* e.g. **U.S.—Foreign relations;** etc.

Foreign population. *See* **Immigration and emigration;** names of countries with the subdivision *Immigration and emigration* (e.g. **U.S.—Immigration and emigration;** etc.); and names of countries, cities, etc. with the subdivision *Foreign population,* e.g. **Chicago—Foreign population; U.S.—Foreign population;** etc.

Foreign relations. *See* **International relations;** and names of countries with the subdivision *Foreign relations,* e.g. **U.S.—Foreign relations;** etc.

Foreign service. *See* **Diplomatic and consular service**

Foreign students. *See* **Students, Foreign**

Foreign study   370.19
  x Overseas study; Study, Foreign; Study abroad; Study overseas

Foreign trade. *See* **Commerce**

Foreigners. *See* **Aliens; Citizenship; Naturalization;** names of countries, cities, etc. with the subdivision *Foreign population* (e.g. **U.S.—Foreign population;** etc.)

Foremen and foreladies. *See* **Supervisors**

Forenames. *See* **Names, Personal**

236

Forensic medicine. *See* **Medical jurisprudence**
Foreordination. *See* **Predestination**
Forest conservation. *See* **Forests and forestry**
Forest fires 634.9
    xx **Fires**
Forest influences 581.5
    See also **Botany—Ecology; Floods—Control; Forests and forestry; Rain and rainfall**
    x Climate and forests; Floods and forests; Forests and climate; Forests and floods; Forests and rainfall; Forests and water supply; Rainfall and forests
    xx **Climate; Floods—Control; Rain and rainfall; Water supply**
Forest products 634.9; 674
    See also **Gums and resins; Lumber and lumbering; Rubber; Wood**
    xx **Botany, Economic; Commercial products; Raw materials**
Forest reserves 719
    See also **Forests and forestry; National parks and reserves; Wilderness areas**
    x National forests; Public lands
    xx **National parks and reserves**
Forestry. *See* **Forests and forestry**
Forests and climate. *See* **Forest influences**
Forests and floods. *See* **Forest influences**
Forests and forestry (May subdiv. geog.) 634.9
    Use for general materials on forests and on forest conservation
    See also **Lumber and lumbering; Pruning; Rain forests; Reforestation; Tree planting; Trees; Wood;** also headings beginning with the word **Forest**
    x Arboriculture; Conservation of forests; Forest conservation; Forestry; Jungles; Preservation of forests; Timber; Woods
    xx **Agriculture; Forest influences; Forest reserves; Natural resources; Trees; Wildlife—Conservation; Wood**
Forests and forestry—U.S. 634.9
    x U.S.—Forests and forestry
Forests and rainfall. *See* **Forest influences**
Forests and water supply. *See* **Forest influences**
Forgery 332.9; 364.1
    See also **Counterfeits and counterfeiting**
    xx **Crime; Fraud; Impostors and imposture**
Forgery of works of art 751.5
    See also **Literary forgeries**
    x Art—Forgeries; Art forgeries; Art objects, Forgery of
    xx **Art**
Forging 671.3; 682
    See also **Blacksmithing; Ironwork; Welding**
    x Drop forging
    xx **Blacksmithing; Ironwork**

Form, Musical. *See* **Musical form**

Formal gardens. *See* **Gardens**

Formosa. *See* **Taiwan**

Formula translation (Computer program language). *See* **FORTRAN (Computer program language)**

Fortification   623

    See also **Military engineering;** also names of countries with the subdivision *Defenses,* e.g. **U.S.–Defenses;** etc.

    x Forts

    xx **Military art and science; Military engineering**

Fortran (Computer program language). *See* **FORTRAN (Computer program language)**

Forts. *See* **Fortification**

Fortune. *See* **Fate and fatalism; Probabilities; Success; Wealth**

Fortune telling   133.3

    See also **Astrology; Clairvoyance; Dreams; Palmistry**

    xx **Amusements; Clairvoyance; Divination; Occult sciences; Prophecies (Occult sciences); Superstition**

Fortunes. *See* **Income; Wealth**

Forums (Discussions). *See* **Discussion groups**

Fossil mammals; Fossil plants; Fossil reptiles. *See* **Mammals, Fossil; Plants, Fossil; Reptiles, Fossil**

Fossils   560

    See also **Extinct animals; Mammals, Fossil; Plants, Fossil; Reptiles, Fossil**

    x Animals, Fossil; Animals, Prehistoric; Paleontology; Prehistoric animals

    xx **Geology, Stratigraphic; Natural history; Science; Zoology**

Foster home care   362.7

    See also **Adoption; Children–Institutional care**

    x Children—Placing out

    xx **Adoption; Child welfare; Children–Institutional care**

Foundations   624; 721

    See also **Basements; Compressed air; Concrete; Masonry; Soils (Engineering); Walls**

    xx **Architecture–Details; Building; Civil engineering; Masonry; Structural engineering; Walls**

Foundations (Endowments). *See* **Endowments**

Founding   671.2

    Use for materials on the melting and casting of metals

    See also **Brass; Metalwork; Pattern making; Type and type founding**

    x Casting; Foundry practice; Iron founding; Molding (Metal); Moulding (Metal)

    xx **Metalwork; Pattern making**

Foundlings. *See* **Orphans**

Foundry practice. *See* **Founding**

Four-day work week. *See* **Hours of labor**

4-H clubs   630.6

 x Boys' agricultural clubs; Girls' agricultural clubs

 xx **Agriculture—Societies; Boys' clubs; Girls' clubs**

Fourth of July   394.2

 x Anniversaries; Independence Day (U.S.); July Fourth

 xx **Holidays; U.S.—History—Revolution, 1775–1783**

Fractures   617

 xx **Bones**

Framing of pictures. *See* **Picture frames and framing**

France   914.4; 944

 May be subdivided like U.S. except for *History*

France. Army. Foreign Legion   355.3

 x Foreign Legion (French Army)

France—History   944

France—History—To 1328   944

 See also **Celts**

France—History—House of Valois, 1328–1589 944

 See also **Hundred Years' War, 1337–1453**

France—History—Bourbons, 1589–1789   944

France—History—Revolution, 1789–1799 944.04

 x Directory, French, 1795–1799; French Revolution; Napoleonic Wars; Reign of Terror; Revolution, French; Terror, Reign of

 xx **Revolutions**

France—History—1799–1815   944.05

France—History—1815–1914   944

France—History—1914–1940   944.081

France—History—German occupation, 1940–1945   944.081

 x German occupation of France, 1940–1945

France—History—1945–1958   944.082

France—History—1958–1969   944.083

France—History—1969– 944.083

Franchise. *See* **Citizenship; Elections; Suffrage**

Franciscans   271

 x Friars, Gray; Friars, Minor; Gray Friars; Grey Friars; Mendicant orders; Minorites; St. Francis, Order of

 xx **Religious orders for men, Catholic**

Fraternities and sororities   371.8

 x College fraternities; College sororities; Greek letter societies; Sororities

 xx **Colleges and universities; Secret societies; Students—Societies**

Fraud   364.1

 See also **Forgery; Impostors and imposture; Swindlers and swindling**

Fraud—*Continued*
  xx **Impostors and imposture; Swindlers and swindling**
Frauds, Literary. *See* **Literary forgeries**
Fraudulent advertising. *See* **Advertising, Fraudulent**
Freaks. *See* **Monsters**
Free agency. *See* **Free will and determinism**
Free coinage. *See* **Monetary policy**
Free diving. *See* **Scuba diving; Skin diving**
Free fall. *See* **Weightlessness**
Free love   301.41
  xx **Sexual ethics**
Free material   371.3
  x Giveaways
Free press. *See* **Freedom of the press**
Free schools   371
  See also **Open plan schools**
  x Alternative   schools;   Experimental schools
  xx **Education—Experimental methods; Open plan schools**
Free speech   323.44
  See also **Freedom of information; Libel and slander; Freedom of the press**
  x Freedom of speech; Liberty of speech; Speech, Liberty of
  xx **Censorship; Civil rights; Freedom of assembly; Freedom of information; Intellectual freedom; Libel and slander**
Free thought   211
  See also **Agnosticism; Bible—Evidences, authority, etc.; Rationalism; Religious freedom; Skepticism**
  xx **Deism; God; Freedom of conscience; Rationalism**
Free trade and protection   382.7
  See also **Tariff**
  x Fair trade (Tariff); Protection; Tariff question—Free trade and protection
  xx **Commerce; Commercial policy; Economic policy; Economics; Tariff**
Free universities   378
  See also **Colleges and universities—Entrance requirements**
  x Alternative universities; Experimental universities
  xx **Colleges and universities**
Free verse   808.1
  x Vers libre
  xx **Poetry**
Free will and determinism   123
  x Choice, Freedom of; Determinism and indeterminism; Free agency; Freedom of choice; Freedom of the will; Indeterminism; Liberty of the will; Will
  xx **Ethics; Fate and fatalism; Philosophy; Predestination; Sin**
Freebooters. *See* **Pirates**

Freedom   323.44

See also **Anarchism and anarchists; Civil rights; Equality; Intellectual freedom; Religious freedom; Slavery**

x Civil liberty; Liberty; Natural law; Personal freedom

xx **Civil rights; Democracy; Political science**

Freedom   marches—U.S.   *See*   **Blacks—Civil rights**

Freedom of assembly   323.4

See also **Free speech; Public meetings; Riots**

x Assembly, Right of; Right of assembly

xx **Civil rights**

Freedom of choice.   *See* **Free will and determinism**

Freedom of conscience   323.44

See also **Conscientious objectors; Free thought; Persecution; Public opinion; Religious freedom**

x Intolerance; Liberty of conscience

xx **Church and state; Conscience; Persecution; Religious freedom; Toleration**

Freedom of information   323.44

See also **Censorship; Free speech; Freedom of the press; Government and the press**

x Information, Freedom of; Right to know

xx **Censorship; Civil rights; Free speech; Freedom of the press; Intellectual freedom**

Freedom of movement   323.44

x Movement, Freedom of

xx **Civil rights**

Freedom of religion.   *See* **Religious freedom**

Freedom of speech.   *See* **Free speech**

Freedom of teaching.   *See* **Academic freedom**

Freedom of the press   323.44

See also **Books—Censorship; Freedom of information; Libel and slander**

x Free press; Liberty of the press; Press; Press censorship

xx **Censorship; Civil rights; Free speech; Freedom of information; Intellectual freedom; Journalism; Libel and slander; Newspapers; Periodicals**

Freedom of the press and fair trial   323.44; 342.8

x Fair trial and free press; Prejudicial publicity; Trial by publicity

Freedom of the will.   *See* **Free will and determinism**

Freedom of worship.   *See* **Religious freedom**

Freemasons   366

x Masons (Secret order)

xx **Secret societies**

Freeways.   *See* **Express highways**

Freeze dried food.   *See* **Food, Freeze dried**

Freezing.   *See* **Cryobiology; Frost; Ice; Refrigeration and refrigerating machinery**

Freezing of human bodies. *See* **Cryonics**

Freight and freightage   380.5; 385

> *See also* **Aeronautics, Commercial; Railroads—Rates**
>
> *xx* **Maritime law; Materials handling; Railroads; Railroads—Rates; Transportation**

French and Indian War. *See* **U.S.—History—French and Indian War, 1755–1763**

French Canadian literature   810; 840

> May use same subdivisions and names of literary forms as for **English literature**
>
> *x* Canadian literature, French; French literature—Canada
>
> *xx* **Canadian literature**

French Canadians   917.1; 971

> *xx* **Canadians**

French Equatorial Africa. *See* **Africa, French-speaking Equatorial**

French foreign opinion—U.S. *See* **U.S.—Foreign opinion, French**

French language   440

> May be subdivided like **English language**
>
> *xx* **Romance languages**

French language—Conversations and phrases 448

> *x* Conversation in foreign languages; Foreign language phrases

French language—Dictionaries—English   443

> See note under **English language—Dictionaries—French**

French language—Reading materials   448.6

French literature   840

> May use same subdivisions and names of literary forms as for **English literature**
>
> *xx* **Literature; Romance literature**

French literature—Canada. *See* **French Canadian literature**

French poetry   841

> *See also* **Troubadours**

French Revolution. *See* **France—History—Revolution, 1789–1799**

French West Africa. *See* **Africa, French-speaking West**

Frequency modulation, Radio. *See* **Radio frequency modulation**

Fresco painting. *See* **Mural painting and decoration**

Fresh water animals   591.92

> *See also* **Aquariums; Marine animals;** also names of fresh water animals, e.g. **Beavers;** etc.
>
> *x* Animals, Aquatic; Animals, Fresh water; Aquatic animals; Water animals
>
> *xx* **Animals; Fresh water biology; Geographical distribution of animals and plants; Marine animals**

Fresh water aquaculture. *See* **Aquaculture**

242

Fresh water biology 574.92
 See also **Aquariums; Fresh water animals; Fresh water plants; Marine biology**
 xx **Biology; Marine biology; Natural history**
Fresh water plants 581.92
 See also **Aquariums; Marine plants**
 x Aquatic plants; Water plants
 xx **Fresh water biology; Geographical distribution of animals and plants; Marine plants; Plants**
Friars, Black. *See* **Dominicans**
Friars, Gray. *See* **Franciscans**
Friars, Minor. *See* **Franciscans**
Friars preachers. *See* **Dominicans**
Friends, Society of 289.6
 x Quakers; Society of Friends
 xx **Congregationalism**
Friendship 177
 See also **Love; Sympathy**
 x Affection
 xx **Ethics; Human behavior; Love**
Frogmen. *See* **Skin diving**
Frogs 597
 x Tadpoles
 xx **Amphibians**
Frontier and pioneer life (May subdiv. geog. by state and region) **917.8; 978**
 See also **Cowhands; Indians of North America—Captivities; Overland journeys to the Pacific (U.S.); Ranch life**
 x Border life; Pioneer life
 xx **Adventure and adventurers**
Frontiers. *See* **Boundaries;** and names of countries with the subdivision *Boundaries*
Frost 551.3; 551.5
 See also **Ice; Refrigeration and refrigerating machinery**
 x Freezing
 xx **Meteorology; Water**
Frozen food. *See* **Food, Frozen**
Fruit 634; 641.3
 Names of fruits are not included in this list but are to be added as needed, usually in the singular form, e.g. **Apple;** etc.
 See also **Berries; Citrus fruit; Fruit culture;** also names of fruits, e.g. **Apple;** etc.
 xx **Botany; Food**
Fruit—Canning. *See* **Canning and preserving**
Fruit—Diseases and pests 634
 See also **Spraying and dusting**
 x Diseases and pests
 xx **Agricultural pests; Bacteriology, Agricultural; Insects, Injurious and beneficial; Pests; Plants—Diseases**
Fruit—Marketing. *See* **Farm produce—Marketing**
Fruit culture 634
 See also **Berries; Grafting; Nurseries (Horticulture); Plant propagation; Pruning;** also names of fruits

Fruit culture—*Continued*
    x Arboriculture; Orchards
    xx **Agriculture; Fruit; Gardening; Horticulture; Trees**
Fruit flies 595.7
    xx **Flies**
Frustration. *See* **Attitude (Psychology); Emotions**
Fuel 662; 665
    See also **Heating;** also names of fuel, e.g. **Charcoal; Coal; Gas; Petroleum as fuel; Synthetic fuels; Wood;** etc.; and subjects with the subdivision *Fuel consumption,* e.g. **Automobiles—Fuel consumption;** etc.
    xx **Combustion; Engines; Fire; Heating; Home economics; Power resources; Smoke prevention**
Fuel, Liquid. *See* **Gasoline; Petroleum as fuel**
Fuel oil. *See* **Petroleum as fuel**
Fugue 781.4
    xx **Composition (Music); Counterpoint; Music—Theory; Musical form**
Fulfillment, Self. *See* **Self realization**
Fumigation 614.4; 648
    See also **Disinfection and disinfectants**
    xx **Communicable diseases; Disinfection and disinfectants; Insecticides**
Fund raising 361.7
    x Community chests; Money raising
Fundamental theology. *See* **Apologetics**
Fundamentalism 230; 273
    Use for materials on the conservative interpretation of Christianity as opposed to Modernism
    See also **Modernism**
    xx **Modernism**
Funds. *See* **Finance**
Funeral directors. *See* **Undertakers and undertaking**
Funeral rites and ceremonies 393
    See also **Ancestor worship; Cremation**
    x Burial; Ecclesiastical rites and ceremonies; Graves; Mortuary customs; Mourning customs
    xx **Archeology; Cremation; Manners and customs; Rites and ceremonies**
Fungi 589
    See also **Bacteriology; Molds (Botany); Mushrooms; Plants—Diseases**
    x Diseases and pests; Mycology
    xx **Agricultural pests; Molds (Botany); Mushrooms; Pests**
Fungicides 632; 668
    See also **Spraying and dusting**
    x Germicides
    xx **Pesticides; Spraying and dusting**
Funnies. *See* **Comic books, strips, etc.**

Fur   675; 685
>   *See also* **Hides and skins**
>   *xx* **Hides and skins**
Fur seals.   *See* **Seals (Animals)**
Fur trade   338.3
>   *xx* **Trapping**
Furbearing animals   636.08
>   *See also* names of furbearing animals, e.g. **Beavers**; etc.
>   *xx* **Animals; Zoology, Economic**
Furnaces   697
>   *See also* **Blast furnaces; Smelting**
>   *xx* **Heating; Smoke prevention**
Furniture (May subdiv. geog. adjective form, e.g. **Furniture, American**; etc.)   684.1; 747
>   *See also* **Built-in furniture; Cabinet work; Church furniture; Garden ornaments and furniture; Libraries—Equipment and supplies; Schools—Equipment and supplies; Upholstery; Veneers and veneering; Wood carving**; also names of articles of furniture, e.g. **Chairs; Mirrors**; etc.
>   *xx* **Art, Decorative; Art objects; Decoration and ornament; Home economics; Interior decoration; Manufactures; Upholstery; Woodwork**
Furniture, American   684.1; 749
>   *x* American furniture; Colonial furniture (U.S.); Furniture, Colonial; U.S.—Furniture
Furniture, Built-in.   *See* **Built-in furniture**
Furniture, Colonial.   *See* **Furniture, American**
Future.   *See* **Forecasting**
Future life   236
>   Use for materials dealing with the character and form of a future existence. Materials dealing with the question of the endless existence of the soul are entered under **Immortality.** Materials on the philosophical concept of eternity are entered under **Eternity**
>   *See also* **Eternity; Immortality; Millennium; Soul; Spiritualism**
>   *x* Eternal life; Future punishment; Hades; Intermediate state; Life, Future; Life after death; Resurrection; Retribution
>   *xx* **Death; Eschatology; Eternity; Heaven; Immortality; Soul**
Future punishment.   *See* **Future life**
Futurism (Art)   759.06
>   *See also* **Kinetic sculpture; Postimpressionism (Art)**
>   *xx* **Art; Painting; Postimpressionism (Art)**
G.I.s.   *See* **Soldiers—U.S.; Veterans**
Gaels.   *See* **Celts**
Galaxies   523.1

Galaxies—*Continued*

    x Extragalactic nebulae; Nebulae, Extragalactic

    xx **Stars**

Gales. *See* **Winds**

Galleries (Art). *See* **Art—Galleries and museums;** names of countries, cities, etc. with the subdivision *Galleries and museums* (e.g. **U.S.—Galleries and museums;** etc.); and names of galleries and museums

Gambling 175; 795

    See also **Card games; Horse racing; Lotteries; Probabilities**

    x Betting; Gaming; Vice

    xx **Crimes without victims**

Game and game birds 598.2

    See also **Falconry; Game protection; Hunting; Shooting; Trapping;** also names of animals and birds, e.g. **Deer; Pheasants;** etc.

    x Wild fowl

    xx **Animals; Birds; Hunting; Trapping**

Game preserves 333.9

    xx **Hunting; Wildlife—Conservation**

Game protection 333.9; 639

    See also **Birds—Protection**

    x Game wardens; Protection of game

    xx **Birds—Protection; Game and game birds; Hunting; Wildlife—Conservation**

Game wardens. *See* **Game protection**

Games 790

    See also **Amusements; Indians of North America—Games; Kindergarten; Play; Sports;** also names of types of games and of individual games, e.g. **Ball games; Card games; Chess; Indoor games; Olympic games; Singing games; Tennis; Word games;** etc.

    x Pastimes

    xx **Amusements; Entertaining; Physical education and training; Play; Recreation; Sports**

Games, Olympic. *See* **Olympic games**

Gaming. *See* **Gambling**

Gangs. *See* **Criminals; Juvenile delinquency**

Garbage. *See* **Refuse and refuse disposal**

Garden design. *See* **Landscape gardening**

Garden furniture. *See* **Garden ornaments and furniture**

Garden of Eden. *See* **Eden**

Garden ornaments and furniture 717

    See also **Sundials**

    x Garden furniture

    xx **Furniture; Gardens; Landscape architecture**

Garden pests. *See* **Agricultural pests; Insects, Injurious and beneficial; Plants—Diseases**

Gardening   635; 635.9

    Use for practical materials on the practical aspects of the cultivation of flowers, fruits, vegetables, etc.

    See also

Bulbs	**Landscape garden-**
Climbing plants	**ing**
Flower gardening	**Nurseries (Horti-**
Fruit culture	**culture)**
Gardens	**Organiculture**
Grafting	**Plant propagation**
Greenhouses	**Plants**
Grounds mainte-	**Plants, Cultivated**
nance	**Pruning**
Horticulture	**Vegetable gardening**
Insects, Injurious	**Weeds**
and beneficial	**Window gardening**

    x Planting

    xx **Agriculture; Horticulture; Plants**

Gardens   635

    Use for general materials about the history of gardens, various types of gardens, and designs of gardens. Materials limited to the cultivation of gardens are entered under **Gardening**. Materials limited to garden design are entered under **Landscape gardening**

    See also **Botanical gardens; Garden ornaments and furniture; Rock gardens**

    x Formal gardens

    xx **Gardening**

Gardens, Miniature   635.9

    x Miniature gardens; Miniature objects; Tray gardens

    xx **Terrariums**

Garment making.   *See* **Dressmaking; Tailoring**

Garments, Leather.   *See* **Leather Garments**

Gas   665

    See also **Coal tar products; Gases; Petroleum**

    x Coal gas; Illuminating gas

    xx **Coal tar products; Fuel; Public utilities**

Gas, Natural   665

    See also **Boring**

    x Natural gas

    xx **Geology, Economic; Wells**

Gas, Poisonous.   *See* **Gases, Asphyxiating and poisonous**

Gas and oil engines   621.43

    See also **Carburetors; Diesel engines; Farm engines;** also subjects with the subdivision *Engines;* e.g. **Airplanes—Engines; Automobiles—Engines;** etc.

    x Gas engines; Gasoline engines; Internal-combustion engines; Oil engines; Petroleum engines

    xx **Engines**

Gas companies.   *See* **Public utilities**

Gas engines.   *See* **Gas and oil engines**

Gas stations. *See* **Automobiles—Service stations**

Gas turbines 621.4
    xx **Turbines**

Gas warfare. *See* **Gases, Asphyxiating and poisonous—War use**

Gases 530.4
    See also **Pneumatics**; also names of gases, e.g. **Nitrogen**; etc.
    xx **Gas; Hydrostatics; Mechanics; Physics; Pneumatics**

Gases, Asphyxiating and poisonous 614.7
    x Asphyxiating gases; Gas, Poisonous; Poison gases

Gases, Asphyxiating and poisonous—War use 623.4
    x Gas warfare; World War, 1914–1918—Gas warfare
    xx **Chemical warfare**

Gasification of coal. *See* **Coal gasification**

Gasoline 665
    x Fuel, Liquid; Liquid fuel
    xx **Petroleum**

Gasoline engines. *See* **Gas and oil engines**

Gastronomy. *See* **Cookery; Dinners and dining; Food; Menus**

Gauchos. *See* **Cowhands**

Gay liberation movement 301.41
    xx **Homosexuality**

Gay life style. *See* **Homosexuality**

Gay men. *See* **Homosexuals, Male**

Gay women. *See* **Lesbians**

Gazetteers 910
    See also **Names, Geographical**; also names of countries, states, etc. with the subdivision—*Gazetteers*, e.g. **U.S.—Gazetteers**; etc.
    xx **Names, Geographical**

Gearing 621.8
    See also **Automobiles—Transmission devices; Mechanical movements**
    x Bevel gearing; Cog wheels; Gears; Spiral gearing
    xx **Machinery; Mechanical movements; Power transmission; Wheels**

Gears. *See* **Gearing**

Geese 636.5
    x Goose
    xx **Poultry**

Gemini project 629.45
    x Project Gemini
    xx **Orbital rendezvous (Space flight); Space flight**

Gems 736
    Use for materials on cut and polished precious stones treated from the point of view of art or antiquity. Materials on uncut stones treated from the mineralogical point of view are entered under **Precious stones.** Materials on

Gems—*Continued*

gems in which the interest is in the setting are entered under **Jewelry**

See also **Jewelry; Precious stones**

x Jewels

xx **Archeology; Art; Decoration and ornament; Engraving; Jewelry; Mineralogy; Precious stones**

Gemstones. *See* **Precious stones**

Gender identity. *See* **Sex role**

Genealogy 929

See also **Biography; Heraldry; Registers of births, etc.; Wills;** also names of families, e.g. **Lincoln family;** etc.

x Ancestry; Descent; Family histories, Family trees; Pedigrees

xx **Biography; Heraldry; History**

Generals 920; 923

xx **Soldiers**

Generation. *See* **Reproduction**

Generation gap. *See* **Conflict of generations**

Generative organs. *See* **Reproductive system**

Generators, Electric. *See* **Electric generators**

Genes. *See* **Heredity**

Genetics 573.2

Use for comprehensive materials dealing with reproduction, heredity, evolution and variation

See also **Adaptation (Biology); Chromosomes; Eugenics; Evolution; Heredity; Natural selection; Reproduction; Variation (Biology)**

xx **Biology; Chromosomes; Life (Biology)**

Genius 153.9

See also **Creation (Literary, artistic, etc.); Gifted children**

x Talent

xx **Psychology**

Gentiles and Jews. *See* **Jews and Gentiles**

Geochemistry 551.9

See also **Geothermal resources**

x Chemical geology; Earth—Chemical composition; Geological chemistry

xx **Chemistry; Earth sciences; Petrology; Physical geography; Rocks**

Geodesy 526

See also **Latitude; Longitude; Surveying**

x Degrees of latitude and longitude

xx **Earth; Measurement; Surveying**

Geographical atlases. *See* **Atlases**

Geographical distribution of animals and plants 574.9; 581.9; 591.9

See also **Alpine plants; Animals—Migration; Birds—Migration; Desert animals; Desert plants; Fresh water animals; Fresh water plants; Marine animals; Marine plants**

x Animal distribution; Animals—Geographical distribution; Biogeography; Botany—Geographical distribution;

Geographical distribution of animals and plants
—*Continued*

Distribution of animals and plants; Fishes—Geographical distribution; Paleobiogeography; Phytogeography; Plant distribution; Plants—Geographical distribution; Zoogeography; Zoology—Geographical distribution

xx **Animals; Ecology; Natural history; Plants**

Geographical distribution of people. *See* **Anthropogeography; Ethnology**

Geographical names. *See* **Names, Geographical**

Geography 910

Use for general materials, frequently school materials, which describe the surface of the earth with its various peoples, animals, natural products and industries. For travel materials limited to one country or region, use the name of the place with the subdivision *Description and travel.* Materials that treat only of the physical features of the earth's surface and its atmosphere are entered under **Physical geography**

See also **Anthropogeography; Atlases; Boundaries; Discoveries (in geography); Ethnology; Maps; Physical geography; Surveying; Voyages and travels;** also names of countries, states, etc. with the subdivision *Description and travel*, and *Geography*, e.g. **U.S.—Description and travel; U.S.—Geography; etc.**

x Social studies

xx **Earth; Earth sciences; Textbooks; World History**

Geography, Ancient 913

Use for materials on the geography of the ancient world in general

See also names of countries of antiquity with the subdivision *Description and geography*, e.g. **Greece—Description and geography; etc.**

x Ancient geography; Classical geography

xx **Geography, Historical; History, Ancient**

Geography, Biblical. *See* **Bible—Geography**

Geography, Commercial 330.9; 910.1

See also **Economic conditions; Trade routes**

x Commercial geography; Economic geography; Geography, Economic; World economics

xx **Commerce; Commercial products; Economic conditions**

Geography—Dictionaries 910.3

Use for dictionaries of geographic terms. Materials listing names and descriptions of places are entered under **Gazetteers**

250

Geography, Economic. *See* **Geography, Commercial**

Geography, Historical   911

> Use for materials that discuss the extent of territory held by states or nations at a given period of history. When limited to one country or region use the name of the place with the subdivision *Historical geography*. Under names of countries of antiquity use, instead, the subdivision *Description and geography*

> *See also* **Geography, Ancient**; also names of modern countries or regions with the subdivision *Historical geography* (e.g. **U.S.–Historical geography**; etc.); and names of ancient countries with the subdivision *Description and geography*, e.g. **Greece–Description and geography**; etc.

> *x* Historical geography

> *xx* **History**

Geography, Historical—Maps. *See* **Atlases, Historical**

Geography, Military. *See* **Military geography**

Geography, Physical. *See* **Physical geography**

Geography—Pictorial works. *See* **Views**

Geography, Political. *See* **Boundaries; Geopolitics**

Geography, Social. *See* **Anthropogeography**

Geological chemistry. *See* **Geochemistry**

Geological physics. *See* **Geophysics**

Geologists   920; 925

> *xx* **Scientists**

Geology (May subdiv. geog.)   550

> See note under **Earth**

> *See also*

Astrogeology	**Mountains**
Coral reefs and islands	**Oceanography**
	Ore deposits
Creation	**Petrology**
Earth	**Physical geography**
Earthquakes	**Rocks**
Geysers	**Submarine geology**
Glaciers	**Volcanoes**
Mineralogy	

> *x* Geoscience

> *xx* **Creation; Earth; Earth sciences; Natural history; Petrology; Rocks; Science**

Geology, Dynamic. *See* **Geophysics**

Geology, Economic   553

> *See also* **Coal; Gas, Natural; Mines and mineral resources; Ores; Petroleum—Geology; Quarries and quarrying; Soils; Stone**; also names of other geological products, e.g. **Asbestos; Gypsum**; etc.

> *x* Economic geology

Geology, Historical. *See* **Geology, Stratigraphic**

Geology, Lunar. *See* **Lunar geology**

Geology—Maps 550.22
> *xx* **Maps**

Geology—Moon. *See* **Lunar geology**

Geology, Stratigraphic 551.7
> *See also* **Fossils**
> *x* Geology, Historical; Historical geology; Rocks—Age; Stratigraphic geology

Geology, Submarine. *See* **Submarine geology**

Geology—U.S. 557.3
> *x* U.S.—Geology

Geometrical drawing 516; 604.2
> *See also* **Geometry, Descriptive; Graphic methods; Mechanical drawing; Perspective**
> *x* Mathematical drawing; Plans
> *xx* **Drawing; Geometry; Mechanical drawing**

Geometry 516
> *See also* **Geometrical drawing; Topology; Trigonometry**
> *x* Geometry, Plane; Geometry, Solid; Plane geometry; Solid geometry
> *xx* **Mathematics**

Geometry, Analytic 516
> *x* Analytical geometry

Geometry, Descriptive 516
> *See also* **Perspective**
> *x* Descriptive geometry
> *xx* **Geometrical drawing**

Geometry, Plane. *See* **Geometry**

Geometry, Projective 516
> *x* Projective geometry

Geometry, Solid. *See* **Geometry**

Geophysics 551
> *See also* **Auroras; Meteorology; Oceanography; Plate tectonics**
> *x* Geological physics; Geology, Dynamic; Physics, Terrestrial; Terrestrial physics
> *xx* **Earth; Earth sciences; Physical geography; Physics; Space sciences**

Geopolitics 320.1
> *See also* **Anthropogeography; Boundaries; World politics**
> *x* Geography, Political
> *xx* **Anthropogeography; Boundaries; International relations; Political science; World politics**

Geoscience. *See* **Earth sciences; Geology**

Geothermal resources 333.9
> *See also* names of geothermal resources, e.g. **Geysers,** etc.
> *x* Thermal waters
> *xx* **Geochemistry**

Geriatrics. *See* **Elderly—Diseases**

Germ theory. *See* **Life—Origin**

Germ theory of disease 616.01
> *See also* **Bacteriology**
> *x* Bacilli; Disease germs; Germs; Microbes
> *xx* **Bacteriology; Communicable diseases**

Germ warfare. *See* **Biological warfare**

German Baptist Brethren. *See* **Church of the Brethren**

German Hebrew. *See* **Yiddish language**

German language   430

    May be subdivided like **English language**

German literature   830

    May use same subdivisions and names of literary forms as for **English literature**

German occupation of France, [Netherlands, etc.] 1940–1945. *See* **France—History—German occupation, 1940–1945; Netherlands—History—German occupation, 1940–1945;** etc.

Germany   914.3; 943

    May be subdivided like U.S. except for *History*

    See also **Germany, East; Germany, West**

Germany—History   943

Germany—History—To 1517   943

    See also **Holy Roman Empire**

Germany—History—1517–1740   943

    See also **Thirty Years' War, 1618–1648**

Germany—History—1740–1815   943

    See also **Seven Years' War, 1756–1763**

Germany—History—1815–1866   943

Germany—History—Revolution, 1848–1849   943

Germany—History—1866–1918   943.08

Germany—History—1918–1933   943.085

Germany—History—1933–1945   943.086

Germany—History—1945–   943.087

Germany (Democratic Republic). *See* **Germany, East**

Germany, East   914.3; 943

    x East Germany; Germany; Germany (Democratic Republic)

    xx **Germany**

Germany (Federal Republic). *See* **Germany, West**

Germany, West   914.3; 943

    x Germany (Federal Republic); West Germany

    xx **Germany**

Germicides. *See* **Disinfection and disinfectants; Fungicides**

Germination   581.1

    x Seeds—Germination

    xx **Plant physiology**

Germs. *See* **Bacteriology; Germ theory of disease; Microorganisms**

Gerontology   612

    See also **Aging; Elderly; Old age**

Gestalt psychology   150.19

    x Configuration (Psychology); Psychology, Structural; Structural psychology

    xx **Consciousness; Knowledge, Theory of; Perception; Psychology; Senses and sensation**

Gesture. *See* **Nonverbal communication**

Gettysburg, Battle of, 1863   973.9
  xx U.S.–History–Civil War, 1861–1865–
    Campaigns and battles; War
Geysers   551.2
  x Eruptions
  xx **Geology; Geothermal resources; Phys-
    ical geography; Water**
Ghost stories.   *See* **Ghosts–Fiction**
Ghost towns.   *See* **Cities and towns, Ruined,
    extinct, etc.**
Ghosts   133.1
  See also **Apparitions; Demonology; Hal-
    lucinations and illusions; Psychical re-
    search; Spiritualism; Superstition**
  x Haunted houses; Phantoms; Poltergeists;
    Specters; Spirits
  xx **Apparitions; Folklore; Hallucinations
    and illusions; Psychical research; Spir-
    itualism; Superstition**
Ghosts–Fiction   Fic; S C
  x Ghost stories
Giants   398.2
  xx **Animals, Mythical**
Gift wrapping   745.54
  x Wrapping of gifts
  xx **Gifts; Packaging; Paper crafts**
Gifted children   155.4
  See also **Children as artists; Children as
    authors**
  x Bright children; Children, Gifted; Pre-
    cocious children; Superior children;
    Talent
  xx **Exceptional children; Genius**
Gifts
  See also **Gift wrapping**
  x Bequests;   Donations;   Philanthropy;
    Presents
Gipsies.   *See* **Gypsies**
Girl Scouts   369.463
  xx **Girls' clubs; Scouts and scouting**
Girls   301.43
  See also **Children; Young women; Youth**
  xx **Children; Women; Young women;
    Youth**
Girls–Clubs.   *See* **Girls' clubs**
Girls–Education   376
Girls–Employment.   *See* **Child labor; Women
    –Employment**
Girls–Societies and clubs.   *See* **Girls' clubs**
Girls' agricultural clubs.   *See* **Agriculture–So-
    cieties; Girls' clubs; 4-H clubs**
Girls' clubs   369.46
  See also **Camp Fire Girls; 4-H clubs; Girl
    Scouts**
  x Girls–Clubs; Girls–Societies and clubs;
    Girls' agricultural clubs
  xx **Clubs;   Social   settlements;   Societies;
    Women–Societies**
Giveaways.   *See* **Free material**

254

Glacial epoch   551.7
  x Ice age
  xx **Earth**
Glaciers   551.3
  xx **Geology; Ice; Physical geography; Water**
Gladiators   796.8; 920; 927
  x Fighting
Gladness.   *See* **Happiness**
Glands   611; 612
Glands, Ductless   611; 612
  See also **Hormones**
  x Ductless glands
  xx **Endocrinology; Hormones**
Glass   666
  xx **Ceramics; Windows**
Glass, Spun.   *See* **Glass fibers**
Glass, Stained.   *See* **Glass painting and staining**
Glass construction   693.9
  xx **Building materials**
Glass fibers   666
  x Fibers, Glass; Glass, Spun; Spun glass
Glass manufacture   666
  xx **Ceramic industries**
Glass painting and staining   748.5
  x Glass, Stained; Painted glass; Stained glass; Windows, Stained glass
  xx **Art industries and trade; Arts and crafts; Painting**
Glassware   642; 748.2
  See also **Vases**
  x Dishes
  xx **Tableware; Vases**
Glazes   666; 738
  xx **Ceramics; Pottery**
Gliders (Aeronautics)   629.133
  x Aircraft; Sailplanes (Aeronautics)
  xx **Aeronautics; Airplanes**
Gliding and soaring   797.5
  x Air surfing; Soaring flight
Global satellite communications systems.   *See* **Artificial satellites in telecommunication**
Globes   912
Glossaries.   *See* names of languages or subjects with the subdivision *Dictionaries,* e.g. **English language—Dictionaries; Chemistry—Dictionaries;** etc.
Glue   668
  xx **Adhesives**
Gnomes.   *See* **Fairies**
Gnosticism   273
  xx **Church history—Early church ca. 30–600; Philosophy; Religions; Theosophy**
Go karts.   *See* **Karts and karting**
Goblins.   *See* **Fairies**

255

God (May subdiv. by religion)   **211; 212; 231**
  See also

Agnosticism	**Mythology**
Atheism	**Natural theology**
Creation	**Pantheism**
Deism	**Rationalism**
Free thought	**Religion**
Metaphysics	**Theism**

  xx **Creation; Deism; Metaphysics; Philoso-
    phy; Religion; Theism**
God (Christianity)   231
  See also **Christianity; Holy Spirit; Jesus
    Christ; Providence and government
    of God; Theology; Trinity**
  xx **Christianity; Theology; Trinity**
Gods   291; 292
  See also **Mythology; Religions**
  x Deities
  xx **Mythology; Religions**
Gold   332.4; 549; 553; 669
  See also **Coinage; Gold mines and mining;
    Goldwork; Money**
  x Bimetallism; Bullion
  xx **Coinage; Metals; Monetary policy;
    Money; Precious metals**
Gold articles.   *See* **Goldwork**
Gold fish.   *See* **Goldfish**
Gold mines and mining   622
  See also **Prospecting**
  xx **Gold**
Gold plate.   *See* **Plate**
Gold rush.   *See* **California—Gold discoveries;
    Klondike gold fields**
Gold work.   *See* **Goldwork**
Golden Gate Bridge   624.2; 917.94
  xx **Bridges**
Goldfish   597; 639
  x Gold fish
  xx **Aquariums**
Goldsmithing.   *See* **Goldwork**
Goldwork   739.2
  See also **Jewelry; Plate**
  x Gold articles; Gold work; Goldsmithing
  xx **Art metalwork; Arts and crafts; Gold;
    Jewelry; Metalwork**
Golf courses   796.352
  xx **Grounds maintenance**
Good and evil   170; 216
  See also **Sin**
  x Evil
  xx **Ethics; Suffering; Theology**
Good Friday   263
  xx **Holy Week; Lent**
Good grooming.   *See* **Grooming, Personal**
Good Neighbor Policy.   *See* **Pan-Americanism**
Goose.   *See* **Geese**
Gothic architecture.   *See* **Architecture, Gothic**
Gothic fiction   FIC; S C
  x Suspense fiction
Goths.   *See* **Teutonic peoples**

256

Gout   616.3

    See also **Arthritis**

Government.   *See* **Political science;** and names
    of countries, cities, etc. with the sub-
    division *Politics and government,* e.g.
    U.S.–Politics and government; etc.

Government, Comparative.   *See* **Comparative
    government**

Government, Local.   *See* **Local government**

Government, Mandatory.   *See* **Mandates**

Government, Municipal.   *See* **Municipal gov-
    ernment**

Government, Resistance to   322.4

    See also **Insurgency; Passive resistance;
    Revolutions**

    x Civil disobedience; Resistance to govern-
    ment

    xx **Insurgency; Political crimes and offenses;
    Political ethics; Political science; Rev-
    olutions**

Government and business.   *See* **Industry and
    state**

Government and the press   323.44; 342.8

    x Press and government

    xx **Freedom of information; Journalism; Re-
    porters and reporting**

Government buildings.   *See* **Public buildings**

Government by commission.   *See* **Municipal
    government by commission**

Government documents.   *See* **Government pub-
    lications**

Government employess.   *See* **Civil service;** and
    names of countries, cities, etc. with
    the subdivision *Officials and employ-
    ees,* e.g. **U.S.–Officials and employ-
    ees;** etc.

Government investigations.   *See* **Governmental
    investigations**

Government libraries.   *See* **Libraries, Govern-
    mental**

Government ownership   338.9

    See also **Municipal ownership; Railroads
    and state**

    x Nationalization; Public ownership; So-
    cialization of industry; State ownership

    xx **Corporations; Economic policy; Eco-
    nomics; Industry and state; Political
    science; Socialism**

Government ownership of railroads.   *See* **Rail-
    roads and state**

Government publications   025.17

    See also names of countries, cities, etc. with
    the subdivision *Government publica-
    tions,* e.g. **U.S.–Government publica-
    tions;** etc.

    x Documents; Government documents; Of-
    ficial publications; Public documents

Government records—Preservation.   *See* **Ar-
    chives**

Government regulation of commerce. *See* **Commercial policy; Interstate commerce;** and special methods of regulation, e.g. **Tariff;** etc.

Government regulation of industry. *See* **Industry and state**

Government regulation of railroads. *See* **Interstate commerce; Railroads and state**

Government service. *See* **Civil service**

Governmental investigations   328.73; 351.9

Use for materials on investigations initiated by the legislative, executive or judicial branches of the government

  x Congressional investigations; Executive investigations; Government investigations; Investigations, Governmental; Judicial investigations; Legislative investigations

  xx **Justice, Administration of**

Governments in exile. *See* **World War, 1939–1945—Governments in exile**

Governors   920; 923

  xx **State governments**

Graal. *See* **Grail**

Grace (Theology)   234

  xx **Conversion; Theology**

Grading and marking (Students)   371.2

  See also **Ability grouping in education; Mental tests; School reports**

  x Marking (Students); Students—Grading and marking

  xx **Educational tests and measurements; School reports**

Graduation. *See* **Commencements**

Graft in politics. *See* **Corruption in politics**

Grafting   631.5

  xx **Botany; Fruit culture; Gardening; Plant propagation; Trees**

Grail   398.2

  x Graal; Holy Grail

  xx **Folklore; Legends**

Grain   633

  See also names of cereal plants, e.g. **Corn; Wheat;** etc.

  x Breadstuffs; Cereals

  xx **Botany, Economic; Flour mills; Food**

Grammar   415

  See also **Language and languages; Philology, Comparative;** also names of languages with the subdivision *Grammar,* e.g. **English language—Grammar;** etc.

  xx **Language and languages**

Grammar schools. *See* **Education, Elementary; Public schools**

Gramophone. *See* **Phonograph**

Grand opera. *See* **Opera**

Grange   334

  xx **Agriculture—Societies**

Granite 552
    xx **Petrology; Rocks**
Grants. *See* **Subsidies**
Grapes 634
    See also **Wine and wine making**
    x Vineyards
    xx **Wine and wine making**
Graphic arts (May subdiv. geog. adjective form,
        e.g. **Graphic arts, French;** etc.) **760**
    See also types of graphic arts, e.g. **Draw-**
        ing; Engraving; Painting; Printing;
        Prints; etc.
    x Art, Graphic; Arts, Graphic
    xx **Art**
Graphic arts, American 769
    x American graphic arts; U.S.—Graphic
        arts
Graphic methods 001.4
    See also **Statistics—Graphic methods**
    x Graphs
    xx **Drawing; Geometrical drawing; Mechan-**
        ical drawing
Graphite 549; 553
    x Black lead
    xx **Carbon**
Graphology 137
    See note under **Writing**
    x Handwriting
    xx **Penmanship; Writing**
Graphs. *See* **Graphic methods**
Grasses 584; 633
    See also **Feeds; Forage plants; Hay; Pas-**
        tures
    x Herbage
    xx **Botany, Economic; Forage plants; Hay;**
        Lawns; Pastures
Graves. *See* **Cemeteries; Epitaphs; Funeral**
    rites and ceremonies; Mounds and
    mound builders; Tombs
Graveyard of the Atlantic. *See* **Bermuda tri-**
    angle
Graveyards. *See* **Cemeteries**
Gravitation 521; 531
    x Gravity
    xx **Physics**
Gravity. *See* **Gravitation**
Gravity free state. *See* **Weightlessness**
Gray Friars. *See* **Franciscans**
Grease. *See* **Lubrication and lubricants; Oils**
    and fats
Great books program. *See* **Discussion groups**
Great Britain 914.1; 941
    May be subdivided like U.S. except for
    History. The abbreviation Gt. Brit.
    may be used when followed by a sub-
    division. For a list of subjects which
    may be used under either England or
    Great Britain, see **England**

Great Britain—*Continued*

    See also **Commonwealth of Nations; England**

    x United Kingdom

Gt. Brit.—Colonies 325.41

    xx **Colonies; Commonwealth of Nations**

Gt. Brit.—History 941

    x England—History; English history

Gt. Brit.—History—To 1066 941.01

    See also **Anglo-Saxons; Celts**

Gt. Brit.—History—Norman period, 1066–1154 941.02

    See also **Hastings, Battle of, 1066; Normans**

Gt. Brit.—History—Plantagenets, 1154–1399 941.03

Gt. Brit.—History—Lancaster and York, 1399–1485 941.04

    See also **Hundred Years' War, 1339–1453**

Gt. Brit.—History—Wars of the Roses, 1455–1485 941.04

    x Wars of the Roses, 1455–1485

Gt. Brit.—History—Tudors, 1485–1603 941.05

    See also **Armada, 1588**

Gt. Brit.—History—Stuarts, 1603–1714 941.06

    See also **Spanish Succession, War of, 1701–1714**

Gt. Brit.—History—Civil War and Commonwealth, 1642–1660 941.06

    x Civil War—England; Commonwealth of England

Gt. Brit.—History—1714–1837 941.07

    See also **Seven Years' War, 1756–1763**

Gt. Brit.—History—19th century 941.08-941.081

    See also **South African War, 1899–1902**

    x Industrial revolution

Gt. Brit.—History—Crimean War, 1853–1856. *See* **Crimean War, 1853–1856**

Gt. Brit.—History—20th century 941.082

Gt. Brit.—History—1945–1952 941.085

Gt. Brit.—History—1952– 941.085

Gt. Brit.—Kings and rulers 920; 923

    xx **Kings and rulers; Queens**

Greece 938

    Use for materials on ancient Greece from earliest times to 323 A.D. Materials on medieval Greece, 323–1453, are entered under **Greece, Medieval.** Materials on modern Greece from 1453–date are entered under **Greece, Modern**

Greece—Antiquities 913.38

    xx **Classical antiquities**

Greece—Biography 920

    x Classical biography

Greece—Civilization. *See* **Civilization, Greek**

Greece—Description and geography 913.38

    Use for descriptive and geographic materials on ancient Greece instead of the

Greece—Description and geography—*Continued*
  subdivisions *Description and travel*
  and *Historical geography*
  x Description; Historical geography
  xx **Geography, Ancient; Geography, Historical**

Greece—History 938
  Use for materials on ancient Greece from
  earliest times to 323 A.D.

Greece, Medieval 949.5

Greece, Modern 914.95; 949.5
  Use for modern Greece from 1453–date

Greece, Modern—History 949.5

Greece, Modern—History—1967–1974 949.5

Greece, Modern—History—1974– 949.5

Greek antiquities. *See* **Classical antiquities**

Greek architecture. *See* **Architecture, Greek**

Greek art. *See* **Art, Greek**

Greek Church. *See* **Orthodox Eastern Church**

Greek civilization. *See* **Civilization, Greek;**
  Hellenism

Greek language 480
  May be subdivided like **English language**
  See also **Hellenism**
  x Classical languages

Greek language, Modern 489
  May be subdivided like **English language**
  x Romaic language

Greek letter societies. *See* **Fraternities and**
  sororities; Secret societies

Greek literature 880
  May use same subdivisions and names of
  literary forms as for **English literature**
  See also **Classical literature; Hellenism**
  xx **Classical literature**

Greek literature, Modern 889
  x Neo-Greek literature; Romaic literature

Greek mythology. *See* **Mythology, Classical**

Greek philosophy. *See* **Philosophy, Ancient**

Greek sculpture. *See* **Sculpture, Greek**

Greenbacks. *See* **Paper money**

Greenhouses 631.3; 635.9
  x Hothouses
  xx **Flower gardening; Gardening; Horticulture**

Greeting cards 741.68
  x Cards, Greeting; Christmas cards

Gregorian chant. *See* **Chants (Plain, Gregorian, etc.)**

Grey Friars. *See* **Franciscans**

Grief. *See* **Joy and sorrow**

Grinding and polishing 621.9
  x Buffing; Polishing

Grippe. *See* **Influenza**

Grist mills. *See* **Flour mills**

Grocery trade 338.4
  See also **Supermarkets**

Grooming, Personal 646.7
  x Good grooming; Personal appearance;
  Personal grooming

261

Grooming, Personal—*Continued*
    xx **Hygiene**
Grottoes. *See* **Caves**
Ground cushion phenomena 629.3
    See also **Ground** effect **machines**
    x Air bearing lift
    xx **Aerodynamics; Pneumatics**
Ground effect machines 629.3
    See also **Helicopters; Vertically rising airplanes**
    x Air bearing vehicles; Air cushion vehicles; Hovercraft; Ground proximity machines; Surface effect machines
    xx **Ground cushion phenomena**
Ground proximity machines. *See* **Ground effect machines**
Grounds maintenance 712
    Use for materials on maintenance of public, industrial, and institutional grounds and large estates
    See also **Golf courses; Roadside improvement**
    xx **Gardening**
Group discussion. *See* **Discussion groups**
Group health. *See* **Insurance, Health**
Group hospitalization. *See* **Insurance, Hospitalization**
Group insurance. *See* **Insurance, Group**
Group living. *See* **Collective settlements**
Group medical practice, Prepaid. *See* **Health maintenance organizations**
Group medical service. *See* **Insurance, Health**
Group problem solving. *See* **Problem solving, Group**
Group relations training 616.8
    x Encounter groups; Sensitivity training; T groups
    xx **Human relations**
Grouping by ability. *See* **Ability grouping in education**
Groups, Ethnic. *See* **Ethnic groups**
Growth 155.4; 574.3; 591.3; 612.6
    Use for biological and psychological materials on the growth and development of animal and human organisms
    See also **Children—Growth; Growth (Plants)**
    xx **Physiology**
Growth (Plants) 581.3
    x Plants—Growth
    xx **Growth; Plant physiology**
Guaranteed annual income. *See* **Wages—Annual wage**
Guaranteed income. *See* **Wages—Annual wage**
Guerrilla warfare 355.4
    See also **World War, 1939–1945—Underground movements**
    x Unconventional warfare
    xx **Insurgency; Military art and science; Tactics; War**

Guerrillas 356
>*See also* **National liberation movements**
>*x* Partisans

Guests. *See* **Entertaining**

Guidance. *See* **Counseling; Educational counseling; Vocational guidance**

Guide dogs 636.7
>*x* Blind, Dogs for the; Dog guides; Dogs for the blind; Seeing eye dogs
>*xx* **Dogs**

Guide posts. *See* **Signs and signboards**

Guided missiles 623.4
>*See also* **Antimissile missiles; Ballistic missiles;** also names of specific missiles, e.g. **Nike rocket;** etc.
>*x* Bombs, Flying; Flying bombs; Missiles, Guided
>*xx* **Bombs; Projectiles; Rocketry; Rockets (Aeronautics)**

Guides. *See* names of countries, states, etc. with the subdivision *Description and travel—Guides,* e.g. **U.S.–Description and travel–Guides;** etc. and names of cities with the subdivision *Description —Guides,* e.g. **Chicago–Description– Guides;** etc.

Guitar 787
>*xx* **Stringed instruments**

Guitar music 787
>*xx* **Instrumental music**

Gulf States 917.6; 976
>*xx* **United States**

Gums and resins 668
>*x* Resins; Rosin
>*xx* **Chemistry, Technical; Forest products; Plastics**

Gunning. *See* **Hunting; Shooting**

Gunpowder 623.4
>*See also* **Ammunition**
>*x* Powder, Smokeless; Smokeless powder
>*xx* **Ammunition; Explosives; Firearms**

Guns. *See* **Firearms; Ordnance; Rifles; Shotguns**

Guns—Control. *See* **Firearms—Law and legislation**

Gymnastics 796.4
>*See also* **Acrobats and acrobatics; Physical education and training**
>*x* Calisthenics
>*xx* **Acrobats and acrobatics; Athletics; Exercise; Hygiene; Physical education and training; Sports**

Gypsies 301.45
>*x* Gipsies; Romanies

Gypsum 553
>*x* Plaster of paris
>*xx* **Geology, Economic**

Gyroscope 629.135; 681
>*xx* **Aeronautical instruments**

H bomb. *See* **Hydrogen bomb**

HMO. *See* Health maintenance organizations

Habit   152.3

    See also **Instinct**

    xx **Human behavior; Instinct; Psychology**

Habitations, Human. *See* **Architecture, Domestic; Houses; Housing**

Habitations of animals. *See* **Animals—Habitations**

Habits of animals. *See* **Animals—Habits and behavior**

Hades. *See* **Future life; Hell**

Hair   611; 646.7

    Includes works on hairdressing and haircutting

    See also **Wigs**

    xx **Head**

Half-tone process. *See* **Photoengraving**

Hallmarks

    See also **Plate**

    x Marks on plate

    xx **Plate**

Halloween   394.2

    x All Hallows' Eve

    xx **Folklore**

Hallucinations and illusions   616.8

    See also **Apparitions; Ghosts; Magic; Optical illusions; Personality disorders**

    x Delusions; Illusions

    xx **Apparitions; Ghosts; Personality disorders; Psychical research; Psychology, Pathological; Subconsciousness; Visions**

Ham radio stations. *See* **Amateur radio stations**

Hand weaving. *See* **Weaving**

Handbooks, manuals, etc. *See* general subjects with the subdivision *Handbooks, manuals, etc.,* e.g. **Photography—Handbooks, manuals, etc.;** etc.

Handicapped   362

    See also **Mentally handicapped; Physically handicapped; Sick; Socially handicapped**

    x Disabled

Handicapped and architecture. *See* **Architecture and the handicapped**

Handicapped children   362.7

    See also **Hyperactive children; Mentally handicapped children; Physically handicapped children; Socially handicapped children**

    x Abnormal children; Children, Abnormal

    xx **Exceptional children**

Handicraft   745.5

    See also **Hobbies; Industrial arts; Industrial arts education; Occupational therapy;** also names of individual crafts, e.g. **Leather work; Weaving;** etc.

    x Crafts

Handicraft—*Continued*
　　xx **Arts and crafts; Hobbies; Industrial arts education; Occupational therapy**
Handwriting. *See* **Autographs; Graphology; Penmanship; Writing**
Hanging. *See* **Capital punishment**
Happiness **131**
　　See also **Joy and sorrow; Pleasure**
　　x Gladness
　　xx **Ethics; Joy and sorrow; Pleasure**
Harbors **386; 387.1; 627**
　　See also **Docks; Marinas; Pilots and pilotage;** also names of cities with the subdivision *Harbor,* e.g. **Chicago—Harbor;** etc.
　　x Ports
　　xx **Civil engineering; Docks; Hydraulic structures; Merchant marine; Navigation; Shipping; Transportation**
Hard drugs. *See* **Narcotics**
Hares. *See* **Rabbits**
Harmony **781.3**
　　xx **Composition (Music); Music; Music— Study and teaching; Music—Theory**
Harry S. Truman Library, Independence, Mo. **026**
　　xx **Presidents—U.S.—Archives**
Harvesting machinery **631.5**
　　x Reapers
　　xx **Agricultural machinery**
Hastings, Battle of, 1066 **941.02**
　　xx **Gt. Brit.—History—Norman period, 1066–1154**
Hats **391; 646.5; 687**
　　See also **Millinery**
　　xx **Clothing and dress; Costume; Millinery**
Haunted houses. *See* **Ghosts**
Hawking. *See* **Falconry**
Hay **633**
　　See also **Feeds; Grasses;** also names of hay crops, e.g. **Alfalfa;** etc.
　　xx **Farm produce; Feeds; Forage plants; Grasses**
Head **611; 612**
　　See also **Brain; Ear; Eye; Face; Hair; Nose; Phrenology**
　　xx **Brain**
Healing, Mental. *See* **Mental healing**
Health. *See* **Hygiene**
Health, Industrial. *See* **Industrial health and safety**
Health, Mental. *See* **Mental health**
Health, Public. *See* **Public health**
Health boards **614.06**
　　x Boards of health; Public health boards
　　xx **Public health**
Health care. *See* **Medical care**
Health education **371.7; 613.07**
　　See also **School hygiene**
　　x Hygiene—Study and teaching

Health education—*Continued*
> *xx* **Children—Care and hygiene; Physical education and training**

Health food. *See* **Food, Natural**

Health insurance. *See* **Insurance, Health**

Health maintenance organizations 368.3; 610.6
> *x* Comprehensive health care organizations; Group medical practice, Prepaid; HMO; Prepaid group medical practice

> *xx* **Insurance, Health; Medical care**

Health of children. *See* **Children—Care and hygiene**

Health of infants. *See* **Infants—Care and hygiene**

Health resorts, spas, etc. 613.1
> *See also* **Summer resorts; Winter resorts**

> *x* Resorts; Sanatoriums; Spas; Watering places

> *xx* **Hydrotherapy; Medicine; Sick; Summer resorts; Travel; Winter resorts**

Healths, Drinking of. *See* **Toasts**

Hearing 617.8
> *See also* **Deafness; Ear**

> *x* Acoustics

> *xx* **Deafness; Ear; Senses and sensation; Sound**

Hearing aids 617.8
> *xx* **Deafness**

Heart 611; 612
> *See also* **Blood—Circulation**

> *xx* **Anatomy, Human; Physiology**

Heart—Diseases 616.1
> *x* Angina pectoris; Cardiac diseases; Coronary heart diseases; Heart attack

Heart—Surgery 617
> *x* Open heart surgery

> *xx* **Surgery**

Heart—Transplantation 617
> *xx* **Transplantation of organs, tissues, etc.**

Heart attack. *See* **Heart—Diseases**

Heat 536
> *See also* **Combustion; Fire; Steam; Temperature; Thermodynamics; Thermometers and thermometry**

> *xx* **Combustion; Electromagnetic waves; Fire; Temperature; Thermodynamics**

Heat—Conduction 536

Heat—Transmission 536

Heat engines 621.4
> *See also* **Steam engines; Thermodynamics**

> *x* Hot air engines

> *xx* **Engines; Thermodynamics**

Heat insulating materials. *See* **Insulation (Heat)**

Heat pumps 621.4
> *xx* **Pumping machinery; Thermodynamics**

Heathenism. *See* **Paganism**

Heating   644; 697
> *See also* Chimneys; Electric heating; Fireplaces; Fuel; Furnaces; Hot air heating; Hot water heating; Insulation (Heat); Oil burners; Radiant heating; Solar heating; Steam heating; Stoves; Ventilation; also subjects with the subdivision *Heating and ventilation,* e.g. Houses—Heating and ventilation; etc.
> *xx* Fire; Fuel; Home economics; Ventilation

Heaven   236
> *See also* Future life
> *xx* Death; Eschatology

Heavy water.   *See* Deuterium oxide

Hebrew language   492.4
> May be subdivided like English language
> *See also* Yiddish language
> *x* Jewish language; Jews—Language

Hebrew literature   892.4
> May use same subdivisions and names of literary forms as for English literature
> *See also* Bible; Jewish literature; Talmud
> *x* Jews—Literature
> *xx* Jewish literature

Hebrews.   *See* Jews

Heirs.   *See* Inheritance and succession

Helicopters   387.7; 629.133
> *x* Aircraft
> *xx* Aeronautics; Airplanes; Ground effect machines

Helicopters—Piloting   629.132; 629.133
> *xx* Airplanes—Piloting

Heliports   387.7
> *xx* Airports

Helium   546; 553
> *xx* Radioactivity

Hell   236
> *x* Eternal punishment; Hades; Retribution
> *xx* Death; Eschatology

Hellenism   913.38; 938; 939
> *x* Greek civilization
> *xx* Civilization, Greek; Greek language; Greek literature; Humanism

Hemp   677
> *See also* Fibers; Rope
> *xx* Fibers; Linen; Rope

Heraldry   929.6
> *See also* Chivalry; Decorations of honor; Flags; Genealogy; Insignia; Knights and knighthood; Mottoes; Nobility; Seals (Numismatics)
> *x* Arms, Coats of; Coats of arms; Crests; Devices (Heraldry); Emblems; Pedigrees
> *xx* Archeology; Biography; Chivalry; Decorations of honor; Genealogy; Knights and knighthood; Nobility; Signs and symbols; Symbolism

Herbage. *See* Grasses

Herbals. *See* Botany, Medical; Herbs; Materia medica

Herbaria. *See* Plants—Collection and preservation

Herbs 635
   x Herbals

Herbs, Medical. *See* Botany, Medical

Hereditary succession. *See* Inheritance and succession

Heredity 575.1
   See also **Blood groups; DNA; Eugenics; Evolution; Mendel's law; Natural selection; Variation (Biology)**
   x Ancestry; Descent; Genes; Inheritance (Biology)
   xx **Biology; Children; Eugenics; Evolution; Genetics; Man; Mendel's law; Natural selection; Sociology**

Hermeneutics, Biblical. *See* **Bible—Criticism, interpretation, etc.**

Hermetic art and philosophy. *See* **Alchemy; Astrology; Occult sciences**

Hermits 920; 922
   x Recluses
   xx **Religious orders; Saints**

Heroes and heroines 920; 923
   See also **Courage; Explorers; Martyrs; Mythology; Saints**
   x Heroines; Heroism
   xx **Adventure and adventurers; Courage; Mythology**

Heroines. *See* **Heroes and heroines; Women—Biography; Women in literature and art; Women in the Bible**

Heroism. *See* **Courage; Heroes and heroines**

Hertzian waves. *See* **Electric waves**

Hibernation of animals. *See* **Animals—Hibernation**

Hidden treasure. *See* **Buried treasure**

Hides and skins 636.08
   See also **Fur; Leather; Tanning**
   x Animal products; Pelts; Skins
   xx **Fur; Leather; Tanning**

Hieroglyphics 411
   See also **Picture writing; Rosetta stone inscription**
   xx **Inscriptions; Picture writing; Writing**

Hi-fi systems. *See* **High-fidelity sound systems**

High-fidelity sound systems 621.389
   See also **Stereophonic sound systems**
   x Hi-fi systems
   xx **Electronics; Sound—Recording and reproducing**

High-frequency radio. *See* **Radio, Short wave**

High school education. *See* **Education, Secondary**

High school libraries. *See* **School libraries (High school)**

High schools   373.1

>> See also **Commencements; Education, Secondary; Junior high schools;** also names of cities with the subdivision *Schools,* e.g. **Chicago—Schools;** etc.

> *x* Secondary schools

> *xx* **Education, Secondary; Public schools**

High schools, Junior. *See* **Junior high schools**

High schools, Rural. *See* **Rural schools**

High society. *See* **Upper classes**

High speed aerodynamics. *See* **Aerodynamics, Supersonic**

High speed aeronautics   629.132

> *See also* **Aerodynamics, Supersonic; Aerothermodynamics; Rocket planes; Rockets (Aeronautics)**

> *x* Aeronautics, High speed

> *xx* **Aeronautics**

High treason. *See* **Treason**

Higher criticism. *See* **Bible—Criticism, interpretation, etc.**

Higher education. *See* **Education, Higher**

Highjacking of airplanes. *See* **Hijacking of airplanes**

Highland clans. *See* **Clans and clan system**

Highland costume. *See* **Tartans**

Highway accidents. *See* **Traffic accidents**

Highway beautification. *See* **Roadside improvement**

Highway construction. *See* **Roads**

Highway engineering   625.7

> *See also* **Roads; Traffic engineering**

> *x* Road engineering

> *xx* **Civil engineering; Roads**

Highway transportation. *See* **Transportation, Highway**

Highwaymen. *See* **Robbers and outlaws**

Highways. *See* **Roads**

Hijacking of airplanes   364.1

> Use same form for the hijacking of other modes of transportation

> *x* Aeronautics, Commercial—Hijacking; Air lines—Hijacking; Air piracy; Airplane hijacking; Airplanes—Hijacking; Highjacking of airplanes; Sky hijacking; Skyjacking

> *xx* **Offenses against public safety**

Hiking   796.5

> *See also* names of forms of hiking, e.g. **Backpacking; Orienteering; Walking;** etc.

> *xx* **Outdoor life; Walking**

Hindoos. *See* **Hindus**

Hinduism   294.5

> *See also* **Brahmanism; Caste; Vedas; Yoga**

> *xx* **Brahmanism; Religions**

Hindus   572.954

> *See also* **East Indians**

> *x* Hindoos

> *xx* **East Indians**

Hippies (May subdiv. geog.)   **301.44**
   x Yippies
   xx **Bohemianism**
Hippies—U.S.   301.44
   x U.S.—Hippies
Hire-purchase plan.   *See* **Instalment plan**
Hispanic-American literature.   *See* **Latin American literature**
Hispano-American War, 1898.   *See* **U.S.—History—War of 1898**
Histochemistry.   *See* **Physiological chemistry**
Historians (May subdiv. geog. adjective form)
   See also **Archeologists**
   x Writers
   xx **Historiography; History**
Historians, American   920; 923
   x American historians; U.S.—Historians
Historic buildings, etc.   728.09
   See also **Literary landmarks;** also names of countries, cities, etc. with the subdivision *Historic buildings, etc.* e.g. **U.S.—Historic buildings, etc.;** etc.
   x Buildings, Historic; Historic houses; Houses, Historic
   xx **Historic sites**
Historic houses.   *See* **Historic buildings, etc.**
Historic sites
   See also types of historic sites, e.g. **Historic buildings, etc.;** etc.
   x Historical sites
   xx **Archaeology; History**
Historical atlases.   *See* **Atlases, Historical**
Historical chronology.   *See* **Chronology, Historical**
Historical dictionaries.   *See* **History—Dictionaries**
Historical fiction   808.3; 809.3
   Use for materials about historical fiction. For historical novels see names of historical events and characters with the subdivision *Fiction,* e.g. **U.S.—History—Civil War, 1861–1865—Fiction; Slavery in the U.S.—Fiction; Napoléon I, Emperor of the French—Fiction;** etc.
   x Fiction, Historical
   xx **Fiction; History**
Historical geography.   *See* **Atlases, Historical; Geography, Historical;** names of modern countries or regions with the subdivision *Historical geography* (e.g. **U.S.—Historical geography;** etc.); and names of ancient countries with the subdivision *Description and geography,* e.g. **Greece—Description and geography;** etc.
Historical geology.   *See* **Geology, Stratigraphic**
Historical records—Preservation.   *See* **Archives**
Historical sites.   *See* **Historic sites**
Historical societies.   *See* **History—Societies**

Historiography 907

See note under **History**

See also **Historians**; also subjects with the subdivision *Historiography*, e.g. **Philosophy—Historiography; U.S.—History—Historiography;** etc.

x History—Criticism; History—Historiography

History 900

Use for general materials on history as a science. This includes the principles of history, the influence of various factors on history and the relation of the science of history to other subjects. Materials on the interpretation and meaning of history, the course of events and their resulting consequences, are entered under **History—Philosophy.** Materials limited to the study and criticism of sources of history, methods of historical research and writing of history, are entered under **Historiography**

See also

Anthropogeography	**Historic sites**
Archeology	**Historical fiction**
Biography	**Kings and rulers**
Church history	**Man**
Civilization	**Middle Ages—History**
Colonization	**tory**
Constitutional history	**Military history**
tory	**Naval history**
Discoveries (in geography)	**Numismatics**
ography)	**Oral history**
Ethnology	**Political science**
Genealogy	**Seals (Numismatics)**
Geography, Historical	**ics)**
cal	**World history**

Historians

and headings beginning with the word **History;** also names of countries, states, etc. with the subdivisions *Antiquities; Foreign relations; History; Politics and government.* For the history of a subject see the name of the subject with the subdivision *History,* or, for literature, film, and music headings, *History and criticism,* e.g. **Art—History; English language—History; English literature—History and criticism; Music—History and criticism;** etc.

x Social studies

History, Ancient 930

See also **Archeology; Bible; Civilization, Ancient; Classical dictionaries; Geography, Ancient; Inscriptions; Numismatics;** also names of ancient peoples (e.g. **Hittites;** etc.); and names of countries of antiquity

x Ancient history

xx **World history**

271

History—Atlases. *See* **Atlases, Historical**

History, Biblical. *See* **Bible—History of Biblical events**

History—Chronology. *See* **Chronology, Historical**

History, Church. *See* **Church history**

History, Constitutional. *See* **Constitutional history**

History—Criticism. *See* **Historiography**

History—Dictionaries 903
 x Historical dictionaries

History—Historiography. *See* **Historiography**

History, Local. *See* names of countries, states, etc. with the subdvision *History, Local,* e.g. **U.S.—History, Local;** etc.

History, Medieval. *See* **Middle Ages—History**

History, Military. *See* **Military history;** and names of countries with the subdivision *History, Military,* e.g. **U.S.—History, Military;** etc.

History, Modern 909.08–909.83
 Use for materials covering the period after 1453
 See also **Civilization, Modern; Reformation; Renaissance**
 x Modern history
 xx **Civilization, Modern; World history**

History, Modern—19th century 909.81
 See also **Nineteenth century**

History, Modern—20th century 909.82
 See also **Twentieth century; World War, 1914–1918; World War, 1939–1945**

History, Modern—Study and teaching 909.0807
 See also **Current events**

History, Natural. *See* **Natural history**

History, Naval. *See* **Naval history;** and names of countries with the subdivision *History, Naval,* e.g. **U.S.—History, Naval;** etc.

History, Oral. *See* **Oral history**

History—Philosophy 901
 See note under **History**
 See also **Civilization**
 x Philosophy of history
 xx **Philosophy**

History—Societies 906
 See also **U.S.—History—Societies**
 x Historical societies

History—Sources 900
 Use only for documents, records and other source materials upon which narrative history is based.
 See also **Archives; Charters;** also names of countries, states, etc. with the subdivision *History—Sources* (e.g. **U.S.—History—Sources;** etc.); and names of periods of history and names of wars with the subdivision *Sources,* e.g. **U.S.—History—Civil War, 1861–1865—**

History—Sources—*Continued*

Sources; World War, 1939–1945—
Sources; etc.

History, Universal. *See* World history

Histrionics. *See* Acting; Theater

Hittites 939

xx History, Ancient

Hoaxes. *See* Imposters and imposture

Hobbies 790.13

See also Collectors and collecting; Handicraft; also names of hobbies

xx Amusements; Handicraft; Leisure; Recreation

Hoboes. *See* Tramps

Hockey. · *See* Field hockey; Ice hockey

Hogs 636.4

See also Pigs

x Swine

Hoisting machinery 621.8

See also types of hoisting machinery; e.g.
Conveying machinery; Cranes, derricks, etc.; Elevators; etc.

x Lifts

xx Conveying machinery

Holiday decorations 394.2; 745.4

x Decorations, Holiday

xx Decoration and ornament

Holidays 394.2

See also Fasts and feasts; Vacations; also
names of holidays, e.g. Fourth of July;
etc.

x Anniversaries; Days; Legal holidays; National holidays

xx Fasts and feasts; Festivals; Manners
and customs; Vacations

Holland. *See* Netherlands

Holography 774

x Laser photography; Lensless photography; Photography, Laser; Photography, Lensless

Holy Ghost. *See* Holy Spirit

Holy Grail. *See* Grail

Holy Roman Empire 943

xx Europe—History—476–1492; Germany—
History—To 1517; Middle Ages—History

Holy Scriptures. *See* Bible

Holy See 262

See also Papacy; Popes

xx Catholic Church—Relations (Diplomatic); Papacy; Popes

Holy Spirit 231

See also Trinity

x Holy Ghost; Spirit, Holy

xx God (Christianity); Theology; Trinity

Holy Week 263

See also Easter; Good Friday

xx Lent

Home   301.42; 640

    See also **Family; Home economics; Marriage**

    xx **Family; Marriage**

Home and school   371.1

    See also **Parents' and teachers' associations**

    x Parents and teachers; School and home; Teachers and parents

    xx **Parents' and teachers' associations**

Home care services   361; 362.1

    xx **Medical care**

Home decoration.   *See* **Interior decoration**

Home designs.   *See* **Architecture, Domestic—Designs and plans**

Home economics   640

    See also

Consumer education	**House cleaning**
Cookery	**Household employees**
Cost of living	**Household pests**
Dairying	**Interior decoration**
Entertaining	**Laundry**
Food	**Mobile home living**
Fuel	**Sewing**
Furniture	**Shopping**
Heating	**Ventilation**

    x Domestic arts; Efficiency, Household; Homemaking; Household management; Housekeeping

    xx **Family life education; Home**

Home economics—Accounting.   *See* **Budgets, Household**

Home economics—Equipment and supplies.   *See* **Household equipment and supplies**

Home education.   *See* **Correspondence schools and courses**

Home life.   *See* **Family life**

Home missions, Christian.   *See* **Missions, Christian**

Home nursing   649.1

    See also **Sick**

    xx **Nursing; Sick**

Home repairing.   *See* **Houses—Maintenance and repair**

Home study courses.   *See* **Correspondence schools and courses**

Homemaking.   *See* **Home economics**

Homeopathy   615

    xx **Medicine; Medicine—Practice**

Homes.   *See* **Houses**

Homes (Institutions).   *See* **Charities; Institutional care; Orphanages;** also classes of people with the subdivision *Institutional care,* e.g. **Blind—Institutional care; Children—Institutional care; Deaf—Institutional care;** etc.

Homes, Mobile.   *See* **Mobile homes**

Homes for the elderly.   *See* **Elderly—Housing**

Homicide   364.1

    See also **Euthanasia**

Homonyms. *See* names of languages with the
subdivision *Homonyms,* e.g. **English
language—Homonyms;** etc.

Homosexuality 301.41
See also **Gay liberation movement; Lesbianism**
x Gay life style

Homosexuals, Female. *See* **Lesbians**

Homosexuals, Male 301.41
x Gay men

Honesty 179
See also **Business ethics; Truthfulness and
falsehood**
x Dishonesty
xx **Business ethics; Ethics; Human behavior; Truthfulness and falsehood**

Honey 638; 641.3
See also **Bees**
xx **Bees**

Honor system. *See* **Self-government (in education)**

Honorary degrees. *See* **Degrees, Academic**

Hooked rugs. *See* **Rugs, Hooked**

Hoover Dam 627
x Boulder Dam; Colorado River—Hoover
Dam
xx **Dams**

Hormones 574.1; 612
See also **Glands, Ductless**
xx **Endocrinology; Glands, Ductless**

Hornbooks 028.5; 372.4

Horology. *See* **Clocks and watches; Sundials**

Horoscopes
xx **Astrology**

Horror 152.4
xx **Emotions; Fear**

Horror—Fiction Fic
x Horror stories

Horror stories. *See* **Horror—Fiction**

Horse. *See* **Horses**

Horse racing 798
x Racing
xx **Gambling**

Horseback riding 798
See also **Rodeos**
x Equestrianism; Riding

Horsebreaking. *See* **Horses—Training**

Horses 599; 636.1
See also **Ponies**
x Horse

Horses—Diseases 636.089

Horses—Training 636.1
x Horsebreaking
xx **Animals—Training**

Horseshoeing. *See* **Blacksmithing**

Horticulture 635
Use for materials on the scientific and economic aspects of the cultivation of
flowers, fruits, vegetables, etc.

Horticulture—*Continued*

    See also Flower gardening; Fruit culture; Gardening; Greenhouses; Landscape gardening; Organiculture; Vegetable gardening

    xx Agriculture; Gardening; Plants

Hosiery 391; 687

    x Stockings

    xx Clothing and dress; Textile industry

Hospital endowments. *See* Endowments

Hospital libraries 027.6

    x Libraries, Hospital

    xx Libraries

Hospitality. *See* Entertaining

Hospitalization insurance. *See* Insurance, Hospitalization

Hospitals (May subdiv. geog. country or state) 362.1

    See also Life support systems (Medical environment); Nursing; also types of hospitals, e.g. Children's hospitals; Medical centers; Nursing homes; Psychiatric hospitals; also names of cities with the subdivision *Hospitals*, e.g. Chicago—Hospitals; etc., and names of hospitals

    x Infirmaries; Institutions, Charitable and philanthropic; Sanatoriums

    xx Charities, Medical; Institutional care; Medical centers; Medicine; Nursing; Public health; Public welfare; Sick

Hospitals, Military 355.7

    See also First aid; also names of wars with the subdivision *Medical and sanitary affairs,* e.g. World War, 1939–1945—Medical and sanitary affairs; etc.

    x Field hospitals; Military hospitals; Veterans—Hospitals

    xx Medicine, Military; Military art and science; Veterans

Hospitals—U.S. 362.1

    x U.S.—Hospitals

Hostels, Youth. *See* Youth hostels

Hostesses, Air line. *See* Air lines—Flight attendants

Hot air engines. *See* Heat engines

Hot air heating 697

    x Warm air heating

    xx Heating

Hot water heating 697

    xx Heating

Hotels, motels, etc. (May subdiv. geog. country or state) 647; 728.5

    See also names of cities and areas with the subdivision *Hotels, motels, etc.,* e.g. Chicago—Hotels, motels, etc.; etc.

    x Auto courts; Boarding houses; Inns; Lodging houses; Motels; Motor courts; Rooming houses; Tourist accommodations

276

Hotels, motels, etc.–U.S. 647; 728.5
> *x* U.S.—Hotels, motels, etc.

Hothouses. *See* **Greenhouses**

Hotlines (Telephone counseling) 361; 384.6
> *See also* **Crisis centers**
> *x* Crisis counseling; Crisis intervention telephone service; Switchboard hotlines; Telephone counseling
> *xx* **Counseling; Crisis centers; Human relations; Social work**

Hours of labor 331.2
> *See also* **Child labor**
> *x* Eight-hour day; Five-day work week; Flexible hours of labor; Flexitime; Four-day work week; Labor, Hours of; Overtime; Working day
> *xx* **Child labor; Labor and laboring classes**

House boats. *See* **Houseboats**

House cleaning 648
> *xx* **Cleaning; Home economics; Sanitation, Household**

House decoration. *See* **Interior decoration**

House drainage. *See* **Drainage, House**

House flies. *See* **Flies**

House furnishing. *See* **Interior decoration**

House painting 698.1
> *xx* **Painting, Industrial**

House plans. *See* **Architecture, Domestic—Designs and plans**

House plants 635.9
> *xx* **Flower gardening; Plants; Plants, Cultivated; Window gardening**

House repairing. *See* **Houses—Maintenance and repair**

House sanitation. *See* **Sanitation, Household**

House trailers. *See* **Mobile homes; Travel trailers and campers**

Houseboats 728
> *x* House boats
> *xx* **Boats and boating**

Household appliances. *See* **Household equipment and supplies**

Household appliances, Electric 643-644
> *See also* names of specific appliances
> *x* Appliances, Electric; Domestic appliances; Electric apparatus and appliances, Domestic; Electric appliances; Electric household appliances; Electricity in the home; Labor saving devices, Household
> *xx* **Household equipment and supplies**

Household budget. *See* **Budgets, Household**

Household employees 640
> *x* Domestic workers; Housemaids; Servants
> *xx* **Home economics; Labor and laboring classes**

Household equipment and supplies 643
> *See also* **Household appliances, Electric**

Household equipment and supplies—*Continued*
>   *x* Cooking utensils; Domestic appliances; Home economics—Equipment and supplies; Household appliances; Implements, utensils, etc.; Kitchen utensils; Labor saving devices, Household; Utensils, Kitchen

Household finances. *See* **Budgets, Household; Cost of living**

Household management. *See* **Home economics**

Household moving. *See* **Moving, Household**

Household pests 648
>   *See also* names of pests, e.g. **Flies;** etc.
>   *x* Diseases and pests; Vermin
>   *xx* **Home economics; Insects, Injurious and beneficial; Pests; Sanitation, Household**

Household sanitation. *See* **Sanitation, Household**

Housekeeping. *See* **Home economics**

Housemaids. *See* **Household employees**

Houses 728
>   Use for general materials on houses
>   *See also* **Apartment houses; Building; Housing; Tenement houses;** also parts of the house, e.g. **Kitchens;** etc.
>   *x* Cottages; Dwellings; Habitations, Human; Homes; Residences; Summer homes
>   *xx* **Architecture, Domestic**

Houses—Heating and ventilation 644; 697
>   *xx* **Heating**

Houses, Historic. *See* **Historic buildings, etc.**

Houses—Maintenance and repair 643
>   *x* Home repairing; House repairing
>   *xx* **Buildings—Maintenance and repair**

Houses, Prefabricated. *See* **Prefabricated houses**

Houses—Security. *See* **Burglary protection**

Houses of animals. *See* **Animals—Habitations**

Housing 301.5
>   Use for materials on the social and economic aspects of the housing problem
>   *See also* **Apartment houses; City planning; Mobile homes; Tenement houses;** also subjects with the subdivision *Housing,* e.g. **Blacks—Housing; Physically handicapped—Housing;** etc.
>   *x* Habitations, Human
>   *xx* **City planning; Houses; Landlord and tenant; Social problems; Tenement houses; Welfare work in industry**

Housing, Black. *See* **Blacks—Housing**

Housing, Discrimination in. *See* **Discrimination in housing**

Housing for the elderly. *See* **Elderly—Housing**

Housing for the physically handicapped. *See* **Physically handicapped—Housing**

Houston, Tex. Baseball Club (National League). *See* **Houston Astros**

278

Houston Astros   796.357
  x Astros; Houston, Tex. Baseball Club
      (National League)
  xx **Baseball clubs**
Hovercraft.   *See* **Ground effect machines**
Hudson River—Bridges   624.4; 917.47
  xx **Bridges**
Huguenots   284
  xx **Christianity; Reformation**
Hull House, Chicago   361.4
  xx **Social settlements**
Human anatomy.   *See* **Anatomy, Human**
Human behavior   150; 301.1
  See also

Behavior modi-	**Justice**
fication	**Life styles**
Charity	**Love**
Courage	**Loyalty**
Courtesy	**Obedience**
Duty	**Patriotism**
Ethics	**Self-control**
Etiquette	**Social adjustment**
Family life	**Spiritual life**
education	**Sympathy**
Friendship	**Temperance**
Habit	**Truthfulness and**
Honesty	**falsehood**

  Human relations
  x Behavior; Conduct of life; Morals; Per-
      sonal conduct
  xx **Character; Courtesy; Ethics; Human re-
      lations**
Human body.   *See* **Anatomy, Human; Physi-
      ology**
Human cold storage.   *See* **Cryonics**
Human color.   *See* **Color of people**
Human ecology   301.3
  See also **Anthropogeography; Environmen-
      tal policy; Man—Influence of environ-
      ment; Man—Influence on nature; Pop-
      ulation**
  x Ecology, Human; Ecology, Social; Social
      ecology
  xx **Environmental policy; Sociology**
Human engineering   620.8
  Use for materials on engineering design as
      related to human anatomical, physio-
      logical and psychological capabilities
      and limitations
  See also **Life support systems (Space en-
      vironment)**
  x Biomechanics;   Biotechnology;   Ergo-
      nomics
  xx **Design, Industrial; Machinery—Design;
      Psychology, Applied**
Human figure in art.   *See* **Anatomy, Artistic;
      Figure drawing; Figure painting**
Human race.   *See* **Anthropology; Man**
Human relations   158; 301.11
  Use for materials that deal with the in-

Human relations—*Continued*
tegration of people so that they can
live and work together with psychological, social and economic satisfaction

See also **Conflict of generations; Discrimination; Family; Group relations training; Hotlines (Telephone counseling);
Human behavior; Intercultural education; Interfaith relations; Personnel
management; Prejudices and antipathies; Psychology, Applied; Social adjustment; Toleration; Transactional
analysis;** also interpersonal relations
between individuals or group of individuals, e.g. **Jews and Gentiles; Landlord and tenant; Parent and child;** etc.

x Interpersonal relations
xx **Family life education; Human behavior;
Psychology, Applied; Social psychology**

Human resources 331.1

See also **Labor supply; Military service,
Compulsory; Military service, Voluntary;** also names of wars with the subdivision *Human resources,* e.g. **World
War, 1939–1945–Human resources**

x Man power; Manpower; Woman power
xx **Employment; Labor supply**

Human resources development. See **Human
resources policy**

Human resources policy 331.1

See also **Labor supply; Occupational
training; Retraining, Occupational; Vocational education**

x Human resources development; Manpower policy
xx **Economic policy; Labor supply**

Human rights. See **Civil rights**

Humanism 001.2; 144; 880
Use for materials on culture founded on
the study of the classics, sometimes
narrowly for Greek and Roman
scholarship

See also **Classical education; Hellenism;
Humanities; Learning and scholarship;
Renaissance**

xx **Classical education; Culture; Learning
and scholarship; Literature; Philosophy; Renaissance**

Humanism—20th century 144
Use for materials on any intellectual, philo-
sophical or religious movement or system which is centered in people rather
than in nature, the supernatural, or
the absolute

Humanities 001.3
See also **Classical education;** and such subjects as **Art; Literature; Music; Philosophy;** etc.

280

Humanities—*Continued*
    xx **Classical education; Humanism**
Humanities and science. *See* **Science and the humanities**
Humanity, Religion of. *See* **Positivism**
Humans in space. *See* **Space flight**
Humor. *See* **Wit and humor**
Humorists 920; 928
    xx **Wit and humor**
Humorous pictures. *See* **Cartoons and caricatures; Comic books, strips, etc.**
Humorous poetry 808.81; 811.08; etc.
    See also **Limericks; Nonsense verses**
Humorous stories. *See* **Wit and humor**
Hundred Years' War, 1339–1453 944
    xx **Europe—History—476–1492; France—History—House of Valois, 1328–1589; Gt. Brit.—History—Lancaster and York, 1399–1485**
Hungary—History 943.9
Hungary—History—Revolution, 1956 943.9
    xx **Revolutions**
Hunting (May subdiv. geog.) 799.2
    See also **Game and game birds; Game preserves; Game protection;** also types of hunting, e.g. **Falconry; Shooting; Tracking and trailing; Trapping; Whaling; etc.**
    x The chase; Gunning
    xx **Game and game birds; Shooting; Trapping**
Hunting—U.S. 799.2
    x U.S.—Hunting
Hurricanes 551.5
    Use for storms originating in the region of the West Indies
    See also **Cyclones;** also names of areas and cities with the subdivision *Hurricane*, e.g. **New England—Hurricane, 1938;** etc.
    xx **Meteorology; Storms; Winds**
Hybridization. *See* **Plant breeding**
Hydraulic cement. *See* **Cement**
Hydraulic engineering 627
    See also

Boring	**Irrigation**
Drainage	**Pumping machinery**
Dredging	**Reclamation of land**
Floods—Control	**Rivers**
Hydraulic structures	**Turbines**
Hydraulics	**Water**
Hydrodynamics	**Water supply engineering**
Hydrostatics	**Wells**

    xx **Civil engineering; Hydraulics; Rivers; Water; Water power; Water supply engineering**
Hydraulic machinery 621.2
    See also **Turbines**
    xx **Machinery; Water power**

Hydraulic structures 627

> *See also* types of hydraulic structures, e.g.
> **Aqueducts; Canals; Dams; Docks;
> Harbors; Reservoirs;** etc.
>
> *xx* **Hydraulic engineering; Structural engineering**

Hydraulics 621.2; 627

> Use for materials on technical applications
> of the theory of hydrodynamics
>
> *See also* **Hydraulic engineering; Hydrodynamics; Hydrostatics; Water; Water
> power**
>
> *x* Water flow
>
> *xx* **Hydraulic engineering; Liquids; Mechanics; Physics**

Hydrodynamics 532

> Use for materials on the theory of the motion and action of fluids. Materials on
> the experimental investigation and
> technical application of this theory are
> entered under **Hydraulics**
>
> *See also* **Hydrostatics; Viscosity; Waves**
>
> *xx* **Dynamics; Hydraulic engineering; Hydraulics; Liquids; Mechanics**

Hydroelectric power. *See* **Water power**

Hydrofoil boats 629.3

Hydrogen 546

> *xx* **Chemical elements**

Hydrogen bomb 623.4

> *See also* **Atomic bomb; Radioactive fallout**
>
> *x* H bomb; Thermonuclear bomb
>
> *xx* **Atomic bomb; Atomic warfare; Atomic
> weapons; Bombs**

Hydrogen nucleus. *See* **Protons**

Hydrology. *See* **Water**

Hydropathy. *See* **Hydrotherapy**

Hydrophobia. *See* **Rabies**

Hydroponics. *See* **Plants—Soilless culture**

Hydrostatics 532

> *See also* **Gases**
>
> *xx* **Hydraulic engineering; Hydraulics; Hydrodynamics; Liquids; Mechanics;
> Physics; Statics**

Hydrotherapy 615

> *See also* **Baths; Health resorts, spas,** etc.
>
> *x* Hydropathy; Water cure
>
> *xx* **Baths; Physical therapy; Therapeutics;
> Water**

Hygiene 613

> *See also*

Air	**Grooming,**
Baths	**Personal**
Children—Care	**Gymnastics**
and hygiene	**Infants—Care and**
Clothing and dress	**hygiene**
Diet	**Mental health**
Disinfection and	**Military hygiene**
disinfectants	**Narcotics**
Exercise	**Occupational**
Food	**diseases**

Hygiene—*Continued*

Physical education and training
Physiology
Rest
Sanitation
School hygiene
Sleep
Stimulants
Temperance
Ventilation
Water—Pollution

    x Cleanliness; Health; Hygiene, Social; Preventive medicine; Social hygiene

  xx **Medicine; Sanitation**

Hygiene, Industrial. *See* **Industrial health and safety**

Hygiene, Mental. *See* **Mental health**

Hygiene, Military. *See* **Military hygiene**

Hygiene, Public. *See* **Public health**

Hygiene, School. *See* **School hygiene**

Hygiene, Sexual. *See* **Sexual hygiene**

Hygiene, Social. *See* **Hygiene; Prostitution; Public health; Sexual hygiene; Venereal diseases**

Hygiene—Study and teaching. *See* **Health education**

Hymenoptera. *See* **Ants; Bees; Wasps**

Hymnology. *See* **Hymns**

Hymns 245; 783.9

    See also **Carols; Church music; Religious poetry**

    x Hymnology; Psalmody

  xx **Church music; Devotional exercises; Poetry; Religious poetry; Songs; Vocal music**

Hyperactive children 155.4

    See also **Hyperactivity**

    x Children, Hyperactive; Hyperkinetic children; Overactive children

  xx **Handicapped children; Hyperactivity**

Hyperactivity 152.3

    See also **Hyperactive children**

    x Hyperkinesia; Overactivity

  xx **Hyperactive children**

Hyperkinesia. *See* **Hyperactivity**

Hyperkinetic children. *See* **Hyperactive children**

Hypnotism 154.7

    See also **Mental suggestion; Mind and body; Personality disorders; Psychoanalysis; Subconsciousness; Therapeutics, Suggestive**

    x Animal magnetism; Autosuggestion; Mesmerism

  xx **Clairvoyance; Medicine; Mental healing; Mental suggestion; Mind and body; Mind reading; Personality disorders; Psychical research; Psychoanalysis; Psychology, Physiological; Subconciousness; Therapeutics, Suggestive; Thought transference**

IBM 7090 (Computer) 621.3819

  xx **Computers**

ICBM. *See* **Intercontinental ballistic missiles**

IQ tests. *See* **Mental tests**

ISBD. *See* **International Standard Bibliographic Description**

ISBN. *See* **International Standard Book Numbers**

ISSN. *See* **International Standard Serial Numbers**

Ice 551.3
> *See also* **Glaciers; Icebergs**
> *x* Freezing
> *xx* **Cold; Frost; Physical geography; Water**

Ice age. *See* **Glacial epoch**

Ice boats. *See* **Iceboats**

Ice cream, ices, etc. 637; 641.8
> *See also* **Confectionery**
> *x* Ices
> *xx* **Desserts; Food, Frozen**

Ice hockey 796.9
> *x* Hockey
> *xx* **Winter sports**

Ice manufacture. *See* **Refrigeration and refrigerating machinery**

Ice skating 796.9
> *x* Figure skating; Skating
> *xx* **Winter sports**

Ice sports. *See* **Winter sports**

Icebergs 551.3
> *xx* **Ice; Ocean; Physical geography**

Iceboats 623.82
> *x* Ice boats
> *xx* **Boats and boating**

Icelandic and Old Norse languages 439
> *See also* **Scandinavian languages**
> *x* Norse languages; Old Norse language
> *xx* **Scandinavian languages**

Icelandic and Old Norse literature 839
> *See also* **Eddas; Sagas; Scalds and scaldic poetry; Scandinavian literature**
> *x* Norse literature; Old Norse literature
> *xx* **Sagas; Scalds and scaldic poetry; Scandinavian literature**

Ices. *See* **Ice cream, ices, etc.**

Ichthyology. *See* **Fishes**

Iconography. *See* **Art; Christian art and symbolism; Portraits; Religious art and symbolism**

Ideal states. *See* **Utopias**

Idealism 141
> *See also* **Materialism; Realism; Transcendentalism**
> *xx* **Materialism; Philosophy; Positivism; Realism; Transcendentalism**

Identification
> *See also* **Fingerprints;** also subjects with the subdivision *Identification,* e.g. **Airplanes—Identification; Criminals—Identification;** etc.

Identity. *See* **Individuality; Personality**

284

Idioms. *See* names of languages with the subdivision *Idiom*s, e.g. **English language —Idioms;** etc.

Illiteracy 379

  x Literacy

  xx **Education**

Illiterate societies. *See* **Society, Nonliterate folk**

Illuminated manuscripts. *See* **Illumination of books and manuscripts**

Illuminating gas. *See* **Gas**

Illumination. *See* **Lighting**

Illumination of books and manuscripts 096; 745.6

  See also **Initials**

  x Illuminated manuscripts; Manuscripts, Illuminated; Miniatures (Illumination of books and manuscripts); Ornamental alphabets

  xx **Alphabets; Art; Art, Medieval; Arts and crafts; Books; Christian art and symbolism; Decoration and ornament; Design, Decorative; Illustration of books; Initials; Manuscripts**

Illusions. *See* **Hallucinations and illusions; Optical illusions**

Illustration of books 741.64

  See also **Caldecott Medal books; Drawing; Engraving; Illumination of books and manuscripts; Photomechanical processes**

  x Book illustration

  xx **Art; Art, Decorative; Books; Color printing; Decoration and ornament; Drawing**

Illustrations. *See* subjects with the subdivision *Pictorial works;* e.g. **Animals—Pictorial works; U.S.—History—Civil War, 1861–1865—Pictorial works;** etc.

Illustrations, Humorous. *See* **Cartoons and caricatures**

Illustrators (May subdiv. geog. adjective form, e.g. **Illustrators, French;** etc.) **920; 927**

  xx **Artists**

Illustrators, American 920; 927

  x American illustrators; U.S.—Illustrators

Images, National. *See* **National characteristics**

Imaginary animals. *See* **Animals, Mythical**

Imagination 153.3

  See also **Creation (Literary, artistic, etc.); Fantasy**

  xx **Educational psychology; Intellect; Psychology**

Immersion, Baptismal. *See* **Baptism**

Immigrants. *See* **Immigration and emigration**

Immigration and emigration 325

  Use for materials on migration from one country to another. Materials on the movement of population within a

285

Immigration and emigration—*Continued*
country for permanent settlements are
entered under **Migration, Internal**
See also **Aliens; Anthropogeography; Colonization; Naturalization; Refugees;**
also names of countries with the subdivision *Immigration and emigration*
(e.g. **U.S.—Immigration and emigration;** etc.); names of countries, cities,
etc. with the subdivision *Foreign population* (e.g. **U.S.—Foreign population;**
etc.); and names of nationality groups,
e.g. **Mexican Americans; Mexicans in
the U.S.;** etc.

x Emigration; Foreign population; Immigrants; Migration; Population, Foreign

xx **Colonies; Colonization; Race relations;
Social problems; Sociology**

Immoral art. *See* **Erotic art**

Immoral literature. *See* **Erotic literature**

Immortality 129
Use for materials dealing with the question
of the endless existence of the soul.
Materials dealing with the character
and form of a future existence are entered under **Future life**

See also **Future life**

x Life after death

xx **Eschatology; Future life; Soul; Theology**

Immunity 574.2; 612
See also **Allergy; Communicable diseases;
Vaccination**

x Medicine, Preventive; Preventive medicine

xx **Bacteriology; Communicable diseases;
Pathology; Vaccination**

Immunization. *See* **Vaccination**

Impeachments 351.9
See also **Recall (Political science)**
xx **Justice, Administration of**

Imperialism 321; 325
See also names of countries with the sub-
division *Foreign relations,* e.g. **U.S.—
Foreign relations;** etc.

x Colonialism

xx **Political science**

Implements, utensils, etc. *See* **Agricultural machinery; Household equipment and
supplies; Stone implements; Tools**

Imports. *See* **Commerce; Tariff**

Impostors and imposture 364.1
See also **Counterfeits and counterfeiting;
Forgery; Fraud; Quacks and quack-
ery; Swindlers and swindling**

x Charlatans; Hoaxes; Pretenders

xx **Fraud; Swindlers and swindling**

Impregnation, Artificial. *See* **Artificial insemination**

Impressionism (Art) 759.05

    See also **Postimpressionism (Art)**

    x Neo-impressionism (Art)

    xx **Painting; Postimpressionism (Art)**

Imprisonment. *See* **Prisons**

In line data processing. *See* **On line data processing**

Inaudible sound. *See* **Ultrasonics**

Incandescent lamps. *See* **Electric lamps**

Incas 980.3

    xx **Indians of South America**

Incendiary bombs 623.4

    x Bombs, Incendiary; Fire bombs

    xx **Bombs; Incendiary weapons**

Incendiary weapons 623.4

    See also types of incendiary weapons, e.g. **Incendiary bombs;** etc.

    xx **Chemical warfare**

Incineration. *See* **Cremation; Refuse and refuse disposal**

Income 339.2-339.4

    See also **Capital; Profit; Wages—Annual wage**

    x Fortunes

    xx **Economics; Finance; Profit; Property; Wealth**

Income tax 336.2

    x Direct taxation; Payroll taxes; Taxation of income

    xx **Finance; Internal revenue; Taxation; Wealth**

Independence Day (U.S.). *See* **Fourth of July**

Independent schools. *See* **Private schools**

Indeterminism. *See* **Free will and determinism**

Index librorum prohibitorum. *See* **Books—Censorship; Catholic literature**

Indexes

    See also **Subject headings;** also subjects with the subdivision *Indexes,* eg. **Newspapers—Indexes; Periodicals—Indexes; Short stories—Indexes;** etc.

    xx **Bibliography**

Indexing 029.6

    See also **Cataloging; Files and filing**

    xx **Bibliographic control; Bibliography; Cataloging; Files and filing**

India rubber. *See* **Rubber**

Indian folklore. *See* **Folklore, Indian**

Indian languages (North American). *See* **Indians of North America—Languages**

Indian literature (American). *See* **American literature—American Indian authors**

Indian reservations. *See* **Indians of North America—Reservations**

Indians 970.1

    Use for materials which treat of the Indians of both South and North America. Names of peoples and linguistic families are not included in this list but may be added as needed

Indians—*Continued*

　May be subdivided like **Indians of North America**

　See also **Indians of Central America; Indians of Mexico; Indians of North America; Indians of South America**

　x American Indians; Amerindians

Indians (of India). *See* **East Indians**

Indians of Canada. *See* **Indians of North America—Canada**

Indians of Central America 970.4

　May be subdivided like **Indians of North America**

　xx **Indians**

Indians of Mexico 970.4

　May be subdivided like **Indians of North America**

　See also **Aztecs; Mayas**

　xx **Indians**

Indians of North America (May subdiv. geog. state or region) **970.1**

　Names of peoples and linguistic families are not included in this list but may be added as needed, e.g. **Ojibwe Indians;** etc.

　Subdivisions used under this heading may also be used under names of peoples and linguistic families

　See also **Cliff dwellers and cliff dwellings; Mounds and mound builders; Indians of North America—Canada;** and names of peoples and linguistic families, e.g. **Ojibwe Indians;** etc.

　x American Indians; Amerindians; Native Americans; Native peoples; North American Indians; Pre-Columbian Americans

　xx **Ethnology—U.S.; Indians**

Indians of North America—Amusements. *See* **Indians of North America—Games; Indians of North America—Social life and customs**

Indians of North America—Antiquities 917

　See also **Mounds and mound builders**

　x Antiquities

　xx **Archeology; U.S.—Antiquities**

Indians of North America—Art 709.01

　x Art, Indian

Indians of North America—Canada 970.4

　x Canadian Indians; Indians of Canada

　xx **Indians of North America**

Indians of North America—Captivities 970.1

　xx **Frontier and pioneer life**

Indians of North America—Children 301.43

　xx **Children**

Indians of North America—Civilization 970.1

Indians of North America—Claims 970.5

　x Indians of North America—Land claims; Indians of North America—Legal status, laws, etc.

288

Indians of North America—Costume and adorn-
ment 391
   xx Costume
Indians of North America—Customs. *See* In-
dians of North America—Social life
and customs
Indians of North America—Dances 793.3
   xx Folk dancing; Indians of North America
—Religion; Indians of North Amer-
ica—Social life and customs
Indians of North America—Drama 812; 822;
etc.
Indians of North America—Economic conditions 330.9701
Indians of North America—Education 371.9
   See also names of Indian schools
   x Indians of North America—Schools
Indians of North America—Fiction Fic
Indians of North America—Folklore. *See*
Folklore, Indian
Indians of North America—Games 790
   x Indians of North America—Amuse-
ments; Indians of North America—
Recreations; Indians of North Amer-
ica—Sports
   xx Games; Indians of North America—So-
cial life and customs
Indians of North America—Government rela-
tions 970.5
   x Indians of North America—Legal sta-
tus, laws, etc.
Indians of North America—History 970.1
   See also Indians of North America—Wars
Indians of North America—Industries
338.9701; 680
Indians of North America—Land claims. *See*
Indians of North America—Claims
Indians of North America—Languages 497
   See also Indians of North America—Sign
language
   x Indian languages (North American)
Indians of North America—Legal status, laws,
etc. *See* Indians of North America—
Claims; Indians of North America—
Government relations
Indians of North America—Legends 398.2
   Use for collections of Indian legends,
myths, tales, etc. Materials about the
folklore of American Indians are en-
tered under Folklore, Indian
   See also Folklore, Indian
   x Indians of North America—Mythology;
Legends, Indian
   xx Folklore, Indian
Indians of North America—Literature. *See*
American literature—American Indian
authors
Indians of North America—Missions, Christian
266
   x Missions, Indian

289

Indians of North America—Music 781.7

   x Music, Indian

Indians of North America—Mythology. *See* **Folklore, Indian; Indians of North America—Legends; Indians of North America—Religion**

Indians of North America—Names 929.4

Indians of North America—Origin 572.9701

Indians of North America—Poetry 811; 821; etc.

Indians of North America—Recreations. *See* **Indians of North America—Games**

Indians of North America—Religion 299

   See also **Indians of North America—Dances; Totems and totemism**

   x Indians of North America—Mythology; Mythology, Indian

   xx **Mythology; Religion**

Indians of North America—Reservations 333.1; 970.5

   x Indian reservations; Reservations, Indian

Indians of North America—Schools. *See* **Indians of North America—Education;** and names of Indian schools

Indians of North America—Sign language 419

   x Sign language

   xx **Indians of North America—Languages**

Indians of North America—Silverwork 739.2

Indians of North America—Social conditions 309.1701

   xx **Social conditions**

Indians of North America—Social life and customs 309.1701; 970.1

   See also **Indians of North America—Dances; Indians of North America—Games**

   x Customs, Social; Indians of North America—Amusements; Indians of North America—Customs; Social customs; Social life and customs

   xx **Manners and customs**

Indians of North America—Sports. *See* **Indians of North America—Games**

Indians of North America—Treatment 970.5

Indians of North America—Wars 970.5

   See also **Black Hawk War, 1832; King Philip's War, 1675–1676; Pontiac's Conspiracy, 1763–1765; U.S.–History—French and Indian War, 1755–1763; U.S.–History—King William's War, 1689–1697;** etc.

   xx **Indians of North America—History**

Indians of South America (May be subdiv. by country, e.g. **Indians of South America—Peru;** etc.) **980.1**

   May be subdivided like **Indians of North America**

   See also **Incas; Mayas**

   x American Indians; Amerindians

   xx **Indians**

Indigestion   616.3

  x Dyspepsia

  xx **Digestion**

Individualism   141; 330.1

  See also **Communism; Socialism**

  xx **Equality; Socialism; Sociology**

Individuality   155.2

  See also **Conformity; Personality; Self**

  x Identity

  xx **Conformity; Consciousness; Personality; Psychology**

Indochina   915.9; 959

  Use for area comprising Laos, Cambodia, and Vietnam

Indoor games   793

  See also **Amusements**

  xx **Amusements; Games**

Induction coils   537.6; 621.31

  See also **Condensers (Electricity)**

Induction (Logic).   *See* **Logic**

Induction motors.   *See* **Electric motors**

Industrial alcohol.   *See* **Alcohol, Denatured**

Industrial arbitration.   *See* **Arbitration, Industrial**

Industrial arts   600; 660

  See also **Art industries and trade; Arts and crafts; Technology;** also names of specific industries, arts, trades (e.g. **Bookbinding; Printing; Shipbuilding;** etc.); and names of countries, cities, etc. with the subdivision *Industries,* e.g. **U.S.—Industries;** etc.

  x Arts, Useful; Mechanic arts; Trades; Useful arts

  xx **Handicraft; Technology**

Industrial arts education   607

  See also **Arts and crafts; Basket making; Carpentry; Handicraft; Modeling; Technical education; Woodwork**

  x Education, Industrial; Industrial education; Industrial schools; Manual training

  xx **Arts and crafts; Handicraft; Technical education; Vocational education**

Industrial arts shops.   *See* **School shops**

Industrial buildings   725

  See also **Factories; Office buildings; Skyscrapers**

  x Buildings, Industrial

  xx **Architecture; Buildings**

Industrial chemistry.   *See* **Chemical engineering; Chemical industries; Chemistry, Technical**

Industrial combinations.   *See* **Trusts, Industrial**

Industrial conciliation.   *See* **Arbitration, Industrial**

Industrial councils.   *See* **Employees' representation in management**

Industrial design.   *See* **Design, Industrial**

Industrial diseases.   *See* **Occupational diseases**

Industrial disputes. *See* **Labor disputes**
Industrial drawing. *See* **Mechanical drawing**
Industrial education. *See* **Industrial arts education; Technical education**
Industrial efficiency. *See* **Efficiency, Industrial**
Industrial engineering. *See* **Industrial management**
Industrial exhibitions. *See* **Exhibitions**
Industrial health and safety 614.8; 658.38
> *See also* **Occupational diseases; Occupations, Dangerous**
>
> *x* Health, Industrial; Hygiene, Industrial; Industrial safety; Occupational health and safety; Safety, Industrial
>
> *xx* **Industrial management; Public health**

Industrial insurance. *See* **Insurance, Industrial**
Industrial management 658
> Use for general materials on the application of the principles of management to industries, including problems of production, marketing, financial control, office management, etc. Materials limited to technical aspects of manufacturing processes are entered under **Factory management**
>
> *See also*

Business	Machinery
Buying	Marketing
Efficiency, Industrial	Materials handling
Factory management	Office management
	Personnel management
Industrial health and safety	
Industrial relations	Sales management
Job analysis	Welfare work in industry

> *x* Industrial engineering; Industrial organization; Industry—Organization, control, etc.; Management, Industrial
>
> *xx* **Business; Industry; Management**

Industrial materials. *See* **Materials**
Industrial mergers. *See* **Conglomerate corporations; Railroads—Consolidation; Trusts, Industrial**
Industrial mobilization 355.2
> Use for materials dealing with industrial and labor policies and programs for defense mobilization
>
> *See also* **Munitions**
>
> *x* Armaments; Defenses, National; Economic mobilization; Industry and war; Mobilization, Industrial; National defenses
>
> *xx* **Economic policy; Military art and science; War—Economic aspects**

Industrial organization. *See* **Industrial management**
Industrial painting. *See* **Painting, Industrial**
Industrial plants. *See* **Factories**
Industrial psychology. *See* **Psychology, Applied**

Industrial relations   331

Use for general materials on employer-employee relations. Materials on problems of personnel and relations from the employer's point of view are entered under **Personnel management**

See also **Arbitration, Industrial; Collective bargaining; Employees' representation in management; Labor contract; Labor disputes; Labor unions; Personnel management; Strikes and lockouts**

x Capital and labor; Employer-employee relations; Labor and capital; Labor-management relations; Labor relations

xx **Industrial management; Labor and laboring classes**

Industrial revolution. *See* **Gt. Brit.—History—19th century; Industry—History**

Industrial safety. *See* **Industrial health and safety**

Industrial schools. *See* **Industrial arts education; Technical education**

Industrial trusts. *See* **Trusts, Industrial**

Industrial wastes   658.5

See also **Pollution; Refuse and refuse disposal; Waste products; Water—Pollution**

x Factory and trade waste; Factory waste; Trade waste; Waste disposal

xx **Refuse and refuse disposal; Waste products; Water—Pollution**

Industrialization   338

Use for general materials only. Materials on the industrialization of individual countries, regions, etc. are entered under the name of the country, city, etc. with the subdivision *Industries*

See also **Developing areas; Technical assistance**

xx **Economic policy; Industry; Technical assistance**

Industries. *See* **Industry;** names of industries (e.g. **Steel industry and trade;** etc); and names of countries, cities, etc. with the subdivision, *Industries*, e.g. **U.S.—Industries;** etc.

Industries, Chemical. *See* **Chemical industries**

Industries, Electric. *See* **Electric industries**

Industry   338; 600

Use for general materials on manufacturing and mechanical activities. Names of all individual industries are not included in this list but are to be added as needed, e.g. **Steel industry and trade;** etc.

See also **Efficiency, Industrial; Industrial management; Industrialization; Machinery in industry; Manufactures**

x Industries; Production

xx **Civilization; Economics**

Industry—History 609

   x Industrial revolution

Industry—Organization, control, etc. *See* **Industrial management; Industry and state**

Industry and art. *See* **Art industries and trade**

Industry and state (May subdiv. geog.) **338.9**

   Use for materials on the theory of state regulation of industry and for general materials on the relations between government and business

   See also

Agriculture and state	**Public service commissions**
Economic policy	**Railroads and state**
Government ownership	**Subsidies**

   x Business and government; Government and business; Government regulation of industry; Industry—Organization, control, etc.; Laissez faire; Socialization of industry; State and industry; State regulation of industry

   xx **Economic policy; Socialism**

Industry and state—U.S. 338.9

   x U.S.—Industry and state

Industry and war. *See* **Industrial mobilization; War—Economic aspects**

Inebriates. *See* **Alcoholics**

Inequality. *See* **Equality**

Infallibility of the Pope. *See* **Popes—Infallibility**

Infantile paralysis. *See* **Poliomyelitis**

Infants 155.4

   Use for materials about children in the earliest period of life, usually the first two years only

   See also **Children**

   x Babies

   xx **Children**

Infants—Care and hygiene 649

   See also **Baby sitters**

   x Health of infants

   xx **Children—Care and hygiene; Hygiene; Nursing**

Infants—Clothing 646; 649

Infants—Diseases 618.9

Infants—Education. *See* **Education, Preschool**

Infants—Nutrition 641.1; 649

Infection and infectious diseases. *See* **Communicable diseases**

Infirmaries. *See* **Hospitals**

Inflation (Finance) 332.4

   See also **Monetary policy; Paper money; Wage-price policy**

   xx **Finance; Monetary policy**

Influenza 616.2

   x Flu; Grippe

   xx **Cold (Disease)**

Information, Freedom of. *See* **Freedom of information**

Information networks   001.5

    See also types of information networks, e.g. **Library information networks;** etc.

    x Automated information networks; Networks, Information

    xx **Information storage and retrieval systems**

Information science   020

    See also **Documentation; Electronic data processing; Information storage and retrieval systems; Library science**

    xx **Communication**

Information   storage   and   retrieval   systems   001.6; 029.7

    See also **Electronic data processing; Information networks; Libraries—Automation;** and names of specific systems

    x Automatic information retrieval; Data processing; Data storage and retrieval systems; Punched card systems

    xx **Bibliographic   control;   Bibliography; Computers; Documentation; Information science; Libraries—Automation**

Inheritance (Biology).   *See* **Heredity**

Inheritance and succession   346.5

    See also **Executors and administrators; Inheritance and transfer tax; Land tenure; Wills**

    x Bequests; Heirs; Hereditary succession; Intestacy; Legacies; Succession, Intestate

    xx **Parent and child; Wealth; Wills**

Inheritance and transfer tax   343.4

    x Estate tax; Taxation of legacies; Transfer tax

    xx **Estate planning; Inheritance and succession; Internal revenue; Taxation**

Initialisms.   *See* **Acronyms**

Initials   745.6

    See also **Alphabets; Illumination of books and   manuscripts;   Lettering;   Monograms; Printing—Specimens; Type and type founding**

    xx **Alphabets; Illumination of books and manuscripts; Letterings; Monograms; Type and type founding**

Initiative and referendum.   *See* **Referendum**

Injunctions   331.89

    See also **Strikes and lockouts**

    xx **Constitutional law; Labor unions; Strikes and lockouts**

Injuries.   *See* **Accidents; First aid**

Injurious insects.   *See* **Insects, Injurious and beneficial**

Injurious occupations.   *See* **Occupations, Dangerous**

Ink drawing.   *See* **Pen drawing**

Inland navigation   386

    See also **Canals; Lakes; Rivers**

    x Navigation, Inland

    xx **Canals; Navigation; Rivers; Shipping;**

Inland navigation—*Continued*
　　　　Transportation; Water resources de-
　　　　velopment; Waterways
Inns.　*See* Hotels, motels, etc.
Inoculation.　*See* Vaccination
Inorganic chemistry.　*See* Chemistry, Inorganic
Insane.　*See* Mentally ill
Insane—Hospitals.　*See* Mentally ill—Institu-
　　　　tional care; Psychiatric hospitals
Insanity.　*See* Mental illness—Jurisprudence
Inscriptions　417
　　　See also Brasses; Epitaphs; Hieroglyphics;
　　　　Seals (Numismatics)
　　　x Epigraphy
　　　xx Archeology; History, Ancient
Insecticides　668
　　　See also Fumigation; Insects, Injurious and
　　　　beneficial; Spraying and dusting; also
　　　　names of insecticides, e.g. DDT (In-
　　　　secticide); etc.
　　　xx Agricultural chemicals; Insects, Injuri-
　　　　ous and beneficial; Pesticides; Spray-
　　　　ing and dusting
Insecticides—Toxicology　668
　　　xx Poisons
Insects　595.7
　　　See also Fertilization of plants; also names
　　　　of insects, e.g. Ants; Bees; Butterflies;
　　　　Moths; Wasps; etc.
　　　x Entomology
　　　xx Invertebrates
Insects, Destructive and useful.　*See* Insects,
　　　　Injurious and beneficial
Insects, Injurious and beneficial　632
　　　See also Aeronautics in agriculture; Agri-
　　　　cultural pests; Household pests; In-
　　　　secticides; Insects as carriers of dis-
　　　　ease; also names of injurious and
　　　　beneficial insects (e.g. Locusts; Silk-
　　　　worms; etc.); and names of crops,
　　　　trees, etc. with the subdivision *Dis-
　　　　eases and pests*, e.g. Fruit—Diseases
　　　　and pests; etc.
　　　x Diseases and pests; Economic entomol-
　　　　ogy; Entomology, Economic; Garden
　　　　pests; Injurious insects; Insects, De-
　　　　structive and useful
　　　xx Agricultural pests; Gardening; Insecti-
　　　　cides; Parasites; Pests; Zoology, Eco-
　　　　nomic
Insects as carriers of disease　614
　　　See also Flies; Mosquitoes
　　　x Entomology, Medical; Medical entomol-
　　　　ogy
　　　xx Communicable diseases; Insects, Injuri-
　　　　ous and beneficial
Insemination, Artificial.　*See* Artificial insem-
　　　　ination
In-service training.　*See* Employees—Training

Insignia   929

    See also **Decorations of honor; Medals; U.S. Army—Insignia; U.S. Army— Medals, badges, decorations, etc.; U.S. Navy—Insignia; U.S. Navy—Medals, badges, decorations, etc.**

    x Badges of honor; Devices (Heraldry); Emblems

    xx **Decorations of honor; Heraldry; Medals**

Insolvency. *See* **Bankruptcy**

Insomnia   616.8

    See also **Narcotics; Sleep**

    x Sleeplessness; Wakefulness

    xx **Sleep**

Inspection of food. *See* **Food adulteration and inspection**

Inspection of meat. *See* **Meat inspection**

Inspection of schools. *See* **School administration and organization; School supervision**

Inspiration. *See* **Creation (Literary, artistic, etc.)**

Inspiration, Biblical. *See* **Bible—Inspiration**

Instalment plan   658.8

    x Hire-purchase plan

    xx **Business; Buying; Consumer credit; Credit**

Instinct   152.3; 156

    See also **Animal intelligence; Habit; Psychology, Comparative**

    x Animal instinct

    xx **Animal intelligence; Animals—Habits and behavior; Habit; Psychology; Psychology, Comparative**

Institutional care   361

    See also **Hospitals; Nursing homes; Orphanages;** also classes of people with the subdivision *Institutional care,* e.g. **Blind—Institutional care; Children— Institutional care; Mentally ill—Institutional care;** etc.

    x Asylums; Benevolent institutions; Charitable institutions; Homes (Institutions)

    xx **Charities; Charities, Medical; Public welfare**

Institutions, Charitable and philanthropic. *See* **Charities; Children—Institutional care; Hospitals**

Instruction. *See* **Education; Teaching**

Instructional materials centers   021; 371.33

    x Audio-visual materials centers; Curriculum materials centers; Learning resource centers; Media centers (Education); Multi-media centers; School media centers

    xx **Libraries**

Instructional supervision. *See* **School supervision**

Instrumental music 785

> *See also* **Musical instruments**; also types
> of instrumental music, e.g. **Band mu-
> sic; Chamber music; Dance music;
> Guitar music; Orchestral music; Piano
> music;** etc.
>
> *x* Music, Instrumental
> *xx* **Music; Musical instruments**

Instrumentation and orchestration 785

> *See also* **Musical instruments**
> *x* Orchestration
> *xx* **Bands (Music); Composition (Music);
> Music; Musical instruments; Orches-
> tra**

Instruments, Aeronautical. *See* **Aeronautical
instruments**

Instruments, Astronautical. *See* **Astronautical
instruments**

Instruments, Astronomical. *See* **Astronomical
instruments**

Instruments, Engineering. *See* **Engineering instruments**

Instruments, Measuring. *See* **Measuring instruments**

Instruments, Meteorological. *See* **Meteorological instruments**

Instruments, Musical. *See* **Musical instruments**

Instruments, Negotiable. *See* **Negotiable instruments**

Instruments, Scientific. *See* **Scientific apparatus and instruments**

Insulation (Heat) 693.8; 697

> *x* Heat insulating materials; Thermal in-
> sulation
> *xx* **Heating**

Insulation (Sound). *See* **Soundproofing**

Insurance 368

> All types of insurance are not included in
> this list but are to be added as needed
> in inverted form, e.g. **Insurance,
> Automobile;** etc.
>
> *See also* **Saving and thrift**
> *x* Underwriting
> *xx* **Estate planning; Finance; Finance, Per-
> sonal**

Insurance, Accident 368.3

> *See also* **Workers' compensation**
> *x* Accident insurance; Disability insurance;
> Insurance, Disability
> *xx* **Insurance, Casualty**

Insurance, Automobile 368.2

> *x* Automobile insurance; No fault auto-
> mobile insurance

Insurance, Casualty 368.5

> *See also* **Insurance, Accident**
> *x* Casualty insurance

Insurance, Disability. *See* **Insurance, Accident; Insurance, Health**

Insurance, Fire   368.1
>*See also* Fireproofing
>*x* Fire insurance
>*xx* Fires

Insurance, Group   368.3
>Includes group life insurance. Materials on group insurance in other fields are entered under the specific heading, e.g. **Insurance, Health**; etc.
>*x* Group insurance
>*xx* **Insurance, Life**

Insurance, Health   368.3
>*See also* **Health maintenance organizations; Insurance, Hospitalization; Workers' compensation**
>*x* Disability insurance; Group health; Group medical service; Health insurance; Insurance, Disability; Insurance, Sickness; Medical care, Prepaid; Medical service, Prepaid; Prepaid medical care; Sickness insurance; Socialized medicine
>*xx* **Social security**

Insurance, Hospitalization   368.3
>*x* Group hospitalization; Hospitalization insurance; Socialized medicine
>*xx* **Insurance, Health**

Insurance, Industrial   368.3
>Use for materials on insurance as carried on by companies whose agents collect the premiums from policy holders in small weekly payments
>*x* Industrial insurance
>*xx* **Insurance, Life; Labor and laboring classes; Saving and thrift**

Insurance, Life   368.3
>*See also* **Annuities; Insurance, Group; Insurance, Industrial; Probabilities**
>*x* Life insurance
>*xx* **Annuities**

Insurance, Malpractice   368
>*x* Malpractice insurance

Insurance, Marine   368.2
>*x* Marine insurance
>*xx* **Commerce; Maritime law; Merchant marine; Shipping**

Insurance, Old age.   *See* **Old age pensions**

Insurance, Sickness.   *See* **Insurance, Health**

Insurance, Social.   *See* **Social security**

Insurance, State and compulsory.   *See* **Social security**

Insurance, Unemployment   368.4
>*x* Labor and laboring classes—Insurance; Payroll taxes; Unemployment insurance
>*xx* **Social security; Unemployed**

Insurance, Workers'.   *See* **Social security**

Insurance, Workers' compensation.   *See* **Workers' compensation**

Insurgency   322.4; 355.02

    See also **Government, Resistance to; Guerrilla warfare; Internal security; Subversive activities; Terrorism**

    x Rebellions

    xx **Government, Resistance to; Internal security; Revolutions**

Integral calculus. *See* **Calculus**

Integrated churches. *See* **Church and race relations**

Integrated schools. *See* **School integration**

Integration, Racial. *See* **Blacks—Integration; Race relations**

Integration in education. *See* **Articulation (Education); School integration; Segregation in education**

Intellect   153.4

    See also

Creation (Literary, artistic, etc.)
Imagination
Knowledge, Theory of
Logic
Memory
Mental tests
Perception
Reason
Reasoning
Senses and sensation
Thought and thinking

    x Intelligence; Mind; Understanding

    xx **Knowledge, Theory of; Psychology; Reasoning; Thought and thinking**

Intellectual cooperation   370.19

    See also **Congresses and conventions; Cultural relations; International education**

    x Cooperation, Intellectual

    xx **International cooperation; International education**

Intellectual freedom   323.4

    See also **Academic freedom; Censorship; Free speech; Freedom of information; Freedom of the press**

    xx **Freedom**

Intellectual life. *See* **Culture; Learning and scholarship;** and names of countries, cities, etc. with the subdivision *Intellectual life,* e.g. **U.S.—Intellectual life;** etc.

Intellectual property. *See* **Copyright; Inventions; Patents**

Intelligence. *See* **Intellect**

Intelligence, Artificial. *See* **Artificial intelligence**

Intelligence agents. *See* **Spies**

Intelligence of animals. *See* **Animal intelligence**

Intelligence service (May subdiv. geog.)   **327; 355.3**

    See also **Espionage; Secret service**

    x Counterespionage; Counterintelligence

    xx **Secret service**

Intelligence service—U.S. 355.3
  x U.S.—Intelligence service
Intelligence tests. See Mental tests
Intemperance. See Alcoholism; Liquor problem; Temperance
Inter-American relations. See Pan-Americanism
Interchange of teachers. See Teachers, Interchange of
Interchange of visitors. See Exchange of persons programs
Intercollegiate athletics. See Athletics; College sports
Intercommunication systems 621.38; 651.7
  See also Closed circuit television; Microwave communication systems
  x Interoffice communication systems; Loud speakers
  xx Electronic apparatus and appliances; Sound—Recording and reproducing; Telecommunication
Intercontinental ballistic missiles 623.4
  See also names of specific ICBM missiles, e.g. Atlas (Missile); etc.
  x ICBM
  xx Atomic weapons; Ballistic missiles
Intercultural education 370.19
  Use for materials dealing with the eradication of racial and religious prejudices by showing the nature and effects of race, creed and immigrant cultures
  See also Education, Bilingual; International education
  x Education, Intercultural; Education, Multicultural; Multicultural education
  xx Acculturation; Human relations; International education; Race relations
Intercultural relations. See Cultural relations
Interest centers approach to teaching. See Open plan schools
Interest (Economics) 332.8
  xx Banks and banking; Business arithmetic; Capital; Finance; Loans
Interest groups. See Lobbying
Interfaith marriage. See Intermarriage, Religious
Interfaith relations 261; 261.2
  xx Christian unity; Human relations
Intergovernmental tax relations 336.2
  See also Revenue sharing
  x Federal-state tax relations; State-local tax relations; Tax relations, Intergovernmental; Tax sharing
  xx Taxation
Interior decoration 747
  See also

Bedspreads	Mural painting and
Carpets	decoration
Drapery	Paper hanging
Furniture	Quilts

Interior decoration—*Continued*

    Rugs   **Upholstery**

    Tapestry   **Wallpaper**

    x Decoration, Interior; Decorative arts; Home decoration; House decoration; House furnishing

    xx **Decoration and ornament; Home economics**

Interlibrary loans. *See* **Libraries—Circulation, loans**

Interlocking signals. *See* **Railroads—Signalling**

Intermarriage 301.42

    x Marriage, Mixed; Mixed marriage

    xx **Marriage**

Intermarriage, Religious 261.8; 301.42

    Use same form for other types of intermarriage

    x Interfaith marriage

Intermediate state. *See* **Eschatology; Future life**

Intermittent fever. *See* **Malaria**

Internal-combustion engines. *See* **Gas and oil engines**

Internal revenue 336.1-336.2

    See also **Income tax; Inheritance and transfer tax**

    x Revenue, Internal

    xx **Finance; Taxation**

Internal revenue law 343.3

    x Law, Internal revenue

    xx **Law**

Internal security 351.1; 355.4

    See also **Insurgency; Subversive activities**

    x Loyalty oaths; Security, Internal

    xx **Insurgency; Subversive activities**

International agencies 060

    See also names of individual agencies

    x Associations, International; International associations; International organizations

    xx **International cooperation**

International arbitration. *See* **Arbitration, International**

International associations. *See* **International agencies**

International business enterprises 382.1

    See also **Investments, Foreign**

    x Business—International aspects; Business enterprises, International; Corporations, International; Corporations, Multinational; Multinational corporations

    xx **Commerce; Corporations; International economic relations**

International conferences. *See* **Congresses and conventions**

International cooperation 327

    Use for general materials on international cooperative activities, with or without the participation of governments

International cooperation—*Continued*

    See also **Arbitration, International; Congresses and conventions;** Cultural relations; **Economic assistance;** Exchange of persons programs; **Intellectual cooperation;** International agencies; International education; **International organization; International police; League of Nations; Reconstruction (1939–1951); Technical assistance; United Nations;** also subjects with the subdivision *International cooperation,* e.g. **Astronautics—International cooperation; Environmental policy—International cooperation;** etc.

    x Cooperation, International

    xx **Cooperation; International education; International law; International organization; International relations; Reconstruction (1939–1951)**

International copyright. *See* **Copyright**

International economic relations 382.1

    See also **Balance of payments; Commercial policy; Economic assistance; International business enterprises; Technical assistance**

    x Economic relations, Foreign; Foreign economic relations

    xx **Economic policy; International relations**

International education 370.19

    Use for materials on education for international understanding, world citizenship, etc.

    See also **Comparative librarianship;** Intellectual cooperation; **Intercultural education; International cooperation; Teachers, Interchange of**

    x Education, International

    xx **Education; Intellectual cooperation; Intercultural education; International cooperation**

International exchange. *See* **Foreign exchange**

International exhibitions. *See* **Exhibitions;** and names of exhibitions

International federation. *See* **International organization**

International language. *See* **Language, Universal**

International law 341

    See also

Aliens	**International relations**
Arbitration, International	
Asylum, Right of	**Mandates**
Boundaries	**Maritime law**
International cooperation	**Military law**
	Naturalization
International organization	**Neutrality**
	Pirates
	Privateering

303

International law—*Continued*

Refugees, Political   Space law
Salvage   Treaties
Slave trade   War

    x Law, International; Law of nations;
       Nations, Law of; Natural law
   xx **International organization; International
       relations; Law; War**

International organization   341.2

     Use for materials on plans leading towards
       political organizations of nations
     See also **European federation; International
       cooperation; International law; Inter-
       national police; Mandates; World poli-
       tics;** also names of specific organiza-
       tions, e.g. **United Nations;** etc.
    x Federation, International; International
       federation; Organization, International;
       World government; World organiza-
       tion
   xx **Congresses and conventions; Interna-
       tional cooperation; International law;
       International relations; Security, Inter-
       national; World politics**

International organizations. *See* **International
     agencies**

International police   341.77

    x Interpol; Police, International
   xx **International cooperation; International
       organization; International relations;
       Security, International**

International politics. *See* **World politics**

International relations   327

     Use for materials on the theory of interna-
       tional relations. Historical accounts
       are entered under **World politics; Eu-
       rope—Politics and government;** etc.
       Materials limited to relations between
       two countries are entered under the
       name of one or both countries with
       the subdivision *Foreign relations*
     See also

Arbitration, Inter-	**International law**
national	**International or-**
Boundaries	**ganization**
Catholic Church—	**International police**
Relations (Diplo-	**Mandates**
matic)	**Monroe Doctrine**
Cultural relations	**Munitions**
Diplomacy	**National security**
Diplomatic and con-	**Nationalism**
sular service	**Neutrality**
Diplomats	**Peace**
Disarmament	**Refugees, Political**
Geopolitics	**Security, Interna-**
International co-	**tional**
operation	**Treaties**
International eco-	**World politics**
nomic relations	

International relations—*Continued*

　　also names of countries with the subdivision *Foreign relations*, e.g. **U.S.—Foreign relations**; etc.

　　x Foreign relations

　　xx **International law; National security; World politics**

International security. *See* **Security, International**

International space cooperation. *See* **Astronautics—International cooperation**

International Standard Bibliographic Description 070.5

　　x ISBD

International Standard Book Numbers 070.5

　　x ISBN

　　xx **Publishers' standard book numbers**

International Standard Serial Numbers 070.5

　　x ISSN

International trade. *See* **Commerce**

Internationalism. *See* **Nationalism**

Internment camps. *See* **Concentration camps**

Interoffice communication systems. *See* **Intercommunication systems**

Interpersonal relations. *See* **Human relations**

Interplanetary communication. *See* **Interstellar communication**

Interplanetary voyages 629.45

　　See also **Outer space—Exploration; Rockets (Aeronautics); Space flight**

　　x Interstellar voyages; Space travel

　　xx **Astronautics; Space flight**

Interpol. *See* **International police**

Interpreting and translating. *See* **Translating and interpreting**

Interpretive dancing. *See* **Modern dance**

Interracial adoption. *See* **Adoption, Interracial**

Interracial relations. *See* **Race relations**

Interscholastic sports. *See* **School sports**

Interstate commerce 381

　　See also **Railroads and state**

　　x Commerce, Interstate; Government regulation of commerce; Government regulation of railroads

　　xx **Commerce; Railroads—Rates; Railroads and state; Trusts, Industrial**

Interstellar communication 621.38

　　See also **Astronautics—Communication systems; Radio astronomy**

　　x Extraterrestrial communication; Interplanetary communication; Outer space —Communication; Space communication; Space telecommunication

　　xx **Life on other planets; Telecommunication**

Interstellar voyages. *See* **Interplanetary voyages**

Interurban railroads. *See* **Electric railroads; Street railroads**

Interviewing 158

    See also Counseling; Psychology, Applied

    xx Applications for positions; Counseling; Psychology, Applied; Social psychology

Interviewing (Journalism). *See* **Journalism; Reporters and reporting**

Intestacy. *See* **Inheritance and succession**

Intolerance. *See* **Freedom of conscience; Religious freedom; Toleration**

Intoxicants. *See* **Alcohol; Liquors and liqueurs; Stimulants**

Intoxication. *See* **Alcoholism; Liquor problem; Narcotic habit; Temperance**

Intuition 153.4

    See also Perception; Reality

    xx Knowledge, Theory of; Perception; Philosophy; Psychology; Rationalism

Inuits. *See* **Eskimos**

Invalid cookery. *See* **Cookery for the sick**

Invalids. *See* **Physically handicapped; Sick**

Invasion of privacy. *See* **Privacy, Right of**

Inventions 608

    See also Creation (Literary, artistic, etc.); Inventors; Patents

    x Discoveries (in science); Intellectual property

    xx Civilization; Inventors; Machinery; Patents; Technology

Inventors 920; 926

    See also Inventions

    xx Engineers; Inventions

Invertebrates 592

    See also Corals; Crustacea; Insects; Mollusks; Protozoa; Sponges; Worms

    xx Zoology

Investigations, Governmental. *See* **Governmental investigations**

Investment trusts 332.6

    x Mutual funds

    xx **Banks and banking; Trust companies**

Investments 332.6

    See also

Annuities	**Securities**
Bonds	**Speculation**
Mortgages	**Stock exchange**
Saving and thrift	**Stocks**
Savings and loan associations	

    xx **Banks and banking; Capital; Estate planning; Finance; Finance, Personal; Loans; Saving and thrift; Securities; Speculation; Stock exchange; Stocks**

Investments, Foreign 332.6

    x Foreign investments

    xx **International business enterprises**

Iran 915.5; 935; 955

    x Persia

306

Iron   669; 672

See also **Building, Iron and steel; Iron ores; Ironwork**

xx **Steel**

Iron age   913

See also **Archeology; Bronze age**

x Prehistory

xx **Archeology; Bronze age**

Iron and steel building.   See **Building, Iron and steel**

Iron curtain countries.   See **Communist countries**

Iron founding.   See **Founding**

Iron industry and trade   338.2

See also **Steel industry and trade**

xx **Ironwork; Steel industry and trade**

Iron ores   549

xx **Iron; Ore deposits; Ores**

Ironing.   See **Laundry**

Ironwork   669; 672

See also **Blacksmithing; Forging; Iron industry and trade; Metalwork; Steel industry and trade; Welding**

x Wrought iron work

xx **Decoration and ornament; Forging; Iron; Metalwork**

Irrigation (May subdiv. geog.)   **333.9; 631.7**

See also **Dams; Dry farming; Reclamation of land; Water rights; Windmills**

xx **Agricultural engineering; Civil engineering; Hydraulic engineering; Reclamation of land; Reservoirs; Soils; Water resources development; Water supply**

Irrigation—U.S.   333.9; 631.7

x U.S.—Irrigation

Islam   297

Use for materials on the religion. For materials on the believers in this religion use **Muslims**

See also **Bahaism; Koran; Mosques**

x Islamism; Mohammedanism; Moslemism; Muhammedanism; Muslimism

xx **Religions**

Islamism.   See **Islam**

Islands   551.4

See also **Coral reefs and islands;** also names of islands and groups of islands, e.g. **Cuba; Islands of the Pacific;** etc.

Islands, Artificial.   See **Artificial islands**

Islands of the Pacific   919.3-919.6; 993-996

x Oceania; Pacific Islands; South Sea Islands

xx **Islands**

Isotopes   539

See also **Radioisotopes**

Israel   915.694; 956.94

xx **Middle East**

Israel—Collective settlements.   See **Collective settlements—Israel**

Israel-Arab border conflicts. *See* **Israeli-Arab relations**

Israeli-Arab relations 956
> *x* Arab-Israeli relations; Israel-Arab border conflicts; Jewish-Arab relations

Israel-Arab War, 1948–1949 956
> *x* Arab-Israel War, 1948–1949

Israel-Arab War, 1956. *See* **Sinai Campaign, 1956**

Israel-Arab War, 1967 956
> *x* Arab-Israel War, 1967; Six Day War, 1967

Israel-Arab War, 1973 956
> *x* Arab-Israel War, 1973; Yom Kippur War, 1973

Israelis 915.694
> *xx* Jews

Israelites. *See* **Jews**

Italo-Ethiopian War, 1935–1936 963
> *x* Ethiopian-Italian War, 1935–1936

Italy 914.5; 945
> May be subdivided like U.S. except for *History*

Italy—History 945
Italy—History—To 1559 945
Italy—History—1559–1789 945
Italy—History—1789–1815 945
Italy—History—1815–1914 945.09
Italy—History—1914–1945 945.091
Italy—History—1945– 945.092
Ivory 679
> *x* Animal products

Jacobins (Dominicans). *See* **Dominicans**

Jails. *See* **Prisons**

Japan 915.2; 952
Japan—History 952
Japan—History—To 1868 952
Japan—History—1868-1945 952.03
Japan—History—Allied occupation, 1945-1952 952.04
> *xx* **Military occupation; World War, 1939–1945—Occupied territories**

Japan—History—1952– 952.04

Japan World's Exposition, Osaka, 1970. *See* **Expo '70**

Japanese color prints. *See* **Color prints, Japanese**

Japanese paper folding. *See* **Origami**

Japanese prints. *See* **Color prints, Japanese**

Jargon. *See* subjects with the subdivision *Jargon,* e.g. **English language—Jargon;** etc.

Jazz ensembles 785.06
Jazz music 781.5
> *See also* **Blues (Songs, etc.)**
> *xx* **Dance music; Music**

Jesuits 271
> *x* Jesus, Society of; Society of Jesus
> *xx* **Religious orders for men, Catholic**

Jesus, Society of. *See* **Jesuits**

Jesus Christ 232

> See also Atonement, Christian; Christian-
> ity; Lord's Supper; Millennium; Sec-
> ond Advent; Trinity
>
> x Christ; Christology
>
> xx Christianity; God (Christianity); Trinity

Jesus Christ—Art 704.948

> See also Bible—Pictorial works; Christian
> art and symbolism; Mary, Virgin—Art
>
> x Jesus Christ—Iconography; Jesus Christ
> in art
>
> xx Christian art and symbolism; Mary,
> Virgin—Art

Jesus Christ—Atonement. See Atonement,
Christian

Jesus Christ—Biography 232.9

> See also Jesus Christ—Crucifixion; Jesus
> Christ—Nativity

Jesus Christ—Birth. See Jesus Christ—Nativity

Jesus Christ—Crucifixion 232.9

> x Crucifixion of Christ
>
> xx Jesus Christ—Biography

Jesus Christ—Divinity 232

> See also Trinity; Unitarianism
>
> x Divinity of Christ
>
> xx Unitarianism

Jesus Christ—Drama 808.82; 812; etc.

> See also Passion plays

Jesus Christ—Iconography. See Jesus Christ—
Art

Jesus Christ—Last Supper. See Lord's Supper

Jesus Christ—Messiahship 232

Jesus Christ—Nativity 232.9

> See also Christmas
>
> x Jesus Christ—Birth; Nativity of Christ
>
> xx Christmas; Jesus Christ—Biography

Jesus Christ—Parables 232.9

> x Bible—Parables
>
> xx Parables

Jesus Christ—Prayers 232.9

> See also Lord's Prayer

Jesus Christ—Prophecies 232

> xx Bible—Prophecies

Jesus Christ—Resurrection 232.9

> x Resurrection

Jesus Christ—Second Advent. See Second Advent

Jesus Christ—Sermon on the Mount. See Sermon on the Mount

Jesus Christ—Teachings 232.9

> x Teachings of Jesus

Jesus Christ in art. See Jesus Christ—Art

Jesus people 269

> xx Youth—Religious life

Jet planes 629.133

> See also Short take off and landing aircraft
>
> x Airplanes, Jet propelled

Jet propulsion 621.43; 629.47
  See also Rockets (Aeronautics)
  xx Airplanes—Engines; Rockets (Aeronautics)
Jewelry 739.27
  See also Gems; Goldwork; Silverwork; also names of specific jewelry
  x Jewels
  xx Art metalwork; Arts and crafts; Decoration and ornament; Gems; Goldwork; Metalwork; Silver; Silverwork
Jewels. *See* Gems; Jewelry; Precious stones
Jewish-Arab relations. *See* Israeli-Arab relations
Jewish civilization. *See* Jews—Civilization
Jewish holidays. *See* Fasts and feasts—Judaism
Jewish language. *See* Hebrew language; Yiddish language
Jewish literature 839
  See also Bible; Hebrew literature; Talmud; Yiddish literature
  x Jews—Literature
  xx Hebrew literature
Jewish religion. *See* Judaism
Jews 572.917; 909
  See also Israelis
  x Hebrews; Israelites
  xx Church history; Judaism
Jews—Antiquities 913.33
  x Antiquities
Jews—Civilization 909
  x Civilization, Jewish; Jewish civilization
Jews—Colonization 325
  xx Colonization
Jews—Customs. *See* Jews—Social life and customs
Jews—Economic conditions 330.9
Jews—Festivals. *See* Fasts and feasts—Judaism
Jews—Folklore. *See* Folklore, Jewish
Jews—Language. *See* Hebrew language; Yiddish language
Jews—Literature. *See* Hebrew literature; Jewish literature
Jews—Persecutions 272; 909; 933
  xx Persecution
Jews—Political activity 909; 956.94
Jews—Relations with Gentiles. *See* Jews and Gentiles
Jews—Religion. *See* Judaism
Jews—Restoration 956.94
  Use for materials dealing with the belief that the Jews, in fulfillment of Biblical prophecy, would some day return to Palestine
  See also Zionism
  xx Zionism
Jews—Rites and ceremonies 296.4
  xx Rites and ceremonies

310

Jews—Social conditions 309.1

Use for materials relating to social conditions of the Jews themselves. Materials on the relation of the Jews to non-Jews are entered under **Jews and Gentiles**

xx **Social conditions**

Jews—Social life and customs 915.694

x Customs, Social; Jews—Customs; Social customs; Social life and customs

xx **Manners and customs**

Jews and Gentiles 301.6

x Antisemitism; Gentiles and Jews; Jews—Relations with Gentiles

xx **Human relations**

Job analysis 658.3

See also **Motion study; Time study**

x Personnel classification

xx **Efficiency, Industrial; Factory management; Industrial management; Occupations; Personnel management; Wages**

Job applications. *See* **Applications for position**

Job discrimination. *See* **Discrimination in employment**

Job performance standards. *See* **Performance standards**

Job resumés. *See* **Resumés (Employment)**

Job satisfaction 331.2; 658.3

xx **Attitude (Psychology); Employee morale; Personnel management; Work**

Job training. *See* **Occupational training**

Jobs. *See* **Employment agencies; Occupations; Professions**

Joke books. *See* **Jokes**

Jokes 808.7; 808.87; 817; etc.

x Joke books

xx **Wit and humor**

Journalism 070

Use for materials dealing with writing for the periodical press and with the editing of this writing, or for materials on journalism as an occupation. Materials limited to the history, organization and management of newspapers are entered under **Newspapers.** Journalism in a particular field is entered under **Journalism** with adjective modifier, e.g. **Journalism, Scientific;** etc.

See also **College and school journalism; Libel and slander; Freedom of the press; Government and the press; Newspapers; Periodicals; Reporters and reporting**

x Editors and editing; Interviewing (Journalism); Newspaper work; Press; Writing (Authorship)

xx **Authorship; Literature; Newspapers; Reporters and reporting**

311

Journalism—Objectivity 070.4
   x Slanted journalism
Journalism, Scientific 070.4
   x Scientific journalism
Journalistic photography. *See* **Photography, Journalistic**
Journalists 920; 928
   x Columnists; Editors and editing; Writers
Journals (Machinery). *See* **Bearings (Machinery)**
Journeys. *See* **Voyages and travels; Voyages around the world;** and names of countries with the subdivision *Description and travel*, e.g. **U.S.—Description and travel;** etc.
Joy and sorrow 152.4
   See also **Happiness; Pleasure**
   x Affliction; Grief; Sorrow
   xx **Emotions; Ethics; Happiness; Suffering**
Judaeo-German. *See* **Yiddish language**
Judaism 296
   See also **Jews; Sabbath; Synagogues; Talmud**
   x Jewish religion; Jews—Religion
   xx **Religions**
Judges 920; 923
   See also **Courts**
   x Chief justices
   xx **Courts; Lawyers**
Judicial investigations. *See* **Governmental investigations**
Judiciary. *See* **Courts**
Judo 796.8
   See also **Karate**
   xx **Physical education and training; Self-defense; Wrestling**
July Fourth. *See* **Fourth of July**
Jungles. *See* **Forests and forestry; Tropics**
Junior colleges 378.1
   x Community colleges
   xx **Colleges and universities; Education, Higher**
Junior colleges—Directories 378.1025
   xx **Directories**
Junior high schools 373.2
   x High schools, Junior; Secondary schools
   xx **Education, Secondary; High schools; Public schools**
Junk. *See* **Waste products**
Jurisprudence. *See* **Law**
Jurisprudence, Medical. *See* **Medical jurisprudence**
Jurists. *See* **Lawyers**
Jury 345.7; 347.7
   x Trial by jury
   xx **Courts; Criminal law**
Justice 170; 340
   xx **Ethics; Human behavior; Law**

Justice, Administration of 350-353
 See also **Courts; Crime; Governmental investigations; Impeachments**
 x Administration of justice
 xx **Courts; Crime**
Juvenile courts 345.8
 See also **Probation**
 x Children's courts
 xx **Courts; Juvenile delinquency; Probation; Reformatories**
Juvenile delinquency 364.36
 See also **Child welfare; Drugs and youth; Juvenile courts; Narcotics and youth; Reformatories**
 x Children, Delinquent; Delinquency, Juvenile; Delinquents; Gangs
 xx **Child welfare; Crime; Problem children; Reformatories; Social problems**
Juvenile delinquency—Case studies 364.36092
 x Case studies
Juvenile literature. *See* **Children's literature**
K.K.K. *See* **Ku Klux Klan**
Kamuti. *See* **Bonsai**
Karate 796.8
 xx **Judo; Self-defense**
Kart racing. *See* **Karts and karting**
Karts and karting 796.7
 x Go karts; Kart racing
 xx **Automobile racing**
Kennedy, John Fitzgerald, Pres. U.S. 92
 xx **Presidents—U.S.**
Keramics. *See* **Ceramics**
Keys. *See* **Locks and keys**
Kibbutz. *See* **Collective settlements—Israel**
Killing, Mercy. *See* **Euthanasia**
Kindergarten 372.21
 See also **Education, Preschool; Montessori method of education**
 xx **Children; Education, Elementary; Education, Preschool; Games; Nursery schools; Schools; Teaching**
Kindness to animals. *See* **Animals—Treatment**
Kinematics 531
 See also **Mechanical movements; Mechanics; Motion**
 xx **Dynamics; Mechanics; Motion**
Kinesics. *See* **Nonverbal communication**
Kinetic art 701
 See also **Kinetic sculpture**
 x Art, Kinetic; Art in motion
 xx **Art, Abstract; Art, Modern—20th century**
Kinetic sculpture 731
 See also **Mobiles (Sculpture)**
 x Sculpture, Kinetic; Sculpture in motion
 xx **Futurism (Art); Kinetic art**
Kinetics. *See* **Dynamics; Motion**
King Philip's War, 1675–1676 973.2
 x U.S.—History—King Philip's War, 1675–1676

King Philip's War, 1675-1676—*Continued*
>*xx* Indians of North America—Wars; U.S.—
>>History—Colonial period, 1600–1775

King William's War, 1689–1697. *See* U.S.—
>History—King William's War, 1689–
>1697

Kings and rulers   920; 923
>*See also* **Courts and courtiers; Dictators;**
>>**Presidents; Queens; Roman emperors;**
>>also names of countries with the sub-
>>division *Kings and rulers,* (e.g. **Gt.**
>>**Brit.–Kings and rulers;** etc.); also
>>names of individual kings, queens,
>>and rulers, e.g. **Elizabeth II, Queen of**
>>**Great Britain;** etc.

>*x* Emperors; Monarchs; Royalty; Rulers;
>>Sovereigns

>*xx* **Courts and courtiers; History; Mon-**
>>**archy; Political science; Queens**

Kitchen gardens. *See* **Vegetable gardening**
Kitchen utensils. *See* **Household equipment**
>**and supplies**

Kitchens   643
>*xx* **Houses**

Kites   629.133; 796.1
>*xx* **Aeronautics**

Klondike gold fields   979.8
>*x* Gold rush

Knighthood. *See* **Knights and knighthood**
Knights and knighthood   394; 940.1
>*See also* **Chivalry; Heraldry**
>*x* Knighthood
>*xx* **Chivalry; Heraldry; Middle Ages; Nobil-**
>>**ity**

Knitting   746.4
Knots and splices   623.88
>*x* Splicing
>*xx* **Navigation; Rope**

Knowledge, Theory of   001.2-001.4; 120; 153
>Use for materials that treat of the origin,
>>nature, methods and limits of human
>>knowledge

>*See also*

Apperception	**Pragmatism**
Belief and doubt	**Rationalism**
Empiricism	**Reality**
Gestalt psychology	**Senses and sensa-**
Intellect	**sation**
Intuition	**Truth**
Perception	

>*x* Cognition; Epistemology; Understanding
>*xx* **Apperception; Consciousness; Intellect;**
>>**Logic; Metaphysics; Philosophy; Re-**
>>**ality; Truth**

Kodak camera   771.3
>*xx* Cameras

Koran   297
>*x* Alkoran; Qur'an
>*xx* **Islam; Sacred books**

Korean War, 1950–1953   951.9

Ku Klux Klan (1865–1876) 322.4
    x K.K.K.
    xx Reconstruction (1865–1876)
Ku Klux Klan (1915–   ) 322.4
    x K.K.K.
LEM. *See* Lunar excursion module
Labor (Childbirth). *See* Childbirth
Labor, Hours of. *See* Hours of labor
Labor, Migratory. *See* Migrant labor
Labor absenteeism. *See* Absenteeism (Labor)
Labor and capital. *See* Industrial relations
Labor and laboring classes (May subdiv. geog.)
    331
        See also

Absenteeism
    (Labor)
Apprentices
Arbitration, Indus-
    trial
Capitalism
Child labor
Church and labor
Collective bar-
    gaining
Communism
Contract labor
Convict labor
Cost of living
Employees' repre-
    sentation in man-
    agement
Employment
Employment
    agencies
Hours of labor
Household em-
    ployees
Industrial relations
Insurance, Indus-
    trial
Labor unions, and
    other headings be-
    ginning with the
    word Labor
Machinery in
    industry
Men—Employ-
    ment
Middle classes
Migrant labor
Occupational dis-
    eases
Occupations
Occupations,
    Dangerous
Old age pensions
Open and closed
    shop
Peasantry
Peonage
Proletariat
Slavery
Socialism
Strikes and lock-
    outs
Syndicalism
Unemployed
Wages
Welfare work in
    industry
Women—Employ-
    ment
World War, 1939–
    1945—Human re-
    sources

also names of classes of laborers (e.g. Ag-
    ricultural laborers; Miners; etc.); and
    names of countries, cities, etc. with the
    subdivisions *Economic conditions* and
    Social conditions, e.g. U.S.—Economic
    conditions; U.S.—Social conditions;
    etc.
    x Laborers; Working classes
    xx Capital; Economics; Social conditions;
        Socialism; Sociology; Work
Labor and laboring classes—Accidents 331.1
Labor and laboring classes—Education 331.2
    x Education of workers
Labor and laboring classes—Housing 301.5

315

Labor and laboring classes—Insurance. *See*
        Insurance, Unemployment; Old age
        pensions; Social security
Labor and laboring classes—Library service.
        See **Libraries and labor**
Labor and laboring classes—U.S. 331.1
      x U.S.—Labor and laboring classes
Labor and the church. *See* **Church and labor**
Labor arbitration. *See* **Arbitration, Industrial**
Labor contract 331.1
      Use for materials dealing with agreements
        between employer and employee in
        which the latter agrees to perform
        work in return for compensation from
        the former
      See also **Collective bargaining; Open and**
        closed shop; Wages
      x Collective labor agreements; Trade
        agreements (Labor)
      xx **Collective bargaining; Contracts; Indus-**
        trial relations
Labor disputes 331.89
      See also **Arbitration, Industrial; Collective**
        bargaining; Strikes and lockouts
      x Disputes, Labor; Industrial disputes
      xx **Industrial relations**
Labor force. *See* **Labor supply**
Labor-management relations. *See* **Industrial**
        relations
Labor market. *See* **Labor supply**
Labor negotiations. *See* **Arbitration, Indus-**
        trial; Collective bargaining
Labor organizations. *See* **Labor unions**
Labor relations. *See* **Industrial relations**
Labor representation in regulation of industry.
        See **Employees' representation in man-**
        agement
Labor saving devices, Household. *See* **House-**
        hold equipment and supplies; House-
        hold appliances, Electric
Labor supply 331.1
      See also **Child labor; Employment agencies;**
        Human resources; Human resources
        policy; Men—Employment; Retraining,
        Occupational; Unemployed; Women
        —Employment; World War, 1939–
        1945—Human resources
      x Labor force; Labor market
      xx **Economic conditions; Employment; Em-**
        ployment agencies; Human resources;
        Human resources policy; Unemployed
Labor turnover 331.1
      See also **Employment agencies**
      xx **Personnel management**
Labor unions (May subdiv. geog.) 331.88
      See also **Arbitration, Industrial; Collective**
        bargaining; Injunctions; Open and
        closed shop; Sabotage; Strikes and
        lockouts; Syndicalism; also names of
        types of unions and names of individ-

Labor unions—*Continued*
ual labor unions, e.g. **Librarians' unions; United Steelworkers of America;** etc.

x Labor organizations; Organized labor; Trade unions; Unions, Labor

xx **Collective bargaining; Cooperation; Industrial relations; Labor and laboring classes; Socialism; Societies; Strikes and lockouts**

Labor unions—U.S.   331.88

x American labor unions; U.S.—Labor unions

Laboratories, Language.   *See* **Language laboratories**

Laboratories, Space.   *See* **Space stations**

Laboratory guides.   *See* scientific and technical subjects with the subdivision *Laboratory guides*, e.g. **Chemistry—Laboratory guides;** etc.

Laborers.   *See* **Labor and laboring classes;** and names of classes of laborers, e.g. **Agricultural laborers; Miners;** etc.

Lace and lace making   746.2

xx **Crocheting; Needlework; Weaving**

Lacquer and lacquering   667

See also **Varnish and varnishing**

x Finishes and finishing

xx **Arts and crafts; Varnish and varnishing; Wood finishing**

Laissez faire.   *See* **Industry and state**

Lakes   551.5

See also names of lakes

xx **Inland navigation; Physical geography; Water; Waterways**

Lamaze method of childbirth.   *See* **Natural childbirth**

Lamps   621.32; 749

See also types of lamps, e.g. **Electric lamps;** etc.

xx **Lighting**

Land.   *See* **Land use**

Land, Condemnation of.   *See* **Eminent domain**

Land, Reclamation of.   *See* **Reclamation of land**

Land drainage.   *See* **Drainage**

Land question.   *See* **Land tenure**

Land settlement (May subdiv. geog.)   **325**

See also **Colonization; Migration, Internal**

x Resettlement; Settlement of land

xx **Colonies; Migration, Internal**

Land settlement—U.S.   325.73

x U.S.—Land settlement

Land surveying.   *See* **Surveying**

Land tenure   333.3

Use for general and historical discussions on systems of holding land

See also **Farm tenancy; Feudalism; Landlord and tenant; Peasantry; Real estate**

317

Land tenure—*Continued*

   x Agrarian question; Fiefs; Land question; Tenure of land

   xx **Agriculture; Agriculture–Economic aspects; Inheritance and succession; Land use; Peasantry; Real estate**

Land use 333

   Use for general materials which cover such topics as types of land, the utilization, distribution and development of land and the economic factors which affect the value of land. Materials which treat only of ownership of land are entered under **Real estate**

   See also

   Eminent domain   **Land tenure**

   Farms   **Real estate**

   Feudalism   **Reclamation of land**

   x Land

   xx **Agriculture; Economics**

Landlord and tenant 333.5

   See note under **Farm tenancy**

   See also **Apartment houses; Farm tenancy; Housing**

   x Tenant and landlord

   xx **Commercial law; Human relations; Land tenure; Real estate**

Landmarks, Literary. *See* **Literary landmarks**

Landmarks, Preservation of. *See* **Natural monuments**

Landscape architecture 712

   See also **Garden ornaments and furniture; Landscape gardening; Landscape protection; Parks; Patios; Roadside improvement**

   x Landscape design

   xx **Landscape gardening; Landscape protection**

Landscape design. *See* **Landscape architecture**

Landscape drawing 743

   See also **Landscape painting**

   xx **Drawing; Landscape painting**

Landscape gardening 714-716

   See also **Evergreens; Landscape architecture; Parks; Plants, Ornamental; Shrubs; Trees**

   x Garden design; Planting

   xx **Gardening; Horticulture; Landscape architecture; Shrubs; Trees**

Landscape painting 758

   See also **Landscape drawing**

   xx **Landscape drawing; Painting**

Landscape protection 333.7

   See also **Landscape architecture; Natural monuments; Regional planning**

   x Beautification of the landscape; Natural beauty conservation; Preservation of natural scenery; Protection of natural scenery; Scenery

Landscape protection—*Continued*

    xx **Landscape architecture; Nature conservation; Regional planning**

Language, International. *See* **Language, Universal**

Language, Universal   401

    See also **Esperanto**

    x International language; Language, International; Universal language; World language

Language and languages   400's

    Use for general materials on the history, philosophy, origin, etc. of language. Comparative studies of languages are entered under **Philology, Comparative**

    See also

Bilingualism	**Rhetoric**
Conversation	**Semantics**
Grammar	**Speech**
Literature	**Translating and**
Philology, Comparative	**interpreting**
Phonetics	**Voice**
	Writing
Programming languages (Electronic computers)	

    also names of languages or groups of cognate languages, e.g. **English language;** etc.; also classes of people with the subdivision *Language*, e.g. **Children—Language;** etc.

    x Comparative linguistics; Linguistics; Philology

    xx **Anthropology; Communication; Ethnology; Grammar; Philology, Comparative; Speech**

Language and languages—Comparative philology. *See* **Philology, Comparative**

Language arts   400

    See also **Literature; Reading; Speech; Writing**

    x Communication arts

    xx **Communication**

Language laboratories   407

    See also **Languages, Modern—Study and teaching**

    x Foreign language laboratories; Laboratories, Language

    xx **Languages, Modern—Study and teaching**

Languages, Modern   400's

    May be subdivided like **English language.** Use for materials on living literary languages

    x Modern languages

Languages, Modern—Conversations and phrases 438; 448; etc.

    x Conversation in foreign languages; Foreign language phrases

319

Languages, Modern—Study and teaching

    See also **Language laboratories**

    xx **Language laboratories**

Lantern projection. *See* **Projectors**

Lantern slides. *See* **Slides (Photography)**

Large and small. *See* **Size and shape**

Large print books   028

    x Books—Large print; Books for sight saving; Large type books; Sight saving books

    xx **Blind, Books for the**

Large type books. *See* **Large print books**

Laser photography. *See* **Holography**

Lasers   535.5; 621.36

    x Light amplification by stimulated emission of radiation; Masers, Optical; Optical masers

    xx **Light**

Last Supper. *See* **Lord's Supper**

Lathe work. *See* **Lathes; Turning**

Lathes   621.9

    See also **Turning**

    x Lathe work

    xx **Turning; Woodworking machinery**

Latin America   918; 980

    See also **Pan-Americanism; South America;** and names of individual Latin American countries

    x Spanish America

    xx **America**

Latin America—Politics and government   980

    x Politics

Latin American literature   860

    Use for materials on French, Portuguese, and/or Spanish literature of Latin American countries

    May use same subdivisions and names of literary forms as for **English literature**

    See also **Brazilian literature**

    x Hispanic-American literature; South American literature; Spanish American literature

    xx **American literature; Spanish literature**

Latin language   470

    May be subdivided like **English language**

    See also **Romance languages**

    x Classical languages

Latin literature   870

    May use same subdivisions and names of literary forms as for **English literature**

    See also **Christian literature, Early; Classical literature**

    x Roman literature

    xx **Classical literature**

Latitude   526; 527

    x Degrees of latitude and longitude

    xx **Earth; Geodesy; Nautical astronomy**

Latter-Day Saints. *See* **Church of Jesus Christ of Latter-Day Saints**

Laughter 152.4
> *See also* Wit and humor
> *xx* Emotions

Launching of satellites. *See* Artificial satellites
> —Launching

Laundry 648
> *x* Ironing; Washing
> *xx* Cleaning; Home economics; Sanitation, Household

Law (May subdiv. geog.) 340
> *See also*

Courts	Legislation
Justice	Medical jurispru-
Lawyers	dence
Legal ethics	Police

> *also* special branches of law, e.g. Administrative law; Commercial law; Constitutional law; Corporation law; Criminal law; Ecclesiastical law; Internal revenue law; International law; Maritime law; Military law; Space law; etc. For laws on special subjects see names of subjects with the subdivision *Law and legislation*, e.g. Automobiles—Law and legislation; Food—Law and legislation; etc.
> *x* Jurisprudence; Laws; Statutes
> *xx* Legislation; Political science

Law, Administrative. *See* Administrative law

Law, Business. *See* Commercial law

Law, Commercial. *See* Commercial law

Law, Constitutional. *See* Constitutional law

Law, Corporation. *See* Corporation law

Law, Criminal. *See* Criminal law

Law, Ecclesiastical. *See* Ecclesiastical law

Law, Internal revenue. *See* Internal revenue law

Law, International. *See* International law

Law, Maritime. *See* Maritime law

Law, Military. *See* Military law

Law, Space. *See* Space law

Law—U.S. 340
> *x* U.S.—Law

Law—Vocational guidance 340.023
> *xx* Vocational guidance

Law enforcement 363.2
> *See also* Police
> *x* Enforcement of law

Law of nations. *See* International law

Law of the sea. *See* Maritime law

Law reform 340
> *x* Legal reform

Lawn tennis. *See* Tennis

Lawns 716
> *See also* Grasses

Laws. *See* Law; Legislation; and subjects with the subdivision *Law and legislation*, e.g. Automobiles—Law and legislation; Food—Law and legislation; etc.

Lawyers 920; 923
> *See also* **Judges; Legal ethics**
> *x* Attorneys; Bar; Barristers; Jurists; Legal profession
> *xx* **Law**

Layout and typography. *See* **Printing**

Leadership 158
> *xx* **Ability; Executive ability; Success**

League of Nations 341.22
> *xx* **Arbitration, International; International cooperation; Peace; World War, 1914–1918–Peace**

League of Nations—Mandatory system. *See* **Mandates**

Learned societies. *See* **Societies**

Learning, Art of. *See* **Study, Method of**

Learning, Psychology of 153.1
> *See also* **Biofeedback training; Feedback (Psychology); Learning disabilities**
> *x* Psychology of learning
> *xx* **Animal intelligence; Child psychology**

Learning and scholarship 001.2
> *See also* **Culture; Education; Humanism; Professional education; Research**
> *x* Intellectual life; Scholarship
> *xx* **Civilization; Culture; Education; Humanism; Research**

Learning center approach to teaching. *See* **Open plan schools**

Learning disabilities 153.1; 370.15
> *x* Learning disorders
> *xx* **Learning, Psychology of; Slow learning children**

Learning disorders. *See* **Learning disabilities**

Learning resource centers. *See* **Instructional materials centers**

Lease and rental services 333.5
> *x* Lease services; Rental services

Lease services. *See* **Lease and rental services**

Leather 675
> *See also* **Hides and skins; Tanning**
> *xx* **Hides and skins; Tanning**

Leather garments 685
> *x* Clothing, Leather; Garments, Leather; Skin garments
> *xx* **Clothing and dress; Leather work**

Leather industry and trade 338.4
> *See also* **Bookbinding; Shoes and shoe industry**

Leather work 745.53
> *See also* names of leather goods, e.g. **Leather garments;** etc.
> *xx* **Art industries and trade; Arts and crafts; Decoration and ornament; Handicraft**

Leaves 581
> *x* Foliage
> *xx* **Botany; Trees**

Lectures and lecturing 808.51
> Use for general materials on the art of lecturing, effectiveness of the lecture

Lectures and lecturing—*Continued*
method, announcements of lectures, etc. Collections of lectures on several subjects are entered under **Speeches, addresses, etc.** Lectures on one topic are entered under that subject. If it is not treated comprehensively add the subdivision *Addresses and essays*

See also **Radio addresses, debates, etc.;** also general subjects with the subdivision *Addresses and essays,* e.g. **Agriculture—Addresses and essays; U.S.—History—Addresses and essays;** etc.

x Addresses; Speaking

xx **Public speaking; Rhetoric; Speeches, addresses, etc.; Teaching**

Left (Political science). *See* **Right and left (Political science)**

Legacies. *See* **Inheritance and succession; Wills**

Legal aid   362.5
See also types of legal aid, e.g. **Legal assistance to the poor;** etc.

x Charities, Legal

Legal assistance to the poor   362.5
x Legal representative of the poor; Legal service for the poor; Poor—Legal assistance

xx **Legal aid; Public welfare**

Legal ethics   340.1
x Ethics, Legal

xx **Law; Lawyers; Professional ethics**

Legal holidays. *See* **Holidays**

Legal medicine. *See* **Medical jurisprudence**

Legal profession. *See* **Lawyers**

Legal reform. *See* **Law reform**

Legal representative of the poor. *See* **Legal assistance to the poor**

Legal service for the poor. *See* **Legal assistance to the poor**

Legal tender. *See* **Paper money**

Legations. *See* **Diplomatic and consular service**

Legends (May subdiv. geog. noun form (e.g. **Legends—Ireland;** etc.) or, where country subdivision is not applicable, use ethnic or religious subdivision, adjective form, e.g. **Legends, Jewish;** etc.   **398.2**

Use for tales coming down from the past, especially those relating to actual events or persons. Collections of tales written between the eleventh and fourteenth centuries and dealing with the age of chivalry are entered under **Romances**

See also **Fables; Fairy tales; Folklore; Grail; Mythology; Romances; Saints**

Legends—*Continued*
  x Stories; Tales; Tall tales; Traditions
  xx **Fiction; Folklore; Literature; Saints**
Legends, Celtic   398.2
  x Celtic legends
Legends, Indian. *See* **Indians of North America—Legends**
Legends, Norse   398.2
  x Norse legends
Legends—U.S.   398.2
  x U.S.—Legends
Legerdemain. *See* **Magic**
Legislation   328
  Use for materials on the theory of lawmaking and descriptions of the preparation and enactment of laws
  See also **Law; Legislative bodies; Parliamentary practice;** also subjects with the subdivision *Law and legislation,* e.g. **Automobiles—Law and legislation; Food—Law and legislation;** etc.
  x Laws
  xx **Constitutional law; Law; Political science**
Legislation, Direct. *See* **Referendum**
Legislative bodies   328
  Use for descriptions and histories of law making bodies, discussions of one-house legislatures, etc.
  See also **Parliamentary practice;** also names of individual legislative bodies, e.g. **U.S. Congress;** etc.
  x Parliaments; Unicameral legislatures
  xx **Constitutional law; Legislation; Representative government and representation**
Legislative investigations. *See* **Governmental investigations**
Legislative reapportionment. *See* **Apportionment (Election law)**
Leisure   790.01
  See also **Hobbies; Recreation; Retirement**
Lem. *See* **Lunar excursion module**
Lending. *See* **Loans**
Lenses   535
  See also types of lenses, e.g. **Contact lenses;** etc.
Lensless photography. *See* **Holography**
Lent   263
  See also **Easter; Good Friday; Holy Week**
  x Ecclesiastical fasts and feasts
Lepidoptera. *See* **Butterflies; Moths**
Lesbianism   301.41
  xx **Homosexuality**
Lesbians   301.41
  x Gay women; Homosexuals, Female
Letter writing   808.6
  Use for materials on the composition, forms, and etiquette of correspondence. Materials limited to business correspondence are entered under

Letter writing—*Continued*
>> Business letters. Collections of literary letters are entered under Letters
> *See also* Business letters
> *x* Correspondence; Salutations
> *xx* Etiquette; Rhetoric; Style, Literary

Lettering 745.6
> *See also* Alphabets; Initials; Monograms; Sign painting
> *x* Ornamental alphabets
> *xx* Alphabets; Decoration and ornament; Design, Decorative; Initials; Mechanical drawing; Painting, Industrial; Sign painting

Letters 808.86
> Use for collections of letters
> *See also* American letters; English letters; etc.
> *x* Correspondence
> *xx* Literature—Collections

Letters of credit. *See* Credit; Negotiable instruments

Letters of marque. *See* Privateering

Letters of recommendation. *See* Applications for positions

Letters of the alphabet. *See* Alphabet

Leukemia 616.1
> *xx* Blood—Diseases

Levant. *See* Middle East

Lewis and Clark Expedition 973.4
> *x* Exploring expeditions
> *xx* U.S.—Exploring expeditions; U.S.—History—1783–1809

Liability, Professional. *See* Malpractice

Libel and slander 346.3
> *See also* Free speech; Freedom of the press; Privacy, Right of
> *x* Defamation; Slander (Law)
> *xx* Free speech; Freedom of the press; Journalism

Liberalism 320.5
> *See also* Right and left (Political science)
> *xx* Right and left (Political science)

Liberty. *See* Freedom

Liberty of conscience. *See* Freedom of conscience

Liberty of speech. *See* Free speech

Liberty of the press. *See* Freedom of the press

Liberty of the will. *See* Free will and determinism

Librarians 920; 923
> *See also* Library technicians

Librarians—Black. *See* Black librarians

Librarians—Collective bargaining. *See* Collective bargaining—Librarians

Librarians—Education. *See* Library education

Librarians—In-service training 023
> *xx* Library education

Librarians—Recruiting 023
> *xx* Recruiting of employees

Librarians—Training. *See* **Library education**
Librarians' unions 331.88
    x Library unions
    xx **Labor unions**
Librarianship. *See* **Library science**
Librarianship, Comparative. *See* **Comparative librarianship**
Libraries (May subdiv. geog. country or state)
    027
    See also special types of libraries, e.g.
    Archives; Business libraries; Hospital libraries; Instructional materials centers; Music libraries; Public libraries; School libraries; School libraries (High school); names of cities with the subdivision *Libraries* (e.g. **Chicago —Libraries;** etc.); names of individual libraries (e.g. **Library of Congress;** etc.); and headings beginning with the words **Libraries** and **Library**
    xx **Archives; Books; Books and reading; Education**
Libraries—Acquisitions 025.2
    See also **Book selection**
    x Acquisitions (Libraries); Book buying (Libraries); Libraries—Order department; Library acquisitions
    xx **Libraries—Collection development; Libraries—Technical services**
Libraries—Administration. *See* **Library administration**
Libraries—Advertising. *See* **Advertising—Libraries**
Libraries—Automation 029.7
    See also **Information storage and retrieval systems;** also names of projects and systems, e.g. **MARC** system; etc.
    x Library automation
    xx **Automation; Information storage and retrieval systems**
Libraries—Boards of trustees. *See* **Libraries—Trustees**
Libraries, Business. *See* **Business libraries**
Libraries—Catalogs. *See* **Library catalogs**
Libraries—Censorship 021.8
Libraries—Centralization 021.6
    x Library systems
Libraries, Children's 027.62
    See also **Children's literature; Libraries, Young adults'; Libraries and schools; School libraries**
    x Children's libraries
    xx **Children's literature; Libraries, Young adults'; Libraries and schools; School libraries**
Libraries, Church 027.6
    x Church libraries; Parish libraries
Libraries—Circulation, loans 025.6
    x Book lending; Interlibrary loans

Libraries—Classification. *See* **Classification—Books**

Libraries—Collection development 025.2
　　See also **Book selection; Libraries—Acquisitions**
　　x Collection development (Libraries)
　　xx **Libraries—Technical services**

Libraries—Collective bargaining. *See* **Collective bargaining—Librarians**

Libraries, College and university 027.7
　　x College libraries; Libraries, University; University libraries
　　xx **College and universities**

Libraries—Cooperation. *See* **Library cooperation**

Libraries, County 027.4
　　See also **Libraries, Regional**
　　x County libraries
　　xx **Libraries, Regional; Library extension**

Libraries—Equipment and supplies 022
　　x Library equipment and supplies; Library supplies
　　xx **Furniture**

Libraries—Federal aid. *See* **Federal aid to libraries**

Libraries—Finance. *See* **Library finance**

Libraries, Governmental 027.5
　　See also **State libraries**
　　x Federal libraries; Government libraries
　　xx **State libraries**

Libraries, Hospital. *See* **Hospital libraries**

Libraries—Law and legislation 344.9
　　x Library laws; Library legislation

Libraries—Lighting 022
　　xx **Lighting**

Libraries, Music. *See* **Music libraries**

Libraries—Order department. *See* **Libraries—Acquisitions**

Libraries, Presidential. *See* **Presidents—U.S.—Archives**

Libraries, Public. *See* **Public libraries**

Libraries—Public relations. *See* **Public relations—Libraries**

Libraries—Reference service 025.5
　　x Reference service (Libraries)
　　xx **Library service**

Libraries, Regional 027.4
　　See also **Libraries, County**
　　x District libraries; Regional libraries
　　xx **Libraries, County; Library extension**

Libraries, School. *See* **School libraries; School libraries (High school)**

Libraries, Special 026; 027.6
　　See also types of special libraries, e.g. **Business libraries; Music libraries;** etc.
　　x Special libraries

Libraries—Standards 020

Libraries, State. *See* **State libraries**

Libraries—State aid. *See* **State aid to libraries**

Libraries—Statistics 020.21

Libraries—Technical services 025
> *See also* **Cataloging; Classification—Books; Libraries—Acquisitions; Libraries—Collection development**
> *x* Centralized processing (Libraries); Library processing; Processing (Libraries); Technical services (Libraries)
> *xx* **Library science**

Libraries—Trustees 021.8
> *x* Libraries—Boards of trustees; Library boards; Library trustees
> *xx* **Library administration**

Libraries—U.S. 020
> *x* U.S.—Libraries

Libraries, University. *See* **Libraries, College and university**

Libraries, Young adults' 027.62
> *See also* **Libraries, Children's; School libraries (High school)**
> *x* Young people's libraries
> *xx* **Libraries, Children's; School libraries (High school); Youth**

Libraries and blacks 027.6
> *See also* **Black librarians**
> *x* Blacks—Libraries; Blacks and libraries
> *xx* **Black librarians**

Libraries and community 021
> Use same form for libraries and other subjects
> *See also* **Public relations—Libraries**
> *x* Community and libraries

Libraries and labor 027.6
> *x* Labor and laboring classes—Library service

Libraries and motion pictures 021
> *x* Educational films; Motion pictures and libraries
> *xx* **Library service; Motion pictures in education**

Libraries and pictures 021
> *xx* **Pictures**

Libraries and readers 024; 025.5
> See note under **Library education**
> *xx* **Library service**

Libraries and schools 021
> *See also* **Children's literature; Libraries, Children's; Libraries and students; School libraries**
> *x* Schools and libraries
> *xx* **Children's literature; Libraries, Children's; School libraries; Schools**

Libraries and state 021.8
> *See also* **Federal aid to libraries; State aid to libraries; State libraries**

Libraries and students 027.62
> *x* Students and libraries
> *xx* **Libraries and schools**

Libraries and the elderly 027.6
> *x* Elderly—Library service

Library acquisitions. *See* **Libraries—Acquisitions**

Library administration 025.1

See also **Libraries—Trustees; Library finance**

x Libraries—Administration; Library policies

Library advertising. *See* **Advertising—Libraries**

Library architecture 727

x Buildings, Library; Library buildings

xx **Architecture**

Library assistants. *See* **Library technicians**

Library automation. *See* **Libraries—Automation**

Library boards. *See* **Libraries—Trustees**

Library buildings. *See* **Library architecture**

Library catalogs 017-019

See also types of library catalogs, e.g. **Catalogs, Book; Catalogs, Card; Catalogs, Classified; Catalogs, Subject;** etc.

x Catalogs; Catalogs, Library; Libraries—Catalogs

Library classification. *See* **Classification—Books**

Library consortia. *See* **Library cooperation; Library information networks**

Library cooperation 021.6

See also **Library information networks**

x Consortia, Library; Cooperation, Library; Libraries—Cooperation; Library consortia

Library education 020.7

Here are entered materials on the education of librarians. Materials dealing with the instruction of readers in library use are entered under the heading **Libraries and readers**

See also **Librarians—In-service training; Library schools**

x Education for librarianship; Librarians—Education; Librarians—Training; Library science—Study and teaching

xx **Education; Professional education**

Library education—Audio-visual aids 020.7

xx **Audio-visual education; Audio-visual materials**

Library education—Curricula 020.7

x Core curriculum; Courses of study; Curricula (Courses of study); Schools—Curricula; Study, Courses of

xx **Education—Curricula**

Library equipment and supplies. *See* **Libraries—Equipment and supplies**

Library extension 021.6

See also **Bookmobiles; Libraries, County; Libraries, Regional**

Library finance 025.1

See also **Federal aid to libraries; State aid to libraries**

329

Library finance—*Continued*

    x Libraries—Finance

    xx **Library administration**

Library information networks 021.6

    x Consortia, Library; Library consortia; Library networks; Library systems; Networks, Library

    xx **Information networks; Library cooperation**

Library laws. *See* **Libraries—Law and legislation**

Library legislation. *See* **Libraries—Law and legislation**

Library networks. *See* **Library information networks**

Library of Congress 027.5; 027.6

    x U.S. Library of Congress

    xx **Libraries**

Library policies. *See* **Library administration**

Library processing. *See* **Libraries—Technical services**

Library resources 021; 025

Library schools 020.7

    xx **Library education**

Library science 020

    Use for general materials on the organization and administration of libraries. Materials about services offered by libraries to patrons are entered under **Library service**

    See also **Bibliography; Cataloging; Classification—Books; Comparative librarianship; Libraries—Technical services; Library service; Library surveys;** also headings beginning with the words **Libraries** and **Library**

    x Librarianship

    xx **Bibliography; Documentation; Information science**

Library science—Study and teaching. *See* **Library education**

Library service 025.5

    See note under **Library science**

    See also **Libraries—Reference service; Libraries and readers; Libraries and motion pictures**

    xx **Library science**

Library supplies. *See* **Libraries—Equipment and supplies**

Library surveys 020.21

    x Surveys

    xx **Library science**

Library systems. *See* **Libraries—Centralization; Library information networks**

Library technicians 920; 923

    x Library assistants; Nonprofessional library assistants; Paraprofessional librarians; Subprofessional library assistants

Library technicians—*Continued*
> *xx* **Librarians; Paraprofessions and para-professionals**

Library trustees. *See* **Libraries—Trustees**
Library unions. *See* **Librarians' unions**
Librettos 782.1
> *See also* **Operas—Stories, plots, etc.;** also musical forms with the subdivision *Librettos,* e.g. **Operas—Librettos;** etc.

Life 128
> *See also* **Death; Ethics**

Life, Christian. *See* **Christian life**
Life, Future. *See* **Future life**
Life—Origin 113
> *x* Germ theory; Origin of life
> *xx* **Evolution**

Life, Spiritual. *See* **Spiritual life**
Life (Biology) 574; 577
> *See also* **Biology; Genetics; Middle age; Old age; Protoplasm; Reproduction**
> *xx* **Biology**

Life after death. *See* **Future life; Immortality**
Life insurance. *See* **Insurance, Life**
Life on other planets 574.999
> See note under **Space biology**
> *See also* **Interstellar communication**
> *x* Astrobiology; Exobiology; Extraterrestrial life; Planets, Life on other
> *xx* **Astronomy; Planets; Space biology; Universe**

Life quality. *See* **Quality of life**
Life sciences 570
> *See also* **Agriculture; Biology; Medicine**
> *x* Biosciences
> *xx* **Science**

Life sciences ethics. *See* **Bioethics**
Life styles 301.44
> *See also* **Counter culture**
> *x* Alternative life style
> *xx* **Human behavior**

Life support systems (Medical environment) 362.1
> *xx* **Hospitals; Terminal care**

Life support systems (Space environment) 629.47
> *See also* **Astronauts—Clothing; Apollo project; Space ships**
> *xx* **Human engineering; Space medicine**

Life support systems (Submarine environment) 627.7
Lifelong education. *See* **Continuing education**
Lifesaving 614.8
> *See also* **First aid**
> *xx* **First aid; Rescue work**

Lifts. *See* **Elevators; Hoisting machinery**
Light 535
> *See also* **Color; Lasers; Optics; Phosphorescence; Photometry; Radiation; Radioactivity; Refraction; Spectrum; X rays**

Light—*Continued*

    xx **Electromagnetic waves; Optics; Photometry; Physics; Radiation; Spectrum; Vibration; Waves**

Light, Electric. *See* **Electric lighting; Fluorescent lighting; Photometry; Phototherapy**

Light—Therapeutic use. *See* **Phototherapy**

Light amplification by stimulated emission of radiation. *See* **Lasers**

Light and shade. *See* **Shades and shadows**

Light ships. *See* **Lightships**

Lighter than air craft. *See* **Airships**

Lighthouses 623.89

    See also **Lightships**

    xx **Navigation**

Lighting 621.32

    See also **Candles; Electric lighting; Fluorescent lighting; Lamps;** also subjects and names of cities with the subdivision *Lighting,* e.g. **Chicago–Lighting; Libraries–Lighting; Streets–Lighting;** etc.

    x Illumination

Lightning 551.5

    xx **Electricity; Meteorology; Thunderstorms**

Lightships 623.89

    x Light ships

    xx **Lighthouses**

Lime 631.8; 666

    See also **Cement**

    xx **Fertilizers and manures**

Limericks 808.81; 811.08; etc.

    See also **Nonsense verses**

    x Rhymes

    xx **Humorous poetry; Nonsense verses**

Limitation of armament. *See* **Disarmament**

Limited access highways. *See* **Express highways**

Lincoln Day. *See* **Lincoln's Birthday**

Lincoln family 920; 929

    xx **Genealogy**

Lincoln's Birthday 394.2

    x Lincoln Day

Line engraving. *See* **Engraving**

Linear algebras. *See* **Algebras, Linear**

Linear system theory. *See* **System analysis**

Linen 677

    See also **Flax; Hemp**

    xx **Fabrics; Fibers; Flax**

Linguistics. *See* **Language and languages**

Linoleum block printing 761

    x Block printing

    xx **Color prints; Engraving**

Linotype 686.2

    xx **Printing; Type and type founding; Typesetting**

Lip reading. *See* **Deaf–Means of communication**

Liqueurs. *See* **Liquors and liqueurs**
Liquid fuel. *See* **Gasoline; Petroleum as fuel**
Liquids 532
>*See also* **Hydraulics; Hydrodynamics; Hydrostatics**
>*xx* **Mechanics; Physics**

Liquor industry 338.4
>*xx* **Alcohol; Temperance**

Liquor problem 363.4; 351.7
>Use for materials of an administrative character including liquor control
>*See also* **Alcoholism; Prohibition; Temperance**
>*x* Drink question; Drunkenness; Intemperance; Intoxication
>*xx* **Alcohol; Alcoholism; Prohibition; Social problems; Temperance**

Liquors and liqueurs 663
>*See also* **Distillation;** also names of specific liquors and liqueurs
>*x* Drinks; Intoxicants; Liqueurs; Spirits, Alcoholic
>*xx* **Alcohol; Beverages; Distillation; Stimulants**

Listening 152.1
>*See also* **Attention**
>*xx* **Attention**

Listening devices. *See* **Eavesdropping**
Literacy. *See* **Illiteracy**
Literary awards. *See* **Literary prizes;** also names of awards, e.g. **Caldecott Medal books;** etc.
Literary characters. *See* **Characters and characteristics in literature**
Literary criticism. *See* **Criticism; Literature—History and criticism**
Literary forgeries 098
>*x* Frauds, Literary
>*xx* **Forgery of works of art**

Literary landmarks (May subdiv. geog.) **809; 810.9;** etc.
>*x* Authors—Homes and haunts; Landmarks, Literary
>*xx* **Historic buildings, etc.; Literature—History and criticism**

Literary landmarks—U.S. 810.9
>*x* U.S.—Literary landmarks

Literary prizes 807
>*See also* names of awards, e.g. **Caldecott Medal books;** etc.
>*x* Awards, Literary; Book awards; Book prizes; Literary awards; Literature—Prizes; Prizes, Literary
>*xx* **Rewards (Prizes, etc.)**

Literary property. *See* **Copyright**
Literary style. *See* **Style, Literary**
Literature 800's
>Use for materials on literature in general, not limited to history, philosophy or any one aspect

Literature—*Continued*
See also

Authorship	Fiction
Ballads	Humanism
Biography (as a literary form)	Journalism
	Legends
Books	Music and literature
Catholic literature	
Children's literature	Parody
Christian literature, Early	Plots (Drama, fiction, etc.)
Classical literature	Poetry
Criticism	Religious literature
Devotional literature	Romanticism
	Sagas
Drama	Satire
Essay	Short story
Fables	Style, Literary
Fairy tales	Wit and humor

also names of literatures, e.g. **English literature; French literature;** etc.; and subjects and themes in literature, e.g. **Bible in literature; Characters and characteristics in literature; Children in literature and art; Realism in literature; Symbolism in literature; Women in literature and art;** etc.

x Belles-lettres

xx **Books; Books and reading; Humanities; Language and languages; Language arts**

Literature—Bio-bibliography   016.8
See also **Authors**
xx **Authors**

Literature, Classical. *See* **Classical literature**

Literature—Collections   808.8
See also **Essays; Letters; Orations, Parodies; Quotations; Romances; Short stories;** also names of literatures and names of literary forms with the subdivision *Collections*, e.g. **English literature—Collections; Poetry—Collections;** etc.

x Literature—Selections

Literature, Comparative   809
x Comparative literature
xx **Philology, Comparative**

Literature—Competitions   807
x Competitions

Literature—Criticism. *See* **Literature—History and criticism**

Literature—Dictionaries   803
See also **Literature—Indexes**
xx **Literature—Indexes**

Literature, Erotic. *See* **Erotic literature**

Literature—Evaluation. *See* **Books—Reviews; Books and reading; Books and reading—Best books; Criticism; Literature—History and criticism**

Literature—History and criticism 809
  See also **Authors; Criticism; Literary land-**
    marks
  x Appraisal of books; Books—Appraisal;
    Evaluation of literature; Literary
    criticism; Literature—Criticism; Lit-
    erature—Evaluation
  xx **Authors; Style, Literary**
Literature, Immoral. *See* **Erotic literature**
Literature—Indexes 800.1
  See also **Literature—Dictionaries**
  xx **Literature—Dictionaries**
Literature, Medieval 809
  May use same subdivisions as under **Lit-**
    erature
  See also **Christian literature, Early**
  x Medieval literature
  xx **Middle Ages; Renaissance**
Literature—Outlines, syllabi, etc. 802
  See also **English literature—Outlines, syl-**
    labi, etc.
Literature—Prizes. *See* **Literary prizes,** also
    names of prizes, e.g. **Caldecott Medal**
    books; etc.
Literature—Selections. *See* **Literature—Collec-**
    tions
Literature—Stories, plots, etc. 808.8
  Use for collections of stories, plots, etc.
    Materials dealing with the construc-
    tion and analysis of plots as a literary
    technique are entered under **Plots**
    (Drama, fiction, etc.)
Literature—Yearbooks 805
  x Annuals
  xx **Yearbooks**
Literature and communism. *See* **Communism**
    and literature
Lithographers 920; 927
  xx **Engravers**
Lithography 686.2; 763; 764
  See also **Offset printing**
  xx **Color printing; Prints**
Lithoprinting. *See* **Offset printing**
Littering. *See* **Refuse and refuse disposal**
Little league baseball 796.357
  xx **Baseball**
Little theater. *See* **Theater—Little theater**
    movement
Liturgies 264
  See also **Mass**
  x Church service books; Ecclesiastical
    rites and ceremonies; Ritual; Service
    books (Liturgy)
  xx **Church music; Devotional exercises;**
    Theology
Live poliovirus vaccine. *See* **Poliomyelitis vac-**
    cine
Livestock 636
  Use for materials on breeds of livestock
    and on stock raising as an industry.

335

Livestock—*Continued*

General descriptions of farm and other domestic animals are entered under **Domestic animals**

See also

Dairying	**Livestock judging**
Domestic animals	**Veterinary medicine**

Also names of livestock, e.g. **Cattle; Cows; Sheep;** etc.

x Animal husbandry; Animal industry; Breeding; Farm animals; Stock and stock breeding; Stock raising

xx **Cattle; Domestic animals**

Livestock judging 636

x Stock judging

xx **Livestock**

Living, Cost of. *See* **Cost of living**

Living, Standard of. *See* **Standard of living**

Living together. *See* **Unmarried couples**

Lizards 598.1

xx **Reptiles**

Loan associations. *See* **Savings and loan associations**

Loan funds, Student. *See* **Student loan funds**

Loans 332.7

Use for materials on loans, particularly small loans, usually made by finance companies. Materials on government loans are entered under **Debts, Public**

See also **Debts, Public; Interest (Economics); Investments; Savings and loan associations**

x Lending

xx **Credit**

Lobbying 328

See also **Corruption in politics**

x Interest groups; Pressure groups

xx **Corruption in politics; Politics, Practical**

Lobsters 595

xx **Crustacea**

Local government 352

Use for materials about local government of districts, counties, townships, etc. Materials about county government only are entered under **County government;** materials about city government are entered under **Municipal government**

See also **Cities and towns; County government; Metropolitan government; Municipal government; Public administration; Villages**

x Government, Local; Town meeting; Township government

xx **Administrative law; Community organization; Political science; Villages**

Local history. *See* names of countries, states, etc. with the subdivision *History, Local,* e.g. **U.S.—History, Local;** etc.

Local traffic. *See* **City traffic**

Local transit 388.4

See also Buses; Street railroads; Subways; also names of cities and metropolitan areas with the subdivision *Transit systems,* e.g. **Chicago—Transit systems; Chicago metropolitan area—Transit systems;** etc.

x City transit; Mass transit; Municipal transit; Public transit; Rapid transit; Transit systems; Urban transportation

xx **Traffic engineering; Transportation**

Localism. *See* **Sectionalism (U.S.);** and names of languages with the subdivision *Provincialisms,* e.g. **English language—Provincialisms;** etc.

Lockouts. *See* **Strikes and lockouts**

Locks and keys 683

x Keys

xx **Burglary protection**

Locomotion. *See* **Aeronautics; Animal locomotion; Automobiles; Boats and boating; Flight; Navigation; Transportation; Walking**

Locomotives 625.2

x Railroads—Rolling stock; Rolling stock

xx **Machinery; Steam engines**

Locomotives—Models 625.1

xx **Machinery—Models**

Locusts 595.7; 632

x Diseases and pests

xx **Insects, Injurious and beneficial**

Locusts, Seventeen-year. *See* **Cicadas**

Lodging houses. *See* **Hotels, motels, etc.**

Log cabins 728

x Cabins

Logarithms 512.9

See also **Slide rule**

xx **Algebra; Mathematics—Tables, etc.; Trigonometry—Tables, etc.**

Logging. *See* **Lumber and lumbering**

Logic 160

See also **Knowledge, Theory of; Probabilities; Reasoning; Thought and thinking**

x Argumentation; Deduction (Logic); Dialectics; Fallacies; Induction (Logic)

xx **Intellect; Philosophy; Reasoning; Science—Methodology; Thought and thinking**

Logic, Symbolic and mathematical 511

See also **Algebra, Boolean; Set theory**

xx **Mathematics; Set theory**

Longevity. *See* **Old age**

Longitude 526; 527

See also **Time**

x Degrees of latitude and longitude

xx **Earth; Geodesy; Nautical astronomy**

Looking glasses. *See* **Mirrors**

Looms 677; 746

xx **Weaving**

Loran 621.3841

xx **Navigation**

Lord's Day. *See* **Sabbath**
Lord's Prayer   226; 242
    xx **Jesus Christ—Prayers**
Lord's Supper   232.9; 265
    See also **Mass**
    x Communion; Ecclesiastical rites and ceremonies; Eucharist; Jesus Christ—Last Supper; Last Supper
    xx **Jesus Christ; Mass; Sacraments**
Lotteries   336.1
    xx **Gambling**
Loud speakers. *See* **Intercommunication systems**
Louisiana Purchase   973.4; 976.3
    xx **U.S.—History—1783–1809**
Love   152.4; 301.42
    See also **Dating (Social customs); Friendship; Marriage**
    x Affection
    xx **Dating (Social customs); Emotions; Friendship; Human behavior**
Love (Theology)   231
    xx **Christian ethics**
Love poetry   808.1; 811; etc.
    x Poetry of love
    xx **Poetry**
Low sodium diet. *See* **Salt free diet**
Low temperature biology. *See* **Cryobiology**
Low temperature   536; 621.5
    See also **Cold; Cryobiology**
    x Cryogenics; Temperatures, Low
    xx **Cold; Temperature**
Loyalists, American. *See* **American Loyalists**
Loyalty   172
    See also **Patriotism**
    x Faithfulness
    xx **Human behavior; Patriotism**
Loyalty oaths. *See* **Internal security**
Lubrication and lubricants   621.8
    See also **Bearings (Machinery); Oils and fats**
    x Grease
    xx **Bearings (Machinery); Machinery; Oils and fats**
Lullabies   784.6
    x Cradle songs; Slumber songs
    xx **Children's poetry; Children's songs; Songs**
Lumber and lumbering   634.9; 674
    Includes materials on cut timber, its preparation for construction and building purposes, and uses of various kinds of lumber
    x Logging; Timber
    xx **Forest products; Forests and forestry; Trees; Wood**
Luminescence. *See* **Phosphorescence**
Luminescence, Animal. *See* **Bioluminescence**
Lunar bases   629.45
    x Moon bases

Lunar cars. *See* **Moon cars**

Lunar eclipses. *See* **Eclipses, Lunar**

Lunar excursion module   629.45
>   *x* LEM; Lem; Lunar module
>   *xx* **Space vehicles**

Lunar expeditions. *See* **Space flight to the moon**

Lunar exploration. *See* **Moon—Exploration**

Lunar geology   559.9
>   *See also* **Lunar petrology; Lunar soil**
>   *x* Geology, Lunar; Geology—Moon; Moon —Geology
>   *xx* **Astrogeology**

Lunar module. *See* **Lunar excursion module**

Lunar petrology   552
>   *x* Lunar rocks; Moon rocks; Rocks, Moon
>   *xx* **Lunar geology; Petrology**

Lunar photography   778.3
>   *See also* **Moon—Photographs**
>   *x* Moon photography
>   *xx* **Space photography**

Lunar probes   629.43
>   *See also* names of space projects, e.g. **Mariner projects**; etc.
>   *x* Moon probes
>   *xx* **Space probes**

Lunar rocks. *See* **Lunar petrology**

Lunar rover vehicles. *See* **Moon cars**

Lunar soil   631.4
>   *See also* **Moon—Surface**
>   *x* Moon soil; Soils, Lunar
>   *xx* **Lunar geology; Moon—Surface**

Lunar surface. *See* **Moon—Surface**

Lunar surface radio communication. *See* **Radio in astronautics**

Lunar surface vehicles. *See* **Moon cars**

Lunch rooms. *See* **Restaurants, bars, etc.**

Luncheons   642
>   *xx* **Caterers and catering; Cookery; Entertaining; Menus**

Lungs   611; 612
>   *See also* **Respiration**

Lungs—Diseases   616.2
>   *See also* names of diseases, e.g. **Pneumonia; Tuberculosis**; etc.

Lying. *See* **Truthfulness and falsehood**

Lynching   364.1
>   *See also* **Vigilance committees**
>   *xx* **Crime**

Machine design. *See* **Machinery—Design**

Machine intelligence. *See* **Artificial intelligence**

Machine language. *See* **Programming languages (Electronic computers)**

Machine readable catalog system. *See* **MARC system**

Machine shop practice   621.7
>   *x* Shop practice

Machine shops   621.7
>   *x* Shops, Machine

Machine tools   621.9

    See also names of machine tools, e.g. **Planing machines;** etc.

    xx **Machinery; Milling machines; Tools**

Machine translating.   *See* **Translating and interpreting**

Machinery   621.31; 621.8-621.9

    See also

Agricultural machinery	**bricants**
	Machine tools
Bearings (Machinery)	**Mechanical drawing**
	Mechanics
Belts and belting	**Metalworking machinery**
Electric machinery	
Engines	**Milling machines**
Gearing	**Patents**
Hydraulic machinery	**Power transmission**
	Steam engines
Inventions	**Woodworking machinery**
Locomotives	
Lubrication and lu-	

    x Machines

    xx **Industrial management; Manufactures; Mechanical engineering; Mechanics; Mills and millwork; Power (Mechanics); Power transmission; Technology; Tools**

Machinery, Automatic. *See* **Automation**

Machinery—Design   621.8

    See also **Human engineering; Machinery—Models**

    x Machine design

Machinery—Drawing. *See* **Mechanical drawing**

Machinery—Models   621.8-621.9

    See also **Airplanes—Models; Automobiles—Models; Locomotives—Models; Motorboats—Models; Railroads—Models; Ships—Models**

    x Mechanical models; Models, Mechanical

    xx **Machinery—Design**

Machinery in industry   338

    Use for materials on the social and economic aspects of mechanization in the industrial world, the machine age, etc.

    See also **Automation**

    xx **Industry; Labor and laboring classes; Technology and civilization**

Machines. *See* **Machinery**

Madonna. *See* **Mary, Virgin**

Magazines. *See* **Periodicals**

Magic   793.8

    Use for materials dealing with modern ("parlor") magic, legerdemain, etc., as entertainment. Materials on the supernatural not connected with magic tricks are entered under **Occult Sciences**

    See also **Card tricks; Occult sciences; Tricks**

Magic—*Continued*
    x Conjuring; Legerdemain; Sleight of hand
    xx **Amusements; Hallucinations and illusions; Occult sciences; Tricks**
Magna Carta 342.4; 942.03
Magnet winding. *See* **Electromagnets**
Magnetic needle. *See* **Compass**
Magnetic recorders and recording 621.381; 789.9
    x Cassette recorders and recording; Recorders, Tape; Tape recorders
    xx **Sound—Recording and reproducing**
Magnetic resonance accelerator. *See* **Cyclotron**
Magnetism 538
    See also **Compass; Electricity; Electromagnetism; Electromagnets; Magnets**
    xx **Electricity; Physics**
Magnets 538
    See also **Electromagnets**
    xx **Magnetism**
Mail-order business 658.8
    xx **Advertising; Business; Selling**
Mail service. *See* **Postal service**
Maize. *See* **Corn**
Makeup (Cosmetics). *See* **Cosmetics**
Makeup, Theatrical 791.43; 791.45; 792
    x Theatrical makeup
    xx **Amateur theatricals; Costume**
Maladjusted children. *See* **Problem children**
Maladjustment (Psychology). *See* **Adjustment (Psychology)**
Malaria 616.9
    x Ague; Chills and fever; Intermittent fever
    xx **Fever**
Male climacteric. *See* **Climacteric, Male**
Male role. *See* **Sex role**
Malfeasance in office. *See* **Misconduct in office**
Malls, Shopping. *See* **Shopping centers and malls**
Malnutrition 616.3
    xx **Nutrition**
Malpractice 346.3
    See also names of professional people with the subdivision *Malpractice*, e.g. **Physicians—Malpractice**; etc.
    x Liability, Professional; Professional liability; Professions—Tort liability; Tort liability of professions
Malpractice insurance. *See* **Insurance, Malpractice**
Mammals 599
    See also groups of mammals, e.g. **Primates**; etc. also names of mammals, e.g. **Bats; Elephants**; etc.
    xx **Animals; Vertebrates; Zoology**
Mammals, Fossil 569
    See also names of extinct animals, e.g. **Mastodon**; etc.
    x Fossil mammals
    xx **Fossils**

Man 572; 573

 Use this heading only in its generic meaning

 See also **Anthropology; Anthropometry; Creation; Ethnology; Heredity**

 x Human race

 xx **Anthropology; Creation; History**

Man—Antiquity. *See* **Man—Origin and antiquity**

Man—Color. *See* **Color of people**

Man—Influence of environment 301.3; 573

 See also **Color of people; Weightlessness**

 x Acclimatization; Altitude, Influence of

 xx **Adaptation (Biology); Anthropogeography; Evolution; Human ecology**

Man—Influence on nature 301.3; 574.5

 See also **Environmental policy; Pollution**

 x Earth, Effect of man on; Nature, Effect of man on

 xx **Environmental policy; Human ecology**

Man, Nonliterate 301.2

 x Nonliterate man; Preliterate man; Primitive man

 xx **Ethnology; Society, Nonliterate folk**

Man—Origin and antiquity 573.2

 See also **Anatomy, Comparative; Evolution; Man, Prehistoric**

 x Antiquities; Man—Antiquity; Origin of man

 xx **Anatomy, Comparative; Evolution; Man, Prehistoric; Religion and science; Physical anthropology**

Man, Prehistoric 572; 573

 See also **Bronze age; Cave dwellers; Man—Origin and antiquity;** also names of prehistoric people, e.g. **Cro-Magnons;** etc. and names of countries, cities, etc. with the subdivision *Antiquities,* e.g. **U.S.—Antiquities;** etc.

 x Antiquities; Prehistoric man

 xx **Archeology; Civilization, Ancient; Ethnology; Man—Origin and antiquity; Stone age**

Man (Theology) 218; 233

 See also **Soul**

 xx **Theology**

Man in space. *See* **Space flight**

Man power. *See* **Human resources**

Management 658

 Use for general materials on the principles of management in factories, industries, shops, etc. Materials on the application of such principles are entered under the specific headings such as those listed below. Add others as needed

 See also **Efficiency, Industrial; Factory management; Farm management; Industrial management; Office management; Personnel management; Sales management**

Management—*Continued*

   x Administration; Management, Scientific; Organization and management; Scientific management

Management, Employees' representation in. *See* **Employees' representation in management**

Management, Industrial. *See* **Industrial management**

Management, Sales. *See* **Sales management**

Management, Scientific. *See* **Management**

Managers. *See* **Supervisors**

Mandates 321

   x Government, Mandatory; League of Nations—Mandatory system

   xx **International law; International organization; International relations; World War, 1914–1918–Territorial questions**

Manikins (Fashion models). *See* **Models, Fashion**

Manned space flight. *See* **Space flight**

Manned space flight—Rescue work. *See* **Space rescue operations**

Manned undersea research stations. *See* **Undersea research stations**

Mannequins. *See* **Models, Fashion**

Manners. *See* **Courtesy; Etiquette**

Manners and customs 390

   See also

Bohemianism	**Funeral rites and**
Caste	**ceremonies**
Chivalry	**Holidays**
Clothing and dress	**Marriage customs**
Costume	**and rites**
Courts and cour-	**Rites and ceremon-**
tiers	**ies**
Dueling	**Social classes**
Etiquette	**Travel**
Festivals	

   also names of ethnic groups, countries, cities, etc. with the subdivision *Social life and customs,* e.g. **Indians of North America—Social life and customs; Jews—Social life and customs; U.S.—Social life and customs;** etc.

   x Ceremonies; Customs, Social; Folkways; Social customs; Social life and customs

   xx **Civilization; Ethnology; Etiquette; Rites and ceremonies**

Manpower. *See* **Human resources**

Manpower policy. *See* **Human resources policy**

Manslaughter. *See* **Murder**

Manual training. *See* **Industrial arts education**

Manufactures 338.4; 670

   See also **Machinery; Mills and millwork; Patents; Prices; Trademarks; Waste products;** also names of articles manu-

Manufactures—*Continued*

    factured (e.g. **Furniture;** etc.) and names of industries (e.g. **Paper making and trade;** etc.); also names of countries, cities, etc. with the subdivision *Industries,* e.g. **Chicago—Industries;** etc.

  x Consumer goods; Consumer products

  xx **Business; Commercial products; Industry; Technology**

Manures. *See* **Fertilizers and manures**

Manuscripts 091

  See also **Autographs; Charters; Illumination of books and manuscripts**

  xx **Archives; Autographs; Bibliography; Books; Charters**

Manuscripts, Illuminated. *See* **Illumination of books and manuscripts**

Manuscripts—Prices. *See* **Books—Prices**

Map drawing 526.8

  See also **Topographical drawing**

  x Cartography; Chartography; Plans

  xx **Topographical drawing**

Maple sugar 641.3; 664

  xx **Sugar**

Maps 912

  Use for general materials about maps and their history. Materials on the methods of map making and the mapping of areas are entered under **Map drawing.** Collections of maps of several countries are entered under **Atlases**

  See also **Atlases; Automobiles—Road guides; Charts;** also types of maps, e.g. **Road maps;** etc. also subjects with the subdivision *Maps* (e.g. **Geology—Maps;** etc.) and names of countries, cities, etc. with the subdivision *Maps,* e.g. **U.S.—Maps; Chicago—Maps;** etc.

  x Cartography; Chartography; Plans

  xx **Charts; Geography**

Maps, Historical. *See* **Atlases, Historical**

Maps, Military. *See* **Military geography**

Maps, Road. *See* **Road maps**

Marble 553

  xx **Petrology; Stone**

Marc project. *See* **MARC system**

MARC system 029.7

  x Machine readable catalog system; Marc project; Project MARC

  xx **Bibliographic control; Libraries—Automation**

Marches (Demonstrations). *See* **Demonstrations**

Marches (Exercises). *See* **Drill (Nonmilitary)**

Marches (Music) 785.1

  xx **Military music**

Marches for black civil rights—U.S. *See* **Blacks—Civil rights**

Margarine 641.3; 664
> *x* Butter, Artificial; Oleomargarine
> *xx* **Butter**

Mariculture. *See* **Aquaculture**

Marinas 387.1
> *See also* **Docks**
> *x* Yacht basins
> *xx* **Boats and boating; Harbors; Yachts and yachting**

Marine animals 591.92
> *See also* **Corals; Fishes; Fresh water animals**
> *x* Animals, Aquatic; Animals, Marine; Animals, Sea; Aquatic animals; Marine fauna; Marine zoology; Sea animals; Water animals
> *xx* **Animals; Fresh water animals; Geographical distribution of animals and plants; Marine biology**

Marine aquaculture. *See* **Aquaculture**

Marine aquariums 639
> *See also* names of specific marine aquariums, e.g. **Marineland;** etc.
> *x* Aquariums, Saltwater; Oceanariums; Salt water aquariums; Sea water aquariums
> *xx* **Aquariums**

Marine architecture. *See* **Naval architecture; Shipbuilding**

Marine biology 574.92
> *See also* **Fresh water biology; Marine animals; Marine ecology; Marine plants; Marine resources; Ocean bottom; Photography, Submarine**
> *x* Biological oceanography; Biology, Marine; Ocean life
> *xx* **Biology; Fresh water biology; Natural history; Oceanography; Underwater exploration**

Marine ecology 574.5
> *x* Biological oceanography; Ecology, Marine
> *xx* **Ecology; Marine biology**

Marine engineering 623.8
> *x* Naval engineering
> *xx* **Civil engineering; Mechanical engineering; Naval architecture; Naval art and science; Steam navigation**

Marine engines 623.82
> *xx* **Engines; Shipbuilding; Steam engines**

Marine fauna. *See* **Marine animals**

Marine flora. *See* **Marine plants**

Marine geology. *See* **Submarine geology**

Marine insurance. *See* **Insurance, Marine**

Marine law. *See* **Maritime law**

Marine mineral resources 553
> *x* Mineral resources, Marine; Ocean mineral resources
> *xx* **Marine resources; Mines and mineral resources; Ocean bottom**

Marine painting   758

  x Sea in art; Seascapes; Ships in art

  xx **Painting**

Marine plants   581.92

  See also **Algae; Fresh water plants**

  x Aquatic plants; Marine flora; Water plants

  xx **Fresh water plants; Geographical distribution of animals and plants; Marine biology**

Marine pollution   333.9

  See also types of water pollution, e.g. **Oil pollution of rivers, harbors, etc.**

  x Ocean pollution; Offshore water pollution; Sea pollution

  xx **Pollution**

Marine resources   333.9; 574.92

  See also **Aquaculture; Fisheries; Marine mineral resources**

  x Ocean—Economic aspects; Ocean resources; Resources, Marine; Sea resources

  xx **Commercial products; Marine biology; Natural resources; Oceanography**

Marine transportation.   *See* **Shipping**

Marine zoology.   *See* **Marine animals**

Marineland   639

  xx **Marine aquariums**

Mariner project   629.43

  x Project Mariner

  xx **Lunar probes; Space probes**

Mariners.   *See* **Sailors**

Mariner's compass.   *See* **Compass**

Marionettes.   *See* **Puppets and puppet plays**

Marital counseling.   *See* **Marriage counseling**

Maritime discoveries.   *See* **Discoveries (in geography)**

Maritime law   341.42

  See also **Commercial law; Freight and freightage; Insurance, Marine; Merchant marine; Pirates; Salvage; Territorial waters**

  x Law, Maritime; Law of the sea; Marine law; Merchant marine—Law and legislation; Naval law; Navigation—Law and legislation; Sea laws

  xx **Commercial law; International law; Law; Shipping; Territorial waters**

Market gardening.   *See* **Vegetable gardening**

Market surveys   658.8

  See also **Public opinion polls**

  xx **Public opinion polls**

Marketing   380.1; 658.8

  Use for materials on the principles and methods involved in the distribution of merchandise from producer to consumer

  See also **Sales management;** and subjects with the subdivision *Marketing*, e.g. **Farm produce—Marketing;** etc.

346

Marketing—*Continued*

    x Distribution (Economics); Merchandising

    xx **Advertising; Business; Industrial management; Selling**

Marketing (Home economics). *See* **Shopping**

Marketing of farm produce. *See* **Farm produce—Marketing**

Markets 380.1; 658.8

    See also **Fairs**

    xx **Business; Cities and towns; Commerce; Fairs; Food**

Marking (Students). *See* **Grading and marking (Students)**

Marks, Potters'. *See* **Pottery—Marks**

Marks on plate. *See* **Hallmarks**

Marriage 173; 301.42

    See also **Celibacy; Dating (Social customs); Divorce; Domestic relations; Family; Family life education; Home; Intermarriage; Marriage contracts; Marriage counseling; Sex; Sexual ethics**

    x Matrimony

    xx **Divorce; Domestic relations; Family; Home; Love; Sacraments**

Marriage—Annulment 301.42

    See also **Divorce**

    x Annulment of marriage

    xx **Divorce**

Marriage, Mixed. *See* **Intermarriage**

Marriage, Open ended. *See* **Unmarried couples**

Marriage contracts 301.42; 346.1

    x Antenuptial contracts; Prenuptial contracts

    xx **Marriage**

Marriage counseling 362.8

    x Marital counseling; Premarital counseling

    xx **Counseling; Family life education; Marriage**

Marriage customs and rites 392

    x Bridal customs; Weddings

    xx **Manners and customs; Rites and ceremonies**

Marriage registers. *See* **Registers of births, etc.**

Marriage statistics. *See* **Vital statistics**

Mars (Planet) 523.4

    See also **Mars probes**

Mars (Planet)—Exploration 629.43

Mars (Planet)—Geology 559.9

    xx **Astrogeology**

Mars (Planet)—Photographs 778.3

Mars probes 629.43

    x Martian probes

    xx **Mars (Planet); Space probes**

Marshall Plan. *See* **Reconstruction (1939–1951)**

Marshes 333.9; 551.4
    x Bogs; Swamps
    xx **Drainage; Reclamation of land**
Martian probes. *See* **Mars probes**
Martyrs 920; 922
    See also **Persecution; Saints**
    xx **Church history; Heroes and heroines; Persecution; Saints**
Marxism. *See* **Communism; Socialism**
Mary, Virgin 232.91
    x Madonna; Virgin Mary
Mary, Virgin—Art 704.948
    See also **Jesus Christ—Art**
    xx **Christian art and symbolism; Jesus Christ—Art**
Masculine psychology. *See* **Men—Psychology**
Masers 621.381
    x Microwave amplification by stimulated emission of radiation
    xx **Amplifiers (Electronics); Electromagnetism; Microwaves**
Masers, Optical. *See* **Lasers**
Masks (Facial) 391
Masks (Plays) 809.2; 808.82; etc.
    x Masques (Plays)
    xx **Drama; Pageants; Theater**
Masks (Sculpture) 731
    x Death masks
    xx **Sculpture**
Masonry 693
    See also **Bricklaying; Bridges; Cement; Concrete; Foundations; Plaster and plastering; Stonecutting; Walls**
    xx **Bricklaying; Building; Civil engineering; Foundations; Stone; Walls**
Masons (Secret order). *See* **Freemasons**
Masques (Plays). *See* **Masks (Plays)**
Mass 264
    See also **Lord's Supper**
    xx **Liturgies; Lord's Supper**
Mass communication. *See* **Communication; Mass media; Telecommunication**
Mass media 301.16
    See also **Motion pictures; Newspapers; Radio broadcasting; Television broadcasting**
    x Mass communication; Media
    xx **Communication**
Mass psychology. *See* **Social psychology**
Mass transit. *See* **Local transit**
Massage 615
    See also **Electrotherapeutics; Osteopathy**
    xx **Medicine—Practice; Osteopathy; Physical therapy**
Mastodon 599
    xx **Extinct animals; Mammals, Fossil**
Materia medica 615
    See also **Anesthetics; Drugs; Pharmacology; Pharmacy; Poisons; Therapeutics;** also names of classes of drugs

Materia medica—*Continued*

and individual drugs, e.g. **Narcotics;** etc.

x Herbals; Pharmacopoeias

xx **Chemistry, Medical and pharmaceutical; Drugs; Medicine; Pharmacy; Therapeutics**

Materialism 146

See also **Idealism; Realism**

xx **Idealism; Monism; Philosophy; Positivism; Realism**

Materials 620.1

Use for discussions on materials of engineering and industry

See also **Strength of materials;** also types of materials, e.g. **Building materials; Raw materials;** etc.

x Engineering materials; Industrial materials; Strategic materials

Materials, Strength of. *See* **Strength of materials**

Materials handling 380.5; 658.7

See also **Freight and freightage; Trucks**

x Mechanical handling

xx **Industrial management; Trucks**

Maternity. *See* **Mothers**

Mathematical analysis 515

See also **Algebra; Algebras, Linear; Calculus; Programming (Electronic computers)**

x Analysis (Mathematics)

Mathematical drawing. *See* **Geometrical drawing; Mechanical drawing**

Mathematical models 511

See also **Programming (Electronic computers); System analysis;** and subjects with the subdivision *Mathematical models,* e.g. **Pollution—Mathematical models;** etc.

x Models, Mathematical

Mathematical operations 511

See also names of specific operations, e.g. **Subtraction;** etc.

Mathematical recreations 793.7

See also **Number games**

x Recreations, Mathematical

xx **Amusements; Puzzles; Scientific recreations**

Mathematical sets. *See* **Set theory**

Mathematicians 920; 925

xx **Scientists**

Mathematics 510

See also

Algebra	**Geometry**
Arithmetic	**Logic, Symbolic**
Binary system	**and mathematical**
(Mathematics)	**Measurement**
Biomathematics	**Number theory**
Calculus	**Set theory**
Dynamics	**Trigonometry**

349

Mathematics—*Continued*

   also subjects with the subdivision *Mathematics*, e.g. **Astronomy—Mathematics;** etc.

   xx **Science**

Mathematics—Tables, etc. 510.21

   See also **Logarithms; Trigonometry—Tables, etc.**

   x Ready reckoners

Matrimony. *See* **Marriage**

Matter 530; 530.4

   xx **Dynamics; Physics**

Mausoleums. *See* **Tombs**

Maxims. *See* **Proverbs**

Mayas 970.3

   xx **Indians of Mexico; Indians of South America**

Meal planning. *See* **Menus; Nutrition**

Meals for astronauts. *See* **Astronauts—Food**

Meals for school children. *See* **School children—Food**

Measurement 389

   See also **Geodesy; Measuring instruments; Surveying; Weights and measures**

   x Mensuration; Metrology

   xx **Mathematics; Weights and measures**

Measurements, Electric. *See* **Electric measurements**

Measures. *See* **Weights and measures**

Measuring instruments 389; 681

   See also **Slide rule**

   x Instruments, Measuring

   xx **Measurement; Weights and measures**

Meat 641.3; 664

   See also names of meat, e.g. **Beef;** etc.

   xx **Food**

Meat industry and trade 338.1

   See also **Cold storage; Meat inspection**

   x Packing industry; Stockyards

   xx **Food supply**

Meat inspection 614.3

   x Inspection of meat

   xx **Food adulteration and inspection; Meat industry and trade; Public health**

Mechanic arts. *See* **Industrial arts**

Mechanical brains. *See* **Computers; Cybernetics**

Mechanical drawing 604.2

   See also **Architectural drawing; Geometrical drawing; Graphic methods; Lettering**

   x Drafting, Mechanical; Engineering drawing; Industrial drawing; Machinery—Drawing; Mathematical drawing; Plans; Structural drafting

   xx **Drawing; Geometrical drawing; Machinery; Pattern making**

Mechanical engineering 620.1

   See note under **Mechanics, Applied**

   See also **Electric engineering; Engines;**

Mechanical engineering—*Continued*

Machinery; Marine engineering; Mechanical movements; Power (Mechanics); Power transmission; Steam engineering

xx **Civil engineering; Steam engineering**

Mechanical handling. *See* **Materials handling**

Mechanical models. *See* **Machinery—Models**

Mechanical movements 531

See also **Automata; Gearing; Robots**

x Mechanisms (Machinery)

xx **Gearing; Kinematics; Mechanical engineering; Mechanics; Motion**

Mechanical musical instruments. *See* **Musical instruments, Mechanical**

Mechanical painting. *See* **Painting, Industrial**

Mechanical stokers. *See* **Stokers, Mechanical**

Mechanical translating. *See* **Translating and interpreting**

Mechanics 531

See also

Dynamics	**Motion**
Engineering	**Power (Mechanics)**
Force and energy	**Statics**
Gases	**Steam engines**
Hydraulics	**Strains and stresses**
Hydrodynamics	**Strength of materials**
Hydrostatics	**als**
Kinematics	**Vibration**
Liquids	**Viscosity**
Machinery	**Wave mechanics**
Mechanical movements	

xx **Engineering; Force and energy; Kinematics; Machinery; Motion; Physics**

Mechanics, Applied 621

Use for materials on the application of the principles of mechanics to engineering structure other than machinery. Materials on the application of the principles of mechanics to the design, construction and operation of machinery are entered under **Mechanical engineering**

x Applied mechanics

Mechanics (Persons) 920; 926

Mechanisms (Machinery). *See* **Mechanical movements**

Medallions. *See* **Medals**

Medals 355.1; 737

See also **Decorations of honor; Insignia; Numismatics;** also names of military services with the subdivisions *Medals, badges, decorations, etc.,* e.g. **U.S. Army—Medals, badges, decorations, etc.; U.S. Navy—Medals, badges, decorations, etc.;** etc.; and names of specific medals

x Badges of honor; Medallions

Medals—*Continued*

  xx **Decorations of honor; Insignia; Numismatics**

Media. *See* **Mass media**

Media centers (Education). *See* **Instructional materials centers**

Mediation, Industrial. *See* **Arbitration, Industrial**

Medicaid 368.4

  xx **Poor—Medical care**

Medical botany. *See* **Botany, Medical**

Medical care 362.1

  See also **Charities, Medical; Health maintenance organizations; Home care services;** also classes of people with the subdivision *Medical care,* e.g. **Elderly —Medical care;** etc.

  x Health care; Medical service

  xx **Public health**

Medical care—Costs 362.102

  x Cost of medical care; Medical service, Cost of; Medicine—Cost of medical care

  xx **Medical economics**

Medical care, Prepaid. *See* **Insurance, Health**

Medical care for the elderly. *See* **Elderly —Medical care; Medicare**

Medical centers 362.1

  See also **Hospitals; Medicine—Study and teaching**

  xx **Hospitals**

Medical charities. *See* **Charities, Medical**

Medical chemistry. *See* **Chemistry, Medical and pharmaceutical**

Medical colleges. *See* **Medicine—Study and teaching**

Medical economics 338.402

  Use for comprehensive materials on the economic aspects of medical service from the point of view of both the practitioner and the public

  See also **Medical care—Costs**

  x Economics, Medical

Medical education. *See* **Medicine—Study and teaching**

Medical electricity. *See* **Electrotherapeutics**

Medical entomology. *See* **Insects as carriers of disease**

Medical ethics 174

  See also **Euthanasia**

  x Ethics, Medical; Medicine—Moral and social aspects

  xx **Bioethics; Professional ethics**

Medical folklore. *See* **Folk medicine**

Medical jurisprudence 614

  Use for materials that treat of the application of medical knowledge to questions of law. Materials that include laws, or discussion of those laws which affect medicine and the medical

Medical jurisprudence—*Continued*

profession, are entered under **Medicine—Law and legislation**

See also **Medicine—Law and legislation; Murder; Poisons; Suicide;** also subjects with the subdivision *Jurisprudence,* e.g. **Mental illness—Jurisprudence;** etc.

x Forensic medicine; Jurisprudence, Medical; Legal medicine; Medicine, Legal

xx **Criminal investigation; Criminal law; Law; Medicine—Law and legislation; Medicine, State**

Medical law and legislation. *See* **Medicine—Law and legislation**

Medical malpractice. *See* names of groups of people in the medical field with the subdivision *Malpractice,* e.g. **Physicians—Malpractice;** etc.

Medical missions. *See* **Missions, Medical**

Medical photography. *See* **Photography, Medical**

Medical profession. *See* **Medicine; Physicians; Surgeons**

Medical research. *See* **Medicine—Research**

Medical service. *See* **Medical care**

Medical service, Cost of. *See* **Medical care—Costs**

Medical service, Prepaid. *See* **Insurance, Health**

Medical technologists 610.69

xx **Allied health personnel**

Medical technology 610.28

xx **Medicine**

Medical transplantation. *See* **Transplantation of organs, tissues, etc.**

Medicare 368.4

x Medical care for the elderly

xx **Elderly—Medical care**

Medicinal plants. *See* **Botany, Medical**

Medicine (May subdiv. geog.) **610**

See also

Anatomy	**Materia medica**
Acupuncture	**Medical technology**
Aviation medicine	**Mind and body**
Bacteriology	**Missions, Medical**
Botany, Medical	**Nursing**
Chemistry, Medical and pharmaceutical	**Osteopathy**
	Pathology
	Pharmacology
Health resorts, spas, etc.	**Pharmacy**
	Physiology
Homeopathy	**Quacks and quackery**
Hospitals	
Hygiene	**Submarine medicine**
Hypnotism	**Surgery**

also headings beginning with the word **Medical**

x Medical profession

xx **Life sciences; Pathology; Therapeutics**

Medicine, Atomic. *See* **Nuclear medicine**

Medicine, Aviation. *See* **Aviation medicine**

Medicine—Biography 920; 926

Medicine—Cost of medical care. *See* **Medical care—Costs**

Medicine, Dental. *See* **Dentistry; Teeth—Diseases**

Medicine—Law and legislation 344.4
> *See also* **Medical jurisprudence**
> *x* Medical law and legislation
> *xx* **Medical jurisprudence**

Medicine, Legal. *See* **Medical jurisprudence**

Medicine, Military 616.9
> *See also* **Armies—Medical and sanitary affairs; First aid; Hospitals, Military; Military hygiene;** also names of wars with the subdivision *Medical and sanitary affairs,* e.g. **World War, 1939–1945—Medical and sanitary affairs;** etc.
> *x* Field hospitals; Military medicine
> *xx* **Armies—Medical and sanitary affairs; Military hygiene**

Medicine—Miscellanea 610.2
> *x* Miscellanea
> *xx* **Curiosities and wonders**

Medicine—Moral and social aspects. *See* **Medical ethics**

Medicine, Nuclear. *See* **Nuclear medicine**

Medicine, Pediatric. *See* **Children—Diseases**

Medicine—Physiological effect. *See* **Pharmacology**

Medicine, Popular 616
> Use for medical books for the layman
> *See also* **Folk medicine**

Medicine—Practice 616
> *See also*

Childbirth	**Homeopathy**
Children—Diseases	**Massage**
Communicable diseases	**Nursing**
	Osteopathy
Diagnosis	**Therapeutics**

> *also* names of diseases and groups of diseases, e.g. **Smallpox; Fever; Nervous system—Diseases;** etc.
> *xx* **Diseases**

Medicine, Preventive. *See* **Bacteriology; Immunity; Public health**

Medicine, Psychosomatic 616.08
> *x* Psychosomatic medicine
> *xx* **Mind and body; Neuroses; Psychoanalysis; Psychology, Pathological**

Medicine—Research 610.7
> *x* Medical research
> *xx* **Research**

Medicine, Socialized. *See* **Medicine, State**

Medicine, State 614
> Use for general materials on the relations of the state to medicine, public health,

Medicine, State—*Continued*
    medical legislation, examinations of
    physicians by state boards, etc.
    See also **Charities, Medical; Medical juris-
        prudence; Public health**
    x Medicine, Socialized; National health
        service; Socialized medicine; State
        medicine
Medicine—Study and teaching 610.7
    x Education, Medical; Medical colleges;
        Medical education
    xx **Medical centers; Professional education;
        Schools; Vocational education**
Medicine, Submarine. *See* **Submarine medi-
    cine**
Medicine, Tropical. *See* **Tropics—Diseases and
    hygiene**
Medicine—U.S. 610
    x U.S.—Medicine
Medicine, Veterinary. *See* **Veterinary medi-
    cine**
Medicine and religion 615
    See also **Christian Science; Faith healing;
        Mental healing**
    x Religion and medicine
Medicines, Patent. *See* **Patent medicines**
Medieval architecture. *See* **Architecture, Me-
    dieval**
Medieval art. *See* **Art, Medieval**
Medieval civilization. *See* **Civilization, Medi-
    eval**
Medieval history. *See* **Middle Ages—History**
Medieval literature. *See* **Literature, Medieval**
Medieval philosophy. *See* **Philosophy, Medi-
    eval**
Meditation 181; 242
    See also **Transcendental meditation**
    xx **Spiritual life**
Meetings, Public. *See* **Public meetings**
Memoirs. *See* **Autobiographies; Biography**
Memorial Day 394.2
    x Days; Decoration Day; National holi-
        days
    xx **School assembly programs**
Memory 153.1
    See also **Attention**
    x Mnemonics
    xx **Brain; Educational psychology; Intel-
        lect; Psychology; Psychology, Physio-
        logical; Thought and thinking**
Men 301.41
    See also **Boys; Fathers; Single men; Young
        men**
Men—Biography 920
    xx **Biography**
Men—Civil rights 301.41
    See also **Men's Liberation Movement**
    xx **Civil rights; Sex discrimination**
Men—Clothing. *See* **Men's clothing**
Men—Clubs. *See* **Men—Societies**

Men—Diseases 614.4; 616
Men—Education 370
   See also **Coeducation**
   x Education of men
   xx **Coeducation**
Men—Employment 331.1
   xx **Discrimination in employment; Labor and laboring classes; Labor supply**
Men—Psychology 150; 155.3
   x Masculine psychology
Men, Single. *See* **Single men**
Men—Social conditions 301.41
   See also **Divorce; Men—Societies; Men's Liberation Movement**
   xx **Social problems**
Men—Societies 367
   See also **Boys' clubs**
   x Men—Clubs; Men's clubs; Men's organizations
   xx **Clubs; Men—Social conditions; Societies**
Mendel's law 575.1
   See also **Heredity**
   xx **Evolution; Heredity; Variation (Biology)**
Mendicancy. *See* **Begging**
Mendicant orders. *See* **Dominicans; Franciscans**
Mennonites 289.7
   See also **Amish**
   xx **Baptists**
Menopause 618.1
   x Change of life in women; Climacteric, Female; Female climacteric
Men's clothing 646; 687
   x Clothing, Men's; Men—Clothing
   xx **Clothing and dress**
Men's clubs. *See* **Men—Societies**
Men's Liberation Movement 323.4
   xx **Men—Civil rights; Men—Social conditions**
Men's organizations. *See* **Men—Societies**
Menstruation 612.6
   xx **Reproduction**
Mensuration. *See* **Measurement**
Mental deficiency. *See* **Mental retardation**
Mental diseases. *See* **Mental illness; Psychology, Pathological**
Mental healing 615
   See also **Christian Science; Faith healing; Hypnotism; Mental suggestion; Mind and body; New Thought; Psychotherapy; Subconsciousness; Therapeutics, Suggestive**
   x Healing, Mental; Mind cure; Psychic healing
   xx **Christian Science; Faith healing; Medicine and religion; Mental suggestion; Mind and body; Psychotherapy; Subconsciousness; Therapeutics, Suggestive**

Mental health   614.5

> *See also* **Mental illness; Mental retarda-
> tion; Mind and body; Occupational
> therapy; Psychology, Pathological;
> Psychology, Physiological; Worry**
>
> *x* Health, Mental; Hygiene, Mental; Men-
> tal hygiene
>
> *xx* **Hygiene; Mental illness; Mind and
> body; Nervous system—Hygiene**

Mental hospitals. *See* **Mentally ill—Institutional care; Psychiatric hospitals**

Mental hygiene. *See* **Mental health**

Mental illness   614.5

> See note under **Psychiatry**
>
> *See also* **Mental health; Mental retarda-
> tion;** also names of specific illnesses
>
> *x* Diseases, Mental; Mental diseases; Psy-
> choses
>
> *xx* **Mental health; Psychiatry; Psychology,
> Pathological**

Mental illness—Jurisprudence   346

> Use for materials on legal aspects of men-
> tal disorders
>
> *x* Insanity
>
> *xx* **Medical jurisprudence**

Mental institutions. *See* **Mentally ill—Institutional care**

Mental philosophy. *See* **Philosophy; Psychology**

Mental retardation   157; 362.3

> *x* Mental deficiency
>
> *xx* **Mental health; Mental illness**

Mental suggestion   131; 154.7; 615

> *See also* **Brainwashing; Hypnotism; Men-
> tal healing; Therapeutics, Suggestive**
>
> *x* Autosuggestion; Suggestion, Mental
>
> *xx* **Hypnotism; Mental healing; Mind and
> body; Psychical research; Subcon-
> sciousness; Therapeutics, Suggestive;
> Thought transference**

Mental telepathy. *See* **Thought transference**

Mental tests   153.9; 371.2

> *See also* **Ability—Testing; Educational tests
> and measurements**
>
> *x* IQ tests; Intelligence tests; Objective
> tests; Psychological tests; Tests
>
> *xx* **Child psychology; Educational psychol-
> ogy; Educational tests and measure-
> ments; Examinations; Grading and
> marking (Students); Intellect; Psychol-
> ogy, Physiological**

Mentally deranged. *See* **Mentally ill**

Mentally handicapped   362.2-362.3

> *See also* **Mentally retarded**
>
> *xx* **Handicapped; Mentally ill**

Mentally handicapped children   155.4; 362.2-
362.3

> *See also* **Mentally retarded children; Slow
> learning children**
>
> *xx* **Child psychiatry; Handicapped children**

Mentally ill   616.8
> *See also* **Mentally handicapped; Mentally retarded**
> *x* Insane; Mentally deranged; Psychotics
> *xx* **Psychiatry**

Mentally ill—Institutional care   362.2
> *See also* **Psychiatric hospitals**
> *x* Asylums; Charitable institutions; Insane —Hospitals; Mental hospitals; Mental institutions
> *xx* **Institutional care**

Mentally ill children   155.4; 616.8
> *See also* **Mentally retarded children**
> *x* Emotionally disturbed children; Psychotic children
> *xx* **Child psychiatry**

Mentally retarded   157; 362.3
> *xx* **Mentally handicapped; Mentally ill**

Mentally retarded children   155.4
> *x* Children, Retarded; Retarded children
> *xx* **Child psychiatry; Mentally handicapped children; Mentally ill children; Slow learning children**

Menus   642
> *See also* **Caterers and catering; Dinners and dining; Luncheons**
> *x* Bills of fare; Gastronomy; Meal planning
> *xx* **Caterers and catering; Cookery; Diet; Dinners and dining**

Menus for space flight. *See* **Astronauts—Food**

Mercantile law. *See* **Commercial law**

Mercantile marine. *See* **Merchant marine**

Mercenary soldiers   355.3
> *xx* **Soldiers**

Merchandise. *See* **Commercial products**

Merchandising. *See* **Marketing; Retail trade**

Merchant marine (May subdiv. geog.)   **387.5**
> *See also* **Harbors; Insurance, Marine; Shipping**
> *x* Mercantile marine
> *xx* **Maritime law; Sailors; Shipping; Ships; Transportation**

Merchant marine—Law and legislation. *See* **Maritime law**

Merchant marine—U.S.   387.5
> *x* U.S.—Merchant marine

Merchants   920; 923
> *xx* **Business; Commerce**

Mercury   546
> *x* Quicksilver

Mercy killing. *See* **Euthanasia**

Mergers, Conglomerate. *See* **Conglomerate corporations**

Mergers, Industrial. *See* **Railroads—Consolidation; Trusts, Industrial**

Mermaids   398.2
> *xx* **Animals, Mythical**

Mesmerism. *See* **Hypnotism**

358

Messages to Congress. *See* **Presidents—U.S.—Messages**

Metabolism 574.1

See also **Nutrition**

xx **Biochemistry; Nutrition; Physiological chemistry**

Metal work. *See* **Metalwork**

Metallography 669

Use for materials on the science of metal structures and alloys, especially the study of such structures visually, with the microscope. Materials dealing with the science and art of extracting metals from their ores, refining and preparing them for use, are entered under **Metallurgy**

x Analysis, Microscopic; Micrographic analysis; Microscopic analysis

xx **Metals; Microscope and microscopy**

Metallurgy 669

See note under **Metallography**

See also **Alloys; Chemical engineering; Chemistry, Technical; Electrometallurgy; Metals; Smelting**

xx **Alloys; Chemical engineering; Ores; Smelting**

Metals 546; 549

See also **Alloys; Metallography; Mineralogy; Precious metals; Solder and soldering;** also names of metals, e.g. **Gold;** etc.

xx **Chemistry, Inorganic; Metallurgy; Ores**

Metals, Transmutation of. *See* **Transmutation (Chemistry);** and for early works on transmutation of metals, see **Alchemy**

Metalwork 671; 739

See also

Architectural metalwork	**Ironwork**
	Jewelry
Art metalwork	**Plate metalwork**
Bronzes	**Sheet metalwork**
Copperwork	**Silverwork**
Dies (Metalworking)	**Solder and soldering**
Electroplating	**Steel**
Founding	**Tinwork**
Goldwork	**Welding**

x Metal work

xx **Arts and crafts; Decoration and ornament; Founding; Ironwork**

Metalwork, Architectural. *See* **Architectural metalwork**

Metalwork, Art. *See* **Art metalwork**

Metalworking machinery 621.9

xx **Machinery**

Metamorphic rocks. *See* **Rocks**

Metaphysics 110

See also **Existentialism; God; Knowledge, Theory of; Universe**

xx **God; Philosophy**

359

Meteorites 523.5
  xx **Astronomy; Meteors**
Meteorological instruments 551.5
  See also names of meteorological instru-
    ments, e.g. **Barometer; Thermometers
    and thermometry;** etc.
  x Instruments, Meteorological
  xx **Scientific apparatus and instruments**
Meteorological observatories. *See* **Meteorol-
    ogy—Observatories**
Meteorological satellites 629.46
  See also names of satellites, e.g. **Tiros
    (Meteorological satellite);** etc.
  x Weather satellites
  xx **Artificial satellites**
Meteorology—551.5
  See note under **Climate**
  See also

Air	**Rain and rainfall**
Atmosphere	**Seasons**
Auroras	**Snow**
Climate	**Solar radiation**
Clouds	**Storms**
Cyclones	**Sunspots**
Droughts	**Thunderstorms**
Floods	**Tornadoes**
Fog	**Weather**
Frost	**Weather forecasting**
Hurricanes	**Weather lore**
Lightning	**Winds**

  xx **Atmosphere; Climate; Earth; Earth sci-
    ences; Geophysics; Physical geogra-
    phy; Rain and rainfall; Science;
    Storms; Weather**
Meteorology—Observatories 551.5028
  x Meteorological observatories; Observa-
    tories, Meteorological; Weather sta-
    tions
Meteorology—Tables, etc. 551.5021
Meteorology in aeronautics 629.132
  x Aeronautics, Meteorology in
  xx **Aeronautics; Weather forecasting**
Meteors 523.5
  See also **Meteorites**
  x Falling stars; Fire balls; Shooting stars;
    Stars, Falling
  xx **Astronomy; Solar system; Stars**
Meter. *See* **Musical meter and rhythm; Versi-
    fication**
Meters, Electric. *See* **Electric meters**
Method of study. *See* **Study, Method of**
Methodology. *See* special subjects with the
    subdivision *Methodology,* e.g. **Science
    —Methodology;** etc.
Metric system 389
  xx **Weights and measures**
Metrical romances. *See* **Romances**
Metrology. *See* **Measurement; Weights and
    measures**

Metropolitan areas 301.34
> *See also* **Cities and towns; Urban renewal;**
> also names of metropolitan areas,
> e.g. **Chicago metropolitan area;** etc.
>
> *x* Suburban areas; Urban areas

Metropolitan finance 336
> *xx* **Finance; Municipal finance**

Metropolitan government 352
> *See also* **Municipal government;** also
> names of metropolitan areas with the
> subdivision *Politics and government,*
> e.g. **Chicago metropolitan area—Poli-**
> **tics and government;** etc.
>
> *xx* **Local government; Municipal govern-**
> **ment**

Metropolitan planning. *See* **Regional planning**

Mexican Americans 301.45
> Use for materials on American citizens of
> Mexican descent. Materials on non-
> citizens from Mexico are entered un-
> der **Mexicans in the U.S.** Use these
> same patterns for other ethnic groups
> in the U.S. and other countries.
>
> *x* Chicanos
>
> *xx* **Ethnology—U.S.; Immigration and emi-**
> **gration; Minorities; U.S.—Foreign**
> **population; U.S.—Immigration and**
> **emigration**

Mexican literature 860
> May use same subdivisions and names of
> literary forms as for English literature

Mexican War, 1845–1848. *See* **U.S.—History**
—War with Mexico, 1845–1848

Mexicans in the U.S. 301.45
> See note under **Mexican Americans**
>
> *xx* **Aliens; Immigration and emigration;**
> **Minorities; U.S.—Foreign population;**
> **U.S.—Immigration and emigration**

Mexico—Presidents 920; 923
> *xx* **Presidents**

Mezzotint engraving 766
> *xx* **Engraving**

Mice 599; 636.08
> *x* Mouse

Microbes. *See* **Bacteriology; Germ theory of**
disease; Microorganisms; Viruses

Microbiology 576; 616.01
> *See also* **Bacteriology; Microorganisms;**
> **Microscope and microscopy;** also sub-
> jects with the subdivision *Microbiol-*
> *ogy,* e.g. **Air—Microbiology;** etc.
>
> *xx* **Biology; Microorganisms; Microscope**
> **and microscopy**

Microchemistry 544; 547
> *xx* **Chemistry; Microscope and microscopy**

Microcomputers 621.3819
> *xx* **Computers**

Microelectronics 621.381

 x Microminiature electronic equipment; Microminiaturization (Electronics)

 xx **Electronics; Semiconductors**

Microfilming. *See* **Microphotography**

Microfilms 686.4

 x Films

 xx **Microforms**

Microforms 686.4

 See also types of microforms, e.g. **Microfilms;** etc.

 x Micropublications

 xx **Microphotography**

Micrographic analysis. *See* **Metallography; Microscope and microscopy**

Microminiature electronic equipment. *See* **Microelectronics**

Microminiaturization (Electronics). *See* **Microelectronics**

Microorganisms 576; 616.01

 See also **Bacteriology; Microbiology; Microscope and microscopy; Protozoa; Viruses**

 x Germs; Microbes; Microscopic organisms

 xx **Bacteriology; Microbiology**

Microphotography 686.4

 Use for materials dealing with the photographing of objects of any size upon a microscopic or very small scale

 See also **Microforms**

 x Microfilming

 xx **Photography**

Micropublications. *See* **Microforms**

Microscope and microscopy 502.8; 535; 578

 See also **Electron microscope and microscopy; Metallography; Microbiology; Microchemistry**

 x Analysis, Microscopic; Micrographic analysis; Microscopic analysis

 xx **Microbiology; Microorganisms**

Microscopic analysis. *See* **Metallography; Microscope and microscopy**

Microscopic organisms. *See* **Microorganisms**

Microwave amplification by stimulated emission of radiation. *See* **Masers**

Microwave communication systems 621.381

 See also **Closed-circuit television**

 xx **Intercommunication** systems; **Radio, Short wave; Telecommunication; Television**

Microwave cookery. *See* **Cookery, Microwave**

Microwaves 537.5

 See also **Masers**

 xx **Electric waves; Electromagnetic waves; Radio, Short wave**

Middle age 301.43

 See also **Age and employment; Aging; Old age**

Middle age—_Continued_

  _x_ Age

  _xx_ **Life (Biology)**

Middle Ages 909.07

  See also **Architecture, Medieval; Art, Medieval; Chivalry; Church history—Mid-
  dle Ages, 600–1500; Civilization, Medieval; Knights and knighthood; Literature, Medieval; Philosophy, Medieval; Renaissance; Thirteenth century**

  _x_ Dark Ages

  _xx_ **Civilization,   Medieval;   Feudalism;
  Renaissance**

Middle Ages—History   909.07; 940.1

  See also **Civilization, Medieval; Crusades;
  Europe—History—476–1942;   Feudalism; Holy Roman Empire; Monasticism**

  _x_ History, Medieval; Medieval history

  _xx_ **Europe—History—476–1492;   History;
  World history**

Middle Atlantic States. _See_ **Atlantic States**

Middle classes   301.44; 323.3

  _x_ Bourgeoisie; Middle-income class

  _xx_ **Democracy; Labor and laboring classes;
  Social classes**

Middle East   915.6; 956

  See also **Arab countries; Israel**

  _x_ East (Near East); Levant; Near East;
  Orient

  _xx_ **Asia**

Middle-income class. _See_ **Middle classes**

Middle West   917.7; 977

  _x_ Central States; Midwest; North Central
  States

  _xx_ **Mississippi   Valley;   Northwest,   Old;
  United States**

Midgets. _See_ **Dwarfs**

Midwest. _See_ **Middle West**

Midwifery. _See_ **Childbirth**

Migrant labor   331.5-331.6

  Use for materials dealing with casual or
  seasonal workers who move from place
  to place in search of employment.
  Materials on the movement of population within a country for permanent
  settlements are entered under **Migration, Internal**

  _x_ Labor, Migratory; Migratory workers

  _xx_ **Agricultural laborers; Labor and laboring classes; Social problems; Unemployed**

Migration. _See_ **Immigration and emigration**

Migration, Internal   301.32

  See note under **Migrant labor**

  See also **Land settlement**

  _xx_ **Colonization; Land settlement; Population**

Migration of animals. _See_ **Animals—Migration**

Migration of birds. _See_ **Birds—Migration**

Migratory workers. *See* **Migrant labor**

Military aeronautics. *See* **Aeronautics, Military**

Military aid. *See* **Military assistance**

Military air bases. *See* **Air bases**

Military airplanes. *See* **Airplanes, Military**

Military art and science 355

> *See also*

Aeronautics, Military	**Industrial mobilization**
Armies	**Naval art and science**
Arms and armor	
Battles	**Ordnance**
Biological warfare	**Psychological warfare**
Camouflage (Military)	
Camps (Military)	**Signals and signaling**
Chemical warfare	**Soldiers**
Civil defense	**Spies**
Disarmament	**Strategy**
Drill and minor tactics	**Tactics**
Fortification	**Transportation, Military**
Guerrilla warfare	**War**
Hospitals, Military	

> *also* headings beginning with the word **Military**
>
> *x* Army; Fighting; Military power; Military science
>
> *xx* **Armies; Drill and minor tactics; Naval art and science; Soldiers; Strategy; War**

Military art and science—Study and teaching. *See* **Military education**

Military assistance (May subdiv. geog. adjective form) **355.03**

> *x* Arms aid; Military aid; Mutual defense assistance program

Military assistance, American 355.03

> *x* American military assistance

Military atrocities *See* names of wars with the subdivision *Atrocities*, e.g. **World War, 1939–1945–Atrocities;** and names of specific atrocities

Military biography. *See* names of armies and navies with the subdivision *Biography*, e.g. **U.S. Army–Biography; U.S. Navy –Biography;** etc.

Military camps. *See* **Camps (Military)**

Military costume. *See* **Uniforms, Military**

Military courts. *See* **Courts martial and courts of inquiry**

Military crimes. *See* **Military offenses**

Military desertion. *See* **Desertion, Military**

Military draft. *See* **Military service, Compulsory**

Military drill. *See* **Drill and minor tactics**

Military education 355.07

> *See also* **Military training camps;** also names of military schools, e.g. **United**

Military education—*Continued*
　　　States Military Academy, West Point;
　　　etc.
　　x Army schools; Education, Military; Military art and science—Study and teaching; Military schools; Military training; Schools, Military
　xx Education
Military engineering　623
　See also Fortification
　xx Civil engineering; Fortification
Military forces. *See* Armies; Navies; and names of countries with the subdivision *Armed Forces*, e.g. U.S.—Armed Forces; etc.
Military geography　355.4
　x Geography, Military; Maps, Military
Military history　355
　See also Battles; Military policy; Naval history; also names of countries with the subhead *Army* or the subdivision *History, Military* (e.g. U.S. Army; U.S.–History, Military; etc.); and names of wars, battles, sieges, etc.
　x History, Military; Wars
　xx History; Naval history
Military hospitals. *See* Hospitals, Military
Military hygiene　613.6
　See also Armies—Medical and sanitary affairs; Medicine, Military; also names of wars with the subdivision *Medical and sanitary affairs*, e.g. World War, 1939–1945—Medical and sanitary affairs; etc.
　x Hygiene, Military; Soldiers—Hygiene
　xx Armies—Medical and sanitary affairs; Hygiene; Medicine, Military; Sanitation
Military law　343.1
　See also Courts martial and courts of inquiry; Military offenses; Military service, Compulsory; Veterans—Law and legislation
　x Articles of war; Law, Military; War, Articles of
　xx Courts martial and courts of inquiry; International law; Law; War
Military life. *See* Soldiers; and names of countries with the subdivision *Army—Military life*, e.g. U.S. Army—Military life; etc.
Military medicine. *See* Medicine, Military
Military motorization. *See* Transportation, Military
Military music　785.1
　See also Band music; Marches (Music); also names of wars with the subdivision *Songs and music*, e.g. World War, 1939–1945—Songs and music; etc.

Military music—*Continued*
  x Music, Military
  xx **Music**
Military occupation   341.6; 355.4
  See also **World War, 1939–1945—Occupied territories;** also names of occupied countries with the subdivision—*History—German occupation, 1940–1945; History—Allied occupation, 1945– , e.g.* **Netherlands—History—German occupation, 1940–1945; Japan—History—Allied occupation, 1945–1952;** etc.
  x Occupation, Military; Occupied territory
Military offenses (May subdiv. geog.)   **355.1**
  See also names of military offenses, e.g. **Desertion, Military;** etc.
  x Crimes, Military; Military crimes; Naval offenses; Offenses, Military
  xx **Criminal law; Military law**
Military offenses—U.S.   355.1
  x U.S. Army—Crimes and misdemeanors; U.S.—Military offenses
Military pensions.   *See* **Pensions, Military**
Military policy   355.03
  See also **National security;** also names of countries with the subdivision *Military policy*, e.g. **U.S.—Military policy;** etc.
  x Defense policy
  xx **Military history; National security**
Military posts   355.7
  x Army posts
Military power.   *See* **Armies; Disarmament; Military art and science; Navies; Sea power**
Military schools.   *See* **Military education**
Military science.   *See* **Military art and science**
Military service, Compulsory   355.2
  x Compulsory military service; Conscription, Military; Draft, Military; Military draft; Military training, Universal; Selective service; Service, Compulsory military
  xx **Armies; Human resources; Military law**
Military service, Compulsory—Draft resisters   355.2
  See also **Conscientious objectors; Desertion, Military;** also names of wars with subdivision *Draft resisters*, e.g. **World War, 1939–1945—Draft resisters;** etc.
  x Draft dodgers; Draft evaders; Draft resisters
  xx **Conscientious objectors; Desertion, Military**
Military service, Voluntary   355.2
  x Volunteer army
  xx **Armies; Human resources**
Military signaling.   *See* **Signals and signaling**
Military strategy.   *See* **Strategy**

366

Military tactics. *See* **Tactics**

Military training. *See* **Military education**

Military training, Universal. *See* **Military service, Compulsory**

Military training camps 355.7

   x Students' military training camps; Training camp, Military

   xx **Military education**

Military transportation. *See* **Transportation, Military**

Military uniforms. *See* **Uniforms, Military**

Military vehicles. *See* **Vehicles, Military**

Militia. *See* names of countries and states with the subdivision *Militia,* e.g. **U.S.—Militia;** etc.

Milk   637; 641.3

   See also **Butter; Cheese**

   xx **Cows; Dairy products; Dairying**

Milk—Analysis 543

Milk, Dried   637

   x Dehydrated milk; Dried milk; Powdered milk

Milk supply 338.1

   xx **Food adulteration and inspection; Public health**

Mill and factory buildings. *See* **Factories**

Millennium 236

   See also **Second Advent**

   xx **Eschatology; Future life; Jesus Christ; Second Advent**

Millikan rays. *See* **Cosmic rays**

Millinery 646.5; 687

   See also **Hats**

   xx **Costume; Hats**

Milling (Flour). *See* **Flour mills**

Milling machines 621.9

   See also **Machine tools**

   xx **Machinery**

Millionaires 920; 923

   See also **Wealth**

   xx **Capitalists and financiers; Wealth**

Mills and millwork 621.7

   See also **Factories; Flour mills; Machinery**

   xx **Factories; Manufactures; Technology**

Mind. *See* **Intellect; Psychology**

Mind and body 150

   See also

Consciousness	**Phrenology**
Dreams	**Psychoanalysis**
Faith healing	**Psychology, Pathological**
Hypnotism	
Medicine, Psychosomatic	**Psychology, Physiological**
Mental healing	**Sleep**
Mental health	**Subconsciousness**
Mental suggestion	**Temperament**
Nervous system	
Personality disorders	

   x Body and mind; Mind cure

Mind and body—*Continued*
>*xx* Brain; Hypnotism; Medicine; Mental healing; Mental health; Philosophy; Phrenology; Psychical research; Psychoanalysis; Psychology, Physiological; Subconsciousness

Mind cure. *See* Christian Science; Faith healing; Mental healing; Mind and body

Mind reading 133.8
>*See also* Clairvoyance; Hypnotism; Thought transference
>
>*xx* Clairvoyance; Psychical research; Thought transference

Mine surveying 622
>*xx* Mining engineering; Prospecting; Surveying

Mineral industries. *See* Mines and mineral resources

Mineral lands. *See* Mines and mineral resources

Mineral resources. *See* Mines and mineral resources

Mineral resources, Marine. *See* Marine mineral resources

Mineralogy 549
>*See also* Gems; Petrology; Phosphorescence; Precious stones; also names of minerals, e.g. Quartz; etc.
>
>*x* Minerals
>
>*xx* Crystallography; Geology; Metals; Mines and mineral resources; Natural history; Ores; Petrology; Rocks; Science

Minerals. *See* Mineralogy; Mines and mineral resources; and names of minerals, e.g. Quartz; etc.

Miners 920; 926
>*See also* types of miners, e.g. Coal miners; etc.
>
>*x* Laborers
>
>*xx* Labor and laboring classes

Mines and mineral resources (May subdiv. geog.) 338.2; 622
>Use for general descriptive materials and for technical and economic materials on mining, metallurgy and minerals of economic value
>
>*See also* Marine mineral resources; Mineralogy; Mining engineering; Precious metals; Prospecting; also specific types of mines and mining, e.g. Coal mines and mining; etc.
>
>*x* Mineral industries; Mineral lands; Mineral resources; Minerals; Mining
>
>*xx* Geology, Economic; Natural resources; Ores; Raw materials

Mines and mineral resources—U.S. 338.2; 622
>*x* U.S.—Mines and mineral resources

Miniature gardens. *See* Gardens, Miniature

Miniature objects. *See* names of miniature objects, e.g. **Dollhouses; Gardens, Miniature; Models and model making; Toys;** etc. and names of objects with the subdivision *Models,* e.g. **Airplanes—Models;** etc.

Miniature painting 757
See also **Portrait painting**
x Miniatures (Portraits)
xx **Painting; Portrait painting**

Miniatures (Illumination of books and manuscripts). *See* **Illumination of books and manuscripts**

Miniatures (Portraits). *See* **Miniature painting**

Minicomputers 621.3819
xx **Computers**

Minimum wage. *See* Wages—Minimum wage

Mining. *See* **Mines and mineral resources; Mining engineering**

Mining, Electric. *See* **Electricity in mining**

Mining engineering 622
See also **Boring; Electricity in mining; Mine surveying**
x Mining
xx **Civil engineering; Coal mines and mining; Electricity in mining; Mines and mineral resources**

Ministers (Diplomatic agents). *See* **Diplomats**

Ministers of state. *See* **Cabinet officers**

Ministers of the gospel. *See* **Clergy**

Ministry (May subdiv. by religion or denomination) **253-254**
x Clergy—Office

Ministry, Christian 253-254
x Christian ministry

Minor tactics. *See* **Drill and minor tactics**

Minorites. *See* **Franciscans**

Minorities 301.45; 323.1
See also **Discrimination; Nationalism; Race relations; Segregation;** also names of peoples living within a country, state, or city dominated by another nationality (e.g. **Mexican Americans; Mexicans in the U.S.;** etc.); and names of countries with the subdivisions *Foreign population* and *Race relations,* e.g. **U.S.—Foreign population; U.S.—Race relations;** etc.
xx **Discrimination; Ethnic groups; Nationalism; Segregation**

Minstrels 920; 927
See also **Troubadours**
xx **Poets**

Minstrels, Black. *See* **Black minstrels**

Mints 332.4
See also **Coinage**
xx **Coinage; Money**

Miracle plays. *See* **Mysteries and miracle plays**

Miracles 231
　　See also **Supernatural**
　　x Divine healing
　　xx **Apparitions; Faith healing; Shrines; Supernatural**
Miracles (Christianity) 231
　　x Bible—Miracles
　　xx **Bible—Evidences, authority, etc.; Christianity; Church history**
Mirrors 748.2
　　x Looking glasses
　　xx **Furniture**
Miscarriage. *See* **Abortion**
Miscellanea. *See* subjects with the subdivision *Miscellanea,* e.g. **Medicine—Miscellanea;** etc.
Misconduct in office 351.9
　　See also **Corruption in politics; Police corruption;** also names of specific incidents, e.g. **Watergate Affair, 1972– ;** etc.
　　x Malfeasance in office; Official misconduct
　　xx **Conflict of interests; Corruption in politics; Criminal law**
Misdemeanors (Law). *See* **Criminal law**
Misleading advertising. *See* **Advertising, Fraudulent**
Missiles, Ballistic. *See* **Ballistic missiles**
Missiles, Guided. *See* **Guided missiles**
Missionaries, Christian 920; 922
　　xx **Missions, Christian**
Missions, Christian 266
　　See also **Evangelistic work; Missionaries, Christian; Salvation Army;** also names of churches, denominations, religious orders, etc. with the subdivision *Missions,* e.g. **Catholic Church—Missions;** etc.
　　x Christian missions; Foreign missions, Christian; Home missions, Christian
　　xx **Christianity; Church history; Church work; Evangelistic work**
Missions, Indian. *See* **Indians of North America—Missions, Christian**
Missions, Medical 266
　　x Medical missions
　　xx **Medicine**
Mississippi Valley 917.7; 977
　　See also **Middle West**
　　xx **United States**
Mississippi Valley—History 977
　　x New France—History
Mistakes. *See* **Errors**
Mixed marriage. *See* **Intermarriage**
Mnemonics. *See* **Memory**
Mobile home living 728
　　See also **Van life**
　　xx **Home economics**

Mobile home parks 647

    xx **Trailer parks**

Mobile homes 647

    x Homes, Mobile; House trailers; Motor homes; Trailers, Home

    xx **Housing; Travel trailers and campers**

Mobiles (Sculpture) 731

    xx **Kinetic sculpture; Sculpture**

Mobilization, Industrial. *See* **Industrial mobilization**

Mobs. *See* **Crowds; Riots**

Model airplanes; Model cars; etc. *See* **Airplanes—Models; Automobiles—Models; etc.**

Modeling 731.4; 738.1

    See also **Sculpture—Technique; Soap sculpture**

    x Clay modeling

    xx **Arts and crafts; Clay; Industrial arts education; Sculpture; Sculpture—Technique**

Models. *See* **Models and model making;** and names of objects with the subdivision *Models,* e.g. **Airplanes—Models;** etc.

Models, Fashion 659.1

    x Fashion models; Manikins (Fashion models); Mannequins; Style manikins

Models, Mathematical. *See* **Mathematical models**

Models, Mechanical. *See* **Machinery—Models**

Models and model making 688

    See also names of objects with the subdivision *Models,* e.g. **Airplanes—Models; Ships—Models;** etc.

    x Miniature objects; Models

Modern architecture. *See* **Architecture, Modern—20th century**

Modern art. *See* **Art, Modern**

Modern civilization. *See* **Civilization, Modern**

Modern dance 793.3

    x Interpretive dancing

    xx **Dancing**

Modern history. *See* **History, Modern**

Modern languages. *See* **Languages, Modern**

Modern painting. *See* **Painting, Modern**

Modern philosophy. *See* **Philosophy, Modern**

Modern sculpture. *See* **Sculpture, Modern**

Modernism 230

    Use for materials on the movement in the Protestant churches which applies modern critical methods to Biblical study and the history of dogma, and emphasizes the spiritual and ethical side of Christianity rather than historic dogmas and creeds

    See also **Fundamentalism**

    xx **Fundamentalism**

Mohammedan art. *See* **Art, Islamic**

Mohammedanism. *See* **Islam**

Mohammedans. *See* **Muslims**

Mold (Botany). *See* Molds **(Botany)**

Molding (Metal). *See* **Founding**

Molds (Botany) 589

  See also **Fungi**

  x Mold (Botany)

  xx **Fungi**

Molecular biochemistry. *See* **Molecular biology**

Molecular biology 574.8

  x Biology, Molecular; Molecular biochemistry; Molecular biophysics

  xx **Biochemistry; Biophysics**

Molecular biophysics. *See* **Molecular biology**

Molecular physiology. *See* **Biophysics**

Molecules 539; 541

  xx **Chemistry, Physical and theoretical**

Mollusks 594

  See also **Shells**

  xx **Invertebrates; Shellfish; Shells**

Monarchs. *See* **Kings and rulers; Queens**

Monarchy 321.6; 321.8

  See also **Democracy; Kings and rulers; Queens**

  x Sovereigns

  xx **Constitutional history; Constitutional law; Democracy; Executive power; Political science**

Monasteries 255; 271; 726

  See also **Abbeys; Convents; Monasticism**

  x Cloisters

  xx **Abbeys; Convents; Monasticism**

Monastic orders. *See* **Religious orders**

Monasticism 255; 271

  See also **Monasteries; Religious life; Religious orders**

  xx **Civilization, Medieval; Middle Ages—History; Monasteries**

Monetary policy (May subdiv. geog.) **332.4**

  See also **Finance; Fiscal policy; Gold; Inflation (Finance); Money; Silver**

  x Bimetallism; Currency devaluation; Devaluation of currency; Free coinage

  xx **Coinage; Finance; Fiscal policy; Inflation (Finance); Money**

Monetary policy—U.S. 332.4

  x U.S.—Monetary policy

Money 332.4-332.5

  Use for materials on currency as a medium of exchange or measure of value

  See also

Banks and banking	**Foreign exchange**
Capital	**Gold**
Coinage	**Mints**
Coins	**Monetary policy**
Counterfeits and counterfeiting	**Paper money**
	Silver
Credit	**Wealth**

  x Bullion; Currency; Specie; Standard of value

372

Money—*Continued*

    xx **Banks and banking; Coinage; Economics; Exchange; Finance; Gold; Monetary policy; Silver; Wealth**

Money, Paper. *See* **Paper money**

Money raising. *See* **Fund raising**

Monkeys 599

    xx **Animals; Primates**

Monkeys—Habits and behavior 599

    xx **Animals—Habits and behavior**

Monks 255; 271

    xx **Religious orders for men**

Monograms 745.6

    See also **Initials**

    x Ciphers (Lettering)

    xx **Alphabets; Initials; Lettering**

Monologues with music 808.5

    x Declamations, Musical; Recitations with music

Monoplanes. *See* **Airplanes**

Monopolies 338.8

    See also **Capitalism; Competition; Corporation law; Railroads—Consolidation; Trusts, Industrial**

    xx **Capital; Commerce; Competition; Economics; Trusts, Industrial**

Monorail railroads 385

    x Railroads, Single rail; Single rail railroads

    xx **Railroads**

Monroe Doctrine 327.73

    xx **International relations; Pan-Americanism; U.S.—Foreign relations**

Monsters 398; 616.07

    x Freaks; Monstrosities

Monstrosities. *See* **Monsters**

Montessori method of education 371.33; 372.1

    xx **Education, Elementary; Kindergarten; Teaching**

Monumental brasses. *See* **Brasses**

Monuments 725-726; 730

    See also **Obelisks; Pyramids; Tombs**

    x Statues

    xx **Architecture; Sculpture**

Monuments, Natural. *See* **Natural monuments**

Moon 523.3

    See also **Tides**

    xx **Astronomy; Solar system**

Moon—Eclipses. *See* **Eclipses, Lunar**

Moon—Exploration 629.45

    x Lunar exploration

    xx **Space flight to the moon**

Moon—Geology. *See* **Lunar geology**

Moon—Maps 523.3

Moon—Photographs 523.3

    xx **Lunar photography**

Moon—Photographs from space 523.3

    xx **Space photography**

Moon—Surface 523.3
See also **Lunar soil**
x Lunar surface
xx **Lunar soil**
Moon, Voyages to. See **Space flight to the moon**
Moon bases. See **Lunar bases**
Moon cars 629.2
x Lunar cars; Lunar rover vehicles; Lunar surface vehicles
Moon photography. See **Lunar photography**
Moon probes. See **Lunar probes**
Moon rocks. See **Lunar petrology**
Moon soil. See **Lunar soil**
Moorish art. See **Art, Islamic**
Moors 572.917; 909
xx **Arabs**
Moral and religious aspects. See subjects with the subdivision *Moral and religious aspects,* e.g. **Birth control—Moral and religious aspects;** etc.
Moral conditions 309.1
See also names of countries, cities, etc. with the subdivision *Moral conditions,* e.g. **U.S.—Moral conditions;** etc.
x Morals
xx **Social conditions**
Moral education. See **Character education**
Moral philosophy. See **Ethics**
Moral theology, Christian. See **Christian ethics**
Morale 152.4
See also **Psychological warfare;** also types of morale, e.g. **Employee morale;** etc.
xx **Courage**
Moralities. See **Morality plays**
Morality. See **Ethics**
Morality plays 808.2; 808.82; 812; 812.08; etc.
See also **Mysteries and miracle plays**
x Moralities
xx **Drama; English drama; Mysteries and miracle plays; Religious drama; Theater**
Morals. See **Ethics; Human behavior; Moral conditions**
Moravians 284
x United Brethren
Mormon Church. See **Church of Jesus Christ of Latter-Day Saints**
Mormons and Mormonism 289.3
See also **Church of Jesus Christ of Latter-Day Saints**
Morphology. See **Anatomy; Anatomy, Comparative; Biology; Botany—Anatomy**
Morse code. See **Cipher and telegraph codes**
Mortality 312; 614
See also **Death**
x Burial statistics; Death rate; Mortuary statistics
xx **Death; Population; Vital statistics**

Mortar 666; 691
xx **Adhesives; Plaster and plastering**
Mortgages 332.6-332.7
See also **Agricultural credit**
x Chattel mortgages
xx **Commercial law; Contracts; Invest-
ments; Real estate; Securities**
Morticians. *See* **Undertakers and undertaking**
Mortuary customs. *See* **Cremation; Funeral
rites and ceremonies**
Mortuary statistics. *See* **Mortality; Vital sta-
tistics**
Mosaics 729; 738.5; 748.5
See also **Mural painting and decoration**
xx **Art, Decorative; Arts and crafts;
Decoration and ornament; Mural
painting and decoration**
Moslem art. *See* **Art, Islamic**
Moslemism. *See* **Islam**
Moslems. *See* **Muslims**
Mosques 726
xx **Architecture; Architecture, Asian;
Church architecture; Islam; Temples**
Mosquitoes 595.7
x Diptera
xx **Insects as carriers of disease**
Mosquitoes—Control 595.7; 614.4
xx **Pests—Control**
Mosses 588
xx **Plants**
Motels. *See* **Hotels, motels, etc.**
Mothers 301.42
x Maternity
xx **Family; Women**
Mothers, Unmarried. *See* **Unmarried mothers**
Mothers' pensions 362.7
See also **Child welfare**
xx **Child welfare; Pensions**
Moths 595.7
See also **Butterflies; Caterpillars; Silk-
worms**
x Cocoons; Lepidoptera
xx **Butterflies; Insects**
Motion 531
See also **Force and energy; Kinematics;
Mechanical movements; Mechanics;
Speed**
x Kinetics
xx **Dynamics; Force and energy; Kine-
matics; Mechanics**
Motion picture cameras 778.5
x Movie cameras
xx **Cameras; Motion picture photography**
Motion picture cartoons 741.5; 791.43
x Animated cartoons
xx **Cartoons and caricatures**
Motion picture industry 338.4; 791.43
Motion picture photography 778.5
See also **Amateur motion pictures; Motion
picture cameras**

Motion picture photography—*Continued*
> *x* Cinematography; Photography—Motion pictures
> *xx* **Photography**

Motion picture plays 808.2; 808.82; 812; 812.08; etc.
> *x* Photoplays; Play production; Scenarios
> *xx* **Drama; Theater—Production and direction**

Motion picture plays—History and criticism 809.2
> *xx* **Dramatic criticism**

Motion picture plays—Technique 808.2
> *x* Motion pictures—Play writing; Play writing; Playwriting
> *xx* **Drama—Technique**

Motion picture projectors. *See* **Projectors**

Motion pictures 791.43
> *See also* **Experimental films; Sound—Recording and reproducing;** also subjects with the subdivision *Motion pictures,* e.g. **Sculpture—Motion pictures;** etc.
> *x* Cinema; Films; Moving pictures; Movies; Talking pictures
> *xx* **Amusements; Audio-visual materials; Mass media; Theater**

Motion pictures, Amateur. *See* **Amateur motion pictures**

Motion pictures—Biography 920; 927

Motion pictures—Catalogs 016.79143
> *x* Catalogs

Motion pictures—Censorship 791.43
> *xx* **Censorship**

Motion pictures, Documentary 791.43
> *x* Documentary films

Motion pictures, Experimental. *See* **Experimental films**

Motion pictures—Moral and religious aspects 791.43

Motion pictures—Play writing. *See* **Motion picture plays—Technique**

Motion pictures and children 649; 791.43
> Use for works dealing with the effect of motion pictures on children and youth
> Use same form for motion pictures and other subjects
> *See also* **Television and children**
> *x* Children and motion pictures
> *xx* **Children; Television and children**

Motion pictures and libraries. *See* **Libraries and motion pictures**

Motion pictures in education 371.33; 791.43
> Use same form for motion pictures in other subjects
> *See also* **Libraries and motion pictures**
> *x* Educational films
> *xx* **Audio-visual education; Teaching—Aids and devices**

Motion study 658.5

>See also Time study
>
>*xx* Efficiency, Industrial; Factory management; Job analysis; Personnel management; Time study

Motivation (Psychology) 152.5

>*xx* Psychology

Motor boats. *See* Motorboats

Motor buses. *See* Buses

Motor cars. *See* Automobiles

Motor coordination. *See* Creative movement

Motor courts. *See* Hotels, motels, etc.

Motor cycles. *See* Motorcycles

Motor homes. *See* Mobile homes

Motor trucks. *See* Trucks

Motorboat racing. *See* Boat racing

Motorboats 623.82

>*x* Motor boats; Outboard motorboats; Power boats
>
>*xx* Boats and boating

Motorboats—Models 623.82

>*xx* Machinery—Models

Motorcycles 629.22

>*See also* specific makes and models of motorcycles
>
>*x* Cycles, Motor; Cycling; Motor cycles; Motorcycling
>
>*xx* Bicycles and bicycling

Motorcycling. *See* Motorcycles

Motoring. *See* Automobiles—Touring

Motorization, Military. *See* Transportation, Military

Motors. *See* Electric motors; Engines

Motorways. *See* Express highways

Mottoes 808.88; 818; etc.

>*x* Emblems
>
>*xx* Heraldry

Moulding (Metal). *See* Founding

Mounds and mound builders 917; 970.4

>*See also* Excavations (Archeology)
>
>*x* Barrows; Burial; Graves
>
>*xx* Archeology; Cliff dwellers and cliff dwellings; Excavations (Archeology); Indians of North America; Indians of North America—Antiquities; Tombs

Mountain climbing. *See* Mountaineering

Mountain plants. *See* Alpine plants

Mountaineering 796.5

>*x* Mountain climbing; Rock climbing
>
>*xx* Mountains; Outdoor life

Mountains 551.4

>Names of mountain ranges and mountains are not included in this list but are to be added as needed, e.g. **Rocky Mountains; Elk Mountain, Wyo.;** etc.
>
>*See also* **Mountaineering; Volcanoes;** also names of mountain ranges (e.g. **Rocky Mountains;** etc.); and names

377

Mountains—*Continued*

of mountains, e.g. **Elk Mountain, Wyo.;** etc.

xx **Geology; Physical geography**

Mourning customs. *See* **Funeral rites and ceremonies**

Mouse. *See* **Mice**

Movement, Freedom of. *See* **Freedom of movement**

Movement education. *See* **Creative movement**

Movements of animals. *See* **Animal locomotion**

Movie cameras. *See* **Motion picture cameras**

Movies. *See* **Motion pictures**

Moving, Household 643

x Household moving

Moving pictures. *See* **Motion pictures**

Muhammedanism. *See* **Islam**

Muhammedans. *See* **Muslims**

Multi-age grouping. *See* **Nongraded schools**

Multi-media centers. *See* **Instructional materials center**

Multi-media materials. *See* **Audio-visual materials**

Multicultural education. *See* **Intercultural education**

Multinational corporations. *See* **International business enterprises**

Multiple birth. *See* **Birth, Multiple**

Mummies 393

x Burial

xx **Archeology**

Municipal administration. *See* **Municipal government**

Municipal art. *See* **Art, Municipal**

Municipal employees. *See* **Civil service; Municipal government;** and names of cities with the subdivision *Officials and employees,* e.g. **Chicago—Officials and employees;** etc.

Municipal engineering 628

See also **Drainage; Refuse and refuse disposal; Sanitary engineering; Sewerage; Street cleaning; Water supply**

xx **Public works; Sanitary engineering**

Municipal finance 352

See also **Metropolitan finance**

x Finance, Municipal

xx **Finance; Municipal government**

Municipal government (May subdiv. geog.) **352**

Use for materials on the government of cities in general and, when subdivided by country, for general consideration of municipal government of countries, or regions. Materials on the government of individual cities, towns, or areas are entered under the name of city, town, or area with the subdivision *Politics and government*

378

Municipal government—*Continued*

> *See also* **Cities and towns; Metropolitan government; Municipal finance; Public administration;** also names of cities with the subdivision *Politics and government,* e.g. **Chicago—Politics and government;** etc.
>
> *x* City government; Government, Municipal; Municipal administration; Municipal employees; Municipalities
>
> *xx* **Local government; Metropolitan government; Political science**

Municipal government—U.S. 352

> *x* U.S.—Municipal government

Municipal government by city manager 352

> *x* City manager; Commission government with city manager

Municipal government by commission 352

> *x* Commission government; Government by commission

Municipal improvements. *See* **Art, Municipal; Cities and towns—Civic improvement;** and names of cities with the subdivision *Public works,* e.g. **Chicago—Public works;** etc.

Municipal ownership 338.9; 352

> *x* Public ownership
>
> *xx* **Corporations; Economic policy; Government ownership**

Municipal planning. *See* **City planning**

Municipal transit. *See* **Local transit**

Municipalities. *See* **Cities and towns; Municipal government**

Munitions 338.4; 623.4

> *x* Armaments
>
> *xx* **Industrial mobilization; International relations; War; War—Economic aspects**

Mural painting and decoration 729; 751.7

> *See also* **Cave drawings; Mosaics**
>
> *x* Fresco painting; Wall decoration; Wall painting
>
> *xx* **Art, Decorative; Arts and crafts; Interior decoration; Mosaics; Painting; Walls**

Murder 364.1

> *See also* **Assassination; Capital punishment**
>
> *x* Manslaughter
>
> *xx* **Assassination; Crime; Criminal law; Medical jurisprudence; Offenses against the person**

Muscles 611; 612

> *xx* **Physiology**

Museums 069

> *See also* **Art—Galleries and museums;** also names of countries, cities, etc. with the subdivision *Galleries and museums* (e.g. **U.S.—Galleries and museums;** etc.); and names of galleries and museums

379

Museums and schools 069; 371.074
    x Schools and museums
    xx **Schools**
Mushrooms 589
    See also **Fungi**
    x Toadstools
    xx **Fungi**
Music (May subdiv. geog. adjective form, e.g. **Music, American**; etc.) **780**
    All types of music are not included in this list. Add as needed for vocal or instrumental, classical or popular, solo or group music
    See also

Chamber music	**Jazz music**
Church music	**Military music**
Composition (Music)	**Musicians**
Concerts	**Orchestral music**
Dance music	**Organ music**
Electronic music	**Piano music**
Folk music	**Radio and music**
Harmony	**Romanticism**
Instrumental music	**Sound**
Instrumentation and orchestration	**Vocal music**

    also subjects with the subdivision *Songs and music*, e.g. **Aeronautics—Songs and music; Cowhands—Songs and music;** etc.; and headings beginning with the words **Music** and **Musical**
    xx **Humanities**
Music—Acoustics and physics 781
    See also **Sound**
    x Acoustics
    xx **Music—Theory; Physics; Sound**
Music, American 780
    See also **Black songs; Spirituals (Songs)**
    x American music; U.S.—Music
Music—Analysis, appreciation 780.1
    x Appreciation of music; Music—Appreciation; Music appreciation; Musical appreciation
Music—Anecdotes, facetiae, satire, etc. 780.2
    xx **Anecdotes; Wit and humor**
Music—Appreciation. *See* **Music—Analysis, appreciation**
Music, Black. *See* **Black music**
Music—Cataloging. *See* **Cataloging—Music**
Music, Choral. *See* **Choral music**
Music—Composition. *See* **Composition (Music)**
Music—Discography 789.9
    x Discography
Music, Dramatic. *See* **Opera; Operetta**
Music, Electronic. *See* **Electronic music**
Music—Examinations, questions, etc. 780.7
    xx **Examinations; Questions and answers**

Music—History and criticism 780.9
　　x Musical criticism
　　xx **Criticism; History**
Music, Indian *See* **Indians of North America—Music**
Music, Influence of. *See* **Music—Psychology**
Music—Instruction and study. *See* **Music—Study and teaching**
Music, Instrumental. *See* **Instrumental music**
Music, Military. *See* **Military music**
Music—Notation. *See* **Musical notation**
Music, Popular (Songs, etc.) 784
　　See also names of types of popular music, e.g. **Blues (Songs, etc.); Rock music;** etc.
　　x Popular music; Popular songs; Songs, Popular
　　xx **Dance music; Songs**
Music, Popular (Songs, etc.)—Writing and publishing 781
　　x Song writing
　　xx **Composition (Music)**
Music—Psychology 781.7
　　x Music, Influence of; Psychology of music
　　xx **Psychology**
Music, Rock. *See* **Rock music**
Music, Sacred. *See* **Church music**
Music—Study and teaching 780.7
　　See also **Composition (Music); Conducting; Harmony; Musical form**
　　x Education, Musical; Music—Instruction and study; Musical education; Musical instruction; School music
Music—Theory 781
　　See also **Composition (Music); Counterpoint; Fugue; Harmony; Music—Acoustics and physics; Musical form; Musical meter and rhythm**
Music, Vocal. *See* **Vocal music**
Music and literature 780.2
　　x Music and poetry; Poetry and music
　　xx **Literature**
Music and poetry. *See* **Music and literature**
Music and radio. *See* **Radio and music**
Music appreciation. *See* **Music—Analysis, appreciation**
Music box 789.8
　　xx **Musical instruments, Mechanical**
Music conductors. *See* **Conductors (Music)**
Music festivals 780.73
　　x Musical festivals
　　xx **Concerts; Festivals**
Music libraries 026
　　x Libraries, Music
　　xx **Libraries; Libraries, Special**
Musical ability 780.7
　　x Musical talent; Talent
　　xx **Ability**

Musical accompaniment 781.6

   x Accompaniment, Musical

  xx **Composition (Music)**

Musical appreciation. *See* **Music—Analysis, appreciation**

Musical comedies. *See* **Musical revues, comedies, etc.**

Musical composition. *See* **Composition (Music)**

Musical criticism. *See* **Music—History and criticism**

Musical education. *See* **Music—Study and teaching**

Musical festivals. *See* **Music festivals**

Musical form 781.5

   See also names of specific types of musical forms, e.g. **Concerto; Fugue; Opera; Operetta; Sonata; Symphony;** etc. Add names of musical forms as needed for the music itself, e.g. **Concertos; Suites;** etc.

   x Form, Musical

  xx **Music—Study and teaching; Music—Theory**

Musical instruction. *See* **Music—Study and teaching**

Musical instruments 781.9

   See also **Instrumental music; Instrumentation and orchestration; Orchestra; Tuning;** also groups of instruments, e.g. **Percussion instruments; Stringed instruments; Wind instruments;** etc.; also names of specific musical instruments, e.g. **Drum; Organ;** etc.

   x Instruments, Musical

  xx **Instrumental music; Instrumentation and orchestration**

Musical instruments, Electronic 789.9

   x Electronic musical instruments

Musical instruments, Mechanical 789.7-789.9

   See also names of instruments, e.g. **Music box;** etc.

   x Mechanical musical instruments

Musical meter and rhythm 781

   x Meter

  xx **Music—Theory; Rhythm**

Musical notation 781

   x Music—Notation; Notation, Musical

Musical revues, comedies, etc. 782.8

   x Musical comedies; Musicals

  xx **Operas; Operetta**

Musical talent. *See* **Musical ability**

Musicals. *See* **Musical revues, comedies, etc.**

Musicians (May subdiv. geog. adjective form, e.g. **Musicians, American;** etc.) **920; 927**

   See also types of musicians, e.g. **Composers; Conductors (Music); Organists; Pianists; Singers; Violinists, violoncellists, etc.;** etc. also names of musicians

  xx **Music**

Musicians, American 920; 927
   x American musicians; U.S.—Musicians
Musicians—Biography 920; 927
   xx Biography
Musicians, Black. *See* Black musicians
Musicians—Portraits 780.2
   xx Portraits
Muslimism. *See* Islam
Muslims 297
   x Mohammedans; Moslems; Muhamme-
      dans; Mussulmans
Muslims, Black. *See* Black Muslims
Mussulmans. *See* Muslims
Mutation (Biology). *See* Evolution; Variation
      (Biology)
Mutual defense assistance program. *See* Mili-
      tary assistance
Mutual funds. *See* Investment trusts
Mycology. *See* Fungi
Mysteries and miracle plays 808.2; 808.82;
      812; etc.
   See also Morality plays
   x Bible plays; Miracle plays
   xx Bible—Drama; Drama; English drama;
      Morality plays; Pageants; Passion
      plays; Religious drama; Theater
Mystery and detective stories 808.83; 813; Fic
      May be used for single novels as well as
      for collections of stories
   x Detective stories; Stories
   xx Fiction
Mysticism 149; 248
   See also Religious art and symbolism; Spir-
      itual life
   xx Philosophy; Religion; Theology
Mythical animals. *See* Animals, Mythical
Mythology (May use ethnic or geog. subdiv. ad-
      jective form, e.g. Mythology, Celtic;
      etc.) 200.4; 291
   See also

Animals, Mythical	Indians of North
Art and mythology	America—Reli-
Folklore	gion
Gods	Symbolism
Heroes and	Totems and totem-
heroines	ism

   x Myths
   xx Creation; Folklore; God; Gods; Heroes
      and heroines; Legends; Religion; Re-
      ligions
Mythology, Classical 292
   x Classical mythology; Greek mythology;
      Roman mythology
   xx Classical antiquities
Mythology, Indian. *See* Indians of North
      America—Religion
Mythology in art. *See* Art and mythology
Myths. *See* Mythology
NATO. *See* North Atlantic Treaty Organiza-
      tion

Names 929.4

See also types of names, e.g. **Code names; Names, Geographical; Names, Personal; Pseudonyms;** etc.

x Epithets; Nomenclature; Proper names; Terminology

Names, Fictitious. *See* **Pseudonyms**

Names, Geographical (May subdiv. geog.) **910**

See also **Gazetteers**

x Geographical names; Place names

xx **Gazetteers; Names**

Names, Geographical—U.S. 917.3

x U.S.—Geographical names; U.S. Names, Geographical

Names, Personal 929.4

May be subdivided by nationality or by country, e.g. **Names, Personal—Scottish; Names, Personal—U.S.;** etc.

See also **Nicknames; Pseudonyms**

x Christian names; Family names; Forenames; Personal names; Surnames

xx **Names**

Names, Personal—U.S. 929.4

x American names; U.S.—Names, Personal; U.S.—Personal names

Names—Pronunciation 421

x Pronunciation

Napoléon I, Emperor of the French—Drama 812; 822; etc.

xx **Drama**

Napoléon I, Emperor of the French—Fiction 813; 823; etc.

xx **Fiction; Historical fiction**

Napoleonic Wars. *See* **Europe—History—1789–1900; France—History—Revolution, 1789–1799**

Narcotic addicts 613.8; 616.8

x Drug addicts

xx **Narcotic habit; Narcotics and crime**

Narcotic habit 362.2; 613.8; 616.8

See note under **Drug abuse**

See also **Narcotic addicts; Narcotics and youth**

x Drug addiction; Drug habit; Intoxication

xx **Drug abuse; Temperance**

Narcotic traffic 364.1

x Drug pushers; Drug traffic

Narcotics 615

See also **Stimulants;** and names of specific narcotics, e.g. **Opium;** etc.

x Hard drugs; Opiates; Soporifics

xx **Drugs; Hygiene; Insomnia; Materia medica; Stimulants; Therapeutics**

Narcotics and crime 364.1

See also **Narcotic addicts**

x Crime and narcotics

Narcotics and youth 362.2; 613.8; 616.8

See also **Drugs and youth**

x Youth and narcotics

xx **Juvenile delinquency; Narcotic habit**

Nation of Islam. *See* **Black Muslims**

National anthems. *See* **National songs**

National characteristics (May subdiv. geog. adjective form, e.g. **National characteristics, French;** etc.)

   See also **Ethnopsychology**

   x Characteristics, National; Images, National; National images; National psychology; Psychology, National

   xx **Anthropology; Ethnopsychology; Nationalism; Social psychology**

National characteristics, American 155.8; 917.3

   x American characteristics; American national characteristics; U.S.—National characteristics

National consciousness. *See* **Nationalism**

National dances. *See* **Folk dancing**

National debts. *See* **Debts, Public**

National defenses. *See* **Industrial mobilization;** and names of countries with the subdivision *Defenses*, e.g. **U.S.—Defenses;** etc.

National forests. *See* **Forest reserves**

National Guard (U.S.) *See* **U.S.—National Guard**

National health service. *See* **Medicine, State**

National holidays. *See* **Holidays;** and names of national holidays, e.g. **Memorial Day;** etc.

National hymns. *See* **National songs**

National images. *See* **National characteristics**

National liberation movements 320.5

   xx **Colonies; Guerrillas; Nationalism**

National monuments. *See* **National parks and reserves; Natural monuments**

National parks and reserves (May subdiv. geog.) **719; 910**

   See also **Forest reserves; Natural monuments; Wilderness areas;** also names of national parks, e.g. **Yellowstone National Park;** etc.

   x National monuments; Public lands

   xx **Forest reserves; Parks; Wildlife—Conservation**

National parks and reserves—U.S. 917.3

   x U.S.—National parks and reserves

National planning. *See* **Economic policy; Social policy;** and names of countries with the subdivision *Economic policy; Social policy;* e.g. **U.S.—Economic policy; U.S.—Social policy;** etc.

National psychology. *See* **Ethnopsychology; National characteristics**

National resources. *See* **Natural resources;** and names of countries with the subdivision *Economic conditions*, e.g. **U.S.—Economic conditions;** etc.

National security 350; 355

> *See also* **Economic policy; International re-
> lations; Military policy;** also names of
> countries with the subdivision *National
> security*, e.g. **U.S.—National security;**
> etc.
>
> *xx* **Economic policy; International relations;
> Military policy**

National socialism 320.5; 321.9; 335.6

> *See also* **Fascism; Socialism**
>
> *x* Fascism—Germany; Nazi movement
>
> *xx* **Fascism; Socialism; Totalitarianism**

National songs (May subdiv. geog. adjective
form, e.g. **National songs, German;**
etc.) 784.7

> *See also* **Folk songs; Patriotic poetry; War
> songs**
>
> *x* National anthems; National hymns; Pa-
> triotic songs; Songs, National
>
> *xx* **Folk songs; Songs**

National songs, American 784.7

> *x* American national songs; U.S.—Na-
> tional songs
>
> *xx* **Songs, American**

Nationalism 320.5

> *See also* **Minorities; National characteris-
> tics; National liberation movements;
> Patriotism**
>
> *x* Internationalism; National consciousness;
> Regionalism
>
> *xx* **International relations; Minorities; Pa-
> triotism; Political science**

Nationalism, Black. *See* **Black nationalism**

Nationalist China. *See* **Taiwan**

Nationality (Citizenship). *See* **Citizenship**

Nationalization. *See* **Government ownership**

Nationalization of railroads. *See* **Railroads and
state**

Nations, Law of. *See* **International law**

Native Americans. *See* **Indians of North
America**

Native peoples. *See* **Ethnology;** and names of
peoples, e.g. **Africans; Indians of
North America;** etc.

Nativity of Christ. *See* **Jesus Christ—Nativity**

Natural beauty conservation. *See* **Landscape
protection**

Natural Bridge, Va. 917.55

> *xx* **Natural monuments**

Natural childbirth 618.2

> *x* Lamaze method of childbirth
>
> *xx* **Childbirth**

Natural disasters (May subdiv. geog.) 904

> *See also* names of natural disasters, e.g.
> **Earthquakes; Floods;** etc.; and names
> of specific natural disasters, e.g. **New
> England—Hurricane, 1938;** etc.
>
> *xx* **Disasters**

Natural disasters—U.S. 904

> *x* U.S.—Natural disasters

Natural food. *See* **Food, Natural**

Natural gas. *See* **Gas, Natural**

Natural history (May subdiv. geog.) **500.9**

> Use for popular materials describing animals, plants, minerals and nature in general. Guides on the detailed study of birds, flowers, etc. are entered under **Nature study**

> *See also*

Aquariums	**Geology**
Biology	**Marine biology**
Botany	**Mineralogy**
Fossils	**Plant lore**
Fresh water biology	**Zoology**
Geographical distribution of animals and plants	

> *x* Animal lore; History, Natural
> *xx* **Animals; Biology; Science; Zoology**

Natural history, Biblical. *See* **Bible—Natural history**

Natural history—Outdoor guides. *See* **Nature study**

Natural history—U.S. 500.9

> *x* U.S.—Natural history

Natural law. *See* **Civil rights; Ethics; Freedom; International law**

Natural monuments (May subdiv. geog.) **719; 910**

> Use for general materials on natural objects of historic or scientific interest such as caves, cliffs, natural bridges, and for those created as national monuments by presidential proclamation

> *See also* **Wilderness areas;** also names of natural monuments, e.g. **Natural Bridge, Va.;** etc.

> *x* Landmarks, Preservation of; Monuments, Natural; National monuments; Preservation of natural scenery; Protection of natural scenery
> *xx* **Landscape protection; National parks and reserves; Nature conservation**

Natural monuments—U.S. 917.3

> *x* U.S.—Natural monuments

Natural religion. *See* **Natural theology**

Natural resources (May subdiv. geog.) **333**

> *See also* **Conservation of natural resources; Fisheries; Reclamation of land; Soil conservation;** also names of natural resources, e.g. **Forests and forestry; Marine resources; Mines and mineral resources; Power resources;** etc.

> *x* National resources; Resources, Natural
> *xx* **Economic conditions; Environmental policy; Wildlife—Conservation**

Natural resources—U.S. 333
See also **U.S.—Economic conditions**
x U.S.—Natural resources
Natural selection 575.01
See also **Evolution; Heredity**
x Selection, Natural; Survival of the fittest
xx **Evolution; Genetics; Heredity; Variation (Biology)**
Natural theology 210
Use for materials that treat of the knowledge of God's existence obtained by observing the visible processes of nature
See also **Creation; Religion and science**
x Natural religion; Theology, Natural
xx **Apologetics; God; Religion; Religion and science; Theology**
Naturalism in literature. See **Realism in literature**
Naturalists 920; 925
See also names of types of naturalists, e.g. **Biologists; Botanists;** etc.
xx **Scientists**
Naturalization 323.6
See also **Aliens; Citizenship**
x Foreigners
xx **Aliens; Americanization; Citizenship; Immigration and emigration; International law; Suffrage**
Nature, Effect of man on. See **Man—Influence on nature**
Nature conservation 333.7
See also **Landscape protection; Natural monuments; Wildlife—Conservation**
x Conservation of nature; Nature protection; Preservation of natural scenery; Protection of natural scenery
xx **Conservation of natural resources**
Nature in literature
See also **Animals in literature; Birds in literature; Nature in poetry**
Nature in ornament. See **Design, Decorative**
Nature in poetry 809.1
x Nature poetry; Poetry of nature
xx **Nature in literature; Poetry**
Nature photography 778.9
See also **Photography of animals; Photography of birds; Photography of fishes; Photography of plants;** and similar headings
x Photography of nature
xx **Nature study; Photography**
Nature poetry. See **Nature in poetry**
Nature protection. See **Nature conservation**
Nature study (May subdiv. geog.) 372.3; 500.907
See note under **Natural history**
See also **Animals—Habits and behavior; Botany; Nature photography; Zoology**
x Natural history—Outdoor guides

Nature study—*Continued*
> *xx* **Animals–Habits and behavior; Outdoor life; Science–Study and teaching**

Nature study–U.S.   500.973
> *x* U.S.—Nature study

Nautical almanacs   528
> *x* Ephemerides
> *xx* **Almanacs; Navigation**

Nautical astronomy   527
> *See also* **Latitude; Longitude; Navigation**
> *x* Astronomy, Nautical
> *xx* **Astronomy; Navigation**

Naval Academy, Annapolis.   *See* **United States Naval Academy, Annapolis**

Naval administration.   *See* **Naval art and science;** and names of countries with the subhead *Navy*, e.g. **U.S. Navy;** etc.

Naval aeronautics.   *See* **Aeronautics, Military**

Naval air bases.   *See* **Air bases**

Naval airplanes.   *See* **Airplanes, Military**

Naval architecture   623.8
> *See also* **Boatbuilding; Marine engineering; Shipbuilding; Ships; Steamboats; Warships**
> *x* Architecture, Naval; Marine architecture
> *xx* **Architecture; Shipbuilding**

Naval art and science   359
> *See also*

Camouflage (Military)	**Sailors**
	Seapower
Marine engineering	**Shipbuilding**
Military art and science	**Signals and signaling**
Navies	**Strategy**
Navigation	**Submarine warfare**
Navy yards and naval stations	**Submarines**
	Torpedoes
Privateering	**Warships**

> *x* Fighting; Naval administration; Naval science; Naval warfare; Navy
> *xx* **Military art and science; Navies; Navigation; Strategy; War**

Naval art and science—Study and teaching.   *See* **Naval education**

Naval bases.   *See* **Navy yards and naval stations**

Naval battles   359.4; 904
> *See also* **Battles; Naval history;** also names of countries with the subdivision *History, Naval,* e.g. **U.S.—History, Naval;** etc.; and names of naval battles
> *x* Naval warfare
> *xx* **Battles; Sea power**

Naval biography.   *See* names of navies with the subdivision *Biography,* e.g. **U.S. Navy —Biography;** etc.

Naval education   359.07
> *See also* **United States Naval Academy, Annapolis**

Naval education—*Continued*

    x Education, Naval; Naval art and science
        —Study and teaching; Naval schools
    xx **Education**

Naval engineering. *See* **Marine engineering**

Naval history   359.09

    See also **Military history; Pirates; Privateering; Sea power;** also names of countries with the subhead *Navy* or the subdivision *History, Naval*, e.g. **U.S. Navy; U.S.–History, Naval;** etc.

    x History, Naval; Wars

    xx **History; Military history; Naval battles; Sea power**

Naval law. *See* **Maritime law**

Naval offenses. *See* **Military offenses**

Naval pensions. *See* **Pensions, Military**

Naval personnel. *See* **Sailors**

Naval power. *See* **Sea power**

Naval schools. *See* **Naval education**

Naval science. *See* **Naval art and science**

Naval shipyards. *See* **Navy yards and naval stations**

Naval signaling. *See* **Signals and signaling**

Naval strategy. *See* **Strategy**

Naval uniforms. *See* **Uniforms, Military**

Naval warfare. *See* **Naval art and science; Naval battles; Submarine warfare**

Navies   359.3

    See also **Armies; Disarmament; Naval art and science; Sea power; Warships;** also names of countries with the subhead *Navy*, e.g. **U.S. Navy;** etc.

    x Armaments; Armed forces; Military forces; Military power; Navy

    xx **Armies; Naval art and science; Sea power; Ships; War; Warships**

Navigation   527; 623.89

    See also

Compass	**Pilot guides**
Harbors	**Pilots and pilotage**
Inland navigation	**Radar**
Knots and splices	**Sailing**
Lighthouses	**Shipwrecks**
Loran	**Signals and signaling**
Nautical almanacs	
Nautical astronomy	**Steam navigation**
Naval art and science	**Tides**
	Winds

    x Locomotion; Seamanship

    xx **Nautical astronomy; Naval art and science; Oceanography; Pilots and pilotage; Sailing; Ships; Steam navigation**

Navigation (Aeronautics)   629.132

    See also **Airplanes–Piloting; Radio in aeronautics**

    x Aerial navigation; Aeronautics—Navigation; Air navigation; Navigation, Aerial

    xx **Aeronautics**

Navigation (Astronautics) 629.45
　　See also **Astronautical instruments; Space flight; Space vehicles—Piloting**
　　x Astronavigation; Space navigation
　　xx **Astrodynamics; Astronautics; Space flight**
Navigation, Aerial. *See* **Navigation (Aeronautics)**
Navigation, Inland. *See* **Inland navigation**
Navigation—Law and legislation. *See* **Maritime law**
Navigation, Steam. *See* **Steam navigation**
Navigators. *See* **Discoveries (in geography); Explorers; Sailors**
Navy. *See* **Naval art and science; Navies; Sea power;** and names of countries with the subhead *Navy,* e.g. **U.S. Navy;** etc.
Navy Sealab project. *See* **Sealab project**
Navy yards and naval stations 359.7
　　x Naval bases; Naval shipyards
　　xx **Naval art and science**
Nazi movement. *See* **National socialism**
Near East. *See* **Middle East**
Nebulae, Extragalactic. *See* **Galaxies**
Necrologies. *See* **Obituaries**
Necromancy. *See* **Divination; Witchcraft**
Needlepoint 746.2
　　x Canvas embroidery
　　xx **Embroidery; Needlework**
Needlework 746.4
　　See also types of needlework; e.g. **Dressmaking; Embroidery; Lace and lace making; Needlepoint; Sewing; Tapestry;** etc.
　　xx **Art, Decorative; Arts and crafts; Dressmaking; Sewing**
Negotiable instruments 332.4; 332.7
　　See also **Bonds**
　　x Bills and notes; Bills of credit; Commercial paper; Instruments, Negotiable; Letters of credit
　　xx **Banks and banking; Commercial law; Contracts; Credit**
Negritude. *See* **Blacks—Race identity**
Negroes. *See* **Blacks**
Neighborhood. *See* **Community life;** and other headings beginning with the word **Community**
Neighborhood centers. *See* **Social settlements**
Neighborhood schools. *See* **Schools**
Neo-Greek literature. *See* **Greek literature, Modern**
Neo-impressionism (Art). *See* **Impressionism (Art)**
Neo-Latin languages. *See* **Romance languages**
Neolithic period. *See* **Stone age**
Neon tubes 621.32
　　xx **Electric signs**
Nero, Emperor of Rome 92
　　xx **Roman emperors**

Nerves 611; 612
> *See also* Nervous system
> *xx* Nervous system

Nerves—Diseases. *See* **Nervous system—Diseases**

Nervous exhaustion. *See* **Neurasthenia**

Nervous prostration. *See* **Neurasthenia**

Nervous system 611; 612
> *See also* Brain; Nerves; Psychology, Pathological; Psychology, Physiological
> *x* Neurology
> *xx* Anatomy; Brain; Mind and body; Nerves; Physiology

Nervous system—Diseases 616.8
> *See also* Epilepsy; Fear; Neurasthenia; Worry
> *x* Nerves—Diseases; Neuropathology
> *xx* Medicine—Practice; Therapeutics

Nervous system—Hygiene 613
> *See also* Mental health

Nests. *See* Birds—Eggs and nests

Netherlands 914.92; 949.2
> *x* Holland

Netherlands—History 949.2

Netherlands—History—German occupation, 1940–1945 949.2
> *x* German occupation of Netherlands, 1940–1945
> *xx* Military occupation; World War, 1939–1945—Occupied territories

Network theory. *See* System analysis

Networks, Information. *See* Information networks

Networks, Library. *See* Library information networks

Neurasthenia 616.8
> *x* Nervous exhaustion; Nervous prostration
> *xx* Nervous system—Diseases

Neurology. *See* Nervous system

Neuropathology. *See* Nervous system—Diseases

Neuroses 616.8
> *See also* Fear; Medicine, Psychosomatic
> *xx* Psychology, Pathological

Neutrality 327; 341.6
> *See also* names of countries with the subdivision *Neutrality*, e.g. U.S.—Neutrality; etc.
> *x* Nonalignment
> *xx* International law; International relations; Privateering; Security, International

Neutrons 539.7; 541
> *See also* Atoms; Electrons; Protons
> *xx* Nuclear physics; Quantum theory

New England 917.4; 974
> *xx* United States

New England—Hurricane, 1938 551.5; 974
> *xx* Disasters; Natural disasters; Hurricanes

New France—History. *See* **Canada—History—
To 1763 (New France); Mississippi
Valley—History**

New nations. *See* **States, New**

New Testament. *See* **Bible. New Testament**

New Thought **289.9**
xx **Mental healing; Psychology; Therapeutics, Suggestive**

New words. *See* **Words, New**

News agencies **070.4**
x News services; Press

News photography. *See* **Photography, Journalistic**

News services. *See* **News agencies**

Newspaper clippings. *See* **Clippings (Books,
newspapers, etc.)**

Newspaper work. *See* **Journalism; Reporters
and reporting**

Newspapers **070**
See note under **Journalism**
See also **Clippings (Books, newspapers, etc.)
Freedom of the press; Journalism; Periodicals; Reporters and reporting; also
American newspapers; English newspapers;** etc.; and names of individual
newspapers
x Press
xx **Communication; Journalism; Mass media; Periodicals**

Newspapers—Indexes **070.1**
xx **Indexes**

Nicene Creed **238**
xx **Creeds**

Nicknames **929.4**
x Epithets; Sobriquets; Soubriquets
xx **Names, Personal**

Night schools. *See* **Evening and continuation
schools**

Nike rocket **623.4**
xx **Guided missiles**

Nineteenth century **901.93; 909.81**
Use for general materials covering progress
and development during this period in
one or in several countries
xx **History, Modern—19th century**

Nitrates **546; 661**
xx **Fertilizers and manures**

Nitrogen **546; 665**
xx **Gases**

No fault automobile insurance. *See* **Insurance,
Automobile**

Nobel prizes **807**
xx **Rewards (Prizes, etc.)**

Nobility **301.44; 929.7**
See also **Aristocracy; Heraldry; Knights
and knighthood**
x Baronage; Peerage
xx **Aristocracy; Heraldry; Social classes**

    See also subjects with the subdivision *Noise,* e.g. **Airplanes—Noise;** etc.

    xx **Public health; Sound**

Noise pollution 614.7; 620.2

    See also subjects with the subdivision *Noise,* e.g. **Airplanes—Noise;** etc.

    xx **Pollution**

Nomenclature. *See* **Names;** and scientific and technical subjects with the subdivision *Terminology,* e.g. **Botany—Terminology;** etc.

Nomination of presidents. *See* **Presidents—U.S.—Nomination**

Nonalignment. *See* **Neutrality**

Nonbook materials. *See* **Audio-visual materials**

Nonconformity. *See* **Conformity; Counter culture; Dissent**

Nondenominational churches. *See* **Community churches**

Nonfossil fuels. *See* **Synthetic fuels**

Nongraded schools 371.2

    x Multi-age grouping; Schools, Nongraded; Schools, Ungraded; Ungraded schools

    xx **Ability grouping in education; Education—Experimental methods**

Noninstitutional churches 289.9

    x Avant-garde churches; Churches, Avant-garde; Churches, Noninstitutional

Nonliterate folk society. *See* **Society, Nonliterate folk**

Nonliterate man. *See* **Man, Nonliterate**

Nonmarital relations. *See* **Unmarried couples**

Nonobjective art. *See* **Art, Abstract**

Nonprint materials. *See* **Audio-visual materials**

Nonprofessional library assistants. *See* **Library technicians**

Nonproliferation of nuclear weapons. *See* **Disarmament**

Nonpublic schools. *See* **Church schools; Private schools**

Nonsense verses 808.81; 811; 821. etc.

    See also **Limericks**

    x Rhymes

    xx **Humorous poetry; Limericks; Poetry—Collections; Wit and humor**

Nonsupport. *See* **Desertion and nonsupport**

Nonverbal communication 001.54

    See also types of nonverbal communication; e.g. **Body language;** etc.

    x Expression; Gesture; Kinesics

    xx **Communication**

Non-victim crimes. *See* **Crimes without victims**

Nonviolence 172; 322.4

    See also **Pacifism; Passive resistance**

Nonviolence—*Continued*

    xx **Pacifism; Passive resistance; War and religion**

Nonviolent noncooperation. *See* **Passive resistance**

Nonword stories. *See* **Stories without words**

Nordic peoples. *See* **Teutonic peoples**

Normal schools. *See* **Teachers colleges**

Normandy, Attack on, 1944 940.54

    x D Day

Normans 941.02

    See also **Vikings**

    xx **Gt. Brit.–History–Norman period, 1066 –1154; Vikings**

Norse languages. *See* **Icelandic and Old Norse languages; Scandinavian languages**

Norse legends. *See* **Legends, Norse**

Norse literature. *See* **Icelandic and Old Norse literature; Scandinavian literature**

Norsemen. *See* **Vikings**

North Africa. *See* **Africa, North**

North America 917; 970

    xx **America**

North America—Exploration. *See* **America—Exploration**

North American Indians. *See* **Indians of North America**

North Atlantic Treaty, 1949 341.1

    xx **Treaties**

North Atlantic Treaty Organization 341.24

    x NATO

North Central States. *See* **Middle West**

North Pole 919.8; 998

    See also **Arctic regions**

    x Polar expeditions

    xx **Arctic regions; Polar regions**

Northeast Passage 919.8; 998

    xx **Arctic regions; Discoveries (in geography); Voyages and travels**

Northern lights. *See* **Auroras**

Northmen. *See* **Vikings**

Northwest, Canadian 917.12; 971.2

    x Canada, Northwest; Canadian Northwest

    xx **Canada**

Northwest, Old 917.7; 977

    Use for materials on the region between the Ohio and Mississippi Rivers and the Great Lakes

    See also **Middle West**

    xx **United States**

Northwest, Pacific 917.95; 979.5

    Use for materials on the old Oregon country, comprising the present states of Oregon, Washington and Idaho, parts of Montana and Wyoming and the province of British Columbia

    x Pacific Northwest

    xx **United States; The West (U.S.)**

Northwest Passage   917.19; 971.9
  xx America—Exploration; Arctic regions;
      Discoveries (in geography); Voyages
      and travels
Norwegian language   439.8
  May be subdivided like **English language**
  See also **Danish language**
  xx **Scandinavian languages**
Norwegian literature   839.8
  May use same subdivisions and names of
      literary forms as for **English literature**
  xx **Scandinavian literature**
Nose   612
  xx **Face; Head; Smell**
Notation, Musical. *See* **Musical notation**
Novelists (May subdiv. geog. adjective form,
      e.g. **Novelists, French;** etc.)   920; 928
  xx **Authors; Fiction**
Novelists, American   920; 928
  x American novelists; U.S.—Novelists
Novels. *See* **Fiction**
Novels—Plots. *See* **Plots (Drama, fiction, etc.)**
Nuclear energy. *See* **Atomic energy**
Nuclear engineering   621.48
  See also **Nuclear reactors; Radioisotopes**
  xx **Atomic energy; Nuclear physics**
Nuclear medicine   616.9
  x Atomic medicine; Medicine, Atomic;
      Medicine, Nuclear
  xx **Radiation—Physiological effect**
Nuclear physics   539.7
  See also **Atomic energy; Chemistry, Phys-**
      ical and theoretical; Cosmic rays;
      Cyclotron; Electrons; Neutrons; Nu-
      clear engineering; Nuclear reactors;
      Protons; Radioactivity; Radiobiology;
      Transmutation (Chemistry)
  x Atomic nuclei; Physics, Nuclear
  xx **Atoms; Chemistry, Physical and theo-**
      retical; Physics; Radioactivity
Nuclear power. *See* **Atomic energy**
Nuclear power plants. *See* **Atomic power**
      plants
Nuclear propulsion   621.48; 629.47
  See also **Nuclear reactors;** also specific ap-
      plications; e.g. **Atomic submarines;**
      etc.
  x Atomic powered vehicles
  xx **Atomic energy**
Nuclear reactors   621.48
  x Atomic piles; Breeder reactors; Fast
      breeder reactors; Reactors (Nuclear
      physics)
  xx **Atomic energy; Nuclear engineering;**
      Nuclear physics; Nuclear propulsion
Nuclear submarines. *See* **Atomic submarines**
Nuclear test ban. *See* **Disarmament**
Nuclear warfare. *See* **Atomic warfare**
Nuclear weapons. *See* **Atomic weapons**

Nudity in the performing arts 790.2
   xx Performing arts
Number games 793.7
   xx Arithmetic—Study and teaching; Counting; Mathematical recreations
Number theory 510.1
   x Theory of numbers
   xx Algebra; Mathematics; Set theory
Numismatics 737
   Use for materials on coins, medals and tokens considered as works of art, as historical specimens, or as aids to the study of history, archeology, etc.
   See also Coins; Medals; Seals (Numismatics)
   xx Archeology; Coins; History; History, Ancient; Medals
Nunneries. *See* Convents
Nuns 255; 271
   Use only for religious sisters who are cloistered. For others use Sisters; Religious
   xx Religious orders for women; Sisters, Religious
Nurseries (Horticulture) 635
   See also Plant propagation
   xx Fruit culture; Gardening; Trees
Nurseries, Day. *See* Child care centers
Nursery rhymes 398.8
   x Poetry for children; Rhymes
   xx Children's poetry; Children's songs; Folklore
Nursery schools 372.21
   See also Child care centers; Education, Preschool; Kindergarten
   xx Child care centers; Education, Elementary; Education, Preschool
Nurses 920; 926
   See also types of nurses, e.g., Practical nurses; School nurses; etc.
   x District nurses; Trained nurses
Nursing 610.73; 649
   See also Children—Care and hygiene; Cookery for the sick; First aid; Hospitals; Infants—Care and hygiene; Red Cross; Sick; also types of nursing; e.g. Home nursing; Practical nursing; etc.
   xx Children—Care and hygiene; Hospitals; Medicine; Medicine—Practice; Sick; Therapeutics
Nursing homes 362.6
   xx Elderly—Care and hygiene; Hospitals; Institutional care
Nutrition 641.1
   See also Diet; Digestion; Food; Malnutrition; Metabolism; Vitamins; also subjects with the subdivision *Nutrition*, e.g. Astronauts—Nutrition; Children—Nutrition; Plants—Nutrition; etc.
   x Meal planning

Nutrition—*Continued*
  xx **Diet; Digestion; Food; Metabolism; Physiology; Therapeutics**
Nuts 634
  Names of nuts are not included in this list but are to be added as needed, in the singular form, e.g. **Pecan;** etc.
  See also names of nuts, e.g. **Pecan;** etc.
  xx **Trees**
Nylon 677
  xx **Fabrics; Synthetic fabrics**
Oak 582
  xx **Trees; Wood**
Oats 633
  xx **Feeds**
Obedience 179
  x Disobedience
  xx **Human behavior**
Obelisks 721
  xx **Archeology; Architecture; Monuments; Pyramids**
Obesity
  x Corpulence; Fatness; Overweight
Obesity—Control. *See* **Reducing**
Obituaries 920
  x Death notices; Necrologies
  xx **Biography**
Objective tests. *See* **Examinations; Mental tests**
Obscene materials. *See* **Pornography**
Obscenity (Law) 345
  See also **Pornography**
Observatories, Astronomical. *See* **Astronomical observatories**
Observatories, Meteorological. *See* **Meteorology—Observatories**
Obstetrics. *See* **Childbirth**
Occidental civilization. *See* **Civilization, Occidental**
Occult sciences 133
  See also

Alchemy	**Oracles**
Astrology	**Palmistry**
Clairvoyance	**Prophecies (Occult**
Demonology	**sciences)**
Divination	**Spiritualism**
Fortune telling	**Superstition**
Magic	**Witchcraft**

  x Hermetic art and philosophy; Sorcery
  xx **Astrology; Demonology; Divination; Magic; Supernatural; Superstition; Witchcraft**
Occupation, Choice of. *See* **Vocational guidance**
Occupation, Military. *See* **Military occupation**
Occupational diseases 616.9
  See also **Occupations, Dangerous; Workers' compensation**
  x Diseases, Industrial; Diseases, Occupational; Diseases of occupation; Indus-

Occupational diseases—*Continued*
    trial diseases; Occupations—Diseases and hygiene
    xx **Hygiene; Industrial health and safety; Labor and laboring classes; Occupations, Dangerous; Public health**

Occupational health and safety. *See* **Industrial health and safety**

Occupational retraining. *See* **Retraining, Occupational**

Occupational therapy 615
    See also **Handicraft**
    xx **Handicraft; Mental health; Physical therapy; Physically handicapped—Rehabilitation; Therapeutics**

Occupational training 331.2; 331.7
    Use for materials on teaching people a skill after formal education. For teaching a skill during the educational process use **Vocational education.** For on the job training use **Employees—Training.** For retraining use **Retraining, Occupational**
    See also **Employees—Training; Retraining, Occupational**
    x Job training; Training, Occupational; Training, Vocational; Vocational training
    xx **Human resources policy; Technical education; Vocational education**

Occupations 331.7
    Use for descriptions and lists of occupations
    See also **Job analysis; Paraprofessions and paraprofessionals; Professions; Vocational guidance;** also names of countries, cities, etc. with the subdivision *Occupations,* e.g. **U.S.—Occupations; Chicago—Occupations;** etc.; and names of occupations
    x Careers; Jobs; Trades; Vocations
    xx **Business; Labor and laboring classes; Professions; Vocational guidance**

Occupations, Dangerous 331.7
    See also **Occupational diseases**
    x Dangerous occupations; Injurious occupations
    xx **Accidents; Industrial health and safety; Labor and laboring classes; Occupational diseases**

Occupations—Diseases and hygiene. *See* **Occupational diseases**

Occupied territory. *See* **Military occupation**

Ocean 551.4
    See also **Icebergs; Oceanography; Seashore; Storms;** also names of oceans and seas, e.g. **Atlantic Ocean;** etc.
    x Oceans; Sea
    xx **Earth; Physical geography; Water**

Ocean—Economic aspects. *See* **Marine re-
sources; Shipping**
Ocean bottom 551.4
See also **Marine mineral resources**
x Ocean floor; Sea bed
xx **Marine biology; Oceanography; Sub-
marine geology**
Ocean cables. *See* **Cables, Submarine**
Ocean farming. *See* **Aquaculture**
Ocean floor. *See* **Ocean bottom**
Ocean life. *See* **Marine biology**
Ocean mineral resources. *See* **Marine mineral
resources**
Ocean pollution. *See* **Marine pollution**
Ocean resources. *See* **Marine resources**
Ocean routes. *See* **Trade routes**
Ocean transportation. *See* **Shipping**
Ocean travel 910.4
See also **Steamboats; Yachts and yachting**
x Sea travel
xx **Transportation; Travel; Voyages and
travels**
Ocean waves 551.4
x Sea waves; Surf; Tidal waves
xx **Oceanography; Waves**
Oceanariums. *See* **Marine aquariums**
Oceanauts. *See* **Aquanauts**
Oceania. *See* **Islands of the Pacific**
Oceanographic research. *See* **Oceanography—
Research**
Oceanographic submersibles. *See* **Submersibles**
Oceanography (May subdiv. geog. area e.g.
Oceanography—Atlantic Ocean; etc.)
551.4
See also **Marine biology; Marine resources;
Navigation; Ocean bottom; Ocean
waves; Submarine geology; Tides**
x Deep sea technology; Oceanology; Un-
dersea technology
xx **Earth; Earth sciences; Geology; Geo-
physics; Ocean**
Oceanography—Computer programs 551.4028
xx **Computer programs**
Oceanography—Research 551.407
See also **Bathyscaphe; Diving, Submarine;
Skin diving; Submersible; Undersea
research stations; Underwater exploration**
x Oceanographic research
Oceanology. *See* **Oceanography**
Oceans. *See* **Ocean**
Oddities. *See* **Curiosities and wonders**
Offenses, Military. *See* **Military offenses**
Offenses against public safety 364.1
See also names of specific offenses, e.g.
**Hijacking of airplanes; Riots; Sab-
otage;** etc.
x Crimes against public safety; Public
safety, Crimes against
xx **Criminal law**

Offenses against the person 364.1

    See also names of specific offenses, e.g. **Assassination; Murder; Rape;** etc.

    x Crimes against the person; Persons, Crimes against

    xx **Criminal law**

Office, Tenure of. *See* **Civil service**

Office buildings 725

    See also **Skyscrapers;** also names of cities with the subdivision *Office buildings,* e.g. **Chicago—Office buildings;** etc.

    x Buildings, Office

    xx **Industrial buildings**

Office employees. *See* **Clerks**

Office equipment and supplies 651

    See also types of office equipment and supplies, e.g. **Calculating machines; Typewriters;** etc.

    x Business machines; Office machines; Office supplies

    xx **Bookkeeping; Office management**

Office machines. *See* **Office equipment and supplies**

Office management 651

    See also **Office equipment and supplies; Personnel management; Secretaries**

    x Office procedures

    xx **Business; Efficiency, Industrial; Factory management; Industrial management; Management; Personnel management**

Office procedures. *See* **Office management**

Office supplies. *See* **Office equipment and supplies**

Office work—Training. *See* **Business education**

Official misconduct. *See* **Misconduct in office**

Official publications. *See* **Government publications;** and names of countries, cities, etc. with the subdivision *Government publications,* e.g. **U.S.—Government publications;** etc.

Officials. *See* **Civil service;** and names of countries, cities, etc. and organizations with the subdivision *Officials and employees,* e.g. **U.S.—Officials and employees; Chicago—Officials and employees; United Nations—Officials and employees;** etc.

Offset printing 686.2

    x Lithoprinting; Printing, Offset

    xx **Lithography; Printing**

Offshore structures. *See* **Artificial islands**

Offshore water pollution. *See* **Marine pollution**

Ohio 917.71; 977.1

    Subdivisions have been given under this subject to serve as a guide to the subdivisions that may be used under the name of any state or province. The

401

Ohio—*Continued*

subdivisions under **United States** may be consulted as a guide for formulating other references that may be needed

Ohio—Antiquities 917

Ohio—Bibliography 016.9771

Ohio—Bio-bibliography 016.9771

Ohio—Biography 920

Ohio—Biography—Dictionaries 920.03

Ohio—Biography—Portraits 920.22

Ohio—Boundaries 917.71; 977.1

Ohio—Census 317.71

Ohio—Church history 277.71

Ohio—Civilization 917.71

Ohio—Climate 551.6

Ohio—Commerce 381

Ohio. Constitution 342.2

   xx **Constitutions, State**

Ohio—Constitutional history 342.2

Ohio—Description and travel 917.71

Ohio—Description and travel—Guides 917.71

Ohio—Description and travel—Views 917.71

Ohio—Directories 977.1025

Use for lists of names and addresses. Lists of names without addresses are entered under **Ohio—Registers**

   See also **Ohio—Registers**

   xx **Ohio—Registers**

Ohio—Economic conditions 330.9771

Ohio—Economic policy 338.9771

   x State planning

   xx **Economic policy**

Ohio—Executive departments 353.03

Ohio—Foreign population 325.771

Ohio—Galleries and museums 708

Ohio—Gazetteers 917.71

Ohio—Government publications 015.771

Ohio—Historic buildings, etc. 917.71; 977.1

Ohio—History 977.1

Ohio—History, Local 977.1

Ohio—History—Societies 977.106

Ohio—History—Sources 977.1

Ohio—Industries 338.9771

   x Ohio—Manufactures

Ohio—Intellectual life 917.71

Ohio—Manufactures. *See* **Ohio—Industries**

Ohio—Maps 912

Ohio—Militia 355.3

Ohio—Moral conditions 309.1771

Ohio—Occupations 331.7

Ohio—Officials and employees 351.1

Ohio—Politics and government 977.1

   xx **State governments**

Ohio—Population 317.71

Ohio—Public buildings 725

Ohio—Public lands 333.1

Ohio—Public works 351.8

Ohio—Race relations 301.45

Ohio—Registers 929.4

Use for lists of names without addresses. List of names that include addresses are entered under **Ohio—Directories**

See also **Ohio—Directories**

xx **Ohio—Directories**

Ohio—Religion 277.71

Ohio—Social conditions 309.1771

Ohio—Social life and customs 917.71

Ohio—Social policy 309.1771

x State planning

Ohio—Statistics 317.71

Oil. *See* **Oils and fats; Petroleum**

Oil burners 697

xx **Heating; Petroleum as fuel**

Oil engines. *See* **Gas and oil engines**

Oil fuel. *See* **Petroleum as fuel**

Oil painting. *See* **Painting**

Oil pollution of rivers, harbors, etc. 333.9

x Oil spills

xx **Marine pollution**

Oil spills. *See* **Oil pollution of rivers, harbors, etc.**

Oil wells. *See* **Petroleum**

Oils, Essential. *See* **Essences and essential oils**

Oils and fats 665

See also **Essences and essential oils; Lubrication and lubricants; Petroleum**

x Animal oils; Fat; Fats; Grease; Oil; Vegetable oils

xx **Coal tar products; Lubrication and lubricants**

Ojibwe Indians 970.3

x Chippewa Indians

xx **Anthropology; Indians of North America**

Old age 301.43

See also **Age and employment; Aging; Elderly; Old age pensions; Retirement**

x Age; Longevity

xx **Gerontology; Life (Biology); Middle age; Physiology**

Old age homes. *See* **Elderly—Housing**

Old age pensions 331.2; 368.4

x Insurance, Old age; Labor and laboring classes—Insurance; Retirement income

xx **Labor and laboring classes; Old age; Pensions; Saving and thrift; Social problems; Social security; Socialism**

Old English language. *See* **Anglo-Saxon language**

Old English literature. *See* **Anglo-Saxon literature**

Old Norse language. *See* **Icelandic and Old Norse languages**

Old Norse literature. *See* **Icelandic and Old Norse literature**

Old Testament. *See* **Bible. Old Testament**

Older people. *See* **Elderly**

Oleomargarine. *See* **Margarine**

Olympic games 796.4; 796.9
    x Games, Olympic
    xx **Athletics; Games; Sports**

On line data processing 001.6
    x In line data processing
    xx **Electronic data processing**

One act plays 808.82; 812; 812.08; etc.
    x Plays; Short plays
    xx **Amateur theatricals; Drama**

One parent family. *See* **Single parent family**

Opaque projectors. *See* **Projectors**

Open and closed shop 331.88
    x Closed shop; Right to work; Union shop
    xx **Labor and laboring classes; Labor contract; Labor unions**

Open classroom approach to teaching. *See* **Open plan schools**

Open education. *See* **Open plan schools**

Open ended marriage. *See* **Unmarried couples**

Open heart surgery. *See* **Heart—Surgery**

Open housing. *See* **Discrimination in housing**

Open plan schools 371.3
    See also **Free schools**
    x Interest centers approach to teaching; Learning center approach to teaching; Open classroom approach to teaching; Open education
    xx **Education—Experimental methods; Free schools**

Opera 782.1
    See also **Ballet; Operetta**
    x Comic opera; Dramatic music; Grand opera; Music, Dramatic
    xx **Drama; Musical form; Theater**

Opera houses. *See* **Theaters**

Operas 782.1
    See also **Musical revues, comedies, etc.**
    xx **Vocal music**

Operas—Librettos 782.1
    xx **Librettos**

Operas—Stories, plots, etc. 782.1
    x Stories
    xx **Librettos; Plots (Drama, fiction, etc.)**

Operation Pluto. *See* **Cuba—History—Invasion, 1961**

Operation Sail, 1976 973.3
    x Outport visits, 1976; Parade of Sail, 1976; Tall ships, 1976; Tall ships transatlantic race, 1976
    xx **American Revolution Bicentennial, 1776–1976**

Operations, Surgical. *See* **Surgery**

Operations research 658.5
    See also **Systems engineering**
    xx **Research; Systems engineering**

Operetta 782.8
    See also **Musical revues, comedies, etc.**

Operetta—*Continued*

   x Comic opera; Dramatic music; Music, Dramatic

   xx **Musical form; Opera; Vocal music**

Opiates. *See* **Narcotics**

Opinion, Public. *See* **Public opinion**

Opinion polls. *See* **Public opinion polls**

Opium 615

   xx **Narcotics**

Opium—Physiological effect 613.8

   x Physiological effect

   xx **Pharmacology**

Optical data processing 651.8

   x Visual data processing

   xx **Bionics; Electronic data processing**

Optical illusions 535

   x Illusions

   xx **Hallucinations and illusions; Psychology, Physiological; Vision**

Optical masers. *See* **Lasers**

Optics 535; 621.36

   See also **Color; Light; Perspective; Phosphorescence; Photometry; Radiation; Refraction; Spectrum; Vision**

   xx **Light; Photometry; Physics**

Optometry 617.7

   See also **Eye**

   xx **Eye**

Oracles 133.3

   See also **Divination**

   xx **Divination; Occult sciences; Prophecies (Occult sciences)**

Oral history

   Use for materials on recording the oral recollections of events by persons. Use appropriate subject headings for the content of the recollections

   x History, Oral

   xx **History**

Orange 634

   xx **Citrus fruit**

Orations 808.85

   Use for collections of orations by several authors, especially those delivered on formal occasions and in a more formal manner than those entered under **Speeches, addresses, etc.**

   See also **After-dinner speeches;** also **American orations; English orations;** etc.

   x Addresses

   xx **Literature—Collections; Public speaking; Speeches, addresses, etc.**

Oratorios 782.7

   xx **Church music; Vocal music**

Oratory. *See* **Public speaking**

Orbital laboratories. *See* **Space stations**

Orbital rendezvous (Space flight) 629.45

   See also names of projects, e.g. **Apollo project; Gemini project;** etc.; also names of space ships

Orbital rendezvous (Space flight)—*Continued*

    x Rendezvous in space; Space orbital rendezvous

    xx **Space flight; Space ships; Space stations**

Orbiting vehicles. *See* **Artificial satellites**

Orchards. *See* **Fruit culture**

Orchestra 785.06

    See also **Bands (Music); Conducting; Conductors (Music); Instrumentation and orchestration; Orchestral music;** and names of types of orchestras

    xx **Bands (Music); Conducting; Musical instruments**

Orchestral music 785

    See also types of orchestral music, e.g. **Chamber music; Concertos; Quintets; Sonatas; String orchestra music; Suites; Symphonies;** etc.

    xx **Instrumental music; Music; Orchestra**

Orchestration. *See* **Instrumentation and orchestration**

Orders, Architectural. *See* **Architecture—Orders**

Orders, Monastic. *See* **Religious orders**

Ordination 253

    xx **Rites and ceremonies; Sacraments**

Ordination of men 253

Ordination of women 253

Ordnance 355.8; 623.4

    See also names of general and specific military ordnance, e.g. **Atomic weapons; Bombs; Projectiles;** etc.; also names of armies with the subdivision *Ordnance and ordnance stores,* e.g. **U.S. Army—Ordnance and ordnance stores;** etc.

    x Cannon; Guns

    xx **Arms and armor; Artillery; Firearms; Military art and science; Projectiles**

Ore deposits 553

    See also **Ores;** also names of ores, e.g. **Iron ores;** etc.

    xx **Geology; Ores**

Ore dressing 622

    x Dressing of ores

    xx **Smelting**

Oregon Trail 917.8; 978

    xx **Overland journeys to the Pacific (U.S.); United States**

Ores 553

    See also **Metallurgy; Metals; Minerology; Mines and mineral resources; Ore deposits;** also names of ores, e.g. **Iron ores;** etc.

    xx **Geology, Economic; Ore deposits**

Organ 786.5

    x Pipe organ

    xx **Musical instruments**

Organ music 786.5

    xx **Church music; Music**

Organ preservation. *See* **Preservation of organs, tissues, etc.**

Organ transplantation. *See* **Transplantation of organs, tissues, etc.**

Organic chemistry. *See* **Chemistry, Organic**

Organic farming. *See* **Organiculture**

Organic food. *See* **Food, Natural**

Organic gardening. *See* **Organiculture**

Organiculture 631.5

    x Organic farming; Organic gardening

    xx **Agriculture; Gardening; Horticulture**

Organists 920; 927

    xx **Musicians**

Organization, International. *See* **International organization**

Organization and management. *See* **Management**

Organizations. *See* **Associations**

Organized crime 364.1

    See also types of organized crime, e.g. **Racketeering;** etc.

    x Crime syndicates

    xx **Crime**

Organized labor. *See* **Labor unions**

Organs, Artificial. *See* **Artificial organs**

Organs, Preservation. *See* **Preservation of organs, tissues, etc.**

Orient. *See* **Asia; Far East; Middle East**

Oriental architecture. *See* **Architecture, Asian**

Oriental art. *See* **Art, Asian**

Oriental civilization. *See* **Civilization, Asian**

Oriental rugs. *See* **Rugs, Oriental**

Orientation. *See* **Orienteering**

Orienteering 152.1; 796.5

    x Direction sense; Orientation; Sense of direction

    xx **Hiking**

Origami 745.54

    x Japanese paper folding

    xx **Paper crafts**

Origin of life. *See* **Life—Origin**

Origin of man. *See* **Man—Origin and antiquity**

Origin of species. *See* **Evolution**

Ornament. *See* **Decoration and ornament**

Ornamental alphabets. *See* **Illumination of books and manuscripts; Lettering**

Ornamental design. *See* **Design, Decorative**

Ornamental plants. *See* **Plants, Ornamental**

Ornithology. *See* **Birds**

Orphanages 362.7

    See also **Child welfare**

    x Charitable institutions; Homes (Institutions)

    xx **Charities; Child welfare; Children—Institutional care; Institutional care; Public welfare**

Orphans 362.7

    x Dependent children; Foundlings

    xx **Children**

Orthodox Eastern Church 281.9
>   *x* Greek Church
>   *xx* **Eastern churches**

Orthodox Eastern Church, Russian 281.9
>   *x* Russian Church

Orthography. *See* **Spelling reform;** and names of languages with the subdivision *Spelling,* e.g. **English language—Spelling;** etc.

Orthopedic surgery. *See* **Orthopedics**

Orthopedics 617
>   *See also* **Physically handicapped**
>   *x* Orthopedic surgery; Surgery, Orthopedic
>   *xx* **Physically handicapped; Surgery**

Osaka. World's Fair, 1970. *See* **Expo '70**

Osteology. *See* **Bones**

Osteopathy 615
>   *See also* **Massage**
>   *xx* **Massage; Medicine; Medicine—Practice**

Ostrogoths. *See* **Teutonic peoples**

Outboard motorboats. *See* **Motorboats**

Outdoor cookery. *See* **Cookery, Outdoor**

Outdoor life 796.54
>   *See also* types of outdoor life and activities, e.g. **Camping; Country life; Hiking; Mountaineering; Nature study; Sports; Wilderness survival;** etc.
>   *x* Rural life
>   *xx* **Camping; Country life; Sports**

Outdoor recreation 796
>   *See also* **Parks; Recreational vehicles;** also types of outdoor recreation, e.g. **Camping;** etc.
>   *xx* **Recreation**

Outdoor survival. *See* **Wilderness survival**

Outer space 523.1
>   *See also* **Space environment**
>   *x* Space, Outer
>   *xx* **Astronautics; Astronomy; Space sciences**

Outer space—Colonies. *See* **Space colonies**

Outer space—Communication. *See* **Intersteller communication**

Outer space—Exploration 629.4
>   *See also* **Space probes**
>   *x* Exploration, Space; Space exploration (Astronautics); Space research
>   *xx* **Interplanetary voyages; Space flight**

Outer space and civilization. *See* **Astronautics and civilization**

Outlaws. *See* **Robbers and outlaws**

Outlines, syllabi, etc. *See* general subjects with the subdivision *Outlines, syllabi, etc.* e.g. **English literature—Outlines, syllabi, etc.;** etc.

Outport visits, 1976. *See* **Operation Sail, 1976**

Overactive children. *See* **Hyperactive children**

Overactivity. *See* **Hyperactivity**

Overland journeys to the Pacific (U.S.) 917.8; 978
>   Use for materials on the pioneers' crossing

Overland journeys to the Pacific (U.S.)
—*Continued*
of the continent toward the Pacific by foot, horseback, wagon, etc.

See also **Oregon Trail**

x Transcontinental journeys (U.S.); Travels

xx **Frontier and pioneer life; Voyages and travels**

Overseas study. *See* **Foreign study**

Overtime. *See* **Hours of labor; Wages**

Overweight. *See* **Obesity**

Overweight—Control. *See* **Reducing**

Ownership. *See* **Property**

Oxyacetylene welding. *See* **Welding**

Oxygen 546; 547

See also **Ozone**

Oysters, Pearl. *See* **Pearlfisheries**

Ozone 665

xx **Oxygen**

POW. *See* **Prisoners of war**

PTA. *See* **Parents' and teachers' associations**

Pacific cable. *See* **Cables, Submarine**

Pacific islands. *See* **Islands of the Pacific**

Pacific Northwest. *See* **Northwest, Pacific**

Pacific States 917.9; 979

xx **The West (U.S.)**

Pacifism 341.73

See also **Conscientious objectors; Nonviolence**

xx **Conscientious objectors; Nonviolence; Peace; War and religion**

Pack transportation. *See* **Backpacking**

Packaged houses. *See* **Prefabricated houses**

Packaging 658.5; 658.7-658.8

See also types of packaging and packaging materials; e.g. **Aluminum foil; Gift wrapping**; etc.

xx **Advertising; Retail trade**

Packing industry. *See* **Meat industry and trade**

Paganism 291

x Heathenism

xx **Christianity and other religions; Religions**

Pageants 394; 791.6

See also **Festivals; Masks (Plays); Mysteries and miracle plays**

xx **Acting; Festivals**

Pain 152.1; 612

See also **Anesthetics; Pleasure; Suffering**

xx **Diagnosis; Emotions; Pleasure; Psychology, Physiological; Senses and sensation; Suffering**

Paint 645; 667

See also **Corrosion and anticorrosives; Pigments**

x Finishes and finishing

xx **Corrosion and anticorrosives; Painting, Industrial; Pigments**

Painted glass. *See* **Glass painting and staining**

Painters (May subdiv. geog. adjective form, e.g.
    Painters, French; etc.) **920; 927**
    See also **Artists;** also names of individual
      painters
  xx **Artists**
Painters, American 920; 927
    x American painters; U.S.—Painters
Painters' materials. *See* **Artists' materials**
Painting (May subdiv. geog. adjective form, e.g.
    Painting, Dutch; etc.) **750; 751**
    Names of all types of painting are not in-
      cluded in this list. Add others as
      needed
    See also

Animal painting and	**Landscape painting**
illustration	**Marine painting**
China painting	**Miniature painting**
Color	**Mural painting and**
Composition (Art)	**decoration**
Cubism	**Perspective**
Expressionism	**Portrait painting**
(Art)	**Postimpressionism**
Figure painting	**(Art)**
Finger painting	**Preraphaelitism**
Flower painting and	**Scene painting**
illustration	**Stencil work**
Futurism (Art)	**Textile painting**
Glass painting and	**Water color paint-**
staining	**ing**
Impressionism	
(Art)	

    x Oil painting; Paintings
    xx **Art; Composition (Art); Decoration**
         and ornament; Drawing; Esthetics;
         Graphic arts; Pictures
Painting, Abstract. *See* **Art, Abstract**
Painting, American 759.13
    x American painting; U.S.—Painting
Painting—Collections 759
    x Collections of art, painting, etc.
Painting—Color reproductions. *See* **Color**
        prints
Painting—Conservation and restoration 751.6
    x Conservation of works of art; Preserva-
      tion of works of art; Restoration of
      works of art
Painting, Finger. *See* **Finger painting**
Painting, Industrial 698.1
    See also **House painting; Lettering; Paint;**
      Sign painting; Varnish and varnishing;
      Wood finishing
    x Finishes and finishing; Industrial paint-
      ing; Mechanical painting; Painting,
      Mechanical
Painting, Mechanical. *See* **Painting, Industrial**
Painting, Modern 759.06
    x Modern painting
Painting, Modern—19th century 759.05
Painting, Modern—20th century 759.06

Painting, Religious. *See* **Religious art and symbolism**

Painting, Romanesque   759.02
  x Romanesque painting
  xx **Art, Romanesque**
Painting—Technique   751.4
  x Technique
Paintings. *See* **Painting**
Pair system. *See* **Binary system (Mathematics)**
Palaces   728.8
  xx **Architecture**
Paleobiogeography. *See* **Geographical distribution of animals and plants**
Paleobotany. *See* **Plants, Fossil**
Paleolithic period. *See* **Stone age**
Paleontology. *See* **Fossils**
Palmistry   133.6
  xx **Divination; Fortune telling; Occult sciences**
Palsy, Cerebral. *See* **Cerebral palsy**
Pamphlets   025.17
Pan-Africanism   320.5
  x African relations
  xx **Africa**
Pan-Americanism   327.7
  Use for materials on the relations and cooperation between the countries of the Americas
  See also **America—Politics and government; Monroe Doctrine**
  x Good Neighbor Policy; Inter-American relations
  xx **America—Politics and government; Latin America**
Panama Canal   918.3; 983
  xx **Canals**
Panarabism   320.5
Panel discussions. *See* **Discussion groups**
Panel heating. *See* **Radiant heating**
Paneuropean federation. *See* **European Federation**
Panics, Economic. *See* **Depressions, Economic**
Pantheism   147; 212
  See also **Deism; Theism**
  xx **God; Philosophy; Religion; Theism; Theology**
Pantomimes   792.3
  See also **Shadow pantomimes and plays**
  xx **Acting; Amateur theatricals; Ballet; Drama; Theater**
Papacy   262
  See also **Holy See; Popes**
  xx **Catholic Church; Church history; Church history—Middle Ages, 600–1500; Holy See; Popes**
Papal encyclicals. *See* **Encyclicals, Papal**
Paper   676
  xx **Fibers**
Paper bound books. *See* **Paperback books**

Paper crafts 745.54

    See also **Gift wrapping;** also names of paper crafts, e.g. **Decoupage; Origami;** etc.

    x Paper folding; Paper sculpture; Paper work; Papier-mâché

Paper folding. *See* **Paper crafts**

Paper hanging 698.6

    See also **Wallpaper**

    xx **Interior decoration; Wallpaper**

Paper making and trade 338.4; 676

    See also **Book industries and trade**

    xx **Book industries and trade; Chemical industries; Manufactures**

Paper money 332.4

    x Bills of credit; Fiat money; Greenbacks; Legal tender; Money, Paper

    xx **Finance; Inflation (Finance); Money**

Paper sculpture. *See* **Paper crafts**

Paper work. *See* **Paper crafts**

Paperback books 070.5

    x Books, Paperback; Paper bound books

    xx **Bibliography—Editions; Books; Publishers and publishing**

Papier-mâché. *See* **Paper crafts**

Parables 226

    See also **Allegories; Fables; Jesus Christ—Parables**

    xx **Allegories; Fables**

Parachute troops 356

    See also names of armies with the subdivision *Parachute troop*s, e.g. **U.S. Army—Parachute troops;** etc.

    x Paratroops

    xx **Aeronautics, Military; Parachutes**

Parachutes 623.74; 629.134

    See also **Parachute troops**

    xx **Aeronautics**

Parade of Sail, 1976. *See* **Operation Sail, 1976**

Parades 791.6

    x Floats (Parades); Processions

Paralysis, Anterior spinal. *See* **Poliomyelitis**

Paralysis, Cerebral. *See* **Cerebral palsy**

Paralysis, Infantile. *See* **Poliomyelitis**

Paralysis, Spastic. *See* **Cerebral palsy**

Paramedical personnel. *See* **Allied health personnel**

Paraprofessional librarians. *See* **Library technicians**

Paraprofessions and paraprofessionals 331.7

    See also names of paraprofessions and paraprofessional personnel, e.g. **Library technicans;** etc.

    xx **Occupations; Professions; Vocational guidance**

Parapsychology. *See* **Psychical research**

Parasites 574.5

    See also **Bacteriology; Insects, Injurious and beneficial**

Parasites—*Continued*

    x Animal parasites; Diseases and pests; Entozoa; Epizoa

    xx **Pests**

Parasols. *See* **Umbrellas and parasols**

Paratroops. *See* **Parachute troops**

Parcel post. *See* **Postal service**

Pardon 364.6

    See also **Amnesty**

    xx **Amnesty; Criminal justice, Administration of; Parole**

Parent and child 301.42

    See also **Child abuse; Conflict of generations; Inheritance and succession**

    x Child and parent

    xx **Conflict of generations; Domestic relations; Family; Human relations**

Parents and teachers. *See* **Home and school**

Parents' and teachers' associations 370.19

    See also **Home and school**

    x PTA; Teachers and parents

    xx **Community and school; Educational associations; Home and school; Societies**

Parents without partners. *See* **Single parent family**

Parish libraries. *See* **Libraries, Church**

Parish registers. *See* **Registers of births, etc.**

Parks (May subdiv. geog. country or state) **719; 910**

    See also **Amusement parks; Botanical gardens; Landscape gardening; National parks and reserves; Playgrounds; Zoological gardens;** also names of cities with the subdivision *Parks*, e.g. **Chicago—Parks;** etc.

    xx **Cities and towns; Landscape architecture; Outdoor recreation; Playgrounds**

Parks—U.S. 719; 917.3

    x U.S.—Parks

Parkways. *See* **Express highways**

Parliamentary government. *See* **Representative government and representation**

Parliamentary practice 060.4

    x Rules of order

    xx **Debates and debating; Legislation; Legislative bodies; Public meetings**

Parliaments. *See* **Legislative bodies**

Parochial schools. *See* **Church schools**

Parodies 808.87

    May be used for collections by one author as well as for collections by several authors

    See also names of prominent authors with the subdivision *Parodies, travesties, etc.* e.g. **Shakespeare, William—Parodies, travesties, etc.;** etc.

    x English parodies; Travesties

    xx **English literature; Literature—Collections**

Parody 808.7

Use for materials about parody. Collections of parodies are entered under **Parodies**

x Comic literature

xx **Literature; Poetry; Satire; Wit and humor**

Parole 364

See also **Pardon; Probation**

xx **Crime; Criminal justice, Administration of; Probation; Social case work**

Part time employment. *See* **Employment, Part time**

Participatory management. *See* **Employee's representation in management**

Parties 793.2

See also types of parties, e.g. **Showers (Parties);** etc.

xx **Entertaining**

Parties, Political. *See* **Political parties**

Partisans. *See* **Guerrillas**

Passion plays 792.1

See also **Mysteries and miracle plays**

xx **Drama; Jesus Christ—Drama; Religious drama; Theater**

Passions. *See* **Emotions**

Passive resistance 172; 322.4

See also **Boycott; Nonviolence**

x Civil disobedience; Nonviolent noncooperation

xx **Government, Resistance to; Nonviolence**

Pastel drawing 741.2

See also **Crayon drawing**

xx **Crayon drawing; Drawing; Portrait painting**

Pastels 741.9

Pastimes. *See* **Amusements; Games; Recreation**

Pastoral psychiatry. *See* **Psychology, Pastoral**

Pastoral psychology. *See* **Psychology, Pastoral**

Pastoral theology. *See* **Pastoral work**

Pastoral work 253

See also **Church work; Clergy; Preaching; Psychology, Pastoral**

x Pastoral theology; Theology, Pastoral

Pastors. *See* **Clergy; Priests**

Pastry 641.8

xx **Baking; Cookery**

Pastures 333.7

See also **Forage plants; Grasses**

xx **Agriculture; Cattle; Forage plants; Grasses**

Patchwork quilts. *See* **Quilts**

Patent medicines 615

x Medicines, Patent

xx **Quacks and quackery**

Patents 608

See also **Inventions; Trademarks**

x Discoveries (in science); Intellectual property

Patents—*Continued*
    xx **Inventions; Machinery; Manufactures; Trademarks**
Pathological botany. *See* **Plants—Diseases**
Pathological chemistry. *See* **Chemistry, Medical and pharmaceutical; Physiological chemistry**
Pathological psychology. *See* **Psychology, Pathological**
Pathology 616.07
    See also **Bacteriology; Diagnosis; Immunity; Medicine; Physiological chemistry; Therapeutics**
    x Disease (Pathology)
    xx **Diagnosis; Medicine**
Pathology, Vegetable. *See* **Plants—Diseases**
Patience (Game). *See* **Solitaire (Game)**
Patients. *See* **Sick**
Patios 712
    xx **Landscape architecture**
Patriotic poetry 808.81; 811; etc.
    xx **National songs; Poetry—Collections**
Patriotic songs. *See* **National songs**
Patriotism 172
    See also **Loyalty; Nationalism**
    xx **Citizenship; Human behavior; Loyalty; Nationalism**
Pattern making 671.2
    See also **Design; Founding; Mechanical drawing**
    xx **Design; Founding**
Patterns. *See* subjects with the subdivision *Patterns*, e.g. **Dressmaking—Patterns;** etc.
Pauperism. *See* **Poverty**
Pavements 625.8
    See also **Asphalt; Roads; Streets**
    xx **Cement; Concrete; Roads; Streets**
Pay television. *See* **Subscription television**
Payroll taxes. *See* **Income tax; Insurance, Unemployment**
Peace 172; 327; 341.73
    See also **Arbitration, International; Disarmament; League of Nations; Pacifism; Security, International; War;** also names of wars with the subdivision *Peace*, e.g. **World War, 1939–1945—Peace;** etc.
    xx **Arbitration, International; Disarmament; International relations; Reconstruction (1914–1939); Reconstruction (1939–1951); Security, International; War**
Peace keeping forces. *See* **United Nations—Armed Forces**
Pearl diving and divers 338.3
    x Ama
Pearl Harbor, Attack on, 1941 940.54
    xx **World War, 1939–1945; World War, 1939–1945—Campaigns and battles**

Pearlfisheries 338.3; 639
 x Oysters, Pearl
 xx **Fisheries**
Peasant art. *See* **Art industries and trade; Folk art**
Peasantry 301.44
 See also **Agricultural laborers; Land tenure; Sociology, Rural**
 x Rural life
 xx **Agricultural laborers; Feudalism; Labor and laboring classes; Land tenure; Sociology, Rural**
Pecan 634
 xx **Nuts**
Pedagogy. *See* **Education; Education—Study and teaching; Teaching**
Peddlers and peddling 658.85
 x Door to door selling
 xx **Sales personnel; Selling**
Pediatric psychiatry. *See* **Child psychiatry**
Pediatrics. *See* **Children—Care and hygiene; Children—Diseases**
Pedigrees. *See* **Genealogy; Heraldry**
Peerage. *See* **Nobility**
Pelts. *See* **Hides and skins**
Pen drawing 741.2
 x Ink drawing
 xx **Drawing**
Pen names. *See* **Pseudonyms**
Penal codes. *See* **Criminal law**
Penal colonies 365
 x Convicts
 xx **Colonies; Colonization; Criminals; Prisons; Punishment**
Penal institutions. *See* **Correctional institutions; Prisons; Reformatories**
Penal law. *See* **Criminal law**
Penal reform. *See* **Prison reform**
Pencil drawing 741.2
 xx **Drawing**
Penicillin 615
 xx **Antibiotics**
Penitentiaries. *See* **Prisons**
Penmanship 372.6; 652
 Use for practical materials. Information on the history and art of writing are entered under **Writing**. Materials on handwriting as an expression of the writer's character are entered under **Graphology**
 See also **Calligraphy; Graphology; Writing**
 x Copybooks; Handwriting
 xx **Business education; Writing**
Pennsylvania Dutch 301.45; 917.48; 974.8
 x Pennsylvania Germans
Pennsylvania Germans. *See* **Pennsylvania Dutch**
Penology. *See* **Prisons; Punishment; Reformatories**

Pensions 331.2; 351.5

    See also **Mothers' pensions; Old age pensions; Social security**

    x Compensation; Retirement income

  xx **Annuities**

Pensions, Military 355.1

    See also **Veterans**

    x Bonus, Soldiers'; Military pensions; Naval pensions; Pensions, Naval; Soldiers' bonus; War pensions

  xx **Veterans**

Pensions, Naval. *See* **Pensions, Military**

Peonage 333.1

    See also **Contract labor; Convict labor**

    x Compulsory labor; Forced labor; Servitude

  xx **Contract labor; Convict labor; Labor and laboring classes; Slavery**

People, Single. *See* **Single people**

People in space. *See* **Space flight**

People's banks. *See* **Banks and banking, Co-operative**

People's democracies. *See* **Communist countries**

People's Republic of China. *See* **China**

Perception 152.1; 153.7

    See also **Apperception; Concepts; Consciousness; Gestalt psychology; Intuition**

    x Feeling

  xx **Apperception; Educational psychology; Intellect; Intuition; Knowledge, Theory of; Psychology; Thought and thinking**

Percussion instruments 789

    See also names of percussion instruments, e.g. **Drums;** etc.

  xx **Musical instruments**

Perennials 635.9

  xx **Flower gardening; Flowers**

Performance standards 658.3

    x Job performance standards; Work performance standards

Performing arts 790.2

    See also **Centers for the performing arts; Nudity in the performing arts; Theater;** also art forms performed on stage or screen, e.g. **Ballet;** etc.

    x Show business

Perfumes 391; 668

  xx **Cosmetics; Essences and essential oils**

Periodic law 541

  xx **Chemical elements; Chemistry, Physical and theoretical**

Periodicals 050

    See also **Freedom of the press; Newspapers;** also **American periodicals; English periodicals;** etc.; and general subjects with the subdivision *Periodicals*, e.g. **Engineering—Periodicals;** etc.

Periodicals—*Continued*
> *x* Magazines; Press; Serials
> *xx* **Journalism; Newspapers**

Periodicals—Indexes 050.1
> *xx* **Indexes**

Periodicity 574.1; 574.5
> *See also* **Biology—Periodicity; Rhythm; Time**
> *x* Cycles
> *xx* **Rhythm; Time**

Permanent education. *See* **Continuing education**

Persecution 272
> *See also* **Freedom of conscience; Jews—Persecutions; Martyrs; Religious freedom**
> *xx* **Atrocities; Church history; Church history—Early church, ca. 30–600; Freedom of conscience; Martyrs; Religious freedom**

Persia. *See* **Iran**

Persian rugs. *See* **Rugs, Oriental**

Personal appearance. *See* **Grooming, Personal**

Personal conduct. *See* **Human behavior**

Personal development. *See* **Personality; Success**

Personal films. *See* **Amateur motion pictures; Experimental films**

Personal finance. *See* **Finance, Personal**

Personal freedom. *See* **Freedom**

Personal grooming. *See* **Grooming, Personal**

Personal names. *See* **Names, Personal**

Personal narratives. *See* subjects with the subdivision *Biography* or *Correspondence* and where these do not fit use the subdivision *Personal narratives,* e.g. **Drug abuse—Personal narratives;** etc.

Personality 155.2
> *See also* **Character; Individuality; Self; Soul**
> *x* Identity; Personal development
> *xx* **Consciousness; Individuality; Psychology; Soul**

Personality disorders 157; 616.8
> *See also* **Hallucinations and illusions; Hypnotism**
> *xx* **Hallucinations and illusions; Hypnotism; Mind and body; Psychical research; Psychology, Pathological; Subconsciousness**

Personnel administration. *See* **Personnel management**

Personnel classification. *See* **Job analysis**

Personnel management 658.3
> Use for materials dealing with problems of personnel in factories, business, etc., hiring and dismissing employees, and general questions of relationship between officials and employees

Personnel management—*Continued*

See also

Absenteeism (Labor)

Affirmative action programs

Applications for positions

Counseling

Efficiency, Industrial

Employee morale

Employees—Dismissal

Employees—Training

Employees' representation in management

Employment agencies

Factory management

Job analysis

Job satisfaction

Labor turnover

Motion study

Office management

Recruiting of employees

Supervisors

Time study

   x Employment management; Personnel administration; Supervision of employees

   xx Efficiency, Industrial; Factory management; Human relations; Industrial management; Industrial relations; Management; Office management

Personnel service in education. *See* **Educational counseling**

Persons, Crimes against. *See* **Offenses against the person**

Persons, Single. *See* **Single people**

Perspective 701

   See also **Drawing**

   x Architectural perspective

   xx **Drawing; Geometrical drawing; Geometry, Descriptive; Optics; Painting**

Persuasion (Rhetoric). *See* **Public speaking; Rhetoric**

Pest control. *See* **Pests—Control**

Pesticide pollution. *See* **Pesticides—Environmental aspects**

Pesticides 668

   See also **Fungicides; Insecticides**

   xx **Agricultural chemicals; Pests—Control; Poisons**

Pesticides—Environmental aspects 574.5-574.6; 632

   See also **Pesticides and wildlife**

   x Environment and pesticides; Pesticide pollution

   xx **Pollution**

Pesticides and wildlife 574.5

   x Wildlife and pesticides

   xx **Pesticides—Environmental aspects; Wildlife—Conservation**

Pestilences. *See* **Epidemics**

Pests 632

   See also types of pests, e.g. **Agricultural pests; Fungi; Household pests; Insects, Injurious and beneficial; Parasites;**

Pests—*Continued*

also names of crops, trees, etc. with the subdivision *Diseases and pests,* e.g. **Fruit—Diseases and pests;** etc.; and names of pests, e.g. **Flies;** etc.

x Vermin

xx **Zoology, Economic**

Pests—Biological control 574.5

x Agricultural pests—Biological control; Biological control of pests

Pests—Control 632

See also **Pesticides;** also names of specific pests with the subdivision *Control,* e.g. **Mosquitoes—Control;** etc.

x Control; Extermination of pests; Pest control; Pests—Extermination

xx **Agricultural pests; Zoology, Economic**

Pests—Extermination. *See* **Pests—Control**

Petroleum (May subdiv. geog.) **665**

See also **Boring; Coal tar products; Gasoline**

x Coal oil; Crude oil; Oil; Oil wells

xx **Gas; Oils and fats; Wells**

Petroleum—Geology 553

xx **Geology, Economic; Prospecting**

Petroleum—Pipe lines 338.2

x Pipe lines, Petroleum

Petroleum—U.S. 665

x U.S.—Petroleum

Petroleum as fuel 665

See also **Oil burners**

x Fuel, Liquid; Fuel oil; Liquid fuel; Oil fuel

xx **Fuel**

Petroleum engines. *See* **Gas and oil engines**

Petroleum industry and trade 338.2

Petroleum pollution of water 628.1

x Water—Petroleum pollution

xx **Water—Pollution**

Petrology 552

See also **Crystallography; Geochemistry; Geology; Lunar petrology; Mineralogy; Rocks; Stone;** also varieties of rocks, e.g. **Granite; Marble;** etc.

xx **Geology; Mineralogy; Rocks; Science; Stone**

Pets 636.08

See also **Domestic animals;** also names of animals, e.g. **Cats; Dogs;** etc.

xx **Animals; Domestic animals**

Pewter 673

xx **Alloys; Plate; Tin**

Phantoms. *See* **Apparitions; Ghosts**

Pharmaceutical chemistry. *See* **Chemistry, Medical and pharmaceutical**

Pharmaceuticals. *See* **Drugs**

Pharmacodynamics. *See* **Pharmacology**

Pharmacology 615

Use for materials on the action of drugs in general. For action of specific drugs

Pharmacology—*Continued*

    see name of drug with the subdivision *Physiological effect,* e.g. **Opium—Physiological effect;** etc.

    See also **Chemotherapy; Drugs; Pharmacy**

    x Medicine—Physiological effect; Pharmacodynamics

    xx **Drugs; Materia medica; Medicine; Pharmacy; Physiological chemistry**

Pharmacopoeias. *See* **Materia medica**

Pharmacotherapy. *See* **Chemotherapy**

Pharmacy **615**

    See also **Botany, Medical; Chemistry, Medical and pharmaceutical; Drugs; Materia medica; Pharmacology**

    xx **Chemistry; Chemistry, Medical and pharmaceutical; Drugs; Materia medica; Medicine; Pharmacology**

Pheasants **598.2**

    xx **Game and game birds**

Phenomenology **142**

    See also **Existentialism**

    xx **Philosophy, Modern**

Philanthropists **920; 923**

Philanthropy. *See* **Charities; Charity organization; Endowments; Gifts; Social work**

Philately. *See* **Postage stamps—Collectors and collecting**

Philology. *See* **Language and languages; Philology, Comparative**

Philology, Comparative **410**

    Use for comparative studies of languages. General materials on the history, philosophy, origin, etc. of languages are entered under **Language and languages**

    See also **Language and languages; Literature, Comparative**

    x Comparative philology; Language and languages—Comparative philology; Philology

    xx **Grammar; Language and languages**

Philosophers (May subdiv. geog. adjective form, e.g. **Philosophers, German;** etc.) **920; 921**

Philosophers, American **920; 921**

    x American philosophers; U.S.—Philosophers

Philosophers' stone. *See* **Alchemy**

Philosophy (May subdiv. geog. adjective form, e.g. **Philosophy, French;** etc.) **100**

    See also

Belief and doubt	**God**
Empiricism	**Humanism**
Ethics	**Idealism**
Fate and fatalism	**Intuition**
Free will and determinism	**Knowledge, Theory of**
Gnosticism	**Logic**

Philosophy—*Continued*

Materialism	**Realism**
Metaphysics	**Reality**
Mind and body	**Skepticism**
Mysticism	**Soul**
Pantheism	**Theism**
Positivism	**Transcendentalism**
Pragmatism	**Truth**
Psychology	**Universe**
Rationalism	

    also subjects with the subdivision *Philos-ophy,* e.g. **History—Philosophy;** etc.

    x Mental philosophy

    xx **Humanities**

Philosophy, American   191

    x American philosophy; U.S.—Philosophy

Philosophy, Ancient   180

    See also **Stoics**

    x Ancient philosophy; Greek philosophy; Philosophy, Greek; Philosophy, Roman; Roman philosophy

Philosophy, Greek.   *See* **Philosophy, Ancient**

Philosophy, Hindu   181

    See also **Yoga**

Philosophy—Historiography   107

    xx **Historiography**

Philosophy, Medieval   189

    x Medieval philosophy

    xx **Middle Ages**

Philosophy, Modern   190

    See also **Evolution; Existentialism; Phe-nomenology**

    x Modern philosophy

Philosophy, Moral.   *See* **Ethics**

Philosophy, Roman.   *See* **Philosophy, Ancient**

Philosophy and religion   210

    See also **Religion—Philosophy**

    x Religion and philosophy

    xx **Religion—Philosophy**

Philosophy of history.   *See* **History—Philoso-phy**

Philosophy of religion.   *See* **Religion—Philoso-phy**

Phonetic spelling.   *See* **Spelling reform**

Phonetics   414

    See also **Speech; Voice;** also names of languages with the subdivision *Pro-nunciation,* e.g. **English language—Pronunciation;** etc.

    x Phonics; Phonology

    xx **Language and languages; Sound; Speech; Voice**

Phonics.   *See* **Phonetics**

Phonodiscs.   *See* **Sound recordings**

Phonograph   789.9

    See also **Sound—Recording and repro-ducing**

    x Gramophone; Record players

Phonograph records.   *See* **Sound recordings**

422

Phonology. *See* **Phonetics;** and names of languages with the subdivision *Pronunciation,* e.g. **English language—Pronunciation;** etc.

Phonorecords. *See* **Sound recordings**

Phosphates 546; 631.8
　　xx **Fertilizers and manures**

Phosphorescence 535; 574.1
　　See also **Bioluminescence**
　　x Luminescence
　　xx **Light; Mineralogy; Optics; Radiation; Radioactivity**

Photocopying machines. *See* **Copying processes and machines**

Photoelectric cells 537.5; 621.381
　　See also **Electronics**
　　x Electric eye

Photoengraving 686.2
　　See also **Photomechanical processes**
　　x Half-tone process
　　xx **Engraving; Photomechanical processes**

Photographic chemistry 771
　　Use for materials on the chemical processes employed in photography
　　See also **Photography—Processing**
　　x Chemistry, Photographic
　　xx **Chemistry**

Photographic film. *See* **Photography—Film**

Photographic slides. *See* **Slides (Photography)**

Photographic supplies. *See* **Photography—Equipment and supplies**

Photography 770
　　See also

Astronomical photography	**Nature photography**
Cameras	**Photomechanical processes**
Color photography	**Slides (Photography)**
Filmstrips	
Microphotography	**Space photography**
Motion picture photography	**Telephotography**

Photography, Aerial 778.3
　　Includes photography from airplanes, balloons, high buildings, etc.
　　x Aerial photography

Photography, Artistic 778
　　x Artistic photography; Photography—Esthetics
　　xx **Art**

Photography, Astronomical. *See* **Astronomical photography**

Photography, Color. *See* **Color photography**

Photography, Commercial 778
　　x Commercial photography

Photography—Darkroom technique. *See* **Photography—Processing**

Photography—Developing and developers 771
　　xx **Photography—Processing**

Photography—Enlarging 770.28
　　x Enlarging (Photography)

Photography—Equipment and supplies 771
See also **Cameras**
x Photographic supplies

Photography—Esthetics. *See* **Photography, Artistic**

Photography—Film 771
x Photographic film

Photography—Handbooks, manuals, etc. 770.2
x Handbooks, manuals, etc.

Photography, Journalistic 070.4
x Journalistic photography; News photography

Photography, Laser. *See* **Holography**

Photography, Lensless. *See* **Holography**

Photography—Lighting 770.2

Photography, Medical 621.36; 778.3
x Medical photography
xx **Photography—Scientific applications**

Photography—Motion pictures. *See* **Motion picture photography**

Photography—Portraits 778.9
xx **Portraits**

Photography—Printing processes 772-773
xx **Photography—Processing**

Photography—Processing 770.28
See also names of special techniques, e.g. **Photography—Developing and developers; Photography—Printing processes; etc.**
x Darkroom technique in photography; Photography—Darkroom technique
xx **Photographic chemistry**

Photography—Retouching 770.2
x Retouching (Photography)

Photography—Scientific applications 778.3
See also specific applications, e.g. **Photography, Medical; etc.**

Photography, Space. *See* **Space photography**

Photography, Stereoscopic 778.4
x Stereophotography

Photography, Submarine 778.7
x Submarine photography; Underwater photography
xx **Marine biology**

Photography in astronautics. *See* **Space photography**

Photography of animals 778.9
Use for materials on the technique and accounts of photographing animals. Materials consisting of photographs and pictures of animals are entered under **Animals—Pictorial works**
See also **Animal painting and illustration; Animals—Pictorial works**
x Animal photography; Animals—Photography
xx **Animal painting and illustration; Animals—Pictorial works; Nature photography**

424

Photography of birds 778.9
Use same form for photography of other subjects
x Bird photography; Birds—Photography
xx **Nature photography**

Photography of fishes 778.9
x Fishes—Photography
xx **Nature photography**

Photography of nature. *See* **Nature photography**

Photography of plants 778.9
x Plants—Photography
xx **Nature photography**

Photomechancial processes 686.2
See also types of photomechancial processes, e.g. **Photoengraving;** etc.
xx **Illustration of books; Photoengraving; Photography**

Photometry 535
See also **Color; Light; Optics**
x Electric light; Light, Electric
xx **Light; Optics**

Photoplays. *See* **Motion picture plays**

Photosynthesis 581

Phototherapy 615
See also **Radiotherapy; Ultraviolet rays**
x Electric light; Light, Electric; Light—Therapeutic use
xx **Physical therapy; Radiotherapy; Therapeutics**

Phrenology 139
See also **Mind and body; Physiognomy**
xx **Brain; Head; Mind and body; Physiognomy; Psychology**

Physical anthropology 573
See also **Color of people; Man—Origin and antiquity**
x Anthropology, Physical; Biological anthropology; Somatology
xx **Anthropology; Ethnology**

Physical chemistry. *See* **Chemistry, Physical and theoretical**

Physical culture. *See* **Physical education and training**

Physical education and training 613.7
See also

Athletics	**Gymnastics**
Coaching (Athletics)	**Health education**
	Physical fitness
Drill (Nonmilitary)	**Posture**
Exercise	**Sports**
Games	

also names of kinds of exercises, e.g. **Fencing; Judo;** etc.
x Calisthenics; Education, Physical; Physical culture; Physical training
xx **Athletics; Education; Exercise; Gymnastics; Hygiene; Sports**

425

Physical fitness 613.7

   x Endurance, Physical; Physical stamina; Stamina, Physical

   xx **Exercise; Physical education and training**

Physical geography (May subdiv. geog.) **551**

   See note under Geography

   See also

Climate	**Lakes**
Earth	**Meteorology**
Earthquakes	**Mountains**
Geochemistry	**Ocean**
Geophysics	**Rivers**
Geysers	**Tides**
Glaciers	**Volcanoes**
Ice	**Winds**
Icebergs	

   x Geography, Physical; Physiography

   xx **Earth; Geography; Geology**

Physical geography—U.S. 551

   x U.S.—Physical geography

Physical stamina. *See* **Physical fitness**

Physical therapy 615

   See also types of therapy, e.g. **Baths; Electrotherapeutics; Hydrotherapy; Massage; Occupational therapy; Phototherapy; Radiotherapy;** etc.

   x Physiotherapy

   xx **Therapeutics**

Physical training. *See* **Physical education and training**

Physically handicapped 362.4

   See also **Orthopedics;** also names of the physically handicapped; e.g. **Blind; Deaf;** etc.

   x Crippled people; Invalids; Soldiers, Disabled; War cripples

   xx **Handicapped; Orthopedics**

Physically handicapped—Housing 301.5; 362.4

   x Dwellings; Housing for the physically handicapped

   xx **Housing**

Physically handicapped—Rehabilitation 362.4

   See also **Occupational therapy**

   x Rehabilitation

Physically handicapped children 155.4; 362.4

   x Children, Crippled; Crippled children

   xx **Handicapped children**

Physicians 920; 926

   See also **Women physicians;** also names of specialists, e.g. **Radiologists; Surgeons;** etc.

   x Doctors; Medical profession

   xx **Surgeons**

Physicians—Directories 610.69025

   xx **Directories**

Physicians—Malpractice 346.3

   x Medical malpractice; Physicians—Tort liability

   xx **Malpractice**

Physicians—Tort liability. *See* **Physicians—Malpractice**

Physicists 920; 925
  xx **Scientists**

Physics 530
  See also

Astrophysics	**Matter**
Biophysics	**Mechanics**
Chemistry, Physical	**Music—Acoustics**
and theoretical	**and physics**
Dynamics	**Nuclear physics**
Electricity	**Optics**
Electrons	**Pneumatics**
Gases	**Quantum theory**
Geophysics	**Radiation**
Gravitation	**Radioactivity**
Hydraulics	**Relativity (Physics)**
Hydrostatics	**Sound**
Light	**Statics**
Liquids	**Thermodynamics**
Magnetism	

  xx **Dynamics; Science**

Physics, Astronomical. *See* **Astrophysics**
Physics, Biological. *See* **Biophysics**
Physics, Nuclear. *See* **Nuclear physics**
Physics, Terrestrial. *See* **Geophysics**

Physiognomy 138
  See also **Face; Phrenology**
  xx **Face; Phrenology; Psychology**

Physiography. *See* **Physical geography**

Physiological chemistry 574.1; 612
  See also **Biochemistry; Cells; Chemistry, Medical and pharmaceutical; Chemistry, Organic; Digestion; Metabolism; Pharmacology; Poisons; Proteins; Vitamins**
  x Animal chemistry; Chemistry, Animal; Chemistry, Pathological; Chemistry, Physiological; Histochemistry; Pathological chemistry
  xx **Biochemistry; Chemistry; Pathology; Physiology**

Physiological effect. *See* appropriate subjects with the subdivision *Physiological effect*, e.g. **Alcohol—Physiological effect; Opium—Physiological effect;** etc.

Physiological psychology. *See* **Psychology, Physiological**

Physiology 612
  See also

Anatomy	**Old age**
Blood	**Physiological chem-**
Bones	**istry**
Cells	**Psychology, Physio-**
Digestion	**logical**
Fatigue	**Reproduction**
Growth	**Respiration**
Muscles	**Senses and sensa-**
Nervous system	**tion**
Nutrition	

427

Physiology—*Continued*
> *also* names of organs of the body, e.g.
> > **Heart;** etc.

> *x* Body, Human; Human body
> *xx* **Anatomy; Biology; Hygiene; Medicine;
> > Science**

Physiology, Comparative 574.1
> *x* Comparative physiology
> *xx* **Zoology**

Physiology, Molecular. *See* **Biophysics**
Physiology of plants. *See* **Plant physiology**
Physiotherapy. *See* **Physical therapy**
Phytogeography. *See* **Geographical distribu-
> tion of animals and plants**

Pianists 920; 927
> *xx* **Musicians**

Piano 786.1
Piano—Tuning 781.9
> *xx* **Tuning**

Piano music 786.1
> *xx* **Instrumental music; Music**

Pickling. *See* **Canning and preserving**
Pickup campers. *See* **Travel trailers and
> campers**

Pictographs. *See* **Picture writing**
Pictorial works. *See* **Pictures;** and subjects
> with the subdivision *Pictorial works,*
> e.g. **Animals—Pictorial works;** etc.

Picture books for children E
> *See also* **Stories without words**
> *xx* **Children's literature**

Picture frames and framing 749
> *x* Framing of pictures

Pictures galleries. *See* **Art—Galleries and mu-
> seums**

Picture posters. *See* **Posters**

Picture writing 411
> *See also* **Cave drawings; Hieroglyphics**
> *x* Pictographs
> *xx* **Hieroglyphics; Writing**

Pictures 025.17; 759; 769; 779
> Use for general materials on the study
> and use of pictures; also for miscel-
> laneous collections of pictures
> *See also* **Cartoons and caricatures; En-
> graving; Etching; Libraries and pic-
> tures; Painting; Portraits;** also sub-
> jects with the subdivision *Pictorial
> works,* e.g. **Animals—Pictorial works;
> U.S.—History—Civil War, 1861–1865
> —Pictorial works;** etc.; also names of
> countries, states, etc. with the sub-
> division *Description and travel—
> Views,* e.g. **U.S.—Description and
> travel—Views;** etc.; and names of
> cities with the subdivision *Description
> —Views,* e.g. **Chicago—Description—
> Views;** etc.
> *x* Pictorial works
> *xx* **Art**

Pictures, Humorous. *See* **Cartoons and caricatures**

Pigmentation. *See* **Color of animals; Color of people**

Pigments 667; 751.2
  See also **Dyes and dyeing; Paint**
  xx **Paint**

Pigs 636.4
  xx **Hogs**

Pilgrims (New England colonists) 974.4
  xx **Puritans; U.S.—History—Colonial period, 1600–1776**

Pilgrims and pilgrimages 248
  See also **Saints; Shrines**
  xx **Shrines; Voyages and travels**

Pilot guides 623.88
  x Coast pilot guides
  xx **Navigation; Pilots and pilotage**

Piloting (Aeronautics). *See* types of aircraft with the subdivision *Piloting,* e.g. **Airplanes—Piloting;** etc.

Piloting (Astronautics). *See* **Space vehicles—Piloting**

Pilots, Airplane. *See* **Air pilots**

Pilots, Ship. *See* **Pilots and pilotage**

Pilots and pilotage 623.88
  See also **Navigation; Pilot guides**
  x Pilots, Ship; Ship pilots
  xx **Harbors; Navigation; Sailors**

Ping-pong 796.34
  x Table tennis

Pioneer life. *See* **Frontier and pioneer life**

Pipe fitting 696
  See also **Plumbing**
  x Steam fitting
  xx **Plumbing**

Pipe lines, Petroleum. *See* **Petroleum—Pipe lines**

Pipe organ. *See* **Organ**

Pipes, Tobacco. *See* **Tobacco pipes**

Pirates 364.1; 910.4
  See also **Privateering; U.S.—History—Tripolitan War, 1801–1805**
  x Barbary corsairs; Buccaneers; Corsairs; Freebooters
  xx **Criminals; International law; Maritime law; Naval history**

Pistols 683; 799.2
  xx **Firearms**

Pity. *See* **Sympathy**

Place names. *See* **Names, Geographical**

Plague 616.9
  x Black death; Bubonic plague

Plain chant. *See* **Chants (Plain, Gregorian, etc.)**

Plainsong. *See* **Chants (Plain, Gregorian, etc.)**

Plane geometry. *See* **Geometry**

Plane trigonometry. *See* **Trigonometry**

Planets   523.4

    See also **Life on other planets; Solar system; Stars;** also names of planets, e.g. **Venus (Planet);** etc.

    xx **Astronomy; Solar system; Stars**

Planets, Life on other.   *See* **Life on other planets**

Planing machines   621.9

    xx **Machine tools**

Planned parenthood.   *See* **Birth control**

Planning, City.   *See* **City planning**

Planning, Economic.   *See* **Economic policy;** and names of countries, states, etc. with the subdivision *Economic policy,* e.g. **U.S.—Economic policy;** etc.

Planning, National.   *See* **Economic policy; Social policy;** and names of countries with the subdivision *Economic policy, Social policy,* e.g. **U.S.—Economic policy; U.S.—Social policy;** etc.

Planning, Regional.   *See* **Regional planning**

Plans.   *See* **Architectural drawing; Geometrical drawing; Map drawing; Maps; Mechanical drawing**

Plant anatomy.   *See* **Botany—Anatomy**

Plant breeding   581.1; 631.5

    Use for materials on that form of plant propagation which aims to improve plants, as by selection after controlled mating, etc.

    See also **Fertilization of plants; Plant propagation**

    x Breeding; Hybridization

    xx **Agriculture; Flower gardening; Plant propagation**

Plant chemistry.   *See* **Botanical chemistry; Plants—Chemical analysis**

Plant diseases.   *See* **Plants—Diseases**

Plant distribution.   *See* **Geographical distribution of animals and plants**

Plant forms in design.   *See* **Design, Decorative**

Plant introduction   581.5

    x Acclimatization

    xx **Botany, Economic**

Plant lore   398

    x Folklore of plants; Plants—Folklore

    xx **Folklore; Natural history; Plant names, Popular; Trees**

Plant names, Popular   581.03

    See also **Botany—Terminology; Plant lore**

    x Botany—Nomenclature

    xx **Botany—Terminology**

Plant names, Scientific.   *See* **Botany—Terminology**

Plant nutrition.   *See* **Plants—Nutrition**

Plant pathology.   *See* **Plants—Diseases**

Plant physiology   581.1

    See also **Fertilization of plants; Germination; Growth (Plants); Plants—Nutrition**

Plant physiology—*Continued*

   x Botany—Physiology; Physiology of plants

   xx **Botany**

Plant propagation 581.1

   Use for materials on the continuance or multiplication of plants by successive production. Materials dealing with methods adopted to secure new and improved varieties are entered under **Plant breeding**

   See also **Grafting; Plant breeding; Seeds**

   x Plants—Propagation; Propagation of plants

   xx **Flower gardening; Fruit culture; Gardening; Nurseries (Horticulture); Plant breeding**

Plantation life 301.34

Planting. *See* **Agriculture; Gardening; Landscape gardening; Tree planting**

Plants 581

   See also **Fertilization of plants; Flower gardening; Gardening; Geographical distribution of animals and plants; Horticulture;** also names of types of plants, e.g. **Alpine plants; Climbing plants; Desert plants; Flowers; Forage plants; Fresh water plants; House plants;** etc.; also names of individual plants, e.g. **Ferns; Mosses;** etc.; and headings beginning with the words **Plant** and **Plants**

   x Flora; Vegetable kingdom

   xx **Botany; Flowers; Gardening; Trees**

Plants—Anatomy. *See* **Botany—Anatomy**

Plants—Chemical analysis 581.1

   See also **Botanical chemistry**

   x Plant chemistry

   xx **Botanical chemistry**

Plants—Collection and preservation 579

   x Botanical specimens—Collection and preservation; Herbaria; Preservation of botanical specimens; Specimens, Preservation of

Plants, Cultivated (May subdiv. geog.) **631.5**

   See also **Annuals (Plants); House plants; Plants, Edible; Plants, Ornamental**

   xx **Gardening**

Plants, Cultivated—U.S. 631.5

   x U.S.—Plants, Cultivated

Plants—Diseases 581.2; 632

   See also names of crops, etc. with the subdivision *Diseases and pests*, e.g. **Fruit—Diseases and pests;** etc.

   x Botany—Pathology; Diseases and pests; Diseases of plants; Garden pests; Pathological botany; Pathology, Vegetable; Plant diseases; Plant pathology; Vegetable pathology

   xx **Agricultural pests; Fungi**

Plants—Ecology. *See* **Botany—Ecology**
Plants, Edible 581.6
> *x* Edible plants; Food plants; Plants, Useful
> *xx* **Botany, Economic; Plants, Cultivated**
Plants, Extinct. *See* **Plants, Fossil**
Plants—Fertilization. *See* **Fertilization of plants**
Plants—Folklore. *See* **Plant lore**
Plants, Fossil 561
> *x* Botany, Fossil; Extinct plants; Fossil plants; Paleobotany; Plants, Extinct
> *xx* **Botany; Fossils**
Plants—Geographical distribution. *See* **Geographical distribution of animals and plants**
Plants—Growth. *See* **Growth (Plants)**
Plants, Medicinal. *See* **Botany, Medical**
Plants—Nutrition 581.1; 631.5
> *x* Plant nutrition
> *xx* **Nutrition; Plant physiology**
Plants, Ornamental 635.9; 715
> *x* Ornamental plants
> *xx* **Flower gardening; Landscape gardening; Plants, Cultivated; Shrubs**
Plants—Photography. *See* **Photography of plants**
Plants—Propagation. *See* **Plant propagation**
Plants—Soilless culture 631.5
> *x* Agriculture, Soilless; Chemiculture; Hydroponics; Soilless agriculture; Water farming
Plants, Useful. *See* **Botany, Economic; Plants, Edible**
Plants in art 704.94
> *See also* **Flower painting and illustration**
> *x* Flowers in art; Trees in art
> *xx* **Art; Decoration and ornament**
Plaster and plastering 693.6
> *See also* **Cement; Concrete; Mortar; Stucco**
> *x* Plastering
> *xx* **Masonry**
Plaster casts 731.4
> *x* Casting; Casts, Plaster
> *xx* **Sculpture**
Plaster of paris. *See* **Gypsum**
Plastering. *See* **Plaster and plastering**
Plastic materials. *See* **Plastics**
Plastic surgery. *See* **Surgery, Plastic**
Plastics 668.4
> *See also* **Chemistry, Organic—Synthesis; Gums and resins; Rubber, Artificial; Synthetic products;** also names of specific plastics
> *x* Plastic materials
> *xx* **Chemistry, Organic—Synthesis; Polymers and polymerization; Synthetic products**
Plate 739.2
> *See also* **Hallmarks; Pewter; Sheffield plate**
> *x* Gold plate

432

Plate—*Continued*
 xx Goldwork; Hallmarks; Silverwork
Plate metalwork   671.7
 xx Metalwork; Sheet metalwork
Plate tectonics   551.4
 See also Continental drift; Submarine geology
 xx Continental drift; Earth—Crust; Geophysics; Submarine geology
Platforms, Drilling.   *See* Artificial islands
Play   790
 See also Amusements; Finger play; Games; Recreation; Sports
 xx Amusements; Children; Games; Recreation
Play centers.   *See* Community centers; Playgrounds
Play direction (Theater).   *See* Theater—Production and direction
Play production.   *See* Amateur theatricals; Motion picture plays; Theater—Production and direction
Play writing.   *See* Drama—Technique; Motion picture plays—Technique; Radio plays —Technique; Television plays—Technique
Playgrounds   796.06
 See also Community centers; Parks; Summer schools
 x Play centers; Public playgrounds; School playgrounds
 xx Child welfare; Children; Community centers; Parks; Recreation; Social settlements
Playhouses.   *See* Theaters
Playing cards.   *See* Card games
Plays.   *See* Drama—Collections; One act plays
Plays, Bible.   *See* Bible—Drama
Plays, Christmas.   *See* Christmas—Drama
Plays, College.   *See* College and school drama—Collections
Plays for children.   *See* Children's plays
Playwrights.   *See* Dramatists
Playwriting.   *See* Drama—Technique; Motion picture plays—Technique; Radio plays —Technique; Television plays—Technique
Pleasure   152.4
 See also Happiness; Pain
 xx Emotions; Happiness; Joy and sorrow; Pain; Senses and sensation
Plots (Drama, fiction, etc.)   808
 Use for materials dealing with the construction and analysis of plots as a literary technique. Collections of plots are entered under Literature—Stories, plots, etc.
 See also literary or musical forms with the subdivision *Stories, plots, etc.* e.g. Bal-

Plots (Drama, fiction, etc.)—*Continued*
　　lets—Stories, plots, etc.; Operas—Sto-
　　ries, plots, etc.; etc.
　　x Drama—Plots; Dramatic plots; Fiction—
　　　Plots; Novels—Plots; Scenarios
　　xx **Authorship; Characters and characteris-
　　　tics in literature; Drama; Fiction;
　　　Literature**
Plows　631.3
　　xx **Agricultural machinery**
Plumbing　696
　　See also **Drainage, House; Gas fitting;
　　　Pipe fitting; Sanitary engineering;
　　　Sanitation, Household; Sewerage; Sol-
　　　der and soldering**
　　xx **Drainage, House; Gas fitting; Pipe fit-
　　　ting; Sanitation, Household**
Pluto operation.　*See* **Cuba—History—Invasion,
　　1961**
Plywood　674
　　xx **Wood**
Pneumatic transmission.　*See* **Compressed air**
Pneumatics　533; 621.5
　　See also **Aerodynamics; Compressed air;
　　　Gases; Ground cushion phenomena;
　　　Sound**
　　xx **Gases; Physics**
Pneumonia　616.2
　　xx **Lungs—Diseases**
Pocket calculators.　*See* **Calculating machines**
Podiatry　617
　　x Chiropody; Foot—Care and hygiene
Poetics　808.1
　　Use for materials on the art and technique
　　　of poetry. Materials on the apprecia-
　　　tion and philosophy of poetry are en-
　　　tered under **Poetry**
　　See also **Rhyme; Rhythm; Versification**
　　x Poetry—Technique
Poetry　808.1
　　See note under **Poetics**
　　Names of all types of poetry are not in-
　　　cluded in this list but are to be added
　　　as needed
　　See also

Ballads	**Hymns**
Children in	**Love poetry**
poetry	**Nature in poetry**
Eddas	**Parody**
Epic poetry	**Scalds and scal-**
Free verse	**dic poetry**

　　also **American poetry; English poetry; etc.;**
　　　and subjects with the subdivision
　　　Poetry, e.g. **Animals—Poetry; Bunker
　　　Hill, Battle of, 1775—Poetry; Chicago
　　　—Poetry; Shakespeare, William—Po-
　　　etry; etc.**
　　x Poetry—Philosophy
　　xx **Esthetics; Literature; Versification**

Poetry—Collections 808.81; 811.08; etc.

> *See also* **American poetry—Collections; English poetry—Collections;** etc.; also **Children's poetry; Christmas—Poetry; Nonsense verses; Patriotic poetry; Religious poetry; School verse; Sea poetry; Songs; War poetry**
>
> *x* Collections of literature; Poetry—Selections; Rhymes
>
> *xx* **Literature—Collections**

Poetry—History and criticism 809.1

> *See also* **American poetry—History and criticism; English poetry—History and criticism;** etc.

Poetry—Philosophy. *See* **Poetry**

Poetry—Selections. *See* **Poetry—Collections**

Poetry—Technique. *See* **Poetics**

Poetry and music. *See* **Music and literature**

Poetry for children. *See* **Children's poetry; Nursery rhymes**

Poetry of love. *See* **Love poetry**

Poetry of nature. *See* **Nature in poetry**

Poets (May subdiv. geog. adjective form, e.g. **Poets, German;** etc.) **920; 928**

> Use for materials dealing with the personal lives of several poets. Materials about their literary productions are entered under **Poetry—History and criticism; English poetry—History and criticism;** etc.
>
> *See also* **Dramatists; Minstrels; Scalds and scaldic poetry; Troubadours**
>
> *xx* **Authors**

Poets, American 920; 928

> *x* American poets; U.S.—Poets

Point Four program. *See* **Reconstruction (1939–1951)**

Poison gases. *See* **Gases, Asphyxiating and poisonous**

Poisonous animals 591.6

> *See also* names of poisonous animals
>
> *xx* **Animals**

Poisonous plants 581.6

> *See also* names of poisonous plants
>
> *xx* **Botany, Economic; Chemistry, Medical and pharmaceutical; Poisons**

Poisons 615.9

> *See also* **Pesticides; Poisonous plants;** and subjects with the subdivision *Toxicology*, e.g. **Insecticides—Toxicology;** etc.
>
> *x* Toxic substances; Venom
>
> *xx* **Accidents; Chemistry; Chemistry, Medical and pharmaceutical; Drugs; Materia medica; Medical jurisprudence; Physiological chemistry**

Polar expeditions. *See* **Antarctic regions; Arctic regions; North Pole; Polar regions; Scientific expeditions; South Pole;** and names of exploring expeditions, and names of explorers

435

Polar lights. *See* **Auroras**
Polar regions   919.8; 998
　　　Use for materials dealing with both the
　　　　Antarctic and Arctic regions
　　See also **Antarctic regions; Arctic regions;**
　　　　North Pole; South Pole
　　x Polar expeditions
Police (May subdiv. geog. country or state)
　　363.2
　　See also **Crime; Criminal investigation; De-**
　　　　tectives; Secret service; also names of
　　　　cities with the subdivision *Police,* e.g.
　　　　Chicago—Police; etc.
　　xx **Crime; Criminal investigation; Detec-**
　　　　tives; Law; Law enforcement
Police, International. *See* **International police**
Police, State   352
　　x State police
Police—U.S.   351.7
　　x U.S.—Police
Police corruption   363.2
　　x Corruption, Police
　　xx **Misconduct in office**
Policewomen   363.2
　　x Women police
Polio. *See* **Poliomyelitis**
Poliomyelitis   616.8
　　x Infantile paralysis; Paralysis, Anterior
　　　　spinal; Paralysis, Infantile; Polio;
　　　　Spinal paralysis, Anterior
Poliomyelitis vaccine   614.4; 615
　　x Live poliovirus vaccine; Sabine vaccine;
　　　　Salk vaccine
Polishing. *See* **Grinding and polishing**
Politeness. *See* **Courtesy; Etiquette**
Political assessments. *See* **Campaign funds**
Political asylum. *See* **Asylum, Right of**
Political boundaries. *See* **Boundaries**
Political behavior. *See* **Political psychology**
Political conventions   329
　　See also **Political parties; Primaries**
　　x Conventions, Political
　　xx **Political parties; Political science**
Political corruption. *See* **Corruption in poli-**
　　tics
Political crimes and offenses   364.1
　　See also **Anarchism and anarchists; Assassi-**
　　　　nation; Concentration camps; Corrup-
　　　　tion in politics; Government, Resis-
　　　　tance to; Political prisoners; Terror-
　　　　ism; Treason
　　x Crimes, Political; Sedition
　　xx **Political ethics; Subversive activities**
Political economy. *See* **Economics**
Political ethics   172
　　See also **Citizenship; Conflict of interest;**
　　　　Corruption in politics; Government,
　　　　Resistance to; Political crimes and of-
　　　　fenses

Political ethics—*Continued*

    x Ethics, Political

    xx **Political science; Social ethics**

Political geography. *See* **Boundaries**

Political parties   329

    See also **Political conventions; Politics, Practical; Right and left (Political science)** also names of parties, e.g. **Democratic Party; Republican Party;** etc.

    x Parties, Political

    xx **Political conventions; Political science**

Political parties—Finance. *See* **Campaign funds**

Political prisoners   365

    x Prisoners, Political

    xx **Political crimes and offenses; Prisoners**

Political psychology   301.1

    See also **Propaganda; Public opinion**

    x Political behavior; Politics, Practical—Psychology; Psychology, Political

    xx **Political science; Psychology; Social psychology**

Political refugees. *See* **Refugees, Political**

Political scandals. *See* **Corruption in politics**

Political science   320

    See also

Anarchism and anarchists	**Municipal government**
Aristocracy	**Nationalism**
Bureaucracy	**Political conventions**
Church and state	
Citizenship	**Political ethics**
Civil rights	**Political parties**
Civil service	**Political psychology**
Communism	
Comparative government	**Politics, Practical**
Constitutional history	**Power (Social sciences)**
Constitutional law	**Public administration**
Constitutions	
Constitutions, State	**Representative government and representation**
Democracy	**Republics**
Executive power	**Revolutions**
Federal government	**Right and left (Political science)**
Freedom	
Geopolitics	**Separation of powers**
Government, Resistance to	
Government ownership	**Socialism**
	The State
Imperialism	**State governments**
Kings and rulers	
Law	**State rights**
Legislation	**Suffrage**
Local government	**Taxation**
Monarchy	**Utopias**
	World politics

    also names of countries and states with

437

Political science—*Continued*

the subhead *Constitution* (e.g. **U.S. Constitution;** etc.); also names of countries, cities, etc. with the subdivision *Politics and government*, e.g. **U.S.— Politics and government;** etc.

x Administration; Civics; Civil government; The Commonwealth; Government

xx **Constitutional history; Constitutional law; History; Social sciences; The State**

Politicians (May subdiv. geog. adjective form) **920; 923**

See also **Diplomats**

x Statesmen

Politicians, American 920; 923

x American politicians; U.S.—Politicians

Politics. *See* names of continents, areas, countries, states, counties, and cities with the subdivision *Politics and government*, e.g. **Asia—Politics and government; Latin America—Politics and government; U.S.—Politics and government; Chicago—Politics and government;** etc.

Politics, Corruption in. *See* **Corruption in politics**

Politics, Practical 329

Use for materials dealing with practical politics in general, such as electioneering, political machines, etc. Materials on the science of politics are entered under **Political science**

See also **Business and politics; Campaign funds; Campaign literature; Corruption in politics; Elections; Lobbying; Primaries; Television in politics;** also names of countries, cities, etc. with the subdivision *Politics and government* (e.g. **U.S.—Politics and government;** etc.); also classes of people with the subdivision *Political activity*, e.g. **College students—Political activity; Women—Political activity;** etc. and headings beginning with the word **Political**

x Campaigns, Political; Electioneering; Practical politics

xx **Political parties; Political science**

Politics, Practical—Psychology. *See* **Political psychology**

Politics and business. *See* **Business and politics**

Politics and Christianity. *See* **Christianity and politics**

Politics and religion. *See* **Religion and politics**

Politics and students. *See* **Students—Political activity**

Pollination. *See* **Fertilization of plants**

Polls, Election. *See* **Elections**

Polls, Public opinion. *See* **Public opinion polls**

438

Pollution 301.31; 333.7-333.9; 614.7

    See also types of pollution, e.g. **Air—Pollution; Marine pollution; Noise pollution; Pesticides—Environmental aspects; Radioactive fallout; Water—Pollution;** etc.

    x Contamination of environment; Environmental pollution

    xx **Environmental policy; Industrial wastes; Man—Influence on nature; Public health; Sanitary engineering; Sanitation**

Pollution—Mathematical models 301.31022

    xx **Mathematical models**

Pollution control devices. (Motor vehicles) *See* **Automobiles—Pollution control devices**

Pollution of air. *See* **Air—Pollution**

Pollution of water. *See* **Water—Pollution**

Poltergeists. *See* **Ghosts**

Polyglot dictionaries. *See* **Dictionaries, Polyglot**

Polymers and polymerization 541; 547

    See also types of polymers, e.g. **Plastics;** etc.

    xx **Chemistry, Organic—Synthesis; Chemistry, Physical and theoretical**

Ponds 551.4

    xx **Water**

Ponies 636.1

    xx **Horses**

Pontiac's Conspiracy, 1763–1765 973.2

    xx **Indians of North America—Wars; U.S.—History—Colonial period, 1600–1775; U.S.—History—French and Indian War, 1755–1763**

Pony express 383

    xx **Express service; Postal service**

Poor 301.44

    See also **Unemployed;** also names of cities with the subdivision *Poor*, e.g. **Chicago—Poor;** etc.

    xx **Poverty; Public welfare**

Poor—Legal assistance. *See* **Legal assistance to the poor**

Poor—Medical care 362.6; 368.4

    See also **Medicaid**

Poor relief. *See* **Charities; Economic assistance, Domestic; Public welfare**

Popes 920; 922

    See also **Holy See; Papacy**

    xx **Church history; Holy See; Papacy**

Popes—Infallibility 262

    x Infallibility of the Pope

Popes—Temporal power 262

    See also **Church and state**

    x Temporal power of the Pope

    xx **Church and state; Church history—Middle Ages, 600–1500**

Popular government. *See* **Democracy**

Popular music. *See* **Music, Popular (Songs, etc.)**

Popular songs. *See* **Music, Popular (Songs, etc.)**

Popularity 158; 301.11

Population 301.32

  See also **Birth control; Birth rate; Census; Eugenics; Migration, Internal; Mortality;** also names of countries, cities, etc. with the subdivision *Population*, e.g. **U.S.—Population; Chicago—Population;** etc.

  xx **Birth rate; Economics; Human ecology; Sociology; Vital statistics**

Population, Foreign. *See* **Immigration and emigration;** names of countries with the subdivision *Immigration and emigration* (e.g. **U.S.—Immigration and emigration;** etc.); and names of countries, cities, etc. with the subdivision *Foreign population*, e.g. **U.S.—Foreign population; Chicago—Foreign population;** etc.

Porcelain 738.2

  See also **China painting**

  x China (Porcelain); Chinaware; Dishes

  xx **Pottery**

Porcelain enamels. *See* **Enamel and enameling**

Porcelain painting. *See* **China painting**

Pornography 176

  See also **Erotica**

  x Obscene materials

  xx **Erotica; Obscenity (Law)**

Portrait painting 757

  See also **Crayon drawing; Figure painting; Miniature painting; Pastel drawing**

  xx **Figure painting; Miniature painting; Painting**

Portraits 704.94; 757; 778.9

  See also **Cartoons and caricatures; Photography—Portraits;** also headings for collective and individual biography and classes of people with the subdivision *Portraits*, e.g. **U.S.—Biography—Portraits; Musicians—Portraits; Shakespeare, William—Portraits;** etc.

  x Iconography

  xx **Art; Biography; Pictures**

Ports. *See* **Harbors**

Portuguese literature 869

  See also **Brazilian literature**

  xx **Brazilian literature**

Position analysis. *See* **Topology**

Positivism 146

  See also **Agnosticism; Idealism; Materialism; Pragmatism; Realism**

  x Humanity, Religion of; Religion of humanity

  xx **Agnosticism; Deism; Philosophy; Rationalism; Realism**

Post-impressionism. *See* **Postimpressionism (Art)**

Post office. *See* **Postal service**

Postage stamps 383; 769

> *x* Stamps, Postage

Postage stamps—Collectors and collecting 769

> *x* Collectibles; Collection of objects; Philately
>
> *xx* **Collectors and collecting**

Postal service (May subdiv. geog.) **383**

> *See also* **Air mail service; Pony express**
>
> *x* Mail service; Parcel post; Post office
>
> *xx* **Communication; Transportation**

Postal service—U.S. 383

> *x* U.S.—Mail; U.S.—Postal service

Posters 741.67

> *See also* **Signs and signboards**
>
> *x* Advertising, Pictorial; Picture posters
>
> *xx* **Advertising; Commercial art; Signs and signboards**

Postimpressionism (Art) 709.04

> *See also* **Cubism; Expressionism (Art); Futurism (Art); Impressionism (Art); Surrealism**
>
> *x* Post-impressionism
>
> *xx* **Art, Modern—19th century; Cubism; Expressionism (Art); Futurism (Art); Impressionism (Art); Painting**

Posture 613.7

> *xx* **Physical education and training**

Potash 631.8; 668

> *xx* **Fertilizers and manures**

Potatoes 633; 635

> *xx* **Vegetables**

Potters 920; 926; 927

> *xx* **Artists**

Pottery (May subdiv. geog. adjective form, e.g. **Pottery, Chinese**; etc.) **666; 738**

> *See also* **Glazes; Porcelain; Terra cotta; Tiles; Vases**
>
> *x* Crockery; Dishes; Earthenware; Faience; Fayence; Stoneware
>
> *xx* **Archeology; Art, Decorative; Art objects; Arts and crafts; Ceramics; Clay industries; Decoration and ornament; Tableware; Vases**

Pottery, American 738

> *x* American pottery; U.S.—Pottery

Pottery—Marks 738

> *x* Marks, Potters'

Poultry 636.5; 641.3

> *See also* names of domesticated birds, e.g. **Ducks; Geese; Turkeys**; etc.
>
> *xx* **Domestic animals**

Poverty 301.44; 362

> *See also* **Charities; Poor; Public welfare**; also names of countries with the subdivisions *Economic conditions* and *Social conditions* (e.g. **U.S.—Economic conditions; U.S.—Social conditions;**

Poverty—*Continued*

etc.); also names of cities with the subdivision *Poor,* e.g. **Chicago—Poor;** etc.

x Destitution; Pauperism

xx **Economic assistance, Domestic; Wealth**

Powder, Smokeless. *See* **Gunpowder**

Powdered milk. *See* **Milk, Dried**

Power (Mechanics) 531; 621

See note under **Power resources**

See also **Compressed air; Electric power; Force and energy; Machinery; Power resources; Power transmission; Steam; Water power; Wind power**

xx **Mechanical   engineering;   Mechanics; Steam engineering**

Power (Social sciences) 301.15

xx **Political science**

Power blackouts. *See* **Electric power failures**

Power boats. *See* **Motorboats**

Power failures. *See* **Electric power failures**

Power plants 621.4

See also types of power plants, e.g. **Atomic power plants; Electric power plants; Steam power plants;** etc.

x Power stations

Power plants, Atomic. *See* **Atomic power plants**

Power plants, Electric. *See* **Electric power plants**

Power plants, Steam. *See* **Steam power plants**

Power politics. *See* **Balance of power; World politics—1945–1965; World politics, 1965–**

Power resources 333.7

Use for materials on the available sources of mechanical power in general. Materials on the physics and engineering aspects of power are entered under **Power (Mechanics)**

See also **Electric power; Energy conservation; Energy consumption; Energy policy; Fuel; Solar energy; Water power; Wind power**

x Energy; Energy resources; Power supply

xx **Natural resources; Power (Mechanics)**

Power resources and state. *See* **Energy policy**

Power resources conservation. *See* **Energy conservation**

Power stations. *See* **Power plants**

Power supply. *See* **Power resources**

Power tools 621.9

xx **Tools**

Power transmission 621.8

See also **Belts and belting; Cables; Electric power distribution; Gearing; Machinery**

x Transmission of power

xx **Belts and belting; Machinery; Mechanical engineering; Power (Mechanics)**

Power transmission, Electric. *See* **Electric lines; Electric power distribution**

Powers, Separation of. *See* **Separation of powers**

Practical nurses 610.73
 xx **Nurses**

Practical nursing 610.73; 649.8
 xx **Nursing**

Practical politics. *See* **Politics, Practical**

Practice teaching. *See* **Student teaching**

Pragmatism 144
 See also **Empiricism; Reality; Truth; Utilitarianism**
 xx **Empiricism; Knowledge, Theory of; Philosophy; Positivism; Realism; Reality; Truth; Utilitarianism**

Prayer 217; 242
 See also **Devotional exercises; Prayers**
 x Devotion
 xx **Devotional exercises; Prayers; Worship**

Prayers 242; 264
 See also **Prayer**
 x Collects; Theology, Devotional
 xx **Prayer**

Prayers in the public schools. *See* **Religion in the public schools**

Preachers. *See* **Clergy**

Preaching 251
 See also **Sermons**
 x Speaking
 xx **Pastoral work; Public speaking; Rhetoric; Sermons**

Preaching friars. *See* **Dominicans**

Precious metals 549; 553
 See also **Gold; Silver**
 xx **Metals; Mines and mineral resources**

Precious stones 549; 553
 Use for mineralogical and technological materials on the subject. Materials treating of stones and jewels from the point of view of art are entered under **Gems**
 See also **Gems;** also names of precious stones, e.g. **Diamonds;** etc.
 x Gemstones; Jewels; Stones, Precious
 xx **Gems; Mineralogy**

Precocious children. *See* **Gifted children**

Pre-Columbian Americans. *See* **Indians of North America**

Predestination 234
 See also **Free will and determinism**
 x Election (Theology); Foreordination
 xx **Calvinism; Fate and fatalism; Theology**

Predictions. *See* **Forecasting; Prophecies (Occult sciences)**

Prefabricated houses 693.9; 728
 x Demountable houses; Dwellings; Houses, Prefabricated; Packaged houses
 xx **Architecture, Domestic; Buildings, Prefabricated**

Pregnancy 612.8; 618
> See also **Childbirth; Prenatal care**
> *xx* **Childbirth; Reproduction**

Prehistoric animals. *See* **Fossils**

Prehistoric man. *See* **Man, Prehistoric**

Prehistory. *See* **Archeology; Bronze age; Iron age; Stone age;** and names of countries, cities, etc. with the subdivision *Antiquities,* e.g. **U.S.–Antiquities;** etc.

Prejudicial publicity. *See* **Freedom of the press and fair trial**

Prejudices and antipathies 152.4; 177
> *See also* types of prejudice, e.g. **Racism; Sexism;** etc.
> *x* Antipathies; Bigotry
> *xx* **Emotions; Human relations; Race awareness**

Preliterate man. *See* **Man, Nonliterate**

Preliterate society. *See* **Society, Nonliterate folk**

Premarital counseling. *See* **Marriage counseling**

Prenatal care 618.2
> *xx* **Pregnancy**

Prenuptial contracts. *See* **Marriage contracts**

Prepaid group medical practice. *See* **Health maintenance organizations**

Prepaid medical care. *See* **Insurance, Health**

Preprimers. *See* **Easy reading materials**

Preraphaelitism 759.05; 759.2
> *xx* **Painting**

Presbyterian Church 285
> *x* Religious denominations

Preschool education. *See* **Education, Preschool**

Preschool reading materials. *See* **Easy reading materials**

Presents. *See* **Gifts**

Preservation of botanical specimens. *See* **Plants–Collection and preservation**

Preservation of buildings. *See* **Architecture–Conservation and restoration**

Preservation of food. *See* **Food–Preservation**

Preservation of forests. *See* **Forests and forestry**

Preservation of historical records. *See* **Archives**

Preservation of natural resources. *See* **Conservation of natural resources**

Preservation of natural scenery. *See* **Landscape protection; Natural monuments; Nature conservation; Wilderness areas**

Preservation of organs, tissues, etc. 617
> *See also* **Transplantation of organs, tissues, etc.**
> *x* Organ preservation; Organs, Preservation

Preservation of wildlife. *See* **Wildlife–Conservation**

Preservation of wood. *See* **Wood—Preservation**

Preservation of works of art. *See* subjects with the subdivision *Conservation and restoration,* e.g. **Painting—Conservation and restoration;** etc.

Preservation of zoological specimens. *See* **Zoological specimens—Collection and preservation**

Preserving. *See* **Canning and preserving**

Presidential aides. *See* **Presidents—U.S.—Staff**

Presidential campaigns—U.S. *See* **Presidents—U.S.—Election**

Presidential libraries. *See* **Presidents—U.S.—Archives;** and names of libraries

Presidents 920; 923

> *See also* **Executive power; Presidents—U.S.;** also names of other countries with the subdivision *Presidents* (e.g. **Mexico—Presidents;** etc.); and names of presidents

xx **Executive power; Kings and rulers**

Presidents—Powers and duties. *See* **Executive power**

Presidents—U.S. 920; 923

> When applicable, the following subdivisions may be used under names of presidents
>
> For materials on presidents of other countries, use names of countries with the subdivision *Presidents,* e.g. **Mexico—Presidents;** etc.
>
> *See also* names of presidents, e.g. **Kennedy, John Fitzgerald, Pres. U.S.;** etc.
>
> *x* U.S.—Presidents
>
> *xx* **Presidents**

Presidents—U.S.—Addresses and essays 353.03

> *See also* **Presidents—U.S.—Inaugural addresses**

Presidents—U.S.—Appointment 353.03

Presidents—U.S.—Archives 026

> *See also* names of libraries, e.g. **Harry S. Truman Library, Independence, Mo.;** etc.
>
> *x* Libraries, Presidential; Presidential libraries

Presidents—U.S.—Assassination 364.1

> *xx* **Assassination**

Presidents—U.S.—Children 920

Presidents—U.S.—Election (May subdiv. by date) **324.73**

> *x* Campaigns, Presidential—U.S.; Electoral college; Presidential campaigns—U.S.
>
> *xx* **Elections**

Presidents—U.S.—Family 920

Presidents—U.S.—Funeral and memorial services 393

> *x* Presidents—U.S.—Memorial services

445

Presidents—U.S.—Health 353.03
   x Presidents—U.S.—Illness
Presidents—U.S.—Homes 728
Presidents—U.S.—Illness. *See* **Presidents—U.S.—Health**
Presidents—U.S.—Impeachment 351.9
Presidents—U.S.—Inability. *See* **Presidents—U.S.—Succession**
Presidents—U.S.—Inaugural addresses 353.03
   xx **Presidents—U.S.—Addresses and essays; Presidents—U.S.—Inauguration**
Presidents—U.S.—Inauguration 353.03
   See also **Presidents—U.S.—Inaugural addresses**
Presidents—U.S.—Medals 353.03
Presidents—U.S.—Memorial services. *See* **Presidents—U.S.—Funeral and memorial services**
Presidents—U.S.—Messages 353.03
   x Messages to Congress; Presidents—U.S.—State of the Union messages; State of the Union messages
Presidents—U.S.—Mothers 920
Presidents—U.S.—Nomination 329
   x Nomination of presidents
Presidents—U.S.—Portraits 353.03
Presidents—U.S.—Power
   See **Executive power—U.S.**
Presidents—U.S.—Protection 353.007
Presidents—U.S.—Quotations 808.88; 818
   xx **Quotations**
Presidents—U.S.—Religion 248
Presidents—U.S.—Resignation 353.03
Presidents—U.S.—Sports 796
Presidents—U.S.—Staff 353.03
   x Presidential aides
   xx **U.S.—Executive departments**
Presidents—U.S.—State of the Union messages. *See* **Presidents—U.S.—Messages**
Presidents—U.S.—Succession 353.03; 342.6
   x Presidents—U.S.—Inability
Presidents—U.S.—Tombs 393
Presidents—U.S.—Travel 353.03; 910
Presidents—U.S.—Wives 920
   x First ladies—U.S.; Presidents' wives—U.S.; Wives of presidents—U.S.
   xx **Women—U.S.**
Presidents' wives—U.S. *See* **Presidents—U.S.—Wives**
Press. *See* **Freedom of the press; Journalism; News agencies; Newspapers; Periodicals; Underground press**
Press, Underground. *See* **Underground press**
Press and government. *See* **Government and the press**
Press censorship. *See* **Freedom of the press**
Press clippings. *See* **Clippings (Books, newspapers, etc.)**
Press working of metal. *See* **Sheet metalwork**
Pressure groups. *See* **Lobbying**

Pressure suits. *See* **Astronauts—Clothing**

Pretenders. *See* **Imposters and imposture**

Prevention of accidents. *See* **Accidents—Prevention**

Prevention of crime. *See* **Crime prevention**

Prevention of cruelty to animals. *See* **Animals —Treatment**

Prevention of fire. *See* **Fire prevention**

Prevention of smoke. *See* **Smoke prevention**

Preventive medicine. *See* **Bacteriology; Hygiene; Immunity; Public health**

Price controls. *See* **Wage-price policy**

Price-wage policy. *See* **Wage-price policy**

Prices 338.5

    See also **Cost of living; Farm produce— Marketing; Wage-price policy; Wages;** also subjects with the subdivision *Prices,* e.g. **Art—Prices; Books—Prices;** etc.

    xx **Commerce; Consumption (Economics); Cost of living; Economics; Finance; Manufactures; Wages**

Priests 253; 920; 922

    See also **Ex-priests**

    x Pastors

    xx **Clergy; Catholic Church—Clergy**

Primaries 329

    See also **Elections**

    x Direct primaries; Elections, Primary

    xx **Elections; Political conventions; Politics, Practical; Representative government and representation**

Primary education. *See* **Education, Elementary**

Primates 599

    See also names of individual primates, e.g. **Monkeys;** etc.

    xx **Animals; Mammals**

Primates—Habits and behavior 599

    xx **Animals—Habits and behavior**

Primers. *See* **Easy reading materials**

Primitive Christianity. *See* **Church history— Early church, ca.30—600**

Primitive man. *See* **Man, Nonliterate**

Primitive society. *See* **Society, Nonliterate folk**

Princes and princesses 920; 923

    x Royalty

Printing 686.2

    See also **Advertising layout and typography; Books; Color printing; Electrotyping; Linotype; Offset printing; Proofreading; Type and type founding; Typesetting**

    x Layout and typography; Typography

    xx **Bibliography; Book industries and trade; Books; Graphic arts; Industrial arts; Publishers and publishing; Typesetting**

447

Printing—Exhibitions 686.2074
> *See also* **Book industries and trade—Exhibitions**
>
> *x* Books—Exhibitions
>
> *xx* **Book industries and trade—Exhibitions; Exhibitions**

Printing, Offset. *See* **Offset printing**

Printing—Specimens 686.2
> *See also* **Type and type founding**
>
> *x* Type specimens
>
> *xx* **Advertising; Initials; Type and type founding**

Printing—Style manuals 686.202
> *See also* **Authorship—Handbooks, manuals, etc.**
>
> *x* Style manuals
>
> *xx* **Authorship—Handbooks, manuals, etc.**

Printing, Textile. *See* **Textile printing**

Prints (May subdiv. geog. adjective form) **769**
> *See also* **Lithography**
>
> *xx* **Graphic arts**

Prints, American 769
> *x* American prints; U.S.—Prints

Prison escapes. *See* **Escapes**

Prison labor. *See* **Convict labor**

Prison reform 365
> *x* Penal reform

Prison schools. *See* **Prisoners—Education**

Prisoners 365
> *See also* **Political prisoners**
>
> *x* Convicts
>
> *xx* **Criminals; Prisons**

Prisoners—Education 365
> *x* Education of criminals; Education of prisoners; Prison schools
>
> *xx* **Adult education; Prisons**

Prisoners, Political. *See* **Political prisoners**

Prisoners of war (May subdiv. geog. adjective form) **341.6**
> *See also* **Concentration camps;** also names of wars with the subdivision *Prisoners and prisons,* e.g. **World War, 1939–1945—Prisoners and prisons;** etc.
>
> *x* Exchange of prisoners of war; POW; War prisoners
>
> *xx* **Concentration camps**

Prisons (May subdiv. geog.) **365**
> *See also* **Convict labor; Crime; Criminal law; Escapes; Penal colonies; Prisoners; Prisoners—Education; Probation; Reformatories;** also names of prisons
>
> *x* Dungeons; Imprisonment; Jails; Penal institutions; Penitentiaries; Penology
>
> *xx* **Convict labor; Correctional institutions; Crime; Criminal justice, Administration of; Punishment**

Prisons—U.S. 365
> *x* U.S.—Prisons

Privacy, Right of 323.44

    See also **Eavesdropping; Wiretapping**

    x Invasion of privacy; Right of privacy

    xx **Libel and slander**

Private schools 371; 372.2; 373.2

    See also **Church schools**

    x Boarding schools; Independent schools;
       Nonpublic schools; Secondary schools

    xx **Education, Secondary**

Private theatricals. *See* **Amateur theatricals**

Privateering 341.77

    See also **Neutrality**

    x Letters of marque

    xx **International law; Naval art and sci-
       ence; Naval history; Pirates**

Prize fighting. *See* **Boxing**

Prizes (Rewards). *See* **Rewards (Prizes, etc.);**
    and names of prizes

Prizes, Literary. *See* **Literary prizes**

Probabilities 519.2

    See also **Sampling (Statistics)**

    x Certainty; Fortune; Statistical inference

    xx **Algebra; Gambling; Insurance, Life;
       Logic; Statistics**

Probation 364.6

    See also **Juvenile courts; Parole**

    x Reform of criminals; Suspended sen-
       tence

    xx **Criminal law; Juvenile courts; Parole;
       Prisons; Punishment; Reformatories;
       Social case work**

Probes, Space. *See* **Space probes**

Problem children 155.4

    Use for materials on children with behavior
       difficulties caused by emotional insta-
       bility or social environment

    See also **Juvenile delinquency**

    x Behavior problems (Children); Chil-
       dren, Emotionally disturbed; Emo-
       tionally disturbed children; Malad-
       justed children

    xx **Exceptional children**

Problem solving 510.76

Problem solving, Group 153.4

    x Brain storming; Group problem solving;
       Think tanks

Problems, exercises, etc. *See* subjects with the
    subdivision *Problems, exercises, etc.,*
    e.g. **Chemistry—Problems, exercises,
    etc.;** etc.

Processing (Libraries). *See* **Libraries—Tech-
    nical services**

Processions. *See* **Parades**

Production. *See* **Economics; Industry**

Production engineering. *See* **Factory manage-
    ment**

Products, Commercial. *See* **Commercial prod-
    ucts**

Products, Dairy. *See* **Dairy products**

Products, Waste. *See* **Waste products**

Profession, Choice of. *See* **Vocational guidance**

Professional associations. *See* **Trade and professional associations**

Professional education 378

 See also **Colleges and universities; Library education; Technical education; Vocational education;** also names of professions with the subdivision *Study and teaching,* e.g. **Medicine—Study and teaching;** etc.

 x Education, Professional

 xx **Education; Education, Higher; Learning and scholarship; Technical education; Vocational education**

Professional ethics 174

 See also **Business ethics; Legal ethics; Medical ethics**

 x Ethics, Professional

Professional liability. *See* **Malpractice**

Professional sports 796

 See also names of specific sports

 xx **Sports**

Professions 331.7

 See also **Occupations; Paraprofessions and paraprofessionals; Vocational guidance;** and names of professions

 x Careers; Jobs; Vocations

 xx **Occupations; Vocational guidance**

Professions—Tort liability. *See* **Malpractice**

Professors. *See* **Teachers**

Profit 332

 See also **Capitalism; Income**

 xx **Business; Capital; Economics; Income; Wealth**

Profit sharing 658.32

 See also **Cooperation**

 xx **Commerce; Cooperation; Wages**

Programmed instruction 371.39

 See also **Teaching machines;** also subjects with the subdivision *Programmed instruction,* e.g. **English language—Programmed instruction;** etc.

 x Programmed textbooks

 xx **Teaching—Aids and devices**

Programmed textbooks. *See* **Progammed instruction**

Programming (Electronic computers) 001.6

 See also **Computer programs; Programming languages (Electronic computers);** also subjects with the subdivision *Computer programs,* e.g. **Oceanography—Computer programs;** etc.

 x Computer programming; Computer software; Computers—Programming; Software, Computer

 xx **Electronic data processing; Mathematical analysis; Mathematical models**

Programming languages (Electronic computers) 400.28

>> *See also* specific languages, e.g. **FORTRAN (Computer program language);** etc.

>> *x* Autocodes; Automatic programming languages; Computer program languages; Computer software; Machine language; Software, Computer

>> *xx* **Electronic data processing; Language and languages; Programming (Electronic computers)**

Programs, Computer. *See* **Computer programs**

Programs, Radio. *See* **Radio programs**

Programs, School assembly. *See* **School assembly programs**

Programs, Television. *See* **Television programs**

Progress 301.24

>> *See also* **Civilization; Science and civilization; Social change; War and civilization**

>> *xx* **Civilization**

Progressive education. *See* **Education—Experimental methods**

Prohibited books. *See* **Books—Censorship**

Prohibition 344.5

>> Use for materials dealing with the legal prohibition of liquor traffic and liquor manufacture

>> *See also* **Liquor problem; Temperance**

>> *xx* **Liquor problem; Temperance**

Project Apollo. *See* **Apollo project**

Project Gemini. *See* **Gemini project**

Project MARC. *See* **MARC system**

Project Mariner. *See* **Mariner project**

Project method in teaching 371.3

>> *xx* **Teaching**

Project Sealab. *See* **Sealab project**

Project Telstar. *See* **Telstar project**

Projectiles 623.4

>> *See also* **Ammunition; Bombs; Guided missiles; Ordnance; Rockets (Aeronautics)**

>> *x* Bullets; Shells (Projectiles)

>> *xx* **Ordnance**

Projective geometry. *See* **Geometry, Projective**

Projectors 778.2

>> *x* Lantern projection; Motion picture projectors; Opaque projectors; Slide projectors

Proletariat 301.44; 323.3

>> *xx* **Labor and laboring classes; Socialism**

Pronunciation. *See* **Names—Pronunciation;** and names of languages with the subdivision *Pronunciation*, e.g. **English language—Pronunciation;** etc.

Proofreading 070.5

>> *xx* **Printing**

Propaganda (May subdiv. geog. adjective form, e.g. **Propaganda, American;** etc.) **301.15**

   See also **Advertising; Psychological warfare; World War, 1939–1945—Propaganda**

   xx **Advertising; Political psychology; Public opinion; Publicity**

Propaganda, American 301.15

   x American propaganda; U.S.—Propaganda

Propagation of plants. *See* **Plant propagation**

Propellers, Aerial 629.134

   x Airplanes—Propellers

   xx **Airplanes**

Proper names. *See* **Names**

Property 330.1

   See also **Eminent domain; Income; Real estate; Wealth**

   x Ownership

   xx **Economics; Wealth**

Property, Literary. *See* **Copyright**

Property, Real. *See* **Real estate**

Prophecies (Bible). *See* **Bible—Prophecies**

Prophecies (Occult sciences) 133.3

   See also **Astrology; Divination; Fortune telling; Oracles**

   x Predictions

   xx **Divination; Occult sciences; Supernatural**

Prophets 920; 922

Proportion (Architecture). *See* **Architecture—Composition, proportion, etc.**

Proportional representation 328

   See also **Elections**

   x Representation, Proportional; Voting, Cumulative

   xx **Constitutional law; Representative government and representation**

Prose literature, American; Prose literature, English; etc. *See* **American prose literature; English prose literature;** etc.

Prosody. *See* **Versification**

Prospecting 622

   See also **Mine surveying; Petroleum—Geology**

   xx **Gold mines and mining; Mines and mineral resources; Silver mines and mining**

Prosthesis. *See* **Artificial organs; Transplantation of organs, tissues, etc.**

Prostitution 176; 301.41; 364.1

   See also **Sexual ethics; Sexual hygiene; Venereal diseases**

   x Hygiene, Social; Social hygiene; Vice

   xx **Crime; Sexual ethics; Sexual hygiene; Social problems; Women—Social conditions**

Protection. *See* **Free trade and protection**

Protection against burglary. *See* **Burglary protection**

Protection of animals. *See* **Animals—Treatment**

Protection of birds. *See* **Birds—Protection**

Protection of children. *See* **Child welfare**

Protection of game. *See* **Game protection**

Protection of natural scenery. *See* **Landscape protection; Natural monuments; Nature conservation; Wilderness areas**

Protection of wildlife. *See* **Wildlife—Conservation**

Proteins 547; 612

xx **Physiological chemistry**

Protest. *See* **Dissent**

Protest marches and rallies. *See* **Demonstrations**

Protest movements (War). *See* names of wars with the subdivision *Protest movements*, e.g. **World War, 1939–1945—Protest movements;** etc.

Protestant churches 280

See also **Protestantism;** also names of churches, e.g. **United Methodist Church (U.S.);** etc.

xx **Church history; Protestantism**

Protestant Episcopal Church in the U.S.A. 283

x Episcopal Church

Protestant Reformation. *See* **Reformation**

Protestantism 280

See also **Protestant churches; Reformation**

xx **Christianity; Church history; Protestant churches; Reformation**

Protests. *See* **Demonstrations**

Protons 539.7

See also **Atoms; Electrons**

x Hydrogen nucleus

xx **Neutrons; Nuclear physics**

Protoplasm 574.8

See also **Cells; Embryology**

xx **Biology; Cells; Embryology; Life (Biology)**

Protozoa 593

xx **Cells; Invertebrates; Microorganisms**

Proverbs 398.9

See also **Epigrams**

x Adages; Maxims; Sayings

xx **Epigrams; Folklore; Quotations**

Providence and government of God 214; 231

xx **God (Christianity); Theology**

Provincialism. *See* **Sectionalism (U.S.);** and names of languages with the subdivision *Provincialisms*, e.g. **English language—Provincialisms;** etc.

Pruning 631.5

xx **Forests and forestry; Fruit culture; Gardening; Trees**

Psalmody. *See* **Church music; Hymns**

Pseudonyms 929.4

x Anonyms; Fictitious names; Names, Fictitious; Pen names

xx **Authors; Names; Names, Personal**

Psychiatric hospitals 362.2

    x Insane—Hospitals; Mental hospitals

    xx **Hospitals; Mentally ill—Institutional care**

Psychiatrists 920; 926

    x Psychopathologists

    xx **Psychologists**

Psychiatry 616.8

    Use for materials on clinical aspects of mental disorders, including therapy. Popular materials and materials on regional or social aspects of mental disorders are entered under **Mental illness.** Systematic descriptions of mental disorders are entered under **Psychology, Pathological**

    See also **Adolescent psychiatry; Child psychiatry; Mental illness; Mentally ill; Psychology, Pathological; Psychotherapy**

    xx **Psychology, Pathological**

Psychiatry, Adolescent. *See* **Adolescent psychiatry**

Psychiatry, Child. *See* **Child psychiatry**

Psychic healing. *See* **Mental healing**

Psychical research 133

    Use for materials on investigations of phenomena that appear to be contrary to physical laws and beyond the normal sense perceptions

    See also

Apparitions

Clairvoyance

Dreams

Extrasensory perception

Ghosts

Hallucinations and illusions

Hypnotism

Mental suggestion

Mind and body

Mind reading

Personality disorders

Psychokinesis

Spiritualism

Subconsciousness

Thought transference

    x Parapsychology

    xx **Ghosts; Psychology; Research; Spiritualism; Supernatural**

Psychoanalysis 616.8

    See also **Dreams; Hypnotism; Medicine, Psychosomatic; Mind and body; Psychology; Psychology, Pathological; Psychology, Physiological; Subconsciousness**

    xx **Dreams; Hypnotism; Mind and body; Psychology; Psychology, Pathological; Psychology, Physiological; Subconsciousness**

Psychokinesis 133.8

    x Telekinesis

    xx **Psychical research; Spiritualism**

Psychological stress. *See* **Stress (Psychology)**

Psychological tests. *See* **Mental tests**

454

Psychological warfare 355.3
>> Use for materials dealing with the methods used to undermine the morale of the civilian population and the military forces of an enemy country
>> *x* Cold war; War of nerves
>> *xx* **Military art and science; Morale; Propaganda; Psychology, Applied; War**

Psychologists 920; 921
>> *See also* **Psychiatrists**

Psychologists, School. *See* **School psychologists**

Psychology 150
>> Names of all psychological subjects are not included in this list. Add as needed
>> *See also*

Adjustment (Psychology)	**Intuition**
Adolescent psychology	**Memory**
Aggressiveness (Psychology)	**Motivation (Psychology)**
Apperception	**New Thought**
Assertiveness (Psychology)	**Perception**
Attention	**Personality**
Attitude (Psychology)	**Phrenology**
Child psychology	**Physiognomy**
Consciousness	**Political psychology**
Educational psychology	**Psychical research**
Emotions	**Psychoanalysis**
Ethnopsychology	**Reasoning**
Genius	**Senses and sensation**
Gestalt psychology	**Social psychology**
Habit	**Stress (Psychology)**
Imagination	**Subconsciousness**
Individuality	**Temperament**
Instinct	**Thought and thinking**
Intellect	**Values**

>> *also* subjects with the subdivision *Psychology,* e.g. **Color—Psychology; Music—Psychology;** etc.
>> *x* Mental philosophy; Mind
>> *xx* **Brain; Philosophy; Psychoanalysis; Soul**

Psychology, Abnormal. *See* **Psychology, Pathological**

Psychology, Adolescent. *See* **Adolescent psychology**

Psychology, Applied 158
>> *See also* **Behavior modification; Counseling; Employee morale; Human engineering; Human relations; Interviewing; Psychological warfare; Psychology, Pastoral;** also subjects with the subdivision *Psychological aspects,* e.g. **Drugs—Psychological aspects;** etc.
>> *x* Applied psychology; Industrial psychol-

Psychology, Applied—*Continued*

    ogy; Psychology, Industrial; Psychology, Practical

    xx **Educational psychology; Human relations; Interviewing; Public relations; Social psychology**

Psychology, Biblical. *See* **Bible—Psychology**

Psychology, Child. *See* **Child psychology**

Psychology, Comparative 156

    See also **Animal intelligence; Instinct;** also names of animals with the subdivision *Psychology,* e.g. **Dogs—Psychology;** etc.

    x Animal psychology; Comparative psychology

    xx **Animal intelligence; Instinct; Zoology**

Psychology, Criminal. *See* **Criminal psychology**

Psychology, Educational. *See* **Educational psychology**

Psychology, Ethnic. *See* **Ethnopsychology**

Psychology, Experimental. *See* **Psychology, Physiological**

Psychology, Industrial. *See* **Psychology, Applied**

Psychology, Medical. *See* **Psychology, Pathological**

Psychology, National. *See* **Ethnopsychology; National characteristics**

Psychology, Pastoral 253.5

    Use for materials on the application of psychology and psychiatry by clergymen to the spiritual problems of individuals

    x Pastoral psychiatry; Pastoral psychology

    xx **Christian ethics; Church work; Psychology, Applied; Pastoral work; Therapeutics, Suggestive**

Psychology, Pathological 157

    See note under **Psychiatry**

    See also **Criminal psychology; Hallucinations and illusions; Medicine, Psychosomatic; Mental illness; Neuroses; Personality disorders; Psychiatry; Psychoanalysis; Subconsciousness**

    x Abnormal psychology; Diseases, Mental; Mental diseases; Pathological psychology; Psychology, Abnormal; Psychology, Medical; Psychopathology; Psycopathy

    xx **Criminal psychology; Mental health; Mind and body; Nervous system; Psychiatry; Psychoanalysis**

Psychology, Physiological 152

    See also

Color sense	**Mind and body**
Dreams	**Optical illusions**
Emotions	**Pain**
Hypnotism	**Psychoanalysis**
Memory	**Senses and sensation**
Mental tests	

Psychology, Physiological—*Continued*
    Sleep   Temperament
      x Experimental psychology; Physiological psychology; Psychology, Experimental; Psychophysics
      xx **Mental health; Mind and body; Nervous system; Physiology; Psychoanalysis**
Psychology, Political. *See* **Political psychology**
Psychology, Practical. *See* **Psychology, Applied**
Psychology, Racial. *See* **Ethnopsychology**
Psychology, Social. *See* **Social psychology**
Psychology, Structural. *See* **Gestalt psychology**
Psychology of color. *See* **Color—Psychology**
Psychology of learning. *See* **Learning, Psychology of**
Psychology of music. *See* **Music—Psychology**
Psychopathologists. *See* **Psychiatrists**
Psychopathology. *See* **Psychology, Pathological**
Psychopathy. *See* **Psychology, Pathological**
Psychophysics. *See* **Psychology, Physiological**
Psychoses. *See* **Mental illness**
Psychosomatic medicine. *See* **Medicine, Psychosomatic**
Psychotherapy 616.8
      See also **Mental healing; Therapeutics, Suggestive**
      xx **Mental healing; Psychiatry; Therapeutics, Suggestive**
Psychotic children. *See* **Mentally ill children**
Psychotics. *See* **Mentally ill**
Public accommodations, Discrimination in. *See* **Discrimination in public accommodations**
Public administration 350
      Use for general materials on the principles and techniques involved in the conduct of public business. Materials limited to the governmental processes of a particular country, state, etc. are entered under the name of the area with the subdivision *Politics and government*
      See also **Administrative law; Bureaucracy; Civil service;** also names of countries, cities, etc. with the subdivision *Politics and government,* e.g. **U.S.—Politics and government;** etc.
      x Administration
      xx **Administrative law; Local government; Municipal government; Political science**
Public assistance. *See* **Public welfare**
Public buildings 725
      See also names of countries, cities, etc. with the subdivision *Public buildings,* e.g. **U.S.—Public buildings; Chicago—Public buildings;** etc.

Public buildings—*Continued*
   x Buildings, Public; Government buildings
   xx **Architecture; Art, Municipal; Public works**
Public charities. *See* **Public welfare**
Public debts. *See* **Debts, Public**
Public demonstrations. *See* **Demonstrations**
Public documents. *See* **Government publications**
Public finance. *See* **Finance**
Public health (May subdiv. geog.) **614**
   See also

Cemeteries	**Medical care**
Charities, Medical	**Milk supply**
Communicable diseases	**Noise**
Community health services	**Occupational diseases**
Cremation	**Pollution**
Disinfection and disinfectants	**Refuse and refuse disposal**
Epidemics	**Sanitary engineering**
Food adulteration and inspection	**Sanitation**
Health boards	**School hygiene**
Hospitals	**Sewage disposal**
Industrial health and safety	**Street cleaning**
Meat inspection	**Vaccination**
	Water—Pollution
	Water supply

   x Health, Public; Hygiene, Public; Hygiene, Social; Medicine, Preventive; Preventive medicine; Social hygiene
   xx **Medicine, State; Sanitation; Social problems**
Public health—U.S. 614
   x U.S.—Public health
Public health boards. *See* **Health boards**
Public lands. *See* **Forest reserves; National parks and reserves;** and names of countries, states, etc. with the subdivision *Public lands,* e.g. **U.S.—Public lands;** etc.
Public libraries 027.4
   See also names of cities with the subdivision *Libraries,* e.g. **Chicago—Libraries;** etc.
   x Libraries, Public
   xx **Libraries**
Public meetings 301.18
   See also **Parliamentary practice**
   x Meetings, Public
   xx **Freedom of assembly**
Public opinion 301.15
   See also **Attitude (Psychology); Propaganda; Public relations; Publicity;** also subjects with the subdivision *Public opinion,* e.g. **World War, 1939–1945 —Public opinion;** etc.; and names of countries with the subdivision *Foreign opinion,* **U.S.—Foreign opinion;** etc.

Public opinion—*Continued*

    x Opinion, Public

    xx **Attitude (Psychology); Freedom of conscience; Political psychology; Public relations**

Public opinion polls 301.15

    See also **Market surveys**

    x Opinion polls; Polls, Public opinion; Straw votes

    xx **Market surveys**

Public ownership. *See* **Government ownership; Municipal ownership**

Public playgrounds. *See* **Playgrounds**

Public records—Preservation. *See* **Archives**

Public relations 659.2

    May be subdivided by topic, e.g. **Public relations—Libraries**; etc.

    See also **Advertising; Psychology, Applied; Public opinion; Publicity**

    xx **Advertising; Public opinion; Publicity**

Public relations—Libraries 021.7

    x Libraries—Public relations

    xx **Libraries and community**

Public safety, Crimes against. *See* **Offenses against public safety**

Public schools (May subdiv. geog. country or state) **371; 372.1; 373.2**

    See also **Evening and continuation schools; High schools; Junior high schools; Rural schools; Schools; Summer schools**; also names of cities with the subdivision *Schools* (e.g. **Chicago—Schools**; etc.); and headings beginning with the word **School**

    x Common schools; Grammar schools; Secondary schools

    xx **Education, Secondary**

Public schools—U.S. 379.73

    x U.S.—Public schools

Public schools and religion. *See* **Religion in the public schools**

Public service commissions 350

    Use for materials on bodies appointed to regulate or control public utilities

    x Public utility commissions

    xx **Corporation law; Corporations; Industry and state**

Public service corporations. *See* **Public utilities**

Public shelters. *See* **Air raid shelters**

Public speaking 808.5

    See also **Acting; Debates and debating; Lectures and lecturing; Orations; Preaching; Voice**

    x Elocution; Oratory; Persuasion (Rhetoric); Speaking

    xx **Voice**

Public transit. *See* **Local transit**

Public utilities 343.9; 351.8; 363.6

    See also **Corporation law; Corporations; Electric industries; Electric railroads; Gas; Railroads; Railroads and state; Street railroads; Telegraph; Telephone; Water supply**

    x Electric utilities; Gas companies; Public service corporations; Utilities, Public

    xx **Corporation law; Corporations**

Public utility commissions. *See* **Public service commissions**

Public welfare 361.6

    Use for materials on tax-supported welfare activities. Materials on privately supported welfare activities are entered under **Charities.** Materials on the methods employed in welfare work, public or private, are entered under **Social work**

    See also

Charities	**Legal assistance**
Child welfare	**to the poor**
Children's hospitals	**Orphanages**
Hospitals	**Poor**
Institutional care	**Unemployed**

    x Charities, Public; Poor relief; Public assistance; Public charities; Relief, Public; Social welfare; Welfare state; Welfare work

    xx **Charities; Poverty; Social work**

Public works 351.8

    See also **Municipal engineering; Public buildings;** also names of countries, cities, etc. with the subdivision *Public works,* e.g. **U.S.—Public works; Chicago—Public works;** etc.

    xx **Civil engineering; Economic assistance, Domestic**

Public worship 264

    x Church attendance

    xx **Worship**

Publicity 659.2

    See also **Advertising; Propaganda; Public relations**

    xx **Advertising; Public opinion; Public relations**

Publishers and authors. *See* **Authors and publishers**

Publishers and publishing 070.5

    See also **Authors and publishers; Book industries and trade; Books; Booksellers and bookselling; Catalogs, Publishers'; Copyright; Paperback books; Printing; Publishers' standard book numbers**

    x Book trade; Editors and editing; Publishing

    xx **Book industries and trade; Books; Booksellers and bookselling; Copyright**

Publishers' catalogs. *See* **Catalogs, Publishers'**

Publishers' standard book numbers 070.5

> *See also* **International Standard Book Numbers**
>
> *x* Book numbers, Publishers' standard; Standard book numbers
>
> *xx* **Publishers and publishing**

Publishing. *See* **Publishers and publishing**

Pugilism. *See* **Boxing**

Pulsars 523

> *x* Pulsating radio sources
>
> *xx* **Stars**

Pulsating radio sources. *See* **Pulsars**

Pumping machinery 621.2; 621.6

> *See* also types of pumping machinery, e.g. **Heat pumps**; etc.
>
> *x* Force pumps; Pumps; Steam pumps
>
> *xx* **Engines; Hydraulic engineering**

Pumps. *See* **Pumping machinery**

Punch and Judy. *See* **Puppets and puppet plays**

Punched card systems. *See* **Information storage and retrieval systems**

Punctuation 421

> *x* English language—Punctuation
>
> *xx* **Rhetoric**

Punishment 364.6

> *See also* **Capital punishment; Crime; Criminal law; Penal colonies; Prisons; Probation; Reformatories**
>
> *x* Penology
>
> *xx* **Crime; Criminal justice, Administration of; Criminal law**

Punishment in schools. *See* **School discipline**

Puppets and puppet plays 791.5

> *See also* **Shadow pantomimes and plays**
>
> *x* Marionettes; Punch and Judy
>
> *xx* **Drama; Folk drama; Theater**

Purchase tax. *See* **Sales tax**

Purchasing. *See* **Buying; Shopping**

Pure food. *See* **Food adulteration and inspection**

Purification of water. *See* **Water—Purification**

Puritans 920; 922

> *See also* **Calvinism; Church of England; Congregationalism; Pilgrims (New England colonists)**
>
> *xx* **Calvinism; Church of England; Congregationalism; U.S.—History—Colonial period, 1600–1775**

Puzzles 793.7

> *See also* **Crossword puzzles; Mathematical recreations; Riddles**
>
> *xx* **Amusements; Riddles**

Pyramids 722

> *See also* **Obelisks**
>
> *xx* **Archeology; Architecture, Ancient; Monuments**

461

Quacks and quackery 615
    See also **Patent medicines**
    xx **Imposters and imposture; Medicine; Swindlers and swindling**
Quakers. *See* **Friends, Society of**
Qualitative analysis. *See* **Chemistry, Analytic**
Quality. *See* subjects with the subdivision *Quality,* e.g. **Air—Quality;** etc.
Quality control 519.8; 658.5
    See also specific industries with the subdivision *Quality control,* e.g. **Steel industry and trade—Quality control;** etc.; also subjects with the subdivision *Quality,* e.g. **Air—Quality;** etc.
    xx **Reliability (Engineering); Sampling (Statistics)**
Quality of life 301; 309
    See also **Social values**
    x Life quality
    xx **Economic conditions; Social conditions; Social values**
Quantitative analysis. *See* **Chemistry, Analytic**
Quantity cookery. *See* **Cookery, Quantity**
Quantum mechanics. *See* **Quantum theory**
Quantum theory 530.1
    See also **Atomic theory; Chemistry, Physical and theoretical; Force and energy; Neutrons; Radiation; Relativity (Physics); Thermodynamics; Wave mechanics**
    x Quantum mechanics
    xx **Atomic theory; Chemistry, Physical and theoretical; Dynamics; Force and energy; Physics; Radiation; Relativity (Physics); Thermodynamics**
Quarantine. *See* **Communicable diseases**
Quarries and quarrying 622
    See also **Stone**
    x Stone quarries
    xx **Geology, Economic; Stone**
Quartz 549
    x Minerals; Rock crystal
    xx **Mineralogy**
Quasars 521; 523
    x Quasi-stellar radio sources
    xx **Astronomy; Radio astronomy**
Quasi-stellar radio sources. *See* **Quasars**
Quebec (Province) 917.14; 971.4
Quebec (Province)—History 971.4
Quebec (Province)—History—Autonomy and independence movements 971.4
    x Quebec (Province)—Separatist movement; Separatist movement in Quebec (Province)
    xx **Canada—English-French relations**
Quebec (Province)—Separatist movement. *See* **Quebec (Province)—History—Autonomy and independence movements**

Queens 920; 923

  See also **Courts and courtiers; Kings and rulers;** also names of countries with the subdivision *Kings and rulers* (e.g. **Gt. Brit.–Kings and rulers;** etc.); and names of queens, e.g. **Elizabeth II, Queen of Great Britain;** etc.

  x Empresses; Monarchs; Royalty; Rulers; Sovereigns

  xx **Courts and courtiers; Kings and rulers; Monarchy**

Queries. *See* **Questions and answers**

Questions and answers 793.73

  Use for informal quizzes of miscellany. Questions and answers on a particular subject are entered under the subject with the subdivision *Miscellanea*, e.g. **Medicine–Miscellanea;** etc. Examination questions on a particular subject are entered under the subject with the subdivision *Examinations, questions, etc.* e.g. **Music–Examinations, questions, etc.;** etc.

  See also subjects with the subdivision *Examinations, questions, etc.*, e.g. **Music–Examinations, questions, etc.;** etc.

  x Answers to questions; Queries; Quizzes

Quicksilver. *See* **Mercury**

Quilting 746.4

Quilts 646.2

  x Coverlets; Patchwork quilts

  xx **Interior decoration**

Quintets 785.7

  xx **Orchestral music**

Quizzes. *See* **Questions and answers**

Qumran texts. *See* **Dead Sea scrolls**

Quotations 080; 808.8

  See also **Proverbs;** also subjects and names of people with the subdivision *Quotations,* e.g. **Presidents–U.S.–Quotations;** etc.

  x Sayings

  xx **Epigrams; Literature–Collections**

Qur'an. *See* **Koran**

R.V. *See* **Recreational vehicles**

Rabbits 599; 636

  x Hares

Rabies 616.9

  x Hydrophobia

Race 572

  xx **Ethnology**

Race awareness 301.45

  See also **Prejudices and antipathies; Blacks –Race identity**

  xx **Race relations**

Race discrimination 301.45

  See also types of discrimination, e.g. **Discrimination in education;** etc.

463

Race discrimination—*Continued*

    x Discrimination, Racial; Racial discrimination

    xx **Discrimination; Race relations; Racism**

Race identity. *See* names of races with the subdivision *Race identity,* e.g. **Blacks —Race identity;** etc.

Race prejudice. *See* **Racism**

Race problems. *See* **Race relations**

Race psychology. *See* **Ethnopsychology**

Race relations 301.45

    See also **Acculturation; Discrimination; Immigration and emigration; Intercultural education; Race awareness; Race discrimination;** also names of countries, cities, etc. with the subdivision *Race relations,* e.g. **U.S.— Race relations; Chicago—Race relations; South Africa—Race relations;** etc.

    x Integration, Racial; Interracial relations; Race problems

    xx **Ethnic groups; Ethnology; Minorities; Social problems; Sociology**

Race relations and the church. *See* **Church and race relations**

Races of people. *See* **Ethnology**

Racial balance in schools. *See* **Busing (School integration); School integration; Segregation in education**

Racial discrimination. *See* **Race discrimination**

Racial identity. *See* names of races with the subdivision *Race identity,* e.g. **Blacks —Race identity;** etc.

Racing. *See* names of type of racing, e.g. **Automobile racing; Bicycle racing; Boat racing; Horse racing; Soap box derbies;** etc.

Racism

    See also **Race discrimination**

    x Race prejudice

    xx **Prejudices and antipathies**

Racketeering 364.1

    x Crime syndicates

    xx **Crime; Organized crime**

Radar 621.3848

    xx **Navigation; Radio**

Radar defense networks 623.7

    See also **Ballistic missile early warning system**

    x Defenses, Radar

    xx **Air defenses**

Radiant heating 697

    x Panel heating

    xx **Heating**

Radiation 539.2

    See also

Cosmic rays	**Light**
Electromagnetic waves	**Phosphorescence**
	Quantum theory

Radiation—*Continued*
  Radioactivity   **Spectrum**
  Radium   **Ultraviolet rays**
  Sound   **X rays**
    xx Light; Optics; Physics; Quantum theory;
      Waves
Radiation—Physiological effect 612
    See also Atomic bomb—Physiological effect; Nuclear medicine
    xx Atomic bomb—Physiological effect
Radiation—Safety measures 612
Radiation, Solar. *See* Solar radiation
Radiation biology. *See* Radiobiology
Radiation therapy. *See* Radiotherapy
Radicals and radicalism 320.5
    x Extremism (Political science)
    xx **Revolutions; Right and left (Political science)**
Radio 621.3841
    See also **Radar; Sound—Recording and reproducing**
    x Wireless
    xx **Electric engineering; Telecommunication**
Radio—Apparatus and supplies 621.3841
    See also Amplifiers, Vacuum tube; Radio—Receivers and reception
    xx **Radio industry and trade**
Radio—Broadcasting. *See* **Radio broadcasting**
Radio—Operators. *See* **Radio operators**
Radio—Receivers and reception 621.3841
    x Radio receivers; Radio reception; Radios
    xx **Radio—Apparatus and supplies**
Radio—Repairing 621.3841
    x Radio repairing; Radio servicing
    xx **Repairing**
Radio, Short wave 621.3841
    See also **Amateur radio stations; Citizens band radio; Microwave communication systems; Microwaves**
    x High-frequency radio; Short wave radio; UHF radio; Ultrahigh frequency radio
    xx **Electric conductors; Electric waves; Radio frequency modulation**
Radio—Stations. *See* **Radio stations**
Radio addresses, debates, etc. 384.54; 808.5; 808.85
    x Radio lectures
    xx **Debates and debating; Lectures and lecturing; Radio broadcasting; Radio scripts**
Radio advertising 659.14
    x Advertising, Radio; Commercials, Radio; Radio commercials
    xx **Advertising; Radio broadcasting; Radio industry and trade**
Radio and music 782.8
    Use same form for radio and other subjects

465

Radio and music—*Continued*

   x Music and radio

   xx **Music**

Radio apparatus industry. *See* **Radio industry and trade**

Radio astronomy 522

   See also names of celestial radio sources, e.g. **Quasars;** etc.

   xx **Astronomy; Interstellar communication**

Radio authorship 808.2

   See also **Radio plays—Technique; Radio scripts**

   x Radio script writing; Radio writing

   xx **Authorship; Radio broadcasting; Radio scripts**

Radio broadcasting 384.54

   See also **Radio addresses, debates, etc.; Radio advertising; Radio authorship; Radio programs; Television broadcasting**

   x Radio—Broadcasting

   xx **Broadcasting; Mass media**

Radio chemistry. *See* **Radiochemistry**

Radio commercials. *See* **Radio advertising**

Radio drama. *See* **Radio plays**

Radio frequency modulation 621.3841

   See also **Radio, Short wave**

   x FM Radio; Frequency modulation, Radio

Radio in aeronautics 629.135

   Use same form for radio in other subjects

   x Aeronautics, Radio in

   xx **Aeronautics; Navigation (Aeronautics)**

Radio in astronautics 629.4

   x Lunar surface radio communication

   xx **Astronautics—Communication systems**

Radio in education 371.33

   x Education and radio

   xx **Audio-visual education; Teaching—Aids and devices**

Radio industry and trade 338.4

   See also **Radio—Apparatus and supplies; Radio advertising**

   x Radio apparatus industry

   xx **Electric industries**

Radio lectures. *See* **Radio addresses, debates, etc.**

Radio operators 621.3841

   x Radio—Operators

Radio plays 808.82; 812; 812.08; etc.

   Use for individual radio plays, for collections of plays, and for works about them. Works on how to write radio plays are entered under **Radio plays—Technique**

   x Radio drama; Scenarios

   xx **Drama; Radio programs; Radio scripts**

Radio plays—Technique 808.2

   See also **Television plays—Technique**

   x Play writing; Playwriting

466

Radio plays—Technique—*Continued*
  xx **Drama—Technique; Radio authorship;**
     Television plays—Technique
Radio programs 384.54
  See also types of programs, and specific
     programs, e.g. **Radio plays;** etc.
  x Programs, Radio
  xx **Radio broadcasting**
Radio receivers. *See* **Radio—Receivers and re-**
     ception
Radio reception. *See* **Radio—Receivers and**
     reception
Radio repairing. *See* **Radio—Repairing**
Radio script writing. *See* **Radio authorship**
Radio scripts 808.82
  See also **Radio addresses, debates, etc.;**
     Radio authorship; Radio plays; Tele-
     vision scripts
  xx **Radio authorship; Television scripts**
Radio servicing. *See* **Radio—Repairing**
Radio stations 384.54
  x Radio—Stations
Radio stations, Amateur. *See* **Amateur radio**
     stations
Radio waves. *See* **Electric waves**
Radio writing. *See* **Radio authorship**
Radioactive fallout 539.7
  x Dust, Radioactive; Fallout, Radioactive
  xx **Atomic bomb; Hydrogen bomb; Pol-**
     lution
Radioactive isotopes. *See* **Radioisotopes**
Radioactive substances. *See* **Radioactivity**
Radioactivity 539.7
  See also

Cosmic rays	**Radiotherapy**
Electrons	**Radium**
Helium	**Transmutation**
Nuclear physics	**(Chemistry)**
Phosphorescence	**Uranium**
Radiobiology	**X-rays**
Radiochemistry	

  x Radioactive substances
  xx **Electricity; Light; Nuclear physics;**
     Physics; Radiation; Radium
Radiobiology 574.1
  x Radiation biology
  xx **Biology; Biophysics; Nuclear physics;**
     Radioactivity
Radiocarbon dating 539.7
  x Carbon 14 dating; Dating, Radiocarbon
  xx **Archeology**
Radiochemistry 541
  x Radio chemistry
  xx **Chemistry, Physical and theoretical;**
     Radioactivity
Radiography. *See* **X rays**
Radioisotopes 621.48
  x Radioactive isotopes
  xx **Isotopes; Nuclear engineering**

467

Radiologists 920; 926
>   *x* Roentgenologists
>   *xx* **Physicians; Radiotherapy; X rays**

Radios. *See* **Radio—Receivers and reception**

Radiotherapy 615
>   *See also* **Phototherapy; Radiologists; Radium; Ultraviolet rays; X rays**
>   *x* Radiation therapy
>   *xx* **Electrotherapeutics;   Phototherapy; Physical therapy; Radioactivity; Radium; Therapeutics; X rays**

Radium 546
>   *See also* **Radioactivity; Radiotherapy**
>   *xx* **Radiation; Radioactivity; Radiotherapy**

Railroad accidents. *See* **Railroads—Accidents**

Railroad construction. *See* **Railroad engineering**

Railroad engineering 625.1
>   *x* Railroad construction
>   *xx* **Civil engineering; Railroads**

Railroad fares. *See* **Railroads—Rates**

Railroad mergers. *See* **Railroads—Consolidation**

Railroad rates. *See* **Railroads—Rates**

Railroad workers. *See* **Railroads—Employees**

Railroads (May subdiv. geog. except U.S.) **385; 625.1**
>   *See also*

Electric railroads	**Railroad engineer-**
Eminent domain	**ing**
Express service	**Railroads and state**
Freight and freight-	**Street railroads**
age	**Subways**
Monorail railroads	

>   *also* names of individual railroads
>   *x* Railways; Trains, Railroad
>   *xx* **Public utilities; Transportation**

Railroads—Accidents 614.8
>   *See also* **Railroads—Safety appliances; Railroads—Signaling**
>   *x* Collisions, Railroad; Derailments; Railroad accidents; Train wrecks; Wrecks
>   *xx* **Accidents; Disasters**

Railroads—Consolidation 338.8
>   *x* Industrial mergers; Mergers, Industrial; Railroad mergers
>   *xx* **Monopolies; Trusts, Industrial**

Railroads, Electric. *See* **Electric railroads**

Railroads—Electrification 621.33
>   *See also* **Electric railroads**
>   *x* Electrification of railroads
>   *xx* **Electric railroads**

Railroads—Employees 385.023; 625.1023
>   *x* Railroad workers

Railroads—Fares. *See* **Railroads—Rates**

Railroads—Finance 385
>   *See also* **Railroads—Rates; Railroads—Statistics**
>   *x* Capitalization (Finance)

Railroads—Government ownership. *See* **Railroads and state**

Railroads—Models 625.1
   xx **Machinery—Models**

Railroads, Nationalization of. *See* **Railroads and state**

Railroads—Rates 385
   See also **Freight and freightage; Interstate commerce**
   x Railroad fares; Railroad rates; Railroads—Fares; Rebates (Railroads)
   xx **Freight and freightage; Railroads—Finance; Railroads and state**

Railroads—Rolling stock. *See* **Locomotives**

Railroads—Safety appliances 625.1
   See also **Brakes; Railroads—Signaling**
   xx **Accidents—Prevention; Railroads—Accidents; Safety appliances**

Railroads—Signaling 625.1
   x Block signal systems; Interlocking signals
   xx **Railroads—Accidents; Railroads—Safety appliances; Signals and signaling**

Railroads, Single rail. *See* **Monorail railroads**

Railroads—Statistics 385.021
   xx **Railroads—Finance**

Railroads, Street. *See* **Street railroads**

Railroads, Underground. *See* **Subways**

Railroads and state 351.8
   See also **Interstate commerce; Railroads—Rates**
   x Government ownership of railroads; Government regulation of railroads; Nationalization of railroads; Railroads—Government ownership; Railroads, Nationalization of; State and railroads; State ownership of railroads
   xx **Government ownership; Industry and state; Interstate commerce; Public utilities; Railroads**

Railways. *See* **Railroads**

Rain and rainfall 551.5
   See also **Droughts; Floods; Forest influences; Meteorology; Snow; Storms**
   x Rainfall
   xx **Climate; Droughts; Forest influences; Meteorology; Storms; Water; Weather**

Rain forests 634.9
   x Tropical rain forests
   xx **Forests and forestry**

Rain making. *See* **Weather—Control**

Rainfall. *See* **Rain and rainfall**

Rainfall and forests. *See* **Forest influences**

Ranch life 630.1; 917.8
   See also **Cowhands**
   x **Farm life; Frontier and pioneer life**

Random sampling. *See* **Sampling (Statistics)**

Rank. *See* **Social classes**

Rape 364.1

   x Assault, Criminal; Criminal assault

   xx **Crime; Offenses against the person**

Rapid reading 372.4

   x Accelerated reading; Faster reading; Speed reading

   xx **Reading—Remedial teaching**

Rapid transit. *See* **Local transit**

Rare animals 591

   See also **Extinct animals**

   x Animals, Rare; Endangered animals; Vanishing animals

   xx **Extinct animals; Wildlife—Conservation**

Rare birds 598.2

   x Birds, Rare; Endangered birds; Vanishing birds

Rare books 090

   x Book rarities; Books, Rare

Rationalism 149; 211

   See also

Agnosticism	**Positivism**
Atheism	**Realism**
Belief and doubt	**Reason**
Deism	**Skepticism**
Free thought	**Theism**
Intuition	

   xx **Agnosticism; Atheism; Belief and doubt; Deism; Free thought; God; Knowledge, Theory of; Philosophy; Realism; Religion**

Raw materials 333

   See also **Farm produce; Forest products; Mines and mineral resources**

   xx **Commercial products; Materials**

Rayon 677

   x Acetate silk; Artificial silk; Silk, Artificial

   xx **Synthetic fabrics; Synthetic products**

Rays, Roentgen. *See* **X rays**

Rays, Ultra-violet. *See* **Ultraviolet rays**

Reactions, Chemical. *See* **Chemical reactions**

Reactors (Nuclear physics). *See* **Nuclear reactors**

Readers. *See* **Reading materials**

Reading 028

   Use for materials on methods of teaching reading, and general materials on the art of reading. Materials on teaching slow readers are entered under **Reading—Remedial teaching.** Materials on the cultural aspects of reading and general discussions of books to read are entered under **Books and reading**

   See also **Books and reading**

   x Children's reading; Reading—Study and teaching

   xx **Language arts**

Reading—Remedial teaching 372.4

   See also **Rapid reading**

   x Reading clinics; Remedial reading

Reading—Study and teaching. *See* **Reading**

Reading clinics. *See* **Reading—Remedial teaching**

Reading interests. *See* **Books and reading**

Reading materials 372.4

> Use for materials in English. For readers in other languages, use the name of the language with the subdivision *Reading materials,* e.g. **French language—Reading materials;** etc.
>
> *See also* **Easy reading materials; Readings and recitations**
>
> *x* English language—Reading materials; Readers
>
> *xx* **Children's literature**

Readings and recitations 808.85

> *x* Recitations and readings; Speakers (Recitation books)
>
> *xx* **Reading materials; School assembly programs**

Ready reckoners. *See* **Mathematics—Tables, etc.**

Real estate 333.3

> Use for general materials on real property in the legal sense, i.e., ownership of land and buildings as opposed to personal property. Materials limited to the buying and selling of real property are entered under **Real estate business.** General materials on land without the ownership aspect are entered under **Land use.** Materials on the assessment of property are entered under **Taxation**
>
> *See also* **Eminent domain; Farms; Land tenure; Landlord and tenant; Mortgages; Real estate business**
>
> *x* Property, Real; Real property; Realty
>
> *xx* **Land use; Land tenure; Property**

Real estate business 333.3

> *xx* **Business; Real estate**

Real property. *See* **Real estate**

Realism 149

> *See also* **Idealism; Materialism; Positivism; Pragmatism; Rationalism**
>
> *xx* **Idealism; Materialism; Philosophy; Positivism; Rationalism**

Realism in literature 809

> Use same form for realism in other forms of the arts
>
> *See also* **Romanticism**
>
> *x* Naturalism in literature
>
> *xx* **Literature; Romanticism**

Reality 111

> *See also* **Empiricism; Knowledge, Theory of; Pragmatism**
>
> *xx* **Intuition; Knowledge, Theory of; Philosophy; Pragmatism; Truth**

Realty. *See* **Real estate**

Reapers. *See* **Harvesting machinery**

Reapportionment (Election law). *See* **Apportionment (Election law)**

Reason 160

   See also **Reasoning**

   xx **Intellect; Rationalism**

Reasoning 153.4; 160

   See also **Intellect; Logic**

   xx **Intellect; Logic; Psychology; Reason; Thought and thinking**

Rebates (Railroads). *See* **Railroads—Rates**

Rebellions. *See* **Insurgency; Revolutions**

Rebels (Social psychology). *See* **Alienation (Social psychology)**

Rebirth. *See* **Reincarnation**

Rebuses. *See* **Riddles**

Recall (Political science) 351.9

   xx **Impeachments; Representative government and representation**

Recipes. *See* **Cookery**

Reciprocity. *See* **Commercial policy**

Recitation with music. *See* **Monologues with music**

Recitations and readings. *See* **Readings and recitations**

Reclamation of land 627; 631.6

   Use for general materials on reclamation, including drainage and irrigation

   See also **Drainage; Irrigation; Marshes; Sand dunes**

   x Clearing of land; Land, Reclamation of

   xx **Agriculture; Civil engineering; Floods; Hydraulic engineering; Irrigation; Land use; Natural resources; soils**

Recluses. *See* **Hermits**

Recommendations for positions. *See* **Applications for positions**

Reconstruction (1865–1876) 973.8

   See also **Ku Klux Klan (1865–1876)**

   x Carpetbag rule; U.S.—History—Civil War, 1861–1865—Reconstruction

   xx **U.S.—History—1865–1898**

Reconstruction (1914–1939) 940.3

   See also **Peace; Veterans—Education; Veterans—Employment; World War, 1914–1918—Economic aspects**

   x World War, 1914–1918—Reconstruction

Reconstruction (1939–1951) (May subdiv. geog. except U.S.) **940.53**

   See also **Economic assistance; International cooperation; Peace; Veterans—Education; Veterans—Employment; World War, 1939–1945—Civilian relief; World War, 1939–1945—Economic aspects; World War, 1939–1945—Reparations**

   x Marshall Plan; Point Four program; World War, 1939–1945—Reconstruction

   xx **Economic assistance; International co-**

Reconstruction (1939–1951)—*Continued*
operation; World War, 1939–1945—
Economic aspects

Record players. *See* **Phonograph**

Recorders, Tape. *See* **Magnetic recorders and recording**

Records, Phonograph. *See* **Sound recordings**

Records—Preservation. *See* **Archives**

Records of births, etc. *See* **Registers of births, etc.; Vital statistics**

Recovery of waste products. *See* **Recycling (Waste, etc.); Salvage (Waste, etc.)**

Recreation 790
Use for materials on the psychological and social aspects of recreation and for materials on organized recreational projects
See also **Amusements; Community centers; Games; Hobbies; Outdoor recreation; Play; Playgrounds; Sports; Vacations;** also classes of people with the subdivision *Recreation,* e.g. **Elderly—Recreation;** etc.
x Pastimes; Relaxation
xx **Amusements; Leisure; Play**

Recreation centers. *See* **Community centers**

Recreational vehicles 629.22
See also types of recreational vehicles, e.g. **Travel trailers and campers;** etc.
x R.V.; Vehicles, Recreational
xx **Outdoor recreation; Vehicles**

Recreations, Mathematical. *See* **Mathematical recreations**

Recreations, Scientific. *See* **Scientific recreations**

Recruiting and enlistment. *See* names of armies and navies with the subdivision *Recruiting, enlistment, etc.;* e.g. **U.S. Army—Recruiting, enlistment, etc.; U.S. Navy—Recruiting, enlistment, etc.;** etc.

Recruiting of employees 659.31
See also **Employment agencies;** also names of occupations and professions with the subdivision *Recruiting,* e.g. **Librarians—Recruiting;** etc.
xx **Personnel management**

Rectors. *See* **Clergy**

Recurrent education. *See* **Continuing education**

Recycling (Waste, etc.) 604.6
Use for materials on the processing of waste paper, cans, bottles, etc. Materials on the recycling or reuse of specific waste products are entered under the products subdivided by the subdivision *Recycling.* Materials on reclaiming and reusing equipment or parts are entered under **Salvage (Waste, etc.)**

473

Recycling (Waste, etc.)—*Continued*

    See also **Refuse and refuse disposal; Salvage (Waste, etc.); Waste products;** and subjects with the subdivision *Recycling,* e.g. **Aluminum—Recycling;** etc.

    x Conversion of waste products; Recovery of waste products; Reuse of waste; Utilization of waste; Waste products—Recycling; Waste reclamation

    xx **Energy conservation; Refuse and refuse disposal; Salvage (Waste, etc.); Waste products**

Red 535.6; 752

    xx **Color**

Red Cross 361.7

    xx **Charities; Nursing**

Redemption. *See* **Atonement; Salvation**

Reducing

    See also **Exercise**

    x Body weight control; Dieting; Obesity—Control; Overweight—Control; Weight control

Reference books 010-016; 028.7

    See also **Books and reading—Best books; Encyclopedias**

    xx **Books and reading**

Reference service (Libraries). *See* **Libraries—Reference service**

Referendum 328

    x Direct legislation; Initiative and referendum; Legislation, Direct

    xx **Constitutional law; Democracy; Elections; Representative government and representation**

Reforestation 634.9

    See also **Tree planting**

    xx **Forests and forestry; Tree planting**

Reform, Social. *See* **Social problems**

Reform of criminals. *See* **Criminals; Probation; Reformatories**

Reform schools. *See* **Reformatories**

Reformation 270.6

    See also **Calvinism; Europe—History—1492–1789; Protestantism; Sixteenth century;** also names of religious sects, e.g. **Huguenots;** etc.

    x Anti-Reformation; Church history—Reformation, 1517–1648; Counter-Reformation; Protestant Reformation

    xx **Christianity; Church history; History, Modern; Protestantism; Sixteenth century**

Reformatories 365

    See also **Juvenile courts; Juvenile delinquency; Probation**

    x Penal institutions; Penology; Reform of criminals; Reform schools

    xx **Children—Institutional care; Correctional institutions; Crime; Juvenile delinquency; Prisons; Punishment**

Reformers 920; 923

> Includes materials about political, social, religious, etc. reformers

Refraction 535

> *x* Dioptrics
> *xx* **Light; Optics**

Refrigeration and refrigerating machinery 621.5

> *See also* **Air conditioning; Cold storage**
> *x* Cooling appliances; Freezing; Ice manufacture
> *xx* **Air conditioning; Cold storage; Frost**

Refugees (May subdiv. geog. or by ethnic groups, adjective form, e.g. **Refugees, Arabic; Refugees, Jewish;** etc.) **325; 920**

> *x* Displaced persons; Exiles
> *xx* **Aliens; Immigration and emigration**

Refugees, American 325.73; 920

> *x* American refugees; U.S.—Refugees

Refugees, Political 341.48

> *See also* names of wars with the subdivision *Refugees*, e.g. **World War, 1939–1945—Refugees;** etc.
> *x* Displaced persons; Political refugees
> *xx* **Asylum, Right of; International law; International relations**

Refuse and refuse disposal 628

> *See also* **Industrial waste; Recycling (Waste, etc.); Salvage (Waste, etc.); Sewage disposal; Street cleaning; Waste products; Water—Pollution**
> *x* Disposal of refuse; Garbage; Incineration; Littering; Solid waste disposal; Waste disposal
> *xx* **Industrial waste; Municipal engineering; Public health; Recycling (Waste, etc.); Salvage (Waste, etc.); Sanitary engineering; Sanitation; Sewage disposal; Street cleaning; Waste products; Water—Pollution**

Regattas. *See* **Rowing; Yachts and yachting**

Regional libraries. *See* **Libraries, Regional**

Regional planning 309.2; 711

> *See also* **City planning; Landscape protection; Social surveys**
> *x* County planning; Metropolitan planning; Planning, Regional; State planning
> *xx* **Landscape protection**

Regionalism. *See* **Nationalism; Sectionalism (U.S.)**

Registers of births, etc. 929

> *See also* **Vital statistics; Wills**
> *x* Birth records; Births, Registers of; Burial statistics; Deaths, Registers of; Marriage registers; Parish registers; Records of births, etc.; Vital records
> *xx* **Genealogy; Vital statistics**

Registers of persons. *See* names of countries, cities, etc. and names of colleges, universities, etc. with the subdivision *Registers*, e.g. **U.S.—Registers; United States Military Academy, West Point —Registers;** etc.

Rehabilitation. *See* groups of people with the subdivision *Rehabilitation*, e.g. **Physically handicapped—Rehabilitation;** etc.

Reign of Terror. *See* **France—History—Revolution, 1789–1799**

Reincarnation   129
   See also **Soul**
   x Rebirth
   xx **Soul; Theosophy**

Reindeer   599; 636.2
   xx **Deer; Domestic animals**

Reinforced concrete. *See* **Concrete, Reinforced**

Relativity (Physics)   530.1
   See also **Quantum theory; Space and time**
   xx **Physics; Quantum theory**

Relaxation. *See* **Recreation; Rest**

Reliability (Engineering)   620
   See also **Quality control**

Relief, Public. *See* **Public welfare**

Religion   200
   See also

Agnosticism	**Religions**
Atheism	**Revelation**
Belief and doubt	**Sacrifice**
Deism	**Skepticism**
Faith	**Spiritual life**
God	**Supernatural**
Mysticism	**Superstition**
Mythology	**Theism**
Natural theology	**Theology**
Pantheism	**Theosophy**
Rationalism	**Worship**

   also names of peoples, ethnic groups, countries, states, etc. with the subdivision *Religion*, e.g. **Indians of North America—Religion; Blacks—Religion; U.S.—Religion;** etc; and headings beginning with the words **Religion** and **Religious**
   xx **God; Religions; Theology**

Religion—Philosophy   200.1
   See also **Philosophy and religion**
   x Philosophy of religion
   xx **Philosophy and religion**

Religion—Study and teaching. *See* **Religious education; Theology—Study and teaching**

Religion and art. *See* **Art and religion**

Religion and astronautics   215
   x Astronautics and religion
   xx **Astronautics and civilization; Religion and science**

Religion and communism. *See* **Communism and religion**

Religion and education. *See* **Church and education**

Religion and literature. *See* **Religion in literature**

Religion and medicine. *See* **Medicine and religion**

Religion and philosophy. *See* **Philosophy and
religion**

Religion and politics 261.8
> *See also* **Christianity and politics**
> *x* Politics and religion

Religion and science 215
> *See also* **Bible and science; Creation; Evo-
> lution; Man—Origin and antiquity;
> Natural theology; Religion and astro-
> nautics**
> *x* Science and religion
> *xx* **Apologetics; Evolution; Natural theol-
> ogy; Theology**

Religion and social problems. *See* **Church and
social problems**

Religion and state. *See* **Church and state**

Religion and war. *See* **War and religion**

Religion in literature 809
> *See also* **Bible in literature**
> *x* Religion and literature
> *xx* **Bible in literature**

Religion in the public schools 377
> *x* Bible in the schools; Prayers in the pub-
> lic schools; Public schools and re-
> ligion; Schools—Prayers
> *xx* **Church and education; Church and state;
> Religious education**

Religion of humanity. *See* **Positivism**

Religions 290-299
> All religions are not included in this list.
> Add as needed
> *See also*

Bahaism	**Islam**
Brahmanism	**Judaism**
Buddhism	**Mythology**
Christianity	**Paganism**
Confucianism	**Religion**
Druids and	**Sects**
Druidism	**Shinto**
Gnosticism	**Taoism**
Gods	**Theosophy**
Hinduism	

> *x* Comparative religion
> *xx* **Civilization; Gods; Religion**

Religions—Biography 920; 922
> *See also* names of religions with the sub-
> division *Biography*, e.g. **Christianity—
> Biography**; etc.
> *x* Religious biography
> *xx* **Biography**

Religious art. *See* **Art, Medieval; Church architecture; Religious art and symbolism**

477

Religious art and symbolism 704.948

> *See also* **Art and religion; Christian art and symbolism**
>
> *x* Iconography; Painting, Religious; Relious art; Religious painting; Religious symbolism; Sacred art; Sculpture, Religious
>
> *xx* **Archeology; Art; Art and religion; Mysticism; Symbolism**

Religious belief. *See* **Faith**

Religious biography. *See* **Christianity—Biography; Religions—Biography**

Religious ceremonies. *See* **Rites and ceremonies**

Religious denominations. *See* **Sects;** and names of churches and sects, e.g. **Presbyterian Church;** etc.

Religious drama 808.82; 812; etc.

> *See also* **Bible—Drama; Christmas—Drama; Morality plays; Mysteries and miracle plays; Passion plays**
>
> *x* Drama, Religious
>
> *xx* **Drama; Drama in education; Religious literature**

Religious education 268; 377

> See note under **Church and education**
>
> *See also* **Character education; Christian education; Religion in the public schools; Sunday schools; Theology—Study and teaching**
>
> *x* Education, Ethical; Education, Religious; Education, Theological; Ethical education; Religion—Study and teaching
>
> *xx* **Education; Theology—Study and teachng**

Religious festivals. *See* **Fasts and feasts;** and names of festivals, e.g. **Christmas; Easter;** etc.

Religious freedom 261.7; 323.44

> *See also* **Church and state; Freedom of conscience; Persecution**
>
> *x* Freedom of religion; Freedom of worship; Intolerance; Religious liberty
>
> *xx* **Church and state; Civil rights; Free thought; Freedom; Freedom of conscience; Persecution; Toleration**

Religious history. *See* **Church history**

Religious liberty. *See* **Religious freedom**

Religious life 248

> *See also* classes of people with the subdivision *Religious life,* e.g. **Family—Religious life;** etc.
>
> *xx* **Christian life; Monasticism; Religious orders**

Religious literature 208; 800

> *See also* **Bible as literature; Religious drama; Religious poetry; Sacred books;** and names of religious and denominational literatures, e.g. **Catholic**

Religious literature—*Continued*
> literature; Christian literature, Early;
> etc.

> *xx* **Bible as literature; Literature**

Religious music. *See* **Church music**

Religious orders **255; 271**
> *See also* **Asceticism; Celibacy; Hermits;
> Religious life**

> *x* Monastic orders; Orders, Monastic
> *xx* **Monasticism**

Religious orders for men (May subdiv. by religion or denomination) **255; 271**
> *See also* **Monks**

Religious orders for men, Catholic **271**
> *See also* names of specific orders, e.g.
> **Dominicans; Franciscans; Jesuits;** etc.

Religious orders for women (May subdiv. by
religion or denomination) **255; 271**
> *See also* **Nuns; Sisters, Religious**

> *x* Sisterhoods
> *xx* **Convents**

Religious orders for women, Catholic **271**
> *See also* names of specific orders

Religious painting. *See* **Religious art and symbolism**

Religious poetry **808.81; 811;** etc.
> *See also* **Carols; Hymns**

> *xx* **Hymns; Poetry—Collections; Religious
> literature**

Religious sisters. *See* **Sisters, Religious**

Religious symbolism. *See* **Religious art and
symbolism**

Remedial reading. *See* **Reading—Remedial
teaching**

Remodeling of buildings. *See* **Buildings—
Maintenance and repair**

Renaissance **940.2**
> *See also* **Architecture, Renaissance; Art,
> Renaissance; Civilization, Medieval;
> Humanism; Literature, Medieval;
> Middle Ages; Sixteenth century**

> *x* Revival of letters
> *xx* **Civilization, Modern; History, Modern;
> Humanism; Middle Ages**

Rendezvous in space. *See* **Orbital rendezvous
(Space flight)**

Rental services. *See* **Lease and rental services**

Repairing **620**
> *See also* **Buildings—Maintenance and re-
> pair;** also names of machines, instru-
> ments, etc. that require maintenance
> with the subdivision *Maintenance and
> repair,* e.g. **Automobiles—Mainte-
> nance and repair;** and names of ob-
> jects that need no maintenance with
> the subdivision *Repairing,* e.g. **Radio
> —Repairing;** etc.

Reparations (World War, 1939–1945). *See*
World War, 1939–1945—Reparations

Report writing 808
  x Reports—Preparation
  xx **Authorship**
Reporters and reporting 070.4
  See also **Government and the press; Journalism**
  x Interviewing (Journalism); Newspaper work
  xx **Journalism; Newspapers**
Reports—Preparation. *See* **Report writing**
Representation. *See* **Representative government and representation**
Representation, Proportional. *See* **Proportional representation**
Representative government and representation 321.8
  See also

Apportionment (Election law)	**Proportional representation**
Constitutions	**Recall (Political science)**
Democracy	
Elections	**Referendum**
Legislative bodies	**Republics**
Primaries	**Suffrage**

  x Parliamentary government; Representation; Self-government
  xx **Constitutional history; Constitutional law; Constitutions; Democracy; Elections; Political science; Republics; Suffrage**
Representatives—U.S. *See* **U.S. Congress. House**
Reprints. *See* **Bibliography—Editions**
Reproduction 574.1; 612.6
  See also **Cells; Embryology; Menstruation; Pregnancy; Sex**
  x Generation
  xx **Biology; Embryology; Genetics; Life (Biology); Physiology; Sex**
Reproduction processes. *See* **Copying processes and machines**
Reproductive system 612.6
  x Generative organs
Reprography. *See* **Copying processes and machines**
Reptiles 598.1
  See also **Crocodiles; Lizards; Snakes; Turtles**
  xx **Vertebrates**
Reptiles, Fossil 568
  See also names of fossil reptiles, e.g. **Dinosaurs;** etc.
  x Fossil reptiles
  xx **Fossils**
Republic of China, 1949–. *See* **Taiwan**
Republic of South Africa. *See* **South Africa**
Republican Party 329.6
  xx **Political parties**

Republics   321.8
> See also **Democracy; Federal government; Representative government and representation**
>
> *x* The Commonwealth
>
> *xx* **Constitutional history; Constitutional law; Democracy; Political science; Representative government and representation**

Rescue operations, Space. *See* **Space rescue operations**

Rescue work   614.8
> See also **First aid; Lifesaving; Space rescue operations**
>
> *x* Search and rescue operations
>
> *xx* **Civil defense**

Research   001.4
> See also **Learning and scholarship; Operations research; Psychical research;** also subjects with the subdivision *Research*, e.g. **Agriculture—Research; Medicine—Research;** etc.
>
> *xx* **Learning and scholarship**

Reservations, Indian. *See* **Indians of North America—Reservations**

Reservoirs   627; 628.1
> See also **Irrigation; Water supply**
>
> *xx* **Hydraulic structures; Water supply**

Resettlement. *See* **Land settlement**

Residences. *See* **Architecture, Domestic; Houses**

Residential security. *See* **Burglary protection**

Resins. *See* **Gums and resins**

Resistance of materials. *See* **Strength of materials**

Resistance to government. *See* **Government, Resistance to**

Resistance welding. *See* **Electric welding**

Resorts. *See* types of resorts, e.g. **Health resorts, spas, etc.; Summer resorts; Winter resorts;** etc.

Resource management. *See* **Conservation of natural resources**

Resources, Marine. *See* **Marine resources**

Resources, Natural. *See* **Natural resources**

Respiration   612
> *x* Breathing
>
> *xx* **Lungs; Physiology; Singing; Voice**

Respiration, Artificial. *See* **Artificial respiration**

Rest   613.7
> See also **Fatigue; Sleep**
>
> *x* Relaxation
>
> *xx* **Fatigue; Hygiene**

Restaurants, bars, etc.   647
> See also **Coffee houses;** also cities with the subdivision *Restaurants, bars, etc.,* e.g. **Chicago—Restaurants, bars, etc.;** etc.
>
> *x* Bars and restaurants; Cafeterias; Din-

Restaurants, bars, etc.—*Continued*
ers; Lunch rooms; Saloons; Taverns; Tea rooms; Tearooms

Restoration of automobiles. *See* **Automobiles —Restoration**

Restoration of buildings. *See* **Architecture— Conservation and restoration**

Restoration of works of art. *See* subjects with the subdivision *Conservation and restoration,* e.g. **Painting—Conservation and restoration**; etc.

Resumés (Employment) 331.1
x Job resumés
xx **Applications for positions**

Resurrection. *See* **Future life; Jesus Christ— Resurrection**

Retail sales tax. *See* **Sales tax**

Retail trade 658.8
See also **Advertising; Chain stores; Department stores; Packaging; Sales personnel; Selling; Shopping centers and malls; Supermarkets**
x Merchandising
xx **Commerce**

Retarded children. *See* **Mentally retarded children; Slow learning children**

Retirement 301.43
xx **Leisure; Old age**

Retirement income. *See* **Annuities; Old age pensions; Pensions**

Retouching (Photography). *See* **Photography —Retouching**

Retraining, Occupational 331.2
See note under **Occupational training**
x Occupational retraining
xx **Employees—Training; Human resources policy; Labor supply; Occupational training; Technical education; Unemployed; Vocational education**

Retribution. *See* **Future life; Hell**

Reuse of waste. *See* **Recycling (Waste, etc.); Salvage (Waste, etc.)**

Revelation 231
xx **Religion; Supernatural; Theology**

Revenue. *See* **Tariff; Taxation**

Revenue, Internal. *See* **Internal revenue**

Revenue sharing 336; 336.1-336.2
x Federal revenue sharing; Tax sharing
xx **Intergovernmental tax relations**

Reviews. *See* subjects with the subdivision *Reviews,* e.g. **Books—Reviews**; etc.

Revival of letters. *See* **Renaissance**

Revivals 269
See also **Evangelistic work**
xx **Christian life; Church history; Church work; Evangelistic work**

Revolution, American. *See* **U.S.—History— Revolution, 1775–1783**

Revolution, French. *See* **France—History— Revolution, 1789–1799**

Revolution, Russian. *See* **Russia—History—Revolution, 1917–1921**

Revolutions 301.6

> *See also* **Insurgency; Government, Resistance to; Radicals and radicalism; Terrorism;** and names of countries with the subdivision *History—Revolution,* e.g. **France—History—Revolution, 1789–1799; Hungary—History—Revolution, 1956; Russia—History—Revolution, 1917–1921; U.S.—History—Revolution, 1775–1783;** etc.

> *x* Coups d'état; Rebellions; Sedition

> *xx* **Government, Resistance to; Political science**

Rewards (Prizes, etc.) 001.4

> *See also* **Literary prizes;** also names of awards and prizes, e.g. **Nobel prizes;** etc.

> *x* Awards; Competitions; Prizes (Rewards)

Rh factor. *See* **Blood groups**

Rhetoric 808

> *See also*

Criticism	**Letter writing**
Debates and debating	**Preaching**
Lectures and lecturing	**Punctuation**
	Satire
	Style, Literary

> *also* names of languages with the subdivision *Composition and exercises,* e.g. **English language—Composition and exercises;** etc.

> *x* Composition (Rhetoric); English language—Rhetoric; Persuasion (Rhetoric); Speaking

> *xx* **English language—Composition and exercises; Language and languages; Style, Literary**

Rheumatism 616.7

> *See also* **Arthritis**

Rhyme 416; 426

> *See also* **Rhythm; Stories in rhyme;** also names of languages with the subdivision *Rhyme,* e.g. **English language—Rhyme;** etc.

> *x* Rime

> *xx* **Poetics; Versification**

Rhymes. *See* **Limericks; Nonsense verses; Nursery rhymes; Poetry—Collections**

Rhythm 416; 426

> *See also* **Musical meter and rhythm; Periodicity; Versification**

> *xx* **Esthetics; Periodicity; Poetics; Rhyme**

Riches. *See* **Wealth**

Riddles 398.6; 793.7

> *See also* **Charades; Puzzles**

> *x* Conundrums; Enigmas; Rebuses

> *xx* **Amusements; Puzzles**

Riding. *See* **Horseback riding**

Rifles 799.2

  x Carbines; Guns

  xx **Arms and armor; Firearms**

Right (Political science). *See* **Right and left (Political science)**

Right and left (Political science) 320.5

  See also **Conservatism; Liberalism; Radicals and radicalism**

  x Extremism (Political science); Left (Political science); Right (Political science)

  xx **Conservatism; Liberalism; Political parties; Political science**

Right of assembly. *See* **Freedom of assembly**

Right of asylum. *See* **Asylum, Right of**

Right of privacy. *See* **Privacy, Right of**

Right to die. *See* **Euthanasia**

Right to know. *See* **Freedom of information**

Right to live. *See* **Abortion; Euthanasia**

Right to work. *See* **Discrimination in employment; Open and closed shop**

Rights, Civil. *See* **Civil rights**

Rights of women. *See* **Women—Civil rights**

Rime. *See* **Rhyme**

Riot control. *See* **Riots—Control**

Riots 301.6

  See also **Crowds; Demonstrations;** also names of cities, and institutions with the subdivision *Riots*, e.g. **Chicago—Riots;** etc.; also names of specific riots

  x Civil disorders; Mobs

  xx **Crime; Demonstrations; Freedom of assembly; Offenses against public safety**

Riots—Control 301.6

  x Riot control

  xx **Crowds**

Rites and ceremonies 390

  See also **Baptism; Fasts and feasts; Funeral rites and ceremonies; Manners and customs; Marriage customs and rites; Ordination; Sacraments; Secret societies;** also classes of people and ethnic groups with the subdivision *Rites and ceremonies*, e.g. **Jews—Rites and ceremonies;** etc.

  x Ceremonies; Ecclesiastical rites and ceremonies; Religious ceremonies; Ritual

  xx **Manners and customs**

Ritual. *See* **Liturgies; Rites and ceremonies**

Rivers 551.4

  See also **Dams; Floods; Hydraulic engineering; Inland navigation; Water—Pollution; Water power; Water rights;** also names of rivers

  xx **Civil engineering; Floods; Floods—Control; Hydraulic engineering; Inland navigation; Physical geography; Water; Waterways**

Rivers—Pollution. *See* **Water—Pollution**

Road construction. *See* **Roads**

Road engineering. *See* **Highway engineering**

Road maps 910.2

> *See also* **Automobiles—Road guides;** also names of countries, areas, states, cities, etc. with the subdivision *Maps,* e.g. **U.S.—Maps; Chicago—Maps;** etc.
>
> *x* Maps, Road; Roads—Maps
>
> *xx* **Automobiles—Road guides; Maps**

Road signs. *See* **Signs and signboards**

Roads 388.1; 625.7

> *See also* **Express highways; Highway engineering; Pavements; Roadside improvement; Soils (Engineering); Street cleaning; Streets**
>
> *x* Construction of roads; Highway construction; Highways; Road construction; Thoroughfares
>
> *xx* **Civil engineering; Highway engineering; Pavements; Streets; Transportation**

Roads—Maps. *See* **Road maps**

Roadside improvement 713

> *x* Highway beautification
>
> *xx* **Grounds maintenance; Landscape architecture; Roads**

Robbers and outlaws 364.1

> *x* Bandits; Brigands; Burglars; Highwaymen; Outlaws; Thieves
>
> *xx* **Criminals**

Robins 598.2

> *xx* **Birds**

Robots 629.8

> See note under **Automata**
>
> *See also* **Automata**
>
> *xx* **Automata; Mechanical movements**

Rochdale system. *See* **Cooperation**

Rock and roll music. *See* **Rock music**

Rock climbing. *See* **Mountaineering**

Rock crystal. *See* **Quartz**

Rock gardens 635.9

> *xx* **Gardens**

Rock music 781.5

> *x* Music, Rock; Rock and roll music
>
> *xx* **Music, Popular (Songs, etc.)**

Rock tombs. *See* **Tombs**

Rocket airplanes. *See* **Rocket planes**

Rocket flight. *See* **Space flight**

Rocket planes 629.133

> *See also* names of rocket planes, e.g. **X-15 (Rocket aircraft);** etc.
>
> *x* Airplanes, Rocket propelled; Rocket airplanes
>
> *xx* **High speed aeronautics; Space ships**

Rocketry 621.43

> *See also* **Ballistic missiles; Guided missiles; Rockets (Aeronautics); Space ships; Space vehicles**
>
> *xx* **Aeronautics; Astronautics**

485

Rockets (Aeronautics)   629.133

>See also **Artificial satellites—Launching; Jet propulsion;** also names of types of rockets, e.g. **Ballistic missiles; Guided missiles;** etc.; and names of specific rockets

>*x* Aerial rockets

>*xx* **Aeronautics; High speed aeronautics; Interplanetary voyages; Jet propulsion; Projectiles; Rocketry**

Rocks   552

>See also **Crystallography; Geochemistry; Geology; Mineralogy; Petrology; Stone;** also varieties of rock, e.g. **Granite;** etc.

>*x* Crystalline rocks; Metamorphic rocks

>*xx* **Geology; Petrology; Stone**

Rocks—Age.   *See* **Geology, Stratigraphic**

Rocks, Moon.   *See* **Lunar petrology**

Rocky Mountains   917.8

>*xx* **Mountains**

Rodeos   791.8

>*xx* **Cowhands; Horseback riding; Sports**

Roentgen rays.   *See* **X rays**

Roentgenologists.   *See* **Radiologists**

Role, Social.   *See* **Social role**

Role conflict   301.11

>See also **Sex role**

>*xx* **Social role**

Role playing   301.11

>*xx* **Social role**

Roller skating   796.2

>*x* Figure skating; Skating

Rolling stock.   *See* **Locomotives**

Romaic language.   *See* **Greek language, Modern**

Romaic literature.   *See* **Greek literature, Modern**

Roman antiquities.   *See* **Classical antiquities; Rome—Antiquities; Rome (City)—Antiquities**

Roman architecture.   *See* **Architecture, Roman**

Roman art.   *See* **Art, Roman**

Roman Catholic Church.   *See* **Catholic Church**

Roman emperors   920; 923

>See also names of Roman emperors, e.g. **Nero, Emperor of Rome;** etc.

>*x* Emperors; Sovereigns

>*xx* **Kings and rulers**

Roman literature.   *See* **Latin literature**

Roman mythology.   *See* **Mythology, Classical**

Roman philosophy.   *See* **Philosophy, Ancient**

Romance languages   440

>See also names of languages belonging to the Romance group, e.g. **French language;** etc.

>*x* Neo-Latin languages

>*xx* **Latin language**

486

Romance literature 840

See also names of literatures belonging to
the Romance group, e.g. **French literature;** etc.

Romances 840

Use for collections of medieval tales dealing with the age of chivalry; they may
be either metrical or prose versions
and may or may not have a factual
basis

See also names of historic persons with the
subdivision *Romances*

x Chivalry—Romances; Metrical romances; Stories

xx **Chivalry; Epic poetry; Fiction; Legends;
Literature—Collections**

Romanesque architecture. *See* **Architecture,
Romanesque**

Romanesque art. *See* **Art, Romanesque**

Romanesque painting. *See* **Painting, Romanesque**

Romanies. *See* **Gypsies**

Romanticism 141; 809

See also **Realism in literature**

xx **Esthetics; Fiction; Literature; Music;
Realism in literature**

Rome 913.37; 937

Use for materials about the Roman Empire.
Materials treating only of the modern
city of Rome are entered under **Rome
(City)**

Rome—Antiquities 913.37

x Roman antiquities

Rome—Biography 920

x Classical biography

Rome—Description and geography 913.37

Use for descriptive and geographic materials on ancient Rome instead of the
subdivisions *Description and travel*
and *Historical geography*

Rome—History 937

Rome—History—Kings, 753–510 B.C. 937

Rome—History—Republic, 510–30 B.C. 937

**Rome—History—Empire, 30 B.C.–476 A.D.
937**

Rome (City) 914.5; 945

See note under **Rome**

Rome (City)—Antiquities 913.37

x Roman antiquities; Ruins

Rome (City)—Description 914.5

Rome (City)—History 945

Roofs 695

xx **Architecture—Details; Building; Building,
Iron and steel; Carpentry**

Rooming houses. *See* **Hotels, motels, etc.**

Root crops 633

See also **Feeds**

xx **Feeds; Vegetables**

Rope   623.88; 677
  See also **Cables; Hemp; Knots and splices**
  xx **Hemp**
Roses   635.9
  xx **Flower gardening; Flowers**
Rosetta stone inscription   493
  xx **Hieroglyphics**
Rosin. *See* **Gums and resins**
Rotation of crops   631.5
  x Crop rotation; Crops, Rotation of
  xx **Agriculture**
Round stage. *See* **Arena theater**
Routes of trade. *See* **Trade routes**
Rowing   797.1
  x Regattas; Sculling
  xx **Athletics; Boats and boating; College
      sports; Exercise; Water sports**
Royalty. *See* **Kings and rulers; Princes and
      princesses; Queens**
Rubber   678
  x India rubber
  xx **Forest products**
Rubber, Artificial   678
  x Artificial rubber; Synthetic rubber
  xx **Plastics; Synthetic products**
Rubber sheet geometry. *See* **Topology**
Rubber tires. *See* **Tires**
Rugs   677; 746.7
  See also **Carpets**
  xx **Arts and crafts; Carpets; Interior decora-
      tion**
Rugs, Hooked   746.7
  x Hooked rugs
Rugs, Oriental   746.7
  x Oriental rugs; Persian rugs
Ruins. *See* **Archeology; Cities and towns,
      Ruined, extinct, etc.; Excavations
      (Archeology);** and names of countries,
      cities, etc. with the subdivision *An-
      tiquities,* e.g. **Rome (City)—Antiquities;**
      etc.
Rulers. *See* **Kings and rulers; Queens;** and
      names of individual rulers
Rules of order. *See* **Parliamentary practice**
Runaways   301.43
  x Adults, Runaway; Children, Runaway;
      Youth, Runaway
  xx **Children; Youth**
Running. *See* **Track athletics**
Rural architecture. *See* **Architecture, Domes-
      tic; Farm buildings**
Rural churches   254.2
  x Church work, Rural; Churches, Country;
      Churches, Rural; Country churches
  xx **Church work**
Rural credit. *See* **Agricultural credit**
Rural electrification. *See* **Electric power distri-
      bution; Electricity in agriculture**
Rural high schools. *See* **Rural schools**

Rural life. *See* **Country life; Farm life; Outdoor life; Peasantry**

Rural schools 371

   x Country schools; District schools; High schools, Rural; Rural high schools

   xx **Public schools**

Rural sociology. *See* **Sociology, Rural**

Russia 914.7; 947

   x Soviet Union; USSR

Russia—Communism. *See* **Communism—Russia**

Russia—History 947

Russia—History—Revolution of 1905 947.08

Russia—History—1917– 947.084

Russia—History—Revolution, 1917–1921 947.08

   x Revolution, Russian; Russian revolution

   xx **Revolutions**

Russia—History—1925–1953 947.084

Russia—History—War with Finland, 1939–1940. *See* **Russo-Finnish War, 1939–1940**

Russia—History—1953– 947.085

Russian artificial satellites. *See* **Artificial satellites, Russian**

Russian Church. *See* **Orthodox Eastern Church, Russian**

Russian communism. *See* **Communism—Russia**

Russian intervention in Czechoslovakia. *See* **Czechoslovakia—History—Intervention, 1968–**

Russian revolution. *See* **Russia—History—Revolution, 1917–1921**

Russian satellite countries. *See* **Communist countries**

Russo-Finnish War, 1939–1940 947.1

   x Finno-Russian War, 1939–1940; Russia—History—War with Finland, 1939–1940

Russo-Turkish War, 1853–1856. *See* **Crimean War, 1853–1856**

Rust. *See* **Corrosion and anticorrosives**

Rustless coatings. *See* **Corrosion and anti-corrosives**

SST. *See* **Supersonic transport planes**

STOL aircraft. *See* **Short take off and landing aircraft**

Sabbath 263; 296.4

   x Lord's Day

   xx **Judaism**

Sabine vaccine. *See* **Poliomyelitis vaccine**

Sabotage 331.89; 355.3; 364.1

   xx **Labor unions; Offenses against public safety; Strikes and lockouts; Subversive activities; Terrorism**

Sacraments 234; 265

   See also **Baptism; Lord's Supper; Marriage; Ordination**

   x Ecclesiastical rites and ceremonies

   xx **Rites and ceremonies; Theology**

Sacred art. *See* **Christian art and symbolism;
Religious art and symbolism**

Sacred books   291.8

> *See also* names of sacred books, e.g. **Bible;
> Koran; Vedas;** etc.
>
> *x* Books, Sacred
>
> *xx* **Religious literature**

Sacred music. *See* **Church music**

Sacrifice   291

> *See also* **Atonement**
>
> *xx* **Ethnology; Religion; Theology; Worship**

Safety, Industrial. *See* **Industrial health and
safety**

Safety appliances   614.8; 620.8

> *See also* **Accidents—Prevention;** also sub-
> jects with the subdivision *Safety ap-
> pliances,* e.g. **Railroads—Safety appli-
> ances;** etc.
>
> *x* Safety devices; Safety equipment
>
> *xx* **Accidents—Prevention**

Safety devices. *See* **Safety appliances**

Safety education   371.7

> *See also* **Accidents—Prevention**
>
> *xx* **Accidents—Prevention**

Safety equipment. *See* **Safety appliances**

Safety measures. *See* **Accidents—Prevention;**
and subjects with the subdivision
Safety measures, e.g. **Aeronautics—
Safety measures;** etc.

Sagas   398.2; 839

> *See also* **Icelandic and Old Norse literature**
>
> *xx* **Folklore; Icelandic and Old Norse liter-
> ature; Literature; Scandinavian litera-
> ture**

Sailing   623.88; 797.1

> *See also* **Boats and boating; Navigation;
> Yachts and yachting**
>
> *xx* **Boats and boating; Navigation; Ships;
> Water sports; Yachts and yachting**

Sailors   920; 926

> *See also* **Merchant marine; Pilots and pilot-
> age; Seafaring life; Veterans;** also
> names of navies, e.g. **U.S. Navy;** etc.
>
> *x* Armed forces; Mariners; Naval person-
> nel; Navigators; Sailors' life; Sea life;
> Seamen
>
> *xx* **Naval art and science; Seafaring life;
> Veterans; Voyages and travels**

Sailors' life. *See* **Sailors; Seafaring life**

Sailors' songs. *See* **Sea songs**

Sailplanes (Aeronautics). *See* **Gliders (Aeronautics)**

St. Dominic, Order of. *See* **Dominicans**

St. Francis, Order of. *See* **Franciscans**

Saints   920; 922

> *See also* **Hermits; Legends; Martyrs;
> Shrines;** also names of saints of differ-
> ent religions, e.g. **Christian saints;** and
> names of individual saints

Saints—*Continued*

    xx **Heroes and heroines; Legends; Martyrs; Pilgrims and pilgrimages; Shrines**

Salads 641.8

    xx **Cookery**

Salamanders 597

    xx **Amphibians**

Sales, Auction. *See* **Auctions**

Sales management 658.8

    x Management, Sales

    xx **Industrial management; Management; Marketing; Selling**

Sales personnel 658.85

    See also **Booksellers and bookselling; Clerks; Peddlers and peddling**

    x Agents, Sales; Clerks (Retail trade); Commercial travelers; Salesmen; Saleswomen

    xx **Clerks; Retail trade**

Sales tax 336.2

    x Purchase tax; Retail sales tax; Taxation of sales

    xx **Taxation**

Salesmanship. *See* **Selling**

Salesmen. *See* **Sales personnel**

Saleswomen. *See* **Sales personnel**

Saline water. *See* **Sea water**

Salk vaccine. *See* **Poliomyelitis vaccine**

Salmon 597

    xx **Fishes**

Saloons. *See* **Restaurants, bars, etc.**

Salt free diet 613.2; 641.5

    x Low sodium diet

    xx **Cookery for the sick; Diet; Diet in disease**

Salt water. *See* **Sea water**

Salt water aquariums. *See* **Marine aquariums**

Salutations. *See* **Etiquette; Letter writing**

Salvage 387.5; 627.7

    See also **Skin diving; Shipwrecks**

    xx **International law; Maritime law; Shipwrecks**

Salvage (Waste, etc.) 604.6

    See note under **Recycling (Waste, etc.)**

    See also **Recycling (Waste, etc.); Refuse and refuse disposal; Waste products**

    x Conversion of waste products; Recovery of waste products; Reuse of waste; Solid waste disposal; Utilization of waste; Waste products—Recycling; Waste reclamation

    xx **Recycling (Waste, etc.); Refuse and refuse disposal; Waste products**

Salvation 234

    See also **Atonement; Sanctification; Sin**

    x Redemption

    xx **Conversion; Faith; Theology**

Salvation Army 267

    xx **Evangelistic work; Missions, Christian**

Sampling (Statistics) 519.5
  See also **Quality control**
  x Random sampling
  xx **Probabilities; Statistics**
San Francisco—Earthquake and fire, 1906
    979.4
  xx **Disasters**
Sanatoriums. *See* **Health resorts, spas, etc.;**
    Hospitals
Sanctification 234
  xx **Salvation; Spiritual life; Theology**
Sanctuary (Law). *See* **Asylum, Right of**
Sand dunes 551.3
  x Dunes
  xx **Reclamation of land; Seashore**
Sandwiches 641.8
  xx **Cookery**
Sanitary affairs. *See* **Sanitary engineering;**
    Sanitation
Sanitary engineering 628
  See also **Drainage; Municipal engineering;**
    Pollution; Refuse and refuse disposal;
    Sanitation; Sewerage; Soils bacteriol-
    ogy; Street cleaning; Water supply
  x Sanitary affairs
  xx **Building; Civil engineering; Drainage,**
    House; Municipal engineering; Plumb-
    ing; Public health; Sanitation
Sanitation 614.7
  See also

  Cemeteries   **School hygiene**
  Cremation   **Ventilation**
  Disinfection and   **Water—Purifica-**
    disinfectants   **tion**
  Hygiene   **Water supply**
  Military hygiene   **World War, 1939–**
  Pollution   **1945—Medical**
  Public health   **and sanitary**
  Refuse and refuse   **affairs**
    disposal
  Sanitary engineer-
    ing

  x Cleanliness; Sanitary affairs
  xx **Hygiene; Public health; Sanitary engi-**
    neering
Sanitation, Household 648
  See also **Drainage, House; House cleaning;**
    Household pests; Laundry; Plumbing;
    Ventilation
  x House sanitation; Household sanitation
  xx **Plumbing**
Santa Claus 394.2
  xx **Christmas**
Satan. *See* **Devil**
Satellite communication system. *See* **Artificial**
    satellites in telecommunication
Satellites, Artificial. *See* **Artificial satellites**
Satire (May subdiv. geog. adjective form, e.g.
    Satire, English, etc.) 808.7; 808.87
  See also **Parody**

492

Satire—*Continued*

    x Comic literature

    xx **Literature; Rhetoric; Wit and humor**

Satire, American   817

    x American satire

    xx **American literature**

Satire, English   827

    x English satire

    xx **English literature**

Saving and thrift   332

    See also **Cost of living; Insurance, Industrial; Investments; Old age pensions; Savings and loan associations**

    x Economy; Thrift

    xx **Cost of living; Economics; Finance, Personal; Insurance; Investments; Success**

Savings and loan associations   332.3

    x Building and loan associations; Cooperative building associations; Loan associations

    xx **Banks and banking; Cooperation; Cooperative societies; Investments; Loans; Saving and thrift**

Savings banks. *See* **Banks and banking**

Saws   621.9; 694

    xx **Carpentry—Tools; Tools**

Saxons. *See* **Anglo-Saxons; Teutonic peoples**

Sayings. *See* **Epigrams; Proverbs; Quotations**

Scalds and scaldic poetry   839.1

    See also **Icelandic and Old Norse literature; Troubadours**

    xx **Icelandic and Old Norse literature; Poetry; Poets**

Scandinavian civilization. *See* **Civilization, Scandinavian**

Scandinavian languages   439

    See also **Danish language; Icelandic and Old Norse languages; Norwegian language; Swedish language**

    x Norse languages

    xx **Icelandic and old Norse languages**

Scandinavian literature   839

    See also **Danish literature; Eddas; Icelandic and Old Norse literature; Norwegian literature; Sagas; Swedish literature**

    x Norse literature

    xx **Icelandic and Old Norse literature**

Scandinavians   572.948; 914.8

    Use for materials on the people since the 10th century. Materials on the early Scandinavians are entered under **Vikings**

    See also **Vikings**

Scenarios. *See* **Motion picture plays; Plots (Drama, fiction, etc.); Radio plays; Television plays**

Scene painting   751.7

    xx **Painting; Theaters—Stage setting and scenery**

Scenery. *See* **Landscape protection; Views;** and names of countries, states, etc. with the subdivision *Description and travel—Views* (e.g. **U.S.—Description and travel—Views;** etc.); and names of cities with the subdivision *Description —Views*, e.g. **Chicago—Description— Views;** etc.

Scenery (Stage). *See* **Theaters—Stage setting and scenery**

Scepticism. *See* **Skepticism**

Scholarship. *See* **Learning and scholarship**

Scholarships, fellowships, etc. 378.3
> *See also* **Student loan funds**
> *x* Fellowships; Student aid
> *xx* **Colleges and universities; Education; Education and state; Endowments; Student loan funds**

School administration and organization 371.2
> See note under **School supervision**
> *See also* **Articulation (Education); School boards; School discipline; School superintendents and principals; School supervision; Self-government (in education); Teaching**
> *x* Educational administration; Inspection of schools; School inspection; School management; School organization; Schools—Administration; Schools— Management and organization

School and community. *See* **Community and school**

School and home. *See* **Home and school**

School architecture. *See* **School buildings**

School assembly programs 372.1; 373
> Use for general materials on school entertainments, literary and otherwise, assembly programs, etc. Collections of prose and poetry for public speaking are entered under **Readings and recitations**
> *See also* **Commencements; Drama in education; Readings and recitations;** also names of days observed, e.g. **Memorial Day;** etc.
> *x* Assembly programs, School; Programs, School assembly; School entertainments; Schools—Exercises and recreations; Schools—Opening exercises
> *xx* **Student activities**

School attendance 371.2
> *See also* **Child labor; Dropouts; Education, Compulsory**
> *x* Absence from school; Absenteeism (School); Attendance, School; Compulsory school attendance; School enrollment; Truancy (Schools)
> *xx* **Education, Compulsory**

494

School boards 379

    x Boards of education

    xx **School administration and organization**

School books. *See* **Textbooks**

School buildings 727

    x Buildings, School; School architecture; School houses; Schoolhouses

    xx **Architecture; Buildings; Schools**

School buildings as recreation centers. *See* **Community centers**

School busing. *See* **Busing (School integration); School children—Transportation**

School children—Food 371.7

    x Food for school children; Meals for school children; School lunches

    xx **Children—Care and hygiene; Diet; Food**

School children—Transportation 371.8

    See also **Busing (School integration)**

    x School busing

    xx **Transportation**

School clubs. *See* **Students—Societies**

School desegregation. *See* **School integration**

School discipline 371.5

    See also **Classroom management; Self-government (in education)**

    x Discipline of children; Punishment in schools

    xx **School administration and organization; Teaching**

School drama. *See* **College and school drama**

School dropouts. *See* **Dropouts**

School endowments. *See* **Endowments**

School enrollment. *See* **School attendance**

School entertainments. *See* **School assembly programs**

School excursions. *See* **Field trips**

School finance. *See* **Education—Finance**

School furniture. *See* **Schools—Equipment and supplies**

School houses. *See* **School buildings**

School hygiene 371.7

    x Children—Health; Hygiene, School

    xx **Children—Care and hygiene; Health education; Hygiene; Public health; Sanitation**

School inspection. *See* **School administration and organization; School supervision**

School integration 344.7; 370.19

    See also **Segregation in education**

    x Desegregated schools; Desegregation in education; Education—Integration; Integrated schools; Integration in education; Racial balance in schools; School desegregation

    xx **Blacks—Education; Blacks—Integration; Segregation in education**

School journalism. *See* **College and school journalism**

School libraries 027.8

See also **Children's literature; Libraries, Children's; Libraries and schools**

x Children's libraries; Libraries, School

xx **Libraries; Libraries, Children's; Libraries and schools**

School libraries (High school) 027.8

See also **Libraries, Young adults'**

x High school libraries; Libraries, School; Secondary school libraries

xx **Libraries; Libraries, young adults'**

School life. See **Students**

School lunches. See **School children—Food**

School management. See **School administration and organization**

School media centers. See **Instructional materials centers**

School music. See **Music—Study and teaching; School songbooks; Singing**

School newspapers. See **College and school journalism**

School nurses 371.7

xx **Children—Care and hygiene; Nurses**

School organization. See **School administration and organization**

School playgrounds. See **Playgrounds**

School plays. See **Children's plays; College and school drama—Collections**

School principals. See **School superintendents and principals**

School psychologists 371.2

x Psychologists, School

xx **Educational counseling**

School reports 371.2

See also **Grading and marking (Students)**

xx **Grading and marking (Students)**

School shops 373.2

x Industrial arts shops

xx **Technical education**

School songbooks 784.6

See also **Children's songs**

x School music; Songbooks, School

xx **Singing; Songbooks; Songs**

School sports 371.8

See also **Coaching (Athletics); College sports**

x Interscholastic sports

xx **Sports; Student activities**

School stories 808.83; 813; etc.; Fic

x Stories

School superintendents and principals 371.2

See also **School supervision**

x School principals; Superintendents of schools

xx **School administration and organization; School supervision; Teachers; Teaching**

School supervision 371.1

Use for materials on the supervision of instruction. Materials on the administra-

School supervision—*Continued*
tive duties of an educator are entered under **School administration and organization**
See also **School superintendents and principals**
x Inspection of schools; Instructional supervision; School inspection; Supervision of schools
xx **School administration and organization; School superintendents and principals; Teaching**
School surveys. *See* **Educational surveys**
School taxes. *See* **Education—Finance**
School teaching. *See* **Teaching**
School trips. *See* **Field trips**
School verse 808.81; 811; etc.
xx **Poetry—Collections**
School withdrawals. *See* **Dropouts**
Schoolhouses. *See* **School buildings**
Schools (May subdiv. geog. country or state) **371**
See also **Education; Libraries and schools; Museums and schools; School buildings;** also types of schools, e.g. **Church schools; Colleges and universities; Kindergarten;** etc.; *also* subjects with the subdivision *Study and teaching* (e.g. **Medicine—Study and teaching;** etc.); names of cities with the subdivision *Schools* (e.g. **Chicago—Schools;** etc.); headings beginning with the word **School;** and names of individual schools
x Community schools; Neighborhood schools
xx **Education; Public schools**
Schools—Administration. *See* **School administration and organization**
Schools—Centralization 379
x Centralization of schools; Consolidation of schools
Schools, Commercial. *See* **Business education**
Schools—Curricula. *See* **Education—Curricula;** also types of education and schools with the subdivision *Curricula,* e.g. **Library education—Curricula; Colleges and universities—Curricula;** etc.
Schools—Decentralization 371.2
x Decentralization of schools
Schools—Equipment and supplies 371.6
x School furniture
xx **Furniture**
Schools—Exercises and recreations. *See* **School assembly programs**
Schools—Management and organization. *See* **School administration and organization**
Schools, Military. *See* **Military education**
Schools, Nongraded. *See* **Nongraded schools**

Schools—Opening exercises. *See* **School assembly programs**

Schools, Parochial. *See* **Church schools**

Schools—Prayers. *See* **Religion in the public schools**

Schools, Ungraded. *See* **Nongraded schools**

Schools—U.S. 371
> *x* U.S.—Schools

Schools and libraries. *See* **Libraries and schools**

Schools and museums. *See* **Museums and schools**

Schools as social centers. *See* **Community centers**

Science (May subdiv. geog.) **500**
> *See also*

Astronomy	**Life sciences**
Bacteriology	**Mathematics**
Biology	**Meteorology**
Botany	**Mineralogy**
Chemistry	**Natural history**
Crystallography	**Petrology**
Earth sciences	**Physics**
Ethnology	**Physiology**
Fossils	**Space sciences**
Geology	**Zoology**

> *also* headings beginning with the word **Scientific**
> *x* Discoveries (in science)

Science—Exhibitions 507.4
> *x* Science fairs

Science—Experiments 507
> *See also* particular branches of science with the subdivision *Experiments*, e.g. **Chemistry—Experiments;** etc.
> *x* Experiments, Scientific; Scientific experiments

Science—Fiction. *See* **Science fiction**

Science—Methodology 501
> *See also* **Logic**
> *x* Methodology; Scientific method

Science—Social aspects. *See* **Science and civilization**

Science—Societies 506
> *x* Scientific societies

Science—Study and teaching 507
> *See also* **Nature study**
> *x* Education, Scientific; Scientific education
> *xx* **Education; Teaching**

Science—U.S. 509
> *x* American science; U.S.—Science

Science and civilization 301.24
> *x* Civilization and science; Science—Social aspects; Science and society
> *xx* **Civilization; Progress**

Science and religion. *See* **Religion and science**

Science and society. *See* **Science and civilization**

Science and space. *See* **Space sciences**

Science and state 351.8

   x Science policy; State and science

Science and the Bible. *See* **Bible and science**

Science and the humanities 001.3

   x Humanities and science

Science fairs. *See* **Science—Exhibitions**

Science fiction 808.83; 813; etc.; Fic

   x Science—Fiction

   xx **Fantastic fiction; Fiction**

Science policy. *See* **Science and state**

Scientific apparatus and instruments 502.8

   See also names of groups of instruments, e.g. **Aeronautical instruments; Astronomical instruments; Chemical apparatus; Electric apparatus and appliances; Electronic apparatus and appliances; Engineering instruments; Meteorological instruments;** etc.; also names of specific instruments

   x Apparatus, Scientific; Instruments, Scientific; Scientific instruments

Scientific education. *See* **Science—Study and teaching**

Scientific expeditions 508.3

   See also names of regions explored, e.g. **Antarctic regions; Arctic regions;** and names of expeditions

   x Expeditions, Scientific; Polar expeditions; Travels

   xx **Antarctic regions; Arctic regions; Discoveries (in geography); Voyages and travels**

Scientific experiments. *See* **Science—Experiments;** and particular branches of science with the subdivision *Experiments,* e.g. **Chemistry—Experiments;** etc.

Scientific instruments. *See* **Scientific apparatus and instruments**

Scientific journalism. *See* **Journalism, Scientific**

Scientific management. *See* **Management**

Scientific method. *See* special subjects with the subdivision *Methodology,* e.g. **Science—Methodology;** etc.

Scientific recreations 793.8

   See also **Mathematical recreations**

   x Recreations, Scientific

   xx **Amusements**

Scientific societies. *See* **Science—Societies**

Scientific writing. *See* **Technical writing**

Scientists 920; 925

   See also types of scientists, e.g. **Astronomers; Chemists; Geologists; Mathematicians; Naturalists; Physicists;** etc. and names of individual scientists

Scottish clans. *See* **Clans and clan system**

Scottish tartans. *See* **Tartans**

Scouts and scouting 369.4

   See also **Boy Scouts; Girl Scouts**

Screen printing. *See* **Silk screen printing**

Scriptures, Holy. *See* **Bible**

Scuba diving 797.2

  Use for free diving with aqualung

  x Diving, Scuba; Free diving

  xx **Diving; Diving, Submarine; Skin diving**

Sculling. *See* **Rowing**

Sculptors (May subdiv. geog. adjective form, e.g. **Sculptors, French;** etc.) **920; 927**

  xx **Artists**

Sculptors, American 920; 927

  x American sculptors; U.S.—Sculptors

Sculpture (May subdiv. geog. adjective form, e.g. **Sculpture, African;** etc.) **730; 731-735**

  See also types of sculpture, e.g. **Brasses; Bronzes; Masks (Sculpture); Mobiles (Sculpture); Modeling; Monuments; Plaster casts; Soap sculpture; Wood carving;** etc.

  x Statues

  xx **Art; Decoration and ornament; Esthetics**

Sculpture, American 730.973

  x American sculpture; U.S.—Sculpture

Sculpture, Greek 730.938; 730.9495

  x Greek sculpture

Sculpture, Kinetic. *See* **Kinetic sculpture**

Sculpture, Modern 735

  x Modern sculpture

Sculpture, Modern—20th century 735

Sculpture—Motion pictures 730.2

  x Films

  xx **Audio-visual materials; Motion pictures**

Sculpture, Religious. *See* **Religious art and symbolism**

Sculpture—Technique 731.4

  See also **Modeling**

  xx **Modeling**

Sculpture in motion. *See* **Kinetic sculpture**

Sea. *See* **Ocean**

Sea animals. *See* **Marine animals**

Sea bed. *See* **Ocean bottom**

Sea farming. *See* **Aquaculture**

Sea fisheries. *See* **Fisheries**

Sea food 597; 641

  See also names of fish used for food

  x Fish as food; Seafood

  xx **Fishes**

Sea in art. *See* **Marine painting**

Sea laboratories. *See* **Undersea research stations**

Sea laws. *See* **Maritime law**

Sea life. *See* **Sailors; Seafaring life;** and names of countries with the subhead *Navy,* e.g. **U.S. Navy;** etc.

Sea lions. *See* **Seals (Animals)**

Sea mosses. *See* **Algae**

Sea poetry 808.81; 811; etc.

    See also **Sea songs**

    xx **Poetry—Collections**

Sea pollution. *See* **Marine pollution**

Sea power 359

    See also **Disarmament; Naval battles; Naval history; Navies; Warships;** also names of countries with the subhead *Navy* or the subdivision *History, Naval,* e.g. **U.S. Navy; U.S.–History, Naval;** etc.

    x Dominion of the sea; Military power; Naval power; Navy

    xx **Disarmament; Naval art and science; Naval history; Navies**

Sea resources. *See* **Marine resources**

Sea routes. *See* **Trade routes**

Sea shells. *See* **Shells**

Sea-shore. *See* **Seashore**

Sea songs 784.7

    x Chanties; Sailors' songs

    xx **Sea poetry; Songs**

Sea stories 808.83; 813; etc.

    x Stories

    xx **Adventure and adventurers**

Sea transportation. *See* **Shipping**

Sea travel. *See* **Ocean travel**

Sea water 551.5

    x Saline water; Salt water

    xx **Water**

Sea water aquariums. *See* **Marine aquariums**

Sea waves. *See* **Ocean waves**

Seafaring life 910.4

    See also **Sailors**

    x Sailors' life; Sea life

    xx **Adventure and adventurers; Sailors; Voyages and travels**

Seafood. *See* **Sea food**

Sealab project 551.4

    x Navy Sealab project; Project Sealab; U.S. Navy—Sealab project

    xx **Undersea research stations**

Seals (Animals) 599

    x Fur seals; Sea lions

Seals (Numismatics) 737

    x Emblems; Signets

    xx **Heraldry; History; Inscriptions; Numismatics**

Seamanship. *See* **Navigation**

Seamen. *See* **Sailors**

Search and rescue operations. *See* **Rescue work**

Seascapes. *See* **Marine painting**

Seashore 551.3; 551.4

    See also **Beaches; Sand dunes**

    x Sea-shore

    xx **Ocean**

Seasons 525

> *See also* names of the seasons, e.g. **Autumn;** etc.

> *xx* **Astronomy; Climate; Meteorology**

Seaweeds. *See* **Algae**

Secession. *See* **State rights; U.S.—History—Civil War, 1861–1865—Causes**

Second Advent 232

> *See also* **Millennium**

> *x* Jesus Christ—Second Advent; Second coming of Christ

> *xx* **Eschatology; Jesus Christ; Millennium**

Second coming of Christ. *See* **Second Advent**

Secondary education. *See* **Education, Secondary**

Secondary school libraries. *See* **School libraries (High school)**

Secondary schools. *See* **Education, Secondary; High schools; Junior high schools; Private schools; Public schools**

Secret service 327; 364.12

> *See also* **Detectives; Espionage; Intelligence service; Spies;** also names of wars with the subdivision *Secret service,* e.g. **World War, 1939–1945—Secret service;** etc.

> *xx* **Detectives; Intelligence service; Police; Spies**

Secret societies 366; 371.8

> *See also* **Fraternities and sororities;** also names of secret societies, e.g. **Freemasons;** etc.

> *x* Greek letter societies

> *xx* **Rites and ceremonies; Societies**

Secret writing. *See* **Cryptography**

Secretaries 651

> *xx* **Business education; Office management**

Sectionalism (U.S.) 917.3; 973

> *x* Localism; Provincialism; Regionalism

Sects 280-289

> *See also* names of churches and sects, e.g. **United Methodist Church (U.S.);** etc.

> *x* Church denominations; Cults and sects; Denominations, Religious; Religious denominations

> *xx* **Church history; Religions**

Securities 332.6

> *See also* types of securities, e.g. **Bonds; Investments; Mortgages; Stocks;** etc.

> *x* Capitalization (Finance); Dividends

> *xx* **Finance; Investments; Speculation; Stock exchange**

Securities exchange. *See* **Stock exchange**

Security, Internal. *See* **Internal security**

Security, International 327; 341.72

> *See also* **Arbitration, International; Disarmament; International organization; International police; Neutrality; Peace**

> *x* Collective security; International security

    xx **Disarmament; International relations; Peace**

Security, Social. *See* **Social security**

Security measures. *See* subjects with the subdivision *Security measures,* e.g. **Atomic power plants—Security measures;** etc.

Sedition. *See* **Political crimes and offenses; Revolutions**

Seeds 581; 631.5

    xx **Botany; Plant propagation**

Seeds—Germination. *See* **Germination**

Seeing eye dogs. *See* **Guide dogs**

Segregation 301.4

    See also **Discrimination; Minorities;** also names of groups of people with the subdivision *Segregation,* e.g. **Blacks—Segregation;** etc.

    x Apartheid

    xx **Discrimination; Minorities**

Segregation in education 370.1

    See also **Busing (School integration); Discrimination in education; School integration**

    x Education, Segregation in; Integration in education; Racial balance in schools

    xx **Discrimination in education; Blacks—Education; Blacks—Segregation; School integration**

Segregation in housing. *See* **Discrimination in housing**

Segregation in public accommodations. *See* **Discrimination in public accommodations**

Seismography. *See* **Earthquakes**

Seismology. *See* **Earthquakes**

Selection, Natural. *See* **Natural selection**

Selective service. *See* **Military service, Compulsory**

Self 126; 155.2

    xx **Consciousness; Individuality; Personality**

Self concept. *See* **Self perception**

Self-consciousness 155.2

Self-control 153.8

    xx **Human behavior**

Self-defense 613.6; 796.8

    See also types of self-defense, e.g. **Boxing; Judo; Karate;** etc.

    x Fighting

Self fulfillment. *See* **Self realization**

Self-government. *See* **Democracy; Representative government and representation**

Self-government (in education) 371.5

    x Honor system; Student councils; Student government; Student self-government

    xx **School administration and organization; School discipline**

Self-instruction. *See* **Correspondence schools and courses;** also names of subjects with subdivision *Programmed instruc-*

Self-instruction—*Continued*

tion, e.g. **English language—Programmed instruction;** etc.

Self perception 155.2

x Self concept

Self realization 155.2

x Fulfillment, Self; Self fulfillment

xx **Success**

Selling 658.85

See also **Advertising; Booksellers and bookselling; Mail-order business; Marketing; Peddlers and peddling; Sales management**

x Salesmanship

xx **Advertising; Business; Department stores; Retail trade**

Semantics 149; 412

See also **Words, New**

xx **Language and languages**

Semiconductors 621.3815

See also **Microelectronics; Transistors**

xx **Electronics**

Semitic peoples 572.9

xx **Anthropology**

Senators—U.S. *See* **U.S. Congress. Senate**

Senior citizens. *See* **Elderly**

Sense of direction. *See* **Orienteering**

Senses and sensation 152.1; 612

See also **Color sense; Gestalt psychology; Hearing; Pain; Pleasure; Smell; Taste; Touch; Vision**

xx **Intellect; Knowledge, Theory of; Physiology; Psychology; Psychology, Physiological**

Sensitivity training. *See* **Group relations training**

Separation (Law). *See* **Divorce**

Separation of powers (May subdiv. geog.) **342.4; 351**

x Division of powers; Powers, Separation of

xx **Constitutional law; Executive power; Political science**

Separation of powers—U.S. 342.4

x U.S.—Separation of powers

Separatism, Black. *See* **Black nationalism**

Separatist movement in Quebec (Province). *See* **Quebec (Province)—History—Autonomy and independence movements**

Sepulchers. *See* **Tombs**

Sepulchral brasses. *See* **Brasses**

Serials. *See* **Periodicals**

Serigraphy. *See* **Silk screen printing**

Sermon on the Mount 226

x Jesus Christ—Sermon on the Mount

Sermons 252

See also **Preaching**

xx **Preaching**

Serpents. *See* **Snakes**

Servants. *See* **Household employees**

Service, Compulsory military. *See* **Military service, Compulsory**

Service books (Liturgy.) *See* **Liturgies**

Service stations, Automobiles. *See* **Automobiles—Service stations**

Servitude. *See* **Peonage; Slavery**

Servomechanisms 629.8

    x Automatic control

    xx **Automation; Feedback control system**

Set theory 511

    See also **Algebra, Boolean; Arithmetic; Logic, Symbolic and mathematical; Number theory; Topology**

    x Aggregates; Classes (Mathematics); Ensembles (Mathematics); Mathematical sets; Sets (Mathematics); Theory of sets

    xx **Logic, Symbolic and mathematical; Mathematics**

Sets (Mathematics). *See* **Set theory**

Settlement of land. *See* **Land settlement**

Settlements, Social. *See* **Social settlements**

Seven Years' War, 1756–1763 940.2

    See also **Europe—History—1492–1789; U.S. —History—French and Indian War, 1755–1763**

    x Silesian War, 3d, 1756–1763

    xx **Europe—History—1492–1789; Germany —History—1740–1815; Gt. Brit.—History—1714–1837**

Seventeen-year locusts. *See* **Cicadas**

Seventeenth century 901.93; 909.08

    See note under **Nineteenth century**

Sewage disposal 628

    See also **Refuse and refuse disposal; Water —Pollution**

    x Waste disposal

    xx **Public health; Refuse and refuse disposal; Water—Pollution**

Sewerage 628

    See also **Drainage**

    x Sewers

    xx **Drainage; Drainage, House; Municipal engineering; Plumbing; Sanitary engineering**

Sewers. *See* **Sewerage**

Sewing 646.2; 646.4

    See also **Dressmaking; Embroidery; Needlework**

    xx **Dressmaking; Home economics; Needlework**

Sex 155.3; 301.41; 612.6

    See also **Reproduction; Transexuality;** also headings beginning with the word **Sexual**

    xx **Biology; Marriage; Reproduction**

Sex change. *See* **Transexuality**

Sex customs. *See* **Sexual behavior**

Sex discrimination   301.41

   See also **Men—Civil rights; Women—Civil rights**

   x Discrimination, Sex

   xx **Discrimination; Sexism**

Sex education   612.6

   See also **Sexual hygiene**

   x Sex instruction

   xx **Family life education; Sexual hygiene**

Sex in art.   *See* **Erotic art**

Sex instruction.   *See* **Sex education**

Sex role   301.41

   x Female role; Gender identity; Male role

   xx **Role conflict; Social role**

Sexism

   See also **Sex discrimination**

   xx **Prejudices and antipathies**

Sexual behavior   155.3

   See also people and animals with the subdivision *Sexual behavior*, e.g. **College students—Sexual behavior;** etc.

   x Sex customs

Sexual ethics   176

   See also **Birth control; Free love; Prostitution; Sexual hygiene; Unmarried couples**

   x Ethics, Sexual

   xx **Marriage; Prostitution; Sexual hygiene; Social ethics**

Sexual hygiene   613.9

   See also **Birth control; Prostitution; Sex education; Sexual ethics; Venereal diseases**

   x Hygiene, Sexual; Hygiene, Social; Social hygiene

   xx **Prostitution; Sex education; Sexual ethics; Venereal diseases**

Shades and shadows   741.2

   x Light and shade; Shadows

   xx **Drawing**

Shadow pantomimes and plays   791.5

   xx **Amateur theatricals; Pantomimes; Puppets and puppet plays; Theater**

Shadows.   *See* **Shades and shadows**

Shaft sinking.   *See* **Boring**

Shakers   289.9

Shakespeare, William   822.3

   When applicable, the following subdivisions may be used for other voluminous authors, e.g. **Dante; Goethe;** etc. The following subjects are to be used for materials about Shakespeare and about his writings. The texts of his plays, etc. are not given subject headings

Shakespeare, William—Adaptations   822.3

   x Shakespeare, William—Paraphrases

Shakespeare, William—Anniversaries   822.3

Shakespeare, William—Authorship   822.3

   x Bacon-Shakespeare controversy

Shakespeare, William—Bibliography   016.8223
   xx **Bibliography**
Shakespeare, William—Biography   92 or **B**
Shakespeare, William—Characters   822.3
   xx **Characters and characteristics in literature**
Shakespeare, William—Collected works   822.3
   x Collections of literature
Shakespeare, William—Comedies   822.3
   Use for criticism, etc. of the comedies, not for the texts of the plays
Shakespeare, William—Concordances   822.3
   x Concordances; Shakespeare, William—Indexes
   xx **Shakespeare, William—Dictionaries**
Shakespeare, William—Contemporary England   822.3; 914.2
Shakespeare, William—Criticism, interpretation, etc.   822.3
   Use for criticism of the plays in general; criticism of the comedies is entered under **Shakespeare, William—Comedies**; criticism of the tragedies under **Shakespeare, William—Tragedies**; criticism of an individual play is entered under **Shakespeare, William**, followed by the title of the play
   xx **Criticism**
Shakespeare, William—Dictionaries   822.3
   See also **Shakespeare, William—Concordances**
   x Shakespeare, William—Indexes
Shakespeare, William—Discography   789.9; 822.3
   x Discography
Shakespeare, William—Drama   812; 822; etc.
   x Shakespeare in fiction, drama, poetry, etc.
Shakespeare, William—Dramatic production   822.3
   x Shakespeare, William—Stage setting and scenery
Shakespeare, William—Fiction   813; Fic
   x Shakespeare in fiction, drama, poetry, etc.
Shakespeare, William—Histories   822.3
   Use for criticism, etc. of the histories, not for the texts of the plays
Shakespeare, William—Indexes. *See* **Shakespeare, William—Concordances; Shakespeare, William—Dictionaries**
Shakespeare, William—Knowledge   822.3
   Use for materials on Shakespeare's knowledge or treatment of specific subjects
   May be subdivided by subject, e.g. **Shakespeare, William—Knowledge—Animals**; etc.
Shakespeare, William—Music. *See* **Shakespeare, William—Songs and music**

507

Shakespeare, William—Paraphrases. *See* **Shakespeare, William—Adaptations**

Shakespeare, William—Parodies, travesties, etc. 822.3

    xx **Parodies**

Shakespeare, William—Poetry   821; 822.3

    x Shakespeare in fiction, drama, poetry, etc.

    xx **Poetry**

Shakespeare, William—Portraits   822.3022

    xx **Portraits**

Shakespeare, William—Quotations   822.3

Shakespeare, William—Religion and ethics 822.3

Shakespeare, William—Songs and music   822.3

    x Shakespeare, William—Music

Shakespeare, William—Sonnets   822.3

Shakespeare, William—Stage history   792; 822.3

    xx **Theater**

Shakespeare, William—Stage setting and scenery. *See* **Shakespeare, William—Dramatic production**

Shakespeare, William—Style. *See* **Shakespeare, William—Technique**

Shakespeare, William—Technique   822.3

    x Shakespeare, William—Style

Shakespeare, William—Tragedies   822.3

    Use for criticism, etc. of the tragedies, not for the texts of the plays

Shakespeare in fiction, drama, poetry, etc. *See* **Shakespeare, William—Drama; Shakespeare, William—Fiction; Shakespeare, William—Poetry**

Shape. *See* **Size and shape**

Sharecropping. *See* **Farm tenancy**

Shares of stock. *See* **Stocks**

Sheep   599; 636

    xx **Livestock**

Sheet metalwork   671.8

    See also **Plate metalwork**

    x Press working of metal

    xx **Metalwork**

Sheffield plate   739.2

    xx **Plate**

Shellfish

    See also **Crustacea; Mollusks**

Shells   564; 594

    See also **Mollusks**

    x Conchology; Sea shells

    xx **Mollusks**

Shells (Projectiles). *See* **Projectiles**

Shelterbelts. *See* **Windbreaks**

Shelters, Air raid. *See* **Air raid shelters**

Shinto   299

    See also **Ancestor worship**

    xx **Religions**

Ship building. *See* **Shipbuilding**

Ship models. *See* **Ships—Models**

Ship pilots. *See* **Pilots and pilotage**

Shipbuilding 623.82

   See also **Boatbuilding; Marine engines; Naval architecture; Ships; Ships—Models; Steamboats**

   x Architecture, Naval; Marine architecture; Ship building; Ships—Construction

   xx **Boatbuilding; Industrial arts; Naval architecture; Naval art and science**

Shipping (May subdiv. geog.) **386; 387**

   See also **Harbors; Inland navigation; Insurance, Marine; Maritime law; Merchant marine; Territorial waters**

   x Marine transportation; Ocean—Economic aspects; Ocean transportation; Sea transportation; Water transportation

   xx **Merchant marine; Transportation**

Shipping—U.S. 386; 387

   x U.S.—Shipping

Ships 387.2; 623.82

   See also **Boats and boating; Merchant marine; Navies; Navigation; Sailing;** also types of ships and vessels, e.g. **Clipper ships; Steamboats; Submarines; Warships; Yachts and yachting;** etc.; *also* names of individual ships

   x Vessels (Ships)

   xx **Boats and boating; Naval architecture; Shipbuilding**

Ships—Construction. *See* **Shipbuilding**

Ships—Models 623.82

   x Ship models

   xx **Machinery—Models; Models and model making; Shipbuilding**

Ships in art. *See* **Marine painting**

Shipwrecks 910.4

   See also **Salvage; Survival (after airplane accidents, shipwrecks, etc.);** also names of wrecked ships

   x Wrecks

   xx **Accidents; Adventure and adventurers; Disasters; Navigation; Salvage; Voyages and travels**

Shoes and shoe industry 338.4; 685

   x Boots

   xx **Clothing and dress; Leather industry and trade**

Shooting 799.3

   Use for materials on the use of firearms. Materials on shooting game are entered under **Hunting**

   See also **Archery; Firearms; Hunting**

   x Gunning

   xx **Firearms; Game and game birds; Hunting**

Shooting stars. *See* **Meteors**

Shop committees. *See* **Employees' representation in management**

Shop management. *See* **Factory management**

Shop practice. *See* **Machine shop practice**

Shop windows. *See* **Show windows**

Shoppers' guides. *See* **Consumer education; Shopping**

Shopping 640.73

Use for materials on buying by the consumer. Materials on buying by government agencies and commercial and industrial enterprises are entered under **Buying**

See also **Buying; Consumer education; Consumers**

x Buyers' guides; Marketing (Home economics); Purchasing; Shoppers' guides

xx **Buying; Consumer education; Home economics**

Shopping centers and malls 658.8

x Malls, Shopping; Shopping malls

xx **Retail trade**

Shopping malls. *See* **Shopping centers and malls**

Shops, Machine. *See* **Machine shops**

Short plays. *See* **One act plays**

Short stories 808.83; 813; etc.; Fic

May be used for collections of short stories by one author as well as for collections by several authors. Materials on the technique of writing short stories are entered under **Short story**

x Collections of literature; Stories

xx **English literature; Literature—Collections**

Short stories—Indexes 808.8301

xx **Indexes**

Short story 808.3

Use for materials on the technique of short story writing. Collections of stories are entered under **Short stories**

See also **Storytelling**

xx **Authorship; Fiction; Literature; Storytelling**

Short take off and landing aircraft 629.133

x STOL aircraft

xx **Jet planes**

Short wave radio. *See* **Radio, Short wave**

Shorthand 653

See also **Abbreviations**

x Stenography

xx **Abbreviations; Business education; Writing**

Shotguns 799.2

x Guns

xx **Firearms**

Show business. *See* **Performing arts**

Show windows 659.1

x Shop windows; Window dressing

xx **Advertising; Windows**

Showers (Parties) 793.2

xx **Parties**

Shrines 291.3; 726
   See also Miracles; Pilgrims and pilgrim-
      ages; Saints; Tombs
   xx Pilgrims and pilgrimages; Saints
Shrubs 582; 635.9
   See also Evergreens; Landscape gardening;
      Plants, Ornamental
   xx Botany; Landscape gardening; Trees
Shyness. *See* Bashfulness
Sick 362.1
   See also Cookery for the sick; First aid;
      Health resorts, spas, etc.; Home nurs-
      ing; Hospitals; Nursing
   x Invalids; Patients
   xx Handicapped; Home nursing; Nursing
Sickness insurance. *See* Insurance, Health
Sidereal system. *See* Stars
Sieges. *See* Battles
Sight. *See* Vison
Sight saving books. *See* Large print books
Sign boards. *See* Signs and signboards
Sign language. *See* Deaf—Means of communi-
      cation; Indians of North America—
      Sign language
Sign painting 667
   See also Alphabets; Lettering; Signs and
      signboards
   xx Advertising; Lettering; Painting, Indus-
      trial; Signs and signboards
Signals and signaling 384
   See also Flags; Railroads—Signaling; Sonar
   x Coastal signals; Fog signals; Military
      signaling; Naval signaling
   xx Flags; Military art and science; Naval
      art and science; Navigation; Signs and
      symbols
Signboards. *See* Signs and signboards
Signers of the Declaration of Independence.
      See U.S. Declaration of Independence
Signets. *See* Seals (Numismatics)
Signs (Advertising). *See* Electric signs; Signs
      and signboards
Signs, Electric. *See* Electric signs
Signs and signboards 659.13
   See also Electric signs; Posters; Sign paint-
      ing
   x Billboards; Guide posts; Road signs;
      Sign boards; Signboards; Signs (Ad-
      vertising)
   xx Advertising; Posters; Sign painting
Signs and symbols 001.54
   See also Abbreviations; Ciphers; Cryptog-
      raphy; Heraldry; Signals and signaling;
      Symbolism; Weather lore
   x Symbols
   xx Abbreviations; Symbolism
Silage and silos 631.2; 633
   x Ensilage; Silos
   xx Feeds; Forage plants

Silesian War, 3d, 1756–1763. *See* **Seven Years'**
    War, 1756–1763
Silk   677
    See also **Silkworms**
    xx **Fibers**
Silk, Artificial. *See* **Rayon**
Silk screen printing   764
    x Screen printing; Serigraphy
    xx **Color printing; Stencil work**
Silkworms   638
    x Cocoons
    xx **Insects, Injurious and beneficial; Moths;**
        Silk
Silos. *See* **Silage and silos**
Silver   669
    See also **Coinage; Jewelry; Money; Silver-**
        work; Silverware
    x Bimetallism; Bullion
    xx **Coinage;   Monetary   policy;   Money;**
        Precious metals
Silver articles. *See* **Silverwork**
Silver mines and mining   622
    See also **Prospecting**
Silver work. *See* **Silverwork**
Silversmithing. *See* **Silverwork**
Silverware   642; 739.2
    x Flatware, Silver
    xx **Silver; Silverwork; Tableware**
Silverwork   739.2
    See also **Jewelry; Plate; Silverware**
    x Silver articles; Silver work; Silversmith-
        ing
    xx **Art metalwork; Arts and crafts; Jewelry;**
        Metalwork; Silver
Sin   170; 231; 241
    See also **Atonement; Free will and deter-**
        minism
    xx **Christian ethics; Ethics; Good and evil;**
        Salvation; Theology
Sinai Campaign, 1956   956
    x Anglo-French   intervention   in   Egypt,
        1956; Arab-Israel War, 1956; Israel-
        Arab War, 1956
    xx **Egypt—History**
Singers   920; 927
    xx **Musicians**
Singing   784.9
    See   also **Choirs   (Music);   Respiration;**
        School songbooks; Vocal music; Voice
    x School music; Vocal culture; Voice cul-
        ture
    xx **Choirs (Music); Vocal music; Voice**
Singing games   796.1
    xx **Games**
Singing societies. *See* **Choral societies**
Single men   301.41
    x Men, Single; Unmarried men
    xx **Men; Single people**

Single parent family 301.42

    x One parent family; Parents without part-
ners

    xx **Family**

Single people 301.41

    See also **Single men; Single women; Un-
married couples**

    x People, Single; Persons, Single; Unmar-
ried people

Single rail railroads. *See* **Monorail railroads**

Single women 301.41

    See also **Unmarried mothers**

    x Unmarried women; Women, Single

    xx **Single people; Women**

Sirius

    xx **Stars**

Sisterhoods. *See* **Religious orders for women**

Sisters, Religious 255; 271

    Use only for uncloistered sisters

    See also **Nuns**

    x Religious sisters

    xx **Religious orders for women**

Sit-down strikes. *See* **Strikes and lockouts**

Six day war, 1967. *See* **Israel-Arab War, 1967**

Sixteenth century 901.93; 909.08

    See note under **Nineteenth century**

    See also **Reformation**

    xx **Reformation; Renaissance**

Size and shape 516

    x Large and small; Shape; Small and large

    xx **Concepts**

Skating. *See* **Ice skating; Roller skating**

Skeletal remains. *See* **Anthropometry**

Skepticism 149; 211

    See also **Agnosticism; Belief and doubt;
Truth**

    x Scepticism; Unbelief

    xx **Agnosticism; Atheism; Belief and doubt;
Faith; Free thought; Philosophy; Rationalism; Religion; Truth**

Sketching. *See* **Drawing**

Skiing, Snow. *See* **Skis and skiing**

Skiing, Water. *See* **Water skiing**

Skin 611; 612

Skin, Color of. *See* **Color of people**

Skin—Diseases 616.5

    See also names of skin diseases, e.g. **Acne;**
etc.

    x Dermatitis

    xx **Diseases**

Skin diving 797.2

    Use for free diving with masks, fins, and
snorkel

    See also **Scuba diving; Undersea research
stations; Underwater exploration**

    x Diving, Skin; Free diving; Frogmen;
Snorkeling; Underwater swimming

    xx **Diving; Diving, Submarine; Oceanog-
raphy—Research; Salvage; Underwater
exploration; Water sports**

Skin garments. *See* **Leather garments**

Skins. *See* **Hides and skins**

Skis and skiing 796.9
　　See also **Water skiing**
　　x Skiing, Snow
　　xx **Winter sports**

Skits 791.1
　　x Entertainments

Sky diving. *See* **Skydiving**

Sky hijacking. *See* **Hijacking of airplanes**

Sky laboratories. *See* **Space stations**

Skydiving 797.5
　　x Sky diving
　　xx **Aeronautical sports**

Skyjacking. *See* **Hijacking of airplanes**

Skyscrapers 690; 725
　　xx **Architecture; Building, Iron and steel;
　　　　Industrial buildings; Office buildings**

Slander (Law). *See* **Libel and slander**

Slang. *See* subjects with the subdivision *Slang*,
　　e.g., **English language—Slang**; etc.

Slanted journalism. *See* **Journalism—Objectiv-
　　ity**

Slave trade 380.1
　　xx **International law; Slavery; Slavery in the
　　　　U.S.**

Slavery 326; 331.1
　　See also **Peonage; Slave trade**
　　x Abolition of slavery; Antislavery; Com-
　　　　pulsory labor; Emancipation of slaves;
　　　　Forced labor; Servitude
　　xx **Contract labor; Freedom; Labor and la-
　　　　boring classes; Sociology**

Slavery in the U.S. 301.45; 326
　　Use same form for slavery in other coun-
　　　　tries
　　See also

Abolitionists	**State rights**
Blacks	**Underground**
Slave trade	**　railroad**
Southern States—	
History	

　　x Emancipation of slaves
　　xx **Blacks; Underground railroad; U.S.—
　　　　History—Civil War, 1861–1865**

Slavery in the U.S.—Fiction Fic
　　x Stories
　　xx **Fiction; Historical fiction**

Sleep 154.6; 613.7
　　See also **Dreams; Insomnia**
　　xx **Brain; Dreams; Hygiene; Insomnia;
　　　　Mind and body; Psychology, Physio-
　　　　logical; Rest; Subconsciousness**

Sleeping sickness 616.8
　　xx **Tropics—Diseases and hygiene**

Sleeplessness. *See* **Insomnia**

Sleight of hand. *See* **Magic**

Slide projectors. *See* **Projectors**

Slide rule 510.28
   xx Calculating machines; Logarithms; Measuring instruments
Slides (Photography) 778.2
   See also Filmstrips
   x Color slides; Lantern slides; Photographic slides
   xx Filmstrips; Photography
Slow learning children 155.4
   See also Learning disabilities; Mentally retarded children
   x Children, Retarded; Retarded children
   xx Exceptional children; Mentally handicapped children
Slum clearance. *See* Urban renewal
Slumber songs. *See* Lullabies
Small and large. *See* Size and shape
Small arms. *See* Firearms
Small business 338.6
   Use for materials on small independent enterprises as contrasted with "big business"
   x Business, Small
   xx Business
Smallpox 614.4; 616.9
   See also Vaccination
   xx Epidemics; Communicable diseases; Medicine—Practice; Therapeutics; Vaccination
Smell 152.1
   See also Nose
   xx Senses and sensation
Smelting 669
   See also Blast furnaces; Electrometallurgy; Metallurgy; Ore dressing
   xx Furnaces; Metallurgy
Smoke prevention 614.7; 628.5
   See also Fuel; Furnaces
   x Prevention of smoke
Smoke stacks. *See* Chimneys
Smokeless powder. *See* Gunpowder
Smoking 178; 613.8
   See also Cigarettes; Cigars; Tobacco; Tobacco habit; Tobacco pipes
   xx Tobacco
Smuggling 364.1
   x Contraband trade
   xx Crime; Tariff
Snakes 598.1
   x Serpents; Vipers
   xx Reptiles
Snorkeling. *See* Skin diving
Snow 551.5
   xx Meteorology; Rain and rainfall; Storms; Water; Weather
Snowmobiles 629.22
   xx All terrain vehicles; Vehicles
Soap 668
   See also Detergents, Synthetic
   xx Cleaning; Cleaning compounds

Soap box derbies   796.6
  x Racing
Soap carving.   *See* **Soap sculpture**
Soap sculpture   736
  x Soap carving
  xx **Modeling; Sculpture**
Soaring flight.   *See* **Gliding and soaring**
Sobriquets.   *See* **Nicknames**
Soccer   796.33
  xx **Ball games; College sports; Football**
Social action   301.1
  See also **Social work;** also subjects with
      subdivision *Citizen participation,* e.g.,
      **City planning–U.S.–Citizen partici-
      pation;** etc.
  x Action, Social; Activism, Social
  xx **Social policy; Social problems; Social
      work**
Social adjustment   158; 301.15
  See also **Socially handicapped**
  x Adjustment, Social
  xx **Human behavior; Human relations; So-
      cial psychology**
Social alienation.   *See* **Alienation (Social psy-
      chology)**
Social aspects.   *See* subjects with subdivision
      Social aspects, e.g., **English language–
      Social aspects;** etc.
Social case work   361.3
  See also **Counseling; Parole; Probation**
  x Case work, Social; Family social work
  xx **Counseling; Social work**
Social centers.   *See* **Community centers**
Social change   301.24; 901.9
  x Change, Social; Cultural change; Social
      evolution
  xx **Anthropology; Evolution; Progress; So-
      cial sciences; Sociology**
Social classes   301.44; 323.3
  See also **Aristocracy; Middle classes; No-
      bility; Upper classes**
  x Class distinction; Rank; Social distinc-
      tions
  xx **Caste; Equality; Manners and customs;
      Social conflict; Sociology**
Social conditions   309
  Use for general materials relating to sev-
      eral or all of the following topics:
      labor, poverty, education, health,
      housing, recreation, moral conditions
  See also **Cost of living; Counter culture;
      Economic conditions; Labor and la-
      boring classes; Moral conditions;
      Quality of life; Social problems; So-
      cial surveys; Standard of living;** and
      names of groups of people and names
      of countries, cities, etc. with the sub-
      division *Social conditions,* e.g. **Indians
      of North America–Social conditions;
      Jews–Social conditions; Blacks–So-**

516

Social conditions—*Continued*
      cial conditions; U.S.–Social conditions; Chicago–Social conditions; etc.
  x Social history
  xx **Social ethics; Sociology**
Social conflict   301.6
      See also **Conflict of generations; Social classes**
  x Class conflict; Class struggle; Conflict, Social
  xx **Social psychology; Sociology**
Social conformity. *See* **Conformity**
Social customs. *See* **Manners and customs;** and names of ethnic groups, countries, cities, etc. with the subdivision *Social life and customs,* e.g. **Indians of North America–Social life and customs; Jews–Social life and customs; U.S. –Social life and customs;** etc.
Social democracy. *See* **Socialism**
Social distinctions. *See* **Social classes**
Social ecology. *See* **Human ecology**
Social equality. *See* **Equality**
Social ethics   177
      See also **Bioethics; Christian ethics; Citizenship; Crime; Political ethics; Sexual ethics; Social conditions; Social problems; Sociology, Christian**
  x Ethics, Social
  xx **Christian ethics; Social problems; Sociology, Christian**
Social evolution. *See* **Social change**
Social history. *See* **Social conditions**
Social hygiene. *See* **Hygiene; Prostitution; Public health; Sexual hygiene; Venereal diseases**
Social insurance. *See* **Social security**
Social life and customs. *See* **Manners and customs;** and names of ethnic groups, countries, cities, etc. with the subdivision *Social life and customs,* e.g. **Indians of North America–Social life and customs; Jews–Social life and customs; U.S.–Social life and customs;** etc.
Social planning. *See* **Social policy**
Social policy   309.2
      See also **Economic policy; Social action;** also names of countries, cities, etc. with the subdivision *Social policy,* e.g. **U.S.–Social policy;** etc.
  x National planning; Planning, National; Social planning; State planning
  xx **Economic policy**
Social problems   362
      See also

Charities	**Discrimination**
Child labor	**Divorce**
Community centers	**Eugenics**
Crime	**Housing**

Social problems—*Continued*

Immigration and emigration	Social action
Juvenile delinquency	Social ethics
	Social surveys
Liquor problem	Standard of living
Men—Social conditions	Suicide
	Tenement houses
Migrant labor	Unemployed
Old age pensions	Women—Employment
Prostitution	Women—Social conditions
Public health	
Race relations	

   x Reform, Social; Social reform; Social
      welfare
   xx **Civilization; Social conditions; Social
      ethics; Sociology**
Social problems and the church. *See* **Church
      and social problems**
Social problems in education. *See* **Educational
      sociology**
Social psychology 301.1
   See also **Alienation (Social psychology);
      Attitude (Psychology); Crowds; Eth-
      nopsychology; Human relations; In-
      terviewing; National characteristics;
      Political psychology; Psychology, Ap-
      plied; Social adjustment; Social con-
      flict; Violence**
   x Mass psychology; Psychology, Social
   xx **Crowds; Ethnopsychology; Psychology;
      Sociology**
Social reform. *See* **Social problems**
Social role 301.11
   See also **Role conflict; Role playing; Sex
      role**
   x Role, Social
Social sciences 300
   Use for general and comprehensive mate-
      rials dealing with sociology, political
      science and economics
   See also **Economics; Political science; So-
      cial change; Sociology**
   x Social studies
Social security 368.4
   See also **Insurance, Health; Insurance, Un-
      employment; Old age pensions;
      Workers' compensation**
   x Insurance, Social; Insurance, State and
      compulsory; Insurance, Workers'; La-
      bor and laboring classes—Insurance;
      Security, Social; Social insurance;
      State and insurance
   xx **Pensions**
Social service. *See* **Social work**
Social settlements 361
   See also **Boys' clubs; Community centers;
      Girls' clubs; Playgrounds;** also names
      of settlements, e.g. **Hull House, Chi-
      cago;** etc.

Social settlements—*Continued*
  x Church settlements; Neighborhood centers; Settlements, Social
  xx **Charities; Social work; Welfare work in industry**
Social studies. *See* **Geography; History; Social sciences**
Social surveys (May subdiv. geog.) **309.1**
  Use for materials on the methods employed in conducting surveys of social and economic conditions of communities and also for surveys of individual regions or cities. In the latter case a second heading may be used for name of region or city followed by the subdivision *Social conditions*
  See also **Educational surveys**
  x Community surveys; Surveys
  xx **City planning; Regional planning; Social conditions; Social problems; Sociology**
Social surveys—U.S. 309.173
  x U.S.—Social surveys
Social values 301.2; 301.24
  See also **Quality of life**
  xx **Conformity; Quality of life; Values**
Social welfare. *See* **Charities; Public welfare; Social problems; Social work**
Social work 361; 362
  Use for materials on the methods employed in welfare work, public or private
  See also **Charities; Community organization; Crisis centers; Hotlines (Telephone counseling); Public welfare; Social action; Social case work; Social settlements; Welfare work in industry**
  x Philanthropy; Social service; Social welfare; Welfare work
  xx **Social action**
Socialism (May subdiv. geog.) **320.5; 335**
  See also

Capitalism	**Labor unions**
Communism	**National socialism**
Equality	**Old age pensions**
Government owner-	**Proletariat**
ship	**Syndicalism**
Individualism	**Utopias**
Industry and state	
Labor and laboring	
classes	

  x Collectivism; Marxism; Social democracy
  xx **Capitalism; Communism; Cooperation; Democracy; Economics; Equality; Individualism; Labor and laboring classes; National socialism; Political science; Sociology; Syndicalism**
Socialism—U.S. 320.5; 335
  x U.S.—Socialism

Socialization of industry. *See* **Government ownership; Industry and state**

Socialized medicine. *See* **Charities, Medical; Insurance, Health; Insurance, Hospitalization; Medicine, State**

Socially handicapped 362

x Culturally deprived; Culturally handicapped; Disadvantaged; Underprivileged

xx **Handicapped; Social adjustment**

Socially handicapped children 362.7

x Culturally deprived children; Culturally handicapped children; Disadvantaged children; Underprivileged children

xx **Handicapped children**

Socials. *See* **Church entertainments**

Societies 060

Use for general materials about societies, etc. The headings enumerated below represent various types of societies and associations. Add others as needed. Materials about, and publications of, societies devoted to specific subjects are entered under the subject with the subdivision *Societies*, e.g. **Agriculture—Societies;** etc.

See also

Associations	**Girls' clubs**
Boys' clubs	**Labor unions**
Choral societies	**Men—Societies**
Clubs	**Parents' and teachers' associations**
Cooperative societies	**Secret societies**
Educational associations	**Women—Societies**

also general subjects with the subdivision *Societies* (e.g. **Agriculture—Societies;** etc.); and names of individual societies

x Learned societies

xx **Associations; Clubs**

Societies, Cooperative. *See* **Cooperative societies**

Society, Nonliterate folk 301.2

See also **Man, Nonliterate**

x Folk society, Nonliterate; Illiterate societies; Nonliterate folk society; Preliterate society; Primitive society

xx **Civilization; Ethnology; Sociology**

Society, Upper. *See* **Upper classes**

Society and art. *See* **Art and society**

Society of Friends. *See* **Friends, Society of**

Society of Jesus. *See* **Jesuits**

Sociology 301

Use for systematic studies on the structure of society. General materials dealing with sociology, political science and economics are entered under **Social sciences**

520

Sociology—*Continued*
   See also

Aristocracy	**Population**
Cities and towns	**Race relations**
Civilization	**Slavery**
Communism	**Social classes**
Educational sociol-	**Social change**
ogy	**Social conditions**
Equality	**Social conflict**
Ethnopsychology	**Social problems**
Family	**Social psychology**
Heredity	**Social surveys**
Human ecology	**Socialism**
Immigration and	**Society, Nonliterate**
emigration	**folk**
Individualism	**Unemployed**
Labor and laboring	
classes	

   xx **Social sciences**

Sociology, Christian   261
    See note under **Church and social prob-**
      lems
    See also **Christianity and economics; Social**
      ethics
    x Christian sociology
    xx **Social ethics**

Sociology, Educational. *See* **Educational so-**
      ciology

Sociology, Rural   301.34
    Use for materials which treat of social or-
      ganization and conditions in rural
      communities. Descriptive, popular and
      literary materials on living in the
      country are entered under **Country**
      life
    See also **Country life; Farm life; Peasantry**
    x Rural sociology
    xx **Country life; Farm life; Peasantry**

Sociology, Urban   301.34
    See also **Cities and towns; City life; Urban**
      renewal
    x Urban sociology
    xx **Cities and towns**

Softball   796.357
    xx **Baseball**

Software, Computer. *See* **Computer pro-**
      grams; Programming (Electronic com-
      puters); Programming languages (Elec-
      tronic computers)

Soil bacteriology. *See* **Soils—Bacteriology**

Soil conservation   631.4
    See also **Erosion; Soil erosion**
    x Conservation of the soil
    xx **Erosion; Natural resources; Soil erosion**

Soil erosion   631.4
    See also **Soil conservation**
    xx **Erosion; Soil conservation**

Soil fertility. *See* **Soils**

Soil mechanics. *See* **Soils (Engineering)**

Soilless agriculture. *See* **Plants—Soilless culture**

Soils 631.4

See also **Agricultural chemistry; Clay; Compost; Drainage; Fertilizers and manures; Irrigation; Reclamation of land; Soils (Engineering);** also headings beginning with the word **Soil**

x Soil fertility

xx **Agricultural chemistry; Agriculture; Geology, Economic**

Soils—Bacteriology 631.4

See also **Bacteriology, Agricultural**

xx **Bacteriology, Agricultural; Sanitary engineering**

Soils (Engineering) 620.1

x Earthwork; Soil mechanics

xx **Foundations; Roads; Soils; Structural engineering**

Soils, Lunar. See **Lunar soil**

Solar batteries 621.47

x Solar cells; Sun powered batteries

xx **Electric batteries; Solar radiation**

Solar cells. See **Solar batteries**

Solar eclipses. See **Eclipses, Solar**

Solar energy 621.47

See also **Solar engines; Solar heating**

x Solar power

xx **Power resources; Solar radiation; Sun**

Solar engines 621.47

xx **Engines; Solar energy**

Solar heat. See **Solar heating**

Solar heating 621.47; 697

See also names of applications, e.g. **Solar homes;** etc.

x Solar heat

xx **Heating; Solar energy**

Solar homes 697; 728

xx **Architecture, Domestic; Solar heating**

Solar physics. See **Sun**

Solar power. See **Solar energy**

Solar radiation 621.47

See also **Solar batteries; Solar energy; Sunspots**

x Radiation, Solar; Sun—Radiation

xx **Meteorology; Space environment**

Solar system 523.2

See also **Comets; Earth; Meteors; Moon; Planets; Sun;** also names of planets, e.g. **Venus (Planet);** etc.

xx **Astronomy; Planets; Stars; Sun**

Solder and soldering 671.5

See also **Alloys; Welding**

x Brazing

xx **Metals; Metalwork; Plumbing; Welding**

Soldiers (May subdiv. geog.) **355-359**

Use for materials dealing with members of the armed forces in general, including the Army, Navy, Marine Corps, etc.

See also **Armies; Generals; Mercenary soldiers; Military art and science; Veterans;** also names of countries with the

Soldiers—*Continued*
　　subdivision *Army—Military life*, e.g.
　　U.S. Army–Military life; etc.
　　x Armed forces; Army life; Military life;
　　　Soldiers' life
　　xx **Armies; Military art and science; Veterans; War**
Soldiers, Disabled. *See* **Physically handicapped**
Soldiers—Hygiene. *See* **Military hygiene**
Soldiers–U.S.　355-359
　　x G.I.s; U.S.—Soldiers
Soldiers' bonus. *See* **Pensions, Military**
Soldiers' handbooks. *See* **U.S. Army–Handbooks, manuals, etc.**
Soldiers' life. *See* **Soldiers;** and names of countries with the subdivision *Army—Military life*, e.g. **U.S. Army–Military life;** etc.
Soldiers' songs. *See* **War songs**
Solid geometry. *See* **Geometry**
Solid waste disposal. *See* **Refuse and refuse disposal; Salvage (Waste, etc.)**
Solitaire (Game)　795.4
　　x Patience (Game)
Somatology. *See* **Physical anthropology**
Sonar　621.389
　　x Echo ranging; Sound navigation
　　xx **Signals and signaling**
Sonata　781.5
　　xx **Musical form**
Sonatas　781.5
　　xx **Orchestral music**
Song books. *See* **Songbooks**
Song writing. *See* **Composition (Music); Music, Popular (Songs, etc.)–Writing and publishing**
Songbooks　784
　　See also **School songbooks**
　　x Community songbooks; Song books
　　xx **Songs**
Songbooks, School. *See* **School songbooks**
Songs (May subdiv. geog. adjective form, e.g. **Songs, American;** etc.)　**784**
　　Use for collections of songs which include both words and music, and for materials about songs. Collections of songs which contain the words but not the music are entered under **Poetry**
　　See also

Ballads	**National songs**
Black songs	**School songbooks**
Carols	**Sea songs**
Children's songs	**Songbooks**
Folk songs	**State songs**
Hymns	**Students' songs**
Lullabies	**War songs**
Music, Popular	
(Songs, etc.)	

　　also general subjects, names of classes of persons and of schools, colleges, etc.

Songs—*Continued*

with the subdivision *Songs and music,* e.g. **Aeronautics—Songs and music; Cowhands—Songs and music; United States Military Academy, West Point—Songs and music;** etc.; and names of individual songs

xx **Poetry—Collections; Vocal music**

Songs, African 784.7

x African songs; Folk songs, African; Folk songs, Black (African)

Songs, American 784.7

See also **Black songs; Folk songs—U.S.; National songs, American**

x American songs; U.S.—Songs

Songs, National. *See* **National songs**

Songs, Popular. *See* **Music, Popular (Songs, etc.)**

Soothsaying. *See* **Divination**

Soporifics. *See* **Narcotics**

Sorcery. *See* **Occult sciences; Witchcraft**

Sororities. *See* **Fraternities and sororities**

Sorrow. *See* **Joy and sorrow**

Soubriquets. *See* **Nicknames**

Soul 128; 233

See also **Future life; Immortality; Personality; Psychology; Reincarnation; Spiritual life**

x Spirit

xx **Future life; Man (Theology); Personality; Philosophy; Reincarnation**

Sound 534; 620.2

See also **Architectural acoustics; Hearing; Music—Acoustics and physics; Noise; Phonetics; Soundproofing; Sounds; Ultrasonics; Vibration**

x Acoustics

xx **Music; Music—Acoustics and physics; Physics; Pneumatics; Radiation**

Sound—Insulation. *See* **Soundproofing**

Sound—Recording and reproducing 621.389

See also **High-fidelity sound systems; Intercommunication systems; Stereophonic sound systems;** also methods of recording, e.g. **Magnetic recorders and recording;** etc.

x Sound recording

xx **Motion pictures; Phonograph; Radio**

Sound effects 534

Sound insulation. *See* **Soundproofing**

Sound navigation. *See* **Sonar**

Sound recording. *See* **Sound—Recording and reproducing**

Sound recordings 789.9

See also **Talking books**

x Audiodiscs; Audiorecords; Discography; Phonodiscs; Phonograph records; Phonorecords; Records, Phonograph

xx **Audio-visual education; Audio-visual materials**

Sound waves   534; 620.2
  See also Ultrasonic waves
  xx Vibration; Waves
Soundproofing   693.8
  x Insulation (Sound); Sound—Insulation;
      Sound insulation
  xx Architectural acoustics; Sound
Sounds   534; 620.2
  xx Sound
Soups   641.8
  xx Cookery
The South. *See* Southern States
South Africa   916.8; 968
  x Africa, South; Republic of South Africa;
      Union of South Africa
South Africa—History   968
  See also South African War, 1899–1902
South Africa—Race relations   320.5; 916.8
  x Apartheid
  xx Race relations
South African War, 1899–1902   968
  x Boer War, 1899-1902; Transvaal War,
      1899–1902
  xx South Africa—History; Gt. Brit.—History
      —19th century
South America   918; 980
  xx America; Latin America
South America—Exploration. *See* America—
      Exploration
South American literature. *See* Latin American
      literature
South Atlantic States. *See* Atlantic States
South Pole   919.8; 998
  See also Antarctic regions
  x Polar expeditions
  xx Antarctic regions; Polar regions
South Sea Islands. *See* Islands of the Pacific
Southeast Asia. *See* Asia, Southeast
Southern Africa. *See* Africa, Southern
Southern States   917.5; 975
  x The South
  xx United States
Southern States—History   975
  xx Slavery in the U.S.
Southwest, New   917.9; 979
      Use for materials on that part of the
        United States which corresponds
        roughly with the old Spanish province
        of New Mexico, including the present
        Arizona, New Mexico, southern Col-
        orado, Utah, Nevada and California
  xx United States
Southwest, Old   917.6; 976
      Use for materials on the section which
        comprised the southwestern part of the
        United States before the cessions of
        land from Mexico following the Mexi-
        can War. It included Louisiana, Texas,
        Arkansas, Tennessee, Kentucky and
        Missouri

525

Southwest, Old—*Continued*

  xx **United States**

Sovereigns. *See* **Kings and rulers; Monarchy; Queens; Roman emperors**

Soviet bloc. *See* **Communist countries**

Soviet invasion of Czechoslovakia. *See* **Czechoslovakia—History—Intervention, 1968–**

Soviet Union. *See* **Russia**

Soybean 633

  xx **Forage plants**

Space, Outer. *See* **Outer space**

Space age. *See* **Astronautics and civilization**

Space and time

  x Time and space

  xx **Relativity (Physics)**

Space biology 574.1

Use for materials on the biology of people, animals, and plants while in outer space. Life indigenous to outer space is entered under **Life on other planets**

  See also **Life on other planets**

  x Astrobiology; Bioastronautics; Cosmobiology; Exobiology; Extraterrestrial life

  xx **Biology; Space sciences**

Space colonies 919.9; 999

Use for materials on communities established in space or on other planets. For bases set up for specific functions other than colonization use **Extraterrestrial bases**

  See also **Extraterrestrial bases**

  x Colonies, Space; Communities, Space; Outer space—Colonies

  xx **Astronautics and civilization; Extraterrestrial bases**

Space communication. *See* **Astronautics—Communication systems; Interstellar communication**

Space craft. *See* **Space ships**

Space environment 629.41

  See also **Cosmic rays; Solar radiation**

  x Environment, Space; Extraterrestrial environment; Space weather

  xx **Astronomy; Outer space**

Space exploration (Astronautics). *See* **Outer space—Exploration**

Space flight 629.4

  See also **Astrodynamics; Astronauts; Extravehicular activity (Space flight); Interplanetary voyages; Navigation (Astronautics); Orbital rendezvous (Space flight); Outer space—Exploration; Space medicine;** also names of projects, e.g. **Gemini project;** etc.

  x Humans in space; Man in space; Manned space flight; People in space; Rocket flight; Space flight, Manned; Space travel

  xx **Aeronautics—Flights; Astrodynamics;**

526

Space flight—*Continued*
> Astronautics; Interplanetary voyages; Navigation (Astronautics); Space medicine

Space flight—Law and legislation. *See* Space law

Space flight, Manned. *See* Space flight

Space flight to the moon   629.45
> Use same form for space flight to other planets
>
> *See also* Apollo project; Moon—Exploration
>
> *x* Flight to the moon; Lunar expeditions; Moon, Voyages to; Voyages to the moon
>
> *xx* Astronautics

Space laboratories. *See* Space stations

Space law   341.4
> *See also* Airspace law
>
> *x* Aerospace law; Artificial satellites—Law and legislation; Astronautics—Law and legislation; Law, Space; Space flight—Law and legislation; Space stations—Law and legislation
>
> *xx* Astronautics and civilization; International law; Law

Space medicine   616.9
> *See also* Aviation medicine; Life support systems (Space environment); Space flight; Weightlessness
>
> *x* Aerospace medicine; Bioastronautics
>
> *xx* Aviation medicine; Space flight; Space sciences

Space navigation. *See* Navigation (Astronautics)

Space nutrition. *See* Astronauts—Nutrition

Space orbital rendezvous. *See* Orbital rendezvous (Space flight)

Space photography   778.3
> *See also* Lunar photography; also objects with the subdivision *Photographs from space*, e.g. Earth—Photographs from space; Moon—Photographs from space; etc.
>
> *x* Astronautics, Photography in; Photography, Space; Photography in astronautics
>
> *xx* Photography

Space platforms. *See* Space stations

Space power. *See* Astronautics and civilization

Space probes   629.43
> Use only for space exploration by remote control from earth
>
> *See also* names of types of probes, e.g. Lunar probes; Mars probes; etc.; also names of space vehicles and space projects, e.g. Mariner project; etc.
>
> *x* Probes, Space
>
> *xx* Outer space—Exploration; Space vehicles

Space rescue operations 629.45

    x Manned space flight—Rescue work; Rescue operations, Space; Space ships—Rescue work

    xx **Rescue work**

Space research. *See* **Outer space—Exploration; Space sciences**

Space rockets. *See* **Space vehicles**

Space sciences 500.5

    Use for general materials for scientific results of space exploration and scientific applications of space flight

    See also **Astronautics; Astronomy; Geophysics; Outer space; Space biology; Space medicine**

    x Science and space; Space research

    xx **Astronautics; Astronomy; Science**

Space sciences—International cooperation 500.5

Space ships 629.45

    Use for materials on space vehicles, with people on board. For materials on spacecraft both with and without people use **Space vehicles**

    See also **Orbital rendezvous (Space flight); Rocket planes**

    x Space craft

    xx **Astronautics; Life support systems (Space environment); Rocketry; Space vehicles**

Space ships—Accidents. *See* **Astronautics—Accidents**

Space ships—Pilots. *See* **Astronauts**

Space ships—Rescue work. *See* **Space rescue operations**

Space stations 629.44

    Use for materials on installations in space established to service space ships in orbit or space colonies or bases

    See also **Orbital rendezvous (Space flight)**

    x Laboratories, Space; Orbital laboratories; Sky laboratories; Space laboratories; Space platforms

    xx **Astronautics; Artificial satellites; Space vehicles**

Space stations—Law and legislation. *See* **Space law**

Space suits. *See* **Astronauts—Clothing**

Space telecommunication. *See* **Interstellar communication**

Space television. *See* **Television in astronautics**

Space travel. *See* **Interplanetary voyages; Space flight**

Space vehicles 629.47

    Use for materials on vehicles with and without people on board

    See also **Artificial satellites; Astronautics; Lunar excursion module; Space probes; Space ships; Space stations**

    x Space rockets

Space vehicles—*Continued*
> *xx* **Artificial satellites; Astronautics; Rocketry**

Space vehicles—Accidents. *See* **Astronautics—Accidents**

Space vehicles—Extravehicular activity. *See* **Extravehicular activity (Space flight)**

Space vehicles—Guidance systems 629.47

Space vehicles—Instruments. *See* **Astronautical instruments**

Space vehicles—Piloting 629.45
> *x* Piloting (Astronautics)
> *xx* **Astronauts; Navigation (Astronautics)**

Space vehicles—Propulsion systems 629.47

Space vehicles—Thermodynamics 629.47
> *xx* **Thermodynamics**

Space vehicles—Tracking 629.47
> *x* Tracking of satellites

Space walk. *See* **Extravehicular activity (Space flight)**

Space weather. *See* **Space environment**

Spain 914.6; 946
> May be subdivided like U.S. except for *History*

Spain—History 946

Spain—History—War of 1898. *See* **U.S.—History—War of 1898**

Spain—History—Civil War, 1936–1939 946.081

Spain—History—1939–1975 946.082

Spain—History—1975– 946.082

Spanish America. *See* **Latin America**

Spanish-American literature. *See* **Latin American literature**

Spanish-American War, 1898. *See* **U.S.—History—War of 1898**

Spanish Armada. *See* **Armada, 1588**

Spanish language 460
> May be subdivided like **English language**

Spanish literature 860
> May use same subdivisions and names of literary forms as for **English literature**
> *See also* **Latin American literature**

Spanish Succession, War of, 1701–1714 940.2
> *x* War of the Spanish Succession, 1701–1714
> *xx* **Europe—History—1492–1789; Gt. Brit.—History—Stuarts, 1603–1714**

Sparring. *See* **Boxing**

Spas. *See* **Health resorts, spas, etc.**

Spastic paralysis. *See* **Cerebral palsy**

Speakers (Recitation books). *See* **Readings and recitations**

Speaking. *See* **Debates and debating; Lectures and lecturing; Preaching; Public speaking; Rhetoric; Voice**

Spear fishing 799.1
> *xx* **Fishing**

Special libraries. *See* **Libraries, Special**

Specialists exchange programs. *See* **Exchange of persons programs**

Specie. *See* **Money**

Specimens, Preservation of. *See* **Taxidermy; Zoological specimens—Collection and preservation;** and names of natural specimens with the subdivision *Collection and preservation,* e.g. **Birds— Collection and preservation; Plants— Collection and preservation;** etc.

Spectacles. *See* **Eyeglasses**

Specters. *See* **Apparitions; Ghosts**

Spectra. *See* **Spectrum**

Spectroscopy. *See* **Spectrum**

Spectrum 535

See also **Light; Ultraviolet rays**

x Analysis, Spectrum; Astronomical spectroscopy; Spectra; Spectroscopy

xx **Astronomy; Chemistry; Light; Optics; Radiation**

Speculation 332.6

See also **Investments; Securities; Stock exchange**

xx **Finance; Investments; Stock exchange**

Speech 372.6; 410; 612

See also **Language and languages; Phonetics; Speech therapy; Voice**

x Talking

xx **Language and languages; Language arts; Phonetics; Voice**

Speech, Liberty of. *See* **Free speech**

Speech correction. *See* **Speech therapy**

Speech disorders 157; 616.8

x Defective speech; Speech pathology; Stammering; Stuttering

Speech pathology. *See* **Speech disorders**

Speech therapy 616.8

x Speech correction

xx **Speech**

Speeches, addresses, etc. 808.85; 815.08; etc.

Use for collections of speeches of a general nature which are less formal than those entered under **Orations** and generally treat of less important subjects

See also **After-dinner speeches; Lectures and lecturing; Orations; Toasts;** also general subjects with the subdivision *Addresses and essays,* e.g. **Agriculture —Addresses and essays; U.S.—History —Addresses and essays;** etc.

x Addresses

xx **After-dinner speeches**

Speed 531

x Velocity

xx **Motion**

Speed, Supersonic. *See* **Aerodynamics, Supersonic**

Speed reading. *See* **Rapid reading**

Speleology. *See* **Caves**

Spellers 421

xx **English language—Spelling**

530

Spelling. *See* names of languages with the subdivision *Spelling,* e.g. **English language—Spelling;** etc.

Spelling reform   421

> *x* English language—Spelling reform; Orthography; Phonetic spelling
>
> *xx* **English language—Spelling**

Spells. *See* **Charms**

Spherical trigonometry. *See* **Trigonometry**

Spices   641.3; 664

> *See also* names of spices

Spiders   595.7

> *x* Arachnida

Spies   327; 355.3

> *See also* **Secret service; World War, 1939–1945—Underground movements**
>
> *x* Intelligence agents
>
> *xx* **Espionage; Military art and science; Secret service; Subversive activities**

Spinal paralysis, Anterior. *See* **Poliomyelitis**

Spinning   677; 746.1

> *xx* **Textile industry**

Spiral gearing. *See* **Gearing**

Spires   726

> *x* Steeples
>
> *xx* **Architecture; Church architecture**

Spirit. *See* **Soul**

Spirit, Holy. *See* **Holy Spirit**

Spiritism. *See* **Spiritualism**

Spirits. *See* **Apparitions; Demonology; Ghosts; Spiritualism; Witchcraft**

Spirits, Alcoholic. *See* **Liquors and liqueurs**

Spiritual healing. *See* **Faith healing**

Spiritual life   248

> *See also* **Christian life; Faith; Meditation; Sanctification**
>
> *x* Life, Spiritual
>
> *xx* **Ethics; Human behavior; Mysticism; Religion; Soul; Theology**

Spiritualism   133.9

> *See also* **Apparitions; Clairvoyance; Ghosts; Psychical research; Psychokinesis**
>
> *x* Spiritism; Spirits
>
> *xx* **Apparitions; Future life; Ghosts; Occult sciences; Psychical research; Supernatural**

Spirituals (Songs)   784.7

> *See also* **Black songs; Blues (Songs, etc.)**
>
> *x* Black spirituals
>
> *xx* **Music, American; Black music; Black songs**

Splicing. *See* **Knots and splices**

Spoils system. *See* **Corruption in politics**

Sponges   593

> *xx* **Invertebrates**

Spontaneous combustion. *See* **Combustion**

Sports   796

> *See also*

Aeronautical sports	**Athletics**
Amusements	**Coaching (Athletics)**

Sports—*Continued*

College sports

Games

Gymnastics

Olympic games

Outdoor life

Physical education
and training

Professional sports

Rodeos

School sports

Water sports

Winter sports

    also names of sports, e.g. **Baseball; Football;** etc.; *also* names of competitions

  xx **Amusements; Athletics; Games; Outdoor life; Physical education and training; Play; Recreation**

Sports—Encyclopedias 796.03

  xx **Encyclopedias**

Sports—Equipment and supplies 796.028

  x Equipment and supplies

Sports cars 629.22

  See also names of specific sports cars

  xx **Automobiles**

Sports coaching. *See* **Coaching (Athletics)**

Spot welding. *See* **Electric welding**

Spraying and dusting 632

  See also **Aeronautics in agriculture; Fungicides; Insecticides**

  xx **Agricultural pests; Fruit—Diseases and pests; Fungicides; Insecticides**

Spun glass. *See* **Glass fibers**

Sputniks. *See* **Artificial satellites, Russian**

Square dancing 793.3

  xx **Folk dancing**

Squirrels 599

  See also **Chipmunks**

Stabilization in industry. *See* **Business cycles; Economic conditions**

Stage. *See* **Acting; Actors and actresses; Drama; Theater**

Stage lighting 792

  x Television—Stage lighting; Theaters—Stage lighting

Stage scenery. *See* **Theaters—Stage setting and scenery**

Stage setting. *See* **Theaters—Stage setting and scenery**

Stagecoaches. *See* **Carriages and carts**

Stained glass. *See* **Glass painting and staining**

Stamina, Physical. *See* **Physical fitness**

Stammering. *See* **Speech disorders**

Stamps, Postage. *See* **Postage stamps**

Standard book numbers. *See* **Publishers' standard book numbers**

Standard of living 339.4

  x Living, Standard of

  xx **Social conditions; Social problems; Wealth**

Standard of value. *See* **Money**

Standard time. *See* **Time**

Stars 523.8

  See also **Astrology; Astronomy, Astrophysics; Galaxies; Meteors; Planets;**

Stars—*Continued*

    Solar system; also names of groups of stars and specific stars, e.g. **Pulsars; Sirius;** etc.

    x Constellations; Double stars; Sidereal system

    xx **Astronomy; Planets**

Stars—Atlases 523.8

    x Astronomy—Atlases; Atlases, Astronomical

    xx **Atlases**

Stars, Falling. *See* **Meteors**

The State 320.1

    See also **Political science**

    x Administration; The Commonwealth; Welfare state

    xx **Political science**

State aid to education 379

    x Education—State aid

    xx **Education—Finance; Education and state**

State aid to libraries 021.8

    x Libraries—State aid

    xx **Libraries and state; Library finance**

State and agriculture. *See* **Agriculture and state**

State and church. *See* **Church and state**

State and education. *See* **Education and state**

State and energy. *See* **Energy policy**

State and environment. *See* **Environmental policy**

State and industry. *See* **Industry and state**

State and insurance. *See* **Social security**

State and railroads. *See* **Railroads and state**

State and science *See* **Science and state**

State and the arts. *See* **Art and state**

State birds 598.2

    xx **Birds**

State church. *See* **Church and state**

State constitutions. *See* **Constitutions, State**

State debts. *See* **Debts, Public**

State encouragement of the arts. *See* **Art and state**

State flowers 582

    Use same form for other state symbols

    x Flowers, State

    xx **Flowers**

State governments 353.9

    Use for general materials on state government. Materials on the government of a particular state are entered under the name of the state with the subdivision *Politics and government*

    See also **Constitutions, State; Federal government; Governors;** and names of states with the subdivision *Politics and government*, e.g. **Ohio—Politics and government;** etc.

    x U.S.—State governments

    xx **Constitutions, State; Federal government; Political science**

State libraries   027.5
    See also **Libraries, Governmental**
    x Libraries, State
    xx **Libraries, Governmental; Libraries and state**

State-local tax relations.   *See* **Intergovernmental tax relations**

State medicine.   *See* **Medicine, State**

State of the Union messages.   *See* **Presidents—U.S.—Messages**

State ownership.   *See* **Government ownership**

State ownership of railroads.   *See* **Railroads and state**

State planning.   *See* **Regional planning; Social policy;** and names of states with the subdivision *Economic policy; Social policy*, e.g. **Ohio—Economic policy; Ohio—Social policy;** etc.

State police.   *See* **Police, State**

State regulation of industry.   *See* **Industry and state**

State rights   320.1; 342.4
    x Secession; States' rights
    xx **Political science; Slavery in the U.S.**

State songs   784.7
    xx **Songs**

States, New   321
    x New nations
    xx **Developing areas**

States' rights.   *See* **State rights**

Statesmen.   *See* **Politicians**

Statics   531
    See also **Dynamics; Hydrostatics; Strains and stresses**
    xx **Dynamics; Mechanics; Physics**

Statistical inference.   *See* **Probabilities**

Statistics   310
    Use for materials on the theory and methods of statistics
    See also **Census; Probabilities; Sampling (Statistics); Vital statistics;** also general subjects and names of countries, cities, etc. with the subdivision *Statistics*, e.g. **Agriculture—Statistics; U.S.—Statistics; Chicago—Statistics;** etc.
    xx **Economics**

Statistics—Graphic methods   001.4
    x Diagrams, Statistical
    xx **Graphic methods**

Statues.   *See* **Monuments; Sculpture**

Statutes.   *See* **Law**

Steam   536
    xx **Heat; Power (Mechanics); Water**

Steam engineering   621.1
    See also **Mechanical engineering; Power (Mechanics); Steam engines; Steam navigation; Steam power plants**
    xx **Mechanical engineering**

Steam engines 621.1

>*See also* **Condensers (Steam); Farm engines; Locomotives; Marine engines; Steam turbines**

>*xx* **Engines; Heat engines; Machinery; Mechanics; Steam engineering**

Steam fitting. *See* **Pipe fitting**

Steam heating 697

>*xx* **Heating**

Steam navigation 386; 387; 623.82

>*See also* **Marine engineering; Navigation; Steam turbines; Steamboats**

>*x* Navigation, Steam

>*xx* **Navigation; Steam engineering; Steamboats; Transportation**

Steam power plants 621.1

>*x* Power plants, Steam

>*xx* **Power plants; Steam engineering**

Steam pumps. *See* **Pumping machinery**

Steam turbines 621.1

>*xx* **Steam engines; Steam navigation; Turbines**

Steamboats 387.2

>*See also* **Steam navigation**

>*x* Steamships

>*xx* **Boats and boating; Naval architecture; Ocean travel; Shipbuilding; Ships; Steam navigation; Transportation**

Steamships. *See* **Steamboats**

Steel 669; 672

>*See also* **Building, Iron and steel; Iron;** also headings beginning with the word **Steel**

>*xx* **Metalwork**

Steel, Structural 691

>*See also* **Building, Iron and steel**

>*x* Steel construction; Structural steel

>*xx* **Building, Iron and steel; Building materials; Civil engineering**

Steel construction. *See* **Building, Iron and steel; Steel, Structural**

Steel engraving. *See* **Engraving**

Steel industry and trade 338.4; 672

>*See also* **Iron industry and trade**

>*x* Industries

>*xx* **Industry; Iron industry and trade; Ironwork**

Steel industry and trade—Quality control 338.4; 672

>*xx* **Quality control**

Steeples. *See* **Spires**

Stencil work 686.2

>*See also* **Silk screen printing**

>*xx* **Arts and crafts; Decoration and ornament; Painting**

Stenography. *See* **Shorthand**

Stereophonic sound systems 621.389

>*xx* **High fidelity sound systems; Sound—Recording and reproducing**

Stereophotography. *See* **Photography, Stereoscopic**

Sterilization (Birth control)   613.9
>   *See also* **Vasectomy**
>   *xx* **Birth control**

Stewardesses, Air line. *See* **Air lines—Flight attendants**

Stewards, Air line. *See* **Air lines—Flight attendants**

Stills. *See* **Distillation**

Stimulants   613.8
>   *See also* **Alcohol; Liquors and liqueurs; Narcotics**
>   *x* Intoxicants
>   *xx* **Hygiene; Narcotics; Temperance; Therapeutics**

Stock and stock breeding. *See* **Livestock**

Stock exchange   332.6
>   *See also* **Bonds; Foreign exchange; Investments; Securities; Speculation; Stocks; Wall Street**
>   *x* Securities exchange; Stock market
>   *xx* **Commerce; Exchange; Finance; Investments; Speculation; Stocks**

Stock judging. *See* **Livestock judging**

Stock market. *See* **Stock exchange**

Stock raising. *See* **Livestock**

Stockings. *See* **Hosiery**

Stocks   332.6
>   *See also* **Bonds; Corporations; Investments; Stock exchange**
>   *x* Dividends; Shares of stock
>   *xx* **Bonds; Commerce; Investments; Securities; Stock exchange**

Stockyards. *See* **Meat industry and trade**

Stoics   188
>   *xx* **Ethics; Philosophy, Ancient**

Stokers, Mechanical   621.1
>   *x* Mechanical stokers

Stomach   612
>   *See also* **Digestion**

Stone   552; 553; 693.1
>   *See also* **Masonry; Petrology; Quarries and quarrying; Rocks; Stonecutting;** also names of stones, e.g. **Marble;** etc.
>   *xx* **Building materials; Geology, Economic; Petrology; Quarries and quarrying; Rocks**

Stone age   913
>   *See also* **Man, Prehistoric; Stone implements**
>   *x* Eolithic period; Neolithic period; Paleolithic period; Prehistory
>   *xx* **Archeology**

Stone-cutting. *See* **Stonecutting**

Stone implements   913
>   *x* Flint implements; Implements, utensils, etc.
>   *xx* **Archeology; Stone age**

Stone quarries. *See* **Quarries and quarrying**

Stonecutting 693.1

    x Stone-cutting

    xx **Masonry; Stone**

Stones, Precious. *See* **Precious stones**

Stoneware. *See* **Pottery**

Storage batteries 621.35

    See also **Electric batteries**

    x Batteries, Electric

    xx **Electric batteries**

Stores. *See* **Chain stores; Cooperative societies; Department stores; Supermarkets**

Stories. *See* **Anecdotes; Fairy tales; Fiction; Legends; Romances; Stories in rhyme; Stories without words; Storytelling;** also literary and musical forms with the subdivision *Stories, plots, etc.,* e.g. **Ballets—Stories, plots, etc.; Operas —Stories, plots, etc.;** also subjects with the subdivision **Fiction,** e.g. **Slavery in the U.S.—Fiction;** etc.; and such phrase headings that do not lend themselves to subdivision, e.g. **Bible stories; Mystery and detective stories; School stories; Sea stories; Short stories;** etc.

Stories in rhyme Fic; E

    x Stories

    xx **Rhyme**

Stories without words E

    x Nonword stories; Stories; Wordless stories

    xx **Picture books for children**

Storms 551.5

    See also **Blizzards; Cyclones; Dust storms; Hurricanes; Meteorology; Rain and rainfall; Snow; Thunderstorms; Tornadoes; Typhoons; Winds;** and other kinds of storms

    xx **Meteorology; Ocean; Rain and rainfall; Tornadoes; Weather; Winds**

Storytelling 027.62; 372.6

    See also **Short story**

    x Stories

    xx **Children's literature; Short story**

Stoves 697

    xx **Heating**

Strain (Psychology). *See* **Stress (Psychology)**

Strains and stresses 531; 620.1; 624.1

    See also **Strength of materials**

    x Architectural engineering; Stresses

    xx **Architecture; Mechanics; Statics; Strength of materials; Structures, Theory of**

Strategic materials. *See* **Materials**

Strategy 355.4

    See also **Armies; Military art and science; Naval art and science; Tactics**

    x Military strategy; Naval strategy

    xx **Military art and science; Naval art and science; War**

Stratigraphic geology. *See* **Geology, Stratigraphic**

Stratosphere 551.5
  xx **Atmosphere, Upper**

Straw votes. *See* **Public opinion polls**

Strawberries 634
  xx **Berries**

Streamlining. *See* **Aerodynamics**

Street cars. *See* **Street railroads**

Street cleaning 628
  See also **Refuse and refuse disposal**
  xx **Cleaning; Municipal engineering; Public health; Refuse and refuse disposal; Roads; Sanitary engineering; Streets**

Street lighting. *See* **Streets—Lighting**

Street railroads 388.4
  See also **Electric railroads; Subways**
  x Interurban railroads; Railroads, Street; Street cars; Trams; Trolley cars
  xx **Electric railroads; Local transit; Public utilities; Railroads; Transportation**

Street traffic. *See* **City traffic; Traffic engineering; Traffic regulations**

Streets 388.4; 625.7
  See also **City traffic; Pavements; Roads; Street cleaning;** also names of cities with the subdivision *Streets*, e.g. **Chicago—Streets;** etc.
  x Alleys; Thoroughfares
  xx **Cities and towns; Civil engineering; Pavements; Roads; Transportation**

Streets—Lighting 628.9
  See also cities with the subdivision *Lighting;* e.g. **Chicago—Lighting;** etc.
  x Cities and towns—Lighting; Street lighting
  xx **Lighting**

Strength of materials 620.1
  See also **Building materials; Strains and stresses;** also special materials and forms with the subdivision *Testing*, e.g. **Concrete—Testing;** etc.
  x Architectural engineering; Materials, Strength of; Resistance of materials
  xx **Architecture; Building; Building, Iron and steel; Building materials; Civil engineering; Materials; Mechanics; Strains and stresses; Structures, Theory of**

Stress (Physiology) 612; 616.8
  x Tension (Physiology)

Stress (Psychology) 131; 157
  x Anxiety; Emotional stress; Psychological stress; Strain (Psychology); Tension (Psychology)
  xx **Psychology**

Stresses. *See* **Strains and stresses**

Strikes and lockouts 331.89

> *See also* **Arbitration, Industrial; Collective bargaining; Injunctions; Labor unions; Sabotage; Syndicalism**
>
> *x* Lockouts; Sit-down strikes; Work stoppages
>
> *xx* **Arbitration, Industrial; Collective bargaining; Industrial relations; Injunctions; Labor and laboring classes; Labor disputes; Labor unions**

String orchestra music 785.06

> *xx* **Orchestral music**

Stringed instruments 787

> *See also* names of stringed instruments, e.g. **Guitar; Violin;** etc.
>
> *x* Bowed instruments
>
> *xx* **Musical instruments**

Strip films. *See* **Filmstrips**

Structural botany. *See* **Botany—Anatomy**

Structural drafting. *See* **Mechanical drawing**

Structural engineering 624

> *See also* **Building; Foundations; Hydraulic structures; Soils (Engineering); Structures, Theory of**
>
> *x* Engineering, Structural
>
> *xx* **Architecture; Building materials; Civil engineering; Structures, Theory of**

Structural materials. *See* **Building materials**

Structural psychology. *See* **Gestalt psychology**

Structural steel. *See* **Steel, Structural**

Structures, Offshore. *See* **Artificial islands**

Structures, Theory of 624

> *See also* **Building; Strains and stresses; Strength of materials; Structural engineering**
>
> *x* Architectural engineering; Theory of structures
>
> *xx* **Building, Iron and steel; Structural engineering**

Stucco 693.6

> *xx* **Building materials; Decoration and ornament; Plaster and plastering**

Student activities 371.8

> *See also* **College and school drama; College and school journalism; School assembly programs; School sports**
>
> *x* Extracurricular activities

Student aid. *See* **Scholarships, fellowships, etc.; Student loan funds**

Student clubs. *See* **Students—Societies**

Student councils. *See* **Self-government (in education)**

Student customs. *See* **Student life**

Student evaluation of teachers 371.1

> *x* Student rating of teachers; Teachers, Rating of (by students)

Student government. *See* **Self-government (in education)**

Student guidance. *See* **Educational counseling; Vocational guidance**

Student life   371.8
>   *x* Student customs
>   *xx* **Students**

Student loan funds   371.2; 378.3
>   *See also* **Scholarships, fellowships, etc.**
>   *x* Loan funds, Student; Student aid
>   *xx* **Scholarships, fellowships, etc.**

Student movement. *See* **Youth movement**

Student protests. *See* **Students—Political activity; Youth movement**

Student rating of teachers. *See* **Student evaluation of teachers**

Student revolt. *See* **Students—Political activity; Youth movement**

Student self-government. *See* **Self-government (in education)**

Student societies. *See* **Students—Societies**

Student teaching   371.1
>   *x* Practice teaching; Teachers—Practice teaching
>   *xx* **Teachers—Training; Teaching**

Students (May subdiv. geog.)   **371.8**
>   *See also* **Student life;** also types of students, e.g. **College students;** etc., also headings beginning with the words **College** and **School**
>   *x* School life

Students—Counseling. *See* **Educational counseling**

Students, Foreign   370.19
>   *x* Foreign students

Students—Grading and marking. *See* **Grading and marking (Students)**

Students—Political activity   322.4; 371.8
>   *x* Politics and students; Student protests; Student revolt
>   *xx* **Youth movement**

Students—Societies   371.8
>   *See also* **Fraternities and sororities**
>   *x* School clubs; Student clubs; Student societies; Students' societies

Students—U.S.   371.8
>   *x* U.S.—Students

Students and libraries. *See* **Libraries and students**

Students' military training camps. *See* **Military training camps**

Students' societies. *See* **Students—Societies**

Students' songs   784.6
>   *x* College songs
>   *xx* **Songs**

Study, Courses of. *See* **Education—Curricula;** also types of education and schools with the subdivision *Curricula,* e.g. **Library education—Curricula; Colleges and universities—Curricula;** etc.

Study, Foreign. *See* **Foreign study**

Study, Method of 371.3

> *See also* subjects with the subdivision *Study and teaching,* e.g. **Art—Study and teaching;** etc.
> *x* Learning, Art of; Method of study
> *xx* **Education; Teaching**

Study abroad. *See* **Foreign study**

Study overseas. *See* **Foreign study**

Stuttering. *See* **Speech disorders**

Style, Literary 808

> *See also* **Criticism; Letter writing; Literature—History and criticism; Rhetoric**
> *x* Literary style
> *xx* **Criticism; Literature; Rhetoric**

Style in dress. *See* **Costume; Fashion**

Style manikins. *See* **Models, Fashion**

Style manuals. *See* **Printing—Style manuals**

Subconsciousness 127; 154.2

> *See also*

Consciousness	**Mind and body**
Dreams	**Personality dis-**
Faith healing	**orders**
Hallucinations and	**Psychoanalysis**
illusions	**Sleep**
Hypnotism	**Thought transfer-**
Mental healing	**ence**
Mental suggestion	

> *xx* **Consciousness; Hypnotism; Mental healing; Mind and body; Psychical research; Psychoanalysis; Psychology; Psychology, Pathological; Therapeutics, Suggestive**

Subgravity state. *See* **Weightlessness**

Subject headings 025.3

> *See also* **Classification—Books**
> *x* Thesauri
> *xx* **Cataloging; Catalogs, Subject; Indexes**

Submarine boats. *See* **Submersibles; Submarines**

Submarine cables. *See* **Cables, Submarine**

Submarine diving. *See* **Diving, Submarine**

Submarine exploration. *See* **Underwater exploration**

Submarine geology 551.4

> *See also* **Ocean bottom; Plate tectonics**
> *x* Geology, Submarine; Marine geology; Underwater geology
> *xx* **Geology; Oceanography; Plate tectonics**

Submarine medicine 616.9

> *x* Medicine, Submarine; Underwater physiology; Underwater medicine
> *xx* **Medicine**

Submarine photography. *See* **Photography, Submarine**

Submarine research stations. *See* **Undersea research stations**

Submarine telegraph. *See* **Cables, Submarine**

Submarine vehicles. *See* **Submersibles**

Submarine warfare 359.4

   See also **Submarines; Torpedoes**

   x Naval warfare; Warfare, Submarine

   xx **Naval art and science; War**

Submarines 359.3; 623.82

   Use for materials on submarines only. Materials on other underwater craft are entered under **Submersibles**

   See also **Atomic Submarines**

   x Boats, Submarine; Submarine boats; U boats

   xx **Boats and boating; Naval art and science; Ships; Submarine warfare; Submersibles; Warships**

Submarines, Atomic. *See* **Atomic submarines**

Submersibles 623.82

   See also types of submersibles, e.g. **Bathyscaphe; Submarines; Undersea research stations;** etc.

   x Boats, Submarine; Deep diving vehicles; Deep sea vehicles; Deep submergence vehicles; Oceanographic submersibles; Submarine boats; Submarine vehicles; Undersea vehicles; Underwater exploration devices

   xx **Oceanography—Research; Underwater—Exploration**

Subprofessional library assistants. *See* **Library technicians**

Subscription television 384.55

   x Pay television; Television, Subscription

   xx **Television**

Subsidies 338.9

   See also headings beginning with **Federal aid to . . .**

   x Bounties; Grants; Subventions

   xx **Economic assistance, Domestic; Economic policy; Industry and state**

Subtraction

   xx **Mathematical operations**

Suburban areas. *See* **Metropolitan areas**

Suburban homes. *See* **Architecture, Domestic**

Suburban life 301.34

   See also names of cities with the subdivision *Suburbs and environs*, e.g. **Chicago—Suburbs and environs;** etc.

Subventions. *See* **Subsidies**

Subversive activities 322.4

   See also **Espionage; Internal security; Political crimes and offenses; Sabotage; Spies; Terrorism**

   x Fifth column

   xx **Insurgency; Internal security**

Subways 388.4

   x Railroads, Underground; Underground railroads

   xx **Civil engineering; Local transit; Railroads; Street railroads; Transportation; Tunnels**

Success 131; 158
>   *See also* **Ability; Business; Leadership;**
>   **Saving and thrift; Self realization**
>   *x* Fortune; Personal development
>   *xx* **Business ethics; Wealth**
Succession, Intestate. *See* **Inheritance and succession**
Suffering 152.1; 214
>   *See also* **Good and evil; Joy and sorrow;**
>   **Pain**
>   *xx* **Pain**
Suffrage 324
>   *See also* **Naturalization; Representative**
>   **government and representation;** also
>   classes of people with the subdivision
>   *Suffrage,* e.g. **Blacks—Suffrage; Women**
>   **—Suffrage;** etc.
>   *x* Franchise; Voting
>   *xx* **Citizenship; Constitutional law; Democ-**
>   **racy; Elections; Political science; Rep-**
>   **resentative government and represen-**
>   **tation**
Suffragettes. *See* **Women—Suffrage**
Sugar 641.3; 664
>   *See also* **Syrups;** also types of sugar, e.g.
>   **Maple sugar;** etc.
Suggestion, Mental. *See* **Mental suggestion**
Suggestive therapeutics. *See* **Therapeutics,**
>   **Suggestive**
Suicide 179; 614.5
>   *xx* **Medical jurisprudence; Social problems**
Suites 785.8
>   *xx* **Musical form; Orchestral music**
Sulfa drugs. *See* **Sulfonamides**
Sulfonamides 615
>   *x* Sulfa drugs
Sulfur. *See* **Sulphur**
Sulphur 546; 553; 661
>   *x* Sulfur
Summer camps. *See* **Camps**
Summer homes. *See* **Architecture, Domestic;**
>   **Houses**
Summer resorts 913-919
>   *See also* **Health resorts, spas, etc.**
>   *x* Resorts
>   *xx* **Health resorts, spas, etc.**
Summer schools 371.2; 371.8
>   *x* Vacation schools
>   *xx* **Playgrounds; Public schools**
Summer schools, Religious 377
>   *x* Bible classes; Vacation church schools;
>   Vacation schools, Religious
Sun 523.7
>   *See also* **Solar energy; Solar system; Sun-**
>   **spots**
>   *x* Solar physics
>   *xx* **Astronomy; Solar system**
Sun—Eclipses. *See* **Eclipses, Solar**
Sun—Radiation. *See* **Solar radiation**
Sun-dials. *See* **Sundials**

Sun-powered batteries. *See* **Solar batteries**

Sun-spots. *See* **Sunspots**

Sunday schools 268

    See also **Bible—Study**

    x Bible classes

    xx **Church work; Religious education**

Sundials 681

    x Horology; Sun-dials

    xx **Clocks and watches; Garden ornaments and furniture; Time**

Sunken cities. *See* **Cities and towns, Ruined, extinct, etc.**

Sunken treasure. *See* **Buried treasure**

Sunspots 523.7

    x Sun-spots

    xx **Meteorology; Solar radiation; Sun**

Super markets. *See* **Supermarkets**

Superhighways. *See* **Express highways**

Superintendents of schools. *See* **School superintendents and principals**

Superior children. *See* **Gifted children**

Supermarkets 658.8

    x Stores; Super markets

    xx **Grocery trade; Retail trade**

Supernatural 133; 398.2

    See also **Divination; Miracles; Occult sciences; Prophecies (Occult sciences); Psychical research; Revelation; Spiritualism; Superstition**

    xx **Miracles; Religion**

Supersonic aerodynamics. *See* **Aerodynamics, Supersonic**

Supersonic airliners. *See* **Supersonic transport planes**

Supersonic transport planes 629.133

    x SST; Supersonic airliners

Supersonic waves. *See* **Ultrasonic waves**

Supersonics. *See* **Ultrasonics**

Superstition 001.9; 398

    See also

Alchemy	**Exorcism**
Apparitions	**Fairies**
Astrology	**Folklore**
Charms	**Fortune telling**
Demonology	**Ghosts**
Divination	**Occult sciences**
Dreams	**Witchcraft**
Errors	

    x Delusions; Traditions

    xx **Demonology; Divination; Errors; Folklore; Ghosts; Occult sciences; Religion; Supernatural**

Supervision of employees. *See* **Personnel management**

Supervision of schools. *See* **School supervision**

Supervisors 331.7

    x Foremen and foreladies; Managers

    xx **Factory management; Personnel management**

Supreme Court—U.S. *See* **U.S. Supreme Court**

Surf. *See* **Ocean waves**

Surf riding. *See* **Surfing**

Surface effect machines. *See* **Ground effect machines**

Surfing 797.1

  x Surf riding

  xx **Water sports**

Surgeons 920; 926

  See also **Physicians**

  x Medical profession

  xx **Physicians**

Surgery 617

  See also **Anesthetics; Antiseptics; Cryosurgery; Orthopedics; Transplantation of organs, tissues, etc.; Vivisection;** also names of organs and regions of the body with the subdivision *Surgery,* e.g. **Heart—Surgery;** etc.

  x Operations, Surgical

  xx **Medicine**

Surgery, Cosmetic. *See* **Surgery, Plastic**

Surgery, Orthopedic. *See* **Orthopedics**

Surgery, Plastic 617

  x Cosmetic surgery; Plastic surgery; Surgery, Cosmetic

  xx **Transplantation of organs, tissues, etc.**

Surgical transplantation. *See* **Transplantation of organs, tissues, etc.**

Surnames. *See* **Names, Personal**

Surrealism 709.04; 759.06

  xx **Art; Postimpressionism (Art)**

Surveillance, Electronic. *See* **Eavesdropping**

Surveying 526.9

  See also **Geodesy; Mine surveying; Topographical drawing**

  x Land surveying

  xx **Civil engineering; Geodesy; Geography; Measurement**

Surveys. *See* types of surveys, e.g. **Educational surveys; Library surveys; Social surveys;** etc.

Survival (after airplane accidents, shipwrecks, etc.) 613.6

  See also **Wilderness survival**

  x Castaways

  xx **Aeronautics—Accidents; Shipwrecks**

Survival of the fittest. *See* **Natural selection**

Suspended sentence. *See* **Probation**

Suspense fiction. *See* **Gothic fiction**

Suspension bridges. *See* **Bridges**

Swamps. *See* **Marshes**

Swedish language 439.7

  May be subdivided like **English language**

  xx **Scandinavian languages**

Swedish literature 839.7

  May use same subdivisions and names of literary forms as for **English literature**

  xx **Scandinavian literature**

Swimming 797.2

See also **Diving; Synchronized swimming**

xx **Water sports**

Swimming pools 614; 725

Swindlers and swindling 364.1

See also **Counterfeits and counterfeiting; Fraud; Impostors and imposture; Quacks and quackery**

x Con game; Confidence game

xx **Crime; Criminals; Fraud; Impostors and imposture**

Swine. *See* **Hogs**

Switchboard hotlines. *See* **Hotlines (Telephone counseling)**

Switches, Electric. *See* **Electric switchgear**

Symbiosis. *See* **Botany—Ecology**

Symbolism 809

See also **Heraldry; Signs and symbols;** also types of symbolism in religions, e.g. **Christian art and symbolism; Religious art and symbolism;** etc.

x Devices (Heraldry); Emblems

xx **Art; Mythology; Signs and symbols**

Symbolism in literature 809

Use same form for symbolism in other subjects

See also **Allegories**

xx **Literature**

Symbols. *See* **Abbreviations; Signs and symbols**

Sympathy 152.4

See also **Bereavement**

x Compassion; Consolation; Pity

xx **Bereavement; Emotions; Friendship; Human behavior**

Symphonic poems 785.3

Symphonies 785.1

Use for musical scores

xx **Orchestral music**

Symphony 785.1

Use for materials on the symphony as a musical form

xx **Musical form**

Symptoms. *See* **Diagnosis**

Synagogues 726

See also names of cities with the subdivision *Synagogues*, e.g. **Chicago—Synagogues;** etc.

xx **Architecture; Judaism**

Synchronized swimming 797.2

x Ballet, Water; Water ballet

xx **Swimming**

Syndicalism 335

See also **Anarchism and anarchists; Communism; Socialism**

xx **Labor and laboring classes; Labor unions; Socialism; Strikes and lockouts**

Synods. *See* **Councils and synods**

546

Synonyms. *See* names of languages with the subdivision *Synonyms and antonyms*, e.g. **English language—Synonyms and antonyms;** etc.

Synthesizer music. *See* **Electronic music**

Synthetic chemistry. *See* **Chemistry, Organic—Synthesis**

Synthetic detergents. *See* **Detergents, Synthetic**

Synthetic fabrics   677

> *See also* names of synthetic fabrics, e.g. **Nylon; Rayon;** etc.
> *x* Fabrics, Synthetic
> *xx* **Fabrics; Synthetic products**

Synthetic food. *See* **Food, Artificial**

Synthetic fuels   662

> *x* Artificial fuels; Nonfossil fuels
> *xx* **Fuel; Synthetic products**

Synthetic products   677; 678

> *See also* **Chemurgy;** also names of types of synthetic products and names of specific products; e.g. **Plastics; Rayon; Rubber, Artificial; Synthetic fabrics; Synthetic fuels;** etc.
> *xx* **Chemistry, Organic—Synthesis; Chemistry, Technical; Chemurgy; Plastics**

Synthetic rubber. *See* **Rubber, Artificial**

Syphilis   616.9

> *xx* **Venereal diseases**

Syrups   641.3

> *xx* **Sugar**

System analysis   001.6

> *See also* **Systems engineering**
> *x* Linear system theory; Network theory; Systems analysis
> *xx* **Cybernetics; Mathematical models**

Systems analysis. *See* **System analysis**

Systems design. *See* **Systems engineering**

Systems engineering   620

> *See also* **Bionics; Operations research**
> *x* Systems design
> *xx* **Automation; Cybernetics; Design, Industrial; Operations research; System analysis**

T groups. *See* **Group relations training**

TIROS (Meteorological satellite). *See* **Tiros (Meteorological satellite)**

TV. *See* **Television**

Table decoration. *See* **Table setting and decoration**

Table etiquette   395

> *xx* **Etiquette**

Table setting and decoration   642

> *See also* **Flower arrangement; Tableware**
> *x* Table decoration
> *xx* **Decoration and ornament**

Table talk. *See* **Conversation**

Table tennis. *See* **Ping-pong**

Tables (Systematic lists). *See* scientific and economic subjects with the subdivision

Tables (Systematic lists)—*Continued*
>> *Tables, etc.,* e.g. **Trigonometry—Ta-
bles, etc.;** etc.

Tableware   642; 738; 739; 748.2
>> *See also* **Glassware; Pottery; Silverware**
>> *xx* **Table setting and decoration**

Tactics   355.4
>> *See also* **Biological warfare; Guerrilla war-
fare**
>> *x* Military tactics
>> *xx* **Military art and science; Strategy**

Tadpoles.   *See* **Frogs**

Tailoring   646.4; 687
>> *See also* **Dressmaking; Uniforms, Military**
>> *x* Garment making
>> *xx* **Clothing and dress; Clothing trade;
Dressmaking; Fashion**

Taiwan   915.1; 951
>> *x* China (Republic of China, 1949–   );
Formosa; Nationalist China; Republic
of China, 1949–

Talent.   *See* **Genius; Gifted children; Musical
ability**

Tales.   *See* **Fables; Fairy tales; Folklore; Legends**

Talismans.   *See* **Charms**

Talking.   *See* **Conversation; Speech**

Talking books   027.6
>> *x* Books, Talking; Cassette books
>> *xx* **Blind, Books for the; Sound recordings**

Talking pictures.   *See* **Motion pictures**

Tall ships, 1976.   *See* **Operation Sail, 1976**

Tall ships transatlantic race.   *See* **Operation
Sail, 1976**

Tall tales.   *See* **American wit and humor; Folklore; Legends**

Talmud   296.1
>> *xx* **Hebrew literature; Jewish literature;
Judaism**

Tanks (Military science)   355.8
>> *x* Armored cars (Tanks); Cars, Armored
(Tanks)

Tanning   675
>> *See also* **Hides and skins; Leather**
>> *xx* **Chemistry, Technical; Hides and skins;
Leather**

Taoism   299
>> *xx* **Religions**

Tap dancing   793.3
>> *See also* **Clog dancing**
>> *xx* **Dancing**

Tape recorder music.   *See* **Electronic music**

Tape recorders.   *See* **Magnetic recorders and
recordings**

Tapestry   746.3
>> *xx* **Decoration and ornament; Design, Dec-
orative; Interior decoration; Needlework**

Tariff (May subdiv. geog.) **336.2; 382.7**

>*See also* **Free trade and protection; Smuggling**
>
>*x* Customs (Tariff); Duties; Exports; Government regulation of commerce; Imports; Revenue
>
>*xx* **Commerce; Commercial policy; Economic policy; Finance; Free trade and protection; Taxation; Trusts, Industrial**

Tariff—U.S. 336.2; 382.7

>*x* U.S.—Tariff

Tariff question—Free trade and protection.

>*See* **Free trade and protection**

Tartans 391

>*x* Highland costume; Scottish tartans
>
>*xx* **Clans and clan system**

Taste 152.1

>*xx* **Senses and sensation**

Taste (Esthetics). *See* **Esthetics**

Taverns. *See* **Restaurants, bars, etc.**

Tax relations, Intergovernmental. *See* **Intergovernmental tax relations**

Tax sharing. *See* **Intergovernmental tax relations; Revenue sharing**

Taxation (May subdiv. geog.) **336.2**

>*See also* **Assessment; Intergovernmental tax relations; Internal revenue;** also types of taxes, e.g. **Income tax; Inheritance and transfer tax; Sales tax; Tariff; Tithes;** etc.
>
>*x* Direct taxation; Duties; Revenue; Taxes
>
>*xx* **Assessment; Estate planning; Finance; Political science**

Taxation—U.S. 336.2

>*x* U.S.—Taxation

Taxation of income. *See* **Income tax**

Taxation of legacies. *See* **Inheritance and transfer tax**

Taxation of sales. *See* **Sales tax**

Taxes. *See* **Taxation**

Taxidermy 579

>*See also* **Zoological specimens—Collection and preservation;** also names of specimens with the subdivision *Collection and preservation*, e.g. **Birds—Collection and preservation;** etc.
>
>*x* Specimens, Preservation of
>
>*xx* **Zoological specimens—Collection and preservation**

Tea rooms. *See* **Restaurants, bars, etc.**

Teacher training. *See* **Teachers—Training; Teachers colleges**

Teachers 920; 923

>*See also* **Educational associations; Educators; School superintendents and principals; Teaching**
>
>*x* College teachers; Faculty (Education); Professors
>
>*xx* **Education; Educators**

Teachers, Exchange of. *See* **Teachers, Interchange of**

Teachers, Interchange of   370.19

    x Exchange of teachers; Interchange of teachers; Teachers, Exchange of

    xx **Exchange of persons programs; International education**

Teachers—Practice teaching. *See* **Student teaching**

Teachers, Rating of (by students). *See* **Student evaluation of teachers**

Teachers—Training   371.1

    Use for materials dealing with the history and methods of training teachers, including the educational functions of teachers colleges. Materials on the study of education as a science are entered under **Education—Study and teaching.** See note under **Teachers colleges**

    See also **Student teaching; Teachers colleges; Teachers' workshops**

    x Teacher training

    xx **Education—Study and teaching; Teachers colleges; Teaching**

Teachers and parents. *See* **Home and school; Parents' and teachers' associations**

Teachers colleges   378

    Use for general and historical materials about teachers colleges. Materials dealing with their educational functions are entered under **Teachers—Training**

    See also **Teachers—Training;** also names of teachers colleges

    x Normal schools; Teacher training; Training colleges for teachers

    xx **Colleges and universities; Education—Study and teaching; Teachers—Training**

Teachers' institutes. *See* **Teachers' workshops**

Teachers' workshops   371.1

    x Teachers' institutes; Workshops, Teachers'

    xx **Teachers—Training**

Teaching   371.1

    Use for materials on the art and method of teaching

    See also

Classroom management	**Project method in teaching**
Education	**School discipline**
Educational psychology	**School superintendents and principals**
Examinations	**School supervision**
Kindergarten	**Student teaching**
Lectures and lecturing	**Study, Method of**
Montessori method of education	**Teachers—Training**
	Teaching teams

Teaching—*Continued*

> *also* subjects with the subdivision *Study and teaching,* e.g. **Science—Study and teaching;** etc.
>
> *x* Instruction; Pedagogy; School teaching
> *xx* **Education; School administration and organization; Teachers**

Teaching—Aids and devices   371.3

> *See also* **Audio-visual materials; Motion pictures in education; Programmed instruction; Radio in education; Teaching machines; Television in education**

Teaching—Experimental methods. *See* **Education—Experimental methods**

Teaching, Freedom of. *See* **Academic freedom**

Teaching machines   371.39

> *x* Automatic teaching; Tutorial machines
> *xx* **Programmed instruction; Teaching—Aids and devices**

Teaching teams   371.1

> *x* Team teaching
> *xx* **Teaching**

Teachings of Jesus. *See* **Jesus Christ—Teachings**

Team teaching. *See* **Teaching teams**

Tearooms. *See* **Restaurants, bars, etc.**

Technical assistance   309.2; 338.91

> See note under **Economic assistance**
> *See also* **Developing areas; Industrialization**
> *x* Aid to developing areas; Assistance to developing areas; Foreign aid program
> *xx* **Developing areas; Economic assistance; Economic policy; Industrialization; International cooperation; International economic relations**

Technical chemistry. *See* **Chemistry, Technical**

Technical education   370.11; 373.2; 374

> *See also* **Apprentices; Correspondence schools and courses; Employees—Training; Evening and continuation schools; Industrial arts education; Occupational training; Professional education; Retraining, Occupational; School shops; Vocational education;** also technical subjects with the subdivision *Study and teaching,* e.g. **Engineering—Study and teaching;** etc.
> *x* Education, Industrial; Education, Technical; Industrial education; Industrial schools; Technical schools; Trade schools
> *xx* **Education; Education, Higher; Employees—Training; Industrial arts education; Professional education; Technology; Vocational education**

Technical schools. *See* **Technical education**

Technical services (Libraries). *See* **Libraries—Technical services**

Technical terms. *See* **Technology—Dictionaries**

551

Technical writing   808
  x Scientific writing
  xx **Authorship; Technology—Language**
Technique.   *See* subjects with the subdivision
        Technique, e.g. **Painting—Technique;**
        Fiction—Technique
Technology   600
  See also

Building	**Inventions**
Chemistry, Techni-	**Machinery**
cal	**Manufactures**
Engineering	**Mills and millwork**
Industrial arts	**Technical education**

  x Applied science; Arts, Useful; Useful
        arts
  xx **Industrial arts**
Technology—Dictionaries   603
  x Technical terms
Technology—Language   601; 603
  See also **Technical writing**
Technology and civilization   301.24
  See also **Machinery in industry**
  x Civilization and technology
  xx **Civilization**
Teen age.   *See* **Adolescence; Youth**
Teen age consumers.   *See* **Young consumers**
Teen age drinking.   *See* **Alcohol and youth**
Teen agers and alcohol.   *See* **Alcohol and**
        youth
Teen agers and drugs.   *See* **Drugs and youth**
Teeth   611; 617.6
  See also **Dentistry**
  x Anatomy, Dental
  xx **Dentistry**
Teeth—Diseases   617.6
  See also **Water—Fluoridation**
  x Medicine, Dental
Telecommunications   384; 621.38
  See also **Artificial satellites in telecommuni-**
        cation; Broadcasting; Cables, Subma-
        rine;   Intercommunication   systems;
        Interstellar   communications;   Micro-
        wave communication systems; Radio;
        Telegraph; Telephone; Television; also
        subjects with the subdivision *Com-*
        munication systems, e.g. **Astronautics**
        —Communication systems; etc.
  x Electric communication; Mass communi-
        cation
  xx **Communication**
Telegraph   384.1; 621.382
  See also **Cables, Submarine; Cipher and**
        telegraph codes
  xx **Electric   engineering;   Electric   wiring;**
        Electricity; Public utilities; Telecom-
        munication
Telegraph, submarine.   *See* **Cables, Submarine**
Telegraph codes.   *See* **Cipher and telegraph**
        codes
Telekinesis.   *See* **Psycokinesis**

Telepathy. *See* **Thought transference**

Telephone 384.6; 621.385

>   *xx* **Electric engineering; Electric wiring; Electricity; Public utilities; Telecommunication**

Telephone—Directories. *See* names of cities with subdivision *Directories—Telephone,* e.g. **Chicago—Directories—Telephone;** etc.

Telephone counseling. *See* **Hotlines (Telephone counseling)**

Telephone directories. *See* names of cities with subdivision *Directories—Telephone,* e.g. **Chicago—Directories—Telephone;** etc.

Telephotography 778.3

>   *xx* **Photography**

Telescope 522

>   *xx* **Astronomical instruments**

Television 384.55; 621.388

>   *See also* **Closed-circuit television; Color television; Microwave communication systems; Subscription television**
>   *x* TV
>   *xx* **Telecommunication**

Television—Apparatus and supplies 621.388

Television—Broadcasting. *See* **Television broadcasting**

Television, Cable. *See* **Community antenna television**

Television—Censorship 384.55

>   *xx* **Censorship**

Television, Closed-circuit. *See* **Closed-circuit television**

Television, Color. *See* **Color television**

Television—Production and direction 384.55; 791.45

Television—Receivers and reception 621.388

Television—Repairing 621.3888

>   *x* Television repairing

Television, Space. *See* **Television in astronautics**

Television—Stage lighting. *See* **Stage lighting**

Television—Stations. *See* **Television stations**

Television, Subscription. *See* **Subscription television**

Television advertising 659.14

>   *x* Advertising, Television; Commercials, Television; Television commercials
>   *xx* **Advertising**

Television and children 384.5502; 791.4502

>   Use same form for television and other subjects
>   Use for materials dealing with the effect of television on children
>   *See also* **Motion pictures and children**
>   *x* Children and television
>   *xx* **Children; Motion pictures and children**

Television and infrared observation satellite. *See* **Tiros (Meteorological satellite)**

Television and youth 384.5502; 791.4502
    x Youth and television
    xx **Youth**
Television authorship 791.45; 808
    See also **Television plays—Technique**
    x Television writing
    xx **Authorship**
Television broadcasting 384.55
    See also **Community antenna television; Television in education; Television in politics; Television programs; Television scripts; Video tape recorders and recording**
    x Television—Broadcasting
    xx **Broadcasting; Mass media; Radio broadcasting**
Television broadcasting—Vocational guidance 384.55
    xx **Vocational guidance**
Television commercials. *See* **Television advertising**
Television drama. *See* **Television plays**
Television in astronautics 629.4
    x Space television; Television, Space
    xx **Astronautics—Communication systems**
Television in education 371.33
    Use same form for television in other subjects
    See also **Closed-circuit television**
    x Education and television; Educational television
    xx **Audio-visual education; Closed-circuit television; Teaching—Aids and devices; Television broadcasting**
Television in politics 329
    xx **Politics, Practical; Television broadcasting**
Television plays 808.82; 812; etc.
    Use for individual television plays, for collections of plays, and for materials about them. Materials on how to write television plays are entered under **Television plays—Technique**
    x Scenarios; Television drama
    xx **Drama; Television programs; Television scripts**
Television plays—Technique 808.2
    See also **Radio plays—Technique**
    x Playwriting
    xx **Drama—Technique; Radio plays—Technique; Television authorship**
Television programs 791.45
    See also types of television programs and specific programs, e.g. **Television plays;** etc.
    x Programs, Television
    xx **Television broadcasting**
Television repairing. *See* **Television—Repairing**

Television scripts 791.45
> See also **Radio scripts; Television plays**
> *xx* **Radio scripts; Television broadcasting**

Television stations 384.55
> *x* Television—Stations

Television writing. *See* **Television authorship**

Telstar project 791.46
> *x* Bell System Telstar satellite; Project Telstar
> *xx* **Artificial satellites in telecommunication**

Temperament 155.2
> *See also* **Character**
> *xx* **Character; Mind and body; Psychology; Psychology, Physiological**

Temperance 178
> Use for general materials on the temperance question and the temperance movement
>
> *See also*
>
> | | |
> |---|---|
> | **Alcohol—Physiological effect** | **Liquor problem** |
> | | **Narcotic habit** |
> | **Alcoholism** | **Prohibition** |
> | **Liquor industry** | **Stimulants** |
>
> *x* Abstinence; Drunkenness; Intemperance; Intoxication; Total abstinence
> *xx* **Alcohol; Alcoholism; Human behavior; Hygiene; Liquor problem; Prohibition**

Temperature 536
> *See also* **Heat; Low temperatures; Thermometers and thermometry**
> *xx* **Heat; Thermometers and thermometry**

Temperatures, Low. *See* **Low temperatures**

Temples 726
> *See also* **Mosques**
> *xx* **Archeology; Architecture; Architecture, Ancient; Architecture, Asian; Church architecture**

Temporal power of the Pope. *See* **Popes—Temporal power**

Temporary employment. *See* **Employment, Temporary**

Ten commandments 222
> *x* Commandments, Ten; Decalogue

Tenant and landlord. *See* **Landlord and tenant**

Tenant farming. *See* **Farm tenancy**

Tenement houses 301.5
> *See also* **City planning; Housing**
> *xx* **Cities and towns; Houses; Housing; Social problems**

Tennis 796.34
> *x* Lawn tennis
> *xx* **Games**

Tenpins. *See* **Bowling**

Tension (Physiology). *See* **Stress (Physiology)**

Tension (Psychology). *See* **Stress (Psychology)**

Tents 796.54
> *xx* **Camping**

Tenure of land. *See* **Land tenure**

Tenure of office. *See* **Civil service**

Terminal care 616
>   *See also* Life support systems (Medical environment)
>   *x* Dying patient
>   *xx* Death

Terminology. *See* Names; and subjects with the subdivision *Terminology*, e.g. Botany—Terminology; etc.

Terns 598.2
>   *xx* Water birds

Terra cotta 620.1; 693.3
>   *xx* Building materials; Decoration and ornament; Pottery

Terrapins. *See* Turtles

Terrariums 635.9
>   *See also* Gardens, Miniature
>   *x* Vivariums

Terrestrial physics. *See* Geophysics

Territorial waters 341.42
>   *See also* Continental shelf; Maritime law
>   *xx* Continental shelf; Maritime law; Shipping

Terror, Reign of. *See* France—History—Revolution, 1789–1799

Terrorism (May subdiv. geog.) **322.4**
>   *See also* Sabotage
>   *xx* Anarchism and anarchists; Assassination; Insurgency; Political crimes and offenses; Revolutions; Subversive activities

Terrorism—U.S. 322.4
>   *x* U.S.—Terrorism

Test pilots. *See* Air pilots; Airplanes—Testing

Tests. *See* Educational tests and measurements; Examinations; Mental tests

Teutonic peoples 572.9363
>   *See also* Anglo-Saxons
>   *x* Goths; Nordic peoples; Ostrogoths; Saxons; Visigoths
>   *xx* Ethnology

Textbooks 371.32
>   Use for materials about textbooks, not for textbooks of a subject. The latter are entered under the name of subject only, e.g. Arithmetic; Geography; etc.
>   *x* School books

Textile chemistry 677
>   *See also* Dyes and dyeing
>   *x* Chemistry, Textile
>   *xx* Chemistry, Technical; Textile industry

Textile design 746
>   *See also* Textile painting
>   *xx* Commercial art; Design; Design, Decorative

Textile fibers. *See* Fibers

Textile industry 677
>   *See also* Bleaching; Cotton manufacture and trade; Dyes and dyeing; Spinning; Textile chemistry; Textile printing; Weaving; Yarn; also names of

Textile industry—*Continued*
    articles manufactured, e.g. **Carpets; Hosiery;** etc.
  xx **Weaving**
Textile painting 746.6
  xx **Painting; Textile design**
Textile printing 746.6
  x Block printing; Printing, Textile
  xx **Textile industry**
Textiles. *See* **Fabrics**
Theater (May subdiv. geog.) **792**
    Use for materials dealing with the drama as acted on the stage, and with the historical, moral, and religious aspects of the theater. Materials treating of the drama from a literary point of view are entered under **Drama; American drama; English drama;** etc.

  See also

Acting	**Opera**
Actors and actresses	**Pantomimes**
Amateur theatricals	**Passion plays**
Arena theater	**Puppets and puppet**
Ballet	**plays**
Children's plays	**Shadow panto-**
Drama	**mimes and plays**
Dramatic criticism	**Shakespeare, Wil-**
Experimental the-	**liam—Stage his-**
ater	**tory**
Masks (Plays)	**Theaters**
Morality plays	**Vaudeville**
Motion pictures	
Mysteries and mir-	
acle plays	

  x Histrionics; Stage
  xx **Acting; Actors and actresses; Amusements; Drama; Drama in education; Performing arts**
Theater—Little theater movement 792
  x Community theater; Little theater
Theater—Production and direction 792
  See also **Motion picture plays**
  x Directing (Theater); Play direction (Theater); Play production
  xx **Amateur theatricals**
Theater—U.S. 792
  x U.S.—Theater
Theater criticism. *See* **Dramatic criticism**
Theater-in-the-round. *See* **Arena theater**
Theaters 725
    Use for materials dealing only with theater buildings, their architecture, construction, decoration, sanitation, etc.
  x Opera houses; Playhouses
  xx **Architecture; Centers for the performing arts; Theater**
Theaters—Stage lighting. *See* **Stage lighting**
Theaters—Stage setting and scenery 792
  See also **Scene painting**

Theaters—Stage setting and scenery—*Continued*
  x Scenery (Stage); Stage scenery; Stage setting; Theatrical scenery
Theatrical costume. *See* **Costume**
Theatrical makeup. *See* **Makeup, Theatrical**
Theatrical scenery. *See* **Theaters—Stage setting and scenery**
Theatricals, Amateur. *See* **Amateur theatricals**
Theatricals, College. *See* **College and school drama**
Thefts, Art. *See* **Art thefts**
Theism 211
  See also **Atheism; Christianity; Deism; God; Pantheism**
  xx **Atheism; Deism; God; Pantheism; Philosophy; Rationalism; Religion; Theology**
Theological education. *See* **Theology—Study and teaching**
Theology 201; 230
  See also

Atheism	**Natural theology**
Atonement	**Pantheism**
Baptism	**Predestination**
Christianity	**Providence and**
Church	**government of**
Conversion	**God**
Creeds	**Religion**
Deism	**Religion and sci-**
Eschatology	**ence**
Ethics	**Revelation**
Faith	**Sacraments**
God (Christianity)	**Sacrifice**
Good and evil	**Salvation**
Grace (Theology)	**Sanctification**
Holy Spirit	**Sin**
Immortality	**Spiritual life**
Liturgies	**Theism**
Man (Theology)	**Trinity**
Mysticism	**Worship**

  xx **Christianity; Creation; God (Christianity); Religion**
Theology, Devotional. *See* **Devotional exercises; Prayers**
Theology, Doctrinal 230; 240
  x Christian doctrine; Doctrinal theology; Dogmatic theology
Theology, Natural. *See* **Natural theology**
Theology, Pastoral. *See* **Pastoral work**
Theology—Philosophy. *See* **Christianity—Philosophy**
Theology—Study and teaching 201.07; 230.7
  See also **Catechisms; Christian education; Church and education; Religious education**
  x Education, Theological; Religion—Study and teaching; Theological education
  xx **Christian education; Church and education; Religious education**

Theoretical chemistry. *See* **Chemistry, Physical and theoretical**

Theory of numbers. *See* **Number theory**

Theory of sets. *See* **Set theory**

Theory of structures. *See* **Structures, Theory of**

Theosophy 147; 212
See also **Buddhism; Gnosticism; Reincarnation; Yoga**
xx **Buddhism; Religion; Religions**

Therapeutics 615
See also

Antiseptics	**Materia medica**
Chemistry, Medical and pharmaceutical	**Medicine**
	Nursing
	Nutrition
Diet in disease	**Stimulants**
Drugs	**X rays**
Electrotherapeutics	

also names of diseases and groups of diseases, e.g. **Smallpox; Fever; Nervous System—Diseases;** etc.; names of drugs, e.g. **Narcotics;** etc.; and names of types of therapy, e.g. **Hydrotherapy; Occupational therapy; Phototherapy; Physical therapy; Radiotherapy;** etc.
x Therapy
xx **Materia medica; Medicine—Practice; Pathology**

Therapeutics, Suggestive 615
See also **Faith healing; Hypnotism; Mental healing; Mental suggestion; New Thought; Psychology, Pastoral; Psychotherapy; Subconsciousness**
x Suggestive therapeutics
xx **Faith healing; Hypnotism; Mental healing; Mental suggestion; Psychotherapy**

Therapy. *See* **Therapeutics**

Thermal insulation. *See* **Insulation (Heat)**

Thermal waters. *See* **Geothermal resources**

Thermoaerodynamics. *See* **Aerothermodynamics**

Thermodynamics 536
See also **Aerothermodynamics; Heat; Heat engines; Heat pumps; Quantum theory;** also subjects with the subdivision *Thermodynamics,* e.g. **Space vehicles —Thermodynamics;** etc.
xx **Chemistry, Physical and theoretical; Dynamics; Heat; Heat engines; Physics; Quantum theory**

Thermometers and thermometry 536
See also **Temperature**
xx **Heat; Meteorological instruments; Temperature**

Thermonuclear bomb. *See* **Hydrogen bomb**

Thesauri. *See* **Subject headings;** also subjects with the subdivision *Synonyms and*

Thesauri—*Continued*

    antonyms, e.g. **English language—Synonyms and antonyms**

Theses. *See* **Dissertations, Academic**

Thieves. *See* **Robbers and outlaws**

Think tanks. *See* **Problem solving, Group**

Thinking. *See* **Thought and thinking**

Third parties (U.S. politics) 329

Third world. *See* **Developing areas**

Thirteenth century 901.92; 909.07

    See note under **Nineteenth century**

    xx **Europe—History—476–1492; Middle Ages**

Thirty Years' War, 1618–1648 909.08; 940.2

    xx **Europe—History—1492–1789; Germany —History—1517–1740**

Thoroughfares. *See* **Roads; Streets**

Thought and thinking 153.4

    See also **Attention; Intellect; Logic; Memory; Perception; Reasoning**

    x Thinking

    xx **Educational psychology; Intellect; Logic; Psychology**

Thought transference 133.8

    See also **Clairvoyance; Extrasensory perception; Hypnotism; Mental suggestion; Mind reading**

    x Mental telepathy; Telepathy

    xx **Clairvoyance; Mind reading; Psychical research; Subconsciousness**

Thrift. *See* **Saving and thrift**

Throat 612

    See also **Voice**

Thunderstorms 551.5

    See also **Lightning**

    xx **Meteorology; Storms**

Tidal waves. *See* **Ocean waves**

Tides 525

    xx **Astronomy; Moon; Navigation; Oceanography; Physical geography**

Tie dyeing 667

    xx **Dyes and dyeing**

Tiles 620.1; 693.3; 738.6

    xx **Bricks; Building materials; Ceramics; Clay industries; Pottery**

Timber. *See* **Forests and forestry; Lumber and lumbering; Trees; Wood**

Time 529

    See also **Calendars; Clocks and watches; Periodicity; Sundials**

    x Standard time

    xx **Longitude; Periodicity**

Time and space. *See* **Space and time**

Time study 658.5

    See also **Motion study**

    xx **Efficiency, Industrial; Factory management; Job analysis; Motion study; Personnel management**

Tin 669

    See also **Pewter**

Tinwork 671
    xx **Metalwork**
Tires 678
    x Rubber tires
    xx **Wheels**
Tiros (Meteorological satellite) 551.6
    x TIROS (Meteorological satellite); Television and infrared observation satellite
    xx **Meteorological satellites**
Tissues—Transplantation. *See* **Transplantation of organs, tissues, etc.**
Tithes 254.8
    xx **Church finance; Ecclesiastical law; Taxation**
Toadstools. *See* **Mushrooms**
Toasts 808.5; 808.85
    See also **After-dinner speeches**
    x Healths, Drinking of
    xx **After-dinner speeches; Epigrams; Speeches, addresses, etc.**
Tobacco 633
    See also **Smoking**
    xx **Smoking**
Tobacco habit 178; 613.8; 616.8
    xx **Smoking**
Tobacco pipes 688
    x Pipes, Tobacco
    xx **Smoking**
Toes. *See* **Foot**
Toilet preparations. *See* **Cosmetics**
Toleration 301.6
    See also **Academic freedom; Discrimination; Freedom of conscience; Religious freedom**
    x Bigotry; Intolerance
    xx **Discrimination; Human relations**
Toll roads. *See* **Express highways**
Tombs 726
    See also **Brasses; Catacombs; Cemeteries; Epitaphs; Mounds and mound builders**
    x Burial; Graves; Mausoleums; Rock tombs; Sepulchers; Vaults (Sepulchral)
    xx **Archeology; Architecture; Cemeteries; Monuments; Shrines**
Tools 621.9
    See also **Agricultural machinery; Carpentry—Tools; Machine tools; Machinery; Power tools;** also names of specific tools, e.g. **Saws;** etc.
    x Implements, utensils, etc.
Topographical drawing 526
    See also **Map drawing**
    xx **Drawing; Map drawing; Surveying**
Topology 512
    See also **Algebras, Linear**
    x Analysis situs; Position analysis; Rubber sheet geometry
    xx **Algebras, Linear; Geometry; Set theory**

Tories, American. *See* **American Loyalists**
Tornadoes 551.5
    See also **Cyclones; Storms**
    xx **Meteorology; Storms; Winds**
Torpedoes 623.4
    xx **Explosives; Naval art and science; Submarine warfare**
Tort liability of professions. *See* **Malpractice**
Tortoises. *See* **Turtles**
Total abstinence. *See* **Temperance**
Totalitarianism 321.9
    See also **Communism; Dictators; Fascism; National socialism**
    x Authoritarianism
Totems and totemism 299
    xx **Ethnology; Indians of North America—Religion; Mythology**
Touch 152.1; 612
    x Feeling
    xx **Senses and sensation**
Tourism. *See* **Tourist trade**
Tourist accommodations. *See* **Hotels, motels, etc.; Youth hostels**
Tourist trade 910.2
    See also **Travel**
    x Tourism
    xx **Travel**
Town life. *See* **City life**
Town meeting. *See* **Local government**
Town planning. *See* **City planning**
Towns. *See* **Cities and towns**
Township government. *See* **Local government**
Toxic substances. *See* **Poisons**
Toys 688.7
    See also **Dollhouses; Dolls; Electric toys**
    x Miniature objects
    xx **Amusements**
Track and field. *See* **Track athletics**
Track athletics 796.4
    See also **Walking**
    x Cross-country running; Field athletics; Running; Track and field
    xx **Athletics; College sports**
Tracking and trailing 799.2-799.3
    x Trailing
    xx **Animals—Habits and behavior; Hunting**
Tracking of satellites. *See* **Artificial satellites—Tracking; Space vehicles—Tracking**
Traction engines. *See* **Tractors**
Tractors 629.22; 631.5
    x Traction engines
    xx **Agricultural machinery; Farm engines**
Trade. *See* **Business; Commerce**
Trade, Boards of. *See* **Chambers of commerce**
Trade agreements (Labor). *See* **Arbitration, Industrial; Labor contract**
Trade and professional associations 380.6; 650.6
    Use for materials on business or professional organizations whose aim is the

Trade and professional associations—*Continued*
protection or advancement of their common interests without regard to the relations of employer and employee
  x Professional associations
  xx **Associations**
Trade barriers. *See* **Commercial policy**
Trade fairs. *See* **Fairs**
Trade routes 387
  x Ocean routes; Routes of trade; Sea routes
  xx **Commerce; Geography, Commercial; Transportation**
Trade schools. *See* **Technical education**
Trade unions. *See* **Labor unions**
Trade waste. *See* **Industrial wastes; Waste products**
Trademarks 341.7
  See also **Patents**
  x Brand names; Company symbols; Corporate symbols
  xx **Commerce; Manufactures; Patents**
Trades. *See* **Industrial arts; Occupations**
Traditions. *See* **Folklore; Legends; Superstition**
Traffic, City. *See* **City traffic**
Traffic accidents 388.3
  x Automobile accidents; Automobiles—Accidents; Highway accidents
  xx **Accidents; Traffic regulations**
Traffic engineering 388
  Use for materials on the planning of the flow of traffic and related topics, largely as they concern street transportation in cities and metropolitan areas
  See also **Car pools; City traffic; Express highways; Local transit**
  x Street traffic
  xx **Highway engineering; Transportation**
Traffic regulations 388
  See also **Automobiles—Law and legislation; Traffic accidents**
  x Street traffic
  xx **Automobiles—Law and legislation; Transportation**
Tragedy 792.1
  xx **Drama**
Trailer parks 796.54
  See also **Mobile home parks**
  xx **Campgrounds**
Trailers. *See* **Automobiles—Trailers; Travel trailers and campers**
Trailers, Home. *See* **Mobile homes**
Trailing. *See* **Tracking and trailing**
Train wrecks. *See* **Railroads—Accidents**
Trained nurses. *See* **Nurses**

563

Training, Occupational. *See* **Occupational training**

Training, Vocational. *See* **Occupational training**

Training camps, Military. *See* **Military training camps**

Training colleges for teachers. *See* **Teachers colleges**

Training of animals. *See* **Animals–Training**

Training of employees. *See* **Employees–Training**

Trains, Railroad. *See* **Railroads**

Tramps 301.44
> *See also* **Begging**
> *x* Hoboes; Vagabonds; Vagrants
> *xx* **Begging**

Trams. *See* **Street railroads**

Transactional analysis 301.11
> *xx* **Human relations**

Transatlantic flights. *See* **Aeronautics–Flights**

Transcendental meditation 294
> *xx* **Meditation**

Transcendentalism 141
> *See also* **Idealism**
> *xx* **Idealism; Philosophy**

Transcontinental journeys (U.S.). *See* **Overland journeys to the Pacific (U.S.)**

Transexuality 612.6
> *x* Change of sex; Sex change
> *xx* **Sex**

Transfer tax. *See* **Inheritance and transfer tax**

Transformers, Electric. *See* **Electric transformers**

Transistors 621.3815
> *xx* **Electronics; Semiconductors**

Transit systems. *See* **Local transit;** and names of cities and metropolitan areas with the subdivision *Transit systems*, e.g. **Chicago–Transit systems; Chicago metropolitan area–Transit systems;** etc.

Translating and interpreting 418
> *x* Interpreting and translating; Machine translating; Mechanical translating
> *xx* **Language and languages**

Transmission of power. *See* **Electric lines; Electric power distribution; Power transmission**

Transmissions, Automobiles. *See* **Automobiles –Transmission devices**

Transmutation (Chemistry) 546; 547
> Use for modern discussions on the transmutation of metals. Materials that treat of the medieval attempts to transmute baser metals into gold are entered under **Alchemy**
> *See also* **Cyclotron**
> *x* Metals, Transmutation of; Transmutation of metals

Transmutation (Chemistry)—*Continued*

xx **Alchemy; Atoms; Nuclear physics; Radioactivity**

Transmutation of metals. *See* **Transmutation (Chemistry);** for early works on transmutation of metals see **Alchemy**

Transplantation of organs, tissues, etc. 617

See also **Surgery, Plastic;** also names of organs of the body with the subdivision *Transplantation*, e.g. **Heart—Transplantation;** etc.

x Medical transplantation; Organ transplantation; Prosthesis; Surgical transplantation; Tissues—Transplantation

xx **Preservation of organs, tissues, etc.; Surgery**

Transplantation of organs, tissues, etc.—Moral and religious aspects

xx **Bioethics**

Transportation 380

Use for general materials on the transportation of persons or goods

See also

Aeronautics, Commercial	**Ocean travel**
Automobiles	**Postal service**
Bridges	**Railroads**
Buses	**Roads**
Canals	**Shipping**
Car pools	**Steam navigation**
Carriages and carts	**Steamboats**
Commerce	**Street railroads**
Electric railroads	**Streets**
Express service	**Subways**
Freight and freightage	**Trade routes**
Harbors	**Traffic engineering**
Inland navigation	**Traffic regulations**
Local transit	**Trucks**
Merchant marine	**Vehicles**
	Waterways

also subjects with the subdivision *Transportation*, e.g. **School children—Transportation; World War, 1939–1945—Transportation;** etc.

x Locomotion

xx **Commerce**

Transportation, Highway 388.3

See also **Automobiles; Buses; Trucks**

x Highway transportation

Transportation, Military 355.8

See also **Vehicles, Military**

x Military motorization; Military transportation; Motorization, Military

xx **Military art and science**

Transvaal War, 1899–1902. *See* **South African War, 1899–1902**

Trapping 639

See also **Fur trade; Game and game birds; Hunting**

xx **Game and game birds; Hunting**

Travel 910.2

Use for the enjoyment of travel, advice to travelers, etc. Descriptions of actual voyages are entered under **Voyages and travels** or under names of places with the subdivision *Description and travel*

See also **Automobiles—Touring; Health resorts, spas, etc.; Ocean travel; Tourist trade; Voyages and travels; Voyages around the world;** also names of countries, states, etc. with the subdivision *Description and travel,* e.g. **U.S.—Description and travel;** etc.

xx **Manners and customs; Tourist trade; Voyages and travels**

Travel trailers and campers 629.22

See also **Mobile homes; Vans**

x Campers and trailers; House trailers; Pickup campers; Trailers

xx **Automobiles—Trailers; Camping; Recreational vehicles**

Travelers (May subdiv. geog. adjective form, e.g. **Travelers, German;** etc.) **920; 923**

See also **Explorers**

x Voyagers

xx **Explorers; Voyages and travels**

Travelers, American 920; 923

x American travelers; U.S.—Travelers

Travelers. *See* **Overland journeys to the Pacific (U.S.); Scientific expeditions; Voyages and travels; Voyages around the world;** and names of countries, states, etc. with the subdivision *Description and travel,* e.g. **U.S.—Description and travel;** etc.

Travesties. *See* **Parodies**

Tray gardens. *See* **Gardens, Miniature**

Treason 364.1

x Collaborationists; High treason

xx **Crime; Political crimes and offenses**

Treasure-trove. *See* **Buried treasure**

Treaties 341.1; 341.6

Names of treaties are not included in this list but are to be added as needed, e.g. **Versailles, Treaty of, 1919;** etc.

See also **Arbitration, International;** also names of treaties (e.g. **North Atlantic Treaty, 1949; Versailles, Treaty of, 1919;** etc.); and names of countries with the subdivision *Foreign relations —Treaties,* e.g. **U.S.—Foreign relations—Treaties;** etc.

xx **Congresses and conventions; Diplomacy; International law; International relations**

Tree planting 635.9

See also **Reforestation; Trees; Windbreaks**

x Planting

Tree planting—*Continued*
  xx **Forests and forestry; Reforestation; Trees**
Trees (May subdiv. geog.) **582; 635.9**
  Use for materials on the structure, care, characteristics and use of trees
  Names of trees are not included in this list but are to be added as needed, in the singular form, e.g. **Oak;** etc.
  See also

Dwarf trees	**Nurseries (Horti-**
Evergreens	**culture)**
Forests and forestry	**Nuts**
Fruit culture	**Plant lore**
Grafting	**Plants**
Landscape garden-	**Pruning**
ing	**Shrubs**
Leaves	**Tree planting**
Lumber and lum-	**Wood**
bering	

  also names of trees, e.g. **Oak;** etc.
  x Arboriculture; Timber
  xx **Botany; Forests and forestry; Landscape gardening; Tree planting**
Trees—U.S. 582
  x U.S.—Trees
Trees in art. *See* **Plants in art**
Trent Affair, 1861 973.7
  xx **U.S.—History—Civil War, 1861–1865**
Trial by jury. *See* **Jury**
Trial by publicity. *See* **Freedom of the press and fair trial**
Trial marriage. *See* **Unmarried couples**
Trials 345.7; 347.7
  See also **Courts martial and courts of inquiry; Crime**
  xx **Crime; Criminal law**
Tricks 793.8
  See also **Card tricks; Magic**
  xx **Magic**
Tricycles. *See* **Bicycles and bicycling**
Trigonometry 516
  x Plane trigonometry; Spherical trigonometry
  xx **Geometry; Mathematics**
Trigonometry—Tables, etc. 516.02
  See also **Logarithms**
  x Tables (Systematic lists)
  xx **Mathematics—Tables, etc.**
Trinity 231
  See also **God (Christianity); Holy Spirit; Jesus Christ**
  xx **God (Christianity); Holy Spirit; Jesus Christ; Jesus Christ—Divinity; Theology; Unitarianism**
Tripoline War. *See* **U.S.—History—Tripolitan War, 1801–1805**
Trolley cars. *See* **Street railroads**
Tropical diseases. *See* **Tropics—Diseases and hygiene**

567

Tropical fish 597
  xx Fishes
Tropical medicine. *See* **Tropics—Diseases and hygiene**
Tropical rain forests. *See* **Rain forests**
Tropics
  See also subjects with the subdivision *Tropics,* e.g. **Agriculture—Tropics**; etc.
  x Jungles
Tropics—Diseases and hygiene 616
  See also names of tropical diseases, e.g. **Sleeping sickness; Yellow fever**; etc.
  x Diseases, Tropical; Medicine, Tropical; Tropical diseases; Tropical medicine
Troubadours 920; 928
  xx **French poetry; Minstrels; Poets; Scalds and scaldic poetry**
Trout fishing 799.1
  xx **Fishing**
Truancy (Schools). *See* **School attendance**
Truck farming. *See* **Vegetable gardening**
Trucks 629.22
  See also **Materials handling**; also names of specific makes and models
  x Automobile trucks; Motor trucks
  xx **Automobiles; Materials handling; Transportation; Transportation, Highway**
Trust companies 338.8; 658
  See also **Banks and banking; Investment trusts**
  x Companies, Trust
  xx **Banks and banking; Business; Corporations**
Trusts, Industrial 338.8; 658
  See also **Antitrust law; Capitalism; Competition; Corporations; Interstate commerce; Monopolies; Railroads—Consolidation; Tariff**
  x Business combinations; Cartels; Combinations, Industrial; Industrial combinations; Industrial mergers; Industrial trusts; Mergers, Industrial
  xx **Capital; Commerce; Competition; Corporation law; Corporations; Economics; Monopolies**
Trusts, Industrial—Law and legislation. *See* **Antitrust law**
Truth 111.8
  See also **Agnosticism; Knowledge, Theory of; Pragmatism; Reality; Skepticism; Truthfulness and falsehood**
  x Certainty
  xx **Belief and doubt; Faith; Knowledge, Theory of; Philosophy; Pragmatism; Skepticism**
Truth in advertising. *See* **Advertising, Fraudulent**
Truthfulness and falsehood 177
  See also **Honesty**

568

Truthfulness and falsehood—*Continued*
　x Credibility; Falsehood; Lying; Untruth
　xx **Honesty; Human behavior; Truth**
Tuberculosis 616.9
　xx **Lungs—Diseases**
Tugboats 623.82
Tuition. *See* **College costs; Colleges and universities—Finance; Education—Finance**
Tumbling 796.4
　xx **Acrobats and acrobatics**
Tumors 616.9
　See also **Cancer**
Tuning 681; 781.9
　See also names of instruments with the subdivision *Tuning,* e.g. **Piano—Tuning;** etc.
　xx **Musical instruments**
Tunnels 624
　See also **Boring; Excavation; Subways**
　xx **Civil engineering**
Turbines 621.2; 621.4
　See also **Gas turbines; Steam turbines**
　xx **Engines; Hydraulic engineering; Hydraulic machinery; Wheels**
Turkeys 636.5
　xx **Poultry**
Turning 621.9
　See also **Lathes; Woodwork**
　x Lathe work; Wood turning
　xx **Carpentry; Lathes; Woodwork**
Turnpikes (Modern). *See* **Express highways**
Turtles 598.1
　x Terrapins; Tortoises
　xx **Reptiles**
Tutorial machines. *See* **Teaching machines**
Twentieth century 901.94; 909.82
　See note under **Nineteenth century**
　xx **History, Modern—20th century**
Twenty-first century 901.94; 909.83
Twins 618.2
　xx **Birth, Multiple**
Type and type founding 686.2
　See also **Advertising layout and typography; Initials; Linotype; Printing—Specimens; Typesetting**
　xx **Founding; Initials; Printing; Printing—Specimens; Typesetting**
Type specimens. *See* **Printing—Specimens**
Typesetting 686.2
　See also **Linotype; Printing; Type and type founding**
　x Composition (Printing)
　xx **Printing; Type and type founding**
Typewriters 652.3; 681
　xx **Office equipment and supplies**
Typewriting 652.3
　xx **Business education; Writing**
Typhoid fever 616.9
　x Enteric fever

Typhoons   551.5

    See note under **Cyclones**

    xx **Storms; Winds**

Typography.   *See* **Printing**

U boats.   *See* **Submarines**

UFO.   *See* **Flying saucers**

UHF radio.   *See* **Radio, Short wave**

U.N.   *See* **United Nations**

USSR.   *See* **Russia**

Ultrahigh frequency radio.   *See* **Radio, Short wave**

Ultrasonic waves   534.5

    x Supersonic waves; Waves, Ultrasonic

    xx **Sound waves; Ultrasonics**

Ultrasonics   534.5

    See also **Ultrasonic waves**

    x Inaudible sound; Supersonics

    xx **Sound**

Ultraviolet rays   535

    x Rays, Ultra-violet

    xx **Electromagnetic waves; Phototherapy; Radiation; Radiotherapy; Spectrum**

Umbrellas and parasols   391; 685

    x Parasols

Unbelief.   *See* **Skepticism**

Unconventional warfare.   *See* **Guerrilla warfare**

Undenominational churches.   *See* **Community churches**

Under water exploration.   *See* **Underwater exploration**

Underdeveloped areas.   *See* **Developing areas**

Undergraduates.   *See* **College students**

Underground, Anticommunist.   *See* **Anticommunist movements**

Underground films.   *See* **Experimental films**

Underground literature   809

    See also **Underground press**

Underground movements (World War, 1939–1945).   *See* **World War, 1939–1945—Underground movements**

Underground press   070.4

    x Alternative press; Press; Press, Underground

    xx **Underground literature**

Underground railroad   326

    See also **Slavery in the U.S.**

    xx **Slavery in the U.S.**

Underground railroads.   *See* **Subways**

Underprivileged.   *See* **Socially handicapped**

Underprivileged children.   *See* **Socially handicapped children**

Undersea exploration.   *See* **Underwater exploration**

Undersea research habitats.   *See* **Undersea research stations**

Undersea research stations   551.4

    See also **Aquanauts;** and names of special research projects and stations, e.g. **Sealab project;** etc.

Undersea research stations—*Continued*

    x Manned undersea research stations; Sea laboratories; Submarine research stations; Undersea research habitats; Underwater research stations

    xx **Oceanography—Research; Skin diving; Submersibles; Underwater exploration**

Undersea technology. *See* **Oceanography**

Undersea vehicles. *See* **Submersibles**

Understanding. *See* **Intellect; Knowledge, Theory of**

Undertakers and undertaking 393

    x Funeral directors; Morticians

Underwater exploration 551.4; 627.7

    See also **Aquanauts; Diving, Submarine; Marine biology; Skin diving; Submersibles; Undersea research stations**

    x Exploration, Submarine; Exploration, Underwater; Submarine exploration; Under water exploration; Undersea exploration

    xx **Adventure and adventurers; Diving, Submarine; Oceanography—Research; Skin diving**

Underwater exploration devices. *See* **Submersibles**

Underwater geology. *See* **Submarine geology**

Underwater medicine. *See* **Submarine medicine**

Underwater photography. *See* **Photography, Submarine**

Underwater physiology. *See* **Submarine medicine**

Underwater research stations. *See* **Undersea research stations**

Underwater swimming. *See* **Skin diving**

Underwriting. *See* **Insurance**

Unemployed 331.1

    See also **Economic assistance, Domestic; Employment, Part time; Employment agencies; Insurance, Unemployment; Labor supply; Migrant labor; Retraining, Occupational**

    x Unemployment

    xx **Charities; Economic assistance, Domestic; Labor and laboring classes; Labor supply; Poor; Public welfare; Social problems; Sociology**

Unemployment. *See* **Unemployed**

Unemployment insurance. *See* **Insurance, Unemployment**

Unfair competition. *See* **Competition, Unfair**

Ungraded schools. *See* **Nongraded schools**

Unicameral legislatures. *See* **Legislative bodies**

Unicorns 398.2

    xx **Animals, Mythical**

Unidentified flying objects. *See* **Flying saucers**

Uniforms, Military   355.1

    x Costume, Military; Military costume; Military uniforms; Naval uniforms; Uniforms, Naval

    xx **Costume; Tailoring**

Uniforms, Naval.   *See* **Uniforms, Military**

Union churches.   *See* **Community churches**

Union of South Africa.   *See* **South Africa**

Union shop.   *See* **Open and closed shop**

Unions, Labor.   *See* **Labor unions**

Unison speaking.   *See* **Choral speaking**

Unitarianism   288

    See also **Jesus Christ—Divinity; Trinity**

    xx **Congregationalism; Jesus Christ—Divinity**

United Brethren.   *See* **Moravians**

United Kingdom.   *See* **Great Britain**

United Methodist Church (U.S.)   287

    xx **Protestant churches; Sects**

United Nations   341.23

    x U.N.

    xx **Arbitration, International; International cooperation; International organization**

United Nations—Armed Forces   341.23

    x Peace keeping forces

United Nations—Finance   341.23

United Nations—Officials and employees   341.23

    x Employees and officials; Officials

United Nations—Yearbooks   341.2305

    x Annuals

    xx **Yearbooks**

United States   917.3; 973

    The abbreviation U.S. may be used when followed by a subdivision

    The subject subdivisions under this heading may be used under the name of any country or region, with the exception of the period divisions of history. For subdivisions that may be used under names of states, see **Ohio**; under names of cities, see **Chicago**

    Most of these subdivisions are examples of the directions given in the general references under various headings throughout the list. *See* references are supplied more liberally than any library may need but they were included here in order to show what subjects are given geographic treatment, not only as a subdivision under the name of a country, but also as a heading subdivided by name of country or by national adjective

    Corporate entries, that is those official bodies which may be used also as author entries, are included only when they have been used as examples or as references or when they are subdivided by subject. Corporate entries are dis-

United States—*Continued*

tinguished by using a period between
parts instead of the dash, e.g. **U.S.
Army**

See also names of regions of the U.S. and
groups of states, e.g. **Atlantic States;
Gulf States; Middle West; Mississippi
Valley; New England; Northwest, Old;
Northwest, Pacific; Oregon Trail;
Southern States; Southwest, New;
Southwest, Old; The West (U.S.);** etc.
and headings beginning with the word
American

U.S.—Actors and actresses. *See* **Actors and
actresses, American**

U.S.—Agriculture. *See* **Agriculture—U.S.**

U.S.—Air—Pollution. *See* **Air—Pollution—
U.S.**

U.S.—Animals. *See* **Animals—U.S.**

U.S.–Antiquities 917.3; 973

See also **Indians of North America—Antiquities**

x Antiquities; Prehistory

xx **Archeology; Man, Prehistoric**

U.S.–Appropriations and expenditures 351.7

xx **Budget–U.S.**

U.S.—Architecture. *See* **Architecture, American**

U.S.—Archives. *See* **Archives—U.S.**

U.S.–Armed Forces 355

See also official names of branches of the
Armed Forces, e.g. **U.S. Army; U.S.
Navy;** etc.

x Armed forces; Military forces

U.S. Army 355

Subdivisions used under this subject may
be used under armies of other countries

x Army

xx **Armies; Military history; U.S.—Armed
Forces**

**U.S. Army–Appointments and retirements
355.1**

x U.S. Army—Retirements

U.S. Army–Biography 920; 923

x Military biography

U.S. Army–Chaplains 355.3; 920; 922

xx **Chaplains**

U.S. Army—Crimes and misdemeanors. *See*
Military offenses—U.S.

U.S. Army–Demobilization 355.2

U.S. Army—Desertions. *See* **Desertion, Military—U.S.**

U.S. Army—Enlistment. *See* **U.S. Army—Recruiting, enlistment, etc.**

U.S. Army–Examinations 355.1

x Army tests

U.S. Army–Handbooks, manuals, etc. 355.02

x Soldiers' handbooks; U.S. Army—Of-

573

U.S. Army–Handbooks, manuals, etc.
—Continued
　　　　ficers' handbooks; U.S. Army—Sol-
　　　　diers' handbooks
U.S. Army–Insignia 355.1
　xx **Insignia**
U.S. Army–Medals, badges, decorations, etc.
　　355.1
　xx **Insignia; Medals**
U.S. Army–Military life 355.1
　x Army life; Military life; Soldiers' life
　xx **Soldiers**
U.S. Army—Music. *See* **U.S. Army–Songs**
　　and music
U.S. Army–Officers 355.3
U.S. Army—Officers' handbooks. *See* **U.S.**
　　Army–Handbooks, manuals, etc.
U.S. Army–Ordnance and ordnance stores
　　355.8
　xx **Ordnance**
U.S. Army–Parachute troops 356
　x U.S.—Parachute troops
　xx **Parachute troops**
U.S. Army–Recruiting, enlistment, etc. 355.2
　x Enlistment; Recruiting and enlistment;
　　　U.S. Army—Enlistment
U.S. Army—Retirements. *See* **U.S. Army–**
　　Appointments and retirements
U.S. Army—Soldiers' handbooks. *See* **U.S.**
　　Army–Handbooks, manuals, etc.
U.S. Army–Songs and music 784.7
　x U.S. Army—Music
U.S.—Art. *See* **Art, American**
U.S.—Art industries and trade. *See* **Art indus-**
　　tries and trade–U.S.
U.S.—Artificial satellites. *See* **Artificial satel-**
　　lites, American
U.S.—Artists. *See* **Artists, American**
U.S.—Astronautics. *See* **Astronautics–U.S.**
U.S.—Atlases. *See* **U.S.–Maps**
U.S.—Authors. *See* **Authors, American**
U.S.—Ballads. *See* **Ballads, American**
U.S.—Banks and banking. *See* **Banks and**
　　banking–U.S.
U.S.–Bibliography 015.73; 016.973
　xx **Bibliography**
U.S.—Bicentennial celebrations. *See* **Ameri-**
　　can Revolution Bicentennial, 1776–
　　1976
U.S.–Bio-bibliography 016.973; 920.03
　x Bio-bibliography
US.–Biography 920
　xx **Biography**
U.S.–Biography–Dictionaries 920.03
　xx **Dictionaries**
U.S.–Biography–Portraits 920.022; 920.03
　x U.S.—History—Portraits
　xx **Portraits**
U.S.—Birds. *See* **Birds–U.S.**
U.S.—Botany. *See* **Botany–U.S.**

U.S.—Boundaries 917.3; 973
    xx **Boundaries**
U.S.—Budget. *See* **Budget—U.S.**
U.S.—Campaign funds. *See* **Campaign funds —U.S.**
U.S.—Cathedrals. *See* **Cathedrals—U.S.**
U.S.—Census 317.3; 351.8
    xx **Census**
U.S.—Centennial celebrations, etc. 351.8
    See also **American Revolution Bicentennial, 1776–1976**
U.S.—Child labor. *See* **Child labor—U.S.**
U.S.—Christmas. *See* **Christmas—U.S.**
U.S.—Church history 277.3
    See also **U.S.—Religion**
    x U.S.—Religious history
    xx **Church history; U.S.—Religion**
U.S.—Churches. *See* **Churches—U.S.**
U.S.—Cities and towns. *See* **Cities and towns —U.S.**
U.S.—City planning. *See* **City planning—U.S.**
U.S.—Civil service. *See* **Civil service—U.S.**
U.S.—Civilization 917.3
    x American civilization
    xx **Civilization**
U.S.—Civilization—Foreign influences 917.3
U.S.—Civilization—1960–1970 917.3
U.S.—Civilization—1970– 917.3
U.S.—Climate 551.6
    xx **Climate; Weather**
U.S.—Collective settlements. *See* **Collective settlements—U.S.**
U.S.—Colleges and universities. *See* **Colleges and universities—U.S.**
U.S.—Colonies 325.73; 973
    x U.S.—Insular possessions; U.S.—Territories and possessions
    xx **Colonies**
U.S.—Commerce 381
    xx **Commerce**
U.S.—Commercial policy 338.973; 381
    xx **Commercial policy; Economic policy**
U.S.—Communism. *See* **Communism—U.S.**
U.S.—Composers. *See* **Composers, American**
U.S. Congress 328.73
    x Congress—U.S.
    xx **Legislative bodies**
U.S. Congress. House 328.73; 342.5
    x Representatives—U.S.
U.S. Congress. Senate 328.73; 342.5
    x Senators—U.S.
U.S. Constitution 342
    x Constitution
    xx **Constitutions; Political science**
U.S. Constitution—Amendments 342.2
    x Bill of rights; Constitutional amendments—U.S.
U.S.—Constitutional history 342.2
    xx **Constitutional history; U.S.—History; U.S.—History—1783–1809**

U.S.—Constitutional law 342

   xx **Constitutional law**

U.S.—Consular service. *See* **U.S.—Diplomatic and consular service**

U.S.—Country life. *See* **Country life—U.S.**

U.S.—Courts. *See* **Courts—U.S.**

U.S.—Crime. *See* **Crime—U.S.**

U.S.—Dancing. *See* **Dancing—U.S.**

U.S.—Debts, Public. *See* **Debts, Public—U.S.**

U.S. Declaration of Independence 973.3

   x Declaration of Independence; Signers of the Declaration of Independence

   xx **U.S.—History—Revolution, 1775–1783**

U.S.—Decoration and ornament. *See* **Decoration and ornament, American**

U.S.—Defenses 355.4

   x Defenses, National; National defenses

   xx **Fortification**

U.S.—Demonstrations. *See* **Demonstrations—U.S.**

U.S.—Description and travel 917.3

   x Description; Journeys; Travels

   xx **Discoveries (in geography); Explorers; Geography; Travel; Voyages and travels**

U.S.—Description and travel—Guides 917.302

   x Guides; U.S.—Guides

U.S.—Description and travel—Maps. *See* **U.S.—Maps**

U.S.—Description and travel—Views 917.3022

   x Scenery

   xx **Pictures; Views**

U.S.—Diplomatic and consular service 327.73; 351.8

   x U.S.—Consular service

   xx **Diplomatic and consular service**

U.S.—Directories 973.05

   Use for lists of names and addresses. Lists of names without addresses are entered under **U.S.—Registers**

   See also **U.S.—Registers**

   xx **Directories; U.S.—Registers**

U.S.—Dramatists. *See* **Dramatists, American**

U.S.—Drawing. *See* **Drawing, American**

U.S.—Earthquakes. *See* **Earthquakes—U.S.**

U.S.—Economic conditions 330.973

   May be subdivided by period using the subdivisions under **U.S.—History,** e.g. **U.S.—Economic conditions—Colonial period;** etc.

   x National resources; U.S.—History, Economic; U.S.—Natural resources

   xx **Economic conditions; Labor and laboring classes; Natural resources—U.S.; Poverty**

U.S.—Economic policy 338.973

   x National planning; Planning, Economic; Planning, National

   xx **Economic policy**

U.S.—Education. *See* **Education—U.S.**

U.S.—Elderly. *See* **Elderly—U.S.**

U.S.—Elections. *See* **Elections—U.S.**

U.S.—Emigration. *See* **U.S.—Immigration and emigration**

U.S.—Employees. *See* **U.S.—Officials and employees**

U.S.—Engraving. *See* **Engraving, American**

U.S.—Environmental policy. *See* **Environmental policy—U.S.**

U.S.—Ethics. *See* **Ethics, American**

U.S.—Ethnology. *See* **Ethnology—U.S.**

U.S.—European War, 1914–1918. *See* **World War, 1914–1918—U.S.**

U.S.—Excavations (Archeology). *See* **Excavations (Archeology)—U.S.**

U.S.—Executive departments 353.03

See also **Presidents—U.S.—Staff**

x Executive departments

U.S.—Executive power. *See* **Executive power —U.S.**

U.S.—Exploration. *See* **America—Exploration; U.S.—Exploring expeditions; The West (U.S.)—Exploration**

U.S.—Exploring expeditions 508.73

Use for materials on exploration within the U.S. and for explorations in other countries which are sponsored by the U.S. Materials on early exploration in territory which became a part of the U.S. are entered under **America—Exploration**

See also names of expeditions (e.g. **Lewis and Clark Expedition;** etc.); and names of explorers

x Explorations; Exploring expeditions; U.S.—Exploration

xx **America—Exploration; Explorers**

U.S.—Famines. *See* **Famines—U.S.**

U.S.—Farm life. *See* **Farm life—U.S.**

U.S.—Fascism. *See* **Fascism—U.S.**

U.S.—Festivals. *See* **Festivals—U.S.**

U.S.—Finance. *See* **Finance—U.S.**

U.S.—Fiscal policy. *See* **Fiscal policy—U.S.**

U.S.—Fisheries. *See* **Fisheries—U.S.**

U.S.—Fishes. *See* **Fishes—U.S.**

U.S.—Fishing. *See* **Fishing—U.S.**

U.S.—Flags. *See* **Flags—U.S.**

U.S.—Flowers. *See* **Flowers—U.S.**

U.S.—Folk art. *See* **Folk art, American**

U.S.—Folk dancing. *See* **Folk dancing, American**

U.S.—Folk music. *See* **Folk music, American**

U.S.—Folk songs. *See* **Folk songs—U.S.**

U.S.—Folklore. *See* **Folklore—U.S.**

U.S.—Foreign opinion (May subdiv. geog. adjective form) **301.15**

x Anti-Americanism; Foreign opinion

xx **Public opinion**

U.S.—Foreign opinion, French 301.15
   x Foreign opinion; French foreign opinion
      —U.S.
U.S.—Foreign policy. *See* **U.S.—Foreign relations**
U.S.—Foreign population 325.73
   See also **U.S.—Immigration and emigration;** also **Mexican Americans; Mexicans in the U.S.;** and similar headings
   x Foreign population; Foreigners; Population, Foreign
   xx **Americanization; Immigration and emigration; Minorities; U.S.—Immigration and emigration**
U.S.—Foreign relations (May subdiv. geog.) 327.73
   See also **Monroe Doctrine; U.S.—Neutrality**
   x Foreign policy; Foreign relations; U.S.—Foreign policy
   xx **Diplomacy; Imperialism; International relations; U.S.—Neutrality; World politics**
U.S.—Foreign relations—Treaties 327.73
   x U.S.—Treaties
   xx **Treaties**
U.S.—Forests and forestry. *See* **Forests and forestry—U.S.**
U.S.—Furniture. *See* **Furniture, American**
U.S.—Galleries and museums 708
   x Galleries (Art); U.S.—Museums
   xx **Art—Galleries and museums; Museums**
U.S.—Gazetteers 910.3; 912
   xx **Gazetteers**
U.S.—Geographical names. *See* **Names, Geographical—U.S.**
U.S.—Geography 917.3
   xx **Geography**
U.S.—Geology. *See* **Geology—U.S.**
U.S.—Government. *See* **U.S.—Politics and government**
U.S.—Government buildings. *See* **U.S.—Public buildings**
U.S.—Government employees. *See* **U.S.—Officials and employees**
U.S.—Government publications 025.17; 070.5
   x Official publications; U.S.—Public documents
   xx **Government publications**
U.S.—Graphic arts. *See* **Graphic arts, American**
U.S.—Guides. *See* **U.S.—Description and travel —Guides**
U.S.—Hippies. *See* **Hippies—U.S.**
U.S.—Historians. *See* **Historians, American**
U.S.—Historic buildings, etc. 720.973; 917.3
   xx **Historic buildings, etc.**
U.S.—Historical geography 557.73
   x Historical geography
   xx **Geography, Historical**

U.S.–Historical geography–Maps 557.73; 912
   xx U.S.–Maps
U.S.–History 973
   The subdivisions by period have been listed after the subject subdivisions of U.S.–History, i.e. following U.S.–History–Study and teaching
   See also U.S.–Constitutional history
   x American history
U.S.–History–Addresses and essays 973.08
   x Addresses
   xx Essays; Lectures and lecturing; Speeches, addresses, etc.
U.S.–History–Bibliography 016.973
U.S.–History–Chronology. *See* Chronology, Historical
U.S.–History–Dictionaries 973.03
U.S.–History–Drama 808.82; 812; etc.
U.S.–History, Economic. *See* U.S.–Economic conditions
U.S.–History–Examinations, questions, etc. 973.076
   See also U.S.–History–Study and teaching
   xx U.S.–History–Study and teaching
U.S.–History–Fiction Fic
U.S.–History–Historiography 973.07
   xx Historiography
U.S.–History, Local 973
   x History, Local; Local history
U.S.–History, Military 355.09
   x History, Military; U.S.—Military history
   xx Military history
U.S.–History, Naval 359.09
   x History, Naval; U.S.—Naval history
   xx Naval battles; Naval history; Sea power
U.S.–History–Outlines, syllabi, etc. 973.02
   xx U.S.–History–Study and teaching
U.S.–History–Periodicals 973.05
U.S.–History–Poetry 808.81; 811; etc.
U.S.—History, Political. *See* U.S.–Politics and government
U.S.—History—Portraits. *See* U.S.–Biography–Portraits
U.S.–History–Societies 973.06
   xx History–Societies
U.S.–History–Sources 973
   xx History–Sources
U.S.–History–Study and teaching 973.07
   See also U.S.–History–Examinations, questions, etc.; U.S.–History–Outlines, syllabi, etc.
   xx U.S.–History–Examinations, questions, etc.
U.S.–History–Colonial period, 1600–1775 973.2
   Use for the period from the earliest permanent English settlements on the Atlantic coast to the American Revolution, i.e. 1600–1775. Materials dealing

U.S.–History–Colonial period, 1600–1775
—Continued

with the period of discovery are entered under **America–Exploration**

See also **Bacon's Rebellion, 1676; King Philip's War, 1675–1676; Pilgrims (New England colonists); Pontiac's Conspiracy, 1763–1765; Puritans; U.S. –History–King William's War, 1689–1697; U.S.–History–French and Indian War, 1755–1763**

x American colonies; Colonial history (U.S.); Colonial life and customs (U.S.)

U.S.—History—King Philip's War, 1675–1676. *See* **King Philip's War, 1675–1676**

U.S.–History–King William's War, 1689–1697 973.2

x King William's War, 1689–1697

xx **Indians of North America–Wars; U.S.– History–Colonial period, 1600–1775**

U.S.–History–French and Indian War, 1755– 1763 973.2

See also **Pontiac's Conspiracy, 1763–1765**

x French and Indian War

xx **Indians of North America–Wars; Seven Years' War, 1756–1763; U.S.–History –Colonial period, 1600–1775**

U.S.–History–Revolution, 1775–1783 973.3

May be subdivided like **U.S.–History– Civil War**

See also **American Loyalists; Canadian Invasion, 1775–1776; Fourth of July; U.S. Declaration of Independence**

x American Revolution; Revolution, American; War of the American Revolution

xx **Revolutions**

U.S.—History—Revolution, 1775–1783—Centennial celebrations, etc. *See* **American Revolution Bicentennial, 1776– 1976**

U.S.–History–1783–1809 973.4

See also **Lewis and Clark Expedition; Louisiana Purchase; U.S.–Constitutional history**

x Confederation of American colonies

U.S.–History–1783–1865 973.5

U.S.–History–Tripolitan War, 1801–1805 973.4

x Tripoline War

xx **Pirates**

U.S.–History–War of 1812 973.5

x War of 1812

U.S.–History–1815–1861 973.5–973.6

See also **Black Hawk War, 1832**

U.S.–History–War with Mexico, 1845–1848 973.6

x Mexican War, 1845–1848

580

U.S.–History–Civil War, 1861–1865 973.7

See also **Confederate States of America;
Slavery in the U.S.; Trent Affair, 1861**

x American Civil War; Civil War—U.S.;
War of Secession (U.S.)

xx **War**

U.S.–History–Civil War, 1861–1865–Biography 920

U.S.–History–Civil War, 1861–1865–Campaigns and battles 973.7

See also names of battles, e.g. **Gettysburg,
Battle of, 1863; etc.**

xx **Battles**

U.S.–History–Civil War, 1861–1865–Causes 973.7

x Secession

U.S.–History–Civil War, 1861–1865–Centennial celebrations, etc. 973.7

U.S.–History–Civil War, 1861–1865–Drama, 808.82; 812; etc.

xx **Drama**

**U.S.–History–Civil War, 1861–1865–Fiction
Fic**

xx **Historical fiction**

U.S.–History–Civil War, 1861–1865–Medical and sanitary affairs 973.7

U.S.–History–Civil War, 1861–1865–Naval operations 973.7

U.S.–History–Civil War, 1861–1865–Personal narratives 973.7

Use for miscellaneous accounts and reports
written by soldiers, officers, journalists and other observers. Accounts limited to a special topic are entered under the specific subject

U.S.–History–Civil War, 1861–1865–Pictorial works 973.7022

x Illustrations

xx **Pictures**

U.S.–History–Civil War, 1861–1865–Prisoners and prisons 973.7

U.S.—History—Civil War, 1861–1865—Reconstruction. *See* **Reconstruction (1865–1876)**

U.S.–History–Civil War, 1861–1865–Sources 973.7

xx **History–Sources**

U.S.–History–1865–1898 973.8

See also **Reconstruction (1865–1876)**

U.S.–History–War of 1898 973.8

x American-Spanish War; 1898; Hispano-American War, 1898; Spain—History—War of 1898; Spanish-American War, 1898

U.S.–History–20th century 973.9

U.S.–History–1898–1919 973.9-973.91

U.S.—History—European War, 1914–1918. *See* **World War, 1914–1918–U.S.**

U.S.–History–1919–1933 973.91

U.S.—History—World War, 1914–1918. *See* **World War, 1914–1918–U.S.**

U.S.–History–1933–1945   973.917

U.S.—History—World War, 1939–1945. *See* **World War, 1939–1945–U.S.**

U.S.–History–1945–1953   973.918

U.S.–History–1953–1961   973.922

U.S.–History–1961–1974   973.92

U.S.–History–1974–   973.924

U.S.—Hospitals. *See* **Hospitals–U.S.**

U.S.—Hotels, motels, etc. *See* **Hotels, motels, etc.–U.S.**

U.S.—Hunting. *See* **Hunting–U.S.**

U.S.—Illustrators. *See* **Illustrators, American**

U.S.–Immigration and emigration   325.73
    See also **U.S.–Foreign population;** and names of nationality groups, e.g. **Mexican Americans; Mexicans in the U.S.;** etc.
    x Foreign population; Population, Foreign; U.S.—Emigration
    xx **Americanization; Colonization; Immigration and emigration; U.S.–Foreign population**

U.S.–Industries   338; 658; 670
    x Industries; U.S.—Manufactures
    xx **Industrial arts**

U.S.—Industry and state. *See* **Industry and state–U.S.**

U.S.—Insular possessions. *See* **U.S.–Colonies**

U.S.–Intellectual life   917.3
    x Intellectual life

U.S.—Intelligence service. *See* **Intelligence service–U.S.**

U.S.—Irrigation. *See* **Irrigation–U.S.**

U.S.—Labor and laboring classes. *See* **Labor and laboring classes–U.S.**

U.S.—Labor unions. *See* **Labor unions–U.S.**

U.S.—Land settlement. *See* **Land settlement– U.S.**

U.S.—Law. *See* **Law–U.S.**

U.S.—Legends. *See* **Legends–U.S.**

U.S.—Libraries. *See* **Libraries–U.S.**

U.S. Library of Congress. *See* **Library of Congress**

U.S.—Literary landmarks. *See* **Literary landmarks–U.S.**

U.S.—Literature. *See* **American literature**

U.S.—Mail. *See* **Postal service–U.S.**

U.S.—Manners and customs. *See* **U.S.–Social life and customs**

U.S.—Manufactures. *See* **U.S.–Industries**

U.S.–Maps   912
    See also **U.S.–Historical geography–Maps**
    x U.S.—Atlases; U.S.—Description and travel—Maps
    xx **Atlases; Maps; Road maps**

U.S.—Medicine. *See* **Medicine–U.S.**

U.S.—Merchant marine. *See* **Merchant marine–U.S.**

U.S.—Military history. *See* **U.S.—History, Military**

U.S.—Military offenses. *See* **Military offenses —U.S.**

U.S.—Military policy 355.03
   xx **Military policy**

U.S.—Militia 355.3
   See also **U.S.—National Guard**
   x Militia

U.S.—Mines and mineral resources. *See* **Mines and mineral resources—U.S.**

U.S.—Monetary policy. *See* **Monetary policy —U.S.**

U.S.—Moral conditions 309.173
   xx **Moral conditions**

U.S.—Municipal government. *See* **Municipal government—U.S.**

U.S.—Museums. *See* **U.S.—Galleries and museums**

U.S.—Music. *See* **Music, American**

U.S.—Musicians. *See* **Musicians, American**

U.S.—Names, Geographical. *See* **Names, Geographical—U.S.**

U.S.—Names, Personal. *See* **Names, Personal —U.S.**

U.S.—National characteristics. *See* **National characteristics, American**

U.S.—National Guard 355.3
   x National Guard (U.S.)
   xx **U.S.—Militia**

U.S.—National parks and reserves. *See* **National parks and reserves—U.S.**

U.S.—National security 351.1; 355.4
   xx **National security**

U.S.—National songs. *See* **National songs, American**

U.S.—Natural disasters. *See* **Natural disasters —U.S.**

U.S.—Natural history. *See* **Natural history— U.S.**

U.S.—Natural monuments. *See* **Natural monuments—U.S.**

U.S.—Natural resources. *See* **Natural resources —U.S.; U.S.—Economic conditions**

U.S.—Nature study. *See* **Nature study—U.S.**

U.S.—Naval history. *See* **U.S.—History, Naval**

U.S. Navy 359
   Subdivisions used under this subject may be used under navies of other countries
   x Naval administration; Navy; Sea life
   xx **Naval history; Navies; Sea power; Sailors; U.S.—Armed Forces; Warships**

U.S. Navy—Biography 920; 923
   x Military biography; Naval biography

U.S. Navy—Enlistment. *See* **U.S. Navy—Recruiting, enlistment, etc.**

U.S. Navy—Handbooks, manuals, etc. 359.02
>   *x* U.S. Navy—Officers' handbooks

U.S. Navy—Insignia 359.1
>   *xx* **Insignia**

U.S. Navy—Medals, badges, decorations, etc. 359.1
>   *xx* **Insignia; Medals**

U.S. Navy—Officers 359.3

U.S. Navy—Officers' handbooks. *See* **U.S. Navy—Handbooks, manuals, etc.**

U.S. Navy—Recruiting, enlistment, etc. 359.2
>   *x* Enlistment; Recruiting and enlistment; U.S. Navy—Enlistment

U.S. Navy—Sealab project. *See* **Sealab project**

U.S.—Neutrality 327
>   *See also* **U.S.—Foreign relations**
>   *xx* **Neutrality; U.S.—Foreign relations**

U.S.—Novelists. *See* **Novelists, American**

U.S.—Occupations 331.7
>   *xx* **Occupations**

U.S.—Officials and employees 351.1
>   *See also* **Civil service—U.S.**
>   *x* Government employees; Officials; U.S.—Employees; U.S.—Government employees
>   *xx* **Civil service—U.S.**

U.S.—Painters. *See* **Painters, American**

U.S.—Painting. *See* **Painting, American**

U.S.—Parachute troops. *See* **U.S. Army—Parachute troops**

U.S.—Parks. *See* **Parks—U.S.**

U.S.—Peoples. *See* **Ethnology—U.S.**

U.S.—Personal names. *See* **Names, Personal —U.S.**

U.S.—Petroleum. *See* **Petroleum—U.S.**

U.S.—Philosophers. *See* **Philosophers, American**

U.S.—Philosophy. *See* **Philosophy, American**

U.S.—Physical geography. *See* **Physical geography—U.S.**

U.S.—Plants, Cultivated. *See* **Plants, Cultivated—U.S.**

U.S.—Poets. *See* **Poets, American**

U.S.—Police. *See* **Police—U.S.**

U.S.—Politicians. *See* **Politicians, American**

U.S.—Politics and government 973
>   May be subdivided by period using the subdivisions under **U.S.—History,** e.g. **U.S.—Politics and government—Colonial period, 1600–1775;** etc.
>   *x* Administration; American government; American politics; Civics; Civil government; Government; Politics; U.S.—Government; U.S.—History, Political
>   *xx* **Comparative government; Political science; Politics, Practical; Public administration; World politics**

U.S.—Population 301.32; 371.3
>   *xx* **Population**

U.S.—Postal service. *See* **Postal service—U.S.**

U.S.—Pottery. *See* **Pottery, American**

U.S.—Presidents. *See* **Presidents—U.S.** For materials on presidents of other countries see names of countries with the subdivision *Presidents,* e.g. **Mexico—Presidents;** etc.

U.S.—Prints. *See* **Prints, American**

U.S.—Prisons. *See* **Prisons—U.S.**

U.S.—Propaganda. *See* **Propaganda, American**

U.S.—Public buildings 725

    x U.S.—Government buildings

    xx **Public buildings**

U.S.—Public debts. *See* **Debts, Public—U.S.**

U.S.—Public documents. *See* **U.S.—Government publications**

U.S.—Public health. *See* **Public health—U.S.**

U.S.—Public lands 333.1

    x Public lands

U.S.—Public schools. *See* **Public schools—U.S.**

U.S.—Public works 351.8

    xx **Public works**

U.S.—Race relations 301.45; 323.1

    See also **Black Muslims**

    xx **Anthropology; Minorities; Race relations**

U.S.—Refugees. *See* **Refugees, American**

U.S.—Registers 973.05

    Use for lists of names without addresses. Lists of names that include addresses are entered under **U.S.—Directories**

    See also **U.S.—Directories**

    x Registers of persons

    xx **U.S.—Directories**

U.S.—Religion 277.3

    See also **U.S.—Church history**

    xx **Religion; U.S.—Church history**

U.S.—Religious history. *See* **U.S.—Church history**

U.S.—Schools. *See* **Schools—U.S.**

U.S.—Science. *See* **Science—U.S.**

U.S.—Sculptors. *See* **Sculptors, American**

U.S.—Sculpture. *See* **Sculpture, American**

U.S.—Separation of powers. *See* **Separation of powers—U.S.**

U.S.—Shipping. *See* **Shipping—U.S.**

U.S.—Social conditions 309.173

    xx **Labor and laboring classes; Poverty; Social conditions**

U.S.—Social life and customs 917.3

    x Customs, Social; Social customs; Social life and customs; U.S.—Manners and customs

    xx **Ethnology; Manners and customs**

U.S.—Social life and customs—Colonial period, 1600–1775 917.3

    x Colonial life and customs (U.S.)

U.S.–Social policy 309.2
    x National planning; Planning, National
    xx **Social policy**
U.S.—Social surveys. *See* **Social surveys–U.S.**
U.S.—Socialism. *See* **Socialism–U.S.**
U.S.—Soldiers. *See* **Soldiers–U.S.**
U.S.—Songs. *See* **Songs, American**
U.S.—State governments. *See* **State govern-
    ments**
U.S.–Statistics 317.3
    x Burial statistics
    xx **Statistics**
U.S.—Students. *See* **Students–U.S.**
U.S. Supreme Court 347.1
    x Supreme Court—U.S.
U.S. Supreme Court–Biography 920; 923
U.S.—Tariff. *See* **Tariff–U.S.**
U.S.—Taxation. *See* **Taxation–U.S.**
U.S.–Territorial expansion 973
U.S.—Territories and possessions. *See* **U.S.–
    Colonies**
U.S.—Terrorism. *See* **Terrorism–U.S.**
U.S.—Theater. *See* **Theater–U.S.**
U.S.—Travelers. *See* **Travelers, American**
U.S.—Treaties. *See* **U.S.–Foreign relations–
    Treaties**
U.S.—Trees. *See* **Trees–U.S.**
U.S.—Universities. *See* **Colleges and univer-
    sities–U.S.**
U.S.—Urban renewal. *See* **Urban renewal–
    U.S.**
U.S.—Vice-Presidents. *See* **Vice-Presidents–
    U.S.**
U.S.—Women. *See* **Women–U.S.**
U.S.—World War, 1914–1918. *See* **World
    War, 1914–1918–U.S.**
U.S.—World War, 1939–1945. *See* **World
    War, 1939–1945–U.S.**
U.S.—Youth. *See* **Youth–U.S.**
U.S.—Zoology. *See* **Zoology–U.S.**
**United States Military Academy, West Point
    355.007**
    x West Point Military Academy
    xx **Military education**
**United States Military Academy, West Point–
    Registers 355.007**
    Use for lists of graduates, etc.
    x Registers of persons
**United States Military Academy, West Point–
    Songs and music 784.7**
    xx **Songs**
**United States Naval Academy, Annapolis
    359.007**
    x Annapolis Naval Academy; Naval Acad-
    emy, Annapolis
    xx **Naval education**
United States of Europe (Proposed). *See*
    European federation
United Steelworkers of America 331.88
    xx **Labor unions**

586

Universal bibliographic control. *See* **Bibliographic control**

Universal history. *See* **World history**

Universal language. *See* **Language, Universal**

Universe 113; 523.1

> *See also* **Astronomy; Creation; Earth; Life on other planets**
>
> *x* Cosmogony; Cosmography; Cosmology
>
> *xx* **Creation; Earth; Metaphysics; Philosophy**

Universities. *See* **Colleges and universities**

University degrees. *See* **Degrees, Academic**

University extension 378.1

> *See also* **Adult education; Correspondence schools and courses**
>
> *xx* **Colleges and universities; Education, Higher**

University libraries. *See* **Libraries, College and university**

University students. *See* **College students**

Unmarried couples 301.41

> *x* Cohabitation; Common law marriage; Living together; Marriage, Open ended; Nonmarital relations; Open ended marriage; Trial marriage; Unmarried people
>
> *xx* **Sexual ethics; Single people**

Unmarried men. *See* **Single men**

Unmarried mothers 301.41

> *x* Mothers, Unmarried; Unwed mothers
>
> *xx* **Single women**

Unmarried people. *See* **Single people; Unmarried couples**

Unmarried women. *See* **Single women**

Untruth. *See* **Truthfulness and falsehood**

Unwed mothers. *See* **Unmarried mothers**

Upholstery 684.1

> *See also* **Drapery; Furniture**
>
> *xx* **Furniture; Interior decoration**

Upper atmosphere. *See* **Atmosphere, Upper**

Upper classes 301.44

> *x* Fashionable society; High society; Society, Upper
>
> *xx* **Aristocracy; Social classes**

Uranium 669

> *xx* **Radioactivity**

Urban areas. *See* **Cities and towns; Metropolitan areas**

Urban life. *See* **City life**

Urban planning. *See* **City planning**

Urban renewal (May subdiv. geog.) **301.34; 309.2**

> Use for materials on urban redevelopment and the economic, sociological and political factors involved. For architectural and engineering aspects use **City planning**
>
> *See also* **City planning; Community organization**
>
> *x* Slum clearance

Urban renewal—*Continued*
    xx City planning; Community organization;
        Metropolitan areas; Sociology, Urban
Urban renewal—Chicago 301.34; 309.2
    x Chicago—Urban renewal
Urban renewal—U.S. 301.34; 309.2
    x U.S.—Urban renewal
Urban sociology. *See* Sociology, Urban
Urban traffic. *See* City traffic
Urban transportation. *See* Local transit
Useful arts. *See* Industrial arts; Technology
Utensils, Kitchen. *See* Household equipment
    and supplies
Utilitarianism 144
    See also Pragmatism
    xx Ethics; Pragmatism
Utilities, Public. *See* Public utilities
Utilization of waste. *See* Recycling (Waste,
    etc.); Salvage (Waste, etc.)
Utopias 321
    x Ideal states
    xx Political science; Socialism
VD. *See* Venereal diseases
VTOL. *See* Vertically rising airplanes
Vacation church schools. *See* Summer schools,
    Religious
Vacation schools. *See* Summer schools
Vacation schools, Religious. *See* Summer
    schools, Religious
Vacations 331.2; 658.31
    See also Holidays
    xx Holidays; Recreation
Vaccination 614.4
    See also Immunity; Smallpox
    x Immunization; Inoculation
    xx Communicable diseases; Immunity; Pub-
    lic health; Smallpox
Vacuum tubes 537.5; 621.3815
    See also Amplifiers, Vacuum tube; Cath-
    ode ray tubes; Electronics
    x Electron tubes
    xx X rays
Vagabonds. *See* Tramps
Vagrants. *See* Tramps
Valuation 338.5
    Use for general materials only. Materials
    on valuation of special classes of prop-
    erty are entered under the class (e.g.
    Real estate; etc.). Materials on valua-
    tion for taxing purposes are entered
    under Assessment
    x Appraisal; Capitalization (Finance)
    xx Assessment
Values 170; 171
    Use for materials on moral and esthetic
    values
    See also Social values
    x Axiology; Worth
    xx Esthetics; Ethics; Psychology

Van life
    x Vanning; Vans—Social aspects
    xx Mobile home living; Vans
Vanishing animals. *See* Rare animals
Vanishing birds. *See* Rare birds
Vanning. *See* Van life
Vans
    See also Van life
    xx Travel trailers and campers
Vans—Social aspects. *See* Van life
Variation (Biology) 575.2
    See also Adaptation (Biology); Color of
        animals; Evolution; Mendel's law; Nat-
        ural selection
    x Mutation (Biology)
    xx Biology; Botany; Evolution; Genetics;
        Heredity; Zoology
Varnish and varnishing 667; 698.3
    See also Lacquer and lacquering
    x Finishes and finishing
    xx Lacquer and lacquering; Painting, Indus-
        trial; Wood finishing
Varsity sports. *See* College sports
Vasectomy 613.9
    xx Sterilization (Birth control)
Vases 666; 731; 738.3
    See also Glassware; Pottery
    xx Glassware; Pottery
Vassals. *See* Feudalism
Vatican Council, 2d, 1962–1965 262
    xx Councils and synods
Vaudeville 792.7
    xx Amusements; Theater
Vaults (Sepulchral). *See* Tombs
Vedas 294
    xx Hinduism; Sacred books
Vegetable anatomy. *See* Botany—Anatomy
Vegetable gardening 635
    See also Vegetables
    x Kitchen gardens; Market gardening;
        Truck farming
    xx Gardening; Horticulture; Vegetables
Vegetable kingdom. *See* Botany; Plants
Vegetable oils. *See* Essences and essential oils;
        Oils and fats
Vegetable pathology. *See* Plants—Diseases
Vegetables 633; 635
    Names of vegetables are not included in
        this list but are to be added as needed,
        e.g. Celery; Potatoes; etc.
    See also Cookery—Vegetables; Root crops;
        Vegetable gardening; Vegetarianism;
        also names of vegetables, e.g. Celery;
        Potatoes; etc.
    xx Botany; Food; Vegetable gardening
Vegetables—Canning. *See* Canning and pre-
        serving
Vegetables—Marketing. *See* Farm produce—
        Marketing
Vegetarian cooking. *See* Cookery—Vegetables

Vegetarianism 613.2
  xx **Diet; Food; Vegetables**
Vehicles 629.2
  See also types of vehicles and individual vehicles, e.g. **All terrain vehicles; Automobiles; Recreational vehicles; Snowmobiles;** etc.
  xx **Transportation**
Vehicles, Military 355.8
  x Army vehicles; Military vehicles
  xx **Transportation, Military**
Vehicles, Recreational. *See* **Recreational vehicles**
Velocity. *See* **Speed**
Veneers and veneering 674; 698.3
  xx **Cabinet work; Furniture**
Venereal diseases 616.9
  See also **Sexual hygiene;** also names of venereal diseases, e.g. **Syphilis;** etc.
  x Hygiene, Social; Social hygiene; VD
  xx **Prostitution; Sexual hygiene**
Venom. *See* **Poisons**
Ventilation 697
  See also **Air conditioning; Chimneys; Heating**
  xx **Air; Air conditioning; Heating; Home economics; Hygiene; Sanitation; Sanitation, Household**
Ventriloquism 793.8
  xx **Amusements; Voice**
Venus (Planet) 523.4
  xx **Planets; Solar system**
Vermin. *See* **Household pests; Pests**
Vers libre. *See* **Free verse**
Versailles, Treaty of, 1919 940.3
  xx **Treaties**
Versification 416; 426
  See also **Poetry; Rhyme**
  x English language—Versification; Meter; Prosody
  xx **Authorship; Poetics; Rhythm**
Vertebrates 596
  See also **Amphibians; Birds; Fishes; Mammals; Reptiles**
  xx **Animals; Zoology**
Vertical take off airplanes. *See* **Vertically rising airplanes**
Vertically rising airplines 629.133
  x Airplanes, Vertically rising; VTOL; Vertical take off airplanes
  xx **Airplanes; Ground effect machines**
Vessels (Ships). *See* **Ships**
Veterans 355.1
  See also **Hospitals, Military; Pensions, Military; Sailors; Soldiers**
  x Ex-service men; G.I.s; War veterans
  xx **Pensions, Military; Sailors; Soldiers**
Veterans—Education 355.1
  x Education of veterans

Veterans—Education—*Continued*
  xx **Reconstruction (1914–1939); Reconstruc-**
    tion (1939–1951)
Veterans—Employment 331.1; 355.1
  x Employment; Employment of veterans
  xx **Reconstruction (1914–1939); Reconstruc-**
    tion (1939–1951)
Veterans—Hospitals. *See* **Hospitals, Military**
Veterans—Law and legislation 343.1
  xx **Military law**
Veterans Day 394.2
  x Armistice Day
Veterinary medicine 636.089
  See also **Animals—Diseases;** and names of
    animals with the subdivision *Diseases,*
    e.g. **Cattle—Diseases;** etc.
  x Medicine, Veterinary
  xx **Livestock**
Viaducts. *See* **Bridges**
Vibration 531; 620.3
  See also **Light; Sound waves; Waves**
  xx **Mechanics; Sound**
Vice. *See* **Crime;** and names of specific vices,
    e.g. **Gambling; Prostitution;** etc.
Vice-Presidents—U.S. 920; 923
  x U.S.—Vice-Presidents
Victimless crimes. *See* **Crimes without victims**
Video tape recorders and recording 384.55;
    621.389
  xx **Television broadcasting**
Vietnam War, 1961–1975. *See* **Vietnamese**
    Conflict, 1961–1975
Vietnamese Conflict, 1961–1975 959.704
  May use appropriate subdivisions under
    World War, 1939–1945
  x Vietnam War, 1961–1975
Views
  Use for collections of pictures of many
    lands
  See also names of countries, states, etc.
    with the subdivision *Description and
    travel—Views* (e.g. **U.S.—Description
    and travel—Views;** etc.); and names of
    cities with the subdivision *Description
    —Views,* e.g. **Chicago—Description—
    Views;** etc.
  x Geography—Pictorial works; Scenery
Vigilance committees 364.1; 364.4
  xx **Crime; Criminal law; Lynching**
Vikings 913.36
  Use for materials on early Scandinavian
    people. Materials on the people since
    the 10th century are entered under
    Scandinavians
  See also **Normans**
  x Norsemen; Northmen
  xx **Normans; Scandinavians**
Villages 301.34
  See also **Local government**
  xx **Cities and towns; Local government**

591

Villas. *See* **Architecture, Domestic**
Vines. *See* **Climbing plants**
Vineyards. *See* **Grapes**
Violence 301.6
    xx **Aggressiveness (Psychology); Social psy-chology**
Violin 787
    x Fiddle
    xx **Stringed instruments**
Violin music 787
Violinists, violoncellists, etc. 920; 927
    x Violoncellists
    xx **Musicians**
Violoncellists. *See* **Violinists, violoncellists, etc.**
Violoncello 787
    x Cello
Vipers. *See* **Snakes**
Virgin Mary. *See* **Mary, Virgin**
Viruses 576
    x Microbes
    xx **Microorganisms**
Visceral learning. *See* **Biofeedback training**
Viscosity 532; 620.1
    xx **Hydrodynamics; Mechanics**
Visigoths. *See* **Teutonic peoples**
Vision 612; 617.7
    See also **Color sense; Eye; Optical illusions**
    x Sight
    xx **Eye; Optics; Senses and sensation**
Vision disorders 362.4; 617.7
    See also **Blind; Color blindness**
    x Defective vision
Visions 133.8
    See also **Apparitions; Dreams; Hallucina-tions and illusions**
    xx **Apparitions**
Visitors' exchange programs. *See* **Exchange of persons programs**
Visual data processing. *See* **Optical data pro-cessing**
Visual instruction. *See* **Audio-visual education**
Vital records. *See* **Registers of births, etc.**
Vital statistics 312
    See also **Census; Mortality; Population; Registers of births, etc.**
    x Burial statistics; Death rate; Marriage statistics; Mortuary statistics; Records of births, etc.
    xx **Registers of births, etc.; Statistics**
Vitamins 574.1; 615; 641.1
    xx **Food; Nutrition; Physiological chemis-try**
Vivariums. *See* **Terrariums**
Vivisection 179
    See also **Animals—Treatment**
    x Antivivisection
    xx **Animals—Treatment; Surgery**

Vocabulary   413; 423; etc.

  See also **Words, New**

  x Words

Vocal culture. *See* **Singing; Voice**

Vocal music   784

  See also **Cantatas; Carols; Choral music; Folk songs; Hymns; Operas; Operetta; Oratorios; Singing; Songs**

  x Music, Vocal

  xx **Music; Singing**

Vocation, Choice of. *See* **Vocational guidance**

Vocational education   370.11

  See note under **Occupational training**

  See also **Blind—Education; Deaf—Education; Employees—Training; Industrial arts education; Occupational training; Professional education; Retraining, Occupational; Technical education; Vocational guidance;** also names of industries, professions, etc. with the subdivision *Study and teaching,* e.g. **Agriculture—Study and teaching; Medicine—Study and teaching;** etc.

  x Career education; Education, Vocational

  xx **Education; Human resources policy; Professional education; Technical education**

Vocational guidance   371.4

  See also **Blind—Education; Deaf—Education; Educational counseling; Employment; Occupations; Paraprofessions and paraprofessionals; Professions;** also fields of knowledge and industries and trades with the subdivision *Vocational guidance,* e.g. **Law—Vocational guidance; Television broadcasting—Vocational guidance;** etc.

  x Business, Choice of; Careers; Choice of profession; Guidance; Occupation, Choice of; Profession, Choice of; Student guidance; Vocation, Choice of

  xx **Educational counseling; Employment; Occupation; Professions; Vocational education**

Vocational training. *See* **Occupational training**

Vocations. *See* **Occupations; Professions**

Voice   784.9

  See also **Phonetics; Public speaking; Respiration; Singing; Speech; Ventriloquism**

  x Speaking; Vocal culture; Voice culture

  xx **Language and languages; Phonetics; Public speaking; Singing; Speech; Throat**

Voice culture. *See* **Singing; Voice**

Volatile oils. *See* **Essences and essential oils**

Volcanoes   551.2

  x Eruptions

  xx **Earthquakes; Geology; Mountains; Physical geography**

593

Volleyball 796.32

Voluntary associations. *See* **Associations**

Voluntary work. *See* **Volunteer workers**

Volunteer army. *See* **Military service, Voluntary**

Volunteer workers 361
  x Voluntary work

Voting. *See* **Elections; Suffrage**

Voting, Cumulative. *See* **Proportional representation**

Voyagers. *See* **Explorers; Travelers**

Voyages and travels 910.4
  See also

Adventure and adventurers	**Sailors**
Aeronautics— Flights	**Scientific expeditions**
Discoveries (in geography)	**Seafaring life**
Explorers	**Shipwrecks**
Northeast Passage	**Travel**
Northwest Passage	**Travelers**
Ocean travel	**Voyages around the world**
Overland journeys to the Pacific (U.S.)	**Whaling**
Pilgrims and pilgrimages	**Yachts and yachting**

  also names of countries, continents, etc.
    with the subdivision *Description and
    travel* (e.g. **U.S.—Description and
    travel;** etc.); also names of regions
    (e.g. **Antarctic regions;** etc.); and
    names of individual ships
  x Journeys; Travels
  xx **Adventure and adventurers; Discoveries (in geography); Explorers; Geography; Travel**

Voyages around the world 910.4
  x Circumnavigation; Journeys; Travels
  xx **Travel; Voyages and travels**

Voyages to the moon. *See* **Space flight to the moon**

Wage-price controls. *See* **Wage-price policy**

Wage-price policy 339.2
  x Price controls; Price-wage policy; Wage-price controls
  xx **Inflation (Finance); Prices; Wages**

Wages 331.2; 658.32
  See also **Cost of living; Equal pay for equal work; Job analysis; Prices; Profit sharing; Wage-price policy**
  x Compensation; Overtime
  xx **Cost of living; Economics; Labor and laboring classes; Labor contracts; Prices**

Wages—Annual wage 331.2
  x Annual income; Annual wage plans;

Wages—Annual wage—*Continued*
>Guaranteed annual income; Guaranteed income

>*xx* **Income**

Wages—Minimum wage 331.2
>*x* Minimum wage

Wagons. *See* **Carriages and carts**

Wakefulness. *See* **Insomnia**

Walking 796.5
>*See also* **Hiking**

>*x* Locomotion

>*xx* **Hiking; Track athletics**

Walking in space. *See* **Extravehicular activity (Space flight)**

Wall decoration. *See* **Mural painting and decoration**

Wall painting. *See* **Mural painting and decoration**

Wall Street 332.6
>Use for materials on the activities of Wall Street as a financial district. Historical and descriptive materials on Wall Street as a street are entered under **New York (City)—Streets**

>*xx* **Stock exchange**

Wallpaper 676
>*See also* **Paper hanging**

>*xx* **Interior decoration; Paper hanging**

Walls 721; 725
>*See also* **Foundations; Masonry; Mural painting and decoration**

>*xx* **Building; Carpentry; Civil engineering; Foundations; Masonry**

War 172
>*See also*

Aeronautics, Military	**Munitions**
Armies	**Naval art and science**
Battles	**Navies**
Chemical warfare	**Peace**
Disarmament	**Psychological warfare**
Guerrilla warfare	**Soldiers**
International law	
Military art and science	**Strategy**
	Submarine warfare

>**Military law**

>*also* names of wars, battles, etc., e.g. **U.S. —History—Civil War, 1861–1865; Gettysburg, Battle of, 1863;** etc.

>*x* Fighting; Wars

>*xx* **Armies; International law; Military art and science; Peace**

War, Articles of. *See* **Military law**

War—Economic aspects 330.1
>Use for materials discussing the economic causes of war and the effect of war on industry and trade

>*See also* **Industrial mobilization; Munitions; World War, 1939–1945—Human resources;** also names of wars with the

War—Economic aspects—*Continued*
  subdivision *Economic aspects,* e.g.
    World War, 1939–1945—Economic aspects; etc.
  x Economics of war; Industry and war; War and industry
War and civilization 172; 301.6
  x Civilization and war
  xx **Civilization; Progress**
War and industry. *See* **War—Economic aspects**
War and religion 201; 261.8
  See also **Conscientious objectors; Nonviolence; Pacifism; World War, 1939–1945—Moral and religious aspects**
  x Christianity and war; Church and war; Religion and war
War crime trials 341.6
  xx **World War, 1939–1945—Atrocities**
War cripples. *See* **Physically handicapped**
War debts. *See* **Debts, Public;** and names of wars with the subdivision *Finance,* e.g. **World War, 1939–1945—Finance;** etc.
War of 1812. *See* **U.S.—History—War of 1812**
War of nerves. *See* **Psychological warfare**
War of 1914. *See* **World War, 1914–1918**
War of 1939–1945. *See* **World War, 1939–1945**
War of Secession (U.S.). *See* **U.S.—History—Civil War, 1861–1865**
War of the American Revolution. *See* **U.S.—History—Revolution, 1775–1783**
War of the Spanish Succession, 1701–1714. *See* **Spanish Succession, War of, 1701–1714**
War pensions. *See* **Pensions, Military**
War poetry 808.81; 811; etc.
  See also **War songs**
  xx **Poetry—Collections; War songs**
War prisoners. *See* **Prisoners of war**
War protest movements. *See* names of wars with the subdivision *Protest movements,* e.g. **World War, 1939–1945—Protest movements;** etc.
War ships. *See* **Warships**
War songs 784.7
  See also **War poetry; World War, 1939–1945—Songs and music**
  x Battle songs; Soldiers' songs
  xx **National songs; Songs; War poetry**
War veterans. *See* **Veterans**
War work. *See* names of wars with the subdivision *War work,* e.g. **World War, 1939–1945—War work;** etc.
Warfare, Submarine. *See* **Submarine warfare**
Warm air heating. *See* **Hot air heating**
Wars. *See* **Military history; Naval history; War;** and names of wars, e.g. **World War, 1939-1945;** etc.

Wars of the Roses, 1455–1485. *See* **Gt. Brit.
—History—Wars of the Roses, 1455–
1485**

Warships 359.3

See also **Aircraft carriers; Navies; Submarines;** also names of countries with the subhead *Navy* (e.g. **U.S. Navy;** etc.); and names of individual warships

x Battle ships; Battleships; War ships

xx **Naval architecture; Naval art and science; Navies; Sea power; Ships**

Washing. *See* **Laundry**

Wasps 595.7

x Hymenoptera

xx **Insects**

Waste disposal. *See* **Industrial waste; Refuse and refuse disposal; Sewage disposal; Waste products**

Waste (Economics) 339.4

xx **Economics**

Waste products 604.6; 628

See also **Industrial waste; Recycling (Waste, etc.); Refuse and refuse disposal; Salvage (Waste, etc.)**

x By-products; Junk; Products, Waste; Trade waste; Waste disposal

xx **Chemistry, Technical; Industrial waste; Manufactures; Recycling (Waste, etc.); Refuse and refuse disposal; Salvage (Waste, etc.)**

Waste products—Recycling. *See* **Recycling (Waste, etc.); Salvage (Waste, etc.)**

Waste reclamation. *See* **Recycling (Waste, etc.); Salvage (Waste, etc.)**

Watches. *See* **Clocks and watches**

Water 551.4; 553

See also

Floods	**Lakes**
Fog	**Ocean**
Frost	**Ponds**
Geysers	**Rain and rainfall**
Glaciers	**Rivers**
Hydraulic engineering	**Sea water**
Hydrotherapy	**Snow**
Ice	**Steam**

x Hydrology

xx **Earth sciences; Hydraulic engineering; Hydraulics**

Water—Analysis 546

x Chemical analysis; Water analysis

xx **Chemistry, Analytic; Water—Pollution**

Water—Conservation. *See* **Water conservation**

Water—Detergent pollution. *See* **Detergent pollution of rivers, lakes, etc.**

Water—Fluoridation 628.1

x Fluoridation of water; Water fluoridation

xx **Teeth—Diseases**

597

Water—Heavy water. *See* **Deuterium oxide**

Water—Petroleum pollution. *See* **Petroleum pollution of water**

Water—Pollution 614.7; 628.1

> *See also* **Industrial waste; Refuse and refuse disposal; Sewage disposal; Water —Analysis; Water supply;** also types of pollution, e.g. **Detergent pollution of rivers, lakes, etc.; Petroleum pollution of water;** etc.
>
> *x* Pollution of water; Rivers—Pollution; Water pollution
>
> *xx* **Industrial waste; Hygiene; Pollution; Public health; Refuse and refuse disposal; Rivers; Sewage disposal; Water supply**

Water—Purification 628.1

> *x* Purification of water; Water purification
> *xx* **Sanitation; Water supply**

Water analysis. *See* **Water—Analysis**

Water animals. *See* **Fresh water animals; Marine animals**

Water ballet. *See* **Synchronized swimming**

Water birds 598.2

> *See also* names of water birds, e.g. **Terns;** etc.
>
> *x* Aquatic birds; Birds, Aquatic; Water fowl; Wild fowl
> *xx* **Birds**

Water color painting 751
> *xx* **Painting**

Water colors 751

Water conduits. *See* **Aqueducts**

Water conservation 333.9

> *See also* **Water supply**
>
> *x* Conservation of water; Water—Conservation
>
> *xx* **Water supply**

Water cure. *See* **Hydrotherapy**

Water farming. *See* **Plants—Soilless culture**

Water flow. *See* **Hydraulics**

Water fluoridation. *See* **Water—Fluoridation**

Water fowl. *See* **Water birds**

Water plants. *See* **Fresh water plants; Marine plants**

Water pollution. *See* **Water—Pollution**

Water power 333.9; 621.2

> *See also* **Dams; Hydraulic engineering; Hydraulic machinery**
>
> *x* Hydroelectric power
>
> *xx* **Hydraulics; Power (Mechanics); Power resources; Rivers; Water resources development**

Water purification. *See* **Water—Purification**

Water resources development 333.9

> *See also* **Inland navigation; Irrigation; Water power; Water supply**

Water rights 333.9
> *xx* **Irrigation; Rivers**

Water skiing 797.1
  x Skiing, Water
  xx **Skiis and skiing**
Water sports 797
    See also **Boats and boating; Canoes and canoeing; Diving; Fishing; Rowing; Sailing; Skin diving; Surfing; Swimming; Yachts and Yachting;** and names of other water sports
  x Aquatic sports
  xx **Sports**
Water supply 627
    See also **Aqueducts; Dams; Forest influences; Irrigation; Reservoirs; Water—Pollution; Water—Purification; Water conservation; Wells;** also names of cities with the subdivision *Water supply,* e.g. **Chicago—Water supply;** etc.
  x Waterworks
  xx **Civil engineering; Municipal engineering; Public health; Public utilities; Reservoirs; Sanitary engineering; Sanitation; Water—Pollution; Water conservation; Water resources development; Wells**
Water supply engineering 628.1
    See also **Boring; Hydraulic engineering**
  xx **Hydraulic engineering**
Water transportation. *See* **Shipping**
Watergate affair, 1972–
  xx **Corruption in politics; Misconduct in office**
Watering places. *See* **Health resorts, spas, etc.**
Waterways 386
    Use for general materials on rivers, lakes, canals as highways for transportation or commerce
    See also **Canals; Inland navigation; Lakes; Rivers**
  xx **Transportation**
Waterworks. *See* **Water supply**
Wave mechanics 530.1
  xx **Mechanics; Quantum theory; Waves**
Waves 551.4
    See also **Electric waves; Light; Ocean waves; Radiation; Sound waves; Wave mechanics**
  xx **Hydrodynamics; Vibration**
Waves, Electromagnetic. *See* **Electromagnetic waves**
Waves, Ultrasonic. *See* **Ultrasonic waves**
Wealth 330.1
  See also

Capital	**Income tax**
Capitalists and financiers	**Inheritance and succession**
Economic conditions	**Millionaires**
Income	**Money**
	Poverty

Wealth—*Continued*
    Profit   **living**
    Property   **Success**
    Standard of
      x Distribution of wealth; Fortunes; Riches
      xx **Capital; Economics; Finance; Million-aires; Money; Property**

Weapons, Atomic. *See* **Atomic weapons**

Weapons and weaponry. *See* **Arms and armor; Firearms**

Weariness. *See* **Fatigue**

Weather 551.6
    See note under **Climate**
    See also **Climate; Meteorology; Rain and rainfall; Snow; Storms; Weather forecasting; Winds;** also names of countries, cities, etc. with the subdivision *Climate,* e.g. **U.S.—Climate;** etc.
    xx **Climate; Meteorology**

Weather—Control 551.6
    x Artificial weather control; Cloud seeding; Control; Rain making; Weather modification

Weather forecasting 551.6
    See also **Meteorology in aeronautics; Weather lore**
    xx **Forecasting; Meteorology; Weather**

Weather lore 551.6
    xx **Folklore; Meteorology; Signs and symbols; Weather forecasting**

Weather modification. *See* **Weather—Control**

Weather satellites. *See* **Meteorological satellites**

Weather stations. *See* **Meteorology—Observatories**

Weaving 746.1; 746.4
    See also **Basket making; Beadwork; Lace and lace making; Looms; Textile industry;** also names of woven articles, e.g. **Carpets;** etc.
    x Hand weaving
    xx **Arts and crafts; Carpets; Handicraft; Textile industry**

Weddings. *See* **Marriage customs and rites**

Weeds 632
    xx **Agricultural pests; Botany; Botany, Economic; Gardening**

Weight control. *See* **Reducing**

Weightlessness 531; 629.41
    x Free fall; Gravity free state; Subgravity state; Zero gravity
    xx **Man—Influence of environment; Space medicine**

Weights and measures 389
    See also **Electric measurements; Measuring instruments; Measurement; Metric system**
    x Cambistry; Measures; Metrology
    xx **Measurement**

Welding 677
>See also **Electric welding; Solder and soldering**
>*x* Oxyacetylene welding
>*xx* **Blacksmithing; Forging; Ironwork; Metalwork; Solder and soldering**

Welding, Electric. *See* **Electric welding**
Welfare agencies. *See* **Charities**
Welfare state. *See* **Economic policy; Public welfare; The State**
Welfare work. *See* **Charities; Public welfare; Social work**
Welfare work in industry 658.38
>*See also* **Counseling; Housing; Social settlements**
>*xx* **Industrial management; Labor and laboring classes; Social work**

Well boring. *See* **Boring**
Wells 627
>*See also* **Boring; Gas, Natural; Petroleum; Water supply**
>*x* Artesian wells
>*xx* **Boring; Hydraulic engineering; Water supply**

The West (U.S.) 917.8; 978
>Use for the region west of the Mississippi River
>*See also* **Northwest, Pacific; Pacific States;** also names of individual states in this region
>*xx* **United States**

The West (U.S.)–Exploration 978
>*x* U.S.—Exploration

West Africa. *See* **Africa, West**
West Germany. *See* **Germany, West**
West Point Military Academy. *See* **United States Military Academy, West Point**
Western civilization. *See* **Civilization, Occidental**
Westminster Abbey 726; 914.2
>*xx* **Abbeys**

Whales 599
Whaling 639
>*xx* **Fisheries; Hunting; Voyages and travels**

Wheat 633
>*See also* **Flour**
>*x* Breadstuffs
>*xx* **Flour; Grain**

Wheels 531; 629.2
>*See also* **Gearing; Tires; Turbines**
>*x* Car wheels

Whittling. *See* **Wood carving**
Wigs 391
>*xx* **Costume; Hair**

Wild animals. *See* **Animals**
Wild flowers 582
>*x* Flowers, Wild; Wildflowers
>*xx* **Flowers**

Wild fowl. *See* **Game and game birds; Water birds**

Wild life—Conservation. *See* **Wildlife—Conservation**

Wilderness areas 333.9

x Preservation of natural scenery; Protection of natural scenery

xx **Forest reserves; National parks and reserves; Natural monuments**

Wilderness survival 796.5

x Bush survival; Outdoor survival

xx **Camping; Outdoor life; Survival (after airplane accidents, shipwrecks, etc.)**

Wildflowers. *See* **Wild flowers**

Wildlife—Conservation 639

See also **Birds—Protection; Forests and forestry; Game preserves; Game protection; National parks and reserves; Natural resources; Pesticides and wildlife; Rare animals;** also names of specific wildlife refuges

x Conservation of wildlife; Preservation of wildlife; Protection of wildlife; Wild life—Conservation

xx **Nature conservation**

Wildlife and pesticides. *See* **Pesticides and wildlife**

Will. *See* **Brainwashing; Free will and determinism**

Wills 346.5

See also **Executors and administrators; Inheritance and succession**

x Bequests; Legacies

xx **Executors and administrators; Genealogy; Inheritance and succession; Registers of births, etc.**

Wind. *See* **Winds**

Wind instruments 788

See also **Bands (Music);** also names of wind instruments, e.g. **Flute;** etc.

x Brass instruments; Woodwind instruments

xx **Bands (Music); Musical instruments**

Wind power 621.4

See also **Windmills**

xx **Power (Mechanics); Power resources; Windmills**

Windbreaks 634.9

x Shelterbelts

xx **Tree planting**

Windmills 621.4

See also **Wind power**

xx **Irrigation; Wind power**

Window dressing. *See* **Show windows**

Window gardening 635

See also **House plants**

xx **Flower gardening; Flowers; Gardening**

Windows 721

See also **Glass; Show windows**

xx **Architecture—Details; Building**

Windows, Stained glass. *See* **Glass painting and staining**

Winds 551.3; 551.5
>See also **Cyclones; Hurricanes; Storms; Tornadoes; Typhoons**
>*x* Gales; Wind
>*xx* **Meteorology; Navigation; Physical geography; Storms; Weather**

Wine and wine making 664
>*See also* **Fermentation; Grapes**
>*xx* **Fermentation; Grapes**

Winter resorts 796.9
>*See also* **Health resorts, spas, etc.**
>*x* Resorts
>*xx* **Health resorts, spas, etc.**

Winter sports 796.9
>*See also* names of winter sports, e.g.; **Ice hockey; Ice skating; Skis and skiing;** etc.
>*x* Ice sports
>*xx* **Sports**

Wireless. *See* **Radio**

Wiretapping 364.12
>*See also* **Eavesdropping**
>*xx* **Criminal investigation; Eavesdropping; Privacy, Right of**

Wiring, Electric. *See* **Electric wiring**

Wit and humor 808.7; 817; etc.
>*See also* **Anecdotes; Comedy; Epigrams; Humorists; Jokes; Nonsense verses; Parody; Satire;** also **American wit and humor; English wit and humor;** etc.; and subjects with the subdivision *Anecdotes, facetiae, satire, etc.,* e.g. **Music—Anecdotes, facetiae, satire, etc.;** etc.
>*x* Facetiae; Humor; Humorous stories
>*xx* **Laughter; Literature**

Witchcraft 133.4
>*See also* **Charms; Demonology; Occult sciences; Witches**
>*x* Black art (Magic); Black magic (Witchcraft); Delusions; Necromancy; Sorcery; Spirits; Wizardry
>*xx* **Demonology; Exorcism; Folklore; Occult sciences; Superstition**

Witches 133.4
>*x* Covens
>*xx* **Witchcraft**

Witnesses 345.6; 347.6
>*x* Cross-examination

Wives of presidents—U.S. *See* **Presidents—U.S.—Wives**

Wizardry. *See* **Witchcraft**

Woman. *See* **Women**

Woman power. *See* **Human resources**

Women (May subdiv. geog.) **301.41**
>*See also* **Girls; Mothers; Single women; World War, 1939–1945—Women; Young women;** also **Women artists; Women authors; Women physicians;** and similar headings; also **Women in**

Women—*Continued*
> aeronautics; **Women in literature and art;** and similar subjects

> *x* Woman

Women—Biography 920
> *x* Heroines

> *xx* **Biography**

Women—Civil rights 301.41; 323.4
> *See also* **Feminism; Women—Suffrage; Women's Liberation Movement**

> *x* Emancipation of women; Rights of women; Women—Emancipation; Women—Equal rights; Women—Rights; Women's rights

> *xx* **Civil rights; Feminism; Sex discrimination; Women—Suffrage**

Women—Clothing. *See* **Women's clothing**

Women—Clubs. *See* **Women—Societies**

Women—Diseases 618.1
> *x* Diseases of women

Women—Dress. *See* **Women's clothing**

Women—Education 376
> *See also* **Coeducation**

> *x* Education of women

> *xx* **Coeducation**

Women—Emancipation. *See* **Women—Civil rights**

Women—Employment 331.4
> *See also* **Equal pay for equal work;** and names of occupations and professions, e.g. **Architecture;** etc.; and such headings as **Women artists; Women physicians;** etc.

> *x* Employment of women; Girls—Employment; Women—Occupations; Working girls; Working women

> *xx* **Discrimination in employment; Labor and laboring classes; Labor supply; Social problems**

Women—Enfranchisement. *See* **Women—Suffrage**

Women—Equal rights. *See* **Women—Civil rights**

Women—Occupations. *See* **Women—Employment**

Women—Political activity 329
> *See also* **Women politicians**

> *xx* **Politics, Practical; Women in public life**

Women—Psychology 155.3
> *x* Feminine psychology

Women—Rights. *See* **Feminism; Women—Civil rights**

Women, Single. *See* **Single women**

Women—Social conditions 301.41
> *See also* **Divorce; Prostitution; Women—Societies; Women in public life; Women's Liberation Movement**

> *xx* **Social problems**

Women—Societies 367
>   *See also* **Girl's clubs**
>   *x* Women—Clubs; Women's clubs; Women's organizations
>   *xx* **Clubs; Societies; Women—Social conditions**
Women—Suffrage 324
>   *See also* **Women—Civil rights**
>   *x* Suffragettes; Women—Enfranchisement
>   *xx* **Suffrage; Women—Civil rights**
Women—U.S. 301.41
>   *See also* **Presidents—U.S.—Wives**
>   *x* U.S.—Women
Women air pilots 629.132
>   *xx* **Air pilots; Women in aeronautics**
Women artists 704
>   Use same form for the attainments of women in other professions and capacities, e.g. **Women scientists**; etc.
>   *xx* **Artists; Women; Women—Employment**
Women authors 809
>   *xx* **Authors; Women**
Women in aeronautics 629.13
>   *See also* **Women air pilots**
>   *xx* **Women**
Women in art. *See* **Women in literature and art**
Women in literature and art 809
>   Use for materials treating of women in literature, and women depicted in works of art. Materials on the attainments of women in literature and art are entered under **Women authors; Women artists**
>   *x* Heroines; Women in art
>   *xx* **Art; Characters and characteristics in literature; Literature; Women**
Women in public life 301.41
>   *See also* **Women—Political activity; Women politicians**
>   *xx* **Women—Social conditions**
Women in the Bible 220.8
>   *x* Bible—Women; Heroines
>   *xx* **Bible—Biography**
Women physicians 610.69
>   *xx* **Physicians; Women; Women—Employment**
Women police. *See* **Policewomen**
Women politicians 920; 923
>   *xx* **Women—Political activity; Women in public life**
Women's clothing 646
>   *x* Women—Clothing; Women—Dress
>   *xx* **Clothing and dress**
Women's clubs. *See* **Women—Societies**
Women's Liberation Movement 323.4
>   *See also* **Feminism**
>   *xx* **Feminism; Women—Civil rights; Women—Social conditions**

Women's organizations. *See* **Women—Societies**

Women's rights. *See* **Feminism; Women—Civil rights**

Wonders. *See* **Curiosities and wonders**

Wood 674

Use for materials on the chemical and physical properties of different kinds of wood and how they are used

See also **Forests and forestry; Lumber and lumbering; Plywood; Woodwork;** also kinds of wood, e.g. **Oak,** etc.

x Timber

xx **Building materials; Forest products; Forests and forestry; Fuel; Trees**

Wood—Preservation 674

x Preservation of wood

Wood block printing. *See* **Wood engraving; Woodcuts**

Wood carving 736

x Carving, Wood; Whittling

xx **Arts and crafts; Decoration and ornament; Furniture; Sculpture; Woodwork**

Wood engraving 761

x Block printing; Wood block printing

xx **Engraving**

Wood finishing 684; 698.3

See also **Lacquer and lacquering; Varnish and varnishing**

x Finishes and finishing

xx **Painting, Industrial**

Wood turning. *See* **Turning**

Woodcuts 761

x Block printing; Wood block printing

Woods. *See* **Forests and forestry**

Woodwind instruments. *See* **Wind instruments**

Woodwork 684

See also **Cabinet work; Carpentry; Furniture; Turning; Wood carving**

xx **Architecture—Details; Cabinet work; Carpentry; Industrial arts education; Turning; Wood**

Woodworking machinery 621.9; 684

See also special kinds of machines, e.g. **Lathes;** etc.

xx **Machinery**

Wool 677

See also **Dyes and dyeing; Yarn**

x Animal products

xx **Fibers; Yarn**

Word games 793.7

See also names of specific word games; e.g. **Crossword puzzles;** etc.

xx **Games**

Wordless stories. *See* **Stories without words**

Words. *See* **Vocabulary**

Words, New 422

x Coinage of words; New words

xx **Semantics; Vocabulary**

Work   331.1
See also **Employee morale; Job satisfaction; Labor and laboring classes**
Work stoppages.   See **Strikes and lockouts**
Workers' compensation   368.4
x Compensation; Employers' liability; Insurance, Workers' Compensation; Workmen's compensation
xx **Insurance, Accident; Insurance, Health; Occupational diseases; Social security**
Workers participation in management.   See **Employees' representation in management**
Working boys.   See **Child labor**
Working classes.   See **Labor and laboring classes**
Working day.   See **Hours of labor**
Working girls.   See **Child labor; Women—Employment**
Working women.   See **Women—Employment**
Workmen's compensation.   See **Workers' compensation**
Workshop councils.   See **Employees' representation in management**
Workshops, Teachers'.   See **Teachers' workshops**
World.   See **Earth**
World, End of the.   See **End of the world**
World economics.   See **Commercial policy; Economic conditions; Economic policy; Geography, Commercial**
World government.   See **International organization**
World history   909
See also **Geography; History, Ancient; History, Modern; Middle Ages—History**
x History, Universal; Universal history
xx **History**
World language.   See **Language, Universal**
World organization.   See **International organization**
World politics   909
See note under **International relations**
See also **World War, 1914–1918; Geopolitics; International organization; International relations; World War, 1939–1945;** also names of countries with the subdivisions *Foreign relations* and *Politics and government*, e.g. **U.S.—Foreign relations; U.S.—Politics and government;** etc.
x International politics
xx **Geopolitics; International organization; International relations; Political science**
World politics—1945–1965   909.82
x Cold war; Power politics
World politics—1965–   909.82
x Power politics

World War, 1914–1918 (May subdiv. geog.)
940.3-940.4

May be subdivided like **World War, 1939–
1945.** Here are listed references applicable only to this war

x European War, 1914–1918; War of 1914

xx **Europe–History–1914–1945; History,
Modern–20th century; World politics**

World War, 1914–1918–Economic aspects
940.3

xx **Reconstruction (1914–1939)**

World War, 1914–1918–Gas warfare 940.4

x Gases, Asphyxiating and poisonous—
War use

World War, 1914–1918–Peace 940.3

See also **League of Nations**

World War, 1914–1918—Reconstruction. *See*
Reconstruction (1914–1918)

**World War, 1914–1918–Territorial questions
940.3**

See also **Mandates**

World War, 1914–1918–U.S. 940.3

x U.S.—European War, 1914–1918; U.S.—
History—European War, 1914–1918;
U.S.—History—World War, 1914–
1918; U.S.—World War, 1914–1918

World War, 1939–1945 (May subdiv. geog.)
940.53-940.54

Subdivisions used under this heading may
be used under other wars

See also names of battles, sieges, etc. e.g.
**Ardennes, Battle of the, 1944–1945;
Pearl Harbor, Attack on, 1941;** etc.

x European War, 1939–1945; War of
1939–1945; Wars

xx **Europe–History–1914–1945; History,
Modern–20th century; World politics**

World War, 1939–1945–Aerial operations
940.54

x Air warfare

xx **Aeronautics, Military**

**World War, 1939–1945–Amphibious opera-
tions 940.54**

xx **World War, 1939–1945–Naval operations**

World War, 1939–1945—Antiwar movements.
See **World War, 1939–1945–Protests
movements**

World War, 1939–1945–Art and war 940.54

World War, 1939–1945–Atrocities 940.54

See also **War crime trials;** also names of
specific atrocities

x Atrocities, Military; Military atrocities

World War, 1939–1945—Battles. *See* **World
War, 1939–1945–Campaigns and battles**

World War, 1939–1945–Biography 920

World War, 1939–1945–Blacks 940.54

World War, 1939–1945–Blockades 940.54

World War, 1939–1945–Campaigns and battles
(May subdiv. geog.) 940.54
See also names of battles, campaigns,
sieges, etc. e.g. **Ardennes, Battle of
the, 1944–1945; Pearl Harbor, Attack
on, 1941;** etc.
x World War, 1939–1945—Battles
xx **Battles**
World War, 1939–1945—Cartoons. *See* **World
War, 1939–1945–Humor, caricatures,
etc.**
World War, 1939–1945–Causes 940.53
World War, 1939–1945–Censorship 940.54
World War, 1939–1945—Charities. *See* **World
War, 1939–1945–Civilian relief;
World War, 1939–1945–War work**
World War, 1939–1945–Children 940.54
xx **Children**
World War, 1939–1945—Civilian defense. *See*
Civil defense
World War, 1939–1945—Civilian evacuation.
See **World War, 1939–1945–Evacua-
tion of civilians**
World War, 1939–1945–Civilian relief 940.54
See also **World War, 1939–1945–Refugees**
x World War, 1939–1945—Charities
xx **Charities; Economic assistance; Recon-
struction (1939–1951); World War,
1939–1945–Food question; World
War, 1939–1945–Medical and sani-
tary affairs; World War, 1939–1945
–Refugees; World War, 1939–1945
–War work**
**World War, 1939–1945–Congresses, confer-
ences, etc. 940.54**
**World War, 1939–1945–Conscientious objec-
tors 940.53**
xx **Conscientious objectors; World War,
1939–1945–Protest movements**
World War, 1939–1945—Correspondents. *See*
World War, 1939–1945–Journalists
World War, 1939–1945—Damage to property.
See **World War, 1939–1945–Destruction and pillage**
World War, 1939–1945–Desertions 940.54
xx **Desertion, Military**
**World War, 1939–1945–Destruction and pil-
lage 940.54**
x World War, 1939–1945—Damage to
property
**World War, 1939–1945–Diplomatic history
940.53**
See also **World War, 1939–1945–Governments in exile**
**World War, 1939–1945–Displaced persons
940.54**
x Displaced persons
xx **World War, 1939–1945–Refugees**

609

World War, 1939–1945—Draft resisters   940.54
  xx Military service, Compulsory—Draft re-
    sisters
World   War,   1939–1945—Economic   aspects
    940.53
    Use for materials treating of the economic
      causes of the war and the effect of the
      war on commerce and industry
    See   also   Reconstruction   (1939–1951);
      World   War,   1939–1945—Finance;
      World War, 1939–1945—Human re-
      sources; World War, 1939–1945—Rep-
      arations
  xx Reconstruction (1939–1951); War—Eco-
    nomic aspects
World War, 1939–1945—Engineering and con-
    struction   940.54
World War, 1939–1945—Evacuation of civilians
    940.54
    x Civilian evacuation; Evacuation of civil-
      ians; World War, 1939–1945—Civil-
      ian evacuation
  xx Civil defense; World War, 1939–1945—
    Refugees
World War, 1939–1945—Finance   940.53
    Use for materials on the cost and financing
      of the war, including war debts, and
      the effect of the war on financial sys-
      tems, including inflation
    x War debts
  xx Debts, Public; World War, 1939–1945—
    Economic aspects
World War, 1939–1945—Food question   940.53
    See also World War, 1939–1945—Civilian
      relief
World War, 1939–1945—Governments in exile
    940.53
    x Governments in exile
  xx World War, 1939–1945—Diplomatic his-
    tory
World   War,   1939–1945—Guerrillas.   *See*
    World War, 1939–1945—Underground
    movements
World War, 1939–1945—Hospitals.   *See* World
    War, 1939–1945—Medical and sani-
    tary affairs
World   War,   1939–1945—Human   resources
    940.54
  xx Armies; Human resources; Labor and
    laboring classes; Labor supply; War—
    Economic aspects; World War, 1939–
    1945—Economic aspects
World War, 1939–1945—Humor, caricatures,
    etc.   940.53
    x World War, 1939–1945—Cartoons
  xx Cartoons and caricatures
World War, 1939–1945—Influence and results
    940.53
World War, 1939–1945—Jews   940.54

World War, 1939–1945–Journalists 940.54

    x World War, 1939–1945—Correspondents; World War, 1939–1945—War correspondents

World War, 1939–1945–Maps 940.54

World War, 1939–1945–Medical and sanitary affairs 940.54

    See also **World War, 1939–1945–Civilian relief**

    x World War, 1939–1945—Hospitals; World War, 1939–1945—Sanitary affairs

    xx **Armies–Medical and sanitary affairs; Hospitals, Military; Medicine, Military; Military hygiene; Sanitation**

World War, 1939–1945–Moral and religious aspects 940.53-940.54

    x World War, 1939–1945—Religious aspects

    xx **War and religion**

World War, 1939–1945–Naval operations 940.54

    See also **World War, 1939–1945–Amphibious operations;** also names of naval battles

World War, 1939–1945–Naval operations– Submarine 940.54

    x World War, 1939–1945—Submarine operations

World War, 1939–1945–Occupied territories 940.54

    Use for general treatment of the subject. For occupation of specific countries, use the name of the country with the subdivision *History—German occupation, 1940–1945* or *History—Allied occupation, 1945–* , e.g. **Netherlands History–German occupation, 1940–1945; Japan–History–Allied occupation, 1945–1952;** etc.

    See also **World War, 1939–1945–Underground movements;** also names of countries with the subdivision *History —German occupation, 1940–1945,* e.g. **Netherlands–History–German occupation, 1940–1945;** etc.

    xx **Military occupation; World War, 1939– 1945–Territorial questions**

World War, 1939–1945–Peace 940.53

    xx **Peace**

World War, 1939–1945–Personal narratives 940.53-940.54

    Use for miscellaneous accounts and reports written by soldiers, officers, journalists and other observers. Accounts limited to a special topic are entered under the specific subject

World War, 1939–1945–Pictorial works 940.53

World War, 1939–1945–Prisoners and prisons 940.54

xx Concentration camps; Prisoners of war

World War, 1939–1945–Propaganda 940.54

xx Propaganda

World War, 1939–1945–Protest movements 940.54

See also World War, 1939–1945–Conscientious objectors

x Antiwar movements; Protest movements (War); War protest movements; World War, 1939–1945–Antiwar movements

World War, 1939–1945–Public opinion 940.54

xx Public opinion

World War, 1939–1945–Railroads. See World War, 1939–1945–Transportation

World War, 1939–1945—Reconstruction. See Reconstruction (1939–1951)

World War, 1939–1945–Refugees 940.54

See also World War, 1939–1945–Civilian relief; World War, 1939–1945–Displaced persons; World War, 1939–1945–Evacuation of civilians

xx Refugees, Political; World War, 1939–1945–Civilian relief

World War, 1939–1945–Regimental histories 940.53

World War, 1939–1945—Religious aspects. See World War, 1939–1945–Moral and religious aspects

World War, 1939–1945–Reparations 940.53

x Reparations (World War, 1939–1945)

xx Reconstruction (1939–1951); World War, 1939–1945–Economic aspects

World War, 1939–1945—Sanitary affairs. See World War, 1939–1945–Medical and Sanitary affairs

World War, 1939–1945–Secret service 940.54

xx Secret service

World War, 1939–1945—Social work. See World War, 1939–1945–War work

World War, 1939–1945–Songs and music 784.6

xx Military music; War songs

World War, 1939–1945–Sources 940.53

xx History–Sources

World War, 1939–1945—Submarine operations. See World War, 1939–1945–Naval operations–Submarine

World War, 1939–1945–Supplies 940.54

World War, 1939–1945–Territorial questions 940.53

See also World War, 1939–1945–Occupied territories

xx Boundaries

World War, 1939–1945–Transportation 940.54

x World War, 1939–1945—Railroads

xx Transportation

World War, 1939–1945—Underground movements 940.54

    x World War, 1939–1945—Guerrillas; Underground movements (World War, 1939–1945)

    xx **Guerrilla warfare; Spies; World War, 1939–1945—Occupied territories**

World War, 1939–1945—U.S. 940.54

    x U.S.—History—World War, 1939–1945; U.S.—World War, 1939–1945

World War, 1939–1945—War correspondents. *See* **World War, 1939–1945—Journalists**

World War, 1939–1945—War work 940.53

    See also **World War, 1939–1945—Civilian relief**

    x War work; World War, 1939–1945—Charities; World War, 1939–1945—Social work

World War, 1939–1945—Women 940.54

    xx **Women**

World's fairs. *See* **Exhibitions; Fairs**

Worms 595

    xx **Invertebrates**

Worry 131

    x Anxiety

    xx **Mental health; Nervous system—Diseases**

Worship 248; 264

    See also **Ancestor worship; Devotional exercises; Prayer; Public worship; Sacrifice**

    x Devotion

    xx **Religion; Theology**

Worth. *See* **Values**

Wounded, First aid to. *See* **First aid**

Wrapping of gifts. *See* **Gift wrapping**

Wrecks. *See* **Shipwrecks;** and subjects with the subdivision *Accidents,* e.g. **Railroads—Accidents;** etc.

Wrestling 796.8

    See also **Judo**

Writers. *See* **Authors;** and special classes of writers, e.g. **Dramatists; Historians; Journalists;** etc.

Writing 411

    Use for general materials on the history and art of writing and on elegant handwriting. Practical guides are entered under **Penmanship.** Materials on handwriting as an expression of the writer's character are entered under **Graphology**

    See also

Abbreviations	**Graphology**
Alphabet	**Hieroglyphics**
Autographs	**Penmanship**
Calligraphy	**Picture writing**
Ciphers	**Shorthand**
Cryptography	**Typewriting**

Writing—*Continued*

   x Handwriting

   xx **Alphabet; Ciphers; Communication; Language and languages; Language arts; Penmanship**

Writing (Authorship). *See* **Authorship; Journalism**

Wrought iron work. *See* **Ironwork**

X-15 (Rocket aircraft) 629.133

   xx **Rocket planes**

X rays 539.7

   See also **Radiologists; Radiotherapy; Vacuum tubes**

   x Radiography; Rays, Roentgen; Roentgen rays

   xx **Electricity; Electromagnetic waves; Light; Radiation; Radioactivity; Radiotherapy; Therapeutics**

Xerography 686.4

   xx **Copying processes and machines**

Yacht basins. *See* **Marinas**

Yacht racing. *See* **Boat racing**

Yachts and yachting 797.1

   See also **Marinas; Sailing**

   x Regattas

   xx **Boatbuilding; Boats and boating; Ocean travel; Sailing; Ships; Voyages and travels; Water sports**

Yarn 677

   See also **Cotton; Flax; Wool**

   xx **Textile industry; Wool**

Yearbooks 050

   See also **Almanacs; Calendars;** and general subjects and names of organizations with the subdivision *Yearbooks,* e.g. **Literature—Yearbooks; United Nations—Yearbooks;** etc.

   x Annuals

   xx **Almanacs**

Yeast 641.3

   xx **Fermentation**

Yellow fever 616.9

   xx **Tropics—Diseases and hygiene**

Yellowstone National Park 917.8; 978

   xx **National parks and reserves**

Yiddish language 437

   May be subdivided like **English language**

   x German Hebrew; Jewish language; Jews—Language; Judaeo-German

   xx **Hebrew language**

Yiddish literature 837

   May use same subdivisions and names of literary forms as for **English literature**

   xx **Jewish literature**

Yippies. *See* **Hippies**

Yoga 181; 613.7

   xx **Hinduism; Philosophy, Hindu; Theosophy**

Yom Kippur 296.4

   xx **Fasts and feasts—Judaism**

Yom Kippur War, 1973. *See* **Israel-Arab War, 1973**

Young adults. *See* **Youth**

Young consumers 640.73; 658.8
> *x* Children as consumers; Teen age consumers; Youth market
> *xx* **Consumers**

Young men 301.43
> *See also* **Boys; Youth**
> *xx* **Boys; Men; Youth**

Young people's libraries. *See* **Libraries, Young adults'**

Young women 301.41
> *See also* **Girls; Youth**
> *xx* **Girls; Women; Youth**

Youth (May subdiv. geog.) **301.43**
> *See also* **Adolescence; Boys; Children; Church work with youth; Dropouts; Girls; Libraries, Young adults'; Runaways; Television and youth; Young men; Young women**
> *x* Adolescents; Age; Teen age; Young adults
> *xx* **Boys; Children; Girls; Young men; Young women**

Youth—Attitudes 301.43
> *xx* **Attitude (Psychology)**

Youth—Religious life 268
> *See also* **Jesus people**

Youth, Runaway. *See* **Runaways**

Youth—U.S. 301.43
> *x* American youth; U.S.—Youth

Youth and alcohol. *See* **Alcohol and youth**

Youth and drugs. *See* **Drugs and youth**

Youth and narcotics. *See* **Narcotics and youth**

Youth and television. *See* **Television and youth**

Youth hostels 647
> *x* Hostels, Youth; Tourist accommodations

Youth market. *See* **Young consumers**

Youth movement 322.4
> *See also* **Students—Political activity**
> *x* Student movement; Student protests; Student revolt
> *xx* **Demonstrations**

Zen Buddhism 294.3
> *xx* **Buddhism**

Zeppelins. *See* **Airships**

Zero gravity. *See* **Weightlessness**

Zinc 669
> *See also* **Brass**

Zionism 956
> *See also* **Jews—Restoration**
> *xx* **Jews—Restoration**

Zodiac 133.5; 523
> *xx* **Astronomy**

Zoning 301.34
> *x* City planning—Zone system; Districting (in city planning)
> *xx* **City planning**

Zoogeography. *See* **Geographical distribution of animals and plants**

Zoological gardens 590.74

> *See also* names of zoological gardens
>
> *x* Zoos
>
> *xx* **Animals; Parks**

Zoological specimens—Collection and preservation 579

> *See also* **Taxidermy;** also names of specimens with the subdivision *Collection and preservation*, e.g. **Birds—Collection and preservation;** etc.
>
> *x* Collections of natural specimens; Preservation of zoological specimens; Specimens, Preservation of
>
> *xx* **Collectors and collecting; Taxidermy**

Zoology (May subdiv. geog.) **590**

> *See also*

Anatomy, Comparative	**Natural history**
Animals	**Physiology, Comparative**
Embryology	**Psychology, Comparative**
Evolution	
Fossils	**Variation (Biology)**

> *also* names of divisions, classes, etc. of the animal kingdom (e.g. **Invertebrates;**

Zoology—*Continued*
       Vertebrates; Birds; Mammals; etc.);
       and names of animals
   x Animal kingdom; Animal physiology;
       Fauna
  xx **Animals; Biology; Natural history; Nature study; Science**

Zoology, Economic 591.6
      Use for general materials on animals injurious and beneficial to man and to agriculture, and for materials on the extermination of wild animals, venemous snakes, etc.
    See also **Agricultural pests; Domestic animals; Furbearing animals; Insects, Injurious and beneficial; Pests; Pests—Control**
   x Animals, Useful and harmful; Biology, Economic; Economic zoology

Zoology—Geographical distribution. *See* **Geographical distribution of animals and plants**

Zoology—U.S. 591.9
   x U.S.—Zoology

Zoology of the Bible. *See* **Bible—Natural history**

Zoos. *See* **Zoological gardens**